PCIP v4.0 Exam Mastery: 800+ Questions Copy

Your Ultimate Q&A Study Companion for the Payment Card Industry Professional (PCIP) Certification

John Meah

Book Cover by John Meah

Illustrations by John Meah

Second edition 2025

Contents

Foreword

This PCIP v4.0 Exam Mastery book serves as an essential companion to "Payment Card Industry PCIP v4.0: Your Ultimate Study Guide to Success, Second Edition." It is specifically designed to be used after you have thoroughly studied the main guide, allowing you to test your knowledge, reinforce key concepts, and identify any areas that may need additional review.

While the main study guide provides comprehensive coverage of PCI DSS v4.0 requirements and concepts, this Q&A companion offers a practical approach to validating your understanding through carefully crafted questions and detailed explanations. Each question has been designed to not only test your knowledge but also to deepen your grasp of the underlying principles that are crucial for both the PCIP examination and real-world application.

To maximize the benefits of this resource, I strongly recommend completing your study of the main guide before diving into these practice questions. This sequential approach will ensure you have the foundational knowledge necessary to fully understand and learn from the scenarios and examples presented here.

Together, these two resources provide a complete preparation system for your PCIP certification journey, combining thorough content coverage with practical application and testing. Let's begin strengthening your PCI DSS expertise and preparing for certification success.

INTRODUCTION

In today's digital economy, where payment card transactions form the backbone of global commerce, securing sensitive payment data has never been more critical. As cyber threats evolve and regulatory requirements become increasingly complex, organizations worldwide are seeking qualified professionals who can navigate the intricate landscape of payment card security and compliance. This is where the Payment Card Industry Professional (PCIP) certification stands as a beacon of expertise and credibility.

Welcome to *PCIP v4.0 Exam Mastery*, your comprehensive companion in the journey toward becoming a certified payment card industry professional. This book represents more than just a collection of practice questions; it's a carefully crafted roadmap to mastering the concepts, requirements, and real-world applications of PCI DSS v4.0.

Why is this book different? Because we understand that authentic learning goes beyond memorizing facts. Each of the 800+ questions in this guide is designed not just to test your knowledge but to deepen your understanding of the underlying principles. The detailed explanations accompanying each question transform every answer into a learning opportunity, helping you grasp the "why" behind the "what" of payment card security.

As you progress through these pages, you'll encounter questions that mirror the complexity and scope of the actual PCIP examination. From fundamental concepts to advanced scenarios, each section builds upon the last, creating a robust foundation of knowledge that you can apply both in the exam room and your professional practice.

This guide aligns perfectly with the latest PCI DSS v4.0 standards, including critical updates like Requirements 6.4.3 and 11.6.1, ensuring you're prepared for the most current industry requirements. Whether you're studying independently or as part of a group, the flexible format allows you to tailor your learning experience to your needs.

Remember, achieving PCIP certification is more than just passing an exam; it's about joining a community of professionals dedicated to protecting payment card data and maintaining the trust of millions of consumers worldwide. Let this book be your trusted companion in that vital journey.

Are you ready to take the next step in your professional development? Turn the page, and let's begin your path to PCIP certification success.

1

ISA, QSA & PCIP - Question Set

Q1: What are the three certifications mentioned in the content that can help advance a career in the payment card industry?

A1: The three certifications mentioned in the content that can help advance a career in the payment card industry are:

1. PCI-QSA (Qualified Security Assessor)
2. PCI-ISA (Internal Security Assessor)
3. PCIP (Payment Card Industry Professional)

These certifications are specifically highlighted as the ones employers are looking for in the payment card industry. They provide professionals with the necessary knowledge and skills to excel in this field, while also boosting their confidence and helping them stand out when applying for jobs. Each certification serves a different purpose and is targeted at professionals in different roles within the payment card industry, but all three are valuable credentials that can enhance career prospects.

Additional Resource: https://www.pcisecuritystandards.org/programs/

Q2: Which of the following statements is TRUE about the PCI-ISA certification?

a) It remains valid even if you change employers b) It is linked to your current employer c) It requires no recertification if you change jobs d) It is only available to large merchants

A2: The correct answer is b) It is linked to your current employer.

According to the content, the ISA certification is tied to your current employer. If you move to a new employer, you will need to retake the ISA examination to maintain your certification. The certification doesn't automatically transfer when you change jobs. The PCI-ISA program is available to information security team members in small, medium, or large merchant environments, acquiring banks, or processors, not just large merchants. Therefore, the certification is employer-specific, requiring recertification when changing employers.

Additional Resource: https://www.pcisecuritystandards.org/programs/isa-program/

Q3: What is the primary role of a Qualified Security Assessor (QSA)?

A3: The primary role of a Qualified Security Assessor (QSA) is to conduct assessments and ensure that organizations comply with PCI standards. However, their role extends beyond merely evaluating an organization's compliance status. QSAs work collaboratively with organizations to help them meet PCI DSS standards by providing recommendations and guidance to remediate non-compliance issues and achieve PCI compliance.

QSAs are certified professionals who have completed an accredited course in PCI data security and are authorized by the PCI Security Standards Council (PCI SSC) to perform these assessments. Their expertise allows them to serve as trusted advisors in helping organizations navigate the complex requirements of PCI DSS compliance. They play a crucial role in the payment card industry's security ecosystem by helping organizations implement appropriate security measures to protect payment card data.

Additional Resource: https://www.pcisecuritystandards.org/programs/qsa-program/

Q4: True or False: The PCIP certification remains with the individual even if they change employers.

A4: True. Unlike the PCI-QSA and PCI-ISA certifications which are tied to employers, the PCIP certification remains with the individual. As stated in the content, "the credential is valid for three years, and as long as you meet the Continuing Professional Education (CPE) requirement, it remains with you for life." This makes the PCIP certification particularly valuable for professionals who may change employers throughout their careers, as they don't need to go through recertification when changing jobs. The individual-based nature of this certification allows professionals to maintain their credential regardless of their employment status, provided they fulfill the CPE requirements to keep their knowledge current.

Additional Resource: https://www.pcisecuritystandards.org/programs/pcip-program/

Q5: What prerequisite knowledge is required before taking the PCIP examination?

A5: Before taking the PCIP examination, candidates are required to have a basic understanding of:

1. Information technology
2. Network security
3. Architecture

These fundamentals are necessary to comprehend the concepts covered in the PCIP examination. Additionally, the content strongly recommends that candidates undertake the PCIP training course(s) provided by the PCI SSC to enhance their knowledge and increase their chances of success in the examination. While these courses aren't explicitly stated as mandatory prerequisites, they are highly recommended preparation tools that help candidates better understand the PCI-DSS Standards and their interrelatedness, which is a core focus of the PCIP certification.

Additional Resource: https://www.pcisecuritystandards.org/programs/pcip-program/

Q6: How long is the PCIP certification valid, and what is required to maintain it?

A6: The PCIP certification is valid for three years. To maintain the certification beyond this period, professionals must meet the Continuing Professional Education (CPE) requirement. As stated in the content, "the credential is valid for three years, and as long as you meet the Continuing Professional Education (CPE) requirement, it remains with you for life."

The CPE requirement ensures that certified professionals stay current with the latest standards, practices, and developments in the payment card industry. This ongoing education is crucial because security standards and threats evolve over time. By fulfilling these CPE requirements, PCIP-certified professionals demonstrate their commitment to maintaining their expertise and knowledge in the field, ensuring they continue to be valuable assets to employers and the industry as a whole.

Additional Resource: https://www.pcisecuritystandards.org/programs/pcip-program/

Q7: Which certification is described as a "foundational certification demonstrating knowledge of the PCI standards and supporting materials"?

a) PCI-QSAb) PCI-ISAc) PCIPd) None of the above

A7: The correct answer is c) PCIP.

According to the content, "The PCIP Qualification is a foundational certification demonstrating knowledge of the PCI standards and supporting materials." The PCIP (Payment Card Industry Professional) certification focuses on relevant PCI-DSS fundamentals and critical areas of expertise required to become a trusted advisor to the payment card industry. It is designed as an entry-level certification that showcases a professional's expertise in PCI-DSS Standards and supporting materials, making it a stepping stone toward more advanced certifications like the PCI-ISA or PCI-QSA.

Additional Resource: https://www.pcisecuritystandards.org/programs/pcip-program/

Q8: What happens to a QSA certification if an individual leaves their employer?

A8: If an individual leaves their employer, their QSA certification will expire. As stated in the content, "if you decide to part ways with your employer, your QSA certification will expire." This is because the QSA certification is tied to the company that conducts PCI-DSS assessments, not just to the individual.

However, the content also mentions that there is a pathway to maintain QSA status: "if you plan to join another company as a qualified QSA, you can go through the recertification process and continue your career in this exciting field." Additionally, the content notes that when looking for new opportunities, "your new employer will likely cover the cost of recertification." This indicates that while the certification does expire upon leaving an employer, professionals can become recertified if they join another company that conducts PCI-DSS assessments, often with the new employer covering the recertification costs.

Additional Resource: https://www.pcisecuritystandards.org/programs/qsa-program/

Q9: Compare and contrast the PCI-ISA and PCI-QSA certifications in terms of their target audience and portability between employers.

A9: PCI-ISA (Internal Security Assessor) and PCI-QSA (Qualified Security Assessor) certifications differ in several important ways:

Target Audience:

- PCI-ISA: Targeted at professionals who are part of information security teams in merchant environments, acquiring banks, or processors. These professionals work internally within their organizations to ensure PCI DSS compliance.
- PCI-QSA: Targeted at professionals who work for companies that conduct PCI-DSS assessments for other organizations. QSAs are external assessors who evaluate and help organizations achieve compliance.

Portability Between Employers:

- PCI-ISA: The certification is tied to the current employer. If the certified professional changes employers, they must retake the ISA examination to maintain certification with the new employer.
- PCI-QSA: Similarly, the QSA certification is linked to the employer. If a QSA leaves their company, their certification expires. To maintain QSA status, they must join another company that conducts PCI-DSS assessments and go through the recertification process.

Both certifications require association with specific types of organizations and both require recertification when changing employers. However, they serve different roles in the PCI compliance ecosystem—ISAs work internally within their organizations, while QSAs provide assessment services to external clients.

Additional Resource: https://www.pcisecuritystandards.org/programs/

Q10: Which of the following best describes the PCIP certification's relationship to other PCI certifications?

a) It is more advanced than both PCI-QSA and PCI-ISA b) It is a prerequisite for obtaining the PCI-QSA certification c) It is a stepping stone toward becoming an ISA or QSA d) It is completely unrelated to other PCI certifications

A10: The correct answer is c) It is a stepping stone toward becoming an ISA or QSA.

According to the content, "The PCIP certification is not just a valuable qualification but also a crucial stepping stone toward becoming an Internal Security Assessor (ISA) or a Qualified Security Assessor (QSA)." This indicates that the PCIP serves as a foundational certification that can lead to more specialized roles within the payment card industry. By obtaining the PCIP certification first, professionals demonstrate their knowledge of PCI standards and supporting materials, which creates a solid knowledge base that can be built upon when pursuing the more role-specific ISA or QSA certifications. The PCIP is not described as more advanced than these other certifications, nor is it explicitly mentioned as a prerequisite, but rather as a beneficial starting point in a professional's certification journey.

Additional Resource: https://www.pcisecuritystandards.org/programs/pcip-program/

Q11: What organization approves and oversees the PCI certifications mentioned in the content?

A11: The organization that approves and oversees the PCI certifications mentioned in the content is the PCI Security Standards Council (PCI SSC). This is explicitly mentioned in the content when discussing the various certifications:

For the PCI-ISA: "The PCI SSC approves this certification and provides rigorous training to professionals like you."

For the PCI-QSA: "The PCI SSC authorizes them to conduct assessments..."

For the PCIP: "The Payment Card Industry Professional (PCIP 4.0) Program offered by the PCI SSC..."

The PCI Security Standards Council is the governing body responsible for developing, maintaining, and promoting the Payment Card Industry Data Security Standards (PCI DSS). It also manages the various certification programs that validate professionals' knowledge and skills in implementing and assessing these standards. The Council ensures that certified professionals meet rigorous requirements and maintain their expertise through continuing education.

Additional Resource: https://www.pcisecuritystandards.org/about_us/

Q12: What benefit of obtaining PCI certifications is specifically mentioned regarding job opportunities?

A12: The specific benefit mentioned regarding job opportunities is that having these certifications on your resume "will set you apart from other candidates" and "help you stand out from the crowd when it comes to landing your dream job." The content explicitly states that these certifications (PCI-QSA, PCI-ISA, and PCIP) are "the ones employers are looking for these days."

These certifications demonstrate to potential employers that you have specialized knowledge and skills in payment card industry security standards. They serve as third-party validation of your expertise, which can give you a competitive edge in the job market. The content also mentions that certifications provide "a significant confidence boost," which can be valuable during job interviews and when taking on new responsibilities. For professionals looking to advance their careers in the payment card industry, these certifications appear to be highly valued credentials that can open doors to new opportunities and positions.

Additional Resource: https://www.pcisecuritystandards.org/programs/

Q13: True or False: A professional must be associated with a company that conducts PCI-DSS assessments to become a certified ISA.

A13: False. According to the content, it is the QSA (Qualified Security Assessor) certification that requires association with a company that conducts PCI-DSS assessments, not the ISA certification.

The content states: "If you're interested in becoming a QSA, you must be associated with a company that conducts PCI-DSS assessments to become a certified QSA."

In contrast, the ISA (Internal Security Assessor) certification is designed for professionals who are "part of an information security team in a small, medium or large merchant environment, acquiring bank, or processor." ISAs work internally within their organizations to ensure PCI DSS compliance, rather than conducting formal assessments for external clients like QSAs do. While the ISA certification is tied to the current employer, the requirement is not specifically that the employer conducts PCI-DSS assessments for other organizations.

Additional Resource: https://www.pcisecuritystandards.org/programs/isa-program/

Q14: What are the key differences between the PCIP certification and the PCI-ISA/PCI-QSA certifications in terms of portability and validity?

A14: The key differences between the PCIP certification and the PCI-ISA/PCI-QSA certifications in terms of portability and validity are:

Portability:

- PCIP: Remains with the individual even when changing employers. As stated in the content, "it remains with you for life" (as long as CPE requirements are met).
- PCI-ISA: Tied to the current employer. If you change employers, you must retake the ISA examination.
- PCI-QSA: Also tied to the employer. If you leave your company, your certification expires and you need to recertify if joining another QSA company.

Validity:

- PCIP: Valid for three years and can be maintained by meeting Continuing Professional Education (CPE) requirements.
- PCI-ISA: Valid as long as you remain with the same employer. Requires recertification if changing employers.
- PCI-QSA: Valid as long as you remain with the same QSA company. Expires upon leaving the company and requires recertification if joining another QSA company.

These differences make the PCIP certification particularly valuable for professionals who anticipate changing employers, as it provides more flexibility and doesn't require recertification with each job change, unlike the PCI-ISA and PCI-QSA certifications.

Additional Resource: https://www.pcisecuritystandards.org/programs/

Q15: Which of the following professionals would most likely benefit from pursuing the PCI-ISA certification?

a) A freelance security consultant who works with multiple clients b) A security team member at a large retail corporation c) A software developer creating payment applications d) A banking customer service representative

A15: The correct answer is b) A security team member at a large retail corporation.

According to the content, the PCI-ISA certification is designed for professionals who are "part of an information security team in a small, medium or large merchant environment, acquiring bank, or processor." A security team member at a large retail corporation fits precisely into this target audience, as retail corporations are merchants that handle payment card data and must comply with PCI DSS requirements.

A freelance consultant (option a) would not be an ideal candidate because the ISA certification is tied to a specific employer and designed for internal team members. A software developer (option c) might benefit more from other PCI certifications specific to payment application development. A customer service representative (option d) typically doesn't have direct responsibilities for information security or PCI compliance implementation.

The ISA certification would help the security team member enhance their knowledge of PCI Security Standards and ensure their retail corporation meets the requirements of PCI DSS efficiently.

Additional Resource: https://www.pcisecuritystandards.org/programs/isa-program/

Q16: Describe the role of Qualified Security Assessors (QSAs) in helping organizations achieve PCI compliance.

A16: Qualified Security Assessors (QSAs) play a multifaceted role in helping organizations achieve PCI compliance:

1. Assessment Conductors: QSAs are authorized by the PCI SSC to conduct formal assessments of an organization's compliance with PCI DSS standards. They evaluate security policies, procedures, and implementations against the required standards.

2. Collaborative Partners: As stated in the content, QSAs "work collaboratively with organizations to help them meet PCI DSS standards." Rather than simply identifying compliance gaps, they actively assist organizations in addressing those gaps.

3. Advisors and Guides: QSAs provide "recommendations and guidance" to organizations, helping them navigate the complex requirements of PCI DSS compliance. Their expertise allows them to suggest appropriate security measures and best practices.

4. Remediation Supporters: QSAs help organizations "remediate non-compliance issues" by identifying practical solutions to security vulnerabilities and compliance gaps.

5. Compliance Facilitators: The ultimate goal of QSAs is to help organizations "achieve PCI compliance," ensuring that payment card data is properly protected according to industry standards.

QSAs serve as trusted external experts who not only evaluate compliance status but also partner with organizations to improve their security posture and meet regulatory requirements. Their role combines assessment, education, and guidance to support organizations throughout their compliance journey.

Additional Resource: https://www.pcisecuritystandards.org/programs/qsa-program/

Q17: What is recommended for candidates to enhance their knowledge and increase their chances of success in the PCIP examination?

A17: The content specifically recommends that candidates undertake the PCIP training course(s) provided by the PCI SSC to enhance their knowledge and increase their chances of success in the PCIP examination.

As stated in the content: "Candidates are highly recommended to undertake the PCIP training course(s) provided by the PCI SSC to enhance their knowledge and increase their chances of success in the examination."

These training courses are designed to help candidates better understand the PCI-DSS Standards and their interrelatedness, which is a core focus of the PCIP certification. While the courses aren't explicitly stated as mandatory prerequisites, they are highly recommended preparation tools that provide structured learning about the key concepts covered in the examination.

Additionally, candidates should already have a basic understanding of information technology, network security, and architecture before taking the PCIP examination, as these are mentioned as prerequisite knowledge areas.

Additional Resource: https://www.pcisecuritystandards.org/programs/pcip-program/

Q18: If a QSA professional is considering changing employers, what information in the content would be most relevant to them?

A18: For a QSA professional considering changing employers, the most relevant information from the content would be:

1. QSA certification expiration: "If you decide to part ways with your employer, your QSA certification will expire." This means they will lose their certification status upon leaving their current employer.
2. Recertification possibility: "If you plan to join another company as a qualified QSA, you can go through the recertification process and continue your career in this exciting field." This indicates they can maintain their QSA status if they join another QSA company and recertify.
3. Job opportunities: "If you're already a QSA and looking for a new challenge, keep an eye out for job postings on LinkedIn! These roles are perfect for individuals contemplating a move to another company or wanting to continue working as QSAs."
4. Recertification costs: "Your new employer will likely cover the cost of recertification." This is important financial information, as it suggests they may not have to personally bear the costs of regaining their certification.

This information outlines the path for QSAs to transition between employers while maintaining their professional credentials, which is crucial for career planning and job searching in this specialized field.

Additional Resource: https://www.pcisecuritystandards.org/programs/qsa-program/

Q19: What value does the PCIP certification provide to professionals in the payment card industry?

A19: The PCIP certification provides multiple values to professionals in the payment card industry:

1. Expertise Demonstration: It allows professionals to "showcase their expertise in PCI-DSS Standards and supporting materials," providing third-party validation of their knowledge.
2. Career Enhancement: The certification can "help enhance their careers" by making them more competitive job candidates and opening doors to advancement opportunities.
3. Knowledge Currency: It helps professionals stay "up-to-date with the latest standards and practices" in the rapidly evolving payment card security field.
4. Foundation for Advanced Certifications: It serves as "a crucial stepping stone toward becoming an Internal Security Assessor (ISA) or a Qualified Security Assessor (QSA)," creating a pathway for career progression.
5. Comprehensive Understanding: It offers "a unique opportunity to comprehend the intricacies of the PCI-DSS Standards and their interrelatedness," providing a holistic view of payment card security.
6. Professional Portability: Unlike some other certifications, the PCIP credential "remains with you for life" (as long as CPE

requirements are met), regardless of employer changes.

7. Trusted Advisor Status: It focuses on developing "critical areas of expertise required to become a trusted advisor to the payment card industry."

The PCIP certification essentially serves as a foundational credential that validates a professional's knowledge, enhances their career prospects, and provides a stepping stone to more specialized roles in the payment card industry.

Additional Resource: https://www.pcisecuritystandards.org/programs/pcip-program/

Q20: True or False: The PCI-ISA certification requires recertification if you change employers, while the PCIP does not.

A20: True. According to the content, the PCI-ISA certification is tied to your current employer, and if you move to a new employer, you need to retake the ISA examination to maintain your certification. The content specifically states: "the ISA certification is tied to your current employer. Still, if you move to a new employer, you can retake the ISA examination to maintain your certification."

In contrast, the PCIP certification remains with the individual regardless of employer changes. As the content explains: "the credential is valid for three years, and as long as you meet the Continuing Professional Education (CPE) requirement, it remains with you for life." This indicates that the PCIP does not require recertification specifically due to changing employers, only ongoing CPE to maintain it over time.

This difference in portability between employers is a significant distinction between these two certifications and may influence which certification a professional chooses to pursue based on their career plans.

Additional Resource: https://www.pcisecuritystandards.org/programs/

Q21: Which certification would be most appropriate for a professional who frequently changes employers but wants to maintain their credentials in the payment card industry?

a) PCI-QSAb) PCI-ISAc) PCIPd) All of the above

A21: The correct answer is c) PCIP.

The PCIP (Payment Card Industry Professional) certification would be most appropriate for a professional who frequently changes employers but wants to maintain their credentials because it's the only certification mentioned that remains with the individual regardless of employer changes. As stated in the content, "the credential is valid for three years, and as long as you meet the Continuing Professional Education (CPE) requirement, it remains with you for life."

In contrast, both the PCI-QSA and PCI-ISA certifications are tied to specific employers:

- The PCI-ISA certification "is tied to your current employer. Still, if you move to a new employer, you can retake the ISA examination to maintain your certification."
- For the PCI-QSA, "if you decide to part ways with your employer, your QSA certification will expire."

For someone who anticipates frequent job changes, the PCIP provides the most stability and continuity in credentials, requiring only ongoing CPE rather than full recertification with each employer change.

Additional Resource: https://www.pcisecuritystandards.org/programs/pcip-program/

Q22: What are the benefits of earning PCI certifications mentioned in the content?

A22: According to the content, earning PCI certifications offers several key benefits:

1. Career Advancement: The certifications "can help you advance your career in the payment card industry" by making you more qualified for positions in this field.
2. Knowledge and Skills Acquisition: By earning these certifications, "you'll gain all the knowledge and skills you need to excel in this field," providing you with the expertise necessary for success.
3. Confidence Boost: The certifications "give you a significant confidence boost," helping you feel more secure in your professional abilities and knowledge.
4. Competitive Advantage: Having these certifications on your resume "will set you apart from other candidates" and "help you stand out from the crowd when it comes to landing your dream job."
5. Employer Recognition: These certifications are "the ones employers are looking for these days," indicating their value in the job market.
6. Up-to-date Knowledge: Certifications help professionals stay "up-to-date with the latest standards and practices" in the payment card industry.
7. Professional Credibility: Certifications allow professionals to "demonstrate their professional knowledge and understanding of the subject," establishing them as credible experts in the field.

These benefits collectively enhance a professional's career prospects, expertise, and marketability in the payment card industry.

Additional Resource: https://www.pcisecuritystandards.org/programs/

Q23: How would you explain the differences between the three PCI certifications to someone new to the payment card industry?

A23: Here's how I would explain the differences between the three PCI certifications to someone new to the payment card industry:

PCIP (Payment Card Industry Professional) This is your foundational certification that demonstrates your knowledge of PCI standards and supporting materials. Think of it as your entry point into PCI certifications. It's ideal if you're starting your career in payment card security or want to validate your understanding of PCI-DSS fundamentals. The best part? This certification stays with you regardless of where you work, as long as you complete ongoing education requirements every three years. It's a great stepping stone if you eventually want to pursue more specialized roles.

PCI-ISA (Internal Security Assessor) This certification is designed for you if you work on an internal security team at a merchant, bank, or payment processor. It helps you ensure your own company complies with PCI standards efficiently. Unlike the PCIP, this certification is tied to your employer—if you change jobs, you'll need to retake the examination. This role focuses on implementing and maintaining compliance within a single organization rather than assessing others.

PCI-QSA (Qualified Security Assessor) This is the certification you need if you want to formally assess other companies' PCI compliance. QSAs are authorized to evaluate organizations and help them remediate issues to achieve compliance. To become a QSA, you must work for a company that performs PCI-DSS assessments. Like the ISA certification, your QSA status expires if you leave your employer, requiring recertification if you join another assessment company.

In summary: PCIP is portable and foundational, ISA is for internal compliance specialists, and QSA is for external assessors. Your career goals and current employment situation should guide which certification you pursue first.

Additional Resource: https://www.pcisecuritystandards.org/programs/

Q24: Which of the following best describes the relationship between the PCIP certification and ongoing education?

a) No continuing education is required once certified b) Continuing education is required annually c) The certification must be completely renewed every three years d) Continuing Professional Education (CPE) is required to maintain the certification

A24: The correct answer is d) Continuing Professional Education (CPE) is required to maintain the certification.

According to the content, "the credential is valid for three years, and as long as you meet the Continuing Professional Education (CPE) requirement, it remains with you for life." This statement clearly indicates that ongoing education in the form of CPE is necessary to maintain the PCIP certification.

The content doesn't specify that no continuing education is required (option a), nor does it mention that continuing education is specifically required on an annual basis (option b). While the certification is valid for three years, the content doesn't state that it must be completely renewed through retesting every three years (option c), but rather that meeting CPE requirements allows it to remain valid.

The CPE requirement ensures that PCIP-certified professionals stay current with evolving standards and practices in the payment card industry, maintaining the relevance and value of their certification over time.

Additional Resource: https://www.pcisecuritystandards.org/programs/pcip-program/

Q25: What role does the PCI SSC play in relation to the certifications discussed in the content?

A25: The PCI Security Standards Council (PCI SSC) plays several crucial roles in relation to the certifications discussed in the content:

1. Approval and Authorization: The PCI SSC "approves" the ISA certification, "authorizes" QSAs to conduct assessments, and "offers" the PCIP program. This indicates that the Council is the governing body that establishes and legitimizes these certifications.

2. Training Provider: The Council "provides rigorous training to professionals" for the ISA program and offers "PCIP training course(s)" that candidates are "highly recommended to undertake." This demonstrates the Council's educational role in preparing professionals for certification.

3. Standards Development: As the name suggests, the PCI SSC is responsible for the PCI Security Standards that these cer-

tifications are based on. Certified professionals demonstrate knowledge of "PCI-DSS Standards and supporting materials" created by the Council.

4. Quality Assurance: The Council ensures that certified professionals meet specific knowledge requirements and maintain their expertise through programs like Continuing Professional Education (CPE).

5. Certification Management: The Council manages the certification programs, including establishing validity periods, renewal requirements, and the scope of knowledge tested.

The PCI SSC essentially serves as the central authority that creates, manages, and validates these certification programs, ensuring they effectively prepare professionals to implement and assess payment card security standards across the industry.

Additional Resource: https://www.pcisecuritystandards.org/about_us/

2

The Evolution of the Payment Card Industry - Question Set

Q1: What year was the PCI Security Standards Council (PCI SSC) established?

A1: The PCI Security Standards Council was established in 2006 as a global non-profit organization. Its primary mission is to oversee the creation, management, education, and promotion of worldwide PCI security standards. The Council was formed to ensure payment transactions across the globe remain secure and protected, especially in response to the increasing threat of cybercrime. This central governing body has been instrumental in creating standardized security protocols and raising awareness about these standards throughout the payment card industry.

Additional resource: pcisecuritystandards.org

Q2: True or False: The PCI-DSS was established through collaboration between the PCI Security Standards Council and the American National Standards Institute (ANSI).

A2: True. According to the provided content, the Payment Card Industry Data Security Standard (PCI-DSS) was established in 2004 through a collaborative effort between the PCI Security Standards Council and the American National Standards Institute (ANSI). This collaboration helped create a comprehensive set of security standards designed to protect credit card information during processing, storage, and transmission.

Additional resource: pcisecuritystandards.org/standards/pci-dss/

Q3: What are the major credit card companies that have adopted the PCI-DSS?

A3: The major credit card companies that have adopted the PCI-DSS include Visa, MasterCard, American Express, Discover, JCB, and UnionPay. These companies have collectively agreed to adopt the PCI-DSS as part of their data security compliance programs to make them more effective. This unified approach ensures consistent security standards across the payment card industry, providing better protection for cardholder data regardless of which card brand is being used for transactions.

Additional resource: securitymetrics.com/blog/what-are-12-requirements-pci-dss-compliance

Q4: Which of the following is NOT a requirement for maintaining PCI-DSS compliance?

a) Implementing robust security controls b) Monitoring and reporting security incidents c) Annual security audits only d) Ensuring network architecture meets security standards

A4: The correct answer is c) Annual security audits only. According to the content, security testing must be a continuous process (business as usual or BAU) rather than just a snapshot taken once a year during an annual audit. The PCI DSS requires organizations to demonstrate compliance over a period of time, not just at a single point in time. Options a, b, and d are all legitimate requirements for maintaining PCI-DSS compliance as organizations must implement robust security controls, monitor and report security incidents, and ensure their network architecture meets stringent security standards.

Additional resource: strikegraph.com/blog/pci-dss-v4

Q5: Explain why PCI DSS v4.0 requires security to be treated as a continuous process rather than an annual event.

A5: PCI DSS v4.0 emphasizes security as a continuous process (Business as Usual or BAU) rather than an annual event because a once-yearly approach provides only a limited snapshot of an organization's security posture at a specific moment in time, which is insufficient for genuine security.

The standard recognizes that threats to payment card data evolve constantly, requiring ongoing vigilance and security measures. Documentation in the standard explicitly directs Qualified Security Assessors (QSAs) to select samples over a period of time to prove compliance, not just at audit time. This approach ensures organizations maintain consistent security practices throughout the year.

Continuous security processes help organizations stay up-to-date with changing threats and vulnerabilities, adapt to new attack vectors, and maintain robust defenses at all times. This approach also allows for the timely detection and remediation of security issues before they can be exploited.

By treating security as an ongoing business function rather than a compliance checkbox, organizations can better protect sensitive information and financial data, ultimately providing more reliable protection for cardholder data and maintaining customer trust.

Additional resource: secureframe.com/blog/pci-compliance-checklist

Q6: What is the minimum password length requirement in PCI DSS v4.0?

a) 8 characters b) 10 characters c) 12 characters d) 16 characters

A6: The correct answer is c) 12 characters. PCI DSS v4.0 has enhanced its authentication requirements to improve security. According to the provided content, passwords must now be at least 12 characters long and must contain a mix of numbers and letters. This change represents a significant improvement over previous versions of the standard and aligns with modern security best practices that recognize longer passwords as being more resistant to brute force attacks and other password cracking techniques.

Additional resource: secureframe.com/en-us/hub/pci-dss/12-requirements

Q7: True or False: Multi-factor authentication (MFA) is optional for accounts that provide access to the card data environment under PCI DSS v4.0.

A7: False. According to the provided content, multi-factor authentication (MFA) will become mandatory for all accounts that provide access to the card data environment under PCI DSS v4.0. This is not optional but a required security measure. The standard now requires users to verify their identity using more than one method, such as a password plus another factor like a fingerprint scan or a security token. This enhanced requirement helps ensure that only authorized users can access cardholder data, significantly improving the security posture of organizations handling payment card information.

Additional resource: pcisecuritystandards.org/standards/pci-dss/

Q8: What significant change does PCI DSS v4.0 make regarding organizational controls?

A8: PCI DSS v4.0 makes a significant change by giving organizations more flexibility to create and implement their own controls. This approach, often referred to as "customized implementation," allows companies to adopt new technologies or security solutions to meet compliance requirements in ways that best suit their specific business models and technical environments.

For example, organizations can now more easily use cloud-based hosting services without being hindered by complicated language or confusing intent statements in the standard. This flexibility opens up possibilities for businesses to leverage various modern technologies such as mobile payments, biometric authentication, and tokenization while still maintaining compliance.

This change represents a shift from a purely prescriptive approach to one that focuses more on security outcomes, allowing organizations to innovate in how they protect cardholder data while still meeting the fundamental security objectives of the PCI DSS.

Additional resource: strikegraph.com/blog/pci-dss-v4

Q9: What is the main goal of the PCI Security Standards Council?

a) To process credit card payments b) To oversee the creation, management, education, and promotion of worldwide PCI security standards c) To issue credit cards to consumers d) To regulate banking institutions

A9: The correct answer is b) To oversee the creation, management, education, and promotion of worldwide PCI security standards. According to the provided content, the PCI Security Standards Council is a global non-profit organization established in 2006 with the main goal of overseeing the creation, management, education, and promotion of the worldwide PCI security standards. Their dedication is to ensuring that payment transactions worldwide are secure and protected, particularly in the face of increasing cybercrime threats.

Additional resource: pcisecuritystandards.org/about_us/

Q10: Discuss the potential consequences an organization might face for failing to comply with PCI-DSS requirements.

A10: Organizations that fail to comply with PCI-DSS requirements face several significant consequences:

1. Financial penalties: Non-compliant organizations may face fines imposed by payment card brands or acquiring banks.

These fines can range from thousands to millions of dollars depending on the organization's size, the severity of non-compliance, and whether a data breach has occurred.

2. Suspension of payment processing privileges: As explicitly mentioned in the content, organizations that fail to comply may have their ability to process credit card payments suspended. This can be devastating for businesses that rely on card payments for revenue.

3. Reputational damage: If an organization suffers a data breach due to PCI-DSS non-compliance, the resulting publicity can severely damage its reputation and customer trust.

4. Increased transaction fees: Card brands may impose higher processing fees on non-compliant merchants as a penalty and to offset increased risk.

5. Legal liability: In the event of a data breach, non-compliant organizations may face lawsuits from affected customers and potentially regulatory action.

6. Business disruption: The remediation efforts required following a compliance failure or breach can significantly disrupt normal business operations.

7. Mandatory forensic investigations: Following a breach, organizations typically must engage (and pay for) a PCI Forensic Investigator to determine the extent of the compromise.

These consequences highlight why compliance with PCI-DSS is not merely optional but essential for any organization handling payment card data.

Additional resource: securitymetrics.com/blog/what-are-12-requirements-pci-dss-compliance

Q11: What services does the PCI Council offer to help organizations comply with PCI-DSS?

A11: The PCI Council offers several services to help organizations comply with PCI-DSS:

1. Training programs: The Council provides extensive training for individuals, merchants, and service providers who must comply with PCI-DSS. These programs help stakeholders understand the requirements and how to implement them effectively.

2. Certification services: The Council offers certification programs that validate an individual's or organization's knowledge and implementation of PCI standards.

3. Validation services: These services help ensure that organizations meet compliance requirements through various assessment methodologies.

4. Educational resources: The Council provides guidance documents, including the PCI DSS Quick Reference Guide mentioned in the content, which offers explanations and implementation advice.

5. Advice and assistance: Beyond mandating adherence, the Council actively offers advice and help to those who need support in understanding or implementing the requirements.

These services collectively demonstrate the Council's commitment not just to enforcing standards but to supporting the payment card ecosystem in achieving and maintaining security compliance.

Additional resource: pcisecuritystandards.org/faq/articles/Frequently_Asked_Question/Where-do-I-direct-questions-about-complying-with-PCI-standards/

Q12: In what year was the Payment Card Industry Data Security Standard (PCI-DSS) established?

a) 2000 b) 2004 c) 2006 d) 2010

A12: The correct answer is b) 2004. According to the provided content, the Payment Card Industry Data Security Standard (PCI-DSS) was established in 2004 through a collaboration between the PCI Security Standards Council and the American National Standards Institute (ANSI). This standard was created to establish a comprehensive framework for protecting credit card information during processing, storage, and transmission, in response to increasing concerns about payment card security and fraud.

Additional resource: pcisecuritystandards.org/standards/pci-dss/

Q13: True or False: Under PCI DSS v4.0, security testing should be conducted as a continuous process rather than just during annual audits.

A13: True. The content explicitly states that "Security testing has to be a continuous process, business as usual (BAU), rather than a snapshot of an organization's PCI DSS compliance taken once a year during the annual audit." This approach ensures that security is maintained consistently throughout the year rather than just at audit time. The standard requires evidence of security measures over a period of time, not just a single point-in-time assessment, emphasizing that genuine security requires ongoing vigilance and continuous testing.

Additional resource: strikegraph.com/blog/pci-dss-v4

Q14: What does PCI DSS v4.0 require regarding password composition?

a) Passwords must contain only letters b) Passwords must be at least 8 characters c) Passwords must contain a mix of numbers and letters and be at least 12 characters long d) Passwords must be changed daily

A14: The correct answer is c) Passwords must contain a mix of numbers and letters and be at least 12 characters long. PCI DSS v4.0 has enhanced its authentication requirements, now requiring passwords to be at least 12 characters long and to contain a mix of numbers and letters. As noted in the content, simple passwords like "1234" or "password" are no longer acceptable under these new requirements. This change reflects the standard's adaptation to current security best practices, which recognize that longer, more complex passwords provide better protection against unauthorized access.

Additional resource: secureframe.com/blog/pci-compliance-checklist

Q15: What does the acronym MFA stand for in the context of PCI DSS v4.0, and why is it important?

A15: MFA stands for Multi-Factor Authentication in the context of PCI DSS v4.0. It is important because it significantly enhances security by requiring users to verify their identity using more than one method of authentication.

According to the content, MFA will become mandatory for all accounts that provide access to the card data environment under PCI DSS v4.0. This means users must authenticate using at least two different factors, such as:

1. Something they know (like a password)

2. Something they have (like a security token or mobile device)

3. Something they are (like a fingerprint or other biometric)

MFA is important because it creates multiple layers of security. Even if one factor is compromised (such as a password being stolen), an attacker would still need to bypass the additional authentication factors to gain access to sensitive cardholder data. This significantly reduces the risk of unauthorized access and potential data breaches, providing much stronger protection than single-factor authentication methods.

Additional resource: secureframe.com/en-us/hub/pci-dss/12-requirements

Q16: Explain how the PCI-DSS contributes to keeping credit card information safe in today's digital world.

A16: The PCI-DSS contributes significantly to keeping credit card information safe in today's digital world through multiple mechanisms:

First, it establishes a comprehensive, standardized security framework that all organizations handling payment card data must follow. This creates a baseline level of security across the entire payment ecosystem, reducing vulnerabilities that could be exploited by cybercriminals.

The standard requires robust security controls including network security, data protection, vulnerability management, access control, monitoring, and information security policies. These requirements work together to form a defense-in-depth approach to security.

PCI-DSS remains relevant by adapting to evolving threats. As noted in the content, the standard is "always up-to-date with industry trends and practices," with regular reviews conducted every three years by the PCI Security Standards Council. This ensures that security requirements evolve alongside new threats and technologies.

Version 4.0 introduces enhanced authentication requirements, including longer passwords (minimum 12 characters) and mandatory multi-factor authentication for access to cardholder data environments. These improvements directly address common attack vectors like password-based breaches.

The standard also emphasizes security as a continuous process rather than a point-in-time compliance exercise. This business-as-usual approach ensures organizations maintain vigilant security practices throughout the year, not just during annual audits.

Furthermore, by mandating compliance and imposing consequences for non-compliance (including potential suspension of payment processing privileges), the standard creates strong incentives for organizations to prioritize payment security.

Through these mechanisms, PCI-DSS plays a crucial role in protecting consumers' credit card information in an increasingly digital and threat-filled environment.

Additional resource: securitymetrics.com/blog/what-are-12-requirements-pci-dss-compliance

Q17: What new approach to security controls does PCI DSS v4.0 introduce?

a) Reduced flexibility for organizations b) Elimination of all custom controls c) Greater flexibility for organizations to create their own controls d) Mandatory cloud-based solutions

A17: The correct answer is c) Greater flexibility for organizations to create their own controls. According to the content, PCI DSS v4.0 "has made a significant change that gives organizations more freedom to create their own controls and put them into action." This approach allows companies to be more flexible in adopting new technologies or security solutions to meet compliance requirements. For example, organizations can now more easily use cloud-based hosting services without being hindered by complicated language or confusing intent statements.

Additional resource: strikegraph.com/blog/pci-dss-v4

Q18: True or False: The PCI Council only mandates adherence to PCI-DSS but does not offer any assistance with compliance.

A18: False. According to the content, "The good news is that the PCI Council not only mandates adherence to the PCI-DSS but also offers advice and help to those who need it." The Council provides extensive training programs for individuals, merchants, and service providers who must comply with PCI-DSS. They also offer certification and validation services to ensure that organizations meet compliance requirements. This demonstrates that the Council takes an active role in supporting compliance efforts, not just in mandating standards.

Additional resource: pcisecuritystandards.org/faq/articles/Frequently_Asked_Question/Where-do-I-direct-questions-about-complying-with-PCI-standards/

Q19: What does the term "BAU" refer to in the context of PCI DSS security testing?

A19: In the context of PCI DSS security testing, "BAU" stands for "Business as Usual." This term refers to the approach that security testing should be integrated into an organization's regular, ongoing operations rather than being treated as a special, isolated event that occurs only during compliance audits.

The content explicitly states that "Security testing has to be a continuous process, business as usual (BAU), rather than a snapshot of an organization's PCI DSS compliance taken once a year during the annual audit." This means organizations should incorporate security testing into their day-to-day operations, making it a normal part of business processes.

This approach ensures continuous monitoring and improvement of security controls, allowing for more effective protection of cardholder data and a more accurate assessment of an organization's security posture over time, rather than just at a single point in time during an annual audit.

Additional resource: secureframe.com/blog/pci-compliance-checklist

Q20: Which of these technologies is specifically mentioned as an example of what organizations can more easily adopt under PCI DSS v4.0's flexible approach?

a) Blockchain b) Artificial intelligence c) Cloud-based hosting services d) Virtual reality

A20: The correct answer is c) Cloud-based hosting services. According to the content, PCI DSS v4.0's more flexible approach allows companies to "use cloud-based hosting services without worrying about complicated language or confusing intent statements." This is mentioned as a specific example of how the new standard's flexibility enables organizations to adopt modern technologies while maintaining compliance with security requirements.

Additional resource: strikegraph.com/blog/pci-dss-v4

Q21: Discuss the benefits of the increased flexibility provided by PCI DSS v4.0 regarding security controls.

A21: PCI DSS v4.0's increased flexibility regarding security controls offers several significant benefits:

1. Technological innovation: Organizations can now more easily adopt cutting-edge technologies and security solutions without being constrained by overly prescriptive requirements. As noted in the content, companies can leverage modern technologies like mobile payments, biometric authentication, and tokenization while maintaining compliance.

2. Customized security approaches: Different organizations have different business models, technologies, and risk profiles. The flexibility allows them to design security controls that address their specific environments while still achieving the security objectives of the standard.

3. Cloud adoption: The content specifically mentions that organizations can now use cloud-based hosting services more easily without being hindered by complicated language or confusing intent statements. This is particularly important as more businesses move their operations to the cloud.

4. Reduced implementation barriers: By focusing more on security outcomes rather than prescriptive methods, the standard reduces unnecessary implementation barriers that may have prevented organizations from adopting the most effective security solutions for their specific circumstances.

5. Better alignment with business objectives: Organizations can align security controls with their business objectives and operational processes, making security more integrated with the business rather than being seen as an obstacle.

6. Adaptability to emerging threats: The flexibility allows organizations to respond more quickly to emerging threats by implementing new controls or technologies without waiting for the standard to be updated.

7. Cost-effectiveness: Organizations can potentially implement more cost-effective security solutions that are tailored to their specific needs while still maintaining compliance.

This approach represents a significant evolution in PCI DSS, moving from a purely prescriptive approach to one that emphasizes security outcomes while giving organizations more freedom in how they achieve those outcomes.

Additional resource: secureframe.com/en-us/hub/pci-dss/12-requirements

Q22: True or False: PCI-DSS compliance is optional for organizations that process a small number of credit card transactions.

A22: False. According to the content, "Every organization that processes these payments must comply with the standard, as failure to do so can lead to penalties or even the suspension of payment processing privileges." The requirement for compliance applies to all organizations that process credit card payments, regardless of volume. There is no exemption mentioned for organizations processing a small number of transactions. While the level of validation required may vary based on transaction volume, the obligation to comply with the standard applies to all merchants and service providers who handle payment card data.

Additional resource: securitymetrics.com/blog/what-are-12-requirements-pci-dss-compliance

Q23: What entities collaborated to establish the PCI-DSS?

a) Visa and MasterCard only b) The PCI Security Standards Council and the American National Standards Institute (ANSI) c) The Federal Trade Commission and major banks d) The International Organization for Standardization (ISO) and the PCI Council

A23: The correct answer is b) The PCI Security Standards Council and the American National Standards Institute (ANSI). According to the provided content, "This comprehensive set of security standards was established in 2004 through a collaboration between the PCI Security Standards Council and the American National Standards Institute (ANSI)." This collaboration brought together industry expertise and standardization experience to create a robust framework for protecting payment card data.

Additional resource: pcisecuritystandards.org/about_us/

Q24: How frequently does the PCI Security Standards Council review the PCI DSS to ensure it remains relevant and effective?

A24: According to the content from the StrikeGraph blog, "Every three years, the Payment Card Industry Security Standards Council (PCI SSC) reviews the Payment Card Industry Data Security Standard (PCI DSS) to ensure the standards remain relevant and effective."

This three-year review cycle is an important aspect of how the PCI SSC maintains the effectiveness of the standard. The regular review process allows the Council to address new threats and supports the evolving payment card landscape by updating requirements, clarifying existing ones, and introducing new controls as necessary.

This approach ensures that the PCI DSS continues to provide adequate protection for cardholder data even as technologies and threat vectors change over time. The development of PCI DSS v4.0 is a result of this periodic review process, introducing enhanced requirements for authentication, continuous security testing, and more flexible implementation options.

Additional resource: strikegraph.com/blog/pci-dss-v4

Q25: Explain the relationship between the major credit card companies and the PCI-DSS, and why this relationship is important.

A25: The relationship between major credit card companies and the PCI-DSS is foundational to the payment card security ecosystem. According to the content, major credit card companies including Visa, MasterCard, American Express, Discover, JCB, and UnionPay have collectively adopted the PCI-DSS as part of their data security compliance programs.

This relationship is important for several key reasons:

1. Unified security approach: By adopting a common standard, these companies ensure consistent security practices across the entire payment card industry. This creates a more reliable security baseline than if each card brand maintained separate, potentially conflicting standards.

2. Mandatory compliance mechanism: The credit card companies serve as the enforcement mechanism for PCI-DSS. They can impose consequences for non-compliance, including financial penalties and the suspension of payment processing privileges, giving the standard real authority.

3. Industry-wide reach: These major card brands collectively dominate the global payment card market, meaning their adoption of PCI-DSS effectively makes it an industry-wide requirement rather than just a suggested best practice.

4. Risk reduction: This relationship helps reduce the overall risk in the payment ecosystem. Since these companies bear significant financial risk from fraud and data breaches, their investment in and support of PCI-DSS serves their business interests while also protecting consumers.

5. Global standardization: The international presence of these credit card companies helps ensure PCI-DSS is implemented globally, creating a worldwide security standard rather than a patchwork of regional approaches.

The relationship between these major card brands and the PCI-DSS represents a rare example of industry-wide collaboration on security standards, demonstrating how competitive companies can work together to address common security challenges that affect the entire industry and its customers.

Additional resource: securitymetrics.com/blog/what-are-12-requirements-pci-dss-compliance

3

The Payment Brands - Question Set

PCI DSS Payment Brands: Question and Answer Set

Q1: Which of the following is NOT one of the six payment brands behind PCI-DSS Compliance? A) American Express B) PayPal C) JCB International D) UnionPay

A1: The correct answer is B) PayPal. The six payment brands that are behind PCI-DSS Compliance are American Express, Discover Financial Services, JCB International, MasterCard Worldwide, Visa International, and UnionPay. PayPal is a payment processor but not one of the six card brands that established or maintain the PCI DSS standards.

For more information: https://www.pcisecuritystandards.org/about_us/

Q2: True or False: Each payment brand has its own PCI DSS compliance program, but the PCI DSS requirements vary between brands.

A2: False. While each of the six payment brands does develop and maintain its own PCI DSS compliance program under its security risk management policies, all PCI DSS requirements are common to all PCI DSS-compliant organizations. The requirements themselves don't vary between brands, although the specific compliance programs and implementation details may differ.

For more information: https://www.pcisecuritystandards.org/pci_security/maintaining_payment_security

Q3: What is the name of Visa Inc.'s PCI DSS compliance program?

A3: Visa Inc.'s PCI DSS compliance program is called the Cardholder Information Security Program (CISP). This is distinct from Visa Europe's program, which is called the Account Information Security (AIS) Program. Each payment brand maintains its own branded compliance program while adhering to the common PCI DSS requirements.

For more information: https://usa.visa.com/partner-with-us/pci-dss-compliance-information.html

Q4: Which payment brand joined the PCI Security Standards Council as a strategic member in 2020? A) JCB International B) UnionPay C) Discover Financial Services D) MasterCard Worldwide

A4: The correct answer is B) UnionPay. According to the provided content, UnionPay became a strategic member of the PCI Security Standards Council (PCI SSC) in 2020. The other five payment brands were part of establishing the council earlier.

For more information: https://www.pcisecuritystandards.org/about_us/member_companies/

Q5: Name three responsibilities encompassed by payment brand compliance programs.

A5: According to the content, payment brand compliance programs encompass several responsibilities including:

1. Tracking and enforcement
2. Penalties, fees, compliance deadlines
3. Validation process and who needs to validate
4. Approval and posting of compliant entities
5. Definition of merchant and service provider levels

Any three of these responsibilities would constitute a correct answer.

For more information: https://www.pcisecuritystandards.org/faqs/

Q6: What is American Express's PCI DSS compliance program called? A) Cardholder Information Security Program B) Site Data Protection C) Data Security Operating Policy D) Account Information Security Program

A6: The correct answer is C) Data Security Operating Policy (DSOP). Each payment brand has its own named compliance program, and American Express's is specifically called the Data Security Operating Policy. This program establishes American Express's requirements for protecting cardholder data in accordance with PCI DSS.

For more information: https://www.americanexpress.com/us/merchant/support/data-security.html

Q7: Describe the role of payment brands in the PCI-DSS validation process and their response to data breaches.

A7: Payment brands play a crucial role in the PCI-DSS validation process and in responding to data breaches. In the validation process, they are the ultimate authority regarding PCI-DSS compliance and accept validation documentation only from trusted QSAs (Qualified Security Assessors) and ASV (Approved Scanning Vendor) companies. They assess the quality of validation documentation to ensure it meets their high standards and give their seal of approval only to entities that have met the rigorous qualifications.

In terms of data breach response, payment brands define rules for forensic analysis to address data breaches. They provide oversight and support investigations of account data compromises. If a data breach occurs, there are specific contacts at each payment brand that affected entities need to reach out to, as listed on the PCI SSC website (FAQ 1142).

Payment brands serve as guardians of account data security, ensuring that businesses maintain top-notch security standards. They monitor and enforce security measures, impose penalties and fees for non-compliance, carry out validation processes, and define the levels of merchants and service providers. Their role extends beyond being figureheads; they actively ensure that all validation documentation is of high quality and that appropriate responses are implemented when data breaches occur.

For more information: https://www.pcisecuritystandards.org/pci_security/responding_to_a_breach

Q8: True or False: The PCI Security Standards Council was initially established by all six payment brands mentioned in the content.

A8: False. According to the content, the Payment Card Industry Security Standards Council was established by five of the biggest payment brands: American Express, Discover Financial Services, JCB International, MasterCard Worldwide, and Visa International. UnionPay is mentioned as a "recent addition," having become a strategic member in 2020, and was not part of the initial establishment of the council.

For more information: https://www.pcisecuritystandards.org/about_us/

Q9: What is Mastercard's PCI DSS compliance program called? A) Data Security Program B) Site Data Protection C) Account Information Security Program D) Cardholder Information Security Program

A9: The correct answer is B) Site Data Protection (SDP). Each payment brand has its own compliance program, and Mastercard's is specifically called Site Data Protection. This program establishes Mastercard's requirements for protecting cardholder data in accordance with PCI DSS.

For more information: https://www.mastercard.us/en-us/business/overview/safety-and-security/security-recommendations/site-data-protection-PCI.html

Q10: Where can one find information about contacts for different payment brands in case of a data breach?

A10: Information about contacts for different payment brands in case of a data breach can be found on the PCI SSC website, specifically in FAQ 1142. This resource provides a list of contacts for different payment brands, along with helpful information on what to do if a data breach occurs, and a list of security do's and don'ts for making online payments safely.

For more information: https://www.pcisecuritystandards.org/faqs/

Q11: Which of the following is NOT a responsibility encompassed by payment brand compliance programs? A) Tracking and enforcement B) Penalties and fees for non-compliance C) Setting interest rates for credit cards D) Definition of merchant and service provider levels

A11: The correct answer is C) Setting interest rates for credit cards. According to the content, payment brand compliance programs encompass responsibilities such as tracking and enforcement, penalties and fees for non-compliance, validation processes, approval and posting of compliant entities, and definition of merchant and service provider levels. Setting interest rates for credit cards is not mentioned as part of their compliance program responsibilities, as this relates to the financial product offerings rather than security compliance.

For more information: https://www.pcisecuritystandards.org/pci_security/standards_overview

Q12: True or False: JCB International's PCI DSS compliance program is called the Site Data Protection.

A12: False. According to the content, JCB International's PCI DSS compliance program is called the Data Security Program, not Site Data Protection. Site Data Protection (SDP) is Mastercard's compliance program. Each payment brand has its own distinct compliance program name.

For more information: https://www.global.jcb/en/products/security/data-security-program.html

Q13: Explain the significance of the six payment brands in the context of PCI-DSS compliance and their role in protecting businesses and consumers.

A13: The six payment brands (American Express, Discover Financial Services, JCB International, MasterCard Worldwide, Visa International, and UnionPay) play a significant role in the context of PCI-DSS compliance and in protecting both businesses and consumers.

These brands serve as the foundation of PCI-DSS compliance, with five of them having established the Payment Card Industry Security Standards Council (with UnionPay joining later as a strategic member). Each brand maintains its own compliance program under its security risk management policies, though all adhere to the common PCI DSS requirements.

The significance of these payment brands lies in their authority and oversight in the compliance process. They act as guardians of payment card security by:

1. Setting and enforcing security standards
2. Determining penalties and fees for non-compliance
3. Defining who needs to validate compliance and through what processes
4. Approving and publicly listing compliant entities
5. Categorizing merchants and service providers into different levels

These brands accept validation documentation only from trusted QSAs and ASV companies, ensuring that only entities meeting rigorous qualifications receive their seal of approval. They assess the quality of validation documentation against their high standards.

In the unfortunate event of a data breach, payment brands define the rules for forensic analysis and provide oversight and support for investigations. They maintain a list of contacts and resources to guide affected entities through the proper response procedures.

Through these roles, the six payment brands protect businesses by ensuring they maintain appropriate security measures, reducing their risk of breaches and associated costs. They protect consumers by safeguarding their payment card data and providing a secure ecosystem for electronic transactions. Their vigilance in monitoring account data security helps maintain trust in the global payment card system, which benefits the entire economy.

For more information: https://www.pcisecuritystandards.org/pci_security/why_security_matters

Q14: What is Visa Europe's PCI DSS compliance program called? A) Cardholder Information Security Program (CISP) B) Account Information Security (AIS) Program C) Site Data Protection (SDP) D) Data Security Operating Policy (DSOP)

A14: The correct answer is B) Account Information Security (AIS) Program. According to the content, Visa Europe's PCI DSS compliance program is specifically called the Account Information Security (AIS) Program, which is distinct from Visa Inc.'s program, the Cardholder Information Security Program (CISP). This reflects the previously separate operational structures of Visa in different regions.

For more information: https://www.visaeurope.com/receiving-payments/security/

Q15: What metaphor does the content use to describe the role of payment brands in PCI-DSS compliance?

A15: The content uses the metaphor of "guardians" to describe the role of payment brands in PCI-DSS compliance. Specifically, it states that the payment brands serve as "guardians of account data security" and that they can be thought of as "guardians who closely monitor account data to ensure that all security standards are met." This metaphor emphasizes their protective and oversight role in maintaining the security of cardholder data.

For more information: https://www.pcisecuritystandards.org/about_us/

Q16: True or False: Payment brands accept validation documentation from any qualified security professional.

A16: False. According to the content, payment brands accept validation documentation only from "the most trusted QSAs and ASV companies." This indicates that there is a specific set of qualified security assessors and approved scanning vendors that are authorized to provide validation documentation that payment brands will accept. These assessors and vendors must be approved by the PCI Security Standards Council.

For more information: https://www.pcisecuritystandards.org/assessors_and_solutions/qualified_security_assessors

Q17: What do payment brands provide in the context of data breach investigations? A) Financial compensation to affected customers B) Oversight and support C) Legal representation D) Technology repair services

A17: The correct answer is B) Oversight and support. According to the content, payment brands "provide oversight and support investigations of account data compromises." They define rules for forensic analysis to address data breaches and offer guidance through their contacts and resources listed on the PCI SSC website. Their role is to guide and oversee the investigation process rather than providing direct financial compensation, legal representation, or technology repair services.

For more information: https://www.pcisecuritystandards.org/pci_security/responding_to_a_breach

Q18: Compare and contrast the compliance programs of two payment brands and discuss why each brand might maintain its own program despite common PCI DSS requirements.

A18: Two payment brands with distinct compliance programs are Visa Inc. with its Cardholder Information Security Program (CISP) and American Express with its Data Security Operating Policy (DSOP).

Visa Inc.'s CISP was one of the earliest payment card security programs, focusing on ensuring merchants and service providers implement measures to protect cardholder data. It includes requirements for secure networks, protection of cardholder data, vulnerability management, access control, monitoring and testing, and maintaining an information security policy.

American Express's DSOP similarly aims to protect cardholder data but may have specific emphases reflecting American Express's business model, which differs from Visa's in that American Express often serves as both the card issuer and the acquiring bank. This integrated approach might influence how American Express structures its compliance program.

While the fundamental PCI DSS requirements are common across all brands, each brand maintains its own program for several reasons:

1. Different business models: Each payment brand has a unique business model and relationship with merchants, acquirers, and issuers, which may require specific implementation approaches.
2. Risk management priorities: Each brand may have different risk assessments and priorities based on their customer base, geographic presence, and past security incidents.
3. Historical development: These programs developed over time, often before the formation of the PCI SSC, and brands maintain them for continuity and to address specific concerns not fully covered by the standardized requirements.
4. Brand-specific requirements: Brands may impose additional requirements beyond the base PCI DSS standards to address specific vulnerabilities or concerns relevant to their payment ecosystem.
5. Enforcement mechanisms: Each brand may have different approaches to enforcement, penalties, and incentives based on their market position and business relationships.

By maintaining their own programs while adhering to common PCI DSS requirements, payment brands can balance standardization (which simplifies compliance for merchants and service providers dealing with multiple card brands) with customization (which allows them to address their specific security needs and business contexts).

For more information: https://www.pcisecuritystandards.org/merchants/process

Q19: Which of the following is a responsibility of payment brands regarding compliant entities? A) Providing direct technical support B) Offering financial incentives for compliance C) Approval and posting of compliant entities D) Managing the entities' customer service operations

A19: The correct answer is C) Approval and posting of compliant entities. According to the content, one of the responsibilities encompassed by payment brand compliance programs is "Approval and posting of compliant entities." This means that payment brands review compliance documentation, approve entities that meet the requirements, and publicly list those compliant entities, creating transparency in the market about which organizations maintain proper security standards.

For more information: https://www.pcisecuritystandards.org/assessors_and_solutions/vpa_agreement

Q20: What does FAQ 1142 on the PCI SSC website provide information about?

A20: According to the content, FAQ 1142 on the PCI SSC website provides information about contacts for different payment brands, what to do if a data breach occurs, and a list of security do's and don'ts to help stay safe while making online payments. This resource is mentioned as a place to learn more about payment brands and their role in data breach response, making it a valuable reference for organizations dealing with security incidents.

For more information: https://www.pcisecuritystandards.org/faqs/

Q21: True or False: Payment brands are responsible for defining merchant and service provider levels in the PCI-DSS ecosystem.

A21: True. According to the content, one of the responsibilities encompassed by payment brand compliance programs is the "Definition of merchant and service provider levels." This means that payment brands establish the criteria for categorizing merchants and service providers into different levels, which often determines their validation requirements. Different merchant levels typically correspond to transaction volume and risk, with higher levels requiring more rigorous validation procedures.

For more information: https://www.pcisecuritystandards.org/merchants/

Q22: How many payment brands initially established the Payment Card Industry Security Standards Council? A) Three B) Four C) Five D) Six

A22: The correct answer is C) Five. According to the content, "Five of the biggest payment brands in the world established the Payment Card Industry Security Standards Council: American Express, Discover Financial Services, JCB International, MasterCard Worldwide, and Visa International." UnionPay is mentioned as a "recent addition," having become a strategic member in 2020, after the initial establishment of the council.

For more information: https://www.pcisecuritystandards.org/about_us/

Q23: What are payment brands described as regarding the validation documentation for PCI-DSS compliance?

A23: Payment brands are described as "the ultimate authority regarding PCI-DSS compliance" in relation to validation documentation. The content states that they "accept validation documentation from only the most trusted QSAs and ASV companies" and "assess the quality of validation documentation, ensuring it meets their high standards." This emphasizes their role as the final arbiters of compliance status and their responsibility to maintain the integrity of the validation process.

For more information: https://www.pcisecuritystandards.org/merchants/process

Q24: Discuss the enforcement aspects of payment brand compliance programs and the potential impact of non-compliance on businesses accepting payment cards.

A24: Payment brand compliance programs include significant enforcement aspects that can have substantial impacts on businesses accepting payment cards. Understanding these enforcement mechanisms is crucial for any organization handling payment card data.

The enforcement aspects of payment brand compliance programs include:

1. Tracking and Enforcement: Payment brands actively monitor compliance status and enforce their security requirements. This may involve regular reporting, scheduled assessments, and verification processes to ensure ongoing adherence to standards.

2. Penalties and Fees: The content explicitly mentions that payment brands establish "penalties, fees, compliance deadlines" as part of their programs. Non-compliant businesses may face financial penalties that vary by brand and can escalate based on factors such as business size, violation severity, duration of non-compliance, and whether breaches have occurred.

3. Compliance Deadlines: Brands set timelines by which merchants and service providers must achieve compliance. Missing these deadlines can trigger penalties or increased scrutiny.

4. Validation Requirements: Payment brands determine who needs to validate compliance and through what processes. Higher-risk or larger-volume merchants and service providers typically face more rigorous validation requirements.

The potential impact of non-compliance on businesses can be severe and multifaceted:

1. Financial Consequences: Direct penalties and fees can range from thousands to millions of dollars depending on the business size and violation severity. These costs can significantly impact profitability.

2. Increased Transaction Fees: Some payment brands may impose higher per-transaction fees on non-compliant merchants, directly affecting operational costs.

3. Reputational Damage: Non-compliant merchants may be publicly listed or have their compliant status revoked, potentially damaging their reputation with customers and partners.

4. Loss of Card Processing Privileges: In extreme cases, payment brands may prohibit non-compliant entities from processing their cards, which could devastate businesses reliant on card payments.

5. Increased Liability: Non-compliant merchants may face increased liability in the event of a data breach, potentially bearing

more of the costs associated with fraud, card reissuance, and customer notification.

6. Operational Disruption: Addressing non-compliance often requires significant operational changes, potentially disrupting business processes and requiring resource reallocation.

The enforcement aspects of payment brand compliance programs serve as powerful motivators for businesses to maintain PCI-DSS compliance, ultimately protecting both their operations and their customers' data.

For more information: https://www.pcisecuritystandards.org/pci_security/maintaining_payment_security

Q25: What is JCB International's PCI DSS compliance program called? A) Cardholder Information Security Program B) Data Security Program C) Site Data Protection D) Data Security Operating Policy

A25: The correct answer is B) Data Security Program. According to the content, JCB International's PCI DSS compliance program is specifically called the Data Security Program. Each payment brand maintains its own named compliance program that implements the PCI DSS requirements within their specific ecosystem and business model.

For more information: https://www.global.jcb/en/products/security/data-security-program.html

4

The Hidden Dangers of Ignoring the PCI-Data Security Standard - Question Set

Q1: According to the content, what percentage of data breaches involving stolen credentials use vendor remote access to infiltrate customers' point of sale systems? A) 75% B) 85% C) 90% D) 95%

A1: The correct answer is D) 95%. According to Verizon's Data Breach Investigation Report 2017 cited in the content, almost all data breaches (95%) involving stolen credentials use vendor remote access to infiltrate their customers' point of sale (PoS) systems. This statistic highlights the critical importance of securing vendor access to payment systems and implementing strong authentication protocols. Businesses must carefully monitor and restrict vendor access to their systems to prevent unauthorized access that could lead to data breaches and financial losses.

For more information: https://www.verizon.com/business/resources/reports/dbir/

Q2: Which of the following is NOT mentioned as an industry that is particularly vulnerable to hacker attacks according to the content? A) Retail B) Food services C) Healthcare D) Financial organizations

A2: The correct answer is C) Healthcare. The content specifically mentions that the industries most vulnerable to hacker attacks include retail, information services, financial organizations, food services, hospitality, and accommodation. While healthcare is indeed a frequently targeted industry in reality, it was not explicitly mentioned in the provided content as one of the most vulnerable industries to hacker attacks in the context of payment card data breaches.

For more information: https://www.pcisecuritystandards.org/documents/PCI_DSS_v4_Industry_Insights.pdf

Q3: TRUE or FALSE: PCI-DSS version 4.0 will require multi-factor authentication only for administrative access to the cardholder data environment.

A3: FALSE. According to the content, PCI-DSS version 4.0 will require merchants to implement multi-factor authentication for ALL access to the cardholder data environment (CDE), not just administrative access. This is a significant security enhancement from previous versions and is designed to prevent unauthorized access to sensitive cardholder data. This requirement recognizes that any access point to the CDE represents a potential security risk that must be protected with strong authentication methods.

For more information: https://blog.pcisecuritystandards.org/preparing-for-pci-dss-v4-0

Q4: What was the total financial loss due to credit card fraud in the United States in 2023 according to the provided statistics? A) $2.1 million B) $8.6 billion C) $14.8 billion D) $21.3 billion

A4: The correct answer is C) $14.8 billion. According to the statistics provided in the content, credit card fraud in the United States reached new heights in 2023 with over 2.1 million reported fraud cases and $14.8 billion in total losses. The content also mentions a 69% increase in digital payment fraud compared to 2022 and that 44% of Americans experienced credit card fraud in the past two years. These statistics emphasize the growing threat of payment card fraud and the urgent need for enhanced security measures.

For more information: https://www.ftc.gov/reports/consumer-sentinel-network-data-book

Q5: What does the acronym CHD stand for in the context of PCI-DSS?

A5: CHD stands for Cardholder Data. This refers to the sensitive information associated with payment cards that needs to be protected under the PCI-DSS framework. Cardholder data includes the primary account number (PAN) along with any of the following elements: cardholder name, expiration date, and service code. The content explains that criminals target CHD to sell it to other fraudsters or to use it for fraudulent transactions. Protecting CHD is a core objective of PCI-DSS compliance and essential for any organization that processes, stores, or transmits payment card information.

For more information: https://www.pcisecuritystandards.org/pci_security/glossary

Q6: Which of the following is described in the content as a social engineering tactic where criminals send messages appearing to come from trusted sources? A) Card skimming B) Phishing C) Malware D) Rootkit

A6: The correct answer is B) Phishing. The content describes phishing as a social engineering tactic that involves sending messages that appear to come from trustworthy sources such as banks, social media platforms, or other providers. These deceptive messages often ask for login credentials or personal information, and when users fall for these scams, their data can be compromised. Cybercriminals using phishing tactics are experts at making their communications appear legitimate while their actual intention is to steal sensitive information.

For more information: https://www.cisa.gov/phishing

Q7: According to the content, what is the estimated worldwide cost of skimming? A) $1 billion B) $2 billion C) $3 billion D) $4 billion

A7: The correct answer is B) $2 billion. The content states that skimming costs an estimated $2 billion worldwide. Skimming is a technique where criminals steal credit or debit card information by copying the data from the magnetic strip on a card using specialized devices placed over legitimate card readers. This significant financial impact underscores why understanding and preventing skimming attacks is crucial for payment card security professionals.

For more information: https://www.uspaymentsforum.org/card-skimming-prevention/

Q8: TRUE or FALSE: In PCI-DSS context, SAD refers to Secure Access Data.

A8: FALSE. In the context of PCI-DSS, SAD stands for Sensitive Authentication Data, not Secure Access Data. As mentioned in the content, SAD is data that criminals can steal and use to create fraudulent cloned cards. Sensitive Authentication Data includes security-related information (like card validation codes/values, full track data from the magnetic stripe or chip, and PINs) that is used to authenticate cardholders during transactions. This data is particularly valuable to criminals because it can be used to create counterfeit payment cards or conduct fraudulent transactions.

For more information: https://www.pcisecuritystandards.org/glossary/sensitive-authentication-data-sad/

Q9: Which of the following is NOT mentioned as a form of malware in the content? A) Spyware B) Rootkits C) Ransomware D) Adware

A9: The correct answer is C) Ransomware. The content mentions various forms of malware including worms, viruses, trojans, spyware, adware, and rootkits, but does not specifically mention ransomware. The content describes how malware can steal sensitive information, bombard users with unwanted ads, spread quickly through systems, and potentially compromise PCI-DSS compliance by allowing unauthorized access to credit card information. While ransomware is indeed a significant type of malware in today's cybersecurity landscape, it was not explicitly mentioned in the provided content.

For more information: https://www.cisa.gov/stopransomware

Q10: Describe at least three methods criminals use to steal payment card data according to the content.

A10: According to the content, criminals use several methods to steal payment card data:

1. Card Skimming: Criminals place skimming devices over legitimate card readers on terminals, ATMs, or kiosks to capture and copy the data from magnetic strips on payment cards. These devices can be small enough to fit in the palm of a hand and difficult to detect.
2. Phishing: This social engineering tactic involves sending deceptive messages that appear to come from trusted sources like banks or social media platforms to trick users into revealing their login credentials or personal information.
3. Malware: Various forms of malicious software (including worms, viruses, trojans, spyware, adware, and rootkits) can be used to infiltrate systems and steal sensitive payment card information from customers making purchases.

4. Insider Threats: Employees or contractors with access to payment systems may intentionally or unintentionally compromise security, such as by mishandling credit card information or stealing data.

5. Code Injection: The content mentions that criminals can inject skimming code into e-commerce sites to steal payment data during online transactions.

6. Exploitation of Weak Passwords: Criminals can gain unauthorized access to payment systems by exploiting weak password policies.

7. Vendor Remote Access Exploitation: Criminals can use stolen credentials to access point of sale systems through vendor remote access channels.

These methods highlight the diverse attack vectors that payment card security professionals must address through proper implementation of PCI-DSS controls.

For more information: https://www.pcisecuritystandards.org/document_library/

Q11: What percentage of Americans experienced credit card fraud in the two years preceding 2023, according to the content? A) 24% B) 34% C) 44% D) 54%

A11: The correct answer is C) 44%. According to the statistics provided in the content, 44% of Americans experienced credit card fraud in the past two years (preceding 2023). This significant percentage demonstrates the widespread nature of payment card fraud and emphasizes why robust security measures like those mandated by PCI-DSS are essential for protecting consumers and businesses alike. This statistic, along with the other fraud data presented (over 2.1 million reported fraud cases and $14.8 billion in total losses), paints a picture of a serious and growing security challenge.

For more information: https://www.ftc.gov/business-guidance/resources/data-breach-response-guide-business

Q12: What significant emphasis does PCI-DSS version 4.0 place that represents a change from previous versions? A) Physical security B) Risk management C) Encryption standards D) Employee training

A12: The correct answer is B) Risk management. According to the content, a significant change in PCI-DSS version 4.0 is the emphasis on risk management. The new version requires merchants to conduct regular risk assessments to identify potential vulnerabilities and take appropriate measures to address them. This shift towards a more risk-based approach allows organizations to better tailor their security controls to their specific environments and threat landscapes, while still maintaining the baseline security requirements that protect cardholder data.

For more information: https://blog.pcisecuritystandards.org/pci-dss-v4-0-resource-hub

Q13: TRUE or FALSE: According to the content, criminals who steal payment card data generally avoid interfering with Point of Sale devices due to their high security.

A13: FALSE. The content explicitly states that criminals who steal payment card data interfere with things like PoS (Point of Sale) devices, ATMs, and kiosks. It further mentions that it can be difficult to spot the difference between legitimate devices and fake fascias installed by criminals. The content also describes how criminals can infiltrate retail stores and gain positions behind counters where they can use skimming devices without being detected. This information contradicts the statement that criminals avoid interfering with PoS devices.

For more information: https://www.fbi.gov/scams-and-safety/common-scams-and-crimes/credit-card-fraud

Q14: What does the content identify as the most common type of identity theft according to the Federal Trade Commission? A) Social Security fraud B) Card fraud C) Tax fraud D) Medical identity theft

A14: The correct answer is B) Card fraud. According to the content, the Federal Trade Commission reports card fraud as the most common type of identity theft. The content specifically mentions that criminals are increasingly targeting digital payments and contactless transactions. This trend highlights the importance of enhanced security protocols and consumer education about payment card security. The fact that card fraud tops the list of identity theft types underscores why PCI-DSS compliance is critical for organizations that handle payment card information.

For more information: https://www.identitytheft.gov/

Q15: Explain what a "skimming device" is and how criminals use it to steal payment card information.

A15: A skimming device is a specialized tool used by criminals to steal credit or debit card information by copying the data from the magnetic strip on payment cards. According to the content, criminals use these devices in the following way:

The skimming devices are physically placed over legitimate card readers on the front of payment terminals, ATMs, or kiosks. These overlay devices are designed to look like part of the original equipment and can be difficult to detect by the average person.

When a customer inserts or swipes their card, the skimming device captures and copies the data from the magnetic strip. This data is then stored or transmitted to the criminal's computer.

The content notes that these devices can be remarkably small - small enough to fit in the palm of a hand - making them easy to install and difficult to notice. Some criminals manage to get trusted positions behind counters in retail stores where they can use these skimming devices without being seen.

With the stolen data, criminals can create fraudulent cloned cards for making unauthorized purchases or sell the information to other fraudsters on the Dark Web. The content mentions that skimming costs an estimated $2 billion worldwide, demonstrating its significance as a threat to payment card security.

For effective protection, PCIP professionals should know how to identify signs of tampering with payment terminals and implement security measures that can detect or prevent the installation of skimming devices.

For more information: https://www.consumer.ftc.gov/articles/how-spot-avoid-and-report-fake-check-scams

Q16: Which of the following is described in the content as a way criminals can use data captured from skimming without having physical cards? A) Face-to-face transactions B) eCommerce transactions C) ATM withdrawals D) Card-present retail purchases

A16: The correct answer is B) eCommerce transactions. The content states that criminals can use captured card data to make fraudulent transactions without having physical cards, specifically mentioning eCommerce or mail-order/telephone order transactions (MOTO) as examples. These types of transactions are often referred to as "card-not-present" transactions because they don't require the physical presence of the payment card. Criminals exploit the fact that these transaction types rely primarily on data rather than the physical card, making them attractive targets for fraud after data has been skimmed or otherwise compromised.

For more information: https://www.pcisecuritystandards.org/pci_security/small_merchant_resources

Q17: According to the content, what was the percentage increase in digital payment fraud in 2023 compared to 2022? A) 29% B) 49% C) 69% D) 89%

A17: The correct answer is C) 69%. According to the statistics provided in the content, there was a 69% increase in digital payment fraud in 2023 compared to 2022. This significant increase reflects the rapidly growing threat landscape for digital payments and highlights why organizations need to maintain robust security measures to protect against evolving threats. This statistic is part of a larger set of concerning fraud metrics for 2023, including over 2.1 million reported fraud cases, $14.8 billion in total losses, and 44% of Americans experiencing credit card fraud in the previous two years.

For more information: https://www.ftc.gov/reports/consumer-protection-data-spotlight

Q18: What real-world example of a data breach is mentioned in the content that illustrates the importance of securing third-party vendor access?

A18: The Target data breach of 2013 is the real-world example mentioned in the content. This breach is used to illustrate the importance of securing third-party vendor access to systems that process or store payment card information. In this incident, hackers were able to steal credit card information from over 40 million Target customers by exploiting vulnerabilities in Target's payment system.

Specifically, the content notes that the hackers gained access by compromising the credentials of an HVAC contractor who had access to Target's network. This highlights the critical need for organizations to secure not only their own systems but also to manage and restrict access for third-party vendors and contractors who might have access to sensitive data.

This example underscores a key aspect of PCI-DSS compliance: the security of the entire payment ecosystem, including all entities that might touch cardholder data, is only as strong as its weakest link. Proper vendor management, including thorough background checks and implementation of appropriate access controls, is essential for protecting cardholder data from compromise.

For more information: https://www.sans.org/blog/target-breach-lessons-learned/

Q19: TRUE or FALSE: According to the content, contactless card payments have no security risks associated with them.

A19: FALSE. The content explicitly states that there are security risks associated with contactless card payments, despite their convenience. The content mentions at least two specific security risks:

1. Card skimming: Thieves can potentially steal card information by reading the data off the card while a purchase is being made.

2. Card cloning: A thief can create a fake card containing stolen Sensitive Authentication Data (SAD) and use it to make contactless payments, giving them access to the victim's money.

The content acknowledges that contactless payments are convenient but emphasizes that users should be aware of these security risks. This information is relevant for PCIP professionals who need to understand the vulnerabilities associated with different payment methods to implement appropriate security controls.

For more information: https://www.pcisecuritystandards.org/documents/Mobile_Payment_Security_Guidelines.pdf

Q20: What is the most significant insider threat to PCI-DSS compliance mentioned in the content?

A20: According to the content, the most significant insider threat to PCI-DSS compliance is when someone within the company (such as an employee or contractor) intentionally or unintentionally causes harm to the organization by mishandling credit card information, stealing data, or selling it on the dark web.

The content explains that insider threats represent a real danger that can compromise sensitive data and put businesses at risk. It emphasizes that these threats come from within the organization itself, making them particularly dangerous because insiders already have authorized access to systems and data.

The content notes that insider threats can lead to:

- Customers' personal and financial information being put at risk
- Hefty fines for the organization
- Damage to the business's reputation
- Significant financial impact (citing that the average cost of a data breach in 2020 was $3.86 million)

To counter insider threats, the content recommends implementing proper security measures such as:

- Strong access controls
- Regularly reviewing and updating security protocols
- Conducting thorough background checks on contractors and vendors
- Training staff on the correct handling of confidential information

This highlights the importance of not only technical controls but also administrative safeguards in maintaining PCI-DSS compliance.

For more information: https://www.cisecurity.org/insights/white-papers/insider-threats-in-the-financial-services-industry

Q21: According to the content, what percentage of organizations is immune to malicious attacks targeting cardholder data? A) 5% B) 10% C) 25% D) None

A21: The correct answer is D) None. The content explicitly states that "no organization is immune to these malicious attacks" when referring to attacks targeting cardholder data (CHD) and sensitive authentication data (SAD). This emphasizes the universal nature of the threat landscape for payment card security and why all organizations that accept payments via credit or debit cards must prioritize security measures. The statement reinforces the idea that cybersecurity is an essential concern for all organizations regardless of their size, industry, or current security posture.

For more information: https://www.pcisecuritystandards.org/about_us/

Q22: Which of the following is NOT mentioned in the content as a method criminals use to form communities? A) Sharing data online B) Sharing information online C) Using reconnaissance tools D) Attending underground conferences

A22: The correct answer is D) Attending underground conferences. While the content mentions that criminals form online communities to share data and information and use reconnaissance and social engineering tools, it does not specifically mention criminals attending underground conferences. The content focuses on digital methods of collaboration and information sharing among cybercriminals rather than physical meetings or conferences. Understanding how criminals operate and collaborate is important for PCIP professionals to better comprehend the threat landscape they're working to mitigate.

For more information: https://www.interpol.int/Crimes/Cybercrime

Q23: Describe the importance of having qualified PCIPs on a team according to the content.

A23: According to the content, having qualified Payment Card Industry Professionals (PCIPs) on a team is crucial for several important reasons:

1. Protection of Data: PCIPs protect an organization's data from the harmful intentions of cybercriminals. They have the specialized knowledge and skills needed to implement effective security controls that safeguard sensitive cardholder information.

2. Customer Data Security: With qualified PCIPs on the team, organizations can be confident that their customers' data is in excellent hands. This ensures that customer information is properly protected throughout its lifecycle within the organization.

3. Business Focus: By having PCIPs handle security concerns, organizations can focus on growing their business without worrying about security breaches. This allows for better allocation of resources and attention to core business functions.

4. Staying Current with PCI Controls: The content mentions that PCIPs ensure organizations stay current with PCI controls and requirements to protect the Cardholder Data Environment (CDE) from digital thieves. This is particularly important

as security threats and compliance requirements evolve over time.

5. Professional Expertise: PCIPs bring specialized expertise in identifying and addressing vulnerabilities in payment systems before they can be exploited by cybercriminals.

The content portrays qualified PCIPs as essential guardians of an organization's payment card data security, providing both technical expertise and peace of mind for businesses that process payment card transactions.

For more information: https://www.pcisecuritystandards.org/programs/pcip/

Q24: According to the content, which of the following is a change in PCI-DSS version 4.0 compared to previous versions? A) Introduction of self-assessment questionnaires B) Requirement for multi-factor authentication for all CDE access C) Elimination of quarterly vulnerability scans D) Reduced emphasis on risk management

A24: The correct answer is B) Requirement for multi-factor authentication for all CDE access. The content specifically states that PCI-DSS version 4.0 "will require merchants to implement multi-factor authentication for all access to the cardholder data environment (CDE) to prevent unauthorized access." This represents a strengthening of authentication requirements compared to previous versions. Additionally, the content mentions an increased emphasis on risk management in version 4.0, not a reduced emphasis, making option D incorrect. The content does not discuss elimination of vulnerability scans or the introduction of self-assessment questionnaires as changes in version 4.0.

For more information: https://blog.pcisecuritystandards.org/first-look-at-pci-dss-v4-0

Q25: Explain how criminals use the Dark Web in relation to payment card data according to the content.

A25: According to the content, criminals use the Dark Web as a marketplace for stolen payment card data in the following ways:

The content explains that after criminals capture card data through methods like skimming, phishing, or malware, they can sell this stolen data on the Dark Web to other fraudsters. This creates a criminal ecosystem where one set of criminals specializes in stealing the data, while others purchase it to commit further fraudulent activities.

Specifically, the content states: "Criminals are always on the lookout to get your card data, which they can sell on the Dark Web to other fraudsters." This indicates that the Dark Web serves as a platform for monetizing stolen cardholder data (CHD) and sensitive authentication data (SAD).

The buyers of this stolen data can then use it to conduct fraudulent transactions without having physical cards, particularly focusing on eCommerce or mail-order/telephone order transactions (MOTO) where the physical card isn't required.

The content emphasizes that criminals "sell them [CHD and SAD] in bulk to other criminals who will use this information to commit their crimes." This suggests that the Dark Web enables large-scale trafficking of payment card information, potentially affecting numerous cardholders with each breach.

Understanding this criminal value chain is important for PCIP professionals as it highlights why cardholder data is so valuable to attackers and why protecting it throughout its lifecycle is critical for organizations that process payment card information.

For more information: https://www.justice.gov/criminal-ccips/cybercrime-dark-web

5

The Payment Card Ecosystem - Question Set

Q1: Which of the following are key stakeholders in the payment card ecosystem? (Select all that apply) a) Cardholders b) Issuers c) Merchants d) Acquirers e) Payment Brands f) All of the above

A1: The correct answer is f) All of the above. The payment card ecosystem includes multiple stakeholders who work together to enable secure card transactions. Cardholders are individuals who own and use payment cards. Issuers (banks like HSBC, Citibank) provide cards to consumers. Merchants are businesses that accept card payments for goods and services. Acquirers (banks and payment processors like WorldPay) help merchants process payments. Payment Brands (Visa, Mastercard, American Express, Discover, JCB, and UnionPay) establish the networks and standards for processing transactions. Understanding how these stakeholders interact is crucial for grasping the full scope of the payment card ecosystem and PCI compliance requirements.

Additional resource: https://www.pcisecuritystandards.org/about/

Q2: TRUE or FALSE: American Express is the only payment brand that issues cards directly to customers.

A2: TRUE. According to the provided material, American Express (AMEX) is unique among payment brands because it is the only card brand that issues cards directly to customers. Other payment brands like Visa and Mastercard work through issuing banks who then provide cards to consumers. This direct issuing model makes American Express both an issuer and a payment brand, giving it a distinctive position in the payment card ecosystem. This distinction is important to understand when studying the different roles and responsibilities within the payment card industry for the PCIP exam.

Additional resource: https://www.americanexpress.com/us/merchant/merchant-support.html

Q3: Explain the importance of the payment card ecosystem to the global economy.

A3: The payment card ecosystem is described as "the backbone of the global economy" because it creates a seamless system for processing payments worldwide. This ecosystem enables consumers to easily shop for goods and services globally without friction. The interconnected network of institutions (including banks, credit card companies, and merchants) collaborates to create a platform where merchants can accept card payments and cardholders can make purchases easily. This system works "seamlessly in the background," allowing consumers to focus on their purchases rather than payment logistics. The efficiency of this ecosystem facilitates global trade, e-commerce, and economic activity by providing secure, reliable payment methods that transcend geographical boundaries. Understanding this ecosystem is essential for professionals working with organizations that handle cardholder data to assess and manage compliance risks effectively.

Additional resource: https://www.visa.com/splisting/searchGrsp.do

Q4: Which of the following entities must comply with PCI-DSS standards? a) Only merchants b) Only payment processors c) Only banks that issue credit cards d) All entities storing, processing, and transmitting cardholder information

A4: The correct answer is d) All entities storing, processing, and transmitting cardholder information. PCI-DSS Compliance Standards apply broadly to all participants in the payment card ecosystem who handle cardholder data, including Merchants, Acquirers, Issuers, card manufacturers, and processors. The standards are designed to ensure that any organization involved in payment card transactions maintains a secure environment to protect cardholder data. This comprehensive approach to security is necessary because vulnerabilities at any point in the transaction chain could potentially compromise sensitive payment information. For professionals pursuing PCIP certification, understanding the scope of PCI-DSS application is fundamental to implementing proper security measures and compliance strategies.

Additional resource: https://www.pcisecuritystandards.org/pci_security/maintaining_payment_security

Q5: What are the six major payment brands that act as pillars for PCI DSS compliance?

A5: The six major payment brands that act as pillars for PCI DSS compliance are:

1. Visa
2. Mastercard
3. American Express
4. Discover
5. JCB (Japan Credit Bureau)
6. UnionPay (more recently added)

These payment brands establish and enforce the PCI DSS requirements for their networks. When a transaction occurs using a card from one of these brands and the merchant uses a payment device that accepts payments from these brands, PCI-DSS standards apply to protect the transaction data. Each of these payment brands has slightly different compliance requirements and reporting procedures, but they all support the core PCI DSS framework to ensure consistent security practices across the payment card industry. Understanding the role of these payment brands is crucial for anyone working in payment card security or preparing for the PCIP exam.

Additional resource: https://www.pcisecuritystandards.org/about/participating_organizations/

Q6: How does understanding the payment card ecosystem benefit professionals working with organizations that handle cardholder data?

A6: Understanding the payment card ecosystem provides several key benefits for professionals working with organizations that handle cardholder data:

1. Risk Assessment: It enables professionals to confidently evaluate potential security and compliance risks by knowing how data flows between different stakeholders.

2. Informed Decision-Making: This knowledge allows professionals to make informed decisions on safeguarding cardholder data based on understanding the entire transaction lifecycle.

3. Compliance Management: It helps in ensuring that organizations remain compliant with PCI-DSS standards by understanding which requirements apply to specific roles in the ecosystem.

4. Strategic Planning: Professionals can develop more effective security strategies when they understand the interconnected components of the payment system.

5. Problem Solving: When issues arise, understanding the ecosystem helps identify where in the chain the problem might be occurring and which stakeholders need to be involved in the resolution.

6. Communication: It improves communication with various stakeholders by using appropriate terminology and understanding each party's responsibilities and challenges.

This comprehensive understanding is described as "crucial" in the provided content, highlighting its importance for PCIP certification and professional practice in payment card security.

Additional resource: https://www.pcisecuritystandards.org/documents/PCI_DSS_v4-0.pdf

Q7: Who are cardholders in the payment card ecosystem, and what is their significance?

A7: Cardholders are individuals who own and use debit and credit cards for making purchases. The content describes cardholders as "the drivers of the economic engine" who keep "the wheels turning and the economy humming with a simple swipe or tap." Their significance in the payment card ecosystem is fundamental as they:

1. Generate the demand for payment card services

2. Initiate transactions that keep the entire ecosystem functioning

3. Provide the economic justification for the payment card infrastructure

4. Are the end users whose data must be protected by PCI-DSS standards

The content emphasizes that cardholders shouldn't underestimate the power of their payment cards, describing them as "worth their weight in gold" due to their importance in facilitating commerce. For PCIP candidates, understanding the cardholder's role is essential because protecting their data is ultimately the primary purpose of PCI compliance measures.

Additional resource: https://www.pcisecuritystandards.org/pci_security/why_security_matters

Q8: What function do Acquirers serve in the payment card ecosystem? a) They issue credit and debit cards to consumers b) They help merchants process payments and manage finances c) They establish the rules for payment card transactions d) They are the end users who make purchases with payment cards

A8: The correct answer is b) They help merchants process payments and manage finances. Acquirers, which include both banks (like HSBC, Citibank, and NatWest) and payment processors (such as WorldPay and GlobalPay), provide merchants with the necessary tools and services to accept and process card payments securely. According to the content, acquirers provide electronic payment devices positioned at checkout counters or self-service areas. Their role is essential as merchants could not accept payments securely without these acquiring banks and payment processors. They offer a range of financial tools and services that make it easier for merchants to do business, including transaction processing, settlement services, and payment security measures. Understanding the role of acquirers is important for the PCIP exam as they are key stakeholders in maintaining PCI compliance.

Additional resource: https://www.pcisecuritystandards.org/merchants/

Q9: TRUE or FALSE: Merchants have no responsibility for offering secure payment processes to their customers.

A9: FALSE. According to the provided content, merchants must understand potential risks and "prioritize offering their customers a hassle-free and secure payment process." The material explicitly states that merchants should "stay up-to-date on the latest secure payment technologies and security protocols" to ensure their customers can "shop confidently and safely." This indicates that merchants have significant responsibility for payment security. As entities that directly interact with customers and process card payments, merchants play a crucial role in the security chain and are subject to PCI-DSS compliance requirements. Securing the point of sale and protecting cardholder data during transactions are essential merchant responsibilities within the payment card ecosystem.

Additional resource: https://www.pcisecuritystandards.org/small_merchant_resources/

Q10: Describe the relationship between payment brands and PCI-DSS compliance.

A10: Payment brands (Visa, Mastercard, American Express, Discover, JCB, and UnionPay) are described as the "sturdy pillars of a castle for PCI DSS." These brands established the Payment Card Industry Security Standards Council (PCI SSC) to develop and maintain the PCI-DSS standards. Their relationship with PCI-DSS compliance is multifaceted:

1. Founders and Enforcers: The payment brands created and continue to enforce PCI-DSS requirements within their networks.

2. Scope Definition: When a transaction uses a card from these brands and the merchant accepts payments from these brands, PCI-DSS applies to that transaction.

3. Compliance Mandates: Payment brands require their participating merchants, processors, and service providers to comply with PCI-DSS as part of their contractual agreements.

4. Security Protection: The content metaphorically describes PCI-DSS as a "knight in shining armor" that protects consumer data from malicious actors, with payment brands being the entities that maintain this protection framework.

5. Validation Requirements: Each payment brand has its own specific requirements for validation of PCI compliance, though they all use the same PCI-DSS standard.

This relationship ensures consistent security practices across the payment card industry while allowing the brands to maintain their distinct network rules.

Additional resource: https://www.pcisecuritystandards.org/pci_security/standards_overview

Q11: What unique characteristic distinguishes American Express from other payment brands? a) It's the only brand that doesn't require PCI compliance b) It's the only brand that issues cards directly to customers c) It's the only brand that works with acquirers d) It's the only brand that operates globally

A11: The correct answer is b) It's the only brand that issues cards directly to customers. According to the provided content, "American Express (AMEX), is the only card brand that issues cards directly to customers." This makes American Express unique in the payment card ecosystem as it serves dual roles - both as a payment brand (like Visa and Mastercard) and as an issuer (like banks such as HSBC or Citibank). Other payment brands work through partner financial institutions who issue their branded cards to consumers. This distinction affects how American Express interacts with other entities in the payment ecosystem and potentially impacts its approach to PCI compliance processes. Understanding these unique characteristics of payment brands is important for professionals studying for the PCIP exam.

Additional resource: https://www.americanexpress.com/us/merchant/payment-processing.html

Q12: How do Issuers contribute to the payment card ecosystem?

A12: Issuers, also known as Banks, contribute to the payment card ecosystem by providing debit and credit cards to consumers. The content describes them as "trusted allies" that offer "a range of financial services to help you manage your money safely and efficiently." Specific contributions of issuers include:

1. Card Distribution: They provide consumers with the physical or digital payment cards needed to make purchases.

2. Financial Services: They offer various financial products and services related to payment cards.

3. Fund Access: They give cardholders access to their funds for making purchases.

4. Security Measures: They implement security features on cards and accounts to protect cardholder data.

5. Transaction Authorization: They approve or decline transactions based on available funds or credit.

The content mentions specific examples of issuers, including HSBC, Citibank, NatWest, and American Express, describing them as "the lifeblood of the financial system." For PCIP candidates, understanding the role of issuers is important because they are key stakeholders subject to PCI-DSS compliance requirements and play a crucial role in securing cardholder data.

Additional resource: https://www.pcisecuritystandards.org/pci_security/

Q13: TRUE or FALSE: PCI-DSS Compliance Standards apply only to merchants who accept payment cards.

A13: FALSE. According to the provided content, "PCI-DSS Compliance Standards apply to Merchants, Acquirers, Issuers, card manufacturers, and processors involved in the Payment card ecosystem." The material explicitly states that "All entities storing, processing, and transmitting cardholder information must comply with PCI-DSS." This clearly indicates that compliance requirements extend far beyond just merchants to include all organizations that handle cardholder data in any capacity. This comprehensive application of the standards ensures that cardholder data is protected throughout the entire payment process, regardless of which entity is handling the information at any given point. This understanding is crucial for professionals pursuing PCIP certification as it establishes the broad scope of PCI compliance.

Additional resource: https://www.pcisecuritystandards.org/documents/PCI_DSS_for_Large_Organizations_v1.pdf

Q14: What tools do Acquirers provide to merchants in the payment card ecosystem? a) Credit risk assessment tools b) Customer loyalty programs c) Electronic payment devices for processing transactions d) Inventory management systems

A14: The correct answer is c) Electronic payment devices for processing transactions. According to the content, acquirers (which include banks like HSBC, NatWest, and Citibank, and processors such as WorldPay and GlobalPay) "provide merchants with tools for safely processing payments" and specifically "provide electronic payment devices, usually positioned at the checkout counter or self-service areas." These devices enable merchants to accept card payments securely. The content emphasizes that "merchants could not accept payments securely without these acquiring banks and payment processors," highlighting the essential role these tools play in the payment card ecosystem. For PCIP certification candidates, understanding the function of these payment devices and the relationship between merchants and acquirers is important for comprehending the overall transaction flow and security requirements.

Additional resource: https://www.pcisecuritystandards.org/pci_security/small_merchant_resources

Q15: Explain why merchants need to stay up-to-date on secure payment technologies and security protocols.

A15: Merchants need to stay up-to-date on secure payment technologies and security protocols for several important reasons:

1. Evolving Threat Landscape: The content states that "in today's world of evolving technologies, potential risks are everywhere," indicating that new security threats emerge continuously that could compromise payment card data.

2. Customer Experience: Merchants must "prioritize offering their customers a hassle-free and secure payment process," which requires implementing current security measures that don't disrupt the shopping experience.

3. Customer Confidence: By staying current with security protocols, merchants enable their "customers to shop confidently and safely," building trust and potentially increasing sales.

4. PCI Compliance: Though not explicitly stated in this section, staying current with security technologies helps merchants maintain compliance with PCI-DSS requirements, which evolve to address new threats.

5. Breach Prevention: Updated security measures help prevent data breaches that could result in financial losses, reputation damage, and legal consequences.

For professionals studying for the PCIP exam, understanding the merchant's responsibility in maintaining security is crucial for implementing effective compliance programs and recognizing potential vulnerabilities in payment processing environments.

Additional resource: https://www.pcisecuritystandards.org/documents/PCI_DSS_SMB_Guide_v4.0.pdf

Q16: What is the primary purpose of the payment card network according to the provided content? a) To generate profits for banks b) To create a seamless system for processing payments globally c) To collect consumer data for marketing purposes d) To reduce the use of cash in society

A16: The correct answer is b) To create a seamless system for processing payments globally. The content explicitly states that "the payment card network is the backbone of the global economy, creating a seamless system for processing payments." It further explains that this network allows people to "easily shop for goods and services worldwide." The payment card network achieves this by connecting various stakeholders (cardholders, merchants, issuers, acquirers, and payment brands) in a way that enables smooth secure transactions across geographical boundaries. This system works "seamlessly in the background," allowing consumers and merchants to focus on their business rather than the complexities of payment processing. For PCIP candidates, understanding this fundamental purpose helps contextualize the importance of protecting the integrity and security of the payment card ecosystem.

Additional resource: https://www.pcisecuritystandards.org/about/

Q17: Which of the following best describes the role of merchants in the payment card ecosystem? a) They issue credit and debit cards to consumers b) They establish the rules for payment card networks c) They accept card payments for goods and services d) They process transactions between banks

A17: The correct answer is c) They accept card payments for goods and services. According to the provided content, merchants are businesses "where we buy goods or services, whether online or in physical stores" using credit or debit cards. The material gives examples such as "your go-to supermarket or trendy boutiques" as businesses that fall under the merchant category. Merchants play a crucial role in the payment card ecosystem as the entities that interact directly with cardholders at the point of sale. The content also highlights that merchants have responsibilities related to security, noting they "must understand this reality and prioritize offering their customers a hassle-free and secure payment process." For the PCIP exam, understanding the merchant's position in the ecosystem is essential for properly assessing compliance requirements and security risks.

Additional resource: https://www.pcisecuritystandards.org/merchants/

Q18: TRUE or FALSE: When a transaction uses a card from one of the six major payment brands and the merchant accepts payments from these brands, PCI-DSS applies to that transaction.

A18: TRUE. The content explicitly states: "When you're making a purchase using a card with one of these five payment brands and the merchant uses a payment device that accepts payments from these brands, then PCI-DSS will apply to your transaction." (Note that the content first mentions six brands but then refers to five; the six major payment brands are Visa, Mastercard, American Express, Discover, JCB, and UnionPay). This statement confirms that PCI-DSS standards apply whenever these specific payment brands are involved in a transaction, regardless of the size or type of merchant. The content describes PCI-DSS as a "knight in shining armor, protecting your data from malicious actors who may try to steal it." This universal application ensures consistent security practices across the payment card industry and is a fundamental concept for the PCIP exam.

Additional resource: https://www.pcisecuritystandards.org/pci_security/why_security_matters

Q19: Why is understanding the payment card ecosystem described as "essential to succeed in the PCIP exam and beyond"?

A19: Understanding the payment card ecosystem is described as essential for PCIP exam success and professional practice because:

1. Risk Evaluation: The content explicitly states this knowledge "will equip you with the tools you need to evaluate potential risks confidently." Understanding how the ecosystem works helps identify where vulnerabilities might exist.

2. Component Interactions: The material notes that "to ace the exam, you need to comprehend how each component interacts with one another." This suggests that questions on the exam will test knowledge of these relationships.

3. Compliance Management: The content emphasizes that this understanding is "crucial when working with organizations that handle cardholder data" and "will prove invaluable in assessing and managing compliance risks."

4. Informed Decision-Making: With this knowledge, professionals can "make informed decisions on how best to safeguard cardholder data and ensure that your organization remains compliant with the PCI-DSS standard."

5. Practical Application: The emphasis on both exam success "and beyond" indicates that this knowledge has real-world application in professional roles related to payment card security.

This comprehensive understanding forms the foundation for all other PCI compliance knowledge and is therefore fundamental to both passing the PCIP exam and implementing effective security practices in professional settings.

Additional resource: https://www.pcisecuritystandards.org/program/pcip/

Q20: Describe the collaborative nature of the payment card ecosystem as presented in the content.

A20: The payment card ecosystem is characterized by extensive collaboration among various stakeholders. The content describes it as "a vast network of institutions and companies working together to streamline card transactions." This collaborative nature is evident in several aspects:

1. Cooperative Structure: Banks, credit card companies, and merchants are described as "just a few players in this ecosystem" who "collaborate to create a seamless platform" for transactions.

2. Seamless Integration: The system works "seamlessly in the background," indicating smooth coordination between different entities that makes the complexity invisible to end users.

3. Interconnected Components: The ecosystem is described as "a complicated web of interconnected parts, all working together seamlessly to keep the system running smoothly."

4. Shared Responsibility: Multiple stakeholders (Merchants, Acquirers, Issuers, card manufacturers, and processors) share responsibility for PCI-DSS compliance, indicating a collaborative approach to security.

5. Complementary Roles: Each stakeholder has a distinct but complementary role - cardholders initiate transactions, issuers provide cards, merchants accept payments, acquirers process transactions, and payment brands establish the standards and networks.

This collaboration enables global commerce by creating a reliable, secure system for card payments that transcends geographical boundaries. Understanding this collaborative ecosystem is crucial for PCIP candidates to comprehend how security measures must function across organizational boundaries.

Additional resource: https://www.pcisecuritystandards.org/about/industry_involvement/

Q21: What is the relationship between cardholders and the economic system according to the provided content? a) Cardholders are passive participants with little economic impact b) Cardholders are the drivers of the economic engine who keep the wheels turning c) Cardholders only impact the economy through high-value purchases d) Cardholders primarily influence the economy through interest payments

A21: The correct answer is b) Cardholders are the drivers of the economic engine who keep the wheels turning. The content directly states: "We cardholders are the drivers of the economic engine! We keep the wheels turning and the economy humming with a simple swipe or tap." This metaphor emphasizes the essential role that cardholders play in initiating transactions that drive economic activity. The material further reinforces this by saying, "don't underestimate the power of those trusty cards in your wallet–they are worth their weight in gold!" This indicates that the collective purchasing power of cardholders has significant economic impact, making them central figures in the payment card ecosystem. For PCIP candidates, understanding the importance of cardholders helps contextualize why protecting their data is so critical to the entire payment system.

Additional resource: https://www.pcisecuritystandards.org/pci_security/why_security_matters

Q22: TRUE or FALSE: UnionPay is one of the six major payment brands that act as pillars for PCI DSS.

A22: TRUE. According to the provided content, six prominent payment brands act as "the sturdy pillars of a castle for PCI DSS," and UnionPay is specifically mentioned as one of them. The content states: "These include Visa, Mastercard, American Express, Discover, JCB and more recently, UnionPay." This indicates that UnionPay has joined the original five payment brands as a major participant in the PCI DSS framework. The inclusion of UnionPay reflects its growing global importance, particularly in Asian markets. For professionals studying for the PCIP exam, it's important to recognize all six major payment brands that support the PCI DSS standards, as transactions involving these brands are subject to PCI compliance requirements.

Additional resource: https://www.pcisecuritystandards.org/about/participating_organizations/

Q23: How does the payment card ecosystem enable global commerce?

A23: The payment card ecosystem enables global commerce in several significant ways:

1. Borderless Transactions: The content states that "thanks to this incredible technology, we can now easily shop for goods and services worldwide," indicating that the payment card network transcends geographical boundaries.

2. Seamless Processing: The ecosystem is described as "creating a seamless system for processing payments," which eliminates friction that might otherwise impede international transactions.

3. Standardized Practices: The existence of global payment brands (Visa, Mastercard, American Express, Discover, JCB, and UnionPay) and universal standards (PCI-DSS) creates consistency in how payments are processed across different countries and currencies.

4. Background Operations: The system works "seamlessly in the background, allowing us to focus on what matters - enjoying our purchases," meaning consumers and merchants can engage in international commerce without worrying about the complex mechanics of cross-border payments.

5. Collaborative Structure: The "vast network of institutions and companies working together" creates an infrastructure that can support transactions regardless of the locations of buyer and seller.

This global payment infrastructure has been instrumental in enabling e-commerce, international travel, and the broader globalization of trade by providing secure, reliable payment methods that work consistently across borders.

Additional resource: https://www.pcisecuritystandards.org/global_initiatives/

Q24: Which of the following entities are subject to PCI-DSS Compliance Standards? (Select all that apply) a) Merchants b) Acquirers c) Issuers d) Card manufacturers e) Processors f) All of the above

A24: The correct answer is f) All of the above. The content explicitly states: "PCI-DSS Compliance Standards apply to Merchants, Acquirers, Issuers, card manufacturers, and processors involved in the Payment card ecosystem." It further emphasizes that "All entities storing, processing, and transmitting cardholder information must comply with PCI-DSS." This comprehensive scope ensures that cardholder data is protected at every stage of its lifecycle, from card production through transaction processing and storage. Each entity has specific compliance responsibilities based on their role in the ecosystem, but all must adhere to the fundamental security principles established by the PCI-DSS. Understanding this broad application of compliance standards is essential for PCIP candidates who need to recognize which organizations are subject to these requirements.

Additional resource: https://www.pcisecuritystandards.org/documents/PCI-DSS-v4-0-ROC-Reporting-Template.pdf

Q25: Compare and contrast the roles of Issuers and Acquirers in the payment card ecosystem.

A25: Issuers and Acquirers play distinct but complementary roles in the payment card ecosystem:

Issuers:

1. Provide debit and credit cards directly to consumers/cardholders

2. Described as "trusted allies" offering financial services to help consumers manage money

3. Include banks such as HSBC, Citibank, NatWest, and card companies like American Express

4. Serve as the "lifeblood of the financial system" by giving consumers access to funds

5. Maintain the accounts that cardholders draw upon when making purchases

Acquirers:

1. Serve merchants rather than consumers
2. Help merchants process payments and manage their finances
3. Include banks (HSBC, Citibank, NatWest) and specialized payment processors (WorldPay, GlobalPay)
4. Provide electronic payment devices positioned at checkout counters
5. Offer tools and services that make it easier for merchants to do business

Key Comparisons:

- Both issuers and acquirers can be banks (e.g., HSBC appears in both categories)
- Issuers focus on the cardholder side of transactions, while acquirers focus on the merchant side
- Both are essential to completing transactions: issuers authorize payments from cardholder accounts, while acquirers enable merchants to accept and process those payments
- Both must comply with PCI-DSS standards as they handle cardholder data

This dual-sided structure ensures that both consumers and merchants have the support they need to participate in the payment card ecosystem securely and efficiently.

Additional resource: https://www.pcisecuritystandards.org/pci_security/standard_overview

6

Connections: Understanding How It All Fits Together - Question Set

Q1: What is the primary function of an Acquiring Bank in the payment card ecosystem?

A. To issue credit cards to consumers B. To hold merchants' funds and process card payments C. To set interchange rates and assessment fees D. To verify cardholder identity

A1: The correct answer is B. To hold merchants' funds and process card payments.

An Acquiring Bank (also called a merchant bank) holds business or merchants' funds and offers them card readers to enable acceptance of card payments. These devices process credit card transactions, and once a transaction is completed, the Acquiring Bank deposits the funds into the merchant's account. This allows merchants to receive customer payments quickly and securely without handling cash or checks. Examples of Acquiring Banks mentioned in the content include HSBC, NatWest, Santander, and Bank of America.

Additional Resource: https://www.pcisecuritystandards.org/merchants/

Q2: Explain how funds flow from a customer's card to a merchant's account during a payment card transaction.

A2: The flow of funds in a payment card transaction follows this sequence:

1. A customer initiates a payment using their card through a merchant's card reader (provided by the Acquiring Bank).
2. The transaction data is sent through the payment brand's network.
3. The Issuing Bank verifies the cardholder's identity and confirms sufficient funds are available.
4. Upon approval, the Issuing Bank releases the funds for the transaction.
5. The Acquiring Bank then deposits these funds into the merchant's account.

This process enables merchants to receive payments quickly and securely without handling cash or checks. The system involves multiple entities (customer, merchant, Acquiring Bank, payment brand, and Issuing Bank) working in coordination to complete the transaction securely.

Additional Resource: https://www.pcisecuritystandards.org/pci_security/

Q3: True or False: HSBC, NatWest, Santander, and American Express are all examples of Acquiring Banks.

A3: False. While HSBC, NatWest, and Santander are examples of Acquiring Banks, American Express is not an Acquiring Bank but a payment brand.

The content specifically lists HSBC, NatWest, Santander, and Bank of America as examples of Acquirers. American Express is mentioned separately as one of the leading global payment brands that form a network connecting major banks worldwide, alongside Visa, Mastercard, Discover, JCB, and UnionPay. Payment brands and Acquiring Banks serve different functions in the payment card ecosystem.

Additional Resource: https://www.pcisecuritystandards.org/about_us/members/

Q4: Which of the following are major global payment brands? (Select all that apply)

A. Visa B. HSBC C. Mastercard D. American Express E. Santander F. JCB

A4: The correct answers are A, C, D, and F (Visa, Mastercard, American Express, and JCB).

According to the content, the leading global payment brands that form a network connecting major banks worldwide include Visa, Mastercard, American Express, Discover, JCB, and UnionPay. HSBC and Santander are examples of Acquiring Banks, not payment brands. Payment brands facilitate transaction data transfers between issuing banks and merchants and have the authority to set interchange rates and assessment fees.

Additional Resource: https://www.pcisecuritystandards.org/about_us/

Q5: What is the role of payment brands in the payment card ecosystem?

A5: Payment brands play several critical roles in the payment card ecosystem:

1. They facilitate transaction data transfers between issuing banks and merchants.
2. They establish and maintain networks that connect major banks worldwide.
3. They have the authority to set interchange rates that apply to transactions.
4. They determine assessment fees charged for their services.
5. They create standards and protocols for secure payment processing.

The major global payment brands (Visa, Mastercard, American Express, Discover, JCB, and UnionPay) form the infrastructure that enables card payments to function across different banks, merchants, and geographical regions. Their networks are essential for the authorization, clearing, and settlement of card transactions worldwide.

Additional Resource: https://www.pcisecuritystandards.org/document_library/

Q6: What factors can affect interchange rates? (Select all that apply)

A. Type of card used B. Transaction amount C. Merchant's annual revenue D. Time of day the transaction occurs

A6: The correct answers are A and B (Type of card used and Transaction amount).

According to the provided content, "interchange rates vary depending on the type of card used, the transaction amount, and other factors." While the content mentions there may be other factors that influence interchange rates, it specifically identifies card type and transaction amount as variables that affect these rates. The merchant's annual revenue and time of day of transactions are not mentioned as factors affecting interchange rates in the provided content.

Additional Resource: https://www.pcisecuritystandards.org/merchants/payment-acceptance/

Q7: Define interchange rates and explain why they are important to merchants.

A7: Interchange rates are fees charged by payment brands for processing transactions between issuing banks and merchants. According to the content, these rates vary depending on the type of card used, the transaction amount, and other factors.

These rates are important to merchants for several key reasons:

1. Financial Impact: They "significantly impact the cost of accepting card payments and can affect their bottom line." Higher interchange rates directly reduce profit margins on sales.

2. Pricing Considerations: Merchants must factor these costs into their pricing strategies to maintain profitability.

3. Business Planning: Understanding interchange rates is essential for accurate financial forecasting and cost management.

4. Payment Method Decisions: Different payment methods have different interchange rates, which may influence which payment types merchants choose to accept.

For merchants to operate profitably while accepting card payments, they must understand these rates and how they apply to their specific business model and transaction types.

Additional Resource: https://www.pcisecuritystandards.org/document_library/

Q8: True or False: Assessment fees and interchange rates are the same thing.

A8: False. Assessment fees and interchange rates are separate and distinct charges in the payment card process.

The content explicitly states: "Assessment fees are additional charges imposed by payment brands for their services. These fees are separate from interchange rates and are charged to merchants for each transaction processed."

While both are costs associated with processing card transactions, they represent different types of fees imposed for different purposes. Interchange rates compensate issuing banks for assuming cardholder risk, while assessment fees are specifically for payment brand services such as network access and fraud prevention.

Additional Resource: https://www.pcisecuritystandards.org/document_library/

Q9: What services might be covered by assessment fees? (Select all that apply)

A. Network access B. Fraud prevention C. Employee training D. Marketing services

A9: The correct answers are A and B (Network access and Fraud prevention).

According to the content, assessment fees "can include charges for network access, fraud prevention, and other services." The content specifically identifies network access and fraud prevention as examples of services covered by assessment fees charged by payment brands. There is no mention of employee training or marketing services being covered by assessment fees in the provided material.

Additional Resource: https://www.pcisecuritystandards.org/merchants/payment-acceptance/

Q10: Compare and contrast interchange rates and assessment fees.

A10: Interchange Rates and Assessment Fees are both transaction costs in card processing but differ in several important ways:

Interchange Rates:

- Charged by payment brands for processing transactions between issuing banks and merchants
- Vary based on factors such as card type and transaction amount
- Represent a major portion of transaction costs
- Primarily compensate the issuing bank for taking on cardholder risk

Assessment Fees:

- Additional charges imposed by payment brands specifically for their services
- Explicitly stated to be "separate from interchange rates"
- Charged to merchants for each transaction processed
- Cover specific services like network access and fraud prevention
- May be more standardized than the variable interchange rates

Key Differences:

1. Purpose: Interchange compensates banks; assessment fees pay for network services
2. Variability: Interchange rates typically vary more based on transaction characteristics

3. Recipients: Interchange primarily benefits issuing banks; assessment fees go to payment brands

4. Structure: They are calculated differently and appear as separate line items on merchant statements

Understanding both fee types is crucial for merchants to accurately assess their total cost of accepting card payments.

Additional Resource: https://www.pcisecuritystandards.org/document_library/

Q11: What is the primary responsibility of an issuing bank during a transaction?

A. Providing card readers to merchants B. Setting interchange rates C. Verifying cardholder identity and fund availability D. Depositing funds into merchant accounts

A11: The correct answer is C. Verifying cardholder identity and fund availability.

The content explicitly states: "The issuing bank verifies the cardholder's identity and confirms whether there are sufficient funds available to cover the transaction." This verification process is a critical security step in the payment card transaction flow that helps prevent fraud and ensures that merchants will receive payment for legitimate transactions.

The other options represent functions performed by different entities: providing card readers is done by Acquiring Banks, setting interchange rates is done by payment brands, and depositing funds into merchant accounts is performed by Acquiring Banks.

Additional Resource: https://www.pcisecuritystandards.org/about_us/

Q12: What services do issuing banks provide to cardholders beyond credit card accounts?

A12: According to the content, issuing banks provide cardholders with access to a variety of financial services beyond just credit card accounts. The content specifically mentions:

1. Current accounts (checking accounts)

2. Savings accounts

3. Mortgage accounts

As stated in the material: "Are you aware that as a cardholder, you have access to more than just an account with this bank? You can also open a current or savings account or even a mortgage account with them!"

This indicates that issuing banks establish broader financial relationships with cardholders, offering a comprehensive suite of banking services rather than just card issuance. These additional services allow banks to serve more of their customers' financial needs through a single institution.

Additional Resource: https://www.pcisecuritystandards.org/pci_security/

Q13: True or False: An issuing bank only verifies cardholder identity during a transaction but does not check for available funds.

A13: False. The issuing bank performs both identity verification and funds availability checks.

According to the content: "The issuing bank verifies the cardholder's identity and confirms whether there are sufficient funds are available to cover the transaction."

This dual verification process is crucial to the security and reliability of the payment system. By verifying both identity and fund availability, the issuing bank helps prevent fraud and ensures that merchants will receive payment for legitimate sales. Both aspects of verification are essential parts of the issuing bank's role in the transaction process.

Additional Resource: https://www.pcisecuritystandards.org/pci_security/

Q14: Which of the following best describes merchants in the payment card ecosystem?

A. Companies that issue credit cards to consumers B. Banks that process payment transactions C. Businesses that accept cards with payment brand logos D. Organizations that set interchange rates

A14: The correct answer is C. Businesses that accept cards with payment brand logos.

According to the content: "In the world of payment cards, merchants or retailers accept cards with logos from American Express, Discover, JCB, Mastercard, and Visa." Merchants are the businesses (either online or brick-and-mortar) that accept payment cards as a form of payment for their goods or services. They are essential to the payment card ecosystem as they drive growth in the industry by generating transaction volume.

Additional Resource: https://www.pcisecuritystandards.org/merchants/

Q15: What type of merchants generate the most spending in the payment card industry?

A15: According to the content, "Merchants who accept cards from all five members of the PCI SSC generate the most spending and are the driving force behind this growth."

These five members are identified in the content as American Express, Discover, JCB, Mastercard, and Visa. Merchants who accept all these major payment brands provide customers with the most payment options, which leads to higher transaction volumes and greater spending.

This indicates that the breadth of payment options a merchant offers correlates directly with their contribution to industry growth. By accepting multiple card brands, merchants maximize the potential customer base that can make purchases using their preferred payment methods.

Additional Resource: https://www.pcisecuritystandards.org/about_us/members/

Q16: True or False: Merchants can only operate in physical locations to accept payment cards.

A16: False. Merchants can operate in both physical and online environments.

The content explicitly states: "These businesses can be online or in traditional brick-and-mortar premises." This clarifies that merchants who accept payment cards are not limited to physical store locations but can also operate in e-commerce or other online environments.

This flexibility allows businesses of various types to participate in the payment card ecosystem, whether they are purely digital businesses, traditional retail stores, or hybrid models that combine both physical and online presence.

Additional Resource: https://www.pcisecuritystandards.org/merchants/

Q17: In the payment card transaction process, which entity deposits funds into the merchant's account?

A. Issuing Bank B. Payment Brand C. Acquiring Bank D. Cardholder

A17: The correct answer is C. Acquiring Bank.

According to the content: "The Acquiring bank will deposit the funds into the merchant's account once the transaction is completed." This is one of the primary functions of the Acquiring Bank in the payment card ecosystem. After a transaction is approved and processed through the payment brand network and the issuing bank has released the funds, the Acquiring Bank is responsible for depositing those funds into the merchant's account.

This enables "merchants to receive customer payments quickly and securely without worrying about handling cash or cheques," as stated in the content.

Additional Resource: https://www.pcisecuritystandards.org/merchants/

Q18: Explain why merchant accounts are considered essential to the payment card ecosystem.

A18: According to the content, "Merchant accounts are essential to the payment card ecosystem because they drive growth in the industry."

Merchant accounts are essential for several key reasons:

1. Industry Growth Driver: As explicitly stated, they drive growth in the payment card industry by generating transaction volume.

2. Revenue Generation: "Merchants who accept cards from all five members of the PCI SSC generate the most spending" - this indicates that merchant accounts create the revenue streams that sustain the ecosystem.

3. Expansion of Card Utility: Each merchant that accepts cards increases the locations where consumers can use their cards, enhancing the value of card ownership.

4. Transaction Volume: Merchants create the demand for card processing services by conducting transactions that utilize the payment infrastructure.

5. Consumer Access: They provide the endpoints where consumers can use their payment cards, making the entire system accessible to end users.

Without merchant participation through merchant accounts, the payment card ecosystem would have no practical application, as there would be nowhere for consumers to use their cards for purchases.

Additional Resource: https://www.pcisecuritystandards.org/merchants/

Q19: What does a card reader enable merchants to do?

A. Issue credit cards to customers B. Set interchange rates C. Process credit card transactions D. Verify cardholder identity

A19: The correct answer is C. Process credit card transactions.

According to the content: "An Acquirer will offer them card readers to enable merchants to accept card payments. These nifty devices are used to process credit card transactions."

Card readers are the hardware that merchants use to capture payment card information from customers. They connect merchants to the payment processing system, allowing them to accept card payments rather than just cash or checks. The Acquiring Bank provides these devices as part of their service to merchants.

Additional Resource: https://www.pcisecuritystandards.org/merchants/payment-acceptance/

Q20: Describe the complete transaction flow from when a customer presents their card until the merchant receives payment.

A20: The complete transaction flow in a payment card transaction follows these steps:

1. Initial Presentation: The customer presents their payment card to the merchant (either physically or online).
2. Card Reading: The merchant uses their card reader (provided by the Acquiring Bank) to capture the payment information
3. Authorization Request: The transaction data is sent through the Acquiring Bank to the appropriate payment brand network.
4. Verification: As stated in the content, "The issuing bank verifies the cardholder's identity and confirms whether there are sufficient funds available to cover the transaction."
5. Authorization Response: Upon approval, the response travels back through the network to the merchant.
6. Fund Release: "Once confirmed, the bank will release the funds to settle the transaction."
7. Settlement: The payment is processed with applicable interchange rates and assessment fees applied.
8. Deposit: Finally, "The Acquiring bank will deposit the funds into the merchant's account once the transaction is completed."

This process allows "merchants to receive customer payments quickly and securely without worrying about handling cash or cheques," as mentioned in the content. The entire flow typically takes seconds for authorization, while final settlement may take 1-3 business days depending on the specific arrangements.

Additional Resource: https://www.pcisecuritystandards.org/document_library/

Q21: Which of the following entities have the authority to set interchange rates and assessment fees?

A. Acquiring Banks B. Issuing Banks C. Payment Brands D. Merchants

A21: The correct answer is C. Payment Brands.

According to the content: "Payment brands... have the authority to set interchange rates and assessment fees, which significantly impact the cost of transactions."

This authority gives payment brands (such as Visa, Mastercard, American Express, Discover, JCB, and UnionPay) considerable influence over the economics of card payments. By setting these rates and fees, they determine much of the cost structure for card processing, which affects both merchants and financial institutions.

Neither Acquiring Banks, Issuing Banks, nor Merchants have the authority to set these rates and fees; they must operate within the framework established by the payment brands.

Additional Resource: https://www.pcisecuritystandards.org/document_library/

Q22: True or False: The acquiring bank and the issuing bank perform the same functions in a card transaction.

A22: False. The acquiring bank and the issuing bank perform different functions in a card transaction.

According to the content:

- The Acquiring Bank "holds business or merchants' funds," "offer[s] them card readers," and "will deposit the funds into the merchant's account once the transaction is completed."
- The Issuing Bank "verifies the cardholder's identity and confirms whether there are sufficient funds are available to cover the transaction" and "will release the funds to settle the transaction."

The Acquiring Bank has a relationship with the merchant and handles the merchant side of the transaction, while the Issuing Bank has a relationship with the cardholder and handles the cardholder side of the transaction. These are distinct roles that work together but serve different purposes in the payment card ecosystem.

Additional Resource: https://www.pcisecuritystandards.org/about_us/

Q23: What is the relationship between payment brands and major banks worldwide?

A23: According to the content, payment brands "form a network connecting major banks worldwide."

This relationship involves payment brands (Visa, Mastercard, American Express, Discover, JCB, and UnionPay) creating the infrastructure and standards that allow different banks to communicate and process transactions with each other. This network enables:

1. Transaction Routing: Payment brands facilitate transaction data transfers between issuing banks and merchants across different financial institutions.
2. Global Connectivity: Their networks connect banks across countries and regions, enabling international card payments.
3. Standardization: They establish common protocols and standards that all participating banks follow.
4. Economic Framework: They set interchange rates and assessment fees that structure the financial relationships between

banks in the network.

This interconnected network is essential for the global functionality of payment cards, allowing consumers to use their cards at merchants around the world regardless of which bank issued their card or which bank the merchant uses.

Additional Resource: https://www.pcisecuritystandards.org/about_us/members/

Q24: How does accepting cards from all five members of the PCI SSC impact merchants?

A24: According to the content, "Merchants who accept cards from all five members of the PCI SSC generate the most spending and are the driving force behind this growth."

Accepting cards from all five members (American Express, Discover, JCB, Mastercard, and Visa) impacts merchants in several significant ways:

1. Increased Revenue: These merchants generate the highest transaction volumes and spending, suggesting that accepting all major card brands leads to greater sales.

2. Broader Customer Base: By accepting all major card brands, merchants can serve customers regardless of their preferred payment method.

3. Competitive Advantage: Offering comprehensive payment options provides a competitive edge over merchants who accept fewer card types.

4. Industry Influence: These merchants become the "driving force" behind industry growth, potentially giving them more influence in the payment card ecosystem.

5. Complex Fee Structure: However, these merchants must also manage the varying interchange rates and assessment fees associated with each payment brand.

By maximizing payment options, these merchants create the most accessible shopping experience for consumers, which translates to higher transaction volumes and greater business success.

Additional Resource: https://www.pcisecuritystandards.org/merchants/

Q25: Explain how the different entities in the payment card ecosystem work together to complete a secure transaction.

A25: The payment card ecosystem functions through the coordinated efforts of multiple entities, each with specific roles in secure transaction processing:

Cardholders initiate transactions with their payment cards. They maintain relationships with Issuing Banks that provide various financial services beyond just card accounts, including "current or savings account or even a mortgage account."

Merchants accept payment cards with logos from major payment brands. They can operate "online or in traditional brick-and-mortar premises" and are "essential to the payment card ecosystem because they drive growth in the industry." They use card readers from their Acquiring Bank to process transactions.

Acquiring Banks "hold business or merchants' funds" and "offer them card readers to enable merchants to accept card payments." After transaction completion, they "deposit the funds into the merchant's account," enabling merchants to "receive customer payments quickly and securely."

Payment Brands (Visa, Mastercard, American Express, Discover, JCB, and UnionPay) "play a crucial role in facilitating transaction data transfers between issuing banks and merchants." They maintain networks connecting banks worldwide and "have the authority to set interchange rates and assessment fees."

Issuing Banks verify "the cardholder's identity and confirms whether there are sufficient funds available to cover the transaction." Once verified, they "release the funds to settle the transaction."

The transaction flow integrates these entities:

1. The cardholder presents their card to the merchant
2. The merchant's card reader captures payment information
3. This data travels through the Acquiring Bank to the payment brand network
4. The payment brand routes the request to the Issuing Bank
5. The Issuing Bank verifies identity and fund availability
6. The approval travels back through the network to the merchant
7. The Issuing Bank releases funds, which flow through the system
8. The Acquiring Bank deposits funds into the merchant's account

Each entity contributes to security: Issuing Banks verify cardholder identity, payment brands maintain secure networks, Acquiring Banks ensure secure fund transfers, and merchants properly handle card data. This collective responsibility creates multiple layers of protection that enable secure electronic payments worldwide.

Additional Resource: https://www.pcisecuritystandards.org/about_us/

7

Secrets of the Card Payment Process - Question Set

Q1: What are the four main steps in the payment card transaction process?

A1: The four main steps in the payment card transaction process are:

1. **Authorization**: When a cardholder presents their card for payment, the merchant requests authorization from the issuing bank through the acquiring bank and payment brand network. This step verifies that the card is valid and has sufficient funds.

2. **Authentication**: The issuing bank validates the card information, including checking the card number, available funds, billing address, and CVV. Based on this validation, the transaction is either approved or declined.

3. **Clearing**: At the end of each day, the merchant batches approved authorizations and sends them to the acquiring bank. The payment brand network then routes these transactions to the respective issuing banks.

4. **Settlement**: The issuing bank transfers funds to the acquiring bank via the payment brand network, typically within 24-48 hours of the transaction. The acquiring bank then credits the merchant's account after fees are deducted.

Understanding these four steps is fundamental to grasping how payment card transactions function in a secure ecosystem.

Additional resource: https://www.pcisecuritystandards.org/document_library/

Q2: What information does the payment brand network analyze when a credit card transaction is processed?

A2: When a credit card transaction is processed, the payment brand network analyzes:

1. Track 1 and Track 2 data from the credit card

2. The first few digits of the card number (BIN - Bank Identification Number)

This information allows the payment brand network to determine:

- Which bank issued the card
- The card type and associated processing requirements
- Where to route the authorization request

The payment brand network acts as an intermediary between the acquiring bank (merchant's bank) and the issuing bank (cardholder's bank), using this data to ensure the transaction is routed correctly for authorization.

Track data contains encoded information on the magnetic stripe of payment cards, with Track 1 typically containing the cardholder's name and account number, while Track 2 contains the account number, expiration date, and service code.

Additional resource: https://www.pcisecuritystandards.org/pci_security/why_security_matters

Q3: True or False: Clearing is considered the final step in the payment card transaction process according to the PCIP exam.

A3: True. According to the exam tip provided in the content, "As far as you are concerned, Clearing is the final step, rather than Settlement." This is a specific exam-related point that candidates should remember, even though the complete process includes settlement after clearing.

In reality, the full process includes:

1. Authorization
2. Authentication
3. Clearing
4. Settlement

However, for the purposes of the PCIP v4.0 exam, clearing is considered the final step that candidates need to focus on. This distinction is important to remember when taking the exam.

Additional resource: https://www.pcisecuritystandards.org/training/

Q4: What four validation checks does the issuing bank perform during the authentication process?

A4: During the authentication process, the issuing bank performs four key validation checks:

1. **Card Number Validation**: Verifies that the credit card number is legitimate, active, and has not been reported lost or stolen.
2. **Available Funds Check**: Confirms that the cardholder has sufficient funds or credit available to cover the transaction amount.
3. **Billing Address Verification**: Matches the billing address provided during the transaction against the address on file with the issuing bank (Address Verification Service or AVS).

4. **CVV Validation**: Verifies that the Card Verification Value (the 3 or 4-digit security code) provided matches the one associated with the physical card.

These four checks work together to authenticate the transaction and reduce the risk of fraud. Only after all these checks are successfully completed will the issuing bank approve the transaction. If any check fails, the transaction will likely be declined.

Additional resource: https://www.pcisecuritystandards.org/merchants/

Q5: What is the timeframe for the issuing bank to transfer funds to the acquiring bank during the settlement process?

A5: According to the content provided, during the settlement process, "The Issuing Bank will transfer the funds to the Acquiring Bank via the Payment Brand network within 24 to 48 hours of the transaction."

This timeframe is the standard industry expectation for settlement between financial institutions. It's important to note that while the authorization and authentication processes happen in real-time during the purchase, the actual movement of funds occurs later during this settlement window.

The settlement timeframe is an important concept in understanding the complete payment card transaction cycle and the float period that exists between when a transaction is approved and when funds actually change hands.

Additional resource: https://www.pcisecuritystandards.org/businesses/

Q6: What action does a merchant take at the End of Day (EoD) regarding payment card transactions?

A6: At the End of Day (EoD), the merchant performs the following actions regarding payment card transactions:

1. The merchant performs an End of Day (EoD) task on the Point of Sale (PoS) terminal

2. This EoD task collects all approved authorizations that occurred during the business day

3. These authorizations are compiled into a batch file

4. The merchant sends this batch file to their acquiring bank or its processor

This process is crucial for initiating the clearing and settlement phases of the payment card transaction cycle. By batching transactions together rather than processing each one individually for settlement, the system becomes more efficient and reduces processing costs for all parties involved.

The EoD process typically occurs automatically at a predetermined time or can be manually initiated by the merchant, depending on their point-of-sale system configuration.

Additional resource: https://www.pcisecuritystandards.org/small_merchant_resources/

Q7: What are the two ways a merchant can provide a receipt to a customer after a transaction is completed?

A7: After a transaction is completed, a merchant can provide a receipt to the customer in one of two ways:

1. **Printed Receipt**: A physical, paper receipt handed directly to the customer at the point of purchase. This tangible record contains transaction details including the date, merchant information, items purchased, and payment method.

2. **Electronic Receipt**: A digital receipt sent via email to the cardholder's email address. This environmentally-friendly option provides the same transaction information as a printed receipt but in digital format.

Both methods serve the important purpose of giving customers a record of their purchase for their personal accounting, potential returns, warranties, or expense reporting. Providing receipts is also a regulatory requirement in many jurisdictions and helps establish a paper trail for both the merchant and customer.

Additional resource: https://www.pcisecuritystandards.org/document_library/

Q8: Multiple Choice: Which of the following entities places a hold on the cardholder's account until the transaction amount is cleared?

A) The merchant B) The acquiring bank C) The payment brand network D) The issuing bank

A8: The correct answer is D) The issuing bank.

As stated in the authentication process description: "The issuing bank places a hold on the cardholder's account until the amount is cleared." This hold ensures that the funds are reserved for the specific transaction, preventing the cardholder from spending the same money elsewhere before the transaction is fully processed and settled.

The hold is not the same as actually removing the funds from the account. Rather, it's a temporary reservation that reduces the available balance until the transaction is fully processed through clearing and settlement, at which point the actual funds transfer occurs.

This is an important distinction in understanding how card payments work from the cardholder's perspective, as they may see a "pending" transaction or a reduced available balance before the transaction is fully settled.

Additional resource: https://www.pcisecuritystandards.org/pci_security/

Q9: Describe the role of the payment brand network in the clearing process.

A9: In the clearing process, the payment brand network plays several crucial roles:

1. **Transaction Routing**: The payment brand network receives batched transaction information from the processor (which got it from the acquiring bank) in the form of clearing messages.

2. **Transaction Distribution**: The network forwards each approved transaction to the corresponding issuing bank, ensuring that transaction details reach the correct financial institution responsible for the cardholder's account.

3. **Facilitating Settlement**: The payment brand network serves as the conduit through which the issuing bank transfers funds to the acquiring bank (within 24-48 hours of the transaction).

4. **Fee Collection and Distribution**: The payment brand network collects its fees from the transaction amount and also ensures the acquiring bank and processor receive their respective fees.

The payment brand network (such as Visa, Mastercard, American Express, etc.) serves as the central infrastructure that connects acquiring banks and issuing banks, making the entire payment ecosystem possible. Without these networks, each bank would need direct relationships with every other bank, which would be impractical and inefficient.

Additional resource: https://www.pcisecuritystandards.org/businesses/

Q10: True or False: During the authorization process, the merchant communicates directly with the issuing bank to get approval for a transaction.

A10: False. During the authorization process, the merchant does not communicate directly with the issuing bank.

Instead, the authorization request follows this path:

1. The merchant's point-of-sale system sends the transaction information to the acquiring bank (the merchant's bank), its processor, or service provider
2. The acquiring bank routes the information to the appropriate payment brand network
3. The payment brand network identifies the issuing bank based on the card's BIN (Bank Identification Number)
4. The payment brand network forwards the authorization request to the issuing bank
5. The issuing bank approves or declines the transaction and sends the response back through the same path in reverse

This multi-step process demonstrates why the payment card industry requires such complex security standards - transaction information passes through multiple entities, each of which must maintain proper security protocols to protect cardholder data.

Additional resource: https://www.pcisecuritystandards.org/documents/PCI_DSS_for_Large_Organizations_v1.pdf

Q11: What actions does an issuing bank take when it receives an authorization request?

A11: When an issuing bank receives an authorization request, it takes the following actions:

1. **Validates the credit card number**: Checks that the card number is legitimate, has not expired, and has not been reported lost or stolen.
2. **Checks available funds**: Verifies that the cardholder has sufficient funds or available credit to cover the transaction amount.
3. **Matches the billing address**: Compares the billing address provided in the transaction with the address on file for the cardholder (Address Verification Service).
4. **Validates the CVV**: Confirms that the Card Verification Value provided matches what's on file for that card.
5. **Approves or declines the transaction**: Based on the results of these checks, the issuing bank makes a decision.
6. **Places a hold on funds**: If approved, the issuing bank places a hold on the cardholder's account for the transaction amount until it is cleared.

These validation steps are critical security measures that help prevent fraudulent transactions and protect both the cardholder and the financial institutions involved in the transaction.

Additional resource: https://www.pcisecuritystandards.org/documents/PCI_DSS_V3.2.1.pdf

Q12: Multiple Choice: In the payment card transaction process, which step occurs immediately after the merchant performs the End of Day (EoD) task?

A) The issuing bank transfers funds to the acquiring bank B) The merchant sends a batch file to the acquiring bank C) The payment brand forwards transactions to the issuing bank D) The acquiring bank credits the merchant's account

A12: The correct answer is B) The merchant sends a batch file to the acquiring bank.

According to the clearing and settlement process described in the content: "The merchant sends a batch file of approved authorizations to the Acquiring bank or its Processor at the end of each day (EoD)."

The sequence of events is:

1. Merchant performs the EoD task on the PoS terminal to collect all approved authorizations
2. Merchant sends the batch file to the acquiring bank or its processor
3. The processor routes the batched information to the payment brand network
4. The payment brand forwards each transaction to the corresponding issuing bank
5. The issuing bank transfers funds to the acquiring bank
6. The acquiring bank credits the merchant's account

Understanding this sequence is important for comprehending the flow of both information and funds in the payment card ecosystem.

Additional resource: https://www.pcisecuritystandards.org/pci_dss_supportive_materials/

Q13: What is the purpose of the Card Verification Value (CVV) in the payment card transaction process?

A13: The Card Verification Value (CVV) serves several important security purposes in the payment card transaction process:

1. **Authentication**: The CVV helps authenticate that the person making the transaction physically possesses the card, as the code is printed on the card (typically on the back for Visa, Mastercard, and Discover, or on the front for American Express).
2. **Fraud Prevention**: Since the CVV is not stored in the magnetic stripe or chip, and should not be stored by merchants after authorization, it provides an additional security layer that helps prevent fraud in card-not-present transactions (like online or phone purchases).
3. **Verification**: During the authentication process, the issuing bank validates the CVV provided by the cardholder against the CVV associated with that specific card.

The CVV is a critical component of the payment card industry's security framework. According to PCI DSS requirements, merchants are prohibited from storing the CVV after transaction authorization, which helps protect this sensitive authentication data from potential data breaches.

Additional resource: https://www.pcisecuritystandards.org/glossary/

Q14: Explain the difference between clearing and settlement in the payment card transaction process.

A14: Clearing and settlement are two distinct phases in the payment card transaction process:

Clearing:

- Occurs after the merchant batches approved authorizations at the end of the day
- Involves the exchange of transaction information between the acquiring bank and the issuing bank via the payment brand network
- The processor routes batched information to the payment brand network as a clearing message
- The payment brand forwards each approved transaction to the corresponding issuing bank
- Essentially, clearing is the process of exchanging transaction details between banks

Settlement:

- Follows the clearing process
- Involves the actual movement of funds between financial institutions
- The issuing bank transfers funds to the acquiring bank via the payment brand network (typically within 24-48 hours)
- The payment brand deducts its fees and the processor's fees from the transaction amount
- The acquiring bank credits the merchant's account with the remaining funds
- Settlement is the actual financial reconciliation of the transaction

An important exam tip mentioned in the content: "As far as you are concerned, Clearing is the final step, rather than Settlement." This suggests that for the PCIP v4.0 exam, candidates should focus on clearing as the concluding step of the process.

Additional resource: https://www.pcisecuritystandards.org/documents/Small_Merchant_Guide_to_Safe_Payments.pdf

Q15: Fill in the blank: During the payment card transaction process, the ______________ pays the acquiring bank and the processor their respective fees from the remaining funds.

A15: During the payment card transaction process, the **payment brand** pays the acquiring bank and the processor their respective fees from the remaining funds.

As described in the settlement process: "The payment Brand pays the Acquiring Bank and the Processor their respective fees from the remaining funds." This occurs after the issuing bank transfers the funds to the acquiring bank via the payment brand network.

The payment brand (such as Visa, Mastercard, American Express, etc.) acts as the central clearinghouse in this process, collecting the total transaction amount from the issuing bank and then distributing the appropriate portions to the various parties involved:

- The bulk of the funds go to the merchant (via the acquiring bank)
- A portion is retained by the payment brand as their fee
- Portions are distributed to the acquiring bank and processor as their fees

This fee structure is a fundamental aspect of how the payment card ecosystem finances itself and continues to operate.

Additional resource: https://www.pcisecuritystandards.org/merchants/process/

Q16: Multiple Choice: Which entity in the payment card ecosystem provides the Point of Sale (POS) device to the merchant?

A) The payment brand network B) The acquiring bank C) The issuing bank D) The cardholder's bank

A16: The correct answer is B) The acquiring bank.

According to the content: "You can use contactless payment by simply tapping your card or inserting/swiping it at the merchant's point of sale (POS) device. The bank provides this device with which the merchant does business, also known as their acquirer."

The acquiring bank (or acquirer) is the financial institution that maintains the merchant's bank account and provides them with the necessary equipment and services to accept card payments. This includes:

- Point of Sale (POS) terminals
- Payment processing services
- Merchant account services
- Settlement of funds to the merchant's account

This relationship between the merchant and their acquiring bank is a critical component of the payment card ecosystem, enabling businesses to accept card payments from customers.

Additional resource: https://www.pcisecuritystandards.org/small_merchant_resources/

Q17: What information is included in Track 1 and Track 2 data on a payment card?

A17: Track 1 and Track 2 data contain encoded information on the magnetic stripe of payment cards:

Track 1 data typically includes:

- Cardholder's name

- Account number (PAN - Primary Account Number)
- Expiration date
- Service code
- Discretionary data (which can include Pin Verification Key Indicator, Pin Verification Value, and Card Verification Value)

Track 2 data typically includes:

- Account number (PAN)
- Expiration date
- Service code
- Discretionary data
- (Track 2 does not include the cardholder's name)

This data is read when a card is swiped through a point-of-sale terminal. The payment brand network analyzes this track data to determine which bank issued the card, primarily by examining the first few digits of the card number (Bank Identification Number or BIN).

It's important to note that under PCI DSS requirements, merchants and service providers should not store the full track data after authorization, as this sensitive authentication data poses security risks if compromised.

Additional resource: https://www.pcisecuritystandards.org/glossary/

Q18: True or False: The acquiring bank transfers funds to the payment brand network, which then forwards them to the issuing bank.

A18: False. The flow of funds moves in the opposite direction.

According to the settlement process described in the content: "The Issuing Bank will transfer the funds to the Acquiring Bank via the Payment Brand network within 24 to 48 hours of the transaction."

The correct flow of funds is:

1. The issuing bank (cardholder's bank) transfers funds to the acquiring bank
2. This transfer happens via the payment brand network
3. The payment brand network deducts its fees and the processor's fees
4. The remaining funds reach the acquiring bank
5. The acquiring bank credits the merchant's account after potentially deducting its own fees

This flow reflects the logical direction of payment - from the customer (via their issuing bank) to the merchant (via their acquiring bank), with the payment brand network facilitating the transfer and collecting fees along the way.

Additional resource: https://www.pcisecuritystandards.org/pci_security/why_security_matters

Q19: What information would the issuing bank include in the cardholder's bill after transactions have been processed?

A19: After transactions have been processed, the issuing bank will include the following information in the cardholder's bill:

1. A statement of all transactions made during the billing cycle
2. The total amount owed
3. The due date for payment
4. Merchant names and locations where purchases were made
5. Transaction dates
6. Individual transaction amounts
7. Any applicable fees or interest charges
8. Available credit remaining (for credit cards)
9. Minimum payment required (for credit cards)

As mentioned in the content: "Once you've made purchases using your credit card, the issuing bank will send you a bill for the total amount owed. This bill will include a statement of all the transactions you made during that billing cycle."

The statement serves as a comprehensive record of the cardholder's activity and obligations. Cardholders are advised to review this statement carefully to ensure all transactions are legitimate and accurate, which serves as an additional security measure to detect potential fraudulent activity.

Additional resource: https://www.pcisecuritystandards.org/consumers/

Q20: Describe the full sequence of steps that occur during the authorization phase of a payment card transaction.

A20: The authorization phase of a payment card transaction follows this sequence of steps:

1. **Card Presentation**: The cardholder approaches the Point of Sale (PoS) device at the merchant's location and presents their credit or debit card.
2. **Card Reading**: The cardholder swipes, inserts, or taps their card on the PoS device, which reads the card information.
3. **Information Transmission**: The card information is transmitted through the internet or by phone to the acquiring bank (merchant's bank), its processor, or service provider.

4. **Routing to Payment Brand**: The acquiring bank routes the transaction information to the appropriate payment brand network (like Visa, Mastercard, etc.).

5. **Payment Brand Analysis**: The payment brand network analyzes the Track 1 and Track 2 data, determining which bank issued the card based on the first few digits of the card number (BIN).

6. **Authorization Request**: The payment brand network sends an authorization request to the identified issuing bank (cardholder's bank).

The authorization phase establishes whether the card is valid and has sufficient funds for the transaction. It's the first critical security checkpoint in the payment process, occurring in real-time while the customer is still at the point of sale.

Additional resource: https://www.pcisecuritystandards.org/documents/Understanding_the_Intent_of_the_Requirements_v1.2.pdf

Q21: Multiple Choice: Which of the following is NOT a step in the authentication process?

A) The issuing bank validates the credit card number B) The payment brand routes the transaction to the processor C) The issuing bank checks for available funds D) The issuing bank validates the CVV

A21: The correct answer is B) The payment brand routes the transaction to the processor.

The authentication process, as described in the content, includes:

1. The issuing bank receiving an authorization request from the payment brand network

2. The issuing bank validating the credit card number

3. The issuing bank checking the available funds

4. The issuing bank matching the billing address

5. The issuing bank validating the CVV

6. The transaction being approved or declined by the issuing bank

7. The issuing bank placing a hold on the cardholder's account

"The payment brand routes the transaction to the processor" is part of the clearing process, not the authentication process. During clearing, the processor routes batched information to the payment brand network, which then forwards transactions to the issuing banks.

Understanding the distinct phases of the payment card transaction process is crucial for the PCIP exam.

Additional resource: https://www.pcisecuritystandards.org/pdfs/pci_ssc_quick_guide.pdf

Q22: What security measures are implemented during a payment card transaction to protect cardholder data?

A22: Several security measures are implemented during a payment card transaction to protect cardholder data:

1. **PIN Authentication**: When using a credit card, the cardholder enters their unique Personal Identification Number (PIN), providing a first layer of authentication.

2. **Card Verification Value (CVV)**: The three or four-digit security code on the card serves as an additional verification method, especially for card-not-present transactions.

3. **Address Verification Service (AVS)**: The issuing bank matches the billing address provided during the transaction against the address on file.

4. **Real-time Authorization**: Transactions are approved or declined in real-time, allowing for immediate detection of potentially fraudulent activity.

5. **Card Data Validation**: The issuing bank validates that the card number is legitimate and has not been reported lost or stolen.

6. **Secure Transmission**: Card data is transmitted through secure channels between the various entities in the payment ecosystem.

7. **Transaction Hold**: The issuing bank places a hold on funds until the transaction is cleared, preventing double-spending.

8. **Batch Processing**: End-of-day batch processing allows for reconciliation and additional security checks.

These measures work together to create a secure environment for payment card transactions, protecting sensitive cardholder data throughout the process.

Additional resource: https://www.pcisecuritystandards.org/pci_security/

Q23: What role does the processor play in the payment card transaction process?

A23: The processor plays several important roles in the payment card transaction process:

1. **Transaction Routing**: The processor may receive transaction information from the merchant's point-of-sale system and route it to the appropriate acquiring bank and payment brand network.

2. **Batch Processing**: As mentioned in the content, "The Processor routes the batched information to the Payment Brand network as a Clearing Message." This occurs after the merchant sends the batch file of approved authorizations to the acquiring bank or its processor at the end of the day.

3. **Technical Infrastructure**: Processors often provide the technical infrastructure that enables the communication between merchants, acquiring banks, and payment brand networks.

4. **Fee Collection**: The processor receives fees for its services, which are paid by the payment brand from the transaction amount during settlement.

5. **Value-Added Services**: Many processors also offer additional services such as fraud detection, reporting, and analytics.

The processor is essentially a technology service provider that facilitates the complex communications required for payment card transactions. Some acquiring banks handle processing functions internally, while others outsource to third-party processors.

Additional resource: https://www.pcisecuritystandards.org/businesses/

Q24: True or False: The acquiring bank is responsible for validating the CVV during a payment card transaction.

A24: False. The issuing bank, not the acquiring bank, is responsible for validating the CVV during a payment card transaction.

As stated in the authentication process section: "The Issuing Bank validates the credit card number, checks the available funds matches the billing address, and validates the CVV."

The roles are clearly defined:

- The acquiring bank (merchant's bank) receives the transaction information from the merchant and routes it to the payment brand network
- The payment brand network forwards the authorization request to the issuing bank
- The issuing bank (cardholder's bank) performs the validation checks, including CVV validation
- The issuing bank then approves or declines the transaction

This division of responsibilities ensures proper security checks while maintaining an efficient transaction process. The issuing bank is best positioned to validate the CVV since it issued the card and has the original CVV value for comparison.

Additional resource: https://www.pcisecuritystandards.org/merchants/

Q25: Scenario-based Question: A customer makes a $100 purchase at a retail store using their credit card. Describe the complete transaction flow from the moment they tap their card until the funds are deposited in the merchant's account.

A25: Complete transaction flow:

At the Point of Sale:

1. The customer selects $100 worth of merchandise and proceeds to checkout.
2. The customer taps their credit card on the merchant's contactless-enabled POS device.
3. The POS device reads the card information and initiates the transaction process.

Authorization Phase: 4. The merchant's POS system transmits the card information and transaction amount to the acquiring bank (merchant's bank) or its processor. 5. The acquiring bank routes this information to the appropriate payment brand network (e.g., Visa, Mastercard). 6. The payment brand network analyzes the card data, identifies the issuing bank based on the card's BIN (first few digits), and forwards the authorization request. 7. The issuing bank (customer's bank) receives the authorization request and performs several checks:

- Validates the credit card number
- Checks that the customer has at least $100 available credit
- Matches the billing address (if provided)
- Validates the CVV (if provided)

1. The issuing bank approves the transaction and places a $100 hold on the customer's account.
2. The approval response travels back through the payment brand network to the acquiring bank and finally to the merchant's POS.
3. The POS displays "Approved" and generates a receipt for the customer.

Clearing Phase: 11. At the end of the business day, the merchant performs an End of Day (EoD) task on the POS terminal. 12. This EoD process collects all approved authorizations, including the $100 purchase. 13. The merchant sends this batch file to their acquiring bank or its processor. 14. The processor routes the batched information to the payment brand network as a clearing message. 15. The payment brand network forwards the transaction to the issuing bank.

Settlement Phase: 16. Within 24-48 hours, the issuing bank transfers $100 (minus interchange fees) to the acquiring bank via the payment brand network. 17. The payment brand deducts its fee (let's say $1.50) and the processor's fee (let's say $0.50). 18. The acquiring bank receives $98 and may deduct its own fee (let's say $1). 19. The acquiring bank deposits the remaining $97 into the merchant's account.

Post-Transaction: 20. The $100 purchase appears on the customer's credit card statement when the issuing bank sends the bill. 21. The customer pays their credit card bill by the due date.

This entire process combines real-time authorization with delayed clearing and settlement, balancing the need for immediate transaction approval with efficient batch processing of funds transfer.

Additional resource: https://www.pcisecuritystandards.org/documents/PCI_DSS_for_Large_Organizations_v1.pdf

8

Understanding Card Security Codes - Question Set

Q1: What is the primary purpose of the Card Validation Code (CVC) or Card Security Code (CSC)?

A1: The primary purpose of the Card Validation Code (CVC) or Card Security Code (CSC) is to add an extra layer of protection for card transactions, particularly for online or card-not-present transactions. This three- or four-digit code helps verify that the person making the transaction actually possesses the physical card, rather than just having the card number. Most online retailers implement security measures that lock an account after multiple failed attempts to enter the correct CVC, providing additional fraud protection. Since this code is not part of the embossed data or magnetic stripe information, it serves as a crucial verification element that's separate from the primary card data.

Additional resource: https://www.pcisecuritystandards.org/pci_security/glossary

Q2: True or False: Merchants are permitted to store the PIN/PIN Block after payment authorization.

A2: False. Merchants are strictly prohibited from storing the PIN/PIN Block after payment authorization. This is explicitly mentioned in the content: "The PIN/PIN Block is the cardholder's personal identification number that you would key into a PoS device. It is not displayed on the physical card (Merchants can't store it after payment authorization)." This prohibition is a critical part of the Payment Card Industry Data Security Standard (PCI DSS) requirements, as PINs are considered Sensitive Authentication Data. Storing this information would create a significant security vulnerability that could be exploited by attackers to perform fraudulent transactions.

Additional resource: https://www.pcisecuritystandards.org/documents/PCI_DSS_v4.0.pdf

Q3: How many digits are typically in a Primary Account Number (PAN)?

A3: According to the content, a Primary Account Number (PAN) is "usually 16 digits long, but in some cases, it can be up to 19 digits." The length of the PAN depends on the card issuer and the type of card. Most major credit card brands like Visa and Mastercard typically use 16-digit PANs, while some other card types might use different lengths within this range. The PAN is a crucial identifier that links the physical card to a specific account in the issuing bank's systems.

Additional resource: https://www.iso.org/standard/70484.html

Q4: Explain the structure and purpose of the Primary Account Number (PAN).

A4: The Primary Account Number (PAN) is the unique number on the front of a payment card (though some cards have it on the back). Its structure and purpose include:

1. Length: Usually 16 digits, but can be up to 19 digits long
2. First digit: Indicates the card provider (e.g., Mastercard starts with 2 or 5, Visa with 4, etc.)
3. First six digits: Known as the Issue Identifier Number (IIN), which identifies the card issuer
4. Middle digits: Account-specific numbers unique to the cardholder
5. Last digit: Called the "Check Digit," calculated using the Luhn algorithm to verify the accuracy of the card number

The PAN serves as the primary identifier for the cardholder's account and enables the processing of transactions through the correct payment network to the appropriate issuing bank. This numbering system was developed by Hans Peter Luhn, an IBM engineer, in 1954, and continues to be the foundation of card payment processing worldwide.

Additional resource: https://www.pcisecuritystandards.org/documents/pci_dss_protection_of_pan.pdf

Q5: Which card brands use a 4-digit security code, and where is it located on the card?

A5: According to the content, American Express and certain Discover payment cards use a 4-digit security code. For American Express cards, this code is called the Card Identification Number (CID) and appears as "an unembossed four-digit number above the PAN, either to the right or to the left" on the face (front) of the card. For Discover cards, their CID is also mentioned as being 4 digits on the front of the card. This contrasts with most other major card brands like Visa, MasterCard, JCB, and UnionPay, which use 3-digit security codes typically located on the back of the card.

Additional resource: https://www.pcisecuritystandards.org/pci_security/small_merchant_resources

Q6: What information is contained in the magnetic stripe's track data, and what are the restrictions on storing this data?

A6: The magnetic stripe contains track data with the following information:

- Credit card account number (PAN)
- Cardholder's name
- Expiration date
- Service code
- Card verification code

- Additional information like country or currency codes (potentially on track 3)

Track 1 data can be up to 79 characters long and includes all fields of both primary tracks.

Regarding storage restrictions, the content explicitly states: "Merchants cannot store complete track data or Sensitive Authentication Data (SAD) after authorization." This is a critical PCI DSS requirement because track data is considered Sensitive Authentication Data (SAD). If this data were compromised, it could potentially be used to create counterfeit cards. The prohibition on storing this data after authorization is a fundamental security control to prevent card fraud.

Additional resource: https://www.pcisecuritystandards.org/documents/PCI_DSS_v4.0.pdf

Q7: What is the difference between the various card security codes used by different card brands?

A7: The different card brands use various names and formats for their security codes, though they all serve the same fundamental purpose of adding authentication for card-not-present transactions:

- CID (Card Identification Number): Used by American Express and Discover - 4 digits on the front of the card
- CAV2 (Card Authentication Value 2): Used by JCB payment cards - 3 digits on the rear of the card
- CVC2 (Card Validation Code 2): Used by MasterCard payment cards - 3 digits on the back of the card
- CVV2 (Card Verification Value 2): Used by Visa payment cards - 3 digits on the back of the card
- CVN (Card Validation Number): Used by UnionPay cards - 3 digits on the back of the card

The main differences are in terminology, location on the card (front vs. back), and the number of digits (3 vs. 4). Despite these differences, all these codes serve the same security purpose: to verify that the person making a transaction has the physical card in their possession. This is particularly important for online or phone transactions where the physical card isn't present.

Additional resource: https://www.pcisecuritystandards.org/glossary/

Q8: True or False: The Primary Account Number (PAN) is always found on the front of payment cards.

A8: False. According to the provided content: "The Primary Account Number (PAN) is usually found on the front of your card but some cards have it on the back." While the vast majority of payment cards do display the PAN on the front, there are exceptions where card issuers place the PAN on the back of the card. This variation in design might be for aesthetic reasons or as an additional security feature, making it less obvious where the card number is located when the card is visible.

Additional resource: https://www.pcisecuritystandards.org/documents/PCI_DSS_v4.0.pdf

Q9: What are the first digits for different card brands, and what do they indicate?

A9: The first digit (or digits) of a payment card's Primary Account Number (PAN) indicates the card provider or payment network According to the content:

- Mastercard numbers start with 2 or 5

- Visa card numbers begin with 4
- Discover starts with 6
- JCB begins with 3, 2, or 1
- American Express numbers start with 3
- UnionPay card numbers begin with 60 or 62

These first digits are part of the Issue Identifier Number (IIN), also known as the Bank Identification Number (BIN), which comprises the first six digits of the card number. The IIN/BIN helps payment systems identify which card network should process the transaction and route it to the appropriate issuing bank. This standardized numbering system enables global interoperability of payment cards across different merchants and payment processors.

Additional resource: https://www.iso.org/standard/70484.html

Q10: What is the purpose of the "Check Digit" in a payment card number?

A10: The "Check Digit" is the last digit of the Primary Account Number (PAN) and serves to "ensure that the credit card number is accurate and in the correct order." It's calculated using the Luhn algorithm (created by IBM engineer Hans Peter Luhn in 1954), which is a mathematical formula that validates the entire card number.

The purpose of the Check Digit is to quickly detect common errors in card number entry, such as a single wrong digit or transposed digits. When a payment system receives a card number, it can immediately validate whether the number could potentially be valid by running the Luhn algorithm. This provides an initial validation check before attempting to process the transaction, helping to catch accidental errors in manual entry and reducing unnecessary processing of obviously invalid numbers.

The Check Digit doesn't provide security against intentional fraud (as someone could generate numbers that pass the Luhn check), but it's effective at catching unintentional mistakes.

Additional resource: https://www.iso.org/standard/70484.html

Q11: Multiple Choice: Which of the following information is NOT considered Sensitive Authentication Data (SAD)?

A) PIN/PIN Block B) Full magnetic stripe data C) Primary Account Number (PAN) D) Card Validation Code (CVC/CVV)

A11: C) Primary Account Number (PAN)

The Primary Account Number (PAN) is not considered Sensitive Authentication Data (SAD). While the PAN is sensitive cardholder data that must be protected according to PCI DSS requirements, it is not classified as SAD.

Sensitive Authentication Data includes:

- Full magnetic stripe data (also called full track data)
- Card Validation Codes (CVC/CVV/etc.)

- PIN/PIN Block data

The key distinction is that SAD is data used specifically for authentication during the transaction process that should never be stored after authorization. While PANs must be protected (through encryption, truncation, etc.), they can be stored by merchants if necessary and if properly secured. The other options (PIN/PIN Block, full magnetic stripe data, and Card Validation Codes) are all explicitly identified as SAD in PCI DSS and must never be stored after transaction authorization.

Additional resource: https://www.pcisecuritystandards.org/documents/PCI_DSS_v4.0.pdf

Q12: True or False: Credit cards typically use all three tracks on the magnetic stripe for transaction processing.

A12: False. According to the content, "Typically, credit cards only use the first two tracks. The third track may contain extra details like a country or currency code." Track 1 and Track 2 contain the essential payment information needed for transaction processing, including the account number, name (on Track 1), expiration date, and service code. Track 3 is rarely used for standard credit card transactions and might contain supplementary information or be left unused. This is consistent with industry standards where Track 1 and Track 2 data are the primary focus of magnetic stripe transactions.

Additional resource: https://www.pcisecuritystandards.org/glossary/

Q13: What is replacing magnetic stripe technology on payment cards and why?

A13: According to the content, "magnetic strips are being replaced by EMV Chips or Chip & Pin for added security and convenience." This replacement is happening because magnetic stripe technology has several disadvantages:

1. Magnetic stripes "can become scratched or damaged," rendering the card unusable
2. The data on magnetic stripes is static and can be easily copied or "skimmed" by fraudsters
3. EMV chip technology provides dynamic authentication, generating unique transaction codes
4. Chip technology is more difficult to counterfeit than magnetic stripes
5. Chip & PIN adds another layer of security by requiring a PIN for transaction authorization

The transition to EMV technology represents a significant security upgrade in the payment card industry. While magnetic stripes contain the same data for every transaction (making them vulnerable to cloning), EMV chips generate unique codes for each transaction, substantially reducing the risk of counterfeit fraud. This technology shift has been a global initiative to reduce payment card fraud and improve the security of the overall payment ecosystem.

Additional resource: https://www.emvco.com/about/deployment-statistics/

Q14: What is the Issue Identifier Number (IIN) and what information does it provide?

A14: The Issue Identifier Number (IIN), also commonly known as the Bank Identification Number (BIN), consists of the first six digits of the Primary Account Number (PAN) on a payment card. According to the content, this number identifies the card issuer.

The IIN/BIN serves several important functions in the payment card ecosystem:

1. It identifies which financial institution issued the card
2. It helps payment networks route transactions to the correct issuing bank
3. It indicates the card brand/network (Visa, Mastercard, etc.)
4. It can provide information about the card type (credit, debit, prepaid, etc.)
5. It may indicate the country where the card was issued

The first digit of the IIN (sometimes called the Major Industry Identifier) specifically indicates the card network or industry (e.g., Mastercard starts with 2 or 5, Visa with 4, etc.), while the complete six-digit IIN provides more specific information about the issuing institution. This standardized numbering system enables the global payment infrastructure to correctly route transactions across different networks, processors, and financial institutions.

Additional resource: https://www.iso.org/standard/70484.html

Q15: Which security features are present on a typical payment card? Describe at least four.

A15: A typical payment card includes multiple security features designed to prevent fraud and verify authenticity:

1. Card Validation Code (CVC) or Card Security Code (CSC): A three- or four-digit code located either on the back (for most cards) or front (for American Express) that provides an additional verification layer for transactions, especially online. This code isn't stored in the magnetic stripe, making it harder for fraudsters to obtain through skimming.
2. Primary Account Number (PAN): The 16-19 digit unique number that includes a check digit (the last digit) calculated using the Luhn algorithm to validate the number's accuracy. The PAN structure follows industry standards with specific digits indicating the card issuer.
3. Magnetic Stripe: Contains encoded track data with payment information, though this is being phased out due to security vulnerabilities. The magnetic stripe includes cardholder data on multiple tracks, with track 1 containing up to 79 characters of data.
4. EMV Chip: The newer security technology replacing magnetic stripes, which generates dynamic data for each transaction, making it much more difficult to clone cards. This chip contains a microprocessor that can perform cryptographic functions.
5. Expiration Date: A validity period displayed as month and year that adds another element of verification for transactions.
6. PIN/PIN Block: A personal identification number that provides an additional authentication factor for ATM transactions and in-person purchases, though this is not physically present on the card.

These multiple layers of security work together to authenticate both the card itself and the person using it, making it more difficult for fraudsters to successfully complete unauthorized transactions.

Additional resource: https://www.pcisecuritystandards.org/pci_security/small_merchant_resources

Q16: True or False: Merchants can store the Card Validation Code (CVC) as long as it's encrypted.

A16: False. Merchants cannot store the Card Validation Code (CVC) under any circumstances after transaction authorization, even if it's encrypted. The content states that "Merchants cannot store complete track data or Sensitive Authentication Data (SAD) after authorization," and the CVC/CVV codes are explicitly considered Sensitive Authentication Data.

This prohibition is a fundamental requirement of the Payment Card Industry Data Security Standard (PCI DSS). The reason for this strict prohibition is that these security codes are specifically designed to verify that the person making a transaction has physical possession of the card. If merchants were allowed to store these codes, it would create a significant security vulnerability, as compromised merchant systems could potentially provide attackers with all the information needed to conduct fraudulent card-not-present transactions.

Additional resource: https://www.pcisecuritystandards.org/documents/PCI_DSS_v4.0.pdf

Q17: What is the difference between Track 1 and Track 2 data on a payment card's magnetic stripe?

A17: According to the content, the key differences between Track 1 and Track 2 data on a payment card's magnetic stripe are:

Track 1 data:

- Can be up to 79 characters long
- Includes all fields of both tracks
- Typically contains the cardholder's name, account number, expiration date, service code, and card verification code

Track 2 data:

- Is more limited in length and data capacity
- Contains similar payment information but without some of the extended data of Track 1
- Is commonly used for transaction processing

The content also mentions that "credit cards only use the first two tracks" for payment processing, with Track 3 sometimes containing supplementary information like country or currency codes but not being essential for standard credit card transactions.

Both Track 1 and Track 2 data are considered Sensitive Authentication Data (SAD), and merchants are prohibited from storing complete track data after authorization under PCI DSS requirements.

Additional resource: https://www.pcisecuritystandards.org/glossary/

Q18: What information does the first digit of a Primary Account Number (PAN) provide? List the first digits for at least three card brands.

A18: The first digit of a Primary Account Number (PAN) indicates the card provider or payment network. According to the content:

- Mastercard numbers start with a 2 or 5
- Visa card numbers begin with a 4
- Discover starts with a 6
- American Express numbers start with a 3
- JCB begins with a 3, 2, or 1
- UnionPay card numbers begin with 60 or 62

This first digit is part of the Issue Identifier Number (IIN), also known as the Bank Identification Number (BIN), which comprises the first six digits of the card number. The first digit helps payment systems quickly identify which card network should process the transaction. This standardized numbering system is crucial for the global interoperability of payment cards and enables merchants and processors to route transactions to the appropriate payment networks.

Additional resource: https://www.iso.org/standard/70484.html

Q19: Explain why merchants are prohibited from storing complete track data after authorization.

A19: Merchants are prohibited from storing complete track data after authorization for several critical security reasons:

1. Fraud Risk: Complete track data (also called full track data or Sensitive Authentication Data) contains all the information needed to create counterfeit physical cards. If compromised, criminals could potentially encode this data onto blank cards, effectively cloning the original cards.

2. PCI DSS Requirement: The Payment Card Industry Data Security Standard explicitly prohibits the storage of Sensitive Authentication Data (SAD) after authorization, which includes full track data, security codes, and PIN data.

3. Unnecessary Risk: Once a transaction is authorized, there is no legitimate business need for merchants to retain the complete track data. Storing this sensitive data creates an unnecessary security risk.

4. Liability: In the event of a data breach, merchants who store prohibited data may face increased liability, fines, and penalties from card brands and regulatory bodies.

5. Protection of the Payment Ecosystem: This prohibition is part of a broader strategy to protect the entire payment card ecosystem by minimizing the locations where sensitive card data is stored.

The content specifically states that "Merchants cannot store complete track data or Sensitive Authentication Data (SAD) after authorization," highlighting this critical security requirement. This restriction is one of the foundational principles of payment card security, designed to reduce the impact of potential data breaches and limit the spread of compromised card data that could be used for fraudulent transactions.

Additional resource: https://www.pcisecuritystandards.org/documents/PCI_DSS_v4.0.pdf

Q20: Multiple Choice: Which of the following describes the Card Security Code for Visa payment cards?

A) CID - 4 digits on the front of the card B) CAV2 - 3 digits on the rear of the card C) CVC2 - 3 digits on the back of the card D) CVV2 - 3 digits on the back of the card

A20: D) CVV2 - 3 digits on the back of the card

According to the content, Visa payment cards use a security code called the Card Verification Value 2 (CVV2), which consists of 3 digits located on the back of the card. This is distinct from the codes used by other card brands:

- American Express uses CID (4 digits on the front)
- JCB uses CAV2 (3 digits on the rear)
- MasterCard uses CVC2 (3 digits on the back)
- Discover uses CID (3 digits on the back)
- UnionPay uses CVN (3 digits on the back)

While these codes serve the same security purpose across all card brands (providing an additional verification element for card-not-present transactions), the specific terminology and sometimes the format/location vary by card brand.

Additional resource: https://usa.visa.com/support/consumer/security.html

Q21: Describe the purpose and limitations of the magnetic stripe on payment cards.

A21: The magnetic stripe on payment cards serves as a data storage mechanism that contains essential account information needed to process transactions. According to the content, it functions similar to "a tiny strip of film" and stores payment information using magnetic fields across three tracks.

Purpose:

- Stores the cardholder's account number, name, expiration date, service code, and card verification code
- Enables card-present transactions by allowing card readers to access account information
- Typically uses only the first two tracks for credit card transactions
- Track 1 can store up to 79 characters of payment information

Limitations:

- "Can become scratched or damaged" easily, rendering the card unusable
- Contains static data that doesn't change between transactions
- Vulnerable to skimming attacks where criminals can copy the data

- Being phased out in favor of more secure EMV chip technology
- Less secure than newer technologies like EMV chips
- Lacks the dynamic authentication capabilities of EMV technology

The magnetic stripe represented an important technological advancement when introduced, but its inherent security limitations have led the payment card industry to transition toward EMV chip technology, which offers enhanced security through dynamic authentication and better protection against card counterfeiting.

Additional resource: https://www.emvco.com/about/deployment-statistics/

Q22: What is the purpose of the Luhn algorithm in payment card security?

A22: The Luhn algorithm (created by IBM engineer Hans Peter Luhn in 1954) is used to validate payment card numbers through a mathematical check. According to the content, the last digit of a Primary Account Number (PAN) is called a "Check Digit," which "helps to ensure that the credit card number is accurate and in the correct order."

The primary purposes of the Luhn algorithm are:

1. Error Detection: It catches common mistakes in manual entry, such as transposed digits or single incorrect digits.
2. Basic Validation: It provides a simple way to determine if a card number could potentially be valid before attempting to process it.
3. Immediate Verification: Systems can quickly verify that a card number follows the proper format without needing to contact the issuing bank.
4. Prevention of Random Numbers: It helps filter out randomly generated numbers that wouldn't pass the mathematical check.

It's important to note that the Luhn algorithm is not a security feature against intentional fraud. Someone could deliberately create a number that passes the Luhn check. Rather, it's designed to catch accidental errors in card number entry or transmission. The algorithm performs a specific mathematical calculation on all digits of the card number, and if the result meets certain criteria (typically being divisible by 10), the number passes the initial validation check.

Additional resource: https://www.iso.org/standard/70484.html

Q23: Compare and contrast the security features of American Express cards versus Visa cards.

A23: American Express and Visa cards have several security features in common, but also some notable differences:

Similarities:

- Both have a Primary Account Number (PAN) that includes a check digit validated using the Luhn algorithm
- Both have a security code used to verify card-not-present transactions
- Both typically include expiration dates and cardholder names

- Both are transitioning from magnetic stripes to EMV chip technology

Key Differences:

1. Security Code:
   - American Express: Uses a 4-digit Card Identification Number (CID) located on the front of the card above the PAN
   - Visa: Uses a 3-digit Card Verification Value 2 (CVV2) located on the back of the card
2. PAN Structure:
   - American Express: Numbers start with 3 and typically have 15 digits
   - Visa: Numbers start with 4 and typically have 16 digits
3. Card Number Position:
   - American Express: The PAN is traditionally centered on the front of the card
   - Visa: The PAN is traditionally aligned to the left on the front of the card (though positioning can vary)
4. Additional Security Features:
   - American Express: Often includes the "Member Since" date as an additional authentication element
   - Visa: Typically includes a hologram dove image as a visual security feature

These differences reflect each card brand's unique approach to security while maintaining the fundamental elements required for secure payment processing. The variation in security code format and placement (4 digits on front vs. 3 digits on back) is particularly notable as it represents different implementations of the same security concept.

Additional resource: https://www.pcisecuritystandards.org/pci_security/small_merchant_resources

Q24: What is Sensitive Authentication Data (SAD) and what are the restrictions regarding its storage?

A24: Sensitive Authentication Data (SAD) refers to security-related information used to authenticate payment card transactions that must be protected with strict security measures. According to the content, SAD is "also called Full Track Data" and is "hidden within the magnetic strip on the back of your card."

SAD includes:

1. Complete magnetic stripe data (full track data)
2. Card security codes (CVC/CVV/CID/CAV2/CVN)
3. PIN/PIN Block data

The restriction regarding SAD storage is explicit and absolute: "Merchants cannot store complete track data or Sensitive Authentication Data (SAD) after authorization." This prohibition is a fundamental requirement of the Payment Card Industry Data Security Standard (PCI DSS).

The rationale behind this restriction is that SAD contains the elements needed to create counterfeit cards or perform fraudulent transactions. If this data were compromised in a breach, criminals could potentially use it to conduct unauthorized transactions or create clone cards. By prohibiting the storage of this data after authorization, the payment card industry significantly reduces the risk of widespread card fraud resulting from merchant data breaches.

This restriction applies regardless of whether the data would be encrypted or otherwise protected - the requirement is that SAD must not be stored after the authorization process is complete.

Additional resource: https://www.pcisecuritystandards.org/documents/PCI_DSS_v4.0.pdf

Q25: Explain how the various security features on a payment card work together to prevent fraud.

A25: Payment cards incorporate multiple security features that work together as a layered defense system to prevent different types of fraud:

1. Primary Account Number (PAN): The 16-19 digit number uniquely identifies the account. Its structure follows the Luhn algorithm, which allows for immediate validation of potential data entry errors through the check digit (last digit). The first digits identify the card brand and issuing bank, enabling proper routing of transactions.

2. Card Security Codes (CVC/CVV/CID): These 3-4 digit codes provide protection for card-not-present transactions like online purchases. Since they're not encoded in the magnetic stripe or EMV chip, they verify that the person has physical possession of the card. Different brands use different terminology (CVV2, CVC2, CID, CAV2, CVN) but they serve the same purpose.

3. Magnetic Stripe: Contains encoded account information on multiple tracks. While being phased out due to security vulnerabilities, it still serves as a data carrier for card-present transactions in regions without full EMV adoption.

4. EMV Chip: Provides enhanced security through dynamic authentication, generating unique transaction codes for each purchase. This prevents the copying or "replay" of transaction data, addressing a key vulnerability of magnetic stripes.

5. PIN/PIN Block: Adds a "something you know" authentication factor for ATM and in-person transactions, requiring knowledge that wouldn't be available to someone who merely found or stole the physical card.

6. Expiration Date: Serves as an additional verification element and ensures cards are periodically replaced with updated security features.

These features create multiple layers of security that address different fraud scenarios:

- Physical counterfeit protection (EMV chip, hologram)
- Lost/stolen card protection (PIN, signature)
- Card-not-present fraud protection (CVV/CVC)
- Data validation (Luhn algorithm, expiration date)

The effectiveness lies in their combination—even if one security element is compromised, others remain as barriers to fraud. For example, a fraudster might obtain the PAN, but without the CVV, expiration date, and/or PIN, different types of transactions would still be prevented. This multi-layered approach means that compromising a single element doesn't provide sufficient information to conduct all types of fraud.

Additional resource: https://www.pcisecuritystandards.org/pci_security/small_merchant_resources

9

PCI-DSS Applicability - Question Set

Q1: Which entities must comply with the Payment Card Industry Data Security Standard?

A1: All entities that store, process, or transmit cardholder data must comply with the Payment Card Industry Data Security Standard (PCI DSS). This includes merchants, service providers, processors, acquirers, and issuers. Additionally, entities that store, process, or transmit sensitive authentication information besides cardholder data are also required to comply with these standards. Compliance is mandatory regardless of the size or volume of transactions handled by the entity, as the primary goal is to ensure secure payment card processing and protect customer data.

Additional resources: https://www.pcisecuritystandards.org/pci_security/maintaining_payment_security

Q2: When displaying a Primary Account Number (PAN), which digits are allowed to be visible?

A2: When displaying a Primary Account Number (PAN), only the first six and last four digits are allowed to be visible. The digits in between must be masked for security purposes. This masking requirement is a fundamental aspect of PCI DSS compliance and helps protect cardholder data from unauthorized access or exposure. For example, if a PAN is "1234567890123456," it should be displayed as "123456XXXXXX3456" when shown on receipts, displays, or reports. Only personnel with a legitimate business need should have access to view the full, unmasked PAN.

Additional resources: https://www.pcisecuritystandards.org/documents/PCI_DSS_for_Large_Organizations_v1.pdf

Q3: True or False: If an organization outsources its payment operations to a third party, it is no longer responsible for PCI DSS compliance.

A3: False. If an organization outsources payment operations or the cardholder data environment (CDE) management to third parties, PCI DSS requirements still apply to the organization. The organization remains responsible for ensuring that account data is protected according to PCI DSS standards. Outsourcing does not transfer compliance responsibility away from the organization. Instead, the organization must ensure that the third party is also compliant with PCI DSS and that appropriate contracts and monitoring are in place to maintain the security of the cardholder data throughout the outsourced relationship.

Additional resources: https://www.pcisecuritystandards.org/documents/Third_Party_Security_Assurance_Info_Supp.pdf

Q4: What is Sensitive Authentication Data (SAD) and why is it important in payment card transactions?

A4: Sensitive Authentication Data (SAD) is data used to authenticate cardholders and/or authorize payment card transactions. It includes data elements stored on the card's magnetic stripe, chip, or elsewhere, such as the full track data, card validation codes/values, and PINs/PIN blocks.

SAD is critically important in payment card transactions because it serves as a unique identifier to authenticate a cardholder and ensure transaction security. It verifies that the person using the card is the legitimate cardholder. However, this same characteristic makes it extremely valuable to attackers, as possession of SAD enables creation of counterfeit cards or fraudulent transactions.

The importance of SAD is highlighted by the strict PCI DSS requirements that prohibit storing this data after authorization, even if encrypted. Protecting SAD is essential for preventing credit card fraud and unauthorized transactions, thus maintaining consumer trust in the payment card ecosystem.

Additional resources: https://www.pcisecuritystandards.org/glossary/sensitive-authentication-data/

Q5: According to PCI DSS, what elements are considered Cardholder Data?

A5: According to PCI DSS, Cardholder Data includes:

1. Primary Account Number (PAN)
2. Cardholder Name (when stored, processed, or transmitted with the PAN)
3. Service Code (when stored, processed, or transmitted with the PAN)
4. Expiration Date (when stored, processed, or transmitted with the PAN)

While the PAN is the most critical element that must always be protected, the other elements require protection only when they are stored, processed, or transmitted together with the PAN. The protection of these data elements is fundamental to PCI DSS compliance and essential for safeguarding customers' financial information from unauthorized access or theft.

Additional resources: https://www.pcisecuritystandards.org/glossary/cardholder-data/

Q6: Which of the following statements is correct regarding storing Sensitive Authentication Data (SAD) after authorization?

A) It can be stored if properly encrypted B) It can be stored for up to 90 days C) It can be stored if the PAN is not present in the environment D) It should not be stored after authorization under any circumstances

A6: The correct answer is D) It should not be stored after authorization under any circumstances.

According to PCI DSS, storing sensitive authentication data after authorization is not permitted under any circumstances, even if it's encrypted. This includes data from the magnetic stripe, chip, card verification codes/values (CAV2, CVC2, CVV2, CID), and PINs/PIN blocks. The prohibition applies even if no Primary Account Number (PAN) is present in the environment. This strict requirement exists because possession of such data enables the creation of counterfeit payment cards and fraudulent transactions, posing significant risks to cardholders and the payment ecosystem.

Additional resources: https://blog.pcisecuritystandards.org/faq-can-sensitive-authentication-data-be-stored-for-troubleshooting-purposes

Q7: True or False: When storing the cardholder name, service code, and expiration date without the PAN, PCI DSS requirements do not apply.

A7: True. PCI DSS requirements for protecting cardholder data elements (cardholder name, service code, and expiration date) apply only when these elements are stored, processed, or transmitted along with the PAN. If these elements are stored without the PAN, they do not fall under PCI DSS protection requirements.

However, it's important to note that while technically true according to PCI DSS, these data elements still constitute personally identifiable information that may be subject to other privacy regulations and security best practices. Organizations should consider implementing appropriate security measures for all customer data, regardless of whether PCI DSS specifically requires it.

Additional resources: https://www.pcisecuritystandards.org/documents/PCI_DSS_Glossary_v3-2-1.pdf

Q8: What is required to make the Primary Account Number (PAN) unreadable according to PCI DSS Requirement 3.5.1?

A8: According to PCI DSS Requirement 3.5.1, the Primary Account Number (PAN) must be made unreadable wherever it is stored. This can be achieved through one of the following methods:

1. One-way hashes based on strong cryptography (the entire PAN must be hashed)
2. Truncation (hashing cannot be used to replace the truncated segment of the PAN)
3. Index tokens and pads (the pad must be securely stored)
4. Strong cryptography with associated key management processes and procedures

This requirement applies to the PAN stored in primary storage (databases, files, etc.) as well as in backup media, logs, and anywhere else the PAN might be stored. It's important to note that only the PAN needs to be made unreadable when stored with other cardholder data elements. The other elements (cardholder name, service code, and expiration date) do not need to be made unreadable if the PAN is properly protected.

Additional resources: https://www.pcisecuritystandards.org/documents/PCI_DSS_v3-2-1.pdf

Q9: Who is permitted to see the full, unmasked Primary Account Number (PAN)?

A9: Only personnel with a legitimate business need or requirement can see the full, unmasked Primary Account Number (PAN). This restriction is an essential part of PCI DSS compliance and helps minimize the exposure of sensitive cardholder data.

"Legitimate business need" refers to situations where access to the full PAN is necessary to complete a specific business function, such as:

- Processing payment transactions
- Resolving disputes or chargebacks
- Fraud investigation and prevention
- Specific customer service scenarios requiring verification

Organizations must implement role-based access control, ensuring that only authorized personnel have access to full PANs. Additionally, the organization should maintain documentation of who has access to full PANs, why they need it, and implement monitoring to detect any unauthorized access attempts. This principle of "least privilege" is a fundamental security concept that reduces the risk of data breaches and insider threats.

Additional resources: https://www.pcisecuritystandards.org/documents/Protecting_Telephone_Based_Payment_Card_Data_v3-0_nov_2018.pdf

Q10: Which of the following data elements is considered Sensitive Authentication Data (SAD)? (Select all that apply)

A) Primary Account Number (PAN) B) Full magnetic stripe data C) Cardholder name D) Card Verification Code (CVV2/CVC2/CID) E) Expiration date F) PIN/PIN Block

A10: The correct answers are B) Full magnetic stripe data, D) Card Verification Code (CVV2/CVC2/CID), and F) PIN/PIN Block.

Sensitive Authentication Data (SAD) specifically includes:

- Full magnetic stripe data (or equivalent data on a chip)
- Card verification codes/values (the three-digit or four-digit number printed on the card)
- PINs/PIN blocks

These data elements are used for authentication purposes during the transaction authorization process and must never be stored after authorization, even if encrypted.

The Primary Account Number (PAN), cardholder name, and expiration date are considered Cardholder Data, not Sensitive Authentication Data. While they must be protected according to PCI DSS requirements, they can be stored after authorization if properly secured (with the PAN rendered unreadable).

Understanding the distinction between Cardholder Data and Sensitive Authentication Data is crucial for proper implementation of PCI DSS controls and ensuring payment card security.

Additional resources: https://www.pcisecuritystandards.org/glossary/sensitive-authentication-data/

Q11: What are the potential consequences for a small business that stores Sensitive Authentication Data after authorization?

A11: A small business that stores Sensitive Authentication Data (SAD) after authorization faces several serious potential consequences:

1. **Security Breaches**: Storing SAD creates an attractive target for hackers, increasing the risk of a data breach. If compromised, attackers can use this data to create counterfeit cards and conduct fraudulent transactions.

2. **Regulatory Penalties**: Non-compliance with PCI DSS can result in fines from payment card brands and acquiring banks. These fines can range from thousands to tens of thousands of dollars, which can be devastating for a small business.

3. **Financial Losses**:

    - Increased transaction fees and processing rates imposed by acquiring banks
    - Costs associated with forensic investigations if a breach occurs
    - Expenses related to notification of affected customers
    - Potential liability for fraud losses resulting from the breach

4. **Reputational Damage**: News of a data breach can severely damage customer trust and the business's reputation. Small businesses often rely heavily on community trust and reputation, making this impact particularly severe.

5. **Loss of Card Processing Privileges**: In extreme cases, a business might lose its ability to accept payment cards altogether, which could be fatal for many modern businesses.

6. **Legal Liability**: Beyond card brand penalties, businesses may face lawsuits from affected customers or banks that issued the compromised cards.

For example, if a small online store unknowingly stores customers' CVV2 codes after authorization and experiences a breach, hackers could use this information to make fraudulent purchases. This could result in numerous chargebacks, financial penalties, investigation costs, and potential loss of customers who no longer trust the business with their payment information.

Small businesses should implement proper payment processing systems that automatically discard SAD after authorization and regularly validate their compliance with PCI DSS requirements.

Additional resources: https://www.pcisecuritystandards.org/small_business_resources/

Q12: According to PCI DSS, which of the following statements is correct about outsourcing the Cardholder Data Environment (CDE)?

A) Outsourcing eliminates the need for PCI DSS compliance B) The merchant is no longer responsible once outsourcing occurs C) PCI DSS requirements still apply and the organization remains responsible D) Only the service provider needs to be PCI DSS compliant

A12: The correct answer is C) PCI DSS requirements still apply and the organization remains responsible.

When an organization outsources payment operations or the management of the Cardholder Data Environment (CDE) to third parties, PCI DSS requirements still apply to the original organization. The organization maintains responsibility for ensuring that account data is protected according to PCI DSS standards throughout the entire payment process, regardless of who handles the data.

This means that organizations must:

- Ensure their service providers are PCI DSS compliant
- Clearly define security responsibilities between parties
- Have written agreements that include acknowledgment of the service provider's responsibility for cardholder data
- Monitor the compliance status of their service providers
- Maintain visibility into how their cardholder data is being handled

While service providers must also be PCI DSS compliant (making option D partially true), the ultimate responsibility for compliance and data protection remains with the organization that collects the payment data. Outsourcing is not a way to transfer compliance obligations or liability.

Additional resources: https://www.pcisecuritystandards.org/documents/PCI_DSS_V3.0_Third_Party_Security_Assurance.pdf

Q13: What does PCI DSS Requirement 3.5.1 specifically mandate regarding cardholder data protection?

A13: PCI DSS Requirement 3.5.1 specifically mandates that only the Primary Account Number (PAN) needs to be made unreadable if it's stored with other cardholder data. This means that when storing cardholder data (which includes PAN, cardholder name, service code, and expiration date), only the PAN must be rendered unreadable through methods such as:

1. One-way hashes based on strong cryptography
2. Truncation (removing a segment of the PAN)
3. Index tokens and pads (with the pads being securely stored)
4. Strong cryptography with associated key management processes

The other elements of cardholder data (name, service code, expiration date) do not need to be made unreadable according to this specific requirement, as long as the PAN is properly protected. However, it's important to note that all cardholder data must be protected according to the appropriate PCI DSS requirements, which include access controls, encryption during transmission, and other security measures.

This requirement helps organizations focus their strongest protection efforts on the most sensitive element of cardholder data—the PAN—while still maintaining appropriate security for all cardholder data.

Additional resources: https://www.pcisecuritystandards.org/documents/Tokenization_Guidelines_Info_Supplement.pdf

Q14: True or False: Sensitive Authentication Data can be stored after authorization if it is properly encrypted.

A14: False. Sensitive Authentication Data (SAD) cannot be stored after authorization, even if it is properly encrypted. This is explicitly prohibited by PCI DSS.

SAD includes:

- Full magnetic stripe data
- Card verification codes/values (CVV2, CVC2, CID, CAV2)
- PINs/PIN blocks

The prohibition on storing this data after authorization is absolute and applies regardless of how securely the data might be encrypted. This strict requirement exists because SAD is specifically designed to verify that a physical card is present during a transaction. If this data were compromised, it would enable criminals to create counterfeit cards or conduct fraudulent transactions.

Even if an organization has strong encryption capabilities, PCI DSS does not allow exceptions to this rule. The safest approach regarding SAD is to never store it after authorization under any circumstances. This applies even if no Primary Account Number (PAN) is present in the environment.

Additional resources: https://www.pcisecuritystandards.org/faq/articles/Frequently_Asked_Question/Protecting-Sensitive-Authentication-Data/

Q15: What specific information is contained in a card's magnetic stripe that makes it part of Sensitive Authentication Data?

A15: A card's magnetic stripe contains several data elements that make it classified as Sensitive Authentication Data (SAD). These include:

1. **Track 1 Data**: Contains the cardholder's name, account number (PAN), expiration date, service code, and discretionary data. It may also include country codes, name format codes, and other sensitive information.
2. **Track 2 Data**: Contains the account number (PAN), expiration date, service code, discretionary data, and in some cases, the CVV1/CVC1 (a card verification value that differs from the printed CVV2/CVC2).
3. **Track 3 Data**: Used less frequently but may contain additional account and authorization information.

The magnetic stripe data is particularly sensitive because it contains all the information needed to create a counterfeit physical card. The service code on the magnetic stripe also indicates whether the card can be used for international transactions, ATM withdrawals, or has specific PIN requirements.

The magnetic stripe may also contain proprietary security codes that are used during the transaction authorization process to verify the authenticity of the physical card. These codes differ from the printed security codes (CVV2/CVC2/CID) visible on the card.

Due to the comprehensive nature of this data and its utility for creating counterfeit cards, PCI DSS strictly prohibits storing full track data after authorization, even if encrypted.

Additional resources: https://www.pcisecuritystandards.org/documents/Accepting_Mobile_Payments_with_a_Smartphone_or_Tablet.pdf

Q16: How does PCI DSS define "making data unreadable" in the context of protecting stored PANs?

A16: PCI DSS defines "making data unreadable" in the context of protecting stored Primary Account Numbers (PANs) as implementing one or more of the following methods:

1. **One-way hashes based on strong cryptography**: Converting the PAN into a fixed-length string of characters using a mathematical algorithm in a way that cannot be reversed. The entire PAN must be hashed.
2. **Truncation**: Removing a segment of the PAN data. Typically, this means only storing a portion of the PAN (such as the first 6 and last 4 digits) and permanently removing the remaining digits. Hashing cannot be used to replace the truncated segment.
3. **Index tokens and pads**: Using a token (a non-sensitive substitute value) that maps back to the original PAN through a tokenization system. The pads used in creating the tokens must be securely stored.
4. **Strong cryptography with associated key management processes and procedures**: Encrypting the PAN data using robust encryption algorithms with proper key management practices, including secure key generation, distribution, storage, and rotation.

The goal of making PANs unreadable is to ensure that even if unauthorized access to stored data occurs, the actual PAN values cannot be determined. The method chosen must be implemented securely and consistently across all storage locations, including databases, backup files, log files, and any other location where PANs might be stored.

It's important to note that making PANs unreadable is just one aspect of PCI DSS compliance. Organizations must also implement other controls such as access restrictions, audit logging, and network segmentation to fully protect cardholder data.

Additional resources: https://www.pcisecuritystandards.org/documents/Tokenization_Product_Security_Guidelines.pdf

Q17: What are the specific risks associated with inadequate protection of cardholder data for:

a) Customers b) Merchants c) Financial institutions

A17: The inadequate protection of cardholder data creates specific risks for different stakeholders in the payment ecosystem:

a) Risks for Customers:

- Identity theft and fraud: Stolen card data can be used to make unauthorized purchases or create counterfeit cards
- Financial losses: While fraud liability protections exist, customers may face temporary loss of funds, time spent resolving fraud claims, and potential impact on credit scores
- Personal data exposure: Beyond financial losses, customers' personal information may be compromised, leading to privacy violations
- Loss of trust in electronic payment systems: Repeated breaches may cause customers to avoid card payments or specific

merchants

- Time and inconvenience: Canceling compromised cards, monitoring credit reports, and disputing fraudulent charges requires significant customer effort

b) Risks for Merchants:

- Financial penalties: Non-compliance with PCI DSS can result in fines ranging from $5,000 to $100,000 per month
- Increased transaction fees: Card brands may impose higher per-transaction fees on non-compliant merchants
- Fraud losses and chargebacks: Merchants often bear the cost of fraudulent transactions
- Remediation costs: Expenses related to investigating breaches, improving security, and notifying affected customers
- Reputational damage: Loss of customer trust and negative publicity can significantly impact business
- Legal liability: Potential lawsuits from affected customers or card-issuing banks
- Loss of ability to process card payments: In severe cases, merchants may lose their card processing privileges

c) Risks for Financial Institutions:

- Card reissuance costs: Expenses related to canceling compromised cards and issuing new ones
- Fraud losses: Financial institutions often absorb fraudulent transaction costs to protect customers
- Customer service burden: Increased support calls and claims processing
- Reputation damage: Customers may blame their financial institution for failing to prevent fraud
- Regulatory scrutiny: Increased attention from financial regulators
- Loss of customer confidence: Customers may switch to other financial institutions perceived as more secure
- Operational disruption: Resources diverted to fraud investigation and remediation

The interconnected nature of the payment ecosystem means that inadequate protection by any one participant can have cascading effects throughout the system, highlighting the importance of universal compliance with PCI DSS requirements.

Additional resources: https://www.pcisecuritystandards.org/documents/PCI_DSS_V3.0_Third_Party_Security_Assurance.pdf

Q18: Which of the following correctly describes the proper handling of the CVV2/CVC2/CID code according to PCI DSS?

A) It can be stored in encrypted format indefinitely B) It can be stored for up to 30 days after authorization C) It can be stored in hashed format indefinitely D) It must not be stored after authorization under any circumstances

A18: The correct answer is D) It must not be stored after authorization under any circumstances.

The Card Verification Value (CVV2/CVC2/CID) is considered Sensitive Authentication Data (SAD) under PCI DSS. This three-digit or four-digit security code printed on payment cards (not encoded on the magnetic stripe) is specifically designed as an authentication element to verify that the person making a transaction has physical possession of the card.

PCI DSS explicitly prohibits storing this data after the authorization process is complete, regardless of how it might be stored:

- It cannot be stored in encrypted format
- It cannot be stored in hashed format
- It cannot be stored for any period after authorization
- No exceptions exist for storing this data, even temporarily

This strict prohibition exists because possession of this code significantly increases the risk of fraudulent card-not-present transactions if stolen. Since the code is designed as a secondary authentication factor, storing it defeats its security purpose.

Merchants and service providers must ensure their payment processing systems automatically discard this data once the authorization process is complete, and they should regularly check that no CVV2/CVC2/CID values are inadvertently being stored in logs, debugging tools, or other systems.

Additional resources: https://www.pcisecuritystandards.org/documents/PCI_DSS_v3_2_1.pdf

Q19: Explain the concept of the Cardholder Data Environment (CDE) and what elements it typically includes.

A19: The Cardholder Data Environment (CDE) refers to the people, processes, and technologies that store, process, or transmit cardholder data or sensitive authentication data. It encompasses all system components that are:

1. **Directly connected to cardholder data systems**: Systems that directly handle payment card information, such as point-of-sale terminals, payment servers, and e-commerce platforms.
2. **Systems in the same network segment**: Any system that shares a network segment with systems that store, process, or transmit cardholder data.
3. **Connected systems that could impact security**: Systems that, while not directly handling cardholder data, could affect the security of the CDE if compromised (such as authentication servers, security systems, or network equipment).

Typical elements of a CDE include:

- **Hardware components**: Servers, workstations, network devices (routers, switches, firewalls), physical payment terminals
- **Virtual components**: Virtual machines, cloud resources, containers
- **Network infrastructure**: Network segments, VLANs, VPNs
- **Applications**: Point-of-sale software, payment applications, e-commerce platforms, database systems
- **Databases**: Storage systems for cardholder data

- **Encryption mechanisms**: Systems that encrypt, decrypt, or transmit encrypted cardholder data
- **Access control systems**: Authentication servers, access management tools
- **Security elements**: Intrusion detection/prevention systems, anti-malware solutions
- **Personnel**: Employees with access to cardholder data or systems within the CDE

Understanding the scope of the CDE is critical for PCI DSS compliance as it defines where security controls must be applied. Organizations should maintain network diagrams that clearly define the CDE boundaries and implement network segmentation to isolate the CDE from less-secure network zones, thereby reducing the compliance scope and enhancing security.

Additional resources: https://www.pcisecuritystandards.org/documents/Guidance-PCI-DSS-Scoping-and-Segmentation_v1.pdf

Q20: True or False: If a merchant outsources payment processing to a PCI-compliant service provider, the merchant no longer needs to worry about compliance.

A20: False. Even if a merchant outsources payment processing to a PCI-compliant service provider, the merchant still maintains responsibility for PCI DSS compliance and must actively ensure that cardholder data is protected.

When outsourcing payment processing, merchants must:

1. **Verify the compliance status** of their service providers, including obtaining evidence of the provider's PCI DSS compliance
2. **Maintain formal agreements** with service providers that clearly outline security responsibilities and include acknowledgment by the service provider of their responsibility for securing cardholder data
3. **Implement their own PCI DSS controls** for any aspect of cardholder data handling that remains within their environment, even if limited
4. **Understand the scope of the service provider's responsibilities** and ensure no gaps exist in the protection of cardholder data throughout its lifecycle
5. **Monitor their service providers' compliance status** on an ongoing basis
6. **Maintain documentation** of which PCI DSS requirements are managed by the service provider versus the merchant

The merchant ultimately remains accountable to their acquiring bank and the payment card brands for any data breaches, regardless of who was processing the data when it was compromised. Outsourcing the processing does not outsource the liability or the compliance obligation.

For example, if a merchant uses a compliant payment gateway but has improperly configured their e-commerce site to temporarily store card verification codes, the merchant would still be non-compliant with PCI DSS, despite using a compliant service provider.

Additional resources: https://www.pcisecuritystandards.org/documents/PCI_DSS_V3.0_Third_Party_Security_Assurance.pdf

Q21: Which of the following scenarios would constitute a violation of PCI DSS requirements regarding the protection of cardholder data?

A) Storing truncated PANs with only the first 6 and last 4 digits visible B) Displaying the full PAN to a fraud analyst with legitimate business need C) Keeping a database of customers' expired credit cards with full PANs in clear text D) Storing cardholder names and expiration dates without the associated PANs

A21: The correct answer is C) Keeping a database of customers' expired credit cards with full PANs in clear text.

This scenario violates PCI DSS requirements because:

- PCI DSS requires that PANs must be rendered unreadable wherever they are stored, regardless of whether the cards are expired or active
- Storing full PANs in clear text (unencrypted, unhashed, untruncated) is explicitly prohibited
- The expiration status of a card does not exempt it from protection requirements

Explanation of the other options:

- Option A (Storing truncated PANs with only the first 6 and last 4 digits visible) is compliant with PCI DSS, as truncation is an acceptable method for making PANs unreadable
- Option B (Displaying the full PAN to a fraud analyst) is compliant if the analyst has a legitimate business need to access the full PAN and appropriate access controls are in place
- Option D (Storing cardholder names and expiration dates without PANs) is compliant because PCI DSS protection requirements for these data elements only apply when they are stored, processed, or transmitted with the PAN

It's important to note that even expired card data remains valuable to attackers and must be protected according to the same standards as active card data. Organizations should implement proper data retention policies to securely delete cardholder data when it is no longer needed for business purposes.

Additional resources: https://www.pcisecuritystandards.org/documents/PCI_Data_Storage_Dos_and_Donts.pdf

Q22: What are the key differences between Cardholder Data and Sensitive Authentication Data, and how do protection requirements differ for each?

A22: **Key Differences Between Cardholder Data and Sensitive Authentication Data:**

Cardholder Data (CHD):

- Primary Account Number (PAN)
- Cardholder Name (when stored with PAN)
- Expiration Date (when stored with PAN)

- Service Code (when stored with PAN)

Sensitive Authentication Data (SAD):

- Full magnetic stripe data (or equivalent on a chip)
- Card validation codes/values (CVV2, CVC2, CID, CAV2)
- PINs/PIN blocks

Functional Difference:

- Cardholder Data primarily identifies the account and basic details
- Sensitive Authentication Data is specifically used to authenticate the cardholder or the physical card during the transaction process

Protection Requirements Differences:

For Cardholder Data:

1. **Storage is permitted** with proper protection
2. **PAN must be rendered unreadable** when stored (using encryption, hashing, truncation, or tokenization)
3. **Access must be restricted** to those with a legitimate business need
4. **Must be encrypted during transmission** over open, public networks
5. **Other CHD elements** (name, expiration date, service code) only need protection when stored with the PAN

For Sensitive Authentication Data:

1. **Storage after authorization is prohibited** under any circumstances
2. **Cannot be stored even if encrypted**
3. **Must be securely deleted** immediately after authorization
4. **Must be protected during the authorization process**
5. **No exceptions exist** for storing this data, regardless of business justification

Practical Application: Organizations can retain cardholder data for legitimate business purposes (such as processing returns or recurring billing) as long as it's properly protected, with the PAN rendered unreadable. However, organizations must ensure their systems never store sensitive authentication data after the authorization process is complete. This often requires careful configuration of payment applications and regular checking of logs and databases to verify compliance.

The strict prohibition on storing SAD exists because this data can be used to create counterfeit cards or conduct fraudulent transactions, while properly protected cardholder data presents a significantly lower risk if compromised.

Additional resources: https://www.pcisecuritystandards.org/glossary/

Q23: A small business owner wants to implement a customer loyalty program that tracks past purchases. Which of the following approaches would be compliant with PCI DSS?

A) Storing full credit card numbers in an encrypted database B) Storing truncated PANs showing only the first 6 and last 4 digits C) Using tokenization to replace the PAN with a token for customer identification D) Both B and C are compliant options

A23: The correct answer is D) Both B and C are compliant options.

Both storing truncated PANs and using tokenization are compliant approaches for implementing a customer loyalty program under PCI DSS:

Truncated PANs (Option B):

- PCI DSS allows storing truncated versions of the PAN where only the first 6 and last 4 digits are visible
- The middle digits must be replaced with masking characters (like X or *)
- This approach reduces risk while still providing enough information to identify the card for loyalty program purposes
- Example: "123456XXXXXX7890"

Tokenization (Option C):

- Tokenization replaces the PAN with a non-sensitive substitute value (token)
- The token cannot be mathematically reversed to obtain the original PAN
- The mapping between tokens and PANs is stored securely in a token vault
- Tokens can be used as unique identifiers for customers in the loyalty program
- This approach significantly reduces the PCI DSS compliance scope

Why Option A is non-compliant: Storing full credit card numbers, even if encrypted, creates unnecessary risk and expands the PCI DSS compliance scope. While encryption is required for stored full PANs, the better practice is to avoid storing full PANs when not needed for business purposes. For a loyalty program, full PANs are not necessary.

For a small business implementing a loyalty program, either truncation or tokenization would be appropriate, with tokenization generally providing the greater security benefit and reduced compliance scope. The business should choose based on their specific needs, technical capabilities, and risk tolerance.

Additional resources: https://www.pcisecuritystandards.org/documents/Tokenization_Guidelines_Info_Supplement.pdf

Q24: What specific requirements apply to the display of PANs on receipts and displays according to PCI DSS?

A24: PCI DSS establishes specific requirements for the display of Primary Account Numbers (PANs) on receipts and displays to minimize the risk of unauthorized exposure. These requirements include:

For Physical Receipts (PCI DSS Requirement 3.3):

- The printed receipt must display no more than the first 6 and last 4 digits of the PAN
- All other digits must be masked with a character such as X, * or #
- This applies to both merchant copies and customer copies of receipts
- This requirement applies to all new systems after January 1, 2005

For Electronic Displays and Reports:

- When displaying PANs on screens, reports, or digital receipts, the same masking rule applies (first 6, last 4 visible maximum)
- Exception: Personnel with a legitimate business need may see the full PAN if proper authentication and access controls are in place

For Email and Other Electronic Communications:

- PANs should never be sent via unencrypted email, instant messaging, or chat
- If PANs must be included in electronic communications, they should be properly masked or the communication should be encrypted

Additional Considerations:

- Receipts must never display the card's security code (CVV2/CVC2/CID)
- The truncation/masking requirements apply even for temporary displays
- Organizations should configure all POS terminals, e-commerce platforms, and reporting systems to automatically mask PANs according to these requirements
- Masked PANs must be used in logs and debugging information

These display requirements are designed to prevent unauthorized individuals from obtaining complete PANs through casual observation or discarded receipts, while still providing enough information for transaction identification purposes.

Additional resources: https://www.pcisecuritystandards.org/documents/PCI_DSS_v3-2-1.pdf

Q25: What steps should a merchant take if they discover they have been inadvertently storing Sensitive Authentication Data after authorization?

A25: If a merchant discovers they have been inadvertently storing Sensitive Authentication Data (SAD) after authorization, they should take the following immediate and systematic steps:

Immediate Actions:

1. **Securely Delete the Data**: Immediately and securely remove all SAD from all storage locations using secure deletion methods that prevent recovery. This includes:
    - Full magnetic stripe data
    - Card verification codes (CVV2/CVC2/CID)
    - PINs/PIN blocks
2. **Expand the Search**: Look for SAD in all possible storage locations, including:
    - Production databases
    - Backup systems and archives
    - Debug logs and error logs
    - Transaction logs
    - Application caches
    - Test/development environments
    - Email systems
    - File shares and individual workstations
3. **Document the Incident**: Record details about what was found, where it was found, how long it was stored, and the secure deletion process used.

Follow-up Actions:

1. **Conduct a Root Cause Analysis**: Determine how and why the SAD was being stored:
    - Was it a misconfiguration of payment applications?
    - Was it caused by custom code?
    - Did it result from debugging or troubleshooting activities?
2. **Implement Preventative Controls**:

- Reconfigure systems to prevent storage of SAD
- Update data handling procedures
- Implement data leakage prevention tools
- Consider implementing tokenization or point-to-point encryption solutions

3. **Notify Relevant Parties**:
    - Inform your acquiring bank about the issue and remediation
    - Consider whether breach notification laws apply
    - Consult with legal counsel about disclosure obligations
4. **Training and Awareness**: Ensure all staff understand SAD handling requirements through updated training.
5. **Verify Remediation**: Conduct thorough testing to ensure that SAD is no longer being stored anywhere in the environment.
6. **Update Policies and Procedures**: Revise documentation to prevent recurrence.
7. **Consider a Full PCI DSS Assessment**: Engage a Qualified Security Assessor (QSA) to perform a comprehensive review of the cardholder data environment.

The key principle is to act quickly to eliminate the risk while also implementing systematic changes to prevent recurrence. Transparency with your payment partners about the issue and its resolution is also important for maintaining trust.

Additional resources: https://www.pcisecuritystandards.org/documents/PCI_DSS_Risk_Assmt_Guidelines_v1.pdf

10

PCI-DSS Standards - Question Set

Q1: What is the primary role of the PCI SSC (Payment Card Industry Security Standards Council)?

A1: The PCI SSC (Payment Card Industry Security Standards Council) serves as the primary resource and authority for organizations that need to follow the PCI-DSS (Payment Card Industry Data Security Standard). Its primary role is to provide guidance, support, and high-quality training for individuals, merchants, and service providers who must comply with these standards.

The PCI SSC also offers certification and validation services to ensure organizations meet all the requirements. They maintain several important resources including:

- Core security standards (PCI-DSS, P2PE, PTS)
- Card production and supporting documents
- Rosters of qualified professionals (QSAs, PCIPs, ASVs)
- Validated payment applications, PTS Devices, and P2PE solutions
- FAQs and educational resources
- Community engagement opportunities through membership and meetings

The PCI SSC essentially functions as an essential partner in helping organizations navigate and maintain compliance with the PCI-DSS, ensuring the security of cardholder data across the payment ecosystem.

For more information: https://www.pcisecuritystandards.org/about_us/

Q2: Which of the following is NOT a resource provided by the PCI SSC?

A) PCI-DSS standards documentation B) Roster of QSAs, PCIPs, and ASVs C) Direct financial compensation for data breaches D) Education & Outreach Programs

A2: The correct answer is C) Direct financial compensation for data breaches.

The PCI SSC provides numerous resources to help organizations comply with security standards, but it does not provide financial compensation for data breaches. This responsibility typically falls to the affected organizations, insurance providers, or might involve legal settlements.

The PCI SSC does provide:

- PCI-DSS, P2PE, PTS and other standards documentation
- Rosters of qualified professionals such as QSAs (Qualified Security Assessors), PCIPs (PCI Professional), and ASVs (Approved Scanning Vendors)
- Educational programs and outreach initiatives
- Community meetings and feedback opportunities
- Validation services for payment applications and solutions

The council's primary focus is on developing, maintaining, and promoting security standards, not on providing financial remediation for security incidents.

For more information: https://www.pcisecuritystandards.org/document_library/

Q3: Explain the relationship between the PCI Software Security Framework (SSF) and PA-DSS.

A3: The PCI Software Security Framework (SSF) is the evolution and replacement of the PA-DSS (Payment Application Data Security Standard). This relationship represents a significant modernization in the PCI Council's approach to payment software security.

The SSF was developed to address limitations in the PA-DSS by creating a more flexible, adaptable framework that aligns with modern software development practices. Key aspects of this relationship include:

1. Replacement: The SSF is designed to eventually fully replace the PA-DSS, which had become less suitable for modern payment technologies and development methodologies.
2. Modernization: While PA-DSS had more rigid requirements based on traditional software development, the SSF features more flexible requirements that allow developers to incorporate payment security into agile and DevOps practices without sacrificing development speed.
3. Scope: The SSF has a broader scope that extends beyond traditional payment applications to encompass various payment software types, including those that operate in cloud environments, mobile platforms, and other modern architectures.
4. Security Focus: Both standards aim to ensure secure payment software, but the SSF puts greater emphasis on secure design principles, threat modeling, and ongoing security throughout the software development lifecycle rather than point-in-time validation.
5. Structure: The SSF consists of two standards - the Secure Software Standard (core security requirements) and the Secure Software Lifecycle Standard (security practices throughout the development lifecycle).

This evolution reflects the PCI SSC's recognition of the changing technology landscape and the need for security standards that can adapt to emerging payment technologies and development practices.

For more information: https://www.pcisecuritystandards.org/pci_security/software_security_framework/

Q4: True or False: A merchant using a PCI SSC-listed P2PE solution will automatically be fully compliant with PCI-DSS.

A4: False. While implementing a PCI SSC-listed P2PE (Point-to-Point Encryption) solution can significantly reduce a merchant's PCI-DSS scope, it does not automatically make a merchant fully compliant with PCI-DSS.

A validated P2PE solution helps protect cardholder data by encrypting it at the point of interaction (POI) and maintaining that encryption until it reaches a secure decryption environment managed by the solution provider. This encryption prevents merchants from accessing unencrypted account data, which can substantially reduce the scope of their PCI-DSS assessment.

However, merchants still have responsibilities under PCI-DSS that extend beyond the P2PE solution, including:

- Securing any systems that might interact with the payment processing environment
- Managing access controls for staff
- Maintaining security policies and procedures
- Ensuring physical security of payment terminals
- Properly implementing and configuring the P2PE solution
- Complying with the P2PE solution provider's requirements

The text specifically states: "Merchants may be able to reduce their PCI-DSS scope by implementing a PCI SSC-listed P2PE solution" - note the focus on scope reduction rather than full automatic compliance.

For more information: https://www.pcisecuritystandards.org/assessors_and_solutions/point_to_point_encryption_solutions/

Q5: What are the key components of a PCI P2PE compliant solution? (Select all that apply)

A) Encryption of cardholder data at the point of interaction B) Secure key management of encryption and decryption devices C) Validation by an independent security assessor D) Merchant involvement in encryption operations E) Merchant access to account data within the encrypted device

A5: The correct answers are A, B, and C.

A PCI P2PE (Point-to-Point Encryption) compliant solution must include:

A) Encryption of cardholder data at the point of interaction (POI) - This is a fundamental requirement of P2PE, where data is encrypted immediately upon entry into the payment system.

B) Secure key management of encryption and decryption devices - P2PE requires rigorous key management practices to ensure encryption keys are properly secured and managed.

C) Validation by an independent security assessor - P2PE solutions must be validated by qualified assessors to confirm they meet all PCI SSC requirements.

Options D and E are incorrect because:

D) Merchant involvement in encryption operations - The provided material explicitly states: "There is no involvement on the merchant's part in the encryption or decryption operations or the management of cryptographic keys."

E) Merchant access to account data within the encrypted device - The text specifically mentions: "A merchant cannot access account data within the encrypted device or decryption environment."

A properly implemented P2PE solution provides multiple layers of protection by encrypting cardholder data and removing merchants from the encryption/decryption processes, thereby reducing PCI-DSS scope for merchants.

For more information: https://www.pcisecuritystandards.org/documents/P2PE_Program_Guide.pdf

Q6: How does the PCI PTS-POI standard relate to the security of payment transactions?

A6: The PCI PTS-POI (Pin Transaction Security - Point of Interaction) standard is a crucial component of payment transaction security that focuses specifically on securing the devices and components where customer-merchant interactions occur.

The PTS-POI standard:

1. Ensures security at the point of interaction: It establishes requirements for devices like card readers, PIN pads, and other hardware components where customers interact with payment systems, protecting this critical interface from potential compromise.
2. Incorporates SRED (Secure Reading and Exchange of Data): When SRED is enabled on a PTS device, it not only protects PIN data (the original objective of PTS) but also encrypts account data, providing comprehensive protection.
3. Provides device validation: The standard ensures that POI devices, such as PIN-entry devices (PEDs), meet rigorous security requirements before they are deployed in payment environments.
4. Reduces PCI-DSS scope: By using PTS-POI compliant devices with SRED enabled, merchants can significantly reduce their PCI-DSS compliance scope since account data is encrypted at the earliest point of capture.
5. Protects against physical and logical attacks: PTS-POI addresses various attack vectors, including physical tampering of devices, logical compromises, and other security vulnerabilities.

The standard essentially serves as the first line of defense in payment security, ensuring that cardholder data is protected from the moment it enters the payment ecosystem, reducing the risk of data compromise during the transaction process.

For more information: https://www.pcisecuritystandards.org/assessors_and_solutions/pin_transaction_devices/

Q7: What is the QIR Program, and what role do QIRs play in payment security?

A7: The QIR (Qualified Integrators and Resellers) Program is a specialized training and certification initiative established by the PCI Security Standards Council. This program focuses on ensuring that professionals who install payment systems for merchants are properly trained in implementing critical security controls.

Role of QIRs in payment security:

1. Secure installation: QIRs are specifically trained to ensure that critical security controls are properly addressed during the installation of merchant payment systems, which helps prevent security vulnerabilities from being introduced during deployment.

2. Risk reduction: By focusing on essential security controls, QIRs help reduce merchant risk by addressing common security weaknesses that could otherwise be exploited.

3. Breach prevention: QIRs work to mitigate the most common causes of payment data breaches by reducing merchant vulnerability through proper implementation of security measures.

4. Implementation expertise: QIRs provide merchants with skilled professionals who understand how to implement payment systems securely, giving merchants peace of mind that their systems meet security requirements.

5. Validation: The PCI SSC maintains a list of QIRs on their website, allowing merchants to verify and select properly qualified professionals for their payment system installations.

The QIR Program essentially bridges the gap between payment security standards and their practical implementation, ensuring that merchants not only have secure technology but also have it installed in a secure manner that maintains its security properties in operation.

For more information: https://www.pcisecuritystandards.org/assessors_and_solutions/qualified_integrators_and_resellers/

Q8: Which of the following statements about Hardware Security Modules (HSMs) in the PCI ecosystem is correct?

A) HSMs do not require specific PCI certification B) HSMs need to be PCI PTS-HSM compliant to be used in the PCI-DSS ecosystem C) HSM certification is optional for card issuers D) HSM requirements are primarily derived from ISO 27001

A8: The correct answer is B) HSMs need to be PCI PTS-HSM compliant to be used in the PCI-DSS ecosystem.

As stated in the provided content: "The thing to remember about HSMs is that they need to be PCI PTS-HSM compliant to be used in the PCI-DSS ecosystem." This is a critical requirement for maintaining the security of cryptographic operations within payment environments.

Hardware Security Modules (HSMs) play a vital role in payment security by:

- Safeguarding cryptographic keys

- Performing secure cryptographic operations

- Supporting PIN processing, card verification, and key generation

The PCI PTS-HSM standard outlines specific security requirements for HSMs throughout their lifecycle and covers various payment processes, including:

- PIN processing
- Card production/verification
- ATM interchange
- Cash-card reloading
- Key generation

The certification requirements for HSMs are primarily derived from FIPS 140-2 (not ISO 27001 as suggested in option D), which is a U.S. government standard for cryptographic modules.

For more information: https://www.pcisecuritystandards.org/documents/PCI_PTS_HSM_Security_Requirements_v3.pdf

Q9: Describe the key security controls required in PCI Card Production environments and explain why they are necessary.

A9: PCI Card Production environments require exceptionally stringent security controls due to the critical nature of producing payment cards and the high value of the assets involved. These controls span both physical and logical security domains:

Key Security Controls:

1. Dual Control (Two-Person Rule): Two people must always be present for daily processes. This prevents any single individual from having complete control over critical operations, reducing the risk of insider threats or unauthorized activities.

2. Device Tamper-Proofing: All devices used in card production must be secured with various tamper-evident and tamper-resistant measures. This ensures that any attempt to physically compromise equipment is detectable and/or preventable.

3. 24-Hour Guard Room: Continuous security monitoring through a permanently staffed guard room is required. This provides constant surveillance and rapid response capability to any security incidents.

4. HSA (High-Security Area) Wall Construction: Walls must be built according to industry standards with appropriate strength and security features. This physical barrier prevents unauthorized access to sensitive areas where card production occurs.

5. Asset Inventory and Firewall Documentation: Maintaining accurate inventories of all assets and documenting firewall locations creates accountability and ensures that all components of the environment are known and properly secured.

Necessity of These Controls:

These rigorous controls are necessary because card production environments:

- Handle extremely sensitive data (payment card information, PINs, etc.)
- Produce high-value instruments (payment cards) that could be used for fraud if compromised
- Create security elements that will protect financial transactions globally
- Are high-value targets for sophisticated attackers
- Represent a critical link in the payment security chain where a single breach could have widespread consequences

The comprehensive nature of these controls reflects the "defense in depth" approach required for environments where payment cards are created, programmed, and prepared for distribution. These measures work together to form a multi-layered security framework that protects against both external threats and insider risks.

For more information: https://www.pcisecuritystandards.org/documents/PCI_Card_Production_Security_Requirements.pdf

Q10: What is the relationship between PCI-DSS and other PCI standards such as P2PE, PTS, SSF, and PCI PIN?

A10: The relationship between PCI-DSS and other PCI standards represents an integrated security framework where each standard serves a specific purpose while collectively supporting comprehensive payment security:

PCI-DSS (Data Security Standard) serves as the foundational standard that applies to all entities involved in payment card processing, including merchants, processors, acquirers, issuers, and service providers. It provides the overarching security requirements for protecting cardholder data throughout the payment ecosystem.

The other standards integrate with PCI-DSS as follows:

1. P2PE (Point-to-Point Encryption): Works as a complementary standard that focuses specifically on encryption of cardholder data from the point of capture to the point of processing. When implemented, P2PE can significantly reduce the scope of PCI-DSS for merchants by removing systems from the cardholder data environment.

2. PTS (PIN Transaction Security): Addresses the security of devices that interact with payment cards and PINs. By ensuring these devices are secure, PTS helps prevent the compromise of account data at the entry point, supporting the goals of PCI-DSS.

3. SSF (Software Security Framework): Focuses on the security of payment software applications, replacing the older PA-DSS. Secure payment applications support PCI-DSS compliance by ensuring that software handling cardholder data does so securely.

4. PCI PIN: Covers the secure management, processing, and transmission of personal identification numbers during payment transactions, addressing a specific high-risk component within the overall payment process.

Together, these standards create a comprehensive security framework that protects account data "from the moment it is captured until it reaches the payment processor." While PCI-DSS provides the broad requirements for data security, these complementary standards address specific technologies, components, and processes within the payment ecosystem, creating multiple layers of protection.

This layered approach ensures that cardholder data is protected through specialized security requirements tailored to each aspect of payment processing, while all working together under the umbrella of PCI-DSS to achieve end-to-end security.

For more information: https://www.pcisecuritystandards.org/pci_security/standards_overview/

Q11: True or False: The PCI Software Security Framework (SSF) is more rigid and less adaptable to modern development practices than the PA-DSS it replaces.

A11: False. The PCI Software Security Framework (SSF) is specifically designed to be more flexible and adaptable to modern development practices compared to the PA-DSS (Payment Application Data Security Standard) that it replaces.

According to the provided content: "The PCI Software Security Framework (SSF) is a set of standards and programs that assist in developing and maintaining secure payment software. It replaces the PA-DSS and is designed with modern, flexible requirements that allow developers to incorporate payment security into their development practices without sacrificing agility or speed."

The SSF was created specifically to address limitations in the PA-DSS, which had become less suitable for contemporary software development methodologies such as Agile and DevOps. Key improvements in the SSF include:

1. Greater flexibility in implementation approaches
2. Better alignment with modern software development lifecycles
3. Focus on security outcomes rather than prescriptive methods
4. Adaptability to diverse technology environments including cloud and mobile
5. Support for continuous development and deployment models

This modernization reflects the PCI SSC's recognition that payment software development has evolved significantly, and security standards needed to evolve as well to remain effective without hindering innovation or time-to-market.

For more information: https://www.pcisecuritystandards.org/pci_security/software_security_framework/

Q12: Which of the following best describes the Secure Reading and Exchange of Data (SRED) module in relation to PCI standards?

A) A software-based encryption protocol used only for online transactions B) A key component of PTS that enables encryption of cardholder data at the terminal C) A document that outlines best practices for data storage D) A certification process for payment application developers

A12: The correct answer is B) A key component of PTS that enables encryption of cardholder data at the terminal.

The Secure Reading and Exchange of Data (SRED) is a crucial module within the PCI PTS (PIN Transaction Security) standard. As described in the provided content: "By incorporating Secure Reading and Exchange of Data (SRED) into PTS devices, the original objective of the PTS standard—protecting the PIN—is achieved. Furthermore, account data is encrypted when SRED is enabled on a PTS device."

SRED serves several important functions:

1. It extends the security capabilities of PTS devices beyond just PIN protection to include encryption of all cardholder data
2. It's a key component of the Point-to-Point Encryption (P2PE) program
3. It ensures that payment terminals are approved for secure encryption of cardholder data at the point of interaction
4. It has been expanded to evaluate non-PIN entry modules, extending protection to non-chip and PIN cards
5. When properly implemented, it helps merchants reduce their PCI-DSS scope by encrypting sensitive data at the earliest possible point

SRED essentially transforms a payment terminal from a device that merely captures data to one that immediately protects that data through encryption, significantly reducing the risk of data compromise even if other systems are breached.

For more information: https://www.pcisecuritystandards.org/documents/PCI_PTS_POI_Security_Requirements_v6-0.pdf

Q13: What is the primary purpose of the PCI PTS-HSM standard and what types of payment processes does it cover?

A13: The primary purpose of the PCI PTS-HSM (PIN Transaction Security-Hardware Security Module) standard is to ensure the protection of Hardware Security Modules (HSMs) throughout their lifecycle by outlining comprehensive security requirements necessary to protect cardholder data.

HSMs are specialized, hardened cryptographic devices that manage and safeguard encryption keys and perform secure cryptographic operations, making them critical to payment security infrastructure. The PTS-HSM standard provides requirements for evaluating these devices to obtain proper accreditation/approval for use in payment environments.

The standard covers a variety of payment processes, including:

1. PIN processing - Securing the verification of Personal Identification Numbers during transactions
2. Card production/verification - Protecting the processes involved in creating and validating payment cards
3. ATM interchange - Securing transactions conducted through automated teller machines
4. Cash-card reloading - Protecting the process of adding funds to prepaid or stored-value cards
5. Key generation - Ensuring cryptographic keys are created securely and with appropriate entropy

These requirements are primarily derived from FIPS 140-2, a U.S. government standard for cryptographic modules, but adapted specifically for payment industry needs. The standard emphasizes that HSMs must be PCI PTS-HSM compliant to be used in the PCI-DSS ecosystem, highlighting their critical role in maintaining the security of payment systems.

By focusing on these specialized security devices, the PTS-HSM standard helps ensure that the fundamental cryptographic infrastructure supporting payment systems maintains the highest levels of security and integrity.

For more information: https://www.pcisecuritystandards.org/documents/PCI_PIN_Security_Requirements.pdf

Q14: How does implementing a PCI SSC-listed P2PE solution affect a merchant's PCI-DSS compliance requirements?

A14: Implementing a PCI SSC-listed Point-to-Point Encryption (P2PE) solution can significantly affect a merchant's PCI-DSS compliance requirements, primarily by reducing the scope of their compliance efforts.

Key impacts include:

1. Scope Reduction: As explicitly stated in the content, "Merchants may be able to reduce their PCI-DSS scope by implementing a PCI SSC-listed P2PE solution." This is the most significant benefit, as it reduces the number of systems and processes that must meet PCI-DSS requirements.

2. Reduced Access to Sensitive Data: When implemented correctly, "A merchant cannot access account data within the encrypted device or decryption environment." This limitation of access to unencrypted cardholder data further reduces compliance obligations.

3. Elimination of Encryption Management: "There is no involvement on the merchant's part in the encryption or decryption operations or the management of cryptographic keys." This transfers the responsibility for these complex security operations to the P2PE solution provider.

4. Multiple Layers of Protection: A properly implemented P2PE solution includes "multiple layers of protection and encryption to ensure the utmost security of cardholder data," creating a more secure environment.

5. Simplified Assessment: Merchants using validated P2PE solutions can typically use simplified validation methods, such as the SAQ P2PE (Self-Assessment Questionnaire) rather than more extensive assessment requirements.

It's important to note that P2PE does not eliminate all PCI-DSS requirements for merchants. They still must:

- Properly implement and maintain the P2PE solution
- Secure any systems that interact with payment terminals
- Follow security practices for the handling of devices
- Maintain appropriate policies and procedures
- Address other applicable PCI-DSS requirements

However, the dramatic reduction in scope makes compliance significantly more manageable, especially for smaller merchants with limited IT security resources.

For more information: https://www.pcisecuritystandards.org/documents/P2PE_v3_Solution_Testing_and_Approval_Program_Guide.pdf

Q15: Explain what the "cardholder data environment" (CDE) refers to in the context of PCI-DSS and why it's important for compliance.

A15: The cardholder data environment (CDE) is a fundamental concept in PCI-DSS that refers to the totality of people, processes, technologies, and systems that store, process, or transmit cardholder data or sensitive authentication data. It encompasses all connected system components that are included in or connected to the environment where cardholder data is present.

Components of the CDE typically include:

- Systems that directly store, process, or transmit cardholder data
- Security systems protecting these environments (firewalls, IDS/IPS, etc.)
- Connected systems that could impact the security of cardholder data
- Network segments containing payment systems
- Supporting infrastructure like authentication servers that manage access to the CDE
- Physical locations where cardholder data is accessible

Importance for PCI-DSS compliance:

1. Scope Definition: The CDE defines the boundaries of what must be protected under PCI-DSS. As the content notes, "To ensure full PCI-DSS compliance, many other elements must be carefully configured and integrated into the cardholder data environment." Properly identifying the CDE is the first step in determining compliance scope.
2. Security Focus: By clearly defining the CDE, organizations can concentrate their security efforts on the most critical areas that contain sensitive payment data.
3. Risk Management: Understanding the CDE helps organizations identify potential vulnerabilities and risk points where cardholder data could be compromised.
4. Comprehensive Protection: The content uses the metaphor of "building a house brick by brick," emphasizing that each element within the CDE "must be meticulously designed and fitted together to create a secure foundation." This highlights the need for a holistic approach to securing the CDE.
5. Compliance Validation: Assessors will review the CDE to ensure all appropriate controls are in place to protect cardholder data.
6. Scope Reduction Strategies: Many PCI-DSS compliance strategies (such as network segmentation, tokenization, or P2PE) are designed to reduce the size and complexity of the CDE.

A properly defined and secured CDE is essential for achieving and maintaining PCI-DSS compliance, as it ensures organizations apply the appropriate security controls to all systems that could affect the security of cardholder data.

For more information: https://www.pcisecuritystandards.org/documents/PCI_DSS_v4-0.pdf

Q16: What are the key differences between the PCI PTS-POI and PCI PTS-PIN Security standards?

A16: The PCI PTS-POI and PCI PTS-PIN Security standards are both part of the PIN Transaction Security (PTS) family of standards but address different aspects of payment security:

PCI PTS-POI (Point of Interaction):

1. Focus: Secures the physical and logical aspects of payment devices where customers interact with the payment system (the "point of interaction")
2. Device-centric: Primarily concerned with the security of hardware devices such as card readers, PIN pads, and point-of-sale terminals
3. Scope: Covers secure components of POI devices including PIN entry capabilities
4. Key objective: Ensures that devices that accept payment cards are designed securely to protect cardholder data at the point of entry
5. SRED component: Includes the Secure Reading and Exchange of Data module which encrypts account data at the device level
6. Application: Applies to device manufacturers and those deploying payment terminals

PCI PTS-PIN Security:

1. Focus: Covers the secure management, processing, and transmission of personal identification numbers (PINs)
2. Process-centric: Concentrates on the secure handling of PIN data throughout its lifecycle
3. Scope: Addresses both online and offline payment card transactions that involve PINs
4. Key objective: Ensures that PINs remain secure from the moment they are entered through processing and verification
5. Broader coverage: Extends beyond just the device to include the entire PIN processing ecosystem
6. Application: Applies to entities involved in PIN processing including issuers, processors, and service providers

The key difference is that PTS-POI focuses on securing the physical devices where payments are initiated (hardware security), while PTS-PIN Security focuses on protecting the PIN data itself throughout the entire transaction process (data security). Together, they form a comprehensive approach to securing PIN-based transactions from the entry point through processing.

For more information: https://www.pcisecuritystandards.org/documents/PCI_PIN_Security_Requirements.pdf

Q17: Which of the following best describes the PCI Security Standards Council's role in developing and maintaining payment security standards?

A) The PCI SSC directly processes payments and manages merchant accounts B) The PCI SSC provides guidelines, training, and certification for payment security C) The PCI SSC is responsible for investigating and penalizing data breaches D) The PCI SSC only focuses on hardware security for payment terminals

A17: The correct answer is B) The PCI SSC provides guidelines, training, and certification for payment security.

According to the provided content: "If your organization needs to follow the PCI-DSS, then the PCI SSC is your go-to resource. They provide guidance, support, and top-notch training for individuals, merchants, and service providers who must comply with these standards. Plus, they offer certification and validation services to ensure you meet all the requirements."

The PCI Security Standards Council (PCI SSC) is the governing body responsible for developing, maintaining, and promoting security standards for the payment card industry. Their core functions include:

1. Developing and updating security standards like PCI-DSS, P2PE, PTS, and others
2. Providing educational resources and training programs for industry professionals
3. Managing certification programs for individuals (like PCIP) and organizations
4. Maintaining rosters of qualified professionals and validated solutions
5. Offering validation services to ensure compliance with standards
6. Facilitating community engagement through meetings and feedback mechanisms

The PCI SSC does not directly process payments (option A), investigate breaches (option C), or focus solely on hardware security (option D). Instead, it serves as the authoritative source for payment security standards and provides the resources necessary for organizations to implement those standards effectively.

For more information: https://www.pcisecuritystandards.org/about_us/

Q18: List and briefly describe the six main resources provided by the PCI SSC to help organizations with compliance.

A18: The PCI Security Standards Council (PCI SSC) provides six main resources to help organizations achieve and maintain compliance with payment security standards:

1. Core Security Standards and Supporting Documents: This includes the primary standards such as PCI-DSS, P2PE and PTS (including POI, HSM, and PIN components), along with supporting implementation guides, information supplements, and technical FAQs. These documents form the foundation of payment security requirements across the industry.
2. Card Production and Supporting Documents: These resources focus specifically on the security requirements for card manufacturing, personalization, and issuance. They outline both physical and logical security controls necessary for secure card production environments, covering the entire lifecycle of payment card creation.

3. Qualified Professional Rosters: The PCI SSC maintains comprehensive listings of validated professionals and organizations including QSAs (Qualified Security Assessors), PCIPs (PCI Professionals), ASVs (Approved Scanning Vendors), and other qualified entities. These rosters help organizations find trusted partners for their compliance efforts.

4. Validated Solutions Directories: These include listings of validated payment applications, PTS Devices, and P2PE solutions that have been assessed and approved by the PCI SSC. Organizations can use these directories to select pre-validated solutions that support compliance.

5. Frequently Asked Questions (FAQs): The PCI SSC maintains an extensive collection of FAQs that address common questions about the standards, implementation challenges, and compliance issues. These resources provide clarification on interpreting and applying the standards.

6. Education & Outreach Programs: The council offers various training programs, webinars, community meetings, and educational resources to help organizations understand the standards and implementation requirements. These include certification programs for individuals and awareness resources for organizations.

These resources collectively form a comprehensive support system for organizations seeking to understand, implement, and maintain compliance with PCI security standards, providing both authoritative guidance and practical assistance throughout the compliance process.

For more information: https://www.pcisecuritystandards.org/document_library/

Q19: What is the purpose of the PCI PTS (PIN Transaction Security) standard and what types of devices does it cover?

A19: The purpose of the PCI PTS (PIN Transaction Security) standard is to prevent theft or fraudulent use of sensitive authentication data and protect cardholder PINs and cryptographic keys from unauthorized access by establishing security requirements for payment processing devices.

The standard was developed specifically in response to the increasing number of attacks on payment systems, serving as a crucial security measure for the various devices involved in payment processing.

The PCI PTS standard covers several types of devices:

1. Point of Interaction (POI) devices - The terminals where customers interact with the payment system

2. Encrypting PIN Pads (EPPs) - Specialized components designed specifically for secure PIN entry

3. Point of Sale (POS) devices - Systems used by merchants to process transactions

4. Hardware Security Modules (HSMs) - Specialized hardware that manages cryptographic keys and operations

5. Unattended Payment Terminals (UPTs) - Self-service payment devices like ATMs and vending machines

6. Non-PIN entry modules - Other components that handle payment data but don't specifically process PINs

A key component of PTS is the Secure Read and Exchange Module (SRED), which ensures that terminals are approved for secure encryption of cardholder data. This extends beyond just PIN protection to encompass all sensitive payment data.

The PTS standard complements the broader Payment Card Industry Data Security Standard (PCI-DSS), working together to provide comprehensive protection for payment processing environments. As the content notes, PCI-DSS is "considered the gold standard for securing payment processing devices," with PTS focusing specifically on the hardware components of the payment ecosystem.

For more information: https://www.pcisecuritystandards.org/documents/PCI_PTS_POI_Security_Requirements.pdf

Q20: In the context of PCI compliance, what are Hardware Security Modules (HSMs) and why are they important?

A20: Hardware Security Modules (HSMs) are specialized, tamper-resistant physical computing devices that safeguard and manage digital keys and perform cryptographic operations within the payment ecosystem. In the context of PCI compliance, they serve as the secure foundation for cryptographic operations that protect sensitive payment data.

Key characteristics and functions of HSMs:

1. Physical Security: HSMs are physically hardened devices designed to detect and respond to tampering attempts, often by erasing sensitive key material if compromised.
2. Key Management: They securely generate, store, and manage cryptographic keys used for encryption, decryption, digital signatures, and other cryptographic functions.
3. Cryptographic Operations: HSMs perform secure cryptographic operations in a protected environment, isolating these operations from potentially vulnerable general-purpose computing systems.
4. Compliance Requirement: As specified in the content, "HSMs need to be PCI PTS-HSM compliant to be used in the PCI-DSS ecosystem," highlighting their mandatory nature for compliant environments.

Importance in PCI compliance:

1. Protection of Cryptographic Keys: HSMs safeguard the encryption keys that protect cardholder data, ensuring these critical security elements aren't exposed to potential compromise.
2. Secure Processing: They enable secure PIN processing, card production/verification, ATM interchange, cash-card reloading, and key generation in a protected environment.
3. Scope Reduction: By isolating cryptographic operations in a secure hardware environment, HSMs can help reduce the PCI-DSS scope of other systems.
4. Standardized Security: PCI PTS-HSM certification requirements (derived primarily from FIPS 140-2) ensure HSMs meet consistent, high-level security standards.
5. Trust Foundation: HSMs provide a hardware root of trust for payment systems, establishing a secure foundation upon which other security controls can build.

HSMs represent a critical control point in payment security, providing hardware-based protection for the cryptographic operations that underpin the entire payment security ecosystem. Their specialized nature and rigorous security requirements make them essential components for achieving and maintaining PCI compliance.

For more information: https://www.pcisecuritystandards.org/documents/PCI_HSM_Security_Requirements_v3.0_Resource_Guide.pdf

Q21: True or False: The PCI Software Security Framework (SSF) is designed primarily for hardware security and has limited application to software development.

A21: False. The PCI Software Security Framework (SSF) is designed specifically for software security, not hardware security, and is intended to be broadly applicable to modern software development practices.

According to the provided content: "The PCI Software Security Framework (SSF) is a set of standards and programs that assist in developing and maintaining secure payment software. It replaces the PA-DSS and is designed with modern, flexible requirements that allow developers to incorporate payment security into their development practices without sacrificing agility or speed."

Key points that refute the statement:

1. Software Focus: As the name indicates, the SSF is explicitly focused on software security, not hardware security.
2. Software Development Integration: The framework is specifically designed to be incorporated into software development practices, making security an integral part of the development process.
3. Modern Development Support: The SSF was created to support modern, agile development methodologies, not to address hardware concerns.
4. PA-DSS Replacement: It replaces the Payment Application Data Security Standard (PA-DSS), which was also focused on software security, not hardware.
5. Flexibility for Developers: The framework provides flexible requirements specifically to allow software developers to maintain agility and speed while incorporating security.

The SSF represents the PCI SSC's recognition that payment software development has evolved significantly, requiring security standards that can adapt to diverse development environments, architectures, and methodologies while still ensuring that payment software is developed securely.

For more information: https://www.pcisecuritystandards.org/pci_security/software_security_framework/

Q22: Which of these is NOT a key component of PCI Card Production security requirements?

A) Two-person rule for daily processes B) 24-hour guard room C) Automated penetration testing of all systems D) HSA walls built to industry standards E) Tamper-proofing of all devices

A22: The correct answer is C) Automated penetration testing of all systems.

Based on the provided content, the key components of PCI Card Production security requirements include:

- "Two people must always be present for daily processes" (two-person rule)
- "Tamper-proofing all devices with various security measures"

- "A 24-hour guard room is necessary for secure card production"
- "HSA walls must be built according to industry standards"
- "Maintaining an accurate inventory of all assets and the location of firewalls"

Automated penetration testing of all systems is not mentioned as a specific requirement for Card Production environments in the provided content. While penetration testing is an important security practice and may be part of broader PCI-DSS requirements, it is not explicitly listed among the key Card Production security controls in the material.

The Card Production security requirements focus heavily on physical security controls, access restrictions, dual control procedures, and asset management - reflecting the high-security needs of environments where payment cards are manufactured and personalized

For more information: https://www.pcisecuritystandards.org/documents/PCI_Card_Production_Security_Requirements.pdf

Q23: How does the PCI PTS-POI standard contribute to reducing a merchant's PCI-DSS scope?

A23: The PCI PTS-POI (PIN Transaction Security - Point of Interaction) standard contributes to reducing a merchant's PCI-DSS scope through several mechanisms that enhance security at the initial point of data capture:

1. SRED Implementation: The primary scope reduction benefit comes through the Secure Reading and Exchange of Data (SRED) capability. As stated in the content: "account data is encrypted when SRED is enabled on a PTS device. As a result merchants can reduce their PCI-DSS scope and protect their customers' data." This encryption at the point of interaction prevents unencrypted cardholder data from entering the merchant's environment.

2. Data Protection at Entry Point: By securing the point of interaction where customers and merchants transact, PTS-POI ensures that payment card data is protected from its initial entry into the payment system. The standard specifically focuses on "protecting cardholder information at the point of interaction."

3. Integrated Security Controls: PTS-POI devices incorporate comprehensive security controls including "using strong cryptography" and "preventing unauthorized access to cardholder information," which reduces the burden on merchants to implement these controls elsewhere in their environment.

4. Device Validation: The standard ensures that Point of Interaction devices, such as PIN-entry devices (PED), meet rigorous security requirements before deployment, providing merchants with assurance that these critical components are secure by design.

5. Complementary to P2PE: PTS-POI with SRED forms a foundational component of Point-to-Point Encryption solutions which can further reduce PCI-DSS scope. The content notes that SRED "is a key component of the Point-to-Point Encryption program."

By implementing PTS-POI compliant devices, particularly those with SRED capabilities, merchants effectively create a security boundary at the point where payment data enters their environment. This boundary prevents unencrypted sensitive data from touching the merchant's systems, thereby reducing the number of systems and processes that fall within PCI-DSS scope and simplifying compliance efforts.

For more information: https://www.pcisecuritystandards.org/documents/PCI_PTS_POI_Security_Requirements_v6.0.pdf

Q24: What is the benefit of using a Qualified Integrator or Reseller (QIR) when implementing payment systems?

A24: The benefit of using a Qualified Integrator or Reseller (QIR) when implementing payment systems centers around enhanced security, reduced risk, and proper implementation of PCI-DSS compliant solutions. Based on the provided content, the specific benefits include:

1. Security-Focused Implementation: QIRs "have been specially trained to ensure that critical security controls are addressed during the installation of merchant payment systems." This specialized training means they understand how to implement payment systems in a manner that prioritizes security from the beginning.
2. Risk Reduction: By focusing on essential security controls, "QIRs reduce merchant risk" by ensuring that payment systems are properly configured and secured according to industry best practices and PCI requirements.
3. Breach Prevention: QIRs "mitigate the most common causes of payment data breaches by reducing merchant vulnerability." Their expertise helps address the security weaknesses that frequently lead to compromises.
4. Proper System Configuration: QIRs understand how to properly configure and integrate payment systems to maintain security controls, which is critical since many breaches occur due to implementation errors rather than product vulnerabilities.
5. Peace of Mind: As stated in the content, "QIRs give merchants the peace of mind that their payment systems are secure." This confidence comes from knowing that a qualified professional with specific training in payment security has handled the implementation.
6. Verified Expertise: The PCI Security Standards Council maintains "a list of QIRs on their website," allowing merchants to verify that they're working with properly qualified professionals who have met the council's requirements.

Using a QIR essentially helps bridge the gap between having secure payment products and having a secure payment implementation. Even the most secure payment solutions can be vulnerable if not properly implemented, and QIRs provide the expertise needed to ensure that security is maintained throughout the installation and configuration process.

For more information: https://www.pcisecuritystandards.org/programs/qualified_integrator_and_reseller/

Q25: Explain how the various PCI standards work together to create a comprehensive approach to payment security.

A25: The various PCI standards work together as an integrated ecosystem to create a comprehensive, multi-layered approach to payment security. Each standard addresses specific aspects of the payment process, and together they form a cohesive framework that protects cardholder data throughout its lifecycle.

Core Integration of PCI Standards:

1. PCI-DSS as the Foundation: The Payment Card Industry Data Security Standard (PCI-DSS) serves as the foundational standard that "applies to all entities involved in payment card processing." It provides the overarching security requirements that govern the entire payment ecosystem, establishing the baseline controls that must be implemented.

2. Protection Across the Transaction Lifecycle: As stated in the content, the various standards work together to ensure that "account data is protected from the moment it is captured until it reaches the payment processor." This end-to-end protection is achieved through the complementary focus of each standard:
    - PCI PTS-POI secures the physical devices where payment data is initially captured
    - PCI P2PE ensures encryption of data from the point of capture to the point of processing
    - PCI SSF ensures payment applications are developed securely
    - PCI PTS-HSM secures the hardware modules that manage cryptographic operations
    - PCI PIN Security protects PIN data throughout transaction processing
    - PCI Card Production secures the creation and personalization of payment cards
3. Layered Security Approach: The content uses the metaphor of "building a house brick by brick" to describe how "each element must be meticulously designed and fitted together to create a secure foundation." This illustrates how the standards create multiple layers of protection, with each standard addressing potential vulnerabilities at different points in the payment process.
4. Complementary Controls: Each standard complements the others by focusing on specific technologies, processes, or components:
    - Hardware security (PTS standards)
    - Software security (SSF)
    - Data protection (P2PE)
    - Process security (PIN Security, Card Production)
    - Environmental security (PCI-DSS)
5. Scope Management: Several standards (particularly P2PE and PTS with SRED) help reduce the scope of PCI-DSS by limiting where unencrypted cardholder data exists, creating a more manageable security perimeter.

This integrated approach ensures that cardholder data is protected by multiple security controls throughout its lifecycle, creating defense in depth. By addressing hardware, software, processes, and environments, the PCI standards collectively establish a comprehensive security framework that protects payment systems from diverse threats and vulnerabilities, while giving organizations flexibility in how they implement specific controls based on their unique environments.

For more information: https://www.pcisecuritystandards.org/pci_security/standards_overview/

11

PCI Code of Professional Responsibility - Question Set

Q1: What are the primary professional standards that a PCIP must uphold according to the certification requirements?

A1: As a Payment Card Industry Professional (PCIP), you must uphold the highest standards of conduct in all professional activities. This specifically includes ensuring strict adherence to all PCI Standards, guidelines, and procedures without exception. The certification requires you to maintain unwavering commitment to providing exceptional customer service while completing all aspects of your work honorably, responsibly, and in compliance with the highest legal standards. The PCIP certification represents not just technical knowledge but a professional commitment to integrity in the payment card industry.

For additional information on PCIP professional standards, visit: https://www.pcisecuritystandards.org/program/pcip/

Q2: True or False: A PCIP may occasionally deviate from PCI Standards when it's more convenient for the customer.

A2: False. The guidance explicitly states that PCIPs "must strive to uphold the highest standards of conduct, ensuring that all PCI Standards, guidelines, and procedures are always followed." The use of the word "always" indicates that there are no acceptable exceptions or situations where deviation is permitted, regardless of convenience. Maintaining the integrity of PCI Standards is a fundamental responsibility of the PCIP certification, and any deviation would compromise both the security framework and the professional's certification status.

For more information on compliance requirements, visit: https://www.pcisecuritystandards.org/document_library/

Q3: Multiple Choice: Which of the following best describes the customer service expectations of a PCIP?

A) Providing adequate service that meets minimum requirements B) Balancing customer needs with personal convenience C) Remaining committed to providing the best in customer service D) Focusing primarily on technical compliance over customer experience

A3: C) Remaining committed to providing the best in customer service

The correct answer is C. The content explicitly states that PCIPs must "remain committed to providing the best in customer service." This emphasizes that PCIPs are expected to go beyond merely adequate service and should strive for excellence in customer interactions. This commitment to superior customer service is positioned as a core professional obligation, alongside technical compliance and ethical conduct, forming the foundation of the PCIP professional standard.

For more on PCIP professional expectations, visit: https://www.pcisecuritystandards.org/program/pcip_agreement/

Q4: Essay Question: Explain how a PCIP's commitment to "highest legal standards" might manifest in day-to-day activities when implementing PCI DSS requirements for a client.

A4: A PCIP's commitment to the "highest legal standards" would manifest in numerous aspects of their daily professional activities when implementing PCI DSS requirements:

First, it requires thorough knowledge of relevant laws and regulations that intersect with payment card security, including data protection laws (like GDPR or CCPA), financial regulations, and industry-specific requirements that vary by jurisdiction. The PCIP must ensure implementations comply with these legal frameworks alongside the PCI Standards.

In practice, this means conducting comprehensive compliance assessments that go beyond technical requirements to include legal considerations. For example, when implementing data retention policies, the PCIP must ensure they meet both PCI DSS requirements and applicable legal retention requirements, which may vary by region.

Documentation practices would reflect this commitment, with meticulous record-keeping that would withstand legal scrutiny. All recommendations and implementations would be clearly justified and linked to specific requirements and legal standards.

When advising clients, a PCIP would refuse requests to implement shortcuts or workarounds, even if pressured. They would clearly explain legal ramifications of non-compliance and insist on proper implementation, documenting any client decisions that might have compliance implications.

The PCIP would also maintain appropriate confidentiality of sensitive information, ensuring all handling of cardholder data follows both PCI requirements and legal obligations regarding data protection.

This commitment extends to continuous education on evolving legal requirements, ensuring implementations remain compliant even as laws change over time.

For resources on legal considerations in PCI compliance, visit: https://www.pcisecuritystandards.org/blog/navigating-legal-and-compliance-requirements/

Q5: What is the ultimate goal of a PCIP regarding customer experience?

A5: The ultimate goal of a Payment Card Industry Professional (PCIP) regarding customer experience is to "ensure every customer experience is exceptional." This standard explicitly establishes that mediocre or merely satisfactory customer experiences are insufficient for a certified PCIP. The professional is expected to consistently deliver service that exceeds expectations and creates positive, memorable interactions. This goal extends beyond technical compliance with PCI standards and reflects the understanding that security implementations affect real people and businesses. By striving for exceptional customer experiences, PCIPs help build trust in the payment card ecosystem while demonstrating that security and positive user experience can coexist with proper implementation.

For more information on customer experience in security implementations, visit: https://www.pcisecuritystandards.org/resources/

Q6: Multiple Choice: How should a PCIP approach the completion of their work according to certification standards?

A) Efficiently, focusing primarily on technical accuracy B) Honorably and responsibly to the highest legal standards C) Quickly, to maximize client satisfaction D) With flexibility, adapting standards to fit each situation

A6: B) Honorably and responsibly to the highest legal standards

The correct answer is B. The certification standards explicitly state that PCIPs must be "honorably and responsibly completing all aspects of your work to the highest legal standards." This comprehensive approach encompasses not just technical accuracy but the manner and integrity with which the work is performed. The emphasis on "honorably" speaks to ethical conduct, while "responsibly" addresses accountability and thoroughness. The requirement to meet "highest legal standards" establishes that mere compliance with minimum legal requirements is insufficient—PCIPs must aspire to exemplary legal conduct in all professional activities.

For more information on PCIP professional responsibilities, visit: https://www.pcisecuritystandards.org/program/pcip_agreement/

Q7: Short Answer: Name three specific behavioral standards explicitly mentioned that PCIPs must adhere to.

A7: Based on the provided content, three specific behavioral standards explicitly mentioned that PCIPs must adhere to are:

1. Upholding the highest standards of conduct in all professional activities

2. Remaining committed to providing the best in customer service

3. Honorably and responsibly completing all aspects of work to the highest legal standards

These standards collectively form the foundation of professional expectations for Payment Card Industry Professionals. They extend beyond technical knowledge to encompass ethical behavior, customer-focused service, and legal compliance—representing the holistic approach required of certified professionals in the payment card security domain.

For more on professional standards for PCIPs, visit: https://www.pcisecuritystandards.org/program/pcip/

Q8: True or False: The PCIP certification focuses exclusively on technical knowledge of PCI Standards.

A8: False. While technical knowledge of PCI Standards is certainly a core component of the PCIP certification, the provided content clearly demonstrates that the certification extends well beyond technical expertise. The PCIP must also uphold the highest standards of professional conduct, demonstrate exceptional customer service skills, and complete work honorably and responsibly to the highest legal standards. The certification represents a holistic professional designation that encompasses technical knowledge, ethical conduct, and service excellence. This comprehensive approach ensures that certified professionals not only understand the standards but implement them with integrity and in a manner that creates exceptional customer experiences.

For a complete overview of PCIP certification requirements, visit: https://www.pcisecuritystandards.org/program/pcip/

Q9: Multiple Choice: Which phrase best captures the PCIP's obligation regarding PCI Standards, guidelines, and procedures?

A) Following them whenever possible B) Implementing them as appropriate to each situation C) Ensuring they are always followed D) Balancing them with business priorities

A9: C) Ensuring they are always followed

The correct answer is C. The content explicitly states that PCIPs must strive to uphold the highest standards of conduct, "ensuring that all PCI Standards, guidelines, and procedures are always followed." The use of "always" indicates an absolute requirement without exceptions or situational flexibility. This strict adherence forms the foundation of the PCIP's professional responsibility and reflects the critical nature of payment card security standards in protecting sensitive financial data.

For more information on PCI Standards implementation, visit: https://www.pcisecuritystandards.org/document_library/

Q10: Essay Question: Describe how a PCIP might balance the potentially competing priorities of strict adherence to PCI Standards while ensuring "exceptional" customer experiences.

A10: Balancing strict PCI Standards adherence while delivering exceptional customer experiences represents a core professional challenge for PCIPs. Rather than viewing these as competing priorities, successful PCIPs integrate them as complementary aspects of professional excellence.

The key to this balance lies in effective communication and education. A PCIP must translate complex technical requirements into understandable business language, helping customers recognize that proper security implementation ultimately protects their business and customers. By explaining the "why" behind requirements, PCIPs transform compliance from a burden into a business asset.

Proactive consultation is essential. By understanding the customer's business model and operations before implementation, PCIPs can design compliant solutions that minimize operational disruption. This might involve phased implementation approaches, identifying compensating controls when appropriate within the standards, or recommending technology solutions that enhance security while improving operational efficiency.

Customer experience excellence also means being responsive to concerns without compromising standards. When customers push back on requirements, the PCIP should listen empathetically, acknowledge challenges, and work collaboratively to find compliant solutions rather than simply citing requirements.

Documentation and training represent another balance point. Exceptional PCIPs create clear, accessible documentation and provide thorough training that empowers customers to maintain compliance independently, fostering a sense of ownership rather than dependency.

Throughout the engagement, the PCIP maintains transparency about timelines, challenges, and requirements, preventing surprises that damage the customer relationship. By positioning themselves as trusted advisors rather than auditors, PCIPs can maintain standards while building positive relationships.

Ultimately, exceptional customer experience in this context means helping customers understand that security and compliance support their business goals rather than hindering them. The PCIP who successfully navigates this balance creates not just compliance, but a security culture that delivers long-term value.

For resources on effective security implementation strategies, visit: https://www.pcisecuritystandards.org/resources/best_practices/

Q11: Multiple Choice: Which aspect of professional conduct is NOT explicitly mentioned as a PCIP requirement in the provided content?

A) Following PCI Standards B) Providing excellent customer service C) Maintaining confidentiality D) Completing work to high legal standards

A11: C) Maintaining confidentiality

The correct answer is C. While maintaining confidentiality is certainly an important aspect of payment card industry work, it is not explicitly mentioned in the provided content. The content specifically references following PCI Standards, providing excellent customer service, and completing work to high legal standards. This doesn't mean confidentiality is unimportant—it's likely covered under other PCIP requirements or within the PCI Standards themselves—but it's not explicitly stated in the provided excerpt about PCIP professional conduct.

For complete PCIP professional requirements, visit: https://www.pcisecuritystandards.org/program/pcip_agreement/

Q12: What does the requirement to complete work "to the highest legal standards" suggest about minimum compliance with laws and regulations?

A12: The requirement to complete work "to the highest legal standards" suggests that minimum compliance with laws and regulations is insufficient for a PCIP. The phrasing deliberately uses the superlative "highest," indicating that PCIPs must go beyond basic legal compliance to exemplary legal conduct.

This standard establishes an aspirational benchmark rather than a minimum threshold. It suggests that PCIPs should be familiar with all applicable laws and regulations affecting payment card security and implementation, including international, federal, state, and industry-specific requirements.

Furthermore, in situations where legal standards might vary by jurisdiction or interpretation, PCIPs are expected to adhere to the most stringent interpretation that best protects cardholder data and the integrity of the payment system. This prevents the practice of seeking out the most lenient legal interpretations or jurisdictions with minimal requirements.

The standard also implies a proactive approach to legal compliance, where PCIPs stay informed about evolving legal requirements and emerging legal precedents rather than merely responding to established regulations.

In practice, this means that PCIPs must be thorough in their legal due diligence, documentation, and implementation practices, creating work product that would withstand the most rigorous legal scrutiny.

For information on legal requirements in payment card security, visit: https://www.pcisecuritystandards.org/blog/legal-considerations-in-pci-dss-compliance/

Q13: True or False: According to the provided content, a PCIP can occasionally prioritize efficiency over customer experience if it ensures better technical compliance.

A13: False. The provided content establishes that PCIPs must "ensure every customer experience is exceptional" without providing exceptions for efficiency or technical considerations. The language is absolute, indicating that exceptional customer experiences are a non-negotiable aspect of PCIP professional conduct. This suggests that PCIPs must find ways to achieve technical compliance while simultaneously delivering exceptional experiences, rather than sacrificing one for the other. This holistic approach recognizes that effective security implementation requires both technical excellence and positive stakeholder engagement. A truly proficient PCIP develops the skills to achieve compliance in ways that enhance rather than detract from the customer experience.

For best practices on balancing compliance and customer experience, visit: https://www.pcisecuritystandards.org/blog/security-and-experience/

Q14: Short Answer: Explain what the phrase "uphold the highest standards of conduct" implies about a PCIP's behavior in challenging professional situations.

A14: The phrase "uphold the highest standards of conduct" implies that in challenging professional situations, a PCIP must maintain exemplary ethical behavior without compromise. This means:

When faced with pressure to implement shortcuts or workarounds to PCI requirements, the PCIP must firmly but respectfully decline, educating stakeholders about requirements while finding compliant alternatives.

In situations where clients or employers request actions that conflict with PCI Standards, the PCIP must navigate these conversations with diplomacy while standing firm on essential compliance requirements.

When discovering compliance issues or vulnerabilities, the PCIP must address them transparently rather than concealing problems even when disclosure might be uncomfortable.

The PCIP must avoid conflicts of interest and maintain objective assessment practices, even when personal or professional relationships might be affected.

If mistakes occur, the PCIP takes responsibility rather than deflecting blame, demonstrating accountability and focusing on remediation.

This phrase establishes an expectation of integrity as the foundation of PCIP professional identity, requiring moral courage to maintain standards even when doing so presents professional challenges.

For guidance on ethical challenges in compliance work, visit: https://www.pcisecuritystandards.org/program/ethical_guidelines/

Q15: Multiple Choice: What is the relationship between PCI Standards and a PCIP's professional conduct according to the content?

A) PCI Standards primarily govern technical implementations, while professional conduct is a separate consideration B) PCIPs must balance PCI Standards with practical business considerations C) PCIPs must ensure PCI Standards, guidelines, and procedures are always followed as part of their professional conduct D) Professional conduct is more important than rigid adherence to PCI Standards

A15: C) PCIPs must ensure PCI Standards, guidelines, and procedures are always followed as part of their professional conduct

The correct answer is C. The content explicitly integrates adherence to PCI Standards into the definition of professional conduct, stating that PCIPs "must strive to uphold the highest standards of conduct, ensuring that all PCI Standards, guidelines, and procedures are always followed." This indicates that following PCI Standards is not separate from professional conduct but is a fundamental component of it. The use of "always" emphasizes that this is an absolute requirement without exceptions, establishing technical compliance as inseparable from professional integrity for certified PCIPs.

For more information on PCIP professional responsibilities, visit: https://www.pcisecuritystandards.org/program/pcip/

Q16: Essay Question: How might a PCIP demonstrate a commitment to "honorably" completing their work in the context of a PCI DSS implementation project?

A16: Demonstrating a commitment to "honorably" completing work in a PCI DSS implementation requires integrity in multiple dimensions throughout the project lifecycle:

At the outset, the PCIP would provide honest assessments of the organization's compliance status and implementation challenges, avoiding both overstatement of problems to inflate services and understatement to win business. They would establish transparent pricing and realistic timelines, refusing to make promises they cannot fulfill.

During scoping, the honorable PCIP ensures all cardholder data environments are properly identified without artificially expanding or contracting scope. They resist any pressure to exclude systems that legitimately process, store, or transmit cardholder data, even when inclusion complicates the project.

In the assessment phase, they conduct thorough, unbiased evaluations without cutting corners on testing procedures. Findings are reported accurately, regardless of whether they reflect positively or negatively on previous work or recommendations.

When designing solutions, honorable PCIPs recommend only necessary controls aligned with actual risk and requirements, avoiding both over-engineering (to increase billable hours) and under-engineering (to reduce project complexity). They clearly distinguish between required controls for compliance and optional enhancements.

Throughout implementation, they maintain detailed documentation of all decisions and changes, creating an auditable trail that demonstrates compliance rationale. When unexpected challenges arise, they communicate promptly rather than hiding difficulties.

If the PCIP identifies errors in their own work, they take responsibility and correct them without additional charges. They refuse to certify compliance for environments that don't genuinely meet requirements, even when under pressure to do so.

Knowledge transfer represents another aspect of honorable work. Rather than creating dependency, the PCIP educates the client's team on maintaining compliance independently, even if this potentially reduces future consulting needs.

Finally, after project completion, they remain available for reasonable follow-up questions without immediate demands for additional fees, demonstrating a commitment to the client's sustainable compliance rather than merely completing contractual obligations.

This honorable approach builds trust in both the individual PCIP and the broader payment card security profession, reinforcing the value of the certification.

For resources on professional ethics in compliance work, visit: https://www.pcisecuritystandards.org/blog/ethical-implementation-guidelines/

Q17: True or False: A PCIP's responsibility to create exceptional customer experiences extends only to direct clients who have hired them.

A17: False. The provided content states that PCIPs must "ensure every customer experience is exceptional" without limiting this obligation to direct clients. This broad phrasing suggests a comprehensive responsibility toward all stakeholders affected by the PCIP's work. This would include not only the organization that hired the PCIP, but also their customers, partners, vendors, and internal teams impacted by PCI implementations.

The inclusive language reflects the understanding that payment card security implementations affect an ecosystem of participants, and the PCIP's work has ripple effects throughout this system. For example, implementation decisions might affect how merchant employees process transactions, how customers experience payment flows, or how service providers interact with the system.

This comprehensive view of "customer experience" aligns with the holistic approach to payment card security, recognizing that security controls affect real people at multiple touchpoints in the payment process.

For more on stakeholder management in security implementations, visit: https://www.pcisecuritystandards.org/blog/stakeholder-engagement-in-security/

Q18: Multiple Choice: Which of the following best describes how a PCIP should approach the implementation of PCI guidelines?

A) Implementing them as closely as possible while allowing for business constraints B) Following them when they align with customer preferences C) Always ensuring they are followed without exception D) Applying them selectively based on risk assessment

A18: C) Always ensuring they are followed without exception

The correct answer is C. The content explicitly states that PCIPs must ensure "all PCI Standards, guidelines, and procedures are always followed." The unambiguous language "always followed" indicates that selective implementation or exceptions based on business constraints, customer preferences, or risk assessments would not meet the professional standard expected of PCIPs. This absolute approach reflects the critical security function of PCI Standards in protecting sensitive payment card data and maintaining the integrity of the payment ecosystem.

For authoritative information on PCI guidelines implementation, visit: https://www.pcisecuritystandards.org/document_library/

Q19: Short Answer: Describe how the dual requirements of "highest standards of conduct" and "exceptional customer experience" might guide a PCIP when delivering difficult news about compliance gaps.

A19: When delivering difficult news about compliance gaps, the dual requirements of "highest standards of conduct" and "exceptional customer experience" would guide a PCIP to approach the situation with both integrity and empathy:

The PCIP would present findings truthfully and completely, without minimizing serious issues or creating unnecessary alarm—upholding the highest standards of conduct requires unflinching honesty about compliance realities.

However, exceptional customer experience would guide the delivery method. The PCIP would schedule appropriate time for the discussion, prepare clear documentation, and present findings in language calibrated to the audience's technical understanding.

Rather than simply identifying problems, the PCIP would come prepared with potential remediation strategies and realistic timelines, transforming a potentially negative conversation into a forward-looking planning session.

The PCIP would acknowledge the challenges and costs associated with remediation while emphasizing the business value of compliance and security, helping stakeholders understand the "why" behind requirements.

Throughout the conversation, the PCIP would maintain a collaborative, problem-solving tone rather than a judgmental one, positioning themselves as a partner in achieving compliance rather than merely an assessor identifying failures.

This balanced approach maintains professional integrity while creating an experience that, while potentially challenging, still demonstrates respect, partnership, and a commitment to the customer's ultimate success.

For guidance on effective compliance communications, visit: https://www.pcisecuritystandards.org/blog/communicating-compliance-findings/

Q20: Multiple Choice: According to the professional standards for PCIPs, what should be the primary motivation behind their work?

A) Technical accuracy and precision B) Ensuring exceptional customer experiences C) Minimizing compliance costs for clients D) Rapid implementation timelines

A20: B) Ensuring exceptional customer experiences

The correct answer is B. The content specifically states that "Your goal as a PCIP is to ensure every customer experience is exceptional." This explicitly positions exceptional customer experiences as the primary goal or motivation for PCIPs. While technical accuracy is certainly important (as implied by following PCI Standards), and cost-effectiveness and timeliness may be components of good service, the content specifically identifies exceptional customer experiences as the overarching goal that should drive all PCIP activities.

For more information on PCIP professional goals, visit: https://www.pcisecuritystandards.org/program/pcip/

Q21: Essay Question: Analyze how the PCIP's obligation to "honorably and responsibly" complete work intersects with situations where clients are resistant to implementing required PCI controls due to cost or operational concerns.

A21: The obligation to complete work "honorably and responsibly" creates a nuanced professional challenge when clients resist implementing required PCI controls due to cost or operational concerns.

The "honorable" dimension requires unflinching truthfulness. The PCIP cannot misrepresent requirements to make implementation more palatable, downplay security risks to accommodate client hesitation, or certify compliance when requirements aren't genuinely met. This may create tension when clients seek shortcuts or exceptions that would compromise security or compliance.

Simultaneously, the "responsible" aspect demands recognition of business realities. A responsible PCIP acknowledges that organizations have legitimate resource constraints and operational concerns. Simply insisting on controls without addressing these realities would reflect an incomplete understanding of professional responsibility.

The intersection of these obligations requires sophisticated professional judgment. The PCIP must maintain the integrity of PCI Standards while demonstrating empathy for the client's position.

In practice, this might involve:

1. Thorough explanation of requirements and their security rationale, helping clients understand the "why" behind controls they perceive as burdensome.
2. Exploring phased implementation approaches that prioritize critical controls while developing realistic timelines for full compliance.
3. Identifying compensating controls that might achieve security objectives while better aligning with operational realities when permitted within the PCI framework.
4. Documenting client decisions and providing clear written guidance about compliance gaps and associated risks, ensuring transparency about implementation choices.
5. Connecting security requirements to business benefits beyond compliance, such as reduced fraud risk, enhanced customer trust, or operational efficiencies.
6. When appropriate, explaining the potential consequences of non-compliance in factual rather than threatening terms helping clients make informed risk decisions.

The honorable and responsible PCIP maintains the courage to refuse requests that would compromise integrity while demonstrating the creativity and patience to help clients navigate legitimate implementation challenges. This balanced approach respects both the letter of PCI requirements and the complex realities of business operations.

For guidance on navigating implementation challenges, visit: https://www.pcisecuritystandards.org/blog/implementation-strategies-for-complex-environments/

Q22: True or False: The PCIP's obligation to follow PCI Standards applies primarily to technical implementation rather than administrative processes.

A22: False. The content states that PCIPs must ensure "all PCI Standards, guidelines, and procedures are always followed" without differentiating between technical and administrative aspects. This comprehensive language encompasses the full spectrum of PCI requirements, including both technical controls (like encryption and access controls) and administrative processes (such as documentation, policy development, and personnel management).

The PCI DSS framework itself addresses both technical and administrative requirements across its twelve requirements, covering everything from network security to policy documentation. The PCIP's obligation to uphold these standards extends equally across all aspects of implementation and compliance.

This comprehensive approach reflects the understanding that effective security requires both technical safeguards and proper administrative governance. A PCIP who focused only on technical implementation while neglecting administrative requirements would not be meeting the professional standard of ensuring all PCI Standards are always followed.

For a complete overview of PCI DSS requirements, visit: https://www.pcisecuritystandards.org/document_library/

Q23: Multiple Choice: Which of the following best characterizes the relationship between legal standards and a PCIP's work?

A) PCIPs should generally align their work with applicable legal requirements B) PCIPs must complete all aspects of work to the highest legal standards C) Legal standards are secondary to technical accuracy in PCI implementations D) PCIPs should balance legal requirements with practical business needs

A23: B) PCIPs must complete all aspects of work to the highest legal standards

The correct answer is B. The content explicitly states that PCIPs must be "honorably and responsibly completing all aspects of your work to the highest legal standards." This unambiguous language establishes that meeting the highest legal standards is a non-negotiable requirement that applies to all aspects of the PCIP's professional activities. The phrasing "highest legal standards" indicates that minimum legal compliance is insufficient—PCIPs must aspire to exemplary legal conduct that exceeds basic requirements. This comprehensive legal obligation reflects the regulated nature of payment card data and the potential legal implications of security breaches.

For information on legal considerations in PCI compliance, visit: https://www.pcisecuritystandards.org/blog/legal-framework/

Q24: Short Answer: Describe three specific ways a PCIP could demonstrate their commitment to providing "the best in customer service" during a PCI implementation project.

A24: Three specific ways a PCIP could demonstrate their commitment to providing "the best in customer service" during a PCI implementation project include:

1. Proactive Communication: The exemplary PCIP establishes clear communication channels at project initiation, provides regular status updates without being prompted, and alerts stakeholders to potential issues before they become problems. They create accessible documentation tailored to different audience needs (executive summaries for leadership, detailed technical guides for implementers) and respond promptly to inquiries with thorough, understandable explanations.

2. Educational Approach: Rather than simply directing compliance activities, the PCIP takes time to explain the rationale behind requirements, helping stakeholders understand how controls protect their business and customers. They conduct knowledge transfer sessions that build internal capability, create customized training materials relevant to the organization's specific environment, and patiently answer questions without technical condescension.

3. Flexible Implementation Support: The PCIP adapts their working style to the organization's culture and processes rather than forcing rigid methodologies. They schedule activities to minimize business disruption, accommodate reasonable timeline adjustments when circumstances change, and provide options when implementation decisions are needed. After formal project completion, they remain available for follow-up questions and guidance, demonstrating commitment to the organization's ongoing compliance success beyond contractual obligations.

These approaches collectively create an experience where compliance becomes a collaborative partnership rather than an imposed burden.

For best practices in client service during security implementations, visit: https://www.pcisecuritystandards.org/blog/client-service-excellence/

Q25: How might the requirement for PCIPs to "ensure every customer experience is exceptional" influence their approach to documentation and knowledge transfer?

A25: The requirement to "ensure every customer experience is exceptional" would significantly influence a PCIP's approach to documentation and knowledge transfer in several ways:

First, documentation would be created with the end user experience as a primary consideration, not merely as a compliance checkbox. This means developing materials that are clear, accessible, and tailored to different stakeholder needs—executive summaries for leadership, detailed technical guides for IT teams, and simplified process documents for general staff.

Documentation would be visually well-organized with consistent formatting, logical structure, and navigational aids that make information easy to locate. The PCIP would invest in creating diagrams, flowcharts, and visual representations that clarify complex concepts rather than relying solely on text.

Language choices would reflect audience needs, avoiding unnecessary technical jargon when communicating with non-technical stakeholders while providing appropriate technical depth for specialist audiences. Documentation would be proactively reviewed for clarity and comprehensibility before delivery.

For knowledge transfer, the exceptional experience standard would drive PCIPs to move beyond one-way information delivery to collaborative learning. This might include interactive training sessions, hands-on workshops, and scenario-based learning that helps stakeholders apply concepts to their specific environment.

The PCIP would assess different learning styles within the organization and adapt delivery methods accordingly—creating video tutorials, written guides, interactive tools, and in-person training to accommodate diverse preferences.

Follow-up support would be built into the knowledge transfer process, with scheduled check-ins, easy-to-access reference materials, and clear channels for questions that might arise after formal training concludes.

Throughout documentation and knowledge transfer, the PCIP would emphasize not just compliance requirements but the business value and security benefits of implementation, helping stakeholders understand why procedures matter rather than simply what they need to do.

This exceptional approach transforms documentation and knowledge transfer from perfunctory deliverables into valuable assets that empower organizations to maintain compliance independently, creating lasting value beyond the immediate engagement.

For resources on effective security documentation practices, visit: https://www.pcisecuritystandards.org/blog/documentation-best-practices/

12

Scoping Your Connected Environment - Question Set

Q1: What does CDE stand for in the context of PCI-DSS, and what elements does it encompass?

A1: CDE stands for Cardholder Data Environment. It encompasses all people, processes, and technologies that store, process, or transmit cardholder data or sensitive authentication data. The CDE also includes all system components that are connected to or could impact the security of cardholder data. These technologies come in various forms, such as network devices, servers, computing devices, and applications. The CDE is essentially the complete ecosystem where payment card data exists or flows through, and every component within this environment must adhere to PCI-DSS security requirements.

For additional information on CDE definition and scope, visit: https://www.pcisecuritystandards.org/document_library/

Q2: True or False: Scoping is optional when preparing for a PCI-DSS assessment.

A2: False. Scoping is a critical and mandatory step in preparing for a PCI-DSS assessment. The content explicitly states that "Understanding what is in scope and what is not is crucial to ensure the safety and security of your cardholder data." Before any annual assessment, entities must verify that the scope of their PCI-DSS is accurate by identifying all locations and flows of cardholder data. Without proper scoping, organizations risk non-compliance, security vulnerabilities, and potential financial penalties. Scoping is described as "the foundation upon which the rest of your PCI-DSS compliance journey is built."

For more details on scoping requirements, visit: https://www.pcisecuritystandards.org/documents/Guidance-PCI-DSS-Scoping-and-Segmentation.pdf

Q3: Which of the following is NOT mentioned as an example of a system component in the CDE?

a) Authentication servers b) Internal firewalls c) Name resolution servers d) Employee mobile phones

A3: The correct answer is d) Employee mobile phones. According to the content, system components in the CDE include authentication servers, security services, internal firewalls that segment the CDE, name resolution or web redirection servers that impact CDE security, and virtualization components like virtual machines, switches/routers, appliances, applications/desktops, and hypervisors. Employee mobile phones are not specifically mentioned in the provided content as examples of system components in the CDE (though they could potentially be in scope if they store, process, or transmit cardholder data).

For a comprehensive list of system components, visit: https://www.pcisecuritystandards.org/glossary/

Q4: Explain the concept of "Connected-to Systems" in PCI-DSS scoping and provide examples.

A4: "Connected-to Systems" in PCI-DSS scoping refers to systems that are connected to the Cardholder Data Environment (CDE) but may not directly store, process, or transmit cardholder data themselves. However, these systems could potentially impact the security of the CDE if compromised.

As explained in the content, these systems are "not directly involved in processing a transaction and do not store any card details" but are connected to the CDE. Examples mentioned include point-of-sale systems, payment gateways, and customer relationship management systems. Other examples might include authentication servers and security services that don't directly handle cardholder data but protect it.

These systems are important to identify during the scoping process because they must be included in the scope of PCI-DSS compliance due to their potential impact on cardholder data security, even though they don't directly handle the data.

For more information on connected-to systems, visit: https://www.pcisecuritystandards.org/document_library/

Q5: What is the SARASR acronym related to in PCI-DSS, and what does each letter stand for?

A5: The SARASR acronym relates to the key steps in the PCI-DSS compliance process. Each letter stands for:

S - Scope: Define the extent of the cardholder data environment, including all payment channels, systems connected to or impacting the CDE, and the overall security of the CDE.

A - Assess: Evaluate the PCI-DSS requirements based on the determined scope.

R - Report: Create a comprehensive report that considers the scope and the evaluation of the CDE.

A - Attest: Ensure that the scope is accurate and up-to-date. A QSA will verify that the scope is correctly defined.

S - Submit: Hand over the completed report to the acquirer or a designated third party.

R - Remediate: Address any identified issues or areas needing improvement in collaboration with the QSA and Acquirer.

This acronym provides a structured approach to remembering the key steps in the PCI-DSS compliance process.

For more on the compliance process, visit: https://www.pcisecuritystandards.org/document_library/

Q6: Which of the following best describes the primary purpose of scoping in PCI-DSS compliance?

a) To reduce the cost of PCI-DSS compliance b) To identify all locations and flows of cardholder data c) To eliminate the need for a Qualified Security Assessor d) To simplify the reporting process

A6: The correct answer is b) To identify all locations and flows of cardholder data. According to the content, the primary purpose of scoping is to "verify that the scope of their PCI-DSS is accurate by identifying all locations and flows of cardholder data." This process helps organizations identify all systems connected to the CDE or systems that could impact it if compromised, ensuring they are included in the scope of PCI-DSS. While scoping may help with cost reduction, eliminating QSA involvement, or simplifying reporting, these are potential benefits rather than the primary purpose.

For comprehensive guidance on scoping, visit: https://www.pcisecuritystandards.org/documents/Guidance-PCI-DSS-Scoping-and-Segmentation.pdf

Q7: Describe the steps an organization should take to confirm the accuracy of their defined Cardholder Data Environment (CDE).

A7: To confirm the accuracy of the defined Cardholder Data Environment (CDE), an organization should:

1. Identify and document all cardholder data in its environment and verify that no cardholder data exists outside the currently defined CDE.
2. Use the results of this identification process to determine whether the PCI-DSS scope is appropriate. This might involve creating a diagram or an inventory of cardholder data locations.
3. Consider any cardholder data found to be in scope of the PCI-DSS assessment as part of the CDE.
4. Retain documentation that shows how the PCI-DSS scope was determined for review by the assessor and for reference during the subsequent annual PCI-DSS scope confirmation.

These steps ensure a comprehensive understanding of where cardholder data resides and flows, which is essential for accurate scoping and effective security controls.

For detailed scoping guidance, visit: https://www.pcisecuritystandards.org/documents/Guidance-PCI-DSS-Scoping-and-Segmentation.pdf

Q8: True or False: A Qualified Security Assessor (QSA) must validate that each PCI-DSS assessment's scope is accurately defined and documented.

A8: True. According to the content, "A QSAs must validate that each PCI-DSS assessments scope is accurately defined and documented." This is an important aspect of the attestation phase in the SARASR process. The QSA plays a critical role in verifying that the entity has properly defined what is in scope for PCI-DSS compliance, ensuring that all systems storing, processing, or transmitting cardholder data, as well as systems connected to the CDE, are appropriately included in the assessment scope.

For more information on the role of QSAs, visit: https://www.pcisecuritystandards.org/assessors_and_solutions/qualified_security_assessors/

Q9: What are the three categories used to classify systems during the scoping task according to the provided content?

A9: According to the content, the three categories used to classify systems during the scoping task are:

1. In Scope: Systems that are directly connected to, have an impact on, or are involved with the cardholder data and the overall security of the cardholder data environment (CDE). This includes all payment channels and systems that interact with

sensitive information.

2. Out of Scope: Systems that are completely isolated and cannot interact with sensitive information. These systems are completely cut off from any access to the CDE.

3. Connected-to: Systems that are connected to the CDE but are not directly involved in processing a transaction and do not store any card details. Despite not handling cardholder data directly, these systems must be considered for their potential impact on CDE security.

This classification helps organizations determine which systems need to comply with PCI-DSS requirements and to what extent.

For more information on scoping categories, visit: https://www.pcisecuritystandards.org/documents/Guidance-PCI-DSS-Scoping-and-Segmentation.pdf

Q10: How can organizations potentially reduce the scope of their PCI-DSS assessment?

A10: Organizations can potentially reduce the scope of their PCI-DSS assessment by introducing specific controls. According to the content, one example is "outsourcing your online ordering to a third-party payment processor," which can reduce scope and simplify compliance efforts.

Other potential scope-reduction strategies (though not all are explicitly mentioned in the content) include:

1. Implementing network segmentation to isolate the CDE from other networks

2. Using tokenization to replace cardholder data with non-sensitive tokens

3. Employing point-to-point encryption (P2PE) solutions

4. Utilizing hosted payment pages where the payment processor handles the card data

5. Implementing data minimization practices to reduce where cardholder data exists

By introducing these controls, organizations can limit the number of systems that store, process, or transmit cardholder data, thereby reducing the scope of their PCI-DSS assessment and potentially simplifying their compliance efforts.

For more information on scope reduction techniques, visit: https://www.pcisecuritystandards.org/documents/Guidance-PCI-DSS-Scoping-and-Segmentation.pdf

Q11: What does the content suggest is the first critical step in achieving PCI-DSS compliance?

a) Hiring a Qualified Security Assessor b) Implementing all applicable PCI requirements c) Developing a comprehensive scope of the Cardholder Data Environment d) Creating a data flow diagram

A11: The correct answer is c) Developing a comprehensive scope of the Cardholder Data Environment. The content explicitly states, "I cannot overstate the importance of developing a comprehensive scope of any organization's Cardholder Data Environment. It is the foundation upon which the rest of your PCI-DSS compliance journey is built." It also mentions that "A comprehensive scope of any organization's Cardholder Data Environment is one of the first steps to take and one you should remember for the PCIP." This emphasizes that proper scoping is the initial critical step before other compliance activities can be effectively undertaken.

For guidance on scoping methodology, visit: https://www.pcisecuritystandards.org/documents/Guidance-PCI-DSS-Scoping-and-Segmentation.pdf

Q12: Which payment channels should be considered when scoping a Cardholder Data Environment?

A12: When scoping a Cardholder Data Environment, all payment channels within the environment should be considered. According to the content, this includes:

1. In-person transactions (such as physical retail locations with payment terminals)
2. Online transactions (e-commerce websites, online ordering systems)
3. Mobile transactions (mobile payment applications, mobile point-of-sale systems)

The content emphasizes the importance of identifying all payment channels to ensure complete compliance. It provides an example of a small retail business that might mistakenly consider only in-person payment terminals as being in scope while failing to recognize that their online payment channel is also in scope. Such an oversight could lead to non-compliance and potential financial penalties. Therefore, a comprehensive identification of all payment channels is crucial for accurate scoping and ensuring full PCI-DSS compliance.

For more information on payment channels and scoping, visit: https://www.pcisecuritystandards.org/document_library/

Q13: Explain the concept of "cardholder data flow" and why mapping it is important for PCI-DSS compliance.

A13: Cardholder data flow refers to the path that payment card data takes as it moves through an organization's systems—where it's stored, how it's processed, and where it's transmitted to. Mapping this flow involves creating a comprehensive visualization or documentation of all the points where cardholder data enters, resides within, and exits the organization's environment.

Mapping cardholder data flow is important for PCI-DSS compliance for several reasons:

1. It helps identify all systems and components that store, process, or transmit cardholder data, ensuring they're included in the PCI-DSS scope.
2. It allows organizations to understand which systems need to be protected according to PCI-DSS requirements.
3. It helps identify potential vulnerabilities or security risks in the data handling process.
4. It provides clarity on which systems are truly in scope for assessment versus those that can be excluded.

The content provides an example of a business owner who, through mapping cardholder data flow, discovers that their point-of-sale system stores cardholder data while their e-commerce platform does not. This information helps determine which devices need to be included in the PCI-DSS assessment and where additional security measures might be needed.

For guidance on mapping data flows, visit: https://www.pcisecuritystandards.org/document_library/

Q14: True or False: Once the scope of PCI-DSS is defined, it remains static and doesn't need to be reviewed again.

A14: False. According to the content, "Once you've scoped your environment and recorded your findings, maintaining the records over time is of the most importance." The content emphasizes that organizations need to "keep track of any changes made to the environment" which will make the "following year's assessment much easier to manage." Additionally, one of the steps in confirming CDE accuracy involves retaining documentation "for reference during the subsequent annual PCI-DSS scope confirmation." This clearly indicates that scope is not static but needs to be monitored, maintained, and reviewed regularly, particularly on an annual basis before assessments.

For best practices on scope maintenance, visit: https://www.pcisecuritystandards.org/document_library/

Q15: What types of systems should be considered during the scoping process according to the content?

A15: According to the content, during the scoping process, organizations should consider:

1. All systems that store, process, or transmit cardholder data
2. Systems connected to the cardholder data environment
3. Systems that could impact the security of the CDE if compromised (such as authentication servers)
4. All types of system components including:
    - Network devices
    - Servers (including authentication servers, security services, name resolution or web redirection servers)
    - Computing devices
    - Applications
    - Virtualization components (virtual machines, switches/routers, appliances, applications/desktops, and hypervisors)
5. Different locations, including backup/recovery sites and fail-over procedures

The content emphasizes the importance of considering "all types of systems and locations" to ensure a comprehensive scope that accounts for all business areas that might impact cardholder data security.

For detailed information on system types in scope, visit: https://www.pcisecuritystandards.org/documents/Guidance-PCI-DSS-Scoping-and-Segmentation.pdf

Q16: Which of the following best describes the relationship between scoping and reporting in PCI-DSS compliance?

a) Scoping has no impact on reporting requirements b) Scoping determines which systems to include in the report c) Scoping determines the reporting obligations such as selecting the appropriate SAQ form or deciding whether an RoC is necessary d) Reporting always precedes scoping in the compliance process

A16: The correct answer is c) Scoping determines the reporting obligations such as selecting the appropriate SAQ form or deciding whether an RoC is necessary. According to the content, "An adequate scope will also determine the reporting obligations for PCI-DSS, such as selecting the appropriate SAQ form or deciding whether an RoC is necessary." This indicates that the scope of an organization's cardholder data environment directly influences what type of reporting will be required for compliance, making scoping a critical prerequisite to the reporting phase.

For more information on reporting requirements, visit: https://www.pcisecuritystandards.org/document_library/

Q17: Describe the relationship between the "Attest" phase and the role of a Qualified Security Assessor (QSA) in the SARASR process.

A17: In the SARASR process, the "Attest" phase involves ensuring that the scope of an organization's cardholder data environment is accurate and up-to-date. According to the content, "As an entity, it is crucial always to ensure that your scope is accurate and up-to-date."

The Qualified Security Assessor (QSA) plays a critical role in this phase by independently verifying and validating that the organization's defined scope is accurate. As stated in the content, "When a Qualified Security Assessor (QSA) evaluates your entity, they will verify that your scope is defined correctly." The content also explicitly mentions that "A QSAs must validate that each PCI-DSS assessments scope is accurately defined and documented."

This relationship establishes a system of checks and balances where the organization first attests to the accuracy of their scope, and then the QSA provides an independent validation of this attestation. This helps ensure the integrity of the compliance process and reduces the risk of overlooking systems or components that should be included in the PCI-DSS assessment.

For more information on the QSA's role, visit: https://www.pcisecuritystandards.org/assessors_and_solutions/qualified_security_assessors/

Q18: What is the purpose of the "Remediate" phase in the SARASR process?

A18: The "Remediate" phase in the SARASR process is the final step that focuses on addressing any issues or areas of improvement identified during the assessment and reporting phases. According to the content, "If the report highlights any areas needing fixing or improving, it is vital to address them promptly and in collaboration with your QSA and Acquirer."

The purpose of this phase is to:

1. Fix any non-compliant aspects of the cardholder data environment

2. Implement necessary security controls or improvements

3. Address vulnerabilities or weaknesses identified during the assessment

4. Work collaboratively with the QSA and Acquirer to ensure issues are properly resolved

5. Ensure the organization progresses toward full PCI-DSS compliance

The content emphasizes that remediation should be done "promptly" and in a collaborative manner to "ensure that your business stays on track" with its compliance efforts. This phase is crucial as it transforms the assessment findings into actionable improvements that enhance the security of cardholder data.

For guidance on remediation strategies, visit: https://www.pcisecuritystandards.org/document_library/

Q19: What documentation should be retained after determining PCI-DSS scope?

A19: According to the content, after determining PCI-DSS scope, the organization should retain "Documentation that shows how the PCI-DSS scope was determined." This documentation serves two important purposes:

1. It is retained "for review by the assessor" – meaning the QSA will need to examine this documentation during the assessment process to validate that the scope was properly determined.

2. It is kept "for reference during the subsequent annual PCI-DSS scope confirmation" – indicating that this documentation serves as a baseline for comparison when conducting the next year's scoping exercise.

While the content doesn't specify the exact format of this documentation, it does mention that when identifying cardholder data locations, the entity might use "a diagram or an inventory of cardholder data locations" to determine if the scope is appropriate. These types of documents would likely be part of the retained documentation, along with any methodology explanations, system classifications, data flow mappings, and justifications for in-scope and out-of-scope determinations.

For documentation requirements, visit: https://www.pcisecuritystandards.org/document_library/

Q20: In the context of PCI-DSS scoping, what distinguishes "Out of Scope" systems from other systems?

A20: According to the content, "Out of Scope" systems are distinguished by being "completely isolated and cannot interact with sensitive information." The key characteristic that sets these systems apart is that they are "completely cut off from any access to the CDE (Cardholder Data Environment)."

This complete isolation means that these systems:

1. Do not store, process, or transmit cardholder data

2. Cannot impact the security of the CDE if compromised

3. Have no connection or communication pathway to the CDE

4. Are entirely separated from systems that handle cardholder data

This strict separation is what allows these systems to be excluded from PCI-DSS compliance requirements. It's important to note that the isolation must be complete; systems that have any ability to interact with or impact the CDE would fall into either the "In Scope" or "Connected-to" categories instead.

For guidance on determining out-of-scope systems, visit: https://www.pcisecuritystandards.org/documents/Guidance-PCI-DSS-Scoping-and-Segmentation.pdf

Q21: Which of the following is NOT mentioned as a step in confirming the accuracy of the defined CDE?

a) Identifying and documenting all cardholder data in the environment b) Verifying that no cardholder data exists outside the currently defined CDE c) Conducting penetration testing on all systems in the CDE d) Retaining documentation that shows how the PCI-DSS scope was determined

A21: The correct answer is c) Conducting penetration testing on all systems in the CDE. While penetration testing is an important aspect of PCI-DSS compliance, it is not specifically mentioned in the content as one of the steps to confirm the accuracy of the defined CDE. The content lists the following steps: identifying and documenting all cardholder data, verifying no cardholder data exists outside the defined CDE, using results to determine if scope is appropriate, considering found cardholder data as part of the CDE, and retaining documentation of how scope was determined. Penetration testing would typically come after the scope is confirmed, as part of the assessment of the in-scope systems.

For information on penetration testing requirements, visit: https://www.pcisecuritystandards.org/document_library/

Q22: True or False: According to the content, virtualization components are excluded from PCI-DSS scope consideration.

A22: False. The content explicitly includes virtualization components as part of the system components that should be considered in PCI-DSS scope. It states, "Virtualization components like virtual machines, switches/routers, appliances, applications/desktops, and hypervisors also play a role." This indicates that virtualization components are not excluded but are specifically mentioned as elements that should be considered during the scoping process, particularly if they are part of the Cardholder Data Environment or could impact its security.

For information on virtualization in PCI-DSS, visit: https://www.pcisecuritystandards.org/document_library/

Q23: Explain how a small business might benefit from understanding payment channels in the scoping process. Include an example from the content.

A23: A small business benefits from understanding payment channels in the scoping process by ensuring comprehensive compliance with PCI-DSS requirements, avoiding potential non-compliance penalties, and appropriately securing all systems that handle cardholder data.

The content provides a specific example: "Imagine you run a small retail business with in-person and online payment channels. Without scoping your cardholder data environment (CDE) ahead of a PCI-DSS assessment, you may mistakenly believe that only your in-person payment terminals are in scope for compliance. However, if you fail to identify your online payment channel as also being in scope, you run the risk of non-compliance and potential financial penalties."

This example illustrates how a small business might overlook certain payment channels (in this case, online transactions) if they don't conduct proper scoping. By understanding all payment channels, the business ensures that they apply appropriate security controls to all systems handling cardholder data, properly comply with all relevant PCI-DSS requirements, and avoid potential penalties for non-compliance.

Additionally, understanding payment channels helps the business identify opportunities for introducing controls that could potentially reduce scope, such as outsourcing their online ordering to a third-party payment processor, which the content mentions could "reduce your scope and simplify your compliance efforts."

For guidance on payment channels in scope, visit: https://www.pcisecuritystandards.org/document_library/

Q24: What is the primary purpose of the book mentioned in the content, and what version of PCI-DSS does it cover?

A24: According to the content, the primary purpose of the book is "to provide as much information as possible to prepare you for PCIP exam day." It specifically aims to help readers prepare for the Payment Card Industry Professional Certification Exam (PCIP 4.0).

The book covers the PCI-DSS v4.01 standard, which is associated with the PCIP 4.0 exam. The content notes that while the book covers this standard, it doesn't attempt to cover every aspect of PCI-DSS v4.01 in exhaustive detail ("is a complex and many-layered subject and would fill too many pages for me to cover here"). Instead, it focuses on the topics, links, and references to other resources that the author found most helpful in passing the exam.

The content positions the book as a "companion" to help readers "navigate the complex and multi-faceted terrain of PCIP 4.0 like a pro," suggesting it serves as a study guide or preparation resource specifically targeted at those taking the PCIP 4.0 certification exam.

For official PCIP certification information, visit: https://www.pcisecuritystandards.org/program_training_and_qualifica tion/

Q25: Describe how an organization would map cardholder data flow and why this is important in the scoping process. Include the example from the content.

A25: Mapping cardholder data flow involves tracing and documenting the complete journey of payment card data throughout an organization's environment—identifying where it enters the system, where it's stored, how it's processed, and where it's transmitted to. This creates a comprehensive visualization of all touchpoints where cardholder data exists.

According to the content, this mapping is important in the scoping process because it helps organizations understand:

- Where cardholder data is stored
- How it is processed
- Where it flows to

The content provides an example: "Imagine you are a business owner who accepts online and in-store credit card payments. Before your PCI-DSS assessment, you must scope your environment and map your cardholder data flow. By doing this, you discover that your point-of-sale (POS) system stores cardholder data, but your e-commerce platform does not. You also learn that your payment gateway is transmitting data to your merchant bank but not storing it."

This example illustrates how mapping cardholder data flow provides critical insights that directly impact scoping decisions:

1. It reveals which systems actually store cardholder data (the POS system) versus those that don't (the e-commerce platform)
2. It identifies systems that transmit but don't store data (payment gateway)
3. It helps determine which devices need to be included in the PCI-DSS assessment
4. It highlights where additional security measures might be needed (e.g., "implementing additional security measures for your POS system, such as encryption or tokenization")

The content concludes that "scoping your environment and mapping your cardholder data flow is critical in ensuring that you comply with PCI-DSS and protect your customers' sensitive information," emphasizing its fundamental importance to the compliance process.

For detailed guidance on data flow mapping, visit: https://www.pcisecuritystandards.org/document_library/

13

Consequences of Non-Compliance to PCI-DSS - Question Set

Q1: What is the legal status of PCI-DSS?

A1: PCI-DSS is not a law but a contractual obligation between merchants, banks, and the six major payment brands (Visa Inc, MasterCard, American Express, Discover Financial Services, JCB International, and UnionPay). It is an agreement that participants in the payment card ecosystem must adhere to as part of their business relationships with these payment brands. While not legally mandated by government legislation, non-compliance can result in contractual penalties, fines, and potentially being prohibited from processing payment card transactions. The contractual nature of PCI-DSS means that enforcement occurs through business relationships rather than through governmental legal systems, though data breaches may still trigger separate legal obligations under various privacy laws.

For more information: https://www.pcisecuritystandards.org/pci_security/standards_overview

Q2: True or False: If a business experiences a breach of personal information, they have 14 days to report it to the Information Commissioners Office (ICO).

A2: False. According to the provided content, if a business experiences a breach of personal information, they have only 72 hours (3 days) to report it to the Information Commissioners Office (ICO). This short timeframe emphasizes the importance of having effective breach detection systems and a well-prepared incident response plan in place. The 72-hour requirement aligns with many modern data protection regulations, including GDPR, and underscores the urgency with which organizations must respond to data breaches to mitigate potential harm to affected individuals.

For more information: https://ico.org.uk/for-organisations/guide-to-data-protection/guide-to-the-general-data-protection-regulation-gdpr/personal-data-breaches/

Q3: What are the potential consequences for merchants who fail to comply with PCI-DSS requirements?

A3: Merchants who fail to comply with PCI-DSS requirements may face several serious consequences:

1. Warnings from payment card brands or acquiring banks

2. Financial penalties or fines of varying severity
3. Prohibition from accepting credit card transactions
4. Mandatory on-site PCI-DSS audit to regain processing privileges
5. Mandatory forensic analysis in case of a breach (which can be costly and time-consuming)
6. Liability for credit card replacement costs transferred from card brands
7. Obligation to notify customers about security breaches
8. Requirement to provide remediation services like credit monitoring
9. Potential liability for fraudulent transactions resulting from data leaks
10. Reputational damage and loss of customer trust
11. Lost business and reduced revenue

These consequences highlight why compliance with PCI-DSS should be treated as a critical business priority rather than just a regulatory checkbox.

For more information: https://www.pcisecuritystandards.org/merchants/process/

Q4: Which of the following is NOT one of the six payment brands that established the PCI-DSS agreement?

A4: a) Visa Inc b) PayPal c) MasterCard d) American Express e) UnionPay

The correct answer is b) PayPal. According to the provided content, PCI-DSS is a contractual obligation between merchants, banks, and the top six payment brands: Visa Inc, MasterCard, American Express, Discover Financial Services (DFS), JCB International, and UnionPay. PayPal, while a significant payment processor, is not one of the six founding payment brands that established the PCI-DSS agreement, though it does require its merchants to be PCI compliant.

For more information: https://www.pcisecuritystandards.org/about_us/

Q5: Explain the concept of the Cardholder Data Environment (CDE) and discuss the best practices for securing it according to PCI-DSS.

A5: The Cardholder Data Environment (CDE) refers to the people, processes, and technology that store, process, or transmit cardholder data or sensitive authentication data, as well as any connected system components included in or connected to that environment.

Best practices for securing the CDE according to PCI-DSS include:

1. Regular testing of systems and applications for vulnerabilities, which should be treated as a Business As Usual (BAU) task rather than just an annual compliance exercise

2. Implementation of comprehensive vulnerability scanning protocols to identify potential security weaknesses
3. Conducting periodic penetration testing to actively identify exploitable vulnerabilities
4. Developing and maintaining a robust incident response (IR) plan to effectively address security breaches
5. Establishing a solid security policy that outlines protection measures and response procedures
6. Treating customer data as if stored in a well-guarded vault, implementing the highest level of security protocols
7. Assuming worst-case scenarios when planning security measures
8. Continuous monitoring of systems for potential vulnerabilities or suspicious activities
9. Limiting the scope of the CDE by segmenting networks to isolate cardholder data
10. Applying the principle of least privilege for access to the CDE
11. Implementing strong encryption for data at rest and in transit
12. Maintaining detailed logs and audit trails for all CDE access and activities

Regular security assessments and continuous vigilance are essential to maintaining the security of the CDE and ensuring compliance with PCI-DSS requirements.

For more information: https://www.pcisecuritystandards.org/documents/PCI_DSS_v4-0.pdf

Q6: How frequently should a business submit its PCI-DSS compliance to an Acquirer?

A6: a) Monthly b) Quarterly c) Annually d) Every two years e) Only after a breach has occurred

The correct answer is c) Annually. According to the provided content, "The actual PCI-DSS compliance submission to an Acquirer is once a year." However, it's important to note that while formal submission occurs annually, security practices like vulnerability scanning and penetration testing should be conducted regularly throughout the year as part of Business As Usual (BAU) operations. PCI-DSS compliance is not just an annual event but requires ongoing security vigilance and maintenance.

For more information: https://www.pcisecuritystandards.org/documents/PCI_DSS_v4-0_ROC_Reporting_Template.pdf

Q7: True or False: If a merchant is found to be non-compliant with PCI-DSS after experiencing a data breach, they may be required to undergo a full on-site audit to regain processing capabilities.

A7: True. According to the provided content, if a merchant doesn't comply with the PCI-DSS agreement and is identified as non-compliant, they "may have to undergo a full PCI-DSS on-site audit to get back in the game." This means that to regain the ability to process payment card transactions after being restricted due to non-compliance, especially following a breach, a comprehensive on-site audit may be mandated. This audit would be more rigorous and intensive than the regular self-assessment questionnaires that many merchants use for annual compliance validation, and would likely involve qualified security assessors examining the merchant's systems, processes, and documentation in person.

For more information: https://www.pcisecuritystandards.org/assessors_and_solutions/qualified_security_assessors/

Q8: What should be included in an effective Incident Response (IR) plan for PCI-DSS compliance?

A8: An effective Incident Response (IR) plan for PCI-DSS compliance should include:

1. Clear definitions of what constitutes a security incident
2. Roles and responsibilities of team members during an incident
3. Communication protocols, including who to notify internally and externally
4. Detailed response procedures for different types of security incidents
5. Steps for containing and mitigating the impact of a breach
6. Procedures for preserving evidence for forensic analysis
7. Documentation requirements throughout the incident
8. Process for reporting breaches to relevant parties (including the 72-hour notification to ICO for personal data breaches)
9. Recovery and restoration procedures
10. Post-incident analysis and lessons learned process
11. Testing and exercise schedules for the IR plan
12. Contact information for all relevant stakeholders
13. Integration with the overall security policy
14. Procedures for updating the IR plan based on new threats or organizational changes
15. Compliance with regulatory requirements for breach notification

The IR plan should be regularly tested, updated, and accessible to all relevant personnel to ensure a quick and effective response to any security incidents, thereby minimizing potential damage and facilitating compliance with PCI-DSS requirements.

For more information: https://www.pcisecuritystandards.org/documents/incident-response-guide.pdf

Q9: What potential financial liability might a merchant face if they experience a cardholder data breach while non-compliant with PCI-DSS?

A9: a) Only the cost of notifying affected customers b) A fixed fine of $50,000 regardless of breach size c) Credit card replacement costs, forensic analysis costs, fraud liability, and potential fines d) No financial liability if the breach was due to sophisticated hackers e) Only the cost of implementing new security measures

The correct answer is c) Credit card replacement costs, forensic analysis costs, fraud liability, and potential fines. According to the provided content, if a merchant is found to be in breach of PCI-DSS requirements during a data security incident, they may face multiple financial consequences. Credit card brands can transfer the cost of credit card replacement to the merchant. Additionally, a mandatory forensic analysis may be required, which can be both time-consuming and expensive. The merchant could also be held liable for any fraudulent transactions resulting from the data leak. Beyond these direct costs, there may be fines from payment card brands and acquiring banks, costs associated with notifying customers and providing remediation services like credit monitoring, and potential revenue losses from reputational damage.

For more information: https://www.pcisecuritystandards.org/documents/PCI_DSS_V4-0_ROC_Template.xlsx

Q10: Describe the approach security professionals should take toward customer data protection according to the provided content.

A10: According to the provided content, security professionals should adopt a comprehensive and proactive approach to customer data protection:

1. View customer data as if stored in a "well-guarded vault" - implementing the highest level of security protocols and procedures to keep it secure from potential invaders.

2. Always assume the worst-case scenario when planning security measures, taking extra steps to ensure data safety rather than implementing only minimum requirements.

3. Treat vulnerability scanning and penetration testing as regular Business As Usual (BAU) tasks, not just annual compliance exercises.

4. Implement continuous monitoring systems to detect potential security issues before they lead to breaches.

5. Develop and maintain robust incident response plans and security policies to respond quickly and effectively to any security threats.

6. Recognize that compliance is not a one-time event but an ongoing process requiring regular testing, updating, and vigilance.

7. Understand that protecting customer data is not just about regulatory compliance but about safeguarding business reputation and customer trust.

8. Take personal responsibility for data security, viewing themselves as guardians of sensitive information.

This approach emphasizes proactive security, continuous improvement, and treating data protection as a core business function rather than merely a compliance requirement.

For more information: https://www.pcisecuritystandards.org/documents/best-practices-securing-ecommerce.pdf

Q11: Within what timeframe must a business report a breach of personal information to the Information Commissioners Office (ICO)?

A11: a) 24 hours b) 48 hours c) 72 hours d) 7 days e) 30 days

The correct answer is c) 72 hours. According to the provided content, "if you experience a breach of personal information, you have only 72 hours to report it to the Information Commissioners Office (ICO)." This 72-hour (3-day) window begins from when the organization becomes aware of the breach, not from when the breach actually occurred. This short timeframe emphasizes the need for organizations to have efficient breach detection systems and clear incident response procedures in place to ensure timely notification to authorities.

For more information: https://ico.org.uk/for-organisations/guide-to-data-protection/guide-to-the-general-data-protection-regulation-gdpr/personal-data-breaches/

Q12: True or False: Credit card brands can transfer the cost of credit card replacement to a merchant if they find the merchant is in breach of PCI-DSS requirements.

A12: True. According to the provided content, "credit card brands can transfer the cost of credit card replacement to you if they find that you're in breach." This means that if a merchant experiences a data breach while not being compliant with PCI-DSS requirements, the payment card brands (such as Visa, MasterCard, etc.) can hold the merchant financially responsible for the costs associated with replacing all affected payment cards. These costs can be substantial, especially in large-scale breaches affecting thousands or millions of cards, as they include the physical production of new cards, distribution costs, and administrative overhead. This potential financial liability is one of the significant incentives for merchants to maintain PCI-DSS compliance.

For more information: https://www.pcisecuritystandards.org/merchants/process/

Q13: What is meant by the statement that vulnerability scanning and penetration testing should be a "BAU task" for businesses seeking to maintain PCI-DSS compliance?

A13: The statement that vulnerability scanning and penetration testing should be a "BAU task" means these security practices should be treated as "Business As Usual" operations—regular, ongoing activities integrated into normal business processes, rather than special or exceptional events.

This implies:

1. Regular scheduling of vulnerability scans and penetration tests throughout the year, not just before annual compliance submissions
2. Integration of security testing into development cycles and system changes
3. Establishing consistent processes for reviewing and remediating identified vulnerabilities
4. Allocating dedicated resources and budget for ongoing security testing
5. Creating standardized procedures for conducting and documenting security tests
6. Training staff to incorporate security testing into their regular workflow
7. Developing metrics to track the effectiveness of security testing over time

The content emphasizes that while PCI-DSS compliance submission occurs annually, the security practices that ensure compliance should be performed continuously as part of regular business operations. This approach ensures more consistent security posture, faster identification and remediation of vulnerabilities, and better overall protection of cardholder data than treating security testing as merely an annual compliance exercise.

For more information: https://www.pcisecuritystandards.org/documents/PCI_DSS_v4-0.pdf

Q14: Which of the following is NOT mentioned as a potential consequence of non-compliance with PCI-DSS?

A14: a) Being banned from accepting credit card transactions b) Mandatory forensic analysis following a breach c) Criminal charges against the company's executives d) Financial penalties or fines e) Having to notify customers about security breaches

The correct answer is c) Criminal charges against the company's executives. While the provided content mentions various serious consequences of PCI-DSS non-compliance including financial penalties, being banned from accepting credit card transactions, mandatory forensic analysis, and customer notification requirements, it does not mention criminal charges against executives. PCI-DSS is described as a contractual obligation rather than a law, so non-compliance typically results in contractual and financial penalties rather than criminal charges. However, it's worth noting that in some jurisdictions, serious data breaches might trigger separate legal obligations under privacy laws that could potentially have criminal implications, but this is not directly tied to PCI-DSS non-compliance itself.

For more information: https://www.pcisecuritystandards.org/faq/

Q15: Discuss the relationship between regular security testing and PCI-DSS compliance, explaining why continuous monitoring is emphasized in the provided content.

A15: The relationship between regular security testing and PCI-DSS compliance is multi-faceted and critical to an effective security program:

Regular security testing serves as the foundation for maintaining PCI-DSS compliance beyond the annual formal submission. While compliance documentation is submitted once a year, the content emphasizes that security testing should be integrated into Business As Usual (BAU) operations. This continuous approach is essential because:

1. Threat landscapes evolve constantly - New vulnerabilities and attack vectors emerge regularly, making point-in-time annual assessments insufficient for adequate protection.

2. System changes create new risks - Every time an organization modifies its environment (new applications, updates, configurations), new vulnerabilities may be introduced that wouldn't be captured by annual testing alone.

3. Early detection minimizes damage - Continuous monitoring and regular testing can identify vulnerabilities before they're exploited, potentially preventing breaches entirely.

4. Compliance vs. Security - The content implicitly distinguishes between formal compliance (annual submission) and actual security posture (continuous monitoring), emphasizing that true security requires ongoing vigilance.

5. Breach prevention is more cost-effective - The significant consequences of breaches (fines, forensic costs, card replacement costs, liability for fraud) make preventative testing more economical than remediation after a breach.

6. Evidence of due diligence - Regular testing demonstrates commitment to security beyond minimum compliance requirements, which could mitigate penalties in case of an incident.

The content emphasizes continuous monitoring because it reflects a security-first rather than compliance-first mentality. It encourages organizations to view security as an ongoing process rather than a periodic event, which better aligns with how actual threats operate and provides more comprehensive protection for cardholder data.

For more information: https://www.pcisecuritystandards.org/documents/PCI_DSS_v4-0_Summary_of_Changes.pdf

Q16: True or False: PCI-DSS compliance requires only an annual submission to an Acquirer, with no other ongoing security obligations throughout the year.

A16: False. While the content does state that "The actual PCI-DSS compliance submission to an Acquirer is once a year," it explicitly emphasizes that this annual submission is not sufficient for maintaining security. The content specifically notes that vulnerability scanning and penetration testing "should be a BAU task for your business," meaning these security activities should be performed regularly throughout the year as part of Business As Usual operations. The content further states that "to keep your business secure and compliant with PCI-DSS, you must constantly monitor your systems for any possible vulnerabilities." This makes it clear that PCI-DSS compliance involves ongoing security obligations throughout the year, not just an annual submission. The annual submission represents formal documentation of compliance, but the actual security practices must be continuous to maintain true compliance and adequate protection of cardholder data.

For more information: https://www.pcisecuritystandards.org/documents/PCI_DSS_v4-0_Report_on_Compliance_Template.pdf

Q17: Which entities are involved in the contractual obligation known as PCI-DSS?

A17: a) Merchants, banks, and payment brands b) Merchants, customers, and government agencies c) Banks, payment brands, and security firms d) Merchants, software vendors, and payment gateways e) Government regulatory bodies and financial institutions

The correct answer is a) Merchants, banks, and payment brands. According to the provided content, "PCI-DSS is not a law but an agreement, a contractual obligation between merchants, banks, and the top six payment brands: Visa Inc, MasterCard, American Express, Discover Financial Services (DFS), JCB International and UnionPay." This establishes that PCI-DSS is fundamentally a contractual arrangement between these three types of entities within the payment card ecosystem, rather than a government regulation or law.

For more information: https://www.pcisecuritystandards.org/about_us/

Q18: What are the potential business impacts of being banned from accepting credit card transactions due to PCI-DSS non-compliance?

A18: Being banned from accepting credit card transactions due to PCI-DSS non-compliance can have several severe business impacts:

1. Lost Revenue: The most immediate impact is the inability to process credit card payments, which for many businesses represents a significant portion of their sales. In today's increasingly cashless economy, this can dramatically reduce transaction volume.

2. Reduced Customer Base: Customers who prefer or exclusively use credit cards will likely shop elsewhere, resulting in customer attrition and difficulty acquiring new customers.

3. Competitive Disadvantage: Competitors who maintain PCI compliance will have a significant advantage in capturing customers who prefer credit card payments.

4. Reputational Damage: News of a payment processing ban often becomes public, damaging the business's reputation for security and reliability.

5. Recovery Costs: As mentioned in the content, regaining the ability to process credit cards would require "a full PCI-DSS on-site audit," which is more rigorous, intrusive, and expensive than standard compliance assessments.

6. Operational Disruption: Businesses would need to quickly implement alternative payment methods and potentially retrain staff, update systems, and change business processes.

7. Cash Flow Issues: The transition period between losing credit card processing capabilities and establishing alternative payment methods can create significant cash flow problems.

8. Long-term Viability Concerns: For businesses heavily dependent on credit card transactions, such a ban could threaten their very existence, potentially leading to bankruptcy if alternative arrangements cannot be established quickly.

The content summarizes these impacts by stating that being banned from accepting credit card transactions "could lead to lost business and reduced revenue," highlighting the serious commercial consequences of non-compliance.

For more information: https://www.pcisecuritystandards.org/merchants/process/

Q19: Outline the key components of an effective security policy for maintaining PCI-DSS compliance, based on the information provided in the content.

A19: Based on the provided content, an effective security policy for maintaining PCI-DSS compliance should include the following key components:

1. Regular Testing Framework: Establish structured protocols for "regularly testing systems and applications for vulnerabilities" as a Business As Usual (BAU) task, not just an annual exercise.

2. Vulnerability Management Program: Implement "vulnerability scanning" as part of ongoing operations, with clear processes for identifying, classifying, and remediating vulnerabilities.

3. Penetration Testing Schedule: Define the scope, frequency, and methodology for penetration testing to "spot any potential security risks" before they can be exploited.

4. Continuous Monitoring System: Establish processes to "constantly monitor systems for any possible vulnerabilities," including automated tools and manual reviews.

5. Incident Response Plan: Develop a comprehensive plan that enables the organization to "quickly and effectively respond to any potential threats" when security incidents occur.

6. Data Protection Standards: Implement the "highest level of security protocols and procedures" for handling customer data, treating it as if it were "stored in a well-guarded vault."

7. Breach Notification Procedures: Establish clear protocols for meeting the 72-hour breach reporting requirement to the Information Commissioners Office (ICO).

8. Security Mindset Guidelines: Foster an organizational culture that "assumes the worst-case scenario" when designing

security controls.

9. Remediation Protocols: Define procedures for addressing identified vulnerabilities, including prioritization frameworks and verification processes.

10. Compliance Documentation Process: Establish procedures for the annual "PCI-DSS compliance submission to an Acquirer" while maintaining continuous compliance.

11. Security Awareness and Training: Ensure all staff understand their role in maintaining data security and compliance.

12. Third-Party Risk Management: Establish standards for ensuring vendors and partners maintain appropriate security controls.

An effective security policy should be comprehensive yet practical, clearly documenting these components while ensuring they're integrated into daily business operations rather than treated as isolated compliance activities.

For more information: https://www.pcisecuritystandards.org/documents/PCI_DSS_v4-0_Best_Practices.pdf

Q20: What is the recommended approach to viewing customer data according to the content?

A20: a) As publicly available information b) As data that requires minimal protection c) As if stored in a well-guarded vault d) As the responsibility of the payment processor only e) As primarily a marketing resource

The correct answer is c) As if stored in a well-guarded vault. According to the provided content, "As an expert in data security, it's your job to view customer data as if stored in a well-guarded vault - keeping it secure and safe from potential invaders." This metaphor emphasizes the high level of protection and security that should be applied to customer data. The content encourages security professionals to implement robust security measures akin to those used to protect valuable assets in a physical vault, highlighting the importance of treating customer data as a critical asset requiring comprehensive protection from unauthorized access.

For more information: https://www.pcisecuritystandards.org/documents/PCI_Data_Storage_Dos_and_Donts.pdf

Q21: True or False: If a merchant experiences a data breach while compliant with PCI-DSS, they cannot be held liable for fraudulent transactions resulting from the breach.

A21: False. The content does not specify that PCI-DSS compliance provides immunity from liability for fraudulent transactions. While the content states that "If a case is brought against you for leaking sensitive client data, you could be held liable for any fraudulent transactions resulting from the leak," it does not explicitly exclude compliant merchants from this liability. PCI-DSS compliance may help mitigate risks and potentially reduce certain penalties, but it does not automatically shield a company from all liability related to fraudulent transactions following a breach. The determining factor mentioned is the leaking of sensitive client data, not the compliance status. Additionally, liability may be governed by various laws, regulations, and contractual agreements beyond just PCI-DSS requirements. Compliance with PCI-DSS is best viewed as a risk reduction measure rather than a liability shield.

For more information: https://www.pcisecuritystandards.org/pci_security/standards_overview

Q22: How should security professionals approach the planning of security measures according to the provided content?

A22: According to the provided content, security professionals should approach the planning of security measures by "always assuming the worst-case scenario and taking extra steps to ensure the safety of customer data." This approach emphasizes:

1. Proactive Risk Assessment: Rather than planning for average or typical scenarios, security professionals should identify and prepare for the most severe potential threats and vulnerabilities.

2. Defense in Depth: The reference to "extra steps" suggests implementing multiple layers of security controls beyond minimum requirements, creating redundancy in protection mechanisms.

3. Prioritizing Customer Data Protection: The specific focus on "safety of customer data" establishes the protection of sensitive information as the primary objective of security planning.

4. Going Beyond Compliance: The language implies that meeting baseline compliance requirements is insufficient; security professionals should exceed these minimums when planning security measures.

5. Anticipatory Planning: By assuming worst-case scenarios, security professionals develop controls that address not just known threats but also potential future risks.

This conservative, protection-focused approach aligns with the content's overall emphasis on treating security as an ongoing, proactive responsibility rather than merely a compliance exercise. By planning for the worst possible outcomes, security professionals create more robust security architectures that are better equipped to handle a range of threats from minor to severe.

For more information: https://www.pcisecuritystandards.org/documents/prioritized-approach-for-pci-dss-v4-0.pdf

Q23: How frequently should vulnerability scanning be conducted for PCI-DSS compliance according to the content?

A23: a) Only once before the annual compliance submission b) Quarterly, as specified in the content c) Regularly as a Business As Usual (BAU) task d) Only after system changes or updates e) Only when required by an auditor

The correct answer is c) Regularly as a Business As Usual (BAU) task. The content states that vulnerability scanning "should be a BAU task for your business" and emphasizes that "to keep your business secure and compliant with PCI-DSS, you must constantly monitor your systems for any possible vulnerabilities." While the content doesn't specify an exact frequency (such as weekly or monthly), it clearly indicates that vulnerability scanning should be conducted regularly as part of normal business operations, not just as a one-time activity before compliance submission. The emphasis on "constantly" monitoring systems further reinforces that this should be an ongoing, regular activity integrated into routine security operations.

For more information: https://www.pcisecuritystandards.org/documents/ASV_Program_Guide_v3.1.pdf

Q24: Explain the relationship between PCI-DSS compliance and data breach response. How does the standard affect how organizations should prepare for and respond to security incidents?

A24: The relationship between PCI-DSS compliance and data breach response is multifaceted, with the standard significantly influencing how organizations should prepare for and respond to security incidents:

Preparation Requirements: PCI-DSS implicitly requires organizations to develop comprehensive incident response plans before breaches occur. The content states that organizations "should have a plan in place for responding to any security breaches" and specifically mentions "an incident response (IR) plan and a solid security policy" as essential tools. This proactive preparation is a key component of PCI-DSS compliance, not just a recommended practice.

Time-Sensitive Notification: The content emphasizes strict timelines for breach notification, noting that organizations have "only 72 hours to report it to the Information Commissioners Office (ICO)" when personal information is compromised. This requirement forces organizations to develop efficient detection, analysis, and notification processes as part of their compliance strategy.

Financial Implications: PCI-DSS compliance significantly affects the financial impact of breaches. The content notes that "credit card brands can transfer the cost of credit card replacement to you if they find that you're in breach," creating a direct financial incentive to maintain compliance and respond effectively to incidents. Additionally, non-compliant merchants may face greater liability "for any fraudulent transactions resulting from the leak."

Forensic Investigation Requirements: The standard creates specific post-breach obligations, with the content noting that "a mandatory forensic analysis may be required" following a breach, particularly for non-compliant organizations. This forensic analysis is described as "time-consuming and expensive," highlighting the importance of both preventing breaches and being prepared to respond appropriately.

Continuous Security Posture: PCI-DSS views breach response not as an isolated event but as part of a continuous security cycle. The content emphasizes that organizations must "constantly monitor systems" and include "vulnerability scanning and penetration testing" in their security plans. This ongoing vigilance helps organizations detect potential breaches earlier and respond more effectively.

Remediation Expectations: Following a breach, the content implies that organizations may need to "implement the highest level of security protocols and procedures" to regain trust and compliance status. This may include providing "services like credit monitoring" to affected customers and undergoing "a full PCI-DSS on-site audit to get back in the game" if processing privileges were suspended.

The standard essentially creates a framework where breach response is not merely reactive but integrated into an organization's overall security program. Organizations that align their incident response capabilities with PCI-DSS requirements will be better positioned to minimize damage, maintain compliance status, and protect both their customers and their reputation when security incidents occur.

For more information: https://www.pcisecuritystandards.org/documents/responding-to-a-breach.pdf

Q25: True or False: According to the content, vulnerability scanning and penetration testing serve the same purpose in a PCI-DSS compliance program.

A25: False. While the content mentions both vulnerability scanning and penetration testing as important security practices, it implicitly distinguishes between them by listing them separately: "you should include vulnerability scanning and penetration testing in your security plan." This indicates they are distinct activities serving different, though complementary, purposes in a PCI-DSS compliance program.

Vulnerability scanning typically involves automated tools that identify known vulnerabilities in systems and applications, providing a broad overview of potential security weaknesses. It's generally more frequent, less intrusive, and can be conducted as part of routine operations.

Penetration testing, on the other hand, involves more active and manual testing where security professionals attempt to exploit vulnerabilities to assess actual security risks. It's typically more thorough, targeted, and simulates real-world attack scenarios.

The content suggests both practices should be part of a comprehensive security approach rather than treating them as interchangeable activities. Together, they help organizations "spot any potential security risks and take action to protect systems and customers from any data breaches that might happen," but they accomplish this through different methodologies and with different scopes of analysis.

For more information: https://www.pcisecuritystandards.org/documents/penetration_testing_guidance_march_2015.pdf

14

Compliance Levels & Requirements - Question Set

Q1: What are the four merchant compliance levels in PCI-DSS, and what transaction volumes define each level?

A1: The PCI-DSS defines four merchant compliance levels based on annual transaction volume:

- Level 1: Merchants processing more than 6 million card transactions annually
- Level 2: Merchants processing between 1 million and 6 million card transactions annually
- Level 3: Merchants processing between 20,000 and 1 million card transactions annually
- Level 4: Merchants processing fewer than 20,000 card transactions annually

These levels help determine the appropriate compliance requirements and validation procedures for each merchant. Understanding these thresholds is crucial for PCIPs to properly categorize merchants and advise on applicable compliance obligations.

For more information: https://www.pcisecuritystandards.org/merchants/

Q2: True or False: Level 4 merchants do not need to conduct quarterly network scans because of their lower transaction volume.

A2: False. All merchant levels, including Level 4 merchants (those processing fewer than 20,000 card transactions annually), must conduct quarterly network scans using an Approved Scanning Vendor (ASV).

Despite having the lowest transaction volume, Level 4 merchants must still meet this requirement to identify security vulnerabilities across their systems, servers, and networks. The PCI DSS does not exempt any merchant level from this fundamental security practice, as even small merchants can be targets for data breaches.

For more information: https://www.pcisecuritystandards.org/documents/ASV_Program_Guide_v3.1.pdf

Q3: Which of the following is NOT required for Level 3 merchants under PCI DSS v4.01?

a) Annual Self-Assessment Questionnaire (SAQ) b) Quarterly network scans by an ASV c) On-site assessment by a QSA d) Annual penetration testing

A3: The correct answer is c) On-site assessment by a QSA.

Level 3 merchants (processing between 20,000 and 1 million transactions annually) are not required to undergo an on-site assessment by a Qualified Security Assessor (QSA). This requirement is specifically mandated only for Level 1 merchants.

Level 3 merchants must still complete:

- Annual Self-Assessment Questionnaire (SAQ)
- Annual Report on Compliance (RoC)
- Quarterly network scans by an Approved Scanning Vendor (ASV)
- Annual penetration testing
- Attestation of Compliance (AoC)

For more information: https://www.pcisecuritystandards.org/documents/PCI-DSS-v4-0.pdf

Q4: What document must be submitted by all merchant levels to confirm the business meets PCI DSS requirements?

A4: The Attestation of Compliance (AoC) must be submitted by all merchant levels to confirm the business meets PCI DSS requirements.

The AoC is a formal declaration document that attests to the merchant's PCI DSS compliance status. It serves as official documentation that the organization has successfully completed the appropriate assessment (whether via on-site assessment for Level 1 or self-assessment for Levels 2-4) and has met all applicable PCI DSS requirements. This document is typically submitted to acquiring banks or payment card brands as evidence of compliance.

For more information: https://www.pcisecuritystandards.org/documents/PCI-DSS-v4-0-AOC-Merchants.pdf

Q5: When determining a merchant's compliance level, what types of transactions should be included in the annual transaction count?

A5: When determining a merchant's compliance level, ALL types of payment card transactions across ALL payment channels must be included in the annual transaction count. This includes:

- Transactions processed over the counter via PIN Entry Devices (PED)
- Transactions through automated payment devices like self-service kiosks
- Transactions from photo booths

- Transactions from supermarket quick scan checkouts
- Online purchases (e-commerce)
- Mail order transactions
- Telephone order (MOTO) transactions

It's critical to obtain a complete picture of ALL card transactions from all channels to accurately determine the merchant's compliance level. The PCIP should consult with the Chief Financial Officer (CFO) or designated finance team member to ensure all transaction types are properly accounted for.

For more information: https://www.pcisecuritystandards.org/faq/articles/Frequently_Asked_Question/How-do-I-determine-my-merchant-level/

Q6: Which of the following professionals can complete the Report on Compliance (RoC) for Level 2 merchants?

a) Only a Qualified Security Assessor (QSA) b) Only an Internal Security Assessor (ISA) c) Either a QSA or an ISA d) None of the above; Level 2 merchants don't require a RoC

A6: The correct answer is c) Either a QSA or an ISA.

According to PCI DSS v4.01, Level 2 merchants (processing between 1 million and 6 million transactions annually) must complete an Annual Report on Compliance (RoC). This report can be completed with either a Qualified Security Assessor (QSA) or an Internal Security Assessor (ISA) to validate PCI DSS adherence.

While Level 2 merchants have the option to use an internal resource (ISA) rather than being required to use an external QSA like Level 1 merchants, they must still complete the RoC as part of their compliance validation.

For more information: https://www.pcisecuritystandards.org/documents/PCI_DSS_Prioritized_Approach_for_DSS_4_0.pdf

Q7: Explain the role of a Qualified Security Assessor (QSA) in PCI DSS compliance for Level 1 merchants.

A7: For Level 1 merchants (processing more than 6 million transactions annually), a Qualified Security Assessor (QSA) plays a critical role in compliance validation through an external audit. The QSA's responsibilities include:

1. Defining the scope of the assessment to determine which systems and processes are in scope for PCI DSS
2. Conducting an on-site assessment of the merchant's environment
3. Reviewing the organization's written records, policies, procedures, and documentation
4. Evaluating data storage practices and cardholder data flows
5. Verifying that technical and operational controls meet PCI DSS requirements

6. Assessing any compensating controls implemented in place of standard controls
7. Providing support and guidance during the compliance process
8. Determining whether the merchant has met all applicable PCI DSS requirements
9. Documenting findings in a detailed Report on Compliance (RoC)
10. Submitting the completed RoC to the merchant's acquiring bank

The QSA serves as an independent, qualified third party who validates compliance, ensuring the assessment is thorough and objective.

For more information: https://www.pcisecuritystandards.org/assessors_and_solutions/qualified_security_assessors/

Q8: What is the primary difference in assessment methodology between Level 1 merchants and Levels 2-4 merchants?

A8: The primary difference in assessment methodology between Level 1 merchants and Levels 2-4 merchants is the requirement for external validation:

- Level 1 merchants (processing more than 6 million transactions annually) must undergo an external on-site audit conducted by a Qualified Security Assessor (QSA). This is a mandatory third-party assessment where the QSA evaluates the merchant's environment in person.
- Levels 2-4 merchants can conduct a self-assessment using the appropriate Self-Assessment Questionnaire (SAQ). This allows these merchants to evaluate their own compliance without mandating an on-site visit from a QSA.

This distinction reflects the risk-based approach of PCI DSS, where entities processing larger volumes of transactions face more stringent external validation requirements due to their potentially higher risk profile. However, it's worth noting that Level 2 merchants, while able to self-assess, must still complete a Report on Compliance (RoC) with either a QSA or Internal Security Assessor (ISA).

For more information: https://www.pcisecuritystandards.org/documents/Understanding_SAQs_PCI_DSS_v4.pdf

Q9: Which of the following statements about PCI DSS compliance levels is correct?

a) Service providers have four compliance levels like merchants b) Compliance levels are determined by the merchant's annual revenue c) Levels 3 and 4 merchants are exempt from quarterly network scans d) Compliance levels are determined by the volume of annual card transactions

A9: The correct answer is d) Compliance levels are determined by the volume of annual card transactions.

PCI DSS compliance levels for merchants are categorized based on the number of card transactions processed annually, not by revenue. According to the provided material, there are four merchant levels and two service provider levels (not four service provider levels). All merchant levels, including Levels 3 and 4, must conduct quarterly network scans using an Approved Scanning Vendor (ASV).

The transaction volume thresholds that determine merchant levels are:

- Level 1: More than 6 million transactions annually
- Level 2: Between 1 million and 6 million transactions annually
- Level 3: Between 20,000 and 1 million transactions annually
- Level 4: Fewer than 20,000 transactions annually

For more information: https://www.pcisecuritystandards.org/documents/PCI_DSS_v4.0_SAQ_Instructions_and_Guidelines.pdf

Q10: What does the acronym "ASV" stand for in PCI DSS compliance, and what is its role?

A10: ASV stands for "Approved Scanning Vendor" in PCI DSS compliance.

An Approved Scanning Vendor is a company that has been qualified by the PCI Security Standards Council to conduct external vulnerability scanning services. The role of an ASV is to:

1. Perform quarterly network vulnerability scans for merchants across all compliance levels
2. Identify security vulnerabilities and weaknesses across systems, servers, and networks
3. Test internet-facing environments for potential entry points that could be exploited by attackers
4. Scan for missing patches, misconfigurations, and other common vulnerabilities
5. Provide detailed reports on identified vulnerabilities and recommendations for remediation
6. Help merchants validate compliance with the external scanning requirements of PCI DSS

These quarterly scans are mandatory for all merchant levels (1 through 4) and are a crucial component of maintaining PCI DSS compliance. The results from ASV scans help merchants identify and address potential security risks before they can be exploited.

For more information: https://www.pcisecuritystandards.org/assessors_and_solutions/approved_scanning_vendors/

Q11: As a PCIP, a merchant asks you which compliance level they fall under if they process 950,000 card transactions annually. What is your answer and why?

A11: Based on the annual transaction volume of 950,000 card transactions, this merchant falls under PCI DSS Compliance Level 3.

Level 3 applies to merchants processing between 20,000 and 1 million card transactions annually. Since 950,000 falls within this range, the merchant is classified as Level 3.

As a PCIP, I would explain that as a Level 3 merchant, they are required to:

- Complete an annual Self-Assessment Questionnaire (SAQ)

- Complete an annual Report on Compliance (RoC) with a QSA or ISA
- Conduct quarterly network scans using an Approved Scanning Vendor (ASV)
- Perform annual penetration testing
- Submit an Attestation of Compliance (AoC)

Unlike Level 1 merchants, they are not required to undergo an on-site assessment by a QSA, which gives them more flexibility in how they validate compliance.

For more information: https://www.pcisecuritystandards.org/documents/PCI_DSS_v4.0_ROC_Reporting_Template.pdf

Q12: True or False: An Internal Security Assessor (ISA) can conduct compliance assessments for Level 1 merchants in place of a Qualified Security Assessor (QSA).

A12: False. According to the provided material, Level 1 merchants (processing more than 6 million transactions annually) must undergo an external audit conducted by a Qualified Security Assessor (QSA).

While an Internal Security Assessor (ISA) can help prepare for the assessment and may assist with completing the Report on Compliance (RoC), the external audit requirement specifically mandates that a QSA conduct the assessment for Level 1 merchants. The material states: "Level 1 merchants must undergo an external audit by a QSA."

This requirement ensures that the highest-volume merchants receive independent, third-party validation of their compliance status due to the increased risk associated with processing large volumes of card transactions.

For more information: https://www.pcisecuritystandards.org/assessors_and_solutions/internal_security_assessors/

Q13: What is the purpose of the Attestation of Compliance (AoC) in PCI DSS compliance?

A13: The Attestation of Compliance (AoC) serves as an official declaration document that confirms a merchant meets the PCI DSS requirements. Its specific purposes include:

1. Formally documenting that an organization has successfully completed the appropriate PCI DSS assessment (whether via on-site assessment or self-assessment)
2. Serving as a summary document that confirms the merchant's compliance status
3. Providing a standardized format for merchants to attest to their compliance
4. Acting as evidence that can be submitted to acquiring banks, payment card brands, or business partners
5. Establishing accountability by requiring official sign-off on compliance status
6. Creating a record that can be referenced in case of disputes or compliance verification

All merchant levels (1-4) are required to submit an AoC as part of their compliance validation process. The AoC complements other documentation such as the Report on Compliance (RoC) or Self-Assessment Questionnaire (SAQ) by providing a concise attestation of the merchant's compliance status.

For more information: https://www.pcisecuritystandards.org/documents/PCI-DSS-v4-0-AOC-Merchants.pdf

Q14: Which of the following must a PCIP consider when determining a merchant's compliance level? (Select all that apply)

a) The merchant's annual revenue b) Transactions processed through PIN Entry Devices (PED) c) Online purchases d) Mail and telephone orders (MOTO) e) The merchant's geographic location

A14: The correct answers are b) Transactions processed through PIN Entry Devices (PED), c) Online purchases, and d) Mail and telephone orders (MOTO).

When determining a merchant's compliance level, a PCIP must consider ALL transaction types across ALL payment channels. According to the provided material, this specifically includes:

- Transactions processed over the counter via PIN Entry Devices (PED)
- Online purchases (e-commerce transactions)
- Mail and telephone orders (MOTO)
- Transactions through automated payment devices (self-service kiosks, photo booths, supermarket quick scan checkouts)

The merchant's annual revenue and geographic location are not relevant factors for determining PCI DSS compliance levels. The only determining factor is the total number of card transactions processed annually across all channels.

For more information: https://www.pcisecuritystandards.org/documents/PCI_DSS_v4_Quick_Reference_Guide.pdf

Q15: What is a Report on Compliance (RoC) and which merchant levels are required to complete one?

A15: A Report on Compliance (RoC) is a comprehensive document that details a merchant's compliance with PCI DSS requirements. It is the formal record of the assessment process, documenting the testing procedures performed, the results of those procedures, and the merchant's compliance status for each PCI DSS requirement.

According to the provided material, ALL merchant levels (1-4) are required to complete an annual Report on Compliance (RoC):

- Level 1 merchants (>6 million transactions annually): Must complete a RoC with a Qualified Security Assessor (QSA)
- Level 2 merchants (1-6 million transactions annually): Must complete a RoC with either a QSA or Internal Security Assessor (ISA)
- Level 3 merchants (20,000-1 million transactions annually): Must complete a RoC with either a QSA or ISA
- Level 4 merchants (<20,000 transactions annually): Must complete a RoC with either a QSA or ISA

The key difference is that Level 1 merchants must have their RoC completed as part of an external audit by a QSA, while merchants in Levels 2-4 have more flexibility in how their RoC is completed.

For more information: https://www.pcisecuritystandards.org/documents/PCI_DSS_v4.0_ROC_Reporting_Template.pdf

Q16: Which professional should a PCIP consult with to ascertain the annual transaction figures for a merchant?

a) Chief Information Officer (CIO) b) Chief Executive Officer (CEO) c) Chief Financial Officer (CFO) d) Chief Technology Officer (CTO)

A16: The correct answer is c) Chief Financial Officer (CFO).

According to the provided material, a PCIP should "ascertain the annual transaction figures for a merchant from the Chief Financial Officer (CFO) or a designated finance team member." The CFO or finance team is most likely to have accurate and comprehensive data on transaction volumes across all payment channels.

This ensures that the PCIP receives complete information about ALL transactions, including those processed through various channels such as PIN Entry Devices, online purchases, automated payment devices, and mail/telephone orders. Getting this information directly from the financial leadership helps ensure accuracy in determining the appropriate compliance level.

For more information: https://www.pcisecuritystandards.org/faq/articles/Frequently_Asked_Question/Who-should-I-contact-to-determine-my-merchant-level/

Q17: Describe the penetration testing requirements for PCI DSS compliance and explain which merchant levels must comply with these requirements.

A17: Penetration testing is a critical security assessment technique required by PCI DSS to identify and address vulnerabilities in a merchant's infrastructure. The requirements include:

1. Purpose: To detect and mitigate infrastructure vulnerabilities that could be exploited by attackers to gain unauthorized access to cardholder data
2. Frequency: Annual penetration testing is required
3. Scope: Testing should cover both internal and external networks, with a focus on systems within the cardholder data environment
4. Methodology: Tests should follow industry-accepted approaches (such as NIST SP 800-115) and include both network-layer and application-layer assessments
5. Results: Findings must be addressed through a formal remediation process

According to the provided material, ALL merchant levels (1-4) must perform annual penetration testing:

- Level 1 merchants (>6 million transactions annually)
- Level 2 merchants (1-6 million transactions annually)
- Level 3 merchants (20,000-1 million transactions annually)
- Level 4 merchants (<20,000 transactions annually)

There are no exemptions from this requirement based on merchant level. Even the smallest merchants (Level 4) must conduct penetration testing to identify and address security vulnerabilities that could lead to a data breach.

For more information: https://www.pcisecuritystandards.org/documents/Penetration-Testing-Guidance-v1_1.pdf

Q18: A merchant processes 6.2 million card transactions annually. Which compliance level do they fall under, and what are their primary assessment requirements?

A18: With 6.2 million card transactions annually, this merchant falls under PCI DSS Compliance Level 1.

Level 1 applies to merchants that process more than 6 million card transactions annually. Since 6.2 million exceeds the 6 million threshold, the merchant is classified as Level 1.

Primary assessment requirements for Level 1 merchants include:

1. External Audit: Must undergo an on-site assessment conducted by a Qualified Security Assessor (QSA)
2. Annual Self-Assessment Questionnaire (SAQ): Must complete the relevant SAQ
3. Annual Report on Compliance (RoC): Must be completed with a QSA
4. Quarterly Network Scans: Must run quarterly vulnerability scans using an Approved Scanning Vendor (ASV)
5. Annual Penetration Testing: Must perform annual testing to detect and mitigate vulnerabilities
6. Attestation of Compliance (AoC): Must submit this document to confirm compliance

The key distinguishing factor for Level 1 merchants is the mandatory external audit by a QSA, which involves an on-site assessment where the QSA defines the scope, reviews documentation, and determines compliance.

For more information: https://www.pcisecuritystandards.org/documents/PCI_DSS_v4.0_Summary_of_Changes.pdf

Q19: What metaphor does the provided material use to describe the importance of understanding compliance levels, and how does this metaphor relate to PCI DSS compliance?

A19: The provided material uses a "treasure map" metaphor to describe the importance of understanding compliance levels.

The material states: "Just like a treasure map, knowing the number of card transactions processed annually will lead you to the appropriate level of compliance and guide you toward the proper audit and self-assessment questionnaires."

This metaphor relates to PCI DSS compliance in several ways:

1. Direction and Guidance: Like a treasure map provides directions to find treasure, transaction volume guides merchants to their proper compliance level
2. Following a Path: The compliance journey requires following specific steps (like following a map)
3. Reaching a Destination: The "treasure" is achieving proper compliance status

4. Using Key Information: Transaction volume serves as the key piece of information (like coordinates on a map)

5. Avoiding Wrong Turns: Proper classification helps avoid taking inappropriate compliance approaches

The metaphor emphasizes that transaction volume is the critical factor that determines the merchant's compliance path, with each level having specific requirements and validation procedures that must be followed to achieve compliance.

For more information: https://www.pcisecuritystandards.org/documents/Prioritized-Approach-for-PCI-DSS-v4_0.pdf

Q20: True or False: For Level 2-4 merchants, the Self-Assessment Questionnaire (SAQ) replaces the need for a Report on Compliance (RoC).

A20: False. According to the provided material, all merchant levels, including Levels 2-4, must complete both an annual Self-Assessment Questionnaire (SAQ) AND an annual Report on Compliance (RoC).

The material explicitly states that for all merchant levels (1-4), the requirements include:

- "Annual Self-Assessment Questionnaire (SAQ): Merchants must complete a relevant SAQ to assess compliance."
- "Annual Report on Compliance (RoC): A RoC must be completed with a Qualified Security Assessor (QSA) or Internal Security Assessor (ISA) to validate PCI DSS adherence."

The key difference is that Level 1 merchants must have their RoC completed by a QSA as part of an external audit, while Levels 2-4 can have their RoC completed with either a QSA or ISA. The SAQ and RoC serve different purposes in the compliance validation process and are both required components for all merchant levels.

For more information: https://www.pcisecuritystandards.org/documents/PCI_DSS_v4.0_SAQ_Instructions_and_Guidelines.pdf

Q21: Which of the following scenarios would require a merchant to undergo an on-site assessment by a Qualified Security Assessor (QSA)?

a) A merchant processing 900,000 transactions annually b) A merchant processing 3 million transactions annually c) A merchant processing 7 million transactions annually d) A merchant processing 15,000 transactions annually

A21: The correct answer is c) A merchant processing 7 million transactions annually.

Only Level 1 merchants (those processing more than 6 million card transactions annually) are required to undergo an on-site assessment conducted by a Qualified Security Assessor (QSA). With 7 million transactions, this merchant exceeds the 6 million threshold and falls into Level 1.

The other options fall into different merchant levels:

- 900,000 transactions: Level 3 (between 20,000 and 1 million transactions)
- 3 million transactions: Level 2 (between 1 million and 6 million transactions)
- 15,000 transactions: Level 4 (fewer than 20,000 transactions)

Merchants in Levels 2-4 can complete a self-assessment rather than requiring an on-site assessment by a QSA.

For more information: https://www.pcisecuritystandards.org/faq/articles/Frequently_Asked_Question/What-are-the-PCI-DSS-compliance-validation-requirements-for-each-level/

Q22: How does a PCIP ensure they have accurate information about a merchant's transaction volume?

A22: A PCIP ensures they have accurate information about a merchant's transaction volume through the following steps:

1. Consulting the right people: The PCIP should obtain transaction figures from the Chief Financial Officer (CFO) or a designated finance team member, as they are most likely to have comprehensive financial data.
2. Ensuring comprehensive coverage: The PCIP must verify that the information presented covers ALL transaction types and ALL payment channels, including:
    - Transactions over the counter via PIN Entry Devices (PED)
    - Automated payment devices (self-service kiosks, photo booths, supermarket quick scan checkouts)
    - Online purchases (e-commerce)
    - Mail order and telephone order (MOTO) transactions
3. Active verification: The material advises "don't be afraid to ask" to ensure all transaction types are included. This suggests PCIPs should actively query and verify the data rather than passively accepting what's initially provided.
4. Explaining the importance: The PCIP should explain that accurate transaction figures are crucial for determining the correct compliance level, which affects the assessment approach and requirements.

The material emphasizes that "the complete picture will give you a much more accurate picture of the merchant's compliance status," highlighting the importance of gathering comprehensive transaction data.

For more information: https://www.pcisecuritystandards.org/documents/PCI_DSS_v4.0_Quick_Reference_Guide.pdf

Q23: Compare and contrast the compliance requirements for Level 1 and Level 4 merchants. What are the key similarities and differences?

A23: Comparison of PCI DSS compliance requirements for Level 1 and Level 4 merchants:

Similarities:

1. Both must complete an annual Self-Assessment Questionnaire (SAQ)
2. Both must complete an annual Report on Compliance (RoC)
3. Both must conduct quarterly network scans by an Approved Scanning Vendor (ASV)
4. Both must perform annual penetration testing

5. Both must submit an Attestation of Compliance (AoC)

Key Differences:

1. Assessment Method:
   - Level 1: Must undergo an external audit by a Qualified Security Assessor (QSA) with on-site assessment
   - Level 4: Can conduct self-assessment without mandatory external QSA audit
2. Transaction Volume:
   - Level 1: Processes more than 6 million transactions annually
   - Level 4: Processes fewer than 20,000 transactions annually
3. Risk Profile:
   - Level 1: Higher risk profile due to large transaction volume
   - Level 4: Lower risk profile due to smaller transaction volume
4. Scrutiny Level:
   - Level 1: Faces higher scrutiny with mandatory external validation
   - Level 4: Has more flexibility in how compliance is validated

Despite the significant difference in transaction volume (300+ times more transactions for Level 1), the core compliance requirements remain largely the same across both levels. The primary distinction is in the validation method, with Level 1 requiring independent external validation through a QSA, while Level 4 can self-validate with more flexibility.

For more information: https://www.pcisecuritystandards.org/documents/PCI-DSS_QRG-v4_0.pdf

Q24: What resource can PCIP candidates use during the Pearson VUE test environment to help remember PCI-DSS merchant levels?

a) A calculator b) A whiteboard c) A reference book d) Internet access

A24: The correct answer is b) A whiteboard.

According to the provided material: "Within the Pearson VUE test environment, you can access a Whiteboard. Here you can make quick notes to help jog your memory. You will have memorized the Merchant Levels, but jotting them down on the Whiteboard will help here."

The whiteboard is a digital tool provided within the Pearson VUE testing environment that allows candidates to make notes during the exam. For the PCIP exam specifically, the material suggests using this whiteboard to jot down merchant levels as a memory aid, even though candidates should have these levels memorized. This can be particularly helpful when answering questions about transaction volume thresholds and corresponding compliance requirements.

For more information: https://home.pearsonvue.com/Test-takers/Resources.aspx

Q25: What is the role of compensating controls in PCI DSS compliance, and who evaluates them during an assessment?

A25: Compensating controls in PCI DSS compliance are alternative security measures implemented when an organization cannot meet a specific PCI DSS requirement exactly as written, usually due to legitimate technical or documented business constraints. These controls provide alternative ways to mitigate the same risk that the original requirement was designed to address.

According to the provided material, compensating controls are evaluated by the Qualified Security Assessor (QSA) during an assessment. The material states that a QSA will "evaluate any compensating controls that your organization may have instead of those deemed applicable by the PCI-DSS."

The role of compensating controls includes:

1. Providing alternative security measures when standard controls cannot be implemented
2. Meeting the intent and rigor of the original PCI DSS requirement
3. Offering "at least an equivalent level of protection" as the original requirement
4. Being documented and justified based on risk analysis
5. Being reviewed and validated by the assessor (QSA)

During an assessment, the QSA will determine if the compensating controls sufficiently address the risk and can be accepted in lieu of the original requirement. This evaluation is particularly important for Level 1 merchants undergoing external audits, but compensating controls may be relevant for all merchant levels.

For more information: https://www.pcisecuritystandards.org/documents/Prioritized_Approach_for_PCI_DSS_v4_0.pdf

15

Service Provider Compliance Levels - Question Set

Q1: According to PCI-DSS, how are service providers categorized and what distinguishes the different levels?

A1: PCI-DSS categorizes service providers into two distinct levels based on transaction volume:

- Level One service providers process more than 300,000 transactions annually
- Level Two service providers process less than 300,000 transactions annually

This categorization determines the compliance validation requirements for each service provider. Level One providers face more rigorous assessment requirements, including a mandatory Report on Compliance (RoC), Attestation of Compliance (AOC), and ASV Scan. Level Two providers have less stringent requirements, typically only needing to complete a Self-Assessment Questionnaire (SAQ) and undergo an ASV Scan.

This distinction recognizes that providers handling larger transaction volumes present a proportionally greater risk to the payment ecosystem if compromised.

Additional resource: https://www.pcisecuritystandards.org/documents/PCI-DSS-v4-0.pdf

Q2: True or False: A Level One service provider processes fewer than 300,000 transactions annually.

A2: False.

According to PCI-DSS, a Level One service provider processes MORE than 300,000 transactions annually, not fewer. The standard specifically defines Level One service providers as those processing over 300,000 transactions per year, while Level Two service providers process less than 300,000 transactions annually. This transaction volume threshold is a critical distinction that determines the compliance validation requirements applicable to the service provider.

Additional resource: https://www.pcisecuritystandards.org/documents/PCI_DSS_v4-0_ROC_Reporting_Template.pdf

Q3: What is the PCI-DSS definition of a "service provider"?

A3: According to PCI-DSS, a "service provider" is defined as a business entity that is not a payment brand but is directly associated with the processing, storing, or transmitting of cardholder data on behalf of another organization.

In simpler terms, service providers are third-party entities that provide services which affect or may affect the security of cardholder data. These organizations support payment card processing operations without being payment brands themselves. Examples include companies offering managed firewalls, IDS/IPS systems, Web Gateway services, and hosting services such as Infrastructure as a Service (IaaS).

The distinction is important because service providers have specific compliance responsibilities under PCI-DSS that differ from merchants or payment brands.

Additional resource: https://www.pcisecuritystandards.org/documents/PCI_DSS_Glossary_v4-0.pdf

Q4: Which of the following would be classified as a Level Two service provider under PCI-DSS?

a) A company processing 350,000 transactions annually b) A company processing 290,000 transactions annually c) A company processing exactly 300,000 transactions annually d) A payment brand processing 200,000 transactions annually

A4: b) A company processing 290,000 transactions annually

According to PCI-DSS, Level Two service providers process less than 300,000 transactions annually. Therefore, a company processing 290,000 transactions would fall into this category.

Option a) is incorrect because 350,000 transactions exceeds the 300,000 threshold, making it a Level One service provider. Option c) is a tricky case, but since the definition specifies "less than" 300,000 for Level Two, exactly 300,000 would technically qualify as Level One. Option d) is incorrect because payment brands are explicitly excluded from the definition of service providers, which are defined as "business entities that are not payment brands."

Additional resource: https://www.pcisecuritystandards.org/documents/PCI_DSS_v4-0_SAQ_D_ServiceProvider.pdf

Q5: Multiple Choice: Which of the following services is NOT explicitly mentioned as a typical service offered by PCI-DSS service providers in the provided content?

a) Managed firewalls b) IDS/IPS c) Web Gateway services d) Point-of-Sale systems

A5: d) Point-of-Sale systems

The provided content explicitly mentions managed firewalls, IDS/IPS, Web Gateway services, and hosting services (such as Infrastructure as a Service) as examples of services typically provided by service providers under PCI-DSS. Point-of-Sale systems are not mentioned in the list of example services.

While service providers might potentially offer Point-of-Sale systems, this wasn't explicitly stated in the provided content, making it the correct answer for a service NOT mentioned.

Additional resource: https://www.pcisecuritystandards.org/documents/Third_Party_Security_Assurance_Info_Supp.pdf

Q6: What is the significance of distinguishing between Level One and Level Two service providers in PCI-DSS?

A6: The distinction between Level One and Level Two service providers is significant for several important reasons:

1. Risk-based approach: The classification acknowledges that providers handling larger transaction volumes (Level One) represent a greater potential risk to the payment ecosystem if compromised, justifying more rigorous security requirements.

2. Compliance validation differences: Level One service providers must undergo more comprehensive assessments, including a Report on Compliance (RoC) conducted by a Qualified Security Assessor (QSA), an Attestation of Compliance (AOC), and ASV scanning. Level Two providers have less stringent requirements, typically only needing a Self-Assessment Questionnaire (SAQ) and ASV scanning.

3. Resource allocation: The tiered approach allows smaller service providers (Level Two) to allocate security resources proportionately to their risk profile while ensuring larger providers face appropriate scrutiny.

4. Industry standardization: This classification creates a clear, consistent framework for organizations to understand their compliance obligations and for their clients to assess risk when selecting service providers.

5. Scalability: As service providers grow and process more transactions, the tiered system provides a clear pathway for when enhanced security measures become necessary.

This differentiation ultimately helps maintain the integrity of the payment card ecosystem while imposing requirements proportionate to risk.

Additional resource: https://www.pcisecuritystandards.org/documents/PCI_DSS_v4-0_Summary_of_Changes.pdf

Q7: True or False: Infrastructure as a Service (IaaS) is one type of service that can be offered by PCI-DSS service providers.

A7: True.

The provided content explicitly states that service providers deliver many services that include "hosting services such as Infrastructure as a Service (IaaS)." IaaS is specifically mentioned as one of the examples of services that service providers may offer.

IaaS providers deliver cloud-based infrastructure resources like virtual servers, storage, and networking components that organizations can use to build their cardholder data environments. When these IaaS environments store, process, or transmit cardholder data, the IaaS provider is considered a service provider under PCI-DSS and must comply with the applicable requirements.

It's important to note that in cloud service models, there is typically a shared responsibility model for PCI compliance, with certain requirements being the responsibility of the service provider and others being the responsibility of the customer.

Additional resource: https://www.pcisecuritystandards.org/documents/Cloud_Computing_Guidelines.pdf

Q8: What criteria is used to determine whether a service provider is classified as Level One or Level Two under PCI-DSS?

A8: The primary criterion used to determine whether a service provider is classified as Level One or Level Two under PCI-DSS is the annual transaction volume:

- Level One service providers process more than 300,000 transactions annually
- Level Two service providers process less than 300,000 transactions annually

This transaction volume refers to the number of payment card transactions that the service provider processes, stores, or transmits on behalf of its clients over a 12-month period. The threshold of 300,000 transactions serves as the clear dividing line between the two levels.

This volume-based classification is designed to ensure that service providers with higher transaction volumes, which present a potentially greater risk to the payment card ecosystem, are subject to more rigorous assessment requirements than those with lower volumes.

Additional resource: https://www.pcisecuritystandards.org/documents/PCI_DSS_for_Large_Organizations.pdf

Q9: Multiple Choice: What compliance documentation is required for a Level One service provider but not for a Level Two service provider?

a) ASV Scan b) Report on Compliance (RoC) c) Self-Assessment Questionnaire (SAQ) d) None of the above

A9: b) Report on Compliance (RoC)

Level One service providers (processing more than 300,000 transactions annually) are required to complete a Report on Compliance (RoC), which must be conducted by a Qualified Security Assessor (QSA). They must also submit an Attestation of Compliance (AOC) and undergo ASV scanning.

In contrast, Level Two service providers (processing less than 300,000 transactions annually) typically only need to complete a Self-Assessment Questionnaire (SAQ) and undergo ASV scanning. They are not required to have a formal RoC performed by a QSA.

Therefore, the RoC is the compliance documentation that is required for Level One service providers but not for Level Two service providers.

Additional resource: https://www.pcisecuritystandards.org/documents/PCI_DSS_v4-0_ROC_Reporting_Template.pdf

Q10: Why is service provider security especially important in the payment card industry?

A10: Service provider security is particularly important in the payment card industry for several critical reasons:

1. Extended security perimeter: Service providers become extensions of an organization's security boundary, potentially creating additional entry points for attackers if not properly secured.

2. Concentration of risk: Service providers often handle cardholder data for multiple clients, creating high-value targets for attackers. A single breach could compromise data from numerous organizations.

3. Shared responsibility: Organizations remain responsible for protecting cardholder data even when outsourcing to service providers, creating complex security dependencies.

4. Access to sensitive data: Service providers often process, store, or transmit cardholder data directly, placing them in a position to potentially compromise data confidentiality, integrity, or availability.

5. Trust relationship: Clients must trust that service providers maintain adequate security controls, often without direct visibility into their security operations.

6. Specialized services: Services like managed firewalls, IDS/IPS, and hosting directly impact the security posture of cardholder data environments.

As noted in the provided content: "A service provider is an organization that provides services that affect or may affect cardholder data security." This emphasizes that service providers' actions (or inactions) can directly impact the security of payment card data, making their security practices a critical component of the overall payment ecosystem's security.

Additional resource: https://www.pcisecuritystandards.org/documents/Third_Party_Security_Assurance_Info_Supp.pdf

Q11: True or False: A business that processes exactly 300,000 transactions annually would be classified as a Level Two service provider.

A11: False.

According to the information provided, Level Two service providers process less than 300,000 transactions annually, while Level One service providers process more than 300,000 transactions annually.

Since the definition for Level Two specifically states "less than 300,000," a business processing exactly 300,000 transactions would not fall into this category. The wording indicates that the threshold is strictly less than 300,000, not less than or equal to.

While the content doesn't explicitly state how to categorize a service provider processing exactly 300,000 transactions, the most reasonable interpretation based on the definitions provided is that they would be classified as a Level One service provider, as they are not processing less than 300,000 transactions.

Additional resource: https://www.pcisecuritystandards.org/documents/PCI_DSS_v4-0_Summary_of_Changes.pdf

Q12: What types of services do PCI-DSS service providers typically offer? Provide examples.

A12: PCI-DSS service providers typically offer a wide range of services that can affect cardholder data security. According to the provided content, these services include, but are not limited to:

1. Managed firewalls: Services that configure, monitor, and maintain firewall infrastructure to protect cardholder data environments.

2. Intrusion Detection Systems/Intrusion Prevention Systems (IDS/IPS): Services that monitor network and system activities for malicious activities or policy violations and take preventative actions when necessary.

3. Web Gateway services: Solutions that control and protect web traffic, often including URL filtering, malware scanning, and data loss prevention capabilities.

4. Hosting services: Including Infrastructure as a Service (IaaS), which provides virtualized computing resources over the internet, potentially hosting systems that store, process, or transmit cardholder data.

Other common services that service providers might offer (though not explicitly mentioned in the provided content) include:

- Payment processing services
- Tokenization and encryption services
- Virtual private networks (VPNs)
- Managed security services
- Cloud services (PaaS, SaaS)
- Data storage and backup solutions

The key characteristic of these services is that they "affect or may affect cardholder data security," making the service providers subject to PCI-DSS requirements when they process, store, or transmit cardholder data on behalf of another organization.

Additional resource: https://www.pcisecuritystandards.org/documents/Cloud_Computing_Guidelines.pdf

Q13: Multiple Choice: Which of the following best describes the relationship between payment brands and service providers according to PCI-DSS?

a) Payment brands are a subset of service providers b) Service providers are a subset of payment brands c) Payment brands and service providers are the same entity d) Service providers are business entities that are not payment brands

A13: d) Service providers are business entities that are not payment brands

According to the provided content, "the term 'service provider' refers to a business entity that is not a payment brand but is directly associated with the processing, storing, or transmitting of cardholder data on behalf of another organization."

This definition explicitly states that service providers are not payment brands, making option d) the correct answer. Payment brands (such as Visa, Mastercard, American Express, Discover, and JCB) establish the PCI-DSS requirements, while service providers are third parties that handle cardholder data while providing services to merchants or other organizations.

The distinction is important because payment brands and service providers have different roles and responsibilities within the payment card ecosystem and are subject to different requirements under PCI-DSS.

Additional resource: https://www.pcisecuritystandards.org/documents/PCI_DSS_Glossary_v4-0.pdf

Q14: What is an ASV Scan, and which levels of service providers require it according to PCI-DSS?

A14: An ASV Scan refers to a vulnerability scan performed by an Approved Scanning Vendor (ASV). These are external vulnerability scans that probe internet-facing environments to identify potential vulnerabilities that could be exploited by attackers to gain unauthorized access to cardholder data.

According to the summary in the provided content, both Level One and Level Two service providers require ASV Scans as part of their compliance validation:

- Level One service providers (processing more than 300,000 transactions annually) require a Report on Compliance (RoC), Attestation of Compliance (AOC), and ASV Scan.
- Level Two service providers (processing less than 300,000 transactions annually) require a Self-Assessment Questionnaire (SAQ) and ASV Scan.

ASV Scans must be performed quarterly by a PCI SSC Approved Scanning Vendor. These scans help identify common vulnerabilities in publicly accessible systems, such as missing security patches, insecure configurations, and other security issues that could compromise cardholder data.

The fact that ASV Scans are required for both levels of service providers underscores their importance in maintaining the security of cardholder data environments, regardless of transaction volume.

Additional resource: https://www.pcisecuritystandards.org/documents/ASV_Program_Guide_v3.1.pdf

Q15: True or False: A managed firewall service is outside the scope of services typically provided by PCI-DSS service providers.

A15: False.

According to the provided content, managed firewalls are specifically mentioned as one of the services that service providers deliver. The text states: "Service providers deliver many services that include but are not limited to managed firewalls, IDS/IPS, Web Gateway services, and hosting services such as Infrastructure as a Service (IaaS)."

Managed firewall services are very much within the scope of services typically provided by PCI-DSS service providers. In fact, they are one of the most common security services offered, as firewalls are a fundamental security control required by PCI-DSS (specifically mentioned in Requirement 1).

Service providers offering managed firewall services would be directly affecting cardholder data security, as firewalls control the flow of traffic to and from cardholder data environments, making these providers subject to PCI-DSS requirements.

Additional resource: https://www.pcisecuritystandards.org/documents/Prioritized_Approach_for_PCI_DSS_v4_0.pdf

Q16: What are the compliance validation requirements for Level One service providers compared to Level Two service providers?

A16: The compliance validation requirements differ significantly between Level One and Level Two service providers:

Level One Service Providers (processing more than 300,000 transactions annually):

1. Report on Compliance (RoC) - A comprehensive assessment conducted by a Qualified Security Assessor (QSA)
2. Attestation of Compliance (AOC) - A formal declaration of compliance status
3. ASV Scan - Quarterly vulnerability scans performed by an Approved Scanning Vendor

Level Two Service Providers (processing less than 300,000 transactions annually):

1. Self-Assessment Questionnaire (SAQ) - A self-validation tool completed by the organization itself
2. ASV Scan - Quarterly vulnerability scans performed by an Approved Scanning Vendor

The key difference is that Level One providers must undergo a more rigorous assessment process conducted by an independent, qualified third party (QSA), resulting in a formal RoC. Level Two providers can self-assess using the appropriate SAQ. This tiered approach balances security requirements with the relative risk posed by service providers of different sizes, applying more stringent validation requirements to those handling larger volumes of transactions.

Both levels still require the ASV scans, highlighting the importance of regular vulnerability assessment regardless of organization size.

Additional resource: https://www.pcisecuritystandards.org/documents/PCI_DSS_v4-0_ROC_Reporting_Template.pdf

Q17: Describe how service providers can impact the security of cardholder data and why PCI-DSS includes specific requirements for them.

A17: Service providers can significantly impact cardholder data security in multiple ways, which is why PCI-DSS includes specific requirements for them:

1. Direct access to sensitive data: Service providers often process, store, or transmit cardholder data on behalf of their clients, giving them direct access to sensitive information that must be protected.
2. Shared infrastructure: Many service providers use shared infrastructure to serve multiple clients, creating potential cross-contamination risks if security controls aren't properly implemented.
3. Extended attack surface: Service providers become an extension of their clients' security perimeters, potentially introducing new vulnerabilities if not properly secured.
4. Concentration of risk: A single service provider may handle cardholder data for dozens or hundreds of clients, creating an attractive target for attackers (high-value target).
5. Varied security capabilities: Service providers have varying levels of security expertise and capabilities, which can directly impact how well cardholder data is protected.

PCI-DSS includes specific requirements for service providers because:

1. Responsibility transfer: While organizations can outsource services, they cannot outsource responsibility for protecting cardholder data.

2. Tiered approach: The two-level classification system ensures proportionate security requirements based on transaction volume and risk.
3. Clear accountability: Service provider requirements clarify who is responsible for which security controls in outsourced relationships.
4. Security consistency: Specific requirements help maintain consistent security practices across the payment ecosystem.
5. Transparency: Requirements promote visibility into service provider security practices for their clients.

The tip in the provided content—"A service provider is an organization that provides services that affect or may affect cardholder data security"—highlights this critical relationship between service providers and the security of cardholder data.

Additional resource: https://www.pcisecuritystandards.org/documents/Third_Party_Security_Assurance_Info_Supp.pdf

Q18: What does IDS/IPS stand for in the context of services offered by PCI-DSS service providers?

A18: In the context of services offered by PCI-DSS service providers, IDS/IPS stands for:

IDS = Intrusion Detection System IPS = Intrusion Prevention System

These are security technologies that monitor network and/or system activities for malicious or unwanted behavior:

- Intrusion Detection Systems (IDS) are designed to detect potential security breaches, violations, or threats. They monitor network traffic and system activities, comparing them against known attack signatures or identifying anomalous behavior, and alert security personnel when suspicious activities are detected.
- Intrusion Prevention Systems (IPS) go a step further by not only detecting potential security threats but also taking automated actions to prevent or block detected threats in real-time.

As mentioned in the provided content, IDS/IPS services are among the common services that PCI-DSS service providers deliver to their clients. These technologies play a crucial role in satisfying several PCI-DSS requirements, particularly those related to network security, monitoring, and threat detection (Requirements 5 and 11 in PCI-DSS v4.0).

Service providers offering managed IDS/IPS services help organizations detect and respond to security incidents that could potentially compromise cardholder data.

Additional resource: https://www.pcisecuritystandards.org/documents/Prioritized_Approach_for_PCI_DSS_v4_0.pdf

Q19: Multiple Choice: A company processes 250,000 transactions annually. According to PCI-DSS, how would this organization be classified if it is a service provider?

a) Level One service provider b) Level Two service provider c) Level Three service provider d) Exempt from service provider requirements

A19: b) Level Two service provider

According to the provided content, PCI-DSS categorizes service providers into two levels based on transaction volume:

- Level One service providers process more than 300,000 transactions annually
- Level Two service providers process less than 300,000 transactions annually

Since the company in question processes 250,000 transactions annually, which is less than the 300,000 threshold, it would be classified as a Level Two service provider.

This classification is important because it determines the compliance validation requirements the organization must meet. As a Level Two service provider, the company would typically need to complete a Self-Assessment Questionnaire (SAQ) and undergo ASV scanning, rather than the more rigorous Report on Compliance (RoC) required for Level One providers.

Additional resource: https://www.pcisecuritystandards.org/documents/PCI_DSS_v4-0_SAQ_D_ServiceProvider.pdf

Q20: True or False: The PCI-DSS defines a service provider as any business entity that is directly involved with cardholder data.

A20: False.

The PCI-DSS definition of a service provider is more specific than just being involved with cardholder data. According to the provided content, "the term 'service provider' refers to a business entity that is not a payment brand but is directly associated with the processing, storing, or transmitting of cardholder data on behalf of another organization."

This definition has two key components:

1. The entity is not a payment brand
2. The entity processes, stores, or transmits cardholder data on behalf of another organization

The definition excludes payment brands (like Visa, Mastercard, etc.) even if they are directly involved with cardholder data. It also specifies that the service provider must be handling the data on behalf of another organization, not just for itself.

Additionally, the supplementary tip clarifies that "a service provider is an organization that provides services that affect or may affect cardholder data security," emphasizing the impact on security rather than just involvement with the data.

Additional resource: https://www.pcisecuritystandards.org/documents/PCI_DSS_Glossary_v4-0.pdf

Q21: What compliance document replaces the Report on Compliance (RoC) for Level Two service providers?

A21: For Level Two service providers, the Self-Assessment Questionnaire (SAQ) replaces the Report on Compliance (RoC) that is required for Level One service providers.

According to the summary in the provided content, Level One service providers (processing more than 300,000 transactions annually) require a Report on Compliance (RoC), Attestation of Compliance (AOC), and ASV Scan. In contrast, Level Two service providers (processing less than 300,000 transactions annually) only require a Self-Assessment Questionnaire (SAQ) and ASV Scan.

The SAQ is a validation tool that enables organizations to self-evaluate their compliance with PCI-DSS requirements. It is less rigorous than a RoC, which must be conducted by a Qualified Security Assessor (QSA). This difference reflects the risk-based approach of PCI-DSS, where organizations handling lower volumes of transactions face less stringent assessment requirements.

For service providers specifically, the appropriate questionnaire is typically SAQ D for Service Providers, which includes all applicable PCI-DSS requirements.

Additional resource: https://www.pcisecuritystandards.org/documents/PCI_DSS_v4-0_SAQ_D_ServiceProvider.pdf

Q22: Multiple Choice: Which of the following would NOT be considered a service provider under PCI-DSS?

a) A company that provides managed firewall services b) A payment brand like Visa or Mastercard c) A company that offers Infrastructure as a Service (IaaS) hosting d) A company that provides Web Gateway services

A22: b) A payment brand like Visa or Mastercard

According to the provided content, "the term 'service provider' refers to a business entity that is not a payment brand but is directly associated with the processing, storing, or transmitting of cardholder data on behalf of another organization."

This definition explicitly excludes payment brands like Visa or Mastercard from being classified as service providers under PCI-DSS. Payment brands establish and enforce the PCI-DSS requirements rather than being subject to them as service providers.

The other options—companies providing managed firewall services, Infrastructure as a Service hosting, and Web Gateway services—are all explicitly mentioned in the content as examples of services that service providers deliver, making them valid examples of service providers under PCI-DSS.

Additional resource: https://www.pcisecuritystandards.org/documents/PCI_DSS_Glossary_v4-0.pdf

Q23: How might an organization determine if it qualifies as a service provider under PCI-DSS, and what are the implications of this classification?

A23: Determining if an organization qualifies as a service provider under PCI-DSS involves examining several key factors:

Assessment Criteria:

1. Is the organization NOT a payment brand? (Must be true)
2. Does the organization process, store, or transmit cardholder data on behalf of another entity? (Must be true)
3. Does the organization provide services that affect or may affect cardholder data security? (Must be true)
4. Do these services include things like managed firewalls, IDS/IPS, Web Gateway services, or hosting services? (Common examples but not exhaustive)

Implications of Service Provider Classification:

1. Compliance Requirements:

- Must determine level (One or Two) based on annual transaction volume (300,000 threshold)
- Level One: Requires RoC, AOC, and ASV Scan
- Level Two: Requires SAQ and ASV Scan

2. Additional Responsibilities:
   - Must comply with service provider-specific requirements in PCI-DSS
   - Must clearly define security responsibilities between the provider and clients
   - May need to provide evidence of compliance to clients
3. Business Impact:
   - Competitive advantage when marketing to PCI-conscious clients
   - Potential contractual obligations to maintain compliance
   - Need for dedicated compliance resources and regular assessments
   - Risk management considerations for handling multiple clients' data
4. Legal and Contractual Considerations:
   - Must establish written agreements with clients defining security responsibilities
   - May face liability if security failures affect client compliance
   - May need to support clients during their own compliance assessments

Understanding this classification is crucial because it determines the specific compliance path an organization must follow and the expectations their clients will have regarding the protection of cardholder data.

Additional resource: https://www.pcisecuritystandards.org/documents/Third_Party_Security_Assurance_Info_Supp.pdf

Q24: True or False: Web Gateway services are among the services typically provided by PCI-DSS service providers.

A24: True.

According to the provided content, "Service providers deliver many services that include but are not limited to managed firewalls, IDS/IPS, Web Gateway services, and hosting services such as Infrastructure as a Service (IaaS)."

Web Gateway services are explicitly mentioned as one of the typical services that PCI-DSS service providers offer. Web Gateways provide security controls for web traffic, often including URL filtering, malware scanning, and data loss prevention capabilities that help protect cardholder data environments from web-based threats.

These services directly affect cardholder data security by controlling and monitoring web traffic that might carry threats or potentially expose sensitive cardholder data, making them a relevant service in the context of PCI-DSS compliance.

Additional resource: https://www.pcisecuritystandards.org/documents/Prioritized_Approach_for_PCI_DSS_v4_0.pdf

Q25: What practical tip is given regarding the use of the Whiteboard during exam preparation for the PCIP v4.0 certification?

A25: The practical tip given in the content regarding the use of the Whiteboard during exam preparation is: "My advice is to make good use of the Whiteboard. It will free your brain up to focus on the questions! However, if you have memorized well and have a clear picture, then great!"

This tip suggests that exam candidates should utilize the whiteboard provided during the exam to:

1. Offload information from working memory, reducing cognitive load
2. Sketch out complex concepts or relationships between PCI-DSS elements
3. Keep track of key points while working through multi-part questions
4. Create a temporary reference for important definitions or thresholds (like the 300,000 transaction threshold for service provider levels)

The tip acknowledges that while using the whiteboard is helpful for most candidates, those who have thoroughly memorized the material may not need this aid. This advice is specifically tailored to the PCIP exam environment, where candidates typically have access to a physical or digital whiteboard during the test.

Using the whiteboard effectively can be particularly helpful for questions about service provider classifications, compliance requirements, and other technical details that might be challenging to keep in working memory while solving complex problems.

Additional resource: https://www.pcisecuritystandards.org/programs/pcip/

16

Card Brand Service Provider Levels - Question Set

Q1: What is the primary reason for a PCIP to understand different service levels expected from service providers by card brands?

A1: Understanding the different service levels expected from service providers by card brands is essential for a PCIP (Payment Card Industry Professional) because it provides critical context for compliance requirements across the payment ecosystem. As a PCIP, you need this knowledge to properly advise organizations on their compliance obligations based on their relationships with various card brands. Different service providers may be subject to different validation requirements depending on their classification level with each card brand, which directly impacts the scope and nature of their PCI DSS implementation. This understanding allows PCIPs to guide service providers in meeting the specific requirements relevant to their business relationships and transaction volumes with each card brand, ensuring appropriate security controls are in place.

Additional resources: https://www.pcisecuritystandards.org/

Q2: Which card brands are mentioned in the content as providing in-depth details about service provider levels on their websites?

A2: The card brands mentioned in the content as providing in-depth details about service provider levels on their websites are Mastercard, Visa, Discover, JCB, UnionPay, and American Express (AMEX). The content specifically states that all these card brands provide detailed information about their service levels on their respective websites. Links are explicitly provided for Mastercard, Visa, Discover, and American Express. This information is valuable for both PCIPs and service providers to understand the specific compliance requirements and expectations set by each card brand, as requirements may vary between brands despite all being based on the PCI DSS framework.

Additional resources: https://www.mastercard.us/en-us/business/overview/safety-and-security/security-recommendations/site-data-protection-PCI/service-providers-need-to-know.html

Q3: True or False: PCIPs need an advanced, detailed understanding of all service provider levels for each card brand.

A3: False. According to the content provided, PCIPs only need "a very basic understanding of the information on these websites." The tip explicitly states not to feel overwhelmed by the amount of content on the card brand websites, indicating that an in-depth, advanced understanding is not required. PCIPs should be familiar with the general concept of service provider levels and know where to find specific information when needed, but don't need to memorize all the detailed requirements for each level across all card brands.

Additional resources: https://www.pcisecuritystandards.org/programs/pcip/

Q4: What types of websites are recommended as resources for understanding card brand service provider levels?

A4: The content recommends visiting the official websites of the major card brands as resources for understanding service provider levels. Specifically, it mentions and provides links to:

1. Mastercard's website for PCI-DSS Service Provider Levels
2. Visa's website for Validation of Compliance
3. Discover's website for Service Provider Compliance
4. American Express's website for Data Security Requirements

These official card brand websites are recommended because they contain authoritative information directly from the source about the different service levels expected from service providers and the specific PCI compliance requirements established by each card brand.

Additional resources: https://www.discoverglobalnetwork.com/solutions/pci-compliance/service-provider-compliance/

Q5: Multiple Choice: Which of the following is NOT listed as a card brand in the content?

a) Mastercard b) PayPal c) UnionPay d) JCB

A5: The correct answer is b) PayPal. The content specifically mentions Mastercard, Visa, Discover, JCB, UnionPay, and AMEX (American Express) as card brands that provide information about service provider levels on their websites. PayPal is not mentioned in the content as a card brand. While PayPal is a significant payment service provider, it is not one of the traditional card brands discussed in the context of setting service provider levels for PCI compliance purposes.

Additional resources: https://www.pcisecuritystandards.org/about_us/members/

Q6: What type of information can service providers expect to find on card brand websites regarding PCI compliance?

A6: Service providers can expect to find information about what they "need to know about PCI Compliance" on card brand websites. Specifically, this includes:

1. Service provider level definitions - how service providers are categorized based on transaction volume or other criteria
2. Compliance validation requirements for each service provider level
3. Reporting requirements specific to each card brand
4. Registration processes for service providers
5. Compliance timelines and deadlines
6. Consequences of non-compliance
7. Resources and tools to assist with compliance
8. Contact information for compliance-related inquiries

This information helps service providers understand their obligations based on their classification level with each card brand and how to properly demonstrate their compliance with PCI DSS requirements.

Additional resources: https://www.visa.com/splisting/searchGrsp.do

Q7: Why might different card brands have different service level classifications for service providers?

A7: Different card brands might have different service level classifications for service providers for several reasons:

1. Risk management strategies: Each card brand has its own approach to managing risk in the payment ecosystem based on their business model and risk tolerance.
2. Market positioning: Card brands may adjust requirements based on their competitive positioning and business relationships with different types of service providers.
3. Transaction volume thresholds: Brands might set different transaction volume thresholds that determine service provider levels based on their own data analysis.
4. Regional considerations: Some card brands have stronger presence in certain regions and may adjust their requirements accordingly.
5. Historical evolution: Requirements have evolved over time as each brand responded to security incidents and developed their compliance programs independently.
6. Business priorities: Each brand may emphasize different aspects of security based on their own business priorities and experiences.

These differences highlight why PCIPs need to be familiar with the various card brand requirements to properly advise service providers on compliance obligations.

Additional resources: https://www.pcisecuritystandards.org/pci_security/maintaining_payment_security

Q8: Multiple Choice: According to the content, how should PCIPs approach the amount of information available on card brand websites?

a) They should memorize all details for the PCIP exam b) They should feel overwhelmed by the comprehensive requirements c) They need only a basic understanding and shouldn't feel overwhelmed d) They should focus exclusively on one card brand's requirements

A8: The correct answer is c) They need only a basic understanding and shouldn't feel overwhelmed. The content explicitly states: "Tip: You only need a very basic understanding of the information on these websites, so don't feel overwhelmed by the amount of content." This guidance indicates that while PCIPs should be familiar with the concept of service provider levels and know where to find the information, they don't need to memorize all the specific details for each card brand. The emphasis is on knowing that these resources exist and having a general understanding of their purpose rather than detailed memorization.

Additional resources: https://www.pcisecuritystandards.org/document_library/

Q9: What is the relationship between card brand service provider levels and PCI DSS compliance?

A9: The relationship between card brand service provider levels and PCI DSS compliance is multi-faceted:

1. Framework vs. Implementation: PCI DSS provides the security framework and standards, while card brands establish service provider levels that determine how compliance with those standards must be validated.

2. Validation Requirements: Different service provider levels have different validation requirements (e.g., self-assessment questionnaires vs. on-site assessments) based on criteria established by each card brand.

3. Enforcement Mechanism: Card brands use service provider levels as an enforcement mechanism for PCI DSS compliance, with specific requirements for each level.

4. Risk-Based Approach: Service provider levels typically reflect a risk-based approach, with more stringent requirements for providers that process higher transaction volumes or provide more critical services.

5. Compliance Programs: Each card brand maintains its own compliance program based on PCI DSS but may add brand-specific requirements or focus areas.

Understanding this relationship is crucial for PCIPs to correctly advise organizations on their compliance obligations and validation procedures.

Additional resources: https://www.pcisecuritystandards.org/pci_security/

Q10: Essay: Explain the importance of card brand websites as resources for PCIPs and service providers.

A10: Card brand websites serve as critical resources for both PCIPs and service providers in the payment card industry ecosystem for several important reasons:

For PCIPs: Card brand websites provide authoritative information directly from the source about service provider levels and compliance requirements. This enables PCIPs to stay current with each brand's specific implementation of PCI DSS requirements, which is essential for providing accurate guidance to clients. These websites help PCIPs understand the nuances between different card brands' approaches to compliance, allowing them to advise organizations on how to efficiently meet all applicable requirements without unnecessary duplication of effort. Additionally, they serve as reference points for verification when questions arise about specific compliance obligations.

For Service Providers: Service providers rely on these websites to understand their specific compliance obligations based on their transaction volumes and services offered. The websites provide clarity on how service providers are categorized (their "level") by each card brand, which directly determines what validation requirements apply to them. They outline reporting requirements, deadlines, and submission processes that service providers must follow to maintain compliance with each card brand. Many also offer tools, resources, and guidance to help service providers implement appropriate security controls.

The centrality of these websites in the compliance ecosystem cannot be overstated. They serve as the definitive source of information regarding each card brand's expectations, helping to reduce ambiguity in compliance requirements. By directing both PCIPs and service providers to these resources, the payment card industry creates a more transparent compliance environment where expectations are clearly communicated. This transparency benefits the entire ecosystem by promoting more consistent security practices and more effective compliance efforts.

Rather than attempting to create a universal standard implementation across all card brands, the industry allows each brand to maintain its own compliance program while adhering to the core PCI DSS framework. This approach recognizes the unique business models and risk profiles of each card brand while still ensuring a baseline level of security across the payment ecosystem.

Additional resources: https://www.pcisecuritystandards.org/pci-perspectives/

Q11: True or False: The content suggests that service providers need to comply with different requirements depending on the card brand.

A11: True. The content strongly implies that service providers need to comply with different requirements depending on the card brand. This is evident from the statement that "it is important to understand the different service levels expected from service providers by the card brands" and the recommendation to visit individual card brand websites to understand "the levels and requirements expected from each card brand." The fact that each card brand maintains its own website with specific information about service provider levels indicates that there are differences in how each brand categorizes service providers and what they require for compliance validation. While all card brands base their requirements on the PCI DSS framework, the implementation details, service provider level thresholds, validation requirements, and reporting processes may vary across Mastercard, Visa, Discover, JCB, UnionPay, and American Express.

Additional resources: https://www.pcisecuritystandards.org/programs/

Q12: Which of the following card brand websites is NOT specifically linked in the provided content?

a) Mastercard b) Visa c) JCB d) Discover

A12: The correct answer is c) JCB. While JCB is mentioned in the content as one of the card brands that provides in-depth details on their websites about service provider levels, a specific link to the JCB website is not provided in the content. The content explicitly provides links for Mastercard, Visa, Discover, and American Express (with a search instruction rather than a direct link for American Express). UnionPay is also mentioned but without a link, similar to JCB.

Additional resources: https://www.global.jcb/en/

Q13: What is the main purpose of understanding card brand service provider levels for a PCIP?

A13: The main purpose of understanding card brand service provider levels for a PCIP (Payment Card Industry Professional) is to effectively advise organizations on their specific compliance obligations and validation requirements. By understanding these levels, a PCIP can:

1. Accurately determine which validation requirements apply to different service providers based on their relationship with each card brand
2. Guide organizations in properly classifying themselves within each card brand's service provider framework
3. Help service providers efficiently meet all applicable requirements without unnecessary compliance efforts
4. Advise on the appropriate documentation and evidence needed for compliance validation based on service provider level
5. Assist in preparing for assessments or completing self-assessment questionnaires that align with the service provider's level
6. Provide strategic guidance on compliance roadmaps that account for differences across card brands
7. Help organizations understand the compliance implications of changes in their business that might affect their service provider level

This knowledge enables PCIPs to serve as effective advisors in navigating the complex landscape of PCI compliance requirements across multiple card brands.

Additional resources: https://www.pcisecuritystandards.org/documents/PCI_DSS_v4-0_ROC_Reporting_Template.pdf

Q14: Multiple Choice: According to the content, which resource would be most helpful for understanding Discover's service provider levels?

a) The PCI Security Standards Council website b) Discover Global Network's Service Provider Compliance webpage c) A third-party compliance consultant d) The provided Mastercard link

A14: The correct answer is b) Discover Global Network's Service Provider Compliance webpage. The content specifically lists 'Discover Service Provider Levels: Service Provider Compliance | Discover Global Network" and provides the URL https://www.discoverglobalnetwork.com/solutions/pci-compliance/service-provider-compliance/ as the resource for understanding Discover's service provider levels. This official Discover Global Network resource would be the most authoritative and helpful source for understanding Discover's specific service provider level classifications and compliance requirements.

Additional resources: https://www.discoverglobalnetwork.com/solutions/pci-compliance/service-provider-compliance/

Q15: Essay: Compare and contrast the importance of understanding card brand service provider levels for PCIPs versus service providers.

A15: Understanding card brand service provider levels holds significant importance for both PCIPs and service providers, though their perspectives and applications of this knowledge differ substantially.

For PCIPs (Payment Card Industry Professionals): PCIPs need to understand card brand service provider levels primarily as consultants and advisors. Their role requires a broad knowledge of how different card brands classify service providers and what compliance requirements apply to each level. This knowledge enables them to guide diverse clients through appropriate compliance pathways. PCIPs must maintain awareness of requirements across all major card brands to provide comprehensive advice, even though they may not need to implement these requirements themselves. Their understanding needs to be sufficient to identify which specific requirements apply to a particular service provider based on their business model, transaction volume, and relationships with card brands. PCIPs use this knowledge diagnostically to assess compliance gaps and prescriptively to recommend remediation strategies.

For Service Providers: Service providers, by contrast, need to understand card brand service provider levels from an implementation perspective. Their focus is typically narrower but deeper, concentrating on the specific requirements that apply to their organization based on their classification with each relevant card brand. Service providers must translate their understanding into operational practices, security controls, and validation procedures. Their knowledge directly informs resource allocation, compliance budgeting, and project planning for security initiatives. The stakes of misunderstanding are potentially higher for service providers, as non-compliance could result in financial penalties, restrictions on processing transactions, or damage to business relationships with clients.

Key Differences:

1. Scope: PCIPs need broader knowledge across multiple service provider types and card brands, while service providers need deeper knowledge of their specific classification.
2. Application: PCIPs apply knowledge consultatively, while service providers apply it operationally.
3. Perspective: PCIPs need to understand the "why" behind requirements to explain them to clients, while service providers focus more on the "how" of implementation.
4. Timeline: PCIPs may engage with requirements periodically during assessments or consultations, while service providers live with the requirements continuously.

Key Similarities:

1. Both need to stay current as card brand requirements evolve.
2. Both benefit from understanding the relationship between PCI DSS and card brand-specific requirements.
3. Both need to recognize how changes in business operations might affect service provider levels.

The complementary nature of these perspectives highlights the importance of collaboration between PCIPs and service providers. PCIPs bring cross-industry expertise and comparative knowledge, while service providers contribute detailed operational understanding of their specific environment. Together, this creates a more robust approach to compliance that addresses both technical requirements and business considerations.

Additional resources: https://www.pcisecuritystandards.org/pci_security/

Q16: True or False: JCB and UnionPay are mentioned as card brands that provide information about service provider levels, but specific links to their websites are not provided in the content.

A16: True. The content does mention both JCB and UnionPay as card brands that provide in-depth details on their websites about service provider levels. Specifically, the content states: "Mastercard, Visa, Discover, JCB, UnionPay and AMEX all provide in-depth details on their websites." However, while the content provides specific links for Mastercard, Visa, Discover, and instructions for finding American Express requirements, it does not include direct links to either JCB or UnionPay websites. This indicates that while these card brands are acknowledged as important sources of information on service provider levels, the content doesn't provide the specific URLs for accessing this information for these two particular card brands.

Additional resources: https://www.global.jcb/en/about-us/compliance/

Q17: What advice does the content provide regarding the amount of information available on card brand websites?

A17: The content provides clear advice regarding the amount of information available on card brand websites in the form of a tip: "You only need a very basic understanding of the information on these websites, so don't feel overwhelmed by the amount of content." This advice acknowledges that card brand websites may contain extensive information about service provider levels and compliance requirements, which could potentially feel overwhelming to someone studying for the PCIP exam. The tip reassures readers that they don't need to master all the details on these websites but rather need only a fundamental understanding of the concepts. This suggests that for the PCIP v4.0 exam, candidates should focus on knowing that different card brands have their own service provider level classifications and requirements, and where to find this information, rather than memorizing all the specific details for each card brand.

Additional resources: https://www.pcisecuritystandards.org/faqs/

Q18: Multiple Choice: As a PCIP, which of the following would be the LEAST important reason to understand card brand service provider levels?

a) To advise clients on their compliance obligations b) To know where to find authoritative information on requirements c) To memorize all specific details for each service provider level d) To understand how service providers are categorized by card brands

A18: The correct answer is c) To memorize all specific details for each service provider level. According to the content, PCIPs only need "a very basic understanding of the information on these websites" and should "not feel overwhelmed by the amount of content." This indicates that memorizing all specific details for each service provider level across all card brands is not necessary. Instead, PCIPs should understand the general concept of service provider levels, how they affect compliance requirements, and where to find specific information when needed. The other options represent legitimate reasons for PCIPs to understand card brand service provider levels: advising clients, knowing where to find information, and understanding categorization frameworks are all important aspects of a PCIP's knowledge base.

Additional resources: https://www.pcisecuritystandards.org/programs/pcip/

Q19: What specific Mastercard resource is mentioned in the content for understanding service provider levels?

A19: The specific Mastercard resource mentioned in the content for understanding service provider levels is "PCI-DSS Service Provider Levels | Mastercard SDP Compliant Service Providers." The content provides the URL https://www.mastercard.us/en-us/business/overview/safety-and-security/security-recommendations/site-data-protection-PCI/service-providers-need-to-know.html for accessing this resource. This Mastercard Site Data Protection (SDP) webpage contains information specifically about Mastercard's classification of service providers and their compliance requirements. The mention of "SDP" refers to Mastercard's Site Data Protection Program, which is their implementation of PCI DSS requirements. This resource would provide authoritative information directly from Mastercard about how they categorize service providers and what validation requirements apply to each level.

Additional resources: https://www.mastercard.us/en-us/business/overview/safety-and-security/security-recommendations/site-data-protection-PCI/service-providers-need-to-know.html

Q20: Short Answer: How many card brands are specifically mentioned in the content as providing information about service provider levels?

A20: Six card brands are specifically mentioned in the content as providing information about service provider levels. The content explicitly states: "Mastercard, Visa, Discover, JCB, UnionPay and AMEX all provide in-depth details on their websites." These six major card brands each maintain their own compliance programs based on the PCI DSS framework but may have different implementations, service provider classifications, and validation requirements. The content emphasizes the importance of understanding these different service levels and directs readers to the respective websites of these card brands for further information. While specific links are provided only for Mastercard, Visa, Discover, and American Express (AMEX), all six brands are acknowledged as important sources of information on service provider levels.

Additional resources: https://www.pcisecuritystandards.org/about_us/members/

Q21: True or False: According to the content, Visa and Mastercard use identical service provider level classifications.

A21: False. While the content doesn't explicitly state whether Visa and Mastercard use identical or different service provider level classifications, it strongly implies differences by noting the importance of understanding "the different service levels expected from service providers by the card brands" and suggesting visiting each card brand's website to understand "the levels and requirements expected from each card brand." The phrasing indicates that service provider levels vary across card brands, including between Visa and Mastercard. If the classifications were identical, there would be less emphasis on checking each card brand's specific requirements. Additionally, the content provides separate links for Visa and Mastercard service provider information, further suggesting that each has its own distinct classification system and requirements.

Additional resources: https://usa.visa.com/partner-with-us/pci-dss-compliance-information.html

Q22: Multiple Choice: Which statement best describes the depth of knowledge a PCIP needs about card brand service provider levels according to the content?

a) In-depth, comprehensive knowledge of all requirements b) Detailed memorization of level thresholds for each brand c) A very basic understanding without feeling overwhelmed d) Advanced knowledge of one primary card brand only

A22: The correct answer is c) A very basic understanding without feeling overwhelmed. The content explicitly states: "Tip: You only need a very basic understanding of the information on these websites, so don't feel overwhelmed by the amount of content." This directly addresses the expected depth of knowledge for PCIPs regarding card brand service provider levels. The tip indicates that while PCIPs should be familiar with the concept of service provider levels and know that different card brands have their own requirements, they don't need to memorize all the specific details or thresholds. Instead, they should know where to find this information when needed and understand its general importance in the PCI compliance ecosystem.

Additional resources: https://www.pcisecuritystandards.org/documents/PCI_DSS_v4.0.pdf

Q23: Essay: Discuss how understanding service provider levels might impact a PCIP's work in the field.

A23: Understanding service provider levels fundamentally shapes a PCIP's effectiveness in navigating the complex landscape of payment card security. This knowledge impacts numerous aspects of their professional practice in the field:

Client Assessment and Scoping: When a PCIP engages with a new client that functions as a service provider, one of their first tasks is determining the organization's service provider level with each relevant card brand. This classification directly influences the scope of compliance activities, validation requirements, and potential risk exposure. Without understanding service provider levels, a PCIP might misclassify an organization, leading to inadequate security controls or excessive compliance efforts. The ability to accurately determine which service provider level applies based on transaction volumes, services offered, and card brand relationships ensures appropriate scoping of compliance activities.

Strategic Compliance Planning: Service provider levels impact timelines, resource requirements, and validation approaches. A PCIP who understands these levels can develop more strategic compliance roadmaps for clients. For example, if a service provider is approaching a transaction volume threshold that would elevate their service provider level with a particular card brand, a knowledgeable PCIP might recommend implementing more robust controls preemptively to ease the eventual transition. This proactive approach transforms compliance from a reactive checkbox exercise to a strategic business function.

Cost-Effective Implementation: Different service provider levels have different validation requirements—some requiring on-site assessments by Qualified Security Assessors (QSAs), others allowing self-assessment questionnaires (SAQs). A PCIP who understands these distinctions can help clients implement right-sized security programs that meet requirements without unnecessary expenditure. They can identify opportunities to harmonize compliance efforts across multiple card brands, reducing duplication while ensuring all requirements are met.

Risk Communication: PCIPs often serve as translators between technical security teams and executive leadership. Understanding service provider levels helps PCIPs articulate compliance obligations in business terms, explaining how classification affects risk exposure, potential penalties for non-compliance, and business relationships. This context helps secure appropriate resources and executive support for security initiatives.

Documentation and Evidence Collection: Different service provider levels require different evidence and documentation. PCIPs with a solid understanding of these requirements can guide clients in establishing appropriate documentation practices from the outset, rather than scrambling to gather evidence during assessment periods. This proactive approach reduces compliance friction and increases the likelihood of successful validation.

Navigating Changes: Card brands periodically update their service provider level requirements. PCIPs who understand the fundamental structure of these levels can more easily interpret and adapt to these changes, providing continuity of guidance to clients through evolving compliance landscapes. This adaptability is particularly valuable when organizations undergo business changes that might affect their service provider classification.

Professional Credibility: While PCIPs don't need exhaustive knowledge of every detail, demonstrating familiarity with service provider levels enhances their credibility with clients, QSAs, and other stakeholders. This knowledge positions them as informed guides through the compliance ecosystem rather than merely technical implementers.

In practice, a PCIP's understanding of service provider levels transforms abstract compliance requirements into practical, contextualized guidance. For example, when advising a client considering a new payment processing service, the PCIP can explain how this business decision might affect their service provider classification with different card brands, potentially triggering new compliance requirements. This business-centric perspective makes security considerations an integral part of strategic decision-making rather than an afterthought.

Additional resources: https://www.pcisecuritystandards.org/pci_security/small_merchant_resources/

Q24: What specific Visa resource is mentioned in the content for understanding service provider levels?

A24: The specific Visa resource mentioned in the content for understanding service provider levels is "Validation of Compliance | Information Security | Visa." The content provides the URL https://bb.visa.com/ for accessing this resource. This Visa webpage would contain information about how Visa categorizes service providers and what validation requirements apply to each level. The term "Validation of Compliance" indicates that this resource likely focuses on the processes and requirements for service providers to demonstrate their compliance with PCI DSS according to Visa's program. This would include information about which validation methods (self-assessment questionnaires, on-site assessments, etc.) apply to different service provider levels, reporting requirements, and compliance deadlines specific to Visa's implementation of PCI DSS for service providers.

Additional resources: https://usa.visa.com/partner-with-us/pci-dss-compliance-information.html

Q25: True or False: The content suggests that PCIPs should focus primarily on Mastercard's service provider requirements since they are listed first.

A25: False. The content does not suggest that PCIPs should focus primarily on Mastercard's service provider requirements despite listing them first. Instead, the content emphasizes the importance of understanding service provider levels across all card brands, stating that "Mastercard, Visa, Discover, JCB, UnionPay and AMEX all provide in-depth details on their websites." The order of listing appears to be arbitrary and not indicative of priority or importance. The content encourages visiting the websites of various card brands to better understand "the levels and requirements expected from each card brand," implying equal importance across all the mentioned card brands. The tip about needing only "a very basic understanding" applies to all the card brand websites, not just Mastercard's, further indicating that no single card brand's requirements should be prioritized above others.

Additional resources: https://www.pcisecuritystandards.org/about_us/members/

17

Approved Scanning Vendor (ASV) - Question Set

Q1: What is an Approved Scanning Vendor (ASV)?

A1: An Approved Scanning Vendor (ASV) is a company that has been certified by the Payment Card Industry (PCI) Security Standards Council to conduct vulnerability scanning services. ASVs specifically focus on identifying and addressing security weaknesses in an organization's Cardholder Data Environment (CDE). These vendors have met rigorous requirements established by the PCI SSC to ensure they can effectively detect vulnerabilities that could potentially compromise cardholder data. ASVs play a critical role in the PCI DSS compliance process by providing independent verification of an organization's external-facing systems.

For more information: https://www.pcisecuritystandards.org/assessors_and_solutions/approved_scanning_vendors

Q2: True or False: Any security company can claim to be an Approved Scanning Vendor without certification from the PCI Security Standards Council.

A2: False. Only companies that have been officially certified by the Payment Card Industry (PCI) Security Standards Council can claim to be Approved Scanning Vendors (ASVs). This certification process ensures that ASVs meet specific technical requirements, follow standardized testing procedures, and maintain the necessary expertise to perform vulnerability scans according to PCI DSS requirements. Organizations should always verify a vendor's ASV status on the official PCI SSC website before engaging their services.

For more information: https://www.pcisecuritystandards.org/program_training_and_qualification/

Q3: What are three primary responsibilities of an Approved Scanning Vendor?

A3: Three primary responsibilities of an Approved Scanning Vendor (ASV) include:

1. Performing external vulnerability scans on an organization's Cardholder Data Environment (CDE) to identify security weaknesses that could be exploited by attackers.

2. Conducting scanning activities without interfering with the organization's production environment to avoid service disruptions.

3. Providing a formal dispute resolution process for organizations that disagree with scan findings or results.

Additional responsibilities include avoiding dangerous testing methods that could harm systems and retaining scan results for at least two years for audit and verification purposes.

For more information: https://www.pcisecuritystandards.org/documents/ASV_Program_Guide_v3.1.pdf

Q4: How long must an ASV retain scan results according to PCI requirements?

A4: According to PCI requirements, an Approved Scanning Vendor (ASV) must retain scan results for at least two years. This retention period is mandatory and ensures that historical vulnerability data is available for:

- Compliance verification during assessments
- Tracking remediation progress over time
- Resolving potential disputes about past scan findings
- Supporting forensic investigations if needed
- Demonstrating consistent compliance to auditors and assessors

This two-year retention requirement helps maintain the integrity of the PCI DSS compliance process and provides an audit trail for both the organization and compliance assessors.

For more information: https://www.pcisecuritystandards.org/documents/ASV_Program_Guide_v3.1.pdf

Q5: Explain the importance of Approved Scanning Vendors in the PCI DSS compliance ecosystem.

A5: Approved Scanning Vendors (ASVs) serve as critical third-party validators within the PCI DSS compliance ecosystem. Their importance stems from several key factors:

1. Independent verification: ASVs provide unbiased assessments of an organization's external security posture, offering objective findings rather than self-assessments.
2. Specialized expertise: ASVs possess the technical knowledge and tools specifically calibrated to detect vulnerabilities that could impact cardholder data security.
3. Standardized methodology: By following PCI SSC requirements, ASVs ensure consistent evaluation across all organizations, creating a level security baseline.
4. Early threat detection: Regular ASV scans help identify emerging vulnerabilities before they can be exploited by malicious actors.
5. Compliance documentation: ASV reports serve as evidence of due diligence for PCI DSS requirements, specifically Requirement 11.3.4.
6. Risk reduction: By identifying and helping remediate vulnerabilities, ASVs directly contribute to reducing the likelihood of data breaches.

7. Industry trust: The ASV program helps maintain confidence in the payment card ecosystem by ensuring organizations regularly test their security controls.

The ASV program represents one of the fundamental external validation mechanisms that helps maintain the integrity and security of the global payment card infrastructure.

For more information: https://www.pcisecuritystandards.org/pci_security/maintaining_payment_security

Q6: How should an organization select an appropriate Approved Scanning Vendor?

A6: When selecting an appropriate Approved Scanning Vendor (ASV), an organization should follow these key steps:

1. Consult the PCI SSC's official list of qualified vendors to ensure the ASV is currently certified and in good standing
2. Evaluate the ASV's experience with organizations of similar size, industry, and technical complexity.
3. Review the ASV's scanning methodology, including scan frequency options, coverage capabilities, and remediation support.
4. Assess the ASV's reporting format and portal capabilities to ensure they meet your organization's needs for clarity and actionable findings.
5. Consider the ASV's dispute resolution process and their reputation for responsiveness to technical questions or disagreements.
6. Compare pricing structures and ensure they align with your budgetary constraints while meeting compliance requirements.
7. Check references from current clients to gauge satisfaction with the ASV's services and support.
8. Evaluate additional services offered, such as remediation guidance, rescanning policies, and educational resources.

The goal is to find an ASV that not only meets the technical requirements for PCI compliance but also works effectively as a partner in your organization's security program.

For more information: https://www.pcisecuritystandards.org/assessors_and_solutions/approved_scanning_vendors

Q7: Which of the following best describes the primary purpose of vulnerability scanning performed by an ASV?

A. To perform penetration testing of the organization's systems B. To identify and address security weaknesses in the Cardholder Data Environment C. To manage firewall configurations D. To implement security patches

A7: The correct answer is B. To identify and address security weaknesses in the Cardholder Data Environment.

The primary purpose of vulnerability scanning performed by an Approved Scanning Vendor (ASV) is to identify and address security weaknesses specifically within the organization's Cardholder Data Environment (CDE). ASVs use specialized tools to detec potential vulnerabilities in external-facing systems that could be exploited by attackers to gain unauthorized access to cardholder data. These scans help organizations locate security gaps in their infrastructure before malicious actors can exploit them.

While vulnerability scanning may indirectly support other security activities like option C (managing firewall configurations) and option D (implementing security patches), these are remediation activities that occur after vulnerabilities are identified. Option A (penetration testing) is a different security assessment methodology that involves actively attempting to exploit vulnerabilities, which goes beyond the scope of standard ASV scanning services.

For more information: https://www.pcisecuritystandards.org/documents/ASV_Program_Guide_v3.1.pdf

Q8: True or False: ASVs are permitted to conduct vulnerability scans in ways that interfere with an organization's production environment.

A8: False. Approved Scanning Vendors (ASVs) are explicitly required to perform vulnerability scans without interfering with an organization's production environment. The PCI Security Standards Council mandates that ASVs conduct their scanning activities in a non-disruptive manner to ensure business continuity while still effectively identifying security vulnerabilities.

This requirement exists because:

- Production environments contain critical systems that process actual business transactions
- Disruptions could lead to financial losses, customer service issues, or data integrity problems
- Organizations need to maintain operations while security assessments take place
- The primary goal is security improvement without causing operational harm

ASVs must use scanning methodologies that minimize the risk of service disruption, system crashes, or other adverse effects. If there's a potential for disruption during certain types of scanning, the ASV should coordinate with the organization to schedule these activities during maintenance windows or other appropriate times.

For more information: https://www.pcisecuritystandards.org/documents/ASV_Program_Guide_v3.1.pdf

Q9: Describe the dispute resolution process that ASVs must provide and why it's important.

A9: Approved Scanning Vendors (ASVs) are required to provide a formal dispute resolution process as part of their services. This process allows organizations to challenge scan findings they believe are inaccurate or require further analysis. The dispute resolution process typically includes:

1. A formal mechanism for organizations to submit disputes about specific findings
2. Technical review by qualified ASV personnel who weren't involved in the original scan
3. Clear documentation of the dispute, including the organization's rationale and evidence
4. Timely investigation and response to the disputed items
5. Final determination with technical justification for either upholding or reversing findings

6. Documentation of the resolution for compliance records

This dispute resolution process is important for several critical reasons:

- Technical Accuracy: It ensures that scan findings truly reflect actual vulnerabilities rather than false positives or misconfigurations.
- Contextual Understanding: Organizations may have compensating controls or business-specific implementations that mitigate reported vulnerabilities, which requires discussion.
- Compliance Fairness: Since ASV scans directly impact PCI DSS compliance status, organizations need recourse if they believe findings are incorrect.
- Knowledge Transfer: The dispute process often educates both parties about specific security implementations and leads to more accurate future scans.
- Continuous Improvement: Feedback from disputes helps ASVs refine their scanning methodologies and reduce false positives.
- Relationship Building: A fair dispute resolution process builds trust between the organization and the ASV, promoting a collaborative security approach.

Without this required process, organizations might be forced to address non-existent issues or face compliance challenges based on technical misunderstandings.

For more information: https://www.pcisecuritystandards.org/documents/ASV_Program_Guide_v3.1.pdf

Q10: Which of the following testing approaches must ASVs avoid?

A. External vulnerability scanning B. Dangerous testing that could harm systems C. Automated scanning tools D. Authenticated scanning

A10: The correct answer is B. Dangerous testing that could harm systems.

Approved Scanning Vendors (ASVs) must specifically avoid dangerous testing that could potentially harm or disrupt an organization's systems or networks. This prohibition is explicitly stated in the ASV requirements established by the PCI Security Standards Council.

Dangerous testing might include:

- Denial of service attacks or tests that could crash production systems
- Exploitation attempts that could damage data or system integrity
- Resource-intensive scans that could overload network capacity
- Tests that might trigger security controls in ways that block legitimate traffic

The other options are either appropriate or potentially appropriate for ASVs:

- Option A (External vulnerability scanning) is the core service that ASVs provide
- Option C (Automated scanning tools) is a standard methodology used by ASVs
- Option D (Authenticated scanning) may be used in some scenarios, though external ASV scans are typically unauthenticated

ASVs must balance thorough security testing with the principle of "do no harm" to the organizations they scan.

For more information: https://www.pcisecuritystandards.org/documents/ASV_Program_Guide_v3.1.pdf

Q11: What does the abbreviation "CDE" stand for in the context of ASV scanning, and what does it encompass?

A11: CDE stands for "Cardholder Data Environment." In the context of ASV scanning, the Cardholder Data Environment encompasses all systems, networks, applications, and processes that store, process, or transmit cardholder data or sensitive authentication data, as well as all connected systems and network components.

The CDE specifically includes:

- Systems directly handling payment card information
- Connected systems that could impact the security of cardholder data
- Network segments containing cardholder data
- Supporting systems that manage access to the cardholder data
- Security systems protecting the CDE (firewalls, IDS/IPS, etc.)
- Virtual components like cloud resources that interact with cardholder data

ASV scanning focuses on the external perimeter of the CDE – specifically targeting internet-facing systems and components that could potentially provide an attacker with access to the cardholder data environment. The goal is to identify vulnerabilities in these external-facing systems before they can be exploited to gain unauthorized access to the protected cardholder data.

Understanding the boundaries and components of the CDE is crucial for organizations to properly scope both their ASV scans and their overall PCI DSS compliance efforts.

For more information: https://www.pcisecuritystandards.org/documents/PCI_DSS_Scoping_Guidance_v1.1.pdf

Q12: True or False: ASVs are required to retain scan results for at least one year.

A12: False. Approved Scanning Vendors (ASVs) are required to retain scan results for at least two years, not one year. This two-year retention requirement is explicitly mandated by the PCI Security Standards Council as part of the ASV Program Guide.

This extended retention period serves several important purposes:

- It provides historical data to track vulnerability remediation over time

- It supports compliance verification during PCI DSS assessments
- It ensures documentation is available for dispute resolution processes
- It helps identify patterns in an organization's security posture
- It satisfies audit requirements that may span multiple assessment cycles

The two-year retention requirement aligns with other documentation retention periods within the PCI DSS framework, creating consistency in the compliance ecosystem. Organizations should confirm that their chosen ASV adheres to this retention requirement as part of their vendor selection process.

For more information: https://www.pcisecuritystandards.org/documents/ASV_Program_Guide_v3.1.pdf

Q13: Which organization certifies and manages the Approved Scanning Vendor program?

A. Payment Card Industry Security Standards Council (PCI SSC) B. National Institute of Standards and Technology (NIST) C. International Organization for Standardization (ISO) D. Center for Internet Security (CIS)

A13: The correct answer is A. Payment Card Industry Security Standards Council (PCI SSC).

The Payment Card Industry Security Standards Council (PCI SSC) is the organization responsible for certifying and managing the Approved Scanning Vendor (ASV) program. The PCI SSC was founded in 2006 by the major payment card brands (American Express, Discover, JCB International, Mastercard, and Visa) to develop, maintain, and promote payment card industry standards for data security.

The PCI SSC:

- Establishes the technical and operational requirements for ASVs
- Manages the certification process for organizations seeking ASV status
- Maintains the official list of qualified ASVs
- Conducts quality assurance reviews of ASV scanning practices
- Updates ASV requirements as security threats and technologies evolve
- Provides guidance on vulnerability scanning methodologies
- Has the authority to revoke ASV status if vendors fail to meet requirements

Organizations seeking PCI DSS compliance must use an ASV that is currently certified by the PCI SSC for their external vulnerability scanning requirements. The PCI SSC website maintains the authoritative list of all approved vendors.

For more information: https://www.pcisecuritystandards.org/about_us/

Q14: Explain the concept of external vulnerability scans in the context of ASV responsibilities and how they differ from internal vulnerability scans.

A14: External vulnerability scans, in the context of ASV responsibilities, are systematic examinations of an organization's internet-facing systems, applications, and network infrastructure conducted from outside the organization's network perimeter. These scans are performed by Approved Scanning Vendors (ASVs) to identify security weaknesses that could potentially be exploited by remote attackers to gain unauthorized access to cardholder data.

Key characteristics of external vulnerability scans conducted by ASVs include:

1. Perspective: They simulate the view of an external attacker by scanning from outside the organization's network.
2. Scope: They focus on internet-facing components like web servers, email gateways, firewalls, and other publicly accessible systems that form the external boundary of the Cardholder Data Environment.
3. Methodology: They use non-intrusive automated tools to detect known vulnerabilities, misconfigurations, outdated software, and other security issues.
4. Authorization: They are performed with the organization's permission but without insider knowledge or credentials.
5. Frequency: PCI DSS requires these scans quarterly and after significant changes to the network.
6. Independence: They must be performed by certified third-party vendors (ASVs) rather than the organization itself.

External vulnerability scans differ from internal vulnerability scans in several important ways:

External Vulnerability ScansInternal Vulnerability ScansPerformed by certified ASVsCan be performed by the organization itself-Scan from outside the networkScan from within the organization's networkFocus on internet-facing systemsExamine all systems in the CDE and connected networksSimulate remote attacker perspectiveDetect vulnerabilities visible to insiders or after perimeter breachLimited to discovering externally visible issuesCan find internal configuration issues and vulnerabilitiesRequired quarterly by PCI DSSAlso required quarterly but don't need ASV certificationTest perimeter defensesTest internal security controls

Both scan types are required for comprehensive PCI DSS compliance, but only external scans must be performed by an Approved Scanning Vendor. Together, they provide a more complete view of an organization's security posture from both external and internal perspectives.

For more information: https://www.pcisecuritystandards.org/documents/ASV_Program_Guide_v3.1.pdf

Q15: What types of security weaknesses do ASVs typically identify in an organization's Cardholder Data Environment?

A15: Approved Scanning Vendors (ASVs) typically identify a wide range of security weaknesses in an organization's Cardholder Data Environment (CDE), focusing particularly on externally accessible vulnerabilities. The most common types of security weaknesses identified include:

1. Software vulnerabilities: Unpatched systems, outdated software versions, and known security flaws in operating systems, web servers, applications, and other components.

2. Misconfigurations: Improperly configured security settings, default credentials, unnecessary open ports, excessive permissions, and insecure protocol usage.
3. TLS/SSL weaknesses: Outdated encryption protocols, weak cipher suites, certificate issues, and vulnerabilities like Heartbleed or POODLE.
4. Authentication problems: Weak password policies, lack of multi-factor authentication on public-facing administrative interfaces, and session management flaws.
5. Information disclosure: Excessive information revealed in error messages, HTTP headers, or other responses that could aid attackers.
6. Cross-site scripting (XSS) and injection vulnerabilities: Flaws in web applications that could allow attackers to inject malicious code or commands.
7. Insecure services: Unnecessarily exposed services like FTP, telnet, SMTP, or database ports that could provide attack vectors.
8. Missing security headers: Absence of security headers like Content-Security-Policy, X-Frame-Options, or HTTP Strict Transport Security.
9. Outdated components: End-of-life software or systems no longer receiving security updates.
10. Cryptographic issues: Weak encryption algorithms, improperly implemented encryption, or insecure key management.

ASVs classify these vulnerabilities according to severity levels, typically aligned with the Common Vulnerability Scoring System (CVSS), to help organizations prioritize remediation efforts. The primary focus is on identifying vulnerabilities that external attackers could potentially exploit to gain unauthorized access to cardholder data.

For more information: https://www.pcisecuritystandards.org/documents/Penetration_Testing_Guidance_March_2015.pdf

Q16: Which of the following is the best resource for finding a qualified Approved Scanning Vendor?

A. General internet search B. Recommendations from IT consulting firms C. The PCI Security Standards Council's list of qualified vendors D. Payment card brand websites

A16: The correct answer is C. The PCI Security Standards Council's list of qualified vendors.

The PCI Security Standards Council (PCI SSC) maintains the official and authoritative list of qualified Approved Scanning Vendors (ASVs). This list is the definitive source for identifying vendors that have been properly certified and are in good standing with the Council. The PCI SSC list provides assurance that listed vendors:

- Have successfully completed the ASV certification process
- Meet the technical and operational requirements established by the Council
- Maintain the necessary expertise and tools to perform compliant scans
- Are subject to ongoing quality assurance reviews

- Follow standardized scanning methodologies
- Are recognized by all major payment card brands

While options A, B, and D might provide some useful information:

- General internet searches (option A) may lead to uncertified vendors or outdated information
- IT consulting recommendations (option B) may be helpful but don't guarantee certification status
- Payment card brand websites (option D) might reference ASVs but typically direct users to the official PCI SSC list

Organizations subject to PCI DSS compliance requirements must use an ASV from the official PCI SSC list to satisfy the external vulnerability scanning requirements. Using an unlisted vendor, even if they claim to provide similar services, will not fulfill compliance obligations.

For more information: https://www.pcisecuritystandards.org/assessors_and_solutions/approved_scanning_vendors

Q17: True or False: ASVs are permitted to perform penetration testing as part of their standard vulnerability scanning services.

A17: False. Approved Scanning Vendors (ASVs) are not permitted to perform penetration testing as part of their standard vulnerability scanning services under their ASV certification.

ASV scanning and penetration testing are distinct security assessment methodologies with different purposes, approaches, and potential impacts:

- ASV scanning is primarily non-intrusive, using automated tools to identify known vulnerabilities without actively exploiting them. It focuses on detecting potential security weaknesses in external-facing systems.
- Penetration testing is an active, controlled attempt to exploit vulnerabilities to determine if unauthorized access or other malicious activities are possible. It may involve manual testing techniques and actual exploitation attempts.

While some security companies may offer both ASV scanning and penetration testing services, these are separate service offerings requiring different qualifications, methodologies, and agreements. The ASV certification specifically covers vulnerability scanning services, not penetration testing.

Organizations often need both types of assessments for comprehensive security and PCI DSS compliance, but they serve different requirements:

- ASV scans satisfy Requirement 11.3.4 (quarterly external vulnerability scanning)
- Penetration testing satisfies Requirements 11.3.1 and 11.3.2 (annual penetration testing)

For more information: https://www.pcisecuritystandards.org/documents/ASV_Program_Guide_v3.1.pdf

Q18: Discuss the required frequency of ASV scans for PCI DSS compliance and why this frequency was established.

A18: For PCI DSS compliance, organizations must undergo ASV scans at least quarterly (every 90 days) and after any significant change to the network or infrastructure. This frequency requirement was established through careful consideration of several key factors:

The quarterly frequency requirement was established based on:

1. Threat Landscape Evolution: New vulnerabilities are discovered constantly. The 90-day window represents a balance between operational feasibility and security vigilance, acknowledging that the threat landscape evolves rapidly.

2. Patch Management Cycles: Most major vendors release security patches monthly or quarterly. The quarterly scan requirement aligns with typical patch management cycles, allowing organizations to implement updates before the next compliance scan.

3. Risk Management: The 90-day interval represents an acceptable level of risk exposure based on industry analysis. Longer intervals would increase the window of vulnerability; shorter intervals would create operational burdens without proportional security benefits.

4. Change Management: Most organizations implement significant changes to their infrastructure within a 90-day window. Quarterly scans help ensure these changes haven't introduced new vulnerabilities.

5. Compliance Verification Lifecycle: The quarterly cadence creates a continuous compliance cycle that keeps security at the forefront of organizational priorities throughout the year.

6. Resource Considerations: The frequency strikes a balance between security needs and the resource requirements (both time and financial) for organizations of various sizes.

The additional requirement for scanning after significant changes acknowledges that:

- Network modifications can introduce new vulnerabilities regardless of the calendar
- Risk exposure begins immediately after changes are implemented
- The standard quarterly schedule might not capture these vulnerabilities in a timely manner

For a scan to be considered compliant, all "high" vulnerabilities identified must be addressed and a passing rescan obtained. If vulnerabilities cannot be remediated, compensating controls must be implemented and documented.

This established frequency helps organizations maintain a reasonably current security posture while acknowledging the practical limitations of more frequent scanning requirements.

For more information: https://www.pcisecuritystandards.org/documents/PCI_DSS_v3-2-1.pdf

Q19: What key factors should be documented when selecting an ASV to perform vulnerability scans?

A19: When selecting an Approved Scanning Vendor (ASV), organizations should document the following key factors to demonstrate due diligence in their vendor selection process:

1. ASV Certification Status: Verification that the vendor appears on the PCI SSC's official list of qualified ASVs and confirmation of their current certification status.
2. Technical Capabilities: Assessment of the ASV's scanning tools, methodologies, and their ability to comprehensively scan the organization's specific environment, including specialized technologies.
3. Scanning Coverage: Documentation of the ASV's ability to scan all required external-facing systems, including web applications, cloud resources, and traditional infrastructure.
4. Reporting Capabilities: Evaluation of report formats, level of detail, remediation guidance, and whether the reports meet PCI DSS documentation requirements.
5. False Positive Rate: Historical data or references regarding the ASV's accuracy and false positive rates.
6. Dispute Resolution Process: Details of the ASV's formal process for addressing disagreements about scan findings.
7. Rescanning Policies: Terms and conditions for rescanning after remediation, including any limitations or additional costs.
8. Support Services: Availability of technical assistance, remediation advice, and general responsiveness.
9. Compliance Expertise: The ASV's demonstrated knowledge of PCI DSS requirements beyond just technical scanning.
10. Cost Structure: Complete pricing information, including baseline services and any potential additional fees.
11. Service Level Agreements: Documented performance guarantees, scheduling flexibility, and response times.
12. Client References: Feedback from organizations of similar size and complexity.

Documenting these factors not only helps make a sound selection decision but also demonstrates to assessors that the organization has taken reasonable steps to select a qualified ASV capable of meeting their compliance needs. This documentation should be maintained as part of the organization's overall PCI DSS compliance records.

For more information: https://www.pcisecuritystandards.org/documents/ASV_Program_Guide_v3.1.pdf

Q20: Which of the following statements is true regarding ASV scan documentation?

A. Scan results can be discarded once remediation is complete B. ASVs must retain scan results for at least two years C. Only failed scans need to be documented D. Organizations are not entitled to copies of their scan reports

A20: The correct answer is B. ASVs must retain scan results for at least two years.

This statement is accurate according to the PCI Security Standards Council requirements for Approved Scanning Vendors. The two-year retention requirement is mandatory and applies to all scan results, regardless of whether the scans passed or failed.

The other options contain inaccurate information:

Option A is incorrect because scan results must be retained even after remediation is complete. These historical records are essential for compliance verification, audit purposes, and tracking security improvements over time.

Option C is incorrect because both passed and failed scans must be documented. Successful scans demonstrate compliance, while failed scans document the identification and remediation process for vulnerabilities.

Option D is incorrect because organizations are absolutely entitled to copies of their scan reports. These reports are essential documentation for the organization's PCI DSS compliance evidence and are typically provided through a portal or direct delivery by the ASV.

The requirement for ASVs to retain scan results for at least two years ensures that adequate historical data is available for compliance assessments, dispute resolution, and security trend analysis.

For more information: https://www.pcisecuritystandards.org/documents/ASV_Program_Guide_v3.1.pdf

Q21: True or False: An organization can become fully PCI DSS compliant by only using an ASV for quarterly external scanning.

A21: False. An organization cannot become fully PCI DSS compliant by only using an Approved Scanning Vendor (ASV) for quarterly external scanning.

ASV scanning satisfies only one specific requirement within the PCI DSS framework - namely, Requirement 11.3.4, which mandates quarterly external vulnerability scanning by a qualified vendor. Full PCI DSS compliance requires adherence to all 12 requirements and their numerous sub-requirements, which address various aspects of cardholder data security:

1. Network security with properly configured firewalls
2. Secure configuration standards for all systems
3. Protection of stored cardholder data
4. Encryption of transmitted cardholder data
5. Malware protection and regular updates
6. Secure systems and applications development
7. Access restriction to cardholder data
8. Unique IDs for all users with system access
9. Physical access restrictions to cardholder data
10. Network monitoring and tracking
11. Regular security systems testing (including but not limited to ASV scanning)
12. Information security policy maintenance

Within Requirement 11 alone, organizations must also conduct internal vulnerability scanning, implement intrusion detection systems, perform penetration testing, deploy file integrity monitoring, and maintain other security testing procedures.

While ASV scanning is an important component of a comprehensive security program, it addresses only external vulnerabilities visible from the internet. Internal vulnerabilities, access controls, encryption, policies, and many other security controls are not evaluated through ASV scanning but are critical for PCI DSS compliance.

For more information: https://www.pcisecuritystandards.org/pci_security/maintaining_payment_security

Q22: Describe the relationship between vulnerability management and ASV scanning, including how organizations should respond to vulnerabilities identified during ASV scans.

A22: Vulnerability management and ASV scanning are intricately connected components within a comprehensive security program, with ASV scanning serving as a specialized external assessment tool within the broader vulnerability management lifecycle.

The Relationship Between Vulnerability Management and ASV Scanning:

Vulnerability management is the systematic, continuous process of identifying, classifying, prioritizing, remediating, and mitigating security vulnerabilities across an organization's systems and applications. This comprehensive process encompasses:

1. Asset inventory and management
2. Risk assessment and classification
3. Vulnerability identification (through various methods)
4. Prioritization based on risk
5. Remediation planning and execution
6. Verification of remediation effectiveness
7. Reporting and documentation
8. Continuous improvement

ASV scanning fits specifically within the "vulnerability identification" phase of this larger process, providing a specialized, PCI-mandated mechanism for detecting external vulnerabilities that could potentially expose cardholder data. ASV scans offer an independent, third-party perspective on external security posture, complementing internal scanning efforts.

Responding to Vulnerabilities Identified During ASV Scans:

When vulnerabilities are identified during ASV scans, organizations should follow a structured response process:

1. **Validation and Analysis:**
    - Verify the vulnerability is legitimate (not a false positive)
    - Determine if the vulnerability affects systems within scope for PCI DSS

- Assess the risk level using the CVSS score and business context

2. **Prioritization:**
    - Address high-severity vulnerabilities first
    - Consider exploitation potential and proximity to cardholder data
    - Factor in business impact of vulnerable systems
3. **Remediation Planning:**
    - Identify appropriate remediation strategies (patching, configuration changes, etc.)
    - Schedule remediation activities with change management approval
    - Consider testing requirements before implementing in production
4. **Implementation:**
    - Apply patches, configuration changes, or other remediation measures
    - Document all actions taken
    - Implement in accordance with change management procedures
5. **Verification:**
    - Request rescanning from the ASV to confirm remediation effectiveness
    - Ensure all high-severity vulnerabilities are resolved
    - Address any new issues identified during rescanning
6. **Compensating Controls (if needed):**
    - If a vulnerability cannot be directly remediated, develop compensating controls
    - Document the business constraints preventing standard remediation
    - Implement mitigating measures that provide similar protection
    - Have these controls verified by the ASV or QSA
7. **Documentation:**
    - Maintain comprehensive records of all identified vulnerabilities
    - Document remediation actions, including who performed them and when
    - Preserve evidence of successful rescans

- Link activities to specific PCI DSS requirements

8. **Process Improvement:**
    - Analyze root causes of significant vulnerabilities
    - Update security standards to prevent similar issues
    - Adjust patch management programs if needed
    - Incorporate lessons learned into security awareness training

For PCI DSS compliance, organizations must achieve a passing ASV scan status, which requires remediation of all high-severity vulnerabilities or implementation of approved compensating controls. The structured approach to vulnerability management ensures that ASV scanning results translate into actual security improvements rather than simply becoming a compliance checkbox exercise.

For more information: https://www.pcisecuritystandards.org/documents/Prioritized-Approach-for-DSS3_2.pdf

Q23: Which vulnerability scanning requirement must be fulfilled specifically by an ASV for PCI DSS compliance?

A. Internal vulnerability scanning B. Web application penetration testing C. External vulnerability scanning D. Wireless network scanning

A23: The correct answer is C. External vulnerability scanning.

For PCI DSS compliance, external vulnerability scanning must be performed specifically by an Approved Scanning Vendor (ASV). This requirement is explicitly stated in PCI DSS Requirement 11.3.4, which mandates that external vulnerability scans be conducted quarterly and after significant changes by a qualified ASV approved by the PCI Security Standards Council.

The other options represent different types of security assessments with different requirements:

Option A (Internal vulnerability scanning) is required by PCI DSS Requirement 11.3.3, but these scans can be performed by qualified internal personnel and do not specifically require an ASV.

Option B (Web application penetration testing) is covered under PCI DSS Requirement 11.3.2 for penetration testing, which requires qualified personnel but not specifically an ASV. Web application testing has distinct methodologies from standard vulnerability scanning.

Option D (Wireless network scanning) is addressed in PCI DSS Requirement 11.1, which requires quarterly wireless scans but does not specify that an ASV must perform them.

External vulnerability scanning by an ASV provides an independent, third-party verification that internet-facing systems are protected against known vulnerabilities that could be exploited by remote attackers. This independence is why the PCI SSC specifically requires certified ASVs for this particular scanning requirement.

For more information: https://www.pcisecuritystandards.org/documents/PCI_DSS_v3-2-1.pdf

Q24: True or False: ASVs are accountable for remediating any vulnerabilities they discover during scanning.

A24: False. Approved Scanning Vendors (ASVs) are not accountable for remediating vulnerabilities they discover during scanning. The responsibility for remediation lies solely with the organization being scanned.

The distinct roles in the vulnerability management process are:

ASV Responsibilities:

- Conducting thorough and accurate vulnerability scans
- Providing detailed reports of identified vulnerabilities
- Assigning appropriate risk ratings to vulnerabilities
- Offering guidance on remediation approaches
- Performing rescans to verify remediation
- Maintaining documentation of scan results
- Providing a dispute resolution process

Organization Responsibilities:

- Reviewing and validating scan findings
- Prioritizing vulnerabilities based on risk
- Implementing necessary patches, configuration changes, or other fixes
- Requesting rescans after remediation
- Implementing compensating controls when direct remediation isn't possible
- Maintaining documentation of remediation efforts
- Managing the overall security of their cardholder data environment

This separation of duties is intentional and ensures that:

1. The ASV maintains independence as an assessment provider
2. The organization retains control over changes to their environment
3. Responsibilities for security remain clearly defined
4. There is no conflict of interest in verification of remediation

While some ASVs may offer remediation services as a separate business offering, such services fall outside their role as an ASV and would be provided under different contractual terms. The core ASV function remains focused on identification and verification, not remediation.

For more information: https://www.pcisecuritystandards.org/documents/ASV_Program_Guide_v3.1.pdf

Q25: What is the ultimate purpose of using an Approved Scanning Vendor in the context of PCI DSS compliance?

A25: The ultimate purpose of using an Approved Scanning Vendor (ASV) in the context of PCI DSS compliance is to identify and address security weaknesses in an organization's Cardholder Data Environment (CDE) before they can be exploited by malicious actors, thereby protecting cardholder data and maintaining trust in the payment card ecosystem.

This purpose encompasses several key objectives:

1. Independent Verification: ASVs provide an unbiased, third-party assessment of external security vulnerabilities, offering an objective perspective that internal teams might not have.
2. Standardized Security Assessment: ASVs follow consistent methodologies established by the PCI SSC, ensuring that all organizations are evaluated against the same security baseline.
3. Early Detection: Regular ASV scans help identify vulnerabilities before attackers can discover and exploit them, reducing the window of exposure.
4. Compliance Validation: ASV scans provide documented evidence that an organization is meeting specific PCI DSS requirements related to external vulnerability management.
5. Security Posture Improvement: The ongoing cycle of scanning and remediation drives continuous improvement in an organization's security controls and configurations.
6. Risk Reduction: By identifying and addressing vulnerabilities in internet-facing systems, organizations reduce the likelihood of successful attacks targeting cardholder data.
7. Industry Trust Maintenance: The ASV program helps ensure that all participants in the payment card industry maintain minimum security standards, preserving consumer confidence in the entire ecosystem.

The ASV requirement recognizes that external security testing by qualified, independent third parties is a crucial component of a comprehensive security strategy. While compliance is an important outcome, the fundamental purpose is to ensure that organizations maintain effective defenses against evolving external threats that could compromise sensitive cardholder data.

For more information: https://www.pcisecuritystandards.org/pci_security/why_security_matters

18

The Six Control Objectives - Question Set

Q1: What is PCI-DSS and what environments is it designed to protect?

A1: PCI-DSS (Payment Card Industry Data Security Standard) is one of the world's most technical and granular security frameworks designed to protect cardholder data environments (CDE). It provides a comprehensive set of requirements organized into six control objectives and twelve main requirements that organizations must implement to secure payment card data. The standard specifically focuses on protecting environments where cardholder data is stored, processed, or transmitted, known as the cardholder data environment (CDE).

Additional resource: https://www.pcisecuritystandards.org/pci_security/

Q2: True or False: PCI-DSS can be applied to organizations outside the payment card industry.

A2: True. According to the provided content, PCI-DSS can be applied to all organizations to secure and protect their environments even if they do not operate within the payment card industry. The content specifically states that "using it as a security standard will go a long way to securing your production environment" even for organizations outside the payment card industry. This makes PCI-DSS a versatile framework that can provide security benefits beyond its primary intended scope.

Additional resource: https://www.pcisecuritystandards.org/documents/PCI_DSS_for_Small_Merchants_Resource_Guide.pdf

Q3: Which of the following best describes the compliance approach of PCI-DSS?

a) Partial compliance is acceptable if documented b) Organizations can choose which requirements to implement c) You either comply with the controls and requirements or you do not d) Compliance is recommended but not mandatory

A3: c) You either comply with the controls and requirements or you do not

The content explicitly states that when adhering to the PCI-DSS framework, "you either comply with the controls and requirements or you do not - there is no in-between." This binary approach to compliance emphasizes the importance of fully implementing all required controls rather than picking and choosing which ones to follow. Partial compliance is not recognized within the PCI-DSS framework.

Additional resource: https://blog.pcisecuritystandards.org/pci-dss-compliance-an-ongoing-process-not-a-one-time-event

Q4: How many control objectives does PCI-DSS consist of?

A4: PCI-DSS consists of six control objectives. The content explicitly mentions "PCI-DSS uses six control objectives that work to secure the whole CDE." These control objectives form the foundational structure of the PCI-DSS framework, and each control objective contains specific requirements that must be met to achieve proper security of cardholder data. The content emphasizes the importance of memorizing these six control objectives for the PCIP exam.

Additional resource: https://www.pcisecuritystandards.org/pci_security/maintaining_payment_security

Q5: What is the relationship between control objectives and requirements in PCI-DSS?

A5: In PCI-DSS, the six control objectives represent the high-level security goals of the framework, while the twelve main requirements provide specific actions that must be taken to achieve these objectives. According to the content, each control objective has specific requirements that must be met to achieve the objective. Furthermore, each of the twelve main requirements has approximately 300 sub-requirements or control measures, creating a hierarchical structure where the control objectives are supported by increasingly detailed and specific requirements.

Additional resource: https://www.pcisecuritystandards.org/document_library/

Q6: Approximately how many sub-requirements or control measures exist across the twelve main PCI-DSS requirements?

a) 30 b) 100 c) 300 d) 3,000

A6: c) 300

According to the content, "Each of the twelve requirements has around three hundred sub-requirements or control measures." This indicates that across all twelve main requirements, there are approximately 300 total sub-requirements that organizations must implement to be compliant with PCI-DSS. This number demonstrates the comprehensive and detailed nature of the framework.

Additional resource: https://www.pcisecuritystandards.org/document_library/

Q7: According to the content, what two factors are equally important in reducing the risk of data breaches?

A7: According to the content, implementing appropriate security measures and correctly configuring those security measures are equally important in reducing the risk of data breaches. The text explicitly states: "Implementing the proper security measures can reduce the risk of data breaches, but equally important is implementing the measures correctly." This highlights that simply having security controls in place is insufficient if they are not properly implemented and configured.

Additional resource: https://www.pcisecuritystandards.org/documents/PCI_DSS_V4_0_At_A_Glance.pdf

Q8: True or False: Even organizations that don't process payment cards can benefit from implementing PCI-DSS as a security standard.

A8: True. The content explicitly states: "Even if you do not operate within the payment card industry, using it as a security standard will go a long way to securing your production environment." This indicates that the comprehensive nature of PCI-DSS makes it valuable as a general security framework, even for organizations that don't directly handle payment card data. Its technical and granular approach provides robust security measures applicable to many types of environments.

Additional resource: https://www.pcisecuritystandards.org/about_us/

Q9: Explain why correctly implementing security measures is as important as choosing appropriate measures according to the content.

A9: According to the content, correctly implementing security measures is as important as choosing appropriate ones because improper implementation can negate the protective benefits of even the most robust security controls. The content states: "Implementing the proper security measures can reduce the risk of data breaches, but equally important is implementing the measures correctly."

This emphasizes that security is not just about selecting the right controls, but also about how those controls are configured, managed, and maintained. Improperly implemented security measures may create a false sense of security while leaving vulnerabilities that could be exploited. For example, having a firewall in place (appropriate measure) is ineffective if it's misconfigured or has permissive rules (incorrect implementation).

The PCI-DSS framework recognizes this reality by establishing a binary compliance model where "you either comply with the controls and requirements or you do not - there is no in-between." This approach ensures that organizations not only implement the required security controls but also implement them correctly according to the standard's specifications.

Additional resource: https://www.pcisecuritystandards.org/pci_security/why_security_matters

Q10: What term does PCI-DSS use to describe the environment that needs to be secured and protected?

A10: PCI-DSS uses the term "cardholder data environment" or "CDE" to describe the environment that needs to be secured and protected. As mentioned in the content, "PCI-DSS is one of the world's most technical and granular security frameworks and can be applied to all organizations to secure and protect their cardholder data environments (CDE)." The CDE encompasses all systems, networks, and processes that store, process, or transmit cardholder data or sensitive authentication data, as well as any connected system components.

Additional resource: https://www.pcisecuritystandards.org/glossary/

Q11: Based on the content, what must an organization ensure to protect cardholder data?

a) Only authorized users have access to the data b) Data is stored in a secure environment c) Both a and b d) Neither a nor b

A11: c) Both a and b

According to the content, "to protect cardholder data, you must ensure that only authorized users have access to the data and that the data is stored in a secure environment." This example highlights two critical aspects of cardholder data protection: access control (limiting who can access the data) and secure storage (ensuring the environment where data is kept is protected). Both elements are necessary for comprehensive cardholder data protection.

Additional resource: https://www.pcisecuritystandards.org/documents/PCI_DSS_V4-0_Summary_of_Changes.pdf

Q12: What does CDE stand for in the context of PCI-DSS?

A12: In the context of PCI-DSS, CDE stands for "Cardholder Data Environment." As mentioned in the content, PCI-DSS is designed to "secure and protect their cardholder data environments (CDE)." The CDE encompasses all the people, processes, and technology that store, process, or transmit cardholder data or sensitive authentication data. It includes systems directly involved in payment card processing as well as connected systems that could impact the security of the cardholder data.

Additional resource: https://www.pcisecuritystandards.org/pci_security/glossary/

Q13: True or False: PCI-DSS allows for flexible interpretation of its requirements depending on the organization's size.

A13: False. According to the content, when it comes to PCI-DSS compliance, "you either comply with the controls and requirements or you do not - there is no in-between." This statement clearly indicates that PCI-DSS does not allow for flexible interpretation of its requirements regardless of an organization's size. The framework is designed to be implemented fully and correctly by all organizations that need to comply with it, without exceptions or partial implementation options.

Additional resource: https://www.pcisecuritystandards.org/pci_security/small_merchant_resources

Q14: How many main requirements does PCI-DSS have?

A14: PCI-DSS has twelve main requirements. The content explicitly states: "Within these six control objectives, there are twelve main requirements." These twelve main requirements form the core of the PCI-DSS framework, with each requirement containing numerous sub-requirements or control measures that provide specific implementation guidance. These twelve requirements are organized under the six control objectives and collectively address the various aspects of securing cardholder data environments.

Additional resource: https://www.pcisecuritystandards.org/pci_security/standard

Q15: Describe the overall goal of the six PCI-DSS control objectives according to the content.

A15: According to the content, the overall goal of the six PCI-DSS control objectives is to "ensure that their payment cardholder data is secure and protected from malicious actors." The content states explicitly: "By adhering to these control objectives, organizations can ensure that their payment cardholder data is secure and protected from malicious actors."

These six control objectives work together to secure the whole Cardholder Data Environment (CDE), creating a comprehensive security framework. Rather than focusing on isolated security measures, the control objectives address different aspects of security that collectively provide robust protection for cardholder data.

The control objectives establish a structured approach to security, with each objective containing specific requirements that must be met. Together, they create multiple layers of defense against potential threats, encompassing preventive, detective, and corrective controls that address the various ways cardholder data could be compromised.

The ultimate aim is to minimize the risk of data breaches and unauthorized access to sensitive payment card information, thereby protecting both the organization and its customers from the consequences of data theft.

Additional resource: https://www.pcisecuritystandards.org/pci_security/maintaining_payment_security

Q16: Which of the following is NOT mentioned as a characteristic of PCI-DSS in the content?

a) Technical b) Granular c) Cost-effective d) Comprehensive

A16: c) Cost-effective

In the content, PCI-DSS is described as "one of the world's most technical and granular security frameworks," but there is no mention of it being cost-effective. The content does imply that PCI-DSS is comprehensive by stating it "can be applied to all organizations to secure and protect their cardholder data environments" and mentioning that it has six control objectives, twelve main requirements, and around three hundred sub-requirements or control measures.

Additional resource: https://www.pcisecuritystandards.org/documents/PCI_DSS_V4_0_At_A_Glance.pdf

Q17: Fill in the blank: "By adhering to these control objectives, organizations can ensure that their payment cardholder data is _________ and _________ from malicious actors."

A17: "By adhering to these control objectives, organizations can ensure that their payment cardholder data is secure and protected from malicious actors."

This direct quote from the content emphasizes the dual goal of the PCI-DSS control objectives: to establish security for cardholder data and to provide protection against potential threats from malicious actors. The terms "secure" and "protected" highlight both the state that should be achieved (security) and the active defense (protection) that the framework provides.

Additional resource: https://www.pcisecuritystandards.org/pci_security/why_security_matters

Q18: What does the content specifically recommend memorizing for the PCIP exam?

A18: The content specifically recommends memorizing the Six Control Objectives for the PCIP exam. This is explicitly stated as a tip: "Memorize the Six Control Objectives for the PCIP exam." This indicates that understanding and being able to recall these six control objectives is likely to be important for success on the PCIP exam. The control objectives provide the high-level structure for the PCI-DSS framework, with specific requirements organized under each objective.

Additional resource: https://www.pcisecuritystandards.org/program/pcip_certification/

Q19: True or False: The content states that PCI-DSS is the only security framework that should be used by organizations handling payment card data.

A19: False. The content does not state that PCI-DSS is the only security framework that should be used. In fact, it implies the opposite by stating, "Keep in mind adopting an industry security standard can help protect your environment, but you must decide which standard best fits your situation." This suggests that organizations should evaluate different security standards and select the one most appropriate for their specific circumstances, rather than assuming PCI-DSS is always the sole or best option.

Additional resource: https://www.pcisecuritystandards.org/pci_security/

Q20: According to the content, what must organizations decide when considering security standards?

a) How much to spend on security b) Which standard best fits their situation c) How many staff to dedicate to security d) Whether to outsource security

A20: b) Which standard best fits their situation

The content explicitly states: "Keep in mind adopting an industry security standard can help protect your environment, but you must decide which standard best fits your situation." This indicates that organizations should evaluate their specific security needs, risks, and circumstances to determine which security standard will be most appropriate and effective for them, rather than applying a one-size-fits-all approach.

Additional resource: https://www.pcisecuritystandards.org/documents/Prioritized-Approach-for-PCI_DSS-v4_0.pdf

Q21: How does the content describe PCI-DSS compared to other security frameworks?

A21: The content describes PCI-DSS as "one of the world's most technical and granular security frameworks." This characterization highlights two key attributes that distinguish PCI-DSS from other security frameworks:

1. Technical: PCI-DSS is described as highly technical, meaning it contains specific, detailed technical requirements rather than just general principles or guidelines. This makes it particularly effective for addressing technical security controls.

2. Granular: The framework is characterized as granular, indicating it provides a high level of detail and specificity in its requirements. This is supported by the mention of "around three hundred sub-requirements or control measures" across the twelve main requirements.

These characteristics position PCI-DSS as a particularly comprehensive and detailed security framework compared to others that might be more principle-based or less specific in their technical requirements.

Additional resource: https://www.pcisecuritystandards.org/documents/PCI_DSS_v4-0.pdf

Q22: Explain the significance of the statement "you either comply with the controls and requirements or you do not - there is no in-between" in the context of PCI-DSS implementation.

A22: The statement "you either comply with the controls and requirements or you do not - there is no in-between" is significant because it establishes PCI-DSS as a binary compliance framework that requires full implementation of all applicable requirements without exception.

This approach is important for several reasons:

1. Consistency and Reliability: It ensures that all organizations claiming PCI-DSS compliance have implemented the same baseline of security controls, making the certification meaningful and reliable.

2. Security Effectiveness: It recognizes that security controls often work as an interconnected system, where partial implementation may leave critical vulnerabilities exposed, potentially rendering the entire security posture ineffective.

3. Rigor and Discipline: It enforces a disciplined approach to security implementation, preventing organizations from selectively implementing only the easiest or least expensive controls.

4. Clear Assessment Criteria: It provides clear criteria for assessors and auditors to evaluate compliance, reducing subjective interpretations.

5. Risk Management: It acknowledges that in security, a single gap or missed control can compromise an entire environment, reflecting the reality that attackers only need to find one vulnerability to succeed.

This binary compliance model contrasts with more flexible frameworks that might allow for risk-based implementation or compensating controls. While potentially more demanding, the PCI-DSS approach helps ensure that cardholder data environments maintain a consistent, comprehensive level of protection against threats.

Additional resource: https://blog.pcisecuritystandards.org/pci-dss-v4-0-resource-guide

Q23: What is emphasized as being "equally important" to implementing appropriate security measures?

A23: According to the content, correctly configuring or implementing those security measures is emphasized as being "equally important" to implementing appropriate security measures. The exact quote is: "Implementing the proper security measures can reduce the risk of data breaches, but equally important is implementing the measures correctly." This highlights that having the right security controls in place is only effective if those controls are properly configured, managed, and maintained. Poorly implemented security measures may create a false sense of security while still leaving vulnerabilities that can be exploited.

Additional resource: https://www.pcisecuritystandards.org/documents/PCI_DSS_V4_0_At_A_Glance.pdf

Q24: True or False: According to the content, the six control objectives of PCI-DSS work independently to secure different parts of the CDE.

A24: False. According to the content, "PCI-DSS uses six control objectives that work to secure the whole CDE." This statement indicates that the six control objectives work together as an integrated approach to secure the entire Cardholder Data Environment, rather than working independently on different parts. This holistic approach ensures comprehensive protection of cardholder data by addressing different aspects of security that collectively provide complete coverage of potential vulnerabilities and threats.

Additional resource: https://www.pcisecuritystandards.org/pci_security/standard

Q25: Based on the example provided in the content, what are two specific measures mentioned for protecting cardholder data?

A25: Based on the example provided in the content, the two specific measures mentioned for protecting cardholder data are:

1. Ensuring only authorized users have access to the data
2. Ensuring the data is stored in a secure environment

The content states explicitly: "For example, to protect cardholder data, you must ensure that only authorized users have access to the data and that the data is stored in a secure environment." These two measures address access control and secure storage respectively, which are fundamental aspects of data protection. Access control limits who can interact with the data, while secure storage ensures the environment containing the data is protected from unauthorized access or compromise.

Additional resource: https://www.pcisecuritystandards.org/documents/PCI_DSS_v4_ROC_Reporting_Template.pdf

19

The 12 PCI-DSS Requirements - Question Set

Q1: How many control objectives does the PCI-DSS framework contain, and how do they relate to the requirements?

A1: The PCI-DSS framework contains six control objectives, which serve as organizing principles for the twelve detailed requirements. Each control objective encompasses specific requirements that work together to address a particular security domain. The twelve requirements are distributed across these six objectives to provide a comprehensive approach to payment card data security. This hierarchical structure helps organizations understand how individual security controls contribute to broader security goals. When studying for the PCIP examination, it's essential to understand not only the individual requirements but also how they fit within the larger control objectives to create a cohesive security framework for protecting cardholder data.

Additional resource: https://www.pcisecuritystandards.org/pci_security/maintaining_payment_security

Q2: Which of the following requirements is specifically focused on cryptography during data transmission?

A) Requirement 2 B) Requirement 3 C) Requirement 4 D) Requirement 6

A2: The correct answer is C) Requirement 4.

Requirement 4 of the PCI-DSS states: "Protect cardholder data with strong cryptography during transmission over open, public networks." This requirement specifically addresses the security of cardholder data while in transit, mandating the use of strong cryptographic protocols, algorithms, and keys to encrypt sensitive information when it travels across public networks. This is distinct from Requirement 3, which focuses on protecting stored account data, and Requirements 2 and 6, which address secure configurations and secure development practices respectively. Properly implemented encryption during transmission prevents data interception and helps maintain the confidentiality of cardholder information.

Additional resource: https://blog.pcisecuritystandards.org/resource-guide-to-pci-dss-4-0

Q3: True or False: PCI-DSS Requirement 7 focuses on implementing antivirus solutions and other anti-malware defenses.

A3: False. PCI-DSS Requirement 7 actually focuses on "Restrict Access to system components and cardholder data on a 'Business Need To Know basis'." This requirement addresses access control policies, procedures, and measures to ensure that only authorized individuals with a legitimate business need can access cardholder data and system components.

The requirement that focuses on anti-malware defenses is Requirement 5: "Protect all systems and networks from malicious software." This requirement mandates the implementation of antivirus solutions, anti-malware programs, and other controls to detect, prevent, and respond to malicious software threats.

Confusing these requirements could lead to significant gaps in a security program, as access control (Requirement 7) and malware protection (Requirement 5) address different types of security risks within the cardholder data environment.

Additional resource: https://www.pcisecuritystandards.org/document_library

Q4: List and briefly explain the twelve requirements of PCI-DSS.

A4: The twelve requirements of PCI-DSS are:

1. Install and maintain network security controls - Implementing firewalls, network segmentation, and other security controls to protect the cardholder data environment from external threats.

2. Apply secure configurations to all system components - Ensuring all systems are configured securely, removing unnecessary functionality, and hardening systems against vulnerabilities.

3. Protect stored account data - Implementing data protection methods including encryption, truncation, and masking to secure stored cardholder data.

4. Protect cardholder data with strong cryptography during transmission - Using encryption and secure protocols when transmitting cardholder data across open, public networks.

5. Protect all systems and networks from malicious software - Implementing antivirus, anti-malware solutions, and keeping them updated to detect and prevent malicious software.

6. Develop and maintain secure systems and software - Following secure coding practices, addressing vulnerabilities promptly, and incorporating security throughout the software development lifecycle.

7. Restrict access to system components and cardholder data on a 'Business Need To Know basis' - Limiting access rights to only what is necessary for job responsibilities.

8. Identify users and authenticate access to system components - Implementing strong authentication methods to verify user identities before granting access.

9. Restrict physical access to cardholder data - Controlling physical access to facilities and systems containing cardholder data.

10. Log and monitor all access to system components and cardholder data - Implementing comprehensive logging mechanisms and regularly reviewing those logs.

11. Regularly test the security of systems and networks - Conducting vulnerability scans, penetration tests, and other security assessments.

12. Support information security with organizational policies and programs - Maintaining a comprehensive security policy and ensuring all personnel are aware of their security responsibilities.

These requirements form the foundation of PCI-DSS compliance and help organizations establish a robust security posture for protecting payment card data.

Additional resource: https://www.pcisecuritystandards.org/pci_security/standards_overview

Q5: Which of the following would be classified under Requirement 8 of PCI-DSS?

A) Encrypting cardholder data during transmission B) Implementing multi-factor authentication for administrators C) Installing and updating anti-virus software D) Conducting quarterly vulnerability scans

A5: The correct answer is B) Implementing multi-factor authentication for administrators.

Requirement 8 of PCI-DSS states: "Identify users and authenticate access to system components." This requirement focuses on authentication mechanisms to verify user identities before granting access to system components. Multi-factor authentication for administrators is a key control under this requirement, as it provides stronger verification of identity by requiring multiple authentication factors.

The other options relate to different PCI-DSS requirements:

- A) Encrypting cardholder data during transmission falls under Requirement 4
- C) Installing and updating anti-virus software falls under Requirement 5
- D) Conducting quarterly vulnerability scans falls under Requirement 11

Proper authentication controls are essential for preventing unauthorized access to sensitive systems and data, making Requirement 8 a critical component of a comprehensive security program.

Additional resource: https://www.pcisecuritystandards.org/documents/PCI_DSS_v4-0_SAQ_D_Merchant.pdf

Q6: Explain the concept of "Business Need to Know" as referenced in Requirement 7 and how organizations should implement it.

A6: The "Business Need to Know" principle, as referenced in PCI-DSS Requirement 7, is a fundamental access control concept that restricts access to system components and cardholder data to only those individuals whose job responsibilities require such access. This principle is based on the premise that excessive access privileges increase security risks.

To implement this principle effectively, organizations should:

1. Establish a formal access control policy that defines job roles, responsibilities, and corresponding access needs.
2. Implement role-based access control (RBAC) where access rights are assigned based on job functions rather than individual identities.

3. Practice the principle of least privilege, granting only the minimum access necessary for employees to perform their job functions.

4. Implement a documented approval process for all access requests that validates the business need.

5. Conduct periodic access rights reviews to identify and remove excessive privileges.

6. Implement procedures for immediate revocation of access when an employee changes roles or leaves the organization.

7. Maintain documentation of all access authorizations and reviews.

8. Segment the cardholder data environment to further restrict access to sensitive data.

By rigorously applying the "Business Need to Know" principle, organizations can significantly reduce the risk of unauthorized access to cardholder data and minimize the potential impact of compromised user accounts.

Additional resource: https://www.pcisecuritystandards.org/documents/Prioritized-Approach-for-PCI-DSS-v4_0.pdf

Q7: True or False: PCI-DSS Requirement 10 requires organizations to retain access logs for at least one year, with a minimum of three months immediately available for analysis.

A7: True. PCI-DSS Requirement 10, which addresses logging and monitoring, specifies that organizations must "Log and monitor all access to system components and cardholder data." As part of this requirement, organizations must retain audit logs for at least one year, with a minimum of three months immediately available for analysis (online, archived, or restorable from backup).

This retention requirement ensures that organizations have sufficient historical data to conduct thorough investigations in case of security incidents. The three-month immediate availability requirement facilitates prompt analysis of recent activities, enabling quicker detection and response to security issues. The full year of retention supports more comprehensive investigations and trend analysis that might require historical data.

Proper implementation of these logging retention requirements is crucial for effective security monitoring, incident response, and compliance validation.

Additional resource: https://blog.pcisecuritystandards.org/pci-dss-v4-0-is-available-now-plan-for-the-transition

Q8: Which of the following requirements focuses on organizational security policies and programs?

A) Requirement 9 B) Requirement 10 C) Requirement 11 D) Requirement 12

A8: The correct answer is D) Requirement 12.

Requirement 12 of PCI-DSS states: "Support information security with organizational policies and programs." This requirement focuses on establishing, maintaining, and communicating comprehensive security policies and programs that support the implementation of all PCI-DSS requirements throughout the organization.

Requirement 12 covers various policy-related aspects including:

- Maintaining an overall security policy

- Implementing risk assessment processes
- Establishing personnel security policies
- Creating incident response procedures
- Managing service providers
- Conducting security awareness training

The other options relate to different PCI-DSS requirements:

- A) Requirement 9 focuses on restricting physical access to cardholder data
- B) Requirement 10 addresses logging and monitoring
- C) Requirement 11 concerns regularly testing security systems and processes

Requirement 12 is often considered the foundation for all other requirements, as it establishes the governance framework for an organization's security program.

Additional resource: https://www.pcisecuritystandards.org/documents/PCI_DSS_v4_ROC_Reporting_Template.pdf

Q9: Describe the primary security controls that should be implemented to satisfy Requirement 1 regarding network security.

A9: To satisfy PCI-DSS Requirement 1, "Install and maintain network security controls," organizations must implement several critical security controls:

1. Network Firewalls: Deploy firewalls at every internet connection and between any demilitarized zone (DMZ) and the internal network to filter unwanted traffic and protect the cardholder data environment.
2. Network Segmentation: Implement network segmentation to isolate the cardholder data environment from other parts of the network, limiting the scope of PCI-DSS compliance and reducing risk.
3. Secure Configuration of Firewalls and Routers: Establish secure configurations for all network security devices, including documentation of security settings, business justification for all services and ports, and secure administration.
4. Inbound and Outbound Traffic Filtering: Configure network security controls to deny all traffic except that which is specifically needed for business purposes.
5. Stateful Inspection: Implement stateful inspection (dynamic packet filtering) to allow only established connections and deny all other traffic.
6. Security Between Wireless Networks: Implement firewalls between all wireless networks and the cardholder data environment, with strict rules restricting traffic to authorized business needs.
7. Regular Review and Documentation: Establish processes for regular review of firewall and router rule sets, with full documentation of network connections and configurations.

8. Personal Firewall Software: For mobile computing devices with direct connectivity to the internet, implement personal firewall software to protect these devices.

Effective implementation of these controls creates multiple layers of defense that significantly reduce the risk of unauthorized access to the cardholder data environment.

Additional resource: https://www.pcisecuritystandards.org/documents/Prioritized-Approach-for-PCI-DSS-v4_0.pdf

Q10: What are the primary differences between Requirement 3 (Protect stored account data) and Requirement 4 (Protect cardholder data during transmission)?

A10: Requirement 3 and Requirement 4 of PCI-DSS address different aspects of cardholder data protection:

Requirement 3: Protect stored account data

- Focuses on data at rest (stored data)
- Addresses protection methods for data that is maintained in databases, files, backups, etc.
- Includes controls such as:
  - Minimizing storage of sensitive authentication data after authorization
  - Masking display of PAN when displayed
  - Secure storage using encryption, truncation, tokenization, or hashing
  - Protecting cryptographic keys used for encryption
  - Implementing key management procedures
  - Documenting all key management operations

Requirement 4: Protect cardholder data during transmission

- Focuses on data in transit (moving across networks)
- Addresses protection methods for data that is being transmitted over open, public networks
- Includes controls such as:
  - Using strong cryptography and security protocols (e.g., TLS, SSH, IPSEC)
  - Ensuring only trusted keys and certificates are accepted
  - Implementing proper TLS protocol configuration
  - Using appropriate encryption strength for the encryption methodology in use
  - Ensuring wireless networks transmitting cardholder data use industry best practices

The key difference is the state of the data being protected: Requirement 3 focuses on protecting data that is stored within the organization's systems, while Requirement 4 focuses on protecting data as it moves between systems, particularly over public networks. Both requirements may use similar technologies (encryption) but apply them to different scenarios and with different implementation details.

Additional resource: https://www.pcisecuritystandards.org/documents/PCI_DSS_v4-0_Summary_of_Changes.pdf

Q11: Which of the following is NOT a primary focus of Requirement 11?

A) Vulnerability scanning B) Penetration testing C) Encryption key management D) Intrusion detection systems

A11: The correct answer is C) Encryption key management.

Requirement 11 of PCI-DSS states: "Regularly test the security of systems and networks." This requirement focuses on implementing regular testing to identify and address vulnerabilities in systems and networks. The primary components of Requirement 11 include:

- Vulnerability scanning (both internal and external)
- Penetration testing
- Intrusion detection/prevention systems
- File integrity monitoring
- Change detection mechanisms

Encryption key management is not part of Requirement 11. Instead, it falls under Requirement 3: "Protect stored account data," which includes specific provisions for secure key management practices when encryption is used to protect stored cardholder data.

Regularly testing security systems and networks is crucial for identifying weaknesses before they can be exploited by attackers, making Requirement 11 an essential component of a proactive security program.

Additional resource: https://blog.pcisecuritystandards.org/understanding-the-intent-of-pci-dss-requirements

Q12: Describe a comprehensive approach to implementing Requirement 6: "Develop and maintain secure systems and software."

A12: A comprehensive approach to implementing PCI-DSS Requirement 6: "Develop and maintain secure systems and software" should include the following key elements:

1. Secure Software Development Lifecycle (SDLC):
    - Incorporate security throughout all phases of the development process
    - Implement formal change control procedures
    - Separate development/test environments from production

- Ensure separation of duties between development and production environments

2. Secure Coding Practices:
    - Develop applications based on secure coding guidelines (e.g., OWASP)
    - Train developers in secure coding techniques
    - Address common coding vulnerabilities (e.g., injection flaws, cross-site scripting)
    - Implement code review practices to identify security issues
3. Vulnerability Management:
    - Establish a process to identify and assign risk rankings to newly discovered security vulnerabilities
    - Ensure security patches are installed within appropriate timeframes based on risk (critical patches within one month)
    - Develop patch management procedures for all system components
4. Security in Custom Software:
    - Prevent common coding vulnerabilities in software development
    - Review custom code prior to release to identify potential coding vulnerabilities
    - Follow change control procedures for all changes to system components
5. Secure Application Management:
    - Remove development, test, and/or custom accounts, user IDs, and passwords before applications become active
    - Review custom code to identify vulnerabilities prior to production deployment or customer release
6. Web Application Security:
    - Protect web-facing applications against known attacks
    - Implement a web application firewall (WAF) or regular security assessments
7. Change Management:
    - Document impact of all changes
    - Obtain appropriate approval before implementing changes
    - Test changes for potential security impacts
8. Security Testing:
    - Conduct security testing after significant changes

- Include regression testing to verify that changes do not adversely affect existing security controls

By implementing these elements, organizations can establish a robust approach to secure systems and software development, reducing the risk of security vulnerabilities that could lead to data breaches.

Additional resource: https://www.pcisecuritystandards.org/documents/Software-Security-Framework-Secure-Software-Requirements.pdf

Q13: True or False: Under PCI-DSS, all twelve requirements must be fully implemented regardless of an organization's size or transaction volume.

A13: False. While all twelve PCI-DSS requirements apply to organizations that store, process, or transmit cardholder data, the specific implementation details and validation requirements can vary based on an organization's size, transaction volume, and processing methods.

The PCI Security Standards Council defines different merchant levels (typically 1-4) based primarily on transaction volume. These levels determine the validation requirements and may affect how organizations implement the twelve requirements:

- Level 1 merchants (highest transaction volume) typically require the most rigorous validation methods, including annual on-site assessments by a Qualified Security Assessor (QSA).
- Lower-level merchants may be eligible to complete Self-Assessment Questionnaires (SAQs), which vary in complexity based on how the organization handles cardholder data.

Additionally, different SAQ types (A, A-EP, B, B-IP, C, C-VT, D, P2PE) represent different implementation scenarios, with some requirements being "not applicable" depending on how cardholder data is handled.

However, it's important to note that while validation requirements differ, the fundamental security principles represented by the twelve requirements still apply to all organizations handling cardholder data. The difference is in how extensively certain controls need to be implemented based on the organization's specific environment and risk profile.

Additional resource: https://www.pcisecuritystandards.org/documents/PCI-DSS-v4-0-SAQs-and-Attestations.zip

Q14: How does Requirement 9 (Restrict physical access to cardholder data) contribute to the overall security posture of an organization?

A14: Requirement 9 of PCI-DSS, "Restrict physical access to cardholder data," significantly strengthens an organization's overall security posture by addressing critical physical security controls that complement technical measures. Its contributions include:

1. Defense-in-Depth Strategy: Creates an additional security layer that attackers must overcome, complementing logical access controls with physical barriers.
2. Prevention of Direct Data Theft: Restricts unauthorized personnel from physically accessing servers, workstations, or media containing cardholder data, preventing direct theft or tampering.
3. Protection Against Hardware Tampering: Prevents the installation of rogue devices (e.g., hardware keyloggers, card skimmers) that could capture cardholder data.

4. Media Protection: Ensures proper management of physical media containing cardholder data through secure storage, classification, and disposal procedures.

5. Visitor Management: Implements controls for identifying and monitoring visitors, reducing the risk of social engineering attacks or unauthorized access.

6. Device Security: Secures point-of-interaction (POI) devices from tampering or substitution through periodic inspections and inventory controls.

7. Documentation Support: Facilitates incident investigations by maintaining logs of physical access to sensitive areas.

8. Environmental Controls: Often includes protection against environmental threats (fire, flood, power failure) that could impact data availability or integrity.

9. Employee Awareness: Reinforces the importance of data protection through visible security measures.

10. Regulatory Compliance: Satisfies both PCI-DSS requirements and often other regulatory mandates that require physical security controls.

By implementing robust physical security controls, organizations ensure that their technical security measures aren't undermined by physical vulnerabilities, creating a more comprehensive security program that protects cardholder data from multiple threat vectors.

Additional resource: https://www.pcisecuritystandards.org/documents/PCI_DSS_v4-0_ROC_Reporting_Template.pdf

Q15: What is the relationship between the six control objectives and the twelve requirements in PCI-DSS?

A15: The relationship between the six control objectives and the twelve requirements in PCI-DSS is hierarchical and organized to provide a comprehensive security framework:

The six control objectives represent broad security goals or categories that organizations should achieve to protect cardholder data. Each control objective encompasses specific requirements (from the twelve requirements) that work together to address a particular security domain:

1. **Build and Maintain a Secure Network and Systems**
    - Requirement 1: Install and maintain network security controls
    - Requirement 2: Apply secure configurations to all system components
2. **Protect Account Data**
    - Requirement 3: Protect stored account data
    - Requirement 4: Protect cardholder data with strong cryptography during transmission over open, public networks
3. **Maintain a Vulnerability Management Program**
    - Requirement 5: Protect all systems and networks from malicious software

- Requirement 6: Develop and maintain secure systems and software

4. **Implement Strong Access Control Measures**
    - Requirement 7: Restrict access to system components and cardholder data on a 'Business Need To Know basis'
    - Requirement 8: Identify users and authenticate access to system components
    - Requirement 9: Restrict physical access to cardholder data
5. **Regularly Monitor and Test Networks**
    - Requirement 10: Log and monitor all access to system components and cardholder data
    - Requirement 11: Regularly test the security of systems and networks
6. **Maintain an Information Security Policy**
    - Requirement 12: Support information security with organizational policies and programs

This structure helps organizations understand how individual requirements contribute to broader security goals. The control objectives provide the "why" (the security goals), while the requirements provide the "what" (specific controls to implement). Together, they create a framework that addresses multiple aspects of information security, from network protection to policy development, ensuring a comprehensive approach to protecting cardholder data.

Additional resource: https://www.pcisecuritystandards.org/pci_security/standards_overview

Q16: In the context of Requirement 5, what are the key controls organizations should implement to protect against malicious software?

A16: In the context of PCI-DSS Requirement 5, "Protect all systems and networks from malicious software," organizations should implement the following key controls:

1. Anti-Virus/Anti-Malware Deployment:
    - Deploy anti-virus/anti-malware solutions on all systems commonly affected by malicious software (particularly personal computers and servers)
    - Ensure coverage extends to all system components in the cardholder data environment
2. Maintenance and Updates:
    - Keep all anti-virus mechanisms current with the latest software versions
    - Install the latest security updates/patches
    - Enable automatic updates where technically feasible
3. Active Running Status:

- Ensure anti-virus engines are actively running at all times
- Implement controls to prevent users from disabling or altering security settings

4. Regular Scanning:
   - Configure solutions to perform periodic scans
   - Generate audit logs that are retained in accordance with Requirement 10
5. Malware Detection and Response:
   - Configure anti-malware solutions to detect all known types of malicious software
   - Remove or quarantine identified malicious software
   - Alert personnel to detected threats
6. Alternative Controls for Systems Not Commonly Affected:
   - For systems not typically affected by malware (e.g., certain mainframes, specialized appliances), perform periodic risk assessments
   - Document results and implement alternative controls if needed
7. Awareness and Training:
   - Educate users about malware risks, particularly from phishing and other social engineering attacks
   - Train users on proper procedures for reporting suspected malware
8. Multi-layered Defense:
   - Implement multiple prevention methods where feasible (e.g., network-based anti-malware, endpoint protection, web filtering)
9. Security Event Monitoring:
   - Integrate anti-malware logs with security monitoring systems
   - Establish procedures for responding to malware alerts
10. Regular Testing and Validation:
    - Periodically test anti-malware effectiveness using test files or simulations
    - Validate that alerts are properly generated and received

Effective implementation of these controls creates a robust defense against malicious software that could compromise the cardholder data environment.

Additional resource: https://blog.pcisecuritystandards.org/pci-dss-v4-0-establishing-evolving-security-programs

Q17: Which of the following is most closely associated with Requirement 10 of PCI-DSS?

A) Implementing secure coding practices B) Conducting penetration testing C) Creating audit trails D) Encrypting transmitted data

A17: The correct answer is C) Creating audit trails.

Requirement 10 of PCI-DSS states: "Log and monitor all access to system components and cardholder data." This requirement is primarily focused on creating and maintaining audit trails through comprehensive logging mechanisms to track user activities, system events, and access to cardholder data. These audit trails serve as evidence for investigating security incidents and demonstrating compliance.

Key components of Requirement 10 include:

- Implementing automated audit trails for all system components
- Recording specific details for each access event
- Synchronizing all system clocks
- Securing audit trails from unauthorized modifications
- Reviewing logs and security events
- Retaining audit trail history for at least one year

The other options relate to different PCI-DSS requirements:

- A) Implementing secure coding practices is associated with Requirement 6
- B) Conducting penetration testing is associated with Requirement 11
- D) Encrypting transmitted data is associated with Requirement 4

Effective logging and monitoring is essential for detecting unauthorized access attempts, tracking user activities, and providing necessary information for security incident investigations.

Additional resource: https://www.pcisecuritystandards.org/documents/PCI_DSS_v4-0_Summary_of_Changes.pdf

Q18: Explain the concept of "defense in depth" as it applies to the PCI-DSS requirements.

A18: Defense in depth is a cybersecurity strategy that employs multiple layers of security controls throughout an organization's systems and processes. When applied to PCI-DSS, this concept is evident across the twelve requirements, which collectively create overlapping layers of protection for cardholder data.

In the context of PCI-DSS, defense in depth manifests in several ways:

1. Multiple Security Layers: The twelve requirements establish different security layers, from network controls (Requirement 1) to application security (Requirement 6) to physical access restrictions (Requirement 9). If one layer is compromised, others remain to protect the data.

2. Preventive, Detective, and Corrective Controls:

   - Preventive controls: Secure configurations (Requirement 2), access restrictions (Requirements 7-9), and encryption (Requirements 3-4)

   - Detective controls: Logging and monitoring (Requirement 10), vulnerability scanning (Requirement 11)

   - Corrective controls: Incident response procedures (Requirement 12), patch management (Requirement 6)

3. Technical and Administrative Safeguards: PCI-DSS combines technical solutions like firewalls and encryption with administrative measures like policies, procedures, and training.

4. Protection at Different Data States:

   - Data at rest: Protected through Requirement 3 (encryption, truncation, etc.)

   - Data in transit: Protected through Requirement 4 (encryption during transmission)

   - Data in use: Protected through Requirements 7-8 (access controls, authentication)

5. Complementary Requirements: Requirements often complement each other. For example, access controls (Requirement 7) are complemented by authentication mechanisms (Requirement 8) and logging (Requirement 10).

6. Internal and External Protection: Defenses address both external threats (firewalls, encryption) and internal threats (access controls, separation of duties).

This layered approach ensures that the compromise of a single control doesn't lead to a complete security failure. By implementing all twelve requirements, organizations create a comprehensive security posture where multiple controls must be bypassed to compromise cardholder data, significantly reducing the risk of successful attacks.

Additional resource: https://www.pcisecuritystandards.org/documents/Prioritized-Approach-for-PCI-DSS-v4_0.pdf

Q19: True or False: PCI-DSS Requirement 2 primarily focuses on implementing strong cryptography for stored cardholder data.

A19: False. PCI-DSS Requirement 2 does not primarily focus on implementing strong cryptography for stored cardholder data. Requirement 2 states: "Apply secure configurations to all system components."

Requirement 2 focuses on ensuring that systems are securely configured by:

- Implementing vendor-supplied security parameter settings or industry-accepted hardening standards

- Changing default passwords and other security parameters

- Implementing necessary security functions on all system components

- Disabling unnecessary services, protocols, and ports
- Implementing secure configuration standards for all system components
- Addressing common security vulnerabilities in system configurations
- Encrypting all non-console administrative access

The requirement that primarily focuses on implementing strong cryptography for stored cardholder data is Requirement 3: "Protect stored account data." Requirement 3 includes specific provisions for encryption, hashing, truncation, or other methods to protect stored cardholder data.

This distinction is important because secure configurations (Requirement 2) and encryption of stored data (Requirement 3) address different aspects of security and require different implementation approaches.

Additional resource: https://www.pcisecuritystandards.org/documents/PCI_DSS_v4-0_Summary_of_Changes.pdf

Q20: Describe how Requirement 8 (Identify users and authenticate access) and Requirement 7 (Restrict access based on need to know) work together to secure cardholder data.

A20: Requirements 7 and 8 of PCI-DSS work together as complementary controls to create a comprehensive access management framework that secures cardholder data:

Requirement 7: Restrict access based on need to know

- Defines WHO should have access to WHAT data or systems
- Establishes the principle that access should be limited to only what is needed for a person's job function
- Implements access control systems to enforce these restrictions
- Focuses on authorization (what a user is allowed to do)

Requirement 8: Identify users and authenticate access

- Defines HOW users prove their identity before access is granted
- Ensures that only legitimate users can access systems by verifying identity
- Implements authentication mechanisms (passwords, MFA, etc.)
- Focuses on authentication (proving who a user is)

How they work together:

1. Sequential Implementation: Authentication (Requirement 8) occurs first to verify identity, then authorization (Requirement 7) determines what the authenticated user can access.
2. Complementary Protection: Requirement 8 ensures only legitimate users gain access, while Requirement 7 ensures those legitimate users can only access appropriate resources.

3. Principle Implementation: Together they implement the security principles of:
    - Identification (claiming an identity)
    - Authentication (proving that identity)
    - Authorization (determining permitted actions)
4. Defense in Depth: If one control fails (e.g., a password is compromised), the other control (limited privileges) can still minimize damage.
5. Comprehensive Coverage:
    - Requirement 7 addresses logical access rights and privileges
    - Requirement 8 addresses account management and authentication methods
    - Together they cover the full spectrum of access control
6. Accountability Support: Both requirements support accountability by ensuring that system access can be attributed to specific, authenticated individuals who have been granted specific permissions.

When properly implemented together, these requirements ensure that only authorized individuals can access cardholder data, and even those individuals can only access what they legitimately need for their business functions, significantly reducing the risk of data breaches.

Additional resource: https://blog.pcisecuritystandards.org/preparing-for-pci-dss-v4-0-authentication-and-access-control

Q21: What types of testing are required under Requirement 11, and what is the purpose of each testing method?

A21: Requirement 11 of PCI-DSS, "Regularly test the security of systems and networks," mandates several types of testing to identify and address security vulnerabilities. Each testing method serves a specific purpose in the overall security assessment strategy:

1. **Wireless Access Point Scanning**
    - Frequency: Quarterly or after significant network changes
    - Purpose: Identify unauthorized wireless access points that could provide uncontrolled access to the cardholder data environment
    - Implementation: Using wireless analyzers, wireless IDS/IPS, or physical site inspections
2. **Internal Vulnerability Scanning**
    - Frequency: Quarterly and after significant changes
    - Purpose: Identify internal vulnerabilities in systems and applications that could be exploited
    - Implementation: Using qualified internal resources or external third parties

- Additional requirement: Rescanning until all "high" vulnerabilities are resolved

3. **External Vulnerability Scanning**
   - Frequency: Quarterly and after significant changes
   - Purpose: Identify vulnerabilities in external-facing systems that could be exploited by attackers
   - Implementation: Must be performed by a PCI SSC Approved Scanning Vendor (ASV)
   - Additional requirement: Rescanning until passing scan results are achieved
4. **Penetration Testing**
   - Frequency: At least annually and after significant changes
   - Purpose: Actively test security controls by attempting to exploit vulnerabilities
   - Types:
     - Network-layer penetration tests (both internal and external)
     - Application-layer penetration tests
   - Implementation: Based on industry-accepted approaches, performed by qualified personnel
5. **Network Intrusion Detection/Prevention Systems (IDS/IPS)**
   - Purpose: Monitor network traffic for suspicious activity indicating potential compromises
   - Implementation: Continuously operating systems that generate alerts when potential intrusions are detected
6. **File Integrity Monitoring**
   - Purpose: Detect unauthorized modifications to critical system files, configuration files, or content files
   - Implementation: Software that alerts personnel to unauthorized modifications
   - Frequency: Run at least weekly, though real-time alerting is recommended
7. **Change Detection Mechanisms**
   - Purpose: Detect unauthorized modifications to critical system files, configuration files, or content files
   - Implementation: Complementary to file integrity monitoring, may include different approaches
   - Frequency: Run at least weekly

Each testing method addresses different aspects of security, from identifying vulnerabilities to detecting potential intrusions or unauthorized changes. Together, they provide a comprehensive approach to security testing that helps organizations maintain a strong security posture and identify weaknesses before they can be exploited by attackers.

Additional resource: https://blog.pcisecuritystandards.org/prepare-for-pci-dss-4-0-implement-a-targeted-risk-analysis

Q22: You are designing a security strategy for a new e-commerce platform that will process credit card transactions. Which PCI-DSS requirements would be most relevant to ensuring secure transmission of cardholder data during online purchases?

A22: When designing a security strategy for a new e-commerce platform focusing on secure transmission of cardholder data during online purchases, the following PCI-DSS requirements are most relevant:

Primary Requirements:

1. **Requirement 4: Protect cardholder data with strong cryptography during transmission**
    - Implement strong TLS/SSL for all web pages that transmit cardholder data
    - Configure TLS with appropriate protocols, encryption strengths, and certificate management
    - Ensure only trusted keys and certificates are accepted
    - Document and verify all transmission processes for cardholder data
2. **Requirement 2: Apply secure configurations to all system components**
    - Implement secure configurations for web servers, application servers, and databases
    - Disable unnecessary services and protocols
    - Configure systems according to industry-accepted hardening standards
    - Ensure TLS is properly configured with secure protocols and cipher suites
3. **Requirement 6: Develop and maintain secure systems and software**
    - Follow secure coding practices for the e-commerce application
    - Address common coding vulnerabilities (e.g., OWASP Top 10)
    - Implement a secure SDLC with security testing before production
    - Consider implementing a WAF to protect web applications

Supporting Requirements:

1. **Requirement 1: Install and maintain network security controls**
    - Implement firewalls to protect the cardholder data environment
    - Configure network security controls to limit inbound and outbound traffic
2. **Requirement 3: Protect stored account data**

    - If temporary storage is needed during transmission, implement encryption
    - Consider tokenization to minimize storage of actual PANs
3. **Requirement 11: Regularly test security of systems and networks**
    - Conduct regular vulnerability scans and penetration tests of the e-commerce platform
    - Implement intrusion detection mechanisms to monitor for suspicious activity
4. **Requirement 10: Log and monitor all access to system components and cardholder data**
    - Implement logging for all transmission-related components
    - Monitor transaction flows for anomalies

This multi-layered approach ensures that cardholder data is protected throughout the transmission process by:

- Encrypting data during transmission (Req. 4)
- Securing the systems handling the transmissions (Req. 2)
- Ensuring the application code is secure (Req. 6)
- Testing and monitoring the environment (Req. 10, 11)

These measures collectively create a comprehensive security strategy specifically focused on the secure transmission of cardholder data during online purchases.

Additional resource: https://www.pcisecuritystandards.org/documents/PCI_DSS_v4-0_E-commerce_Guidelines.pdf

Q23: Compare and contrast the physical security controls in Requirement 9 with the logical access controls in Requirements 7 and 8.

A23: Physical security controls (Requirement 9) and logical access controls (Requirements 7 and 8) represent complementary approaches to protecting cardholder data, each focusing on different aspects of security:

Physical Security Controls (Requirement 9)

Focus:

- Restricts physical access to facilities, equipment, and media containing cardholder data
- Protects tangible assets and physical access points

Key Components:

- Facility entry controls (badges, key cards, biometrics)
- Video monitoring and access logs

- Physical media management and disposal procedures
- Point-of-interaction (POI) device security

Protection Mechanisms:

- Physical barriers (locked doors, cabinets, cages)
- Visitor management procedures
- Employee identification badges
- Device inspection and inventory procedures

Scope:

- Buildings, data centers, server rooms
- Physical media (paper, backup tapes, drives)
- Hardware devices (servers, workstations, POI devices)

Logical Access Controls (Requirements 7 and 8)

Focus:

- Restricts electronic access to systems and data
- Manages digital identities and access privileges

Key Components:

- Requirement 7: Access restriction based on job role and need-to-know
- Requirement 8: User identification and authentication mechanisms

Protection Mechanisms:

- Role-based access control systems
- Authentication factors (passwords, tokens, biometrics)
- Account management procedures
- Privilege assignment and management

Scope:

- Operating systems, applications, databases
- Networks, virtual environments

- Digital data and records

Key Differences:

1. Access Type:
    - Physical controls manage bodily presence and tangible asset access
    - Logical controls manage electronic and network-based access
2. Implementation Methods:
    - Physical controls use tangible mechanisms (locks, badges)
    - Logical controls use digital mechanisms (passwords, access control lists)
3. Circumvention Techniques:
    - Physical controls are bypassed through physical means (tailgating, lock picking)
    - Logical controls are bypassed through digital means (password cracking, privilege escalation)

Key Similarities:

1. Defense-in-Depth Strategy:
    - Both contribute to layered security approach
    - Each provides backup if the other is compromised
2. Principle Application:
    - Both implement least privilege and need-to-know principles
    - Both require identification, authentication, and authorization
3. Documentation Requirements:
    - Both require maintenance of access logs
    - Both require formal authorization processes

Together, physical and logical access controls create a comprehensive security framework that protects cardholder data from both physical and electronic threats, implementing the defense-in-depth concept that is fundamental to PCI-DSS.

Additional resource: https://www.pcisecuritystandards.org/documents/Prioritized-Approach-for-PCI-DSS-v4_0.pdf

Q24: Which of the following would be a violation of Requirement 3 regarding the protection of stored account data?

A) Storing hashed primary account numbers (PANs) using SHA-256 B) Storing full track data after authorization C) Displaying only the last four digits of a card number on receipts D) Using tokenization for stored card data

A24: The correct answer is B) Storing full track data after authorization.

Requirement 3 of PCI-DSS states: "Protect stored account data." This requirement includes specific provisions regarding the storage of sensitive authentication data, including track data. According to Requirement 3, full track data (from the magnetic stripe or chip) must not be stored after authorization, even if encrypted.

The other options are compliant with Requirement 3:

- A) Storing hashed PANs using SHA-256 is an acceptable method of protecting stored primary account numbers, provided a strong cryptographic hash function with appropriate salt is used.
- C) Displaying only the last four digits of a card number on receipts is compliant and is specifically required by PCI-DSS to protect cardholder data.
- D) Using tokenization for stored card data is an acceptable method of protecting cardholder data, as it replaces the PAN with a non-sensitive token value.

Storing sensitive authentication data (including track data, card verification codes/values, and PIN blocks) after authorization is explicitly prohibited by PCI-DSS because this data presents a high risk if compromised. Even with encryption, the storage of this data is not permitted after the authorization process is complete.

Additional resource: https://blog.pcisecuritystandards.org/fact-sheet-from-a-to-z-understanding-pci-dss-4.0-requirement-3.5.1.2

Q25: How does Requirement 12 support and integrate with the other eleven requirements of PCI-DSS?

A25: Requirement 12, "Support information security with organizational policies and programs," serves as the foundational framework that supports and integrates with the other eleven requirements of PCI-DSS in several crucial ways:

1. Policy Framework Integration

- Establishes the overall information security policy that references and incorporates all PCI-DSS requirements
- Creates the governance structure under which the technical and operational requirements operate
- Defines roles and responsibilities for implementing all other requirements

2. Risk Assessment Support

- Requires formal risk assessment processes that help prioritize and focus security efforts across all requirements
- Informs the implementation approach for other requirements based on identified risks

- Supports the justification for security controls and resource allocation

3. Personnel Management

- Establishes security awareness training that educates staff on all security requirements
- Defines background checks and hiring procedures for those handling cardholder data
- Creates accountability for adherence to all security requirements

4. Incident Response Coordination

- Establishes incident response procedures that address security breaches across all requirements
- Coordinates response activities when failures in other requirements occur
- Ensures proper detection, reporting, and remediation of security incidents

5. Vendor Management

- Establishes procedures for managing service providers who may impact multiple requirements
- Ensures third parties adhere to applicable PCI-DSS requirements
- Defines monitoring processes for service provider compliance

6. Operational Procedures

- Documents daily operational security procedures that implement controls from other requirements
- Establishes change management processes that affect system components across multiple requirements
- Creates operational security awareness through daily procedures

7. Documentation and Evidence

- Requires documentation that demonstrates compliance with all other requirements
- Establishes record-keeping procedures for all security activities
- Supports audit trails and compliance validation

8. Security Technology Usage

- Defines acceptable use policies for technologies implemented under other requirements
- Establishes guidelines for remote access technologies, wireless technologies, and portable devices
- Supports proper implementation of technical controls

9. Compliance Monitoring

- Establishes processes to monitor and test security controls implemented under other requirements
- Creates a framework for regular compliance reviews
- Supports ongoing validation of security measures

By establishing the organizational framework, policies, and procedures necessary for a comprehensive security program, Requirement 12 ensures that the technical and operational controls specified in the other eleven requirements are properly implemented, maintained, and monitored. It transforms individual security controls into a cohesive security program with proper governance, oversight, and continuous improvement mechanisms.

Additional resource: https://blog.pcisecuritystandards.org/preparing-for-pci-dss-v4-0-incorporating-security-into-business-as-usual-activities

20

Control Objective 1 - Question Set

Build and Maintain Secure Networks and Systems

Q1: What is the primary purpose of Network Security Controls (NSCs) according to Requirement 1 of PCI DSS?

A1: The primary purpose of Network Security Controls (NSCs) is to restrict network traffic between networks and provide crucial protection against potential threats from untrusted networks. NSCs act as gatekeepers that enforce security policies and decisions specifically at layer 3 of the OSI model. They safeguard sensitive areas, particularly the cardholder data environment (CDE), by preventing unauthorized access through unprotected pathways. NSCs create controlled boundaries between networks of different trust levels, ensuring that only properly authorized traffic passes through based on established security rules. In PCI DSS compliance, NSCs are fundamental components that help organizations maintain a secure network infrastructure for processing, storing, and transmitting cardholder data.

For more information: https://www.pcisecuritystandards.org/documents/PCI_DSS_v4-0.pdf

Q2: True or False: According to PCI DSS, an internal network that is considered trusted from an infrastructure perspective but is out of scope for PCI DSS assessment should still be treated as trusted for PCI DSS purposes.

A2: False. According to the provided content, even if an internal network is considered trusted from an infrastructure perspective, if it's out of scope for PCI DSS assessment, it must still be treated as untrusted for PCI DSS purposes. This is a critical security principle that ensures proper boundaries are maintained between networks that are verified as compliant with PCI DSS requirements and those that haven't been assessed. Treating out-of-scope networks as untrusted ensures that appropriate security controls are implemented to protect the cardholder data environment regardless of internal trust designations within the organization.

For more information: https://www.pcisecuritystandards.org/document_library/

Q3: Which of the following best describes the function of a DMZ in network security architecture?

A) A zone where all cardholder data is stored B) A secure buffer zone between public and private networks C) A type of encryption algorithm for data in transit D) A mandatory wireless network isolation area

A3: The correct answer is B) A secure buffer zone between public and private networks.

A DMZ (Demilitarized Zone) serves as a secure buffer zone or intermediate network segment placed between an organization's public-facing services and its private internal network. The DMZ contains systems that may need to be accessible from untrusted networks (like the internet) while providing a layer of separation from the organization's sensitive internal resources, including the cardholder data environment (CDE).

This architecture allows organizations to place public-facing servers in the DMZ while keeping the most sensitive systems and data in more protected internal network segments. By implementing a DMZ, organizations can add an extra layer of security by ensuring that even if a public-facing system is compromised, attackers still face additional barriers before reaching sensitive cardholder data. The DMZ concept is an important component of defense-in-depth security strategy in PCI DSS compliance.

For more information: https://www.pcisecuritystandards.org/glossary/

Q4: Explain the concept of an "implicit deny all rule" in the context of Network Security Controls and why it's important for PCI DSS compliance.

A4: An "implicit deny all rule" is a fundamental security principle applied to Network Security Controls (NSCs) where the default action is to block or deny all traffic unless specifically allowed by another rule. This means that any network traffic that doesn't match an explicit permission rule is automatically denied.

This approach is critical for PCI DSS compliance because it implements a security posture of "deny by default, allow by exception," which is significantly more secure than trying to identify and block all potential malicious traffic. With an implicit deny all rule in place:

1. Only specifically defined and authorized traffic can pass through the NSC
2. Any new types of traffic are automatically blocked until explicitly allowed
3. The organization maintains complete control over what communication is permitted
4. The risk of overlooking potentially dangerous traffic types is minimized

This principle supports the PCI DSS requirement to restrict traffic to only that which is necessary for business purposes. It places the burden of proof on allowing traffic rather than blocking it, ensuring that all permitted communications have been reviewed and approved. The implicit deny all rule serves as a critical last line of defense against unauthorized access attempts to the cardholder data environment.

For more information: https://www.pcisecuritystandards.org/pci_security/maintaining_payment_security

Q5: Which of the following are considered examples of Network Security Controls (NSCs) according to PCI DSS Requirement 1? (Select all that apply)

A) Physical firewalls B) Software-based firewalls C) Cloud-based firewalls (security groups) D) Antivirus software E) Data loss prevention systems

A5: The correct answers are A) Physical firewalls, B) Software-based firewalls, and C) Cloud-based firewalls (security groups).

According to the content provided, Network Security Controls (NSCs) specifically include:

- Physical firewalls (traditional hardware devices that filter network traffic)
- Software-based firewalls (firewall functionality implemented as software applications)
- Cloud-based firewalls, also known as security groups (SG) (virtual firewalls that operate in cloud environments)

While antivirus software and data loss prevention systems are important security controls that may be required by other PCI DSS requirements, they are not specifically identified as NSCs in Requirement 1. NSCs are distinguished by their role in enforcing policies and decisions at layer 3 of the OSI model to control traffic between networks of different trust levels.

It's important to understand the specific definition of NSCs for PCI DSS compliance purposes, as this determines which systems must comply with the specific configuration, documentation, and review requirements outlined in Requirement 1.

For more information: https://www.pcisecuritystandards.org/document_library/

Q6: How often must network security control rules be reviewed according to PCI DSS Requirement 1?

A) Monthly B) Quarterly C) Every six months D) Annually

A6: The correct answer is C) Every six months.

According to the key takeaways section in the provided content: "conducting firewall rule reviews every six months to meet compliance." This six-month review cycle is a specific requirement under PCI DSS Requirement 1. These regular reviews ensure that the network security control rules remain appropriate, effective, and aligned with the organization's current network architecture and business needs.

During these six-month reviews, organizations should:

1. Verify that all existing rules are still necessary for business operations
2. Confirm that rules have appropriate documentation and justification
3. Remove or update any rules that are no longer needed or require modification
4. Ensure that the rules continue to enforce the organization's security policy
5. Document the review process and its results

Regular reviews of network security control rules help prevent configuration drift, reduce the risk of unauthorized access, and maintain the security posture of the cardholder data environment over time.

For more information: https://www.pcisecuritystandards.org/documents/PCI_DSS_v4-0.pdf

Q7: What documentation is required to justify network traffic allowed through Network Security Controls according to PCI DSS Requirement 1?

A7: According to PCI DSS Requirement 1, organizations must document business justification for all allowed network traffic through Network Security Controls. The key documentation required includes:

1. A data flow diagram that maps the flow of account/cardholder data through the network
2. Specific business justification for each allowed inbound and outbound traffic flow
3. Documentation of the protocols, ports, and services permitted
4. Explanation of why each allowed traffic flow is necessary for business operations

The content specifically mentions that organizations should "maintain a data flow diagram of account data flow" and use this diagram to "justify network traffic." Additionally, organizations must "document business justification for allowing wired or wireless traffic."

This documentation serves multiple purposes:

- Provides clear rationale for why each communication path exists
- Helps identify unnecessary or risky traffic that could be eliminated
- Assists in regular rule reviews (conducted every six months)
- Demonstrates compliance during PCI DSS assessments
- Serves as a reference when evaluating proposed changes to the network

Proper documentation ensures that all allowed traffic has a legitimate business purpose and helps prevent the introduction of unnecessary security risks to the cardholder data environment.

For more information: https://www.pcisecuritystandards.org/documents/Prioritized-Approach-for-PCI-DSS-v4_0.pdf

Q8: Which of the following statements correctly describes how traffic from wireless networks should be handled with respect to the CDE according to PCI DSS Requirement 1?

A) All wireless traffic should be encrypted before entering the CDE B) Wireless traffic should be limited to authorized users only C) All traffic from wireless networks into the CDE should be blocked D) Wireless traffic should be routed through a separate VLAN before reaching the CDE

A8: The correct answer is C) All traffic from wireless networks into the CDE should be blocked.

According to the key takeaways in the provided content, PCI DSS Requirement 1 specifically emphasizes the need to "block all traffic from wireless networks into the CDE." This is a strict control measure designed to protect the cardholder data environment from the inherent risks associated with wireless networks.

Wireless networks are considered particularly vulnerable to various attacks such as eavesdropping, man-in-the-middle attacks, and unauthorized access. By completely blocking traffic from wireless networks into the CDE, organizations create a clear separation that prevents these wireless-specific threats from directly impacting the most sensitive components of their network infrastructure.

If wireless access to systems within the CDE is necessary for business operations, organizations typically need to implement alternative secure access methods, such as requiring users to connect through a VPN or other secure access solution rather than allowing direct wireless traffic into the CDE.

For more information: https://www.pcisecuritystandards.org/document_library/

Q9: What additional security measure is required for mobile and/or employee-owned devices connecting to the CDE according to PCI DSS Requirement 1?

A9: According to PCI DSS Requirement 1, organizations must activate personal firewall software on all devices connected to the CDE, including mobile and/or employee-owned devices. The content specifically states: "By activating personal firewall software on all devices connected to the CDE, you can add an extra layer of protection to your network."

Personal firewall software provides host-based protection that:

1. Controls inbound and outbound traffic at the individual device level
2. Helps protect against malware and unauthorized access attempts
3. Provides an additional security layer beyond network-based controls
4. Maintains protection when devices are used outside the organization's network

This requirement is particularly important for mobile and employee-owned devices (BYOD scenarios) because these devices may connect to multiple networks of varying security levels outside the organization's control. The personal firewall helps ensure that these devices don't become compromised while connected to less secure networks and subsequently introduce threats when reconnecting to the CDE.

Organizations should ensure that personal firewalls are properly configured, actively running, and cannot be altered or disabled by users without proper authorization. This control is an essential component of defense-in-depth strategy for protecting the cardholder data environment.

For more information: https://www.pcisecuritystandards.org/documents/PCI_DSS_v4-0.pdf

Q10: True or False: Under PCI DSS Requirement 2, it is acceptable to retain vendor-supplied default passwords on network devices as long as they are documented properly.

A10: False. PCI DSS Requirement 2 explicitly mandates that organizations must remove vendor defaults and parameters, which includes changing all system default settings, usernames, and passwords. The content clearly states that organizations must "change all system default settings, usernames, and passwords" to protect the environment and cardholder data from potential security vulnerabilities.

Vendor-supplied default passwords are a significant security risk because:

1. They are widely known and often publicly available

2. They are common targets in automated attacks

3. They may be identical across multiple installations of the same product

4. They often do not meet minimum password complexity requirements

Even with proper documentation, retaining default passwords violates a fundamental security principle of PCI DSS. Organizations must change all default passwords to strong, unique credentials as part of the system hardening process before placing systems into production. This applies to all system components including network devices, servers, applications, cloud services, and security systems.

For more information: https://www.pcisecuritystandards.org/glossary/

Q11: Describe the concept of "system hardening" as it relates to PCI DSS Requirement 2 and explain its importance in protecting cardholder data.

A11: System hardening refers to the process of securing a system by reducing its attack surface through the removal or disabling of unnecessary functions, features, accounts, services, ports, and protocols. In the context of PCI DSS Requirement 2, system hardening involves applying secure configurations to ALL system components to eliminate potential security vulnerabilities.

Key aspects of system hardening under Requirement 2 include:

1. Removing vendor defaults and parameters (especially default passwords)

2. Disabling features that are not needed for business operations

3. Removing unnecessary roles, functions, and modules on all system components

4. Eliminating unneeded software from systems

5. Configuring security parameters to prevent misuse

6. Encrypting non-console access with strong cryptography

7. Implementing only necessary services, protocols, and ports with appropriate justification

System hardening is crucial for protecting cardholder data because:

- It minimizes the potential attack vectors available to malicious actors
- It reduces the likelihood of exploitation through unnecessary or insecure services
- It eliminates commonly known vulnerabilities associated with default configurations
- It ensures systems operate with the principle of least functionality
- It creates a more controlled and secure environment for processing card data

The importance of system hardening is highlighted in the real-world example provided, where a company experienced a data breach because they failed to change default SNMP settings, including the default community string "public." This illustrates how unmodified default settings can lead directly to security compromises and data breaches.

System hardening should be implemented through formal build standards and configuration procedures to ensure consistency across the environment.

For more information: https://www.pcisecuritystandards.org/documents/Prioritized-Approach-for-PCI-DSS-v4_0.pdf

Q12: What layer of the OSI model do Network Security Controls (NSCs) primarily operate at according to PCI DSS Requirement 1?

A) Layer 1 (Physical) B) Layer 2 (Data Link) C) Layer 3 (Network) D) Layer 7 (Application)

A12: The correct answer is C) Layer 3 (Network).

According to the content provided, Network Security Controls (NSCs) "enforce policies and decisions at layer 3 of the OSI model to safeguard sensitive areas, such as the cardholder data environment (CDE), from unprotected pathways."

Layer 3 is the Network layer of the OSI model, which is responsible for packet forwarding, routing, and addressing functions. NSCs operating at this layer can:

1. Control traffic based on IP addresses (source and destination)
2. Filter packets based on network protocols
3. Implement routing decisions between different networks
4. Apply access control lists to permit or deny traffic
5. Segment networks based on security requirements

By operating at Layer 3, NSCs can effectively create boundaries between networks of different trust levels and control the movement of traffic between them. This is essential for implementing the network segmentation and access control requirements specified in PCI DSS.

While some modern firewalls and security solutions may incorporate functionality at multiple OSI layers (including application-layer inspection), the fundamental role of NSCs as defined in PCI DSS is focused on their Layer 3 capabilities for controlling traffic between networks.

For more information: https://www.pcisecuritystandards.org/document_library/

Q13: When configuring SNMP for network devices under PCI DSS Requirement 2, which of the following practices should be avoided?

A) Using the latest version of SNMP B) Implementing read-only community strings C) Using the default community string "public" D) Implementing IP-based access restrictions

A13: The correct answer is C) Using the default community string "public".

According to the real-world example provided in the content, a company experienced a data breach because "the system was configured with default SNMP settings, including the use of the default community string 'public'." The key takeaways section further reinforces this by stating the importance of "making sure we set up Simple Network Management Protocol (SNMP) in a way that keeps our data safe. This means using the latest version and not using default settings like 'public' that could be easily guessed by hackers."

Default SNMP community strings like "public" (for read access) and "private" (for write access) are widely known and represent a significant security vulnerability if not changed. Attackers specifically target these default strings in reconnaissance and attack attempts.

To properly secure SNMP under PCI DSS Requirement 2, organizations should:

1. Use the latest version of SNMP (preferably SNMPv3 which includes authentication and encryption)
2. Change default community strings to unique, complex values
3. Implement access controls to restrict which IP addresses can query SNMP
4. Use read-only community strings when write access is not required
5. Consider implementing SNMP over encrypted channels when possible

Properly securing SNMP is an important component of the overall system hardening process required by PCI DSS Requirement 2.

For more information: https://www.pcisecuritystandards.org/documents/PCI_DSS_v4-0.pdf

Q14: What action should be taken regarding encryption keys when an employee with knowledge of those keys leaves the organization according to PCI DSS Requirement 2?

A14: According to PCI DSS Requirement 2, when an employee with knowledge of encryption keys leaves the organization, the encryption keys should be changed. The content specifically states: "changing encryption keys when someone with knowledge leaves the organization further bolsters your security posture."

This requirement is based on the principle that access to encryption keys represents a significant security risk if that access extends beyond an individual's employment with the organization. When an employee departs:

1. There is no longer a business need for that individual to possess the key information
2. The organization cannot guarantee the former employee won't misuse the information
3. Keys that remain unchanged represent a potential security vulnerability
4. The confidentiality of encrypted data could be compromised

The process of changing encryption keys after personnel changes should be:

- Formally documented in the organization's key management procedures

- Executed promptly after the employee's departure
- Verified to ensure all affected systems are using the new keys
- Logged and recorded as part of the key management history

This practice applies to all types of encryption keys, including those used for encrypting stored data, securing communications, accessing systems, and signing code or transactions. By changing keys when personnel with knowledge leave, organizations maintain control over who can access protected information and systems.

For more information: https://www.pcisecuritystandards.org/document_library/

Q15: Requirement 1 of PCI DSS mandates the restriction of traffic between networks. Which statement best describes how inbound and outbound traffic should be handled?

A) All inbound traffic should be blocked, but outbound traffic can flow freely B) Inbound and outbound traffic should be restricted to only that which is necessary for business C) Inbound traffic should be encrypted, while outbound traffic should be logged D) Only traffic from known IP addresses should be allowed in either direction

A15: The correct answer is B) Inbound and outbound traffic should be restricted to only that which is necessary for business.

According to the key takeaways in the provided content, PCI DSS Requirement 1 emphasizes the need to "restrict inbound and outbound traffic to necessary communication only." This principle applies to both directions of traffic flow and implements the concept of least privilege at the network level.

By restricting traffic to only what is necessary for business operations:

1. The potential attack surface is minimized
2. Unnecessary communication paths that could be exploited are eliminated
3. Abnormal traffic patterns become easier to identify
4. The principle of "deny all except that which is explicitly allowed" is enforced
5. Both incoming threats and potential data exfiltration are addressed

This approach requires organizations to identify and document all legitimate business needs for communication across network boundaries. Any traffic that doesn't serve a documented business purpose should be blocked by network security controls. This comprehensive approach to traffic restriction applies to all network boundaries, including those between the internet and DMZ, between the DMZ and internal networks, and between the CDE and other internal networks.

For more information: https://www.pcisecuritystandards.org/documents/PCI_DSS_v4-0.pdf

Q16: What does PCI DSS Requirement 2 specify regarding non-console administrative access to system components?

A) It should be limited to necessary personnel only B) It should be encrypted with strong cryptography C) It should require multi-factor authentication D) It should be logged and monitored

A16: The correct answer is B) It should be encrypted with strong cryptography.

According to the content provided, PCI DSS Requirement 2 specifies that organizations must "encrypt all non-console access with strong cryptography." This is mentioned as one of the proactive measures to protect the environment and cardholder data from potential security vulnerabilities.

Non-console administrative access refers to any administrative access that occurs through a network interface rather than direct physical access to the system (console access). This includes methods such as:

1. SSH (Secure Shell)

2. HTTPS for web-based administration interfaces

3. RDP (Remote Desktop Protocol)

4. VNC (Virtual Network Computing)

5. Other remote administration tools and protocols

By requiring strong cryptography for these connections, PCI DSS ensures that administrative credentials and sensitive configuration information cannot be intercepted in transit. This protection is critical because administrative sessions often include privileged access to systems that process, store, or transmit cardholder data.

While the other options (limiting access to necessary personnel, requiring multi-factor authentication, and logging/monitoring) may be required by other PCI DSS requirements, the specific focus of the encryption requirement in Requirement 2 is to protect the confidentiality of administrative sessions through strong cryptography.

For more information: https://www.pcisecuritystandards.org/documents/Prioritized-Approach-for-PCI-DSS-v4_0.pdf

Q17: When implementing network security controls for PCI DSS compliance, what should be done with wireless networks in relation to the CDE?

A17: According to PCI DSS Requirement 1, organizations must "block all traffic from wireless networks into the CDE." This is a specific control requirement mentioned in the key takeaways section of the provided content.

The complete approach to handling wireless networks in relation to the cardholder data environment (CDE) includes:

1. Implementing a complete block of all traffic originating from wireless networks directly into the CDE

2. Treating all wireless networks as untrusted from a PCI DSS perspective

3. Documenting any business justification for allowing traffic between wireless networks and other segments (outside the

CDE)

4. Implementing personal firewall software on all devices connected to the CDE, which provides an additional layer of protection against wireless-based attacks

5. Creating clear network segmentation between wireless networks and the CDE

If there is a legitimate business need for wireless devices to access resources in the CDE, this should be implemented through indirect, controlled means, such as:

- Requiring VPN connections from wireless networks to establish an encrypted tunnel
- Implementing multi-factor authentication for access
- Using jump servers or secure access workstations as intermediaries
- Applying additional security controls and monitoring for these access paths

The strict separation between wireless networks and the CDE recognizes the inherent security risks associated with wireless communications and prevents these risks from directly affecting the most sensitive cardholder data environment.

For more information: https://www.pcisecuritystandards.org/document_library/

Q18: Multiple choice: According to PCI DSS Requirement 2, which of the following actions should be taken regarding unnecessary software, features, and functionality?

A) They should be documented but can remain enabled B) They should be disabled but not removed C) They should be removed or disabled completely D) They can remain if proper monitoring is in place

A18: The correct answer is C) They should be removed or disabled completely.

According to the content provided, PCI DSS Requirement 2 deals with "the hardening of systems and how organizations must remove vendor defaults and parameters. This includes disabling features that are not needed, such as roles and unnecessary modules on appliances, servers, desktops, laptops, and mobile devices." Additionally, it mentions "removing unnecessary software" as part of the proactive measures to protect the environment.

The requirement to remove or disable unnecessary software, features, and functionality is based on the security principle of reducing attack surface. Each enabled feature, function, or piece of software potentially:

1. Introduces vulnerabilities that could be exploited
2. Requires patching and maintenance
3. May provide unauthorized access paths
4. Increases the complexity of the security environment

By removing or disabling unnecessary components, organizations:

- Reduce potential vulnerabilities

- Simplify maintenance and updates
- Focus security resources on essential functionality
- Implement the principle of least functionality

This requirement applies to all system components in the cardholder data environment, including servers, workstations, network devices, applications, and cloud services. Organizations should develop and follow formal procedures to identify and remove unnecessary functionality as part of their system hardening process.

For more information: https://www.pcisecuritystandards.org/documents/PCI_DSS_v4-0.pdf

Q19: Essay question: Explain the relationship between data flow diagrams and network security control rule justification in PCI DSS Requirement 1. How do these elements work together to improve security?

A19: The relationship between data flow diagrams and network security control rule justification is foundational to implementing PCI DSS Requirement 1 effectively. These elements work together in a complementary fashion to create a comprehensive approach to network security that is both business-aligned and security-focused.

Data Flow Diagrams as the Foundation

Data flow diagrams (DFDs) provide a visual representation of how cardholder data moves through an organization's systems and networks. According to the content, organizations must "maintain a data flow diagram of account data flow" as part of their compliance efforts. These diagrams:

1. Map the complete journey of cardholder data from the point of entry to storage, processing, and transmission
2. Identify all systems, applications, and network segments that interact with cardholder data
3. Document the types of data that traverse each network path
4. Illustrate trust boundaries between different network segments
5. Show connections to external entities and third parties

Network Security Control Rule Justification

The key takeaways mention using the data flow diagram to "justify network traffic." This establishes a direct link between understanding data flows and creating appropriate security rules. Network security control rules must be:

1. Based on legitimate business requirements
2. Explicitly documented with clear justification
3. Reviewed every six months for continued relevance
4. Updated when network and system environments change

How They Work Together to Improve Security

The integration of data flow diagrams and rule justification creates a security approach that is:

1. Business-Aligned: By starting with data flows, security controls are directly tied to actual business processes rather than being arbitrary or disconnected from business needs. This ensures that legitimate business traffic is permitted while unnecessary traffic is blocked.

2. Comprehensive: The data flow diagram provides a complete picture of where protection is needed, helping to identify all required network security control rules. This prevents gaps in coverage where sensitive data might be exposed.

3. Minimal: Understanding the precise paths that cardholder data takes allows organizations to implement the principle of "deny all except that which is explicitly allowed." Only traffic that supports documented business functions is permitted, reducing the attack surface.

4. Justifiable: Each network security control rule has a clear business purpose tied to supporting a specific data flow. This eliminates "mystery rules" that exist without clear reasons and may introduce security weaknesses.

5. Maintainable: When business processes or data flows change, the impact on network security control rules is clear. The organization can update both the diagram and the corresponding rules to maintain alignment.

6. Verifiable: During compliance assessments, auditors can trace from business processes to data flows to security control rules, creating a chain of evidence that demonstrates proper protection.

This integrated approach ensures that network security controls are not implemented as isolated technical configurations but as business-justified security measures directly supporting the protection of cardholder data. By maintaining this relationship between data flows and security rules, organizations create a security posture that is both effective and efficient, blocking unnecessary access while enabling legitimate business operations.

For more information: https://www.pcisecuritystandards.org/documents/Prioritized-Approach-for-PCI-DSS-v4_0.pdf

Q20: True or False: According to PCI DSS Requirement 2, an organization can use default SNMP community strings if they are properly documented in the security policy.

A20: False. According to the content provided, specifically in the real-world example and key takeaways sections, using default SNMP settings, including the default community string "public," is explicitly identified as a security vulnerability that can lead to data breaches.

The content states: "The breach occurred because the system was configured with default SNMP settings, including the use of the default community string 'public.'" It further emphasizes in the key takeaways that organizations should make "sure we set up Simple Network Management Protocol (SNMP) in a way that keeps our data safe. This means using the latest version and not using default settings like 'public' that could be easily guessed by hackers."

Documentation alone does not mitigate the security risk posed by default settings. PCI DSS Requirement 2 focuses on applying secure configurations to all system components, which includes:

1. Removing vendor defaults and default parameters

2. Changing default settings to secure configurations

3. Using strong, unique values instead of known defaults

Default SNMP community strings like "public" are universally known and are among the first values attempted in attacks targeting SNMP. Proper documentation might record what settings are in use, but it does not address the fundamental security vulnerability created by using default values.

For SNMP to be configured securely under PCI DSS Requirement 2, organizations must:

- Change default community strings to unique, complex values
- Preferably use SNMPv3 with authentication and encryption
- Implement access controls to restrict which systems can use SNMP
- Disable SNMP if it is not needed for business operations

For more information: https://www.pcisecuritystandards.org/document_library/

Q21: What are Network Security Controls (NSCs) according to PCI DSS Requirement 1, and what forms can they take in different environments?

A21: According to PCI DSS Requirement 1, Network Security Controls (NSCs) are devices or technologies that enforce security policies and decisions at layer 3 of the OSI model to control traffic between networks of different trust levels. They provide crucial protection for computer networks against potential threats from untrusted networks.

NSCs can take several forms across different environments:

1. **Physical Firewalls**: Traditional hardware devices installed at network boundaries that filter traffic based on defined rule sets. These are typically used in on-premises data centers and corporate networks.

2. **Software-based Firewalls**: Firewall functionality implemented as software applications running on servers or endpoints. These can be used in various environments but are particularly useful for protecting individual systems.

3. **Cloud-based Firewalls/Security Groups (SG)**: Virtual firewalls that operate in cloud environments to control traffic between cloud resources and between the cloud and external networks. Examples include AWS Security Groups, Azure Network Security Groups, and Google Cloud Firewall Rules.

4. **Virtual Firewalls**: Firewall instances that run as virtual appliances in virtualized environments, providing network segmentation and traffic control within virtual infrastructures.

5. **Container Network Policies**: In containerized environments, network policies that control communication between container pods and services.

The content specifically mentions that NSCs "can be physical or virtual devices that enforce policies and decisions at layer 3 of the OSI model to safeguard sensitive areas, such as the cardholder data environment (CDE), from unprotected pathways."

Regardless of their form, all NSCs serve the same fundamental purpose: to restrict traffic between networks based on defined security policies, with an implicit "deny all" approach where only explicitly allowed traffic is permitted. These controls are essential for protecting the cardholder data environment from unauthorized access, particularly from untrusted networks like the internet, wireless networks, and third-party networks beyond an entity's control.

For more information: https://www.pcisecuritystandards.org/glossary/

Q22: Which of the following scenarios would be compliant with PCI DSS Requirement 1's approach to network security? (Select all that apply)

A) Allowing all outbound traffic from the CDE but restricting inbound traffic B) Implementing a DMZ with public-facing web servers separated from the internal network C) Using the same firewall rules for all network segments to ensure consistency D) Blocking all traffic from wireless networks to the CDE E) Documenting business justification for each allowed inbound and outbound connection

A22: The correct answers are B) Implementing a DMZ with public-facing web servers separated from the internal network, D) Blocking all traffic from wireless networks to the CDE, and E) Documenting business justification for each allowed inbound and outbound connection.

Let's analyze each option:

A) Allowing all outbound traffic from the CDE but restricting inbound traffic - This is NOT compliant because Requirement 1 specifies that both inbound AND outbound traffic must be restricted to only what is necessary for business. The key takeaways specifically mention the need to "restrict inbound and outbound traffic to necessary communication only."

B) Implementing a DMZ with public-facing web servers separated from the internal network - This IS compliant. The content states: "With a DMZ, you can create a secure buffer zone between your public and private networks, protecting sensitive data from malicious actors." A DMZ is explicitly mentioned as a recommended security architecture.

C) Using the same firewall rules for all network segments to ensure consistency - This is NOT compliant because different network segments have different security requirements and traffic needs. Using identical rules everywhere would either be too permissive for high-security areas or too restrictive for areas that need broader communication.

D) Blocking all traffic from wireless networks to the CDE - This IS compliant. The key takeaways explicitly state the need to "block all traffic from wireless networks into the CDE."

E) Documenting business justification for each allowed inbound and outbound connection - This IS compliant. The content emphasizes the need to "document business justification for allowing wired or wireless traffic" and mentions "justifying network traffic using the diagram."

For more information: https://www.pcisecuritystandards.org/documents/PCI_DSS_v4-0.pdf

Q23: Multiple choice: According to PCI DSS Requirement 2, what action should be taken when functions with different security levels share the same resource?

A) All functions should operate at the highest security level B) Functions should be separated into different resources C) The resource should default to the highest security requirement D) Additional monitoring should be implemented

A23: The correct answer is C) The resource should default to the highest security requirement.

The content specifically mentions a real-world example where a company "did not default to the highest security requirement when sharing functions with different security levels," which contributed to a data breach. This implies that the proper approach is to configure shared resources to operate at the highest security level required by any function using that resource.

When different functions with varying security requirements share the same system component or resource:

1. The entire resource must be configured to meet the highest security requirements of any function using it
2. Lower-security functions must operate within the higher security parameters
3. Security cannot be selectively lowered for some functions without compromising the overall security posture

This principle ensures that security is not compromised for convenience or to accommodate less-secure functions. It recognizes that a system's security is only as strong as its weakest configuration, so when functions share resources, the highest security standards must prevail.

Examples of this principle in practice include:

- A server hosting both public content and sensitive administrative functions must be configured to the security standards required for the administrative functions
- A database containing both public records and cardholder data must be secured according to the requirements for protecting cardholder data
- A network segment carrying both regular business traffic and cardholder data must be protected according to CDE requirements

For more information: https://www.pcisecuritystandards.org/document_library/

Q24: Explain how the "implicit deny all" approach enhances security in network security controls and how it should be implemented according to PCI DSS Requirement 1.

A24: The "implicit deny all" approach is a fundamental security principle that significantly enhances security in network security controls (NSCs) by establishing a default posture of blocking all traffic unless explicitly permitted. According to PCI DSS Requirement 1, "NSCs should be configured with an implicit 'deny all' rule so that only explicitly allowed traffic is allowed through."

How "Implicit Deny All" Enhances Security:

1. **Comprehensive Protection:** Rather than trying to identify and block all potential threats (which is impossible given the constantly evolving threat landscape), this approach blocks everything by default and only opens specific, necessary pathways.
2. **Reduced Attack Surface:** By allowing only known, necessary traffic, the potential attack surface is minimized. Attackers cannot exploit communication channels that aren't explicitly permitted.
3. **Prevention of Unknown Threats:** New attack vectors or exploitation techniques that haven't been specifically identified yet will still be blocked by default.
4. **Enforced Business Justification:** Every allowed traffic flow must have an explicit rule and justification, ensuring that all

network communication serves a legitimate business purpose.

5. **Simplified Rule Maintenance:** Security administrators focus on defining what should be allowed rather than trying to keep up with an ever-growing list of threats to block.

Implementation According to PCI DSS Requirement 1:

To properly implement the "implicit deny all" approach:

1. **Configure NSCs with a Default Deny Rule:** Every NSC should have a final rule that denies all traffic not explicitly allowed by previous rules. This rule is typically placed at the end of the rule set.

2. **Document Business Justification:** For each allowed traffic flow, document the specific business justification. The content states organizations must "document business justification for allowing wired or wireless traffic."

3. **Specify Exact Requirements:** Rules should be as specific as possible, defining:

    - Source and destination IP addresses/ranges
    - Specific protocols (TCP, UDP, ICMP, etc.)
    - Exact port numbers (not broad ranges)
    - Direction of traffic (inbound/outbound)

4. **Review Regularly:** The content specifies that firewall rule reviews should be conducted every six months to ensure all rules remain necessary and appropriate.

5. **Verify Implementation:** Test that the NSCs are properly configured to deny traffic that doesn't match any allow rules.

6. **Maintain Data Flow Diagrams:** Use data flow diagrams to map legitimate traffic flows, which serves as the basis for determining what traffic should be allowed.

7. **Block Wireless Traffic to CDE:** Specifically block all traffic from wireless networks into the CDE, as explicitly required.

By implementing the "implicit deny all" approach according to these guidelines, organizations create a security posture that allows legitimate business activities while effectively protecting cardholder data from unauthorized access through network pathways.

For more information: https://www.pcisecuritystandards.org/documents/Prioritized-Approach-for-PCI-DSS-v4_0.pdf

Q25: When implementing security controls for both Requirements 1 and 2, what fundamental security principle is being applied when removing unnecessary functionality, restricting traffic to only what is needed, and requiring business justification for allowed traffic?

A) Defense in depth B) Principle of least privilege C) Separation of duties D) Implicit deny all

A25: The correct answer is B) Principle of least privilege.

The principle of least privilege is the fundamental security concept that underlies many of the specific requirements in both Requirements 1 and 2 of PCI DSS. This principle states that users, processes, and systems should have only the minimum privileges necessary to perform their required functions and no more.

In the provided content, we can see this principle applied in multiple ways:

For Requirement 1:

- "Restrict inbound and outbound traffic to necessary communication only"
- "NSCs should be configured with an implicit 'deny all' rule so that only explicitly allowed traffic is allowed through"
- Requiring business justification for allowing any traffic
- Blocking all traffic from wireless networks into the CDE

For Requirement 2:

- "Disabling features that are not needed, such as roles and unnecessary modules"
- "Removing any unnecessary software"
- Applying secure configurations to ALL system components
- Removing vendor defaults and parameters

The principle of least privilege reduces risk by:

1. Minimizing the attack surface available to malicious actors
2. Limiting the potential damage that could result from accidents or attacks
3. Reducing the scope of compliance efforts to only necessary components
4. Simplifying the security environment by eliminating unnecessary elements

While the other options are also important security principles:

- Defense in depth refers to using multiple layers of security controls
- Separation of duties prevents any single individual from controlling an entire process
- Implicit deny all is a specific implementation approach that supports the principle of least privilege

The principle of least privilege is the overarching concept that most comprehensively describes the security approach evident across both Requirements 1 and 2.

For more information: https://www.pcisecuritystandards.org/documents/PCI_DSS_v4-0.pdf

21

CONTROL OBJECTIVE 2 - QUESTION SET

Protect Account Data

Q1: What is the recommended approach to protecting stored cardholder data according to Requirement 3?

A1: The recommended approach to protecting stored cardholder data according to Requirement 3 is the "if you don't need it, don't store it" approach. This simple yet effective rule helps organizations minimize risk by not retaining unnecessary cardholder data. By storing only the minimum required data elements, organizations reduce their attack surface and limit potential exposure in case of a breach. This approach is foundational to PCI DSS compliance and is compared to keeping the gates of a fortress locked when access is not needed. Organizations should regularly review their data storage practices and purge any cardholder data that is not essential for business operations.

Additional Resource: https://www.pcisecuritystandards.org/documents/PCI_DSS_v4-0.pdf

Q2: Which of the following correctly describes how PAN data should be masked according to PCI DSS 4.0? (Multiple Choice)

a) Only the first four and last four digits can be displayed b) Only the first six and last four digits can be displayed c) Only the last four digits can be displayed d) Only the middle six digits can be displayed

A2: The correct answer is b) Only the first six and last four digits can be displayed.

According to PCI DSS 4.0 Requirement 3, when displaying PAN (Primary Account Number) data, the standard permits showing only the first six and last four digits. The digits in between must be masked to protect the full PAN from unauthorized viewing. This masking requirement applies to displays, printouts, and other representations of the PAN. It's important to note that masking is different from truncation, as masked data could potentially be unmasked within the system, while truncated data has portions permanently removed. This requirement helps balance the need for identifying a card while protecting the complete number from unauthorized access.

Additional Resource: https://blog.pcisecuritystandards.org/pci-dss-v4-0-resource-guide

Q3: Explain the difference between masking and truncation as defined in PCI DSS 4.0 Requirement 3.

A3: Masking and truncation are two distinct methods for protecting PAN data, with important differences in their implementation and reversibility:

Masking: This is a method of hiding specific digits when displaying or printing the PAN, typically showing only the first six and last four digits while concealing the rest with symbols like asterisks (e.g., 123456******7890). The key characteristic of masking is that the full PAN data remains stored in the system, and the masked PAN can potentially be unmasked by authorized users with appropriate access rights. Masking is primarily a display control rather than a data storage protection method.

Truncation: This is a process that permanently removes a portion of the PAN, storing only a segment of the original number (e.g., storing only the last four digits). Once truncation occurs, the removed digits cannot be recovered within the system, as they are not stored anywhere. The only way to recreate the complete PAN would be to reference the original source or another system that stores the complete PAN. Truncation is therefore more secure for long-term storage since it eliminates portions of the sensitive data entirely.

Understanding this distinction is crucial for implementing appropriate data protection strategies that comply with PCI DSS requirements while balancing business needs and security concerns.

Additional Resource: https://www.pcisecuritystandards.org/glossary/

Q4: True or False: According to PCI DSS 4.0, service providers are not required to provide guidance on best practices for managing shared cryptographic keys.

A4: False. According to the provided content under the "Key Takeaways" for Requirement 3, service providers must provide guidance on best practices for managing shared keys. The requirement specifically mentions that service providers have a responsibility to offer guidance to their clients on how to properly manage shared cryptographic keys. This guidance helps ensure that all parties involved in the sharing of cryptographic keys understand their responsibilities and implement appropriate security controls. Proper management of shared keys is critical to maintaining the security of encrypted cardholder data, especially in environments where multiple organizations may have access to the same encrypted data. This requirement recognizes the unique position service providers hold in the payment ecosystem and their role in promoting security best practices among their clients.

Additional Resource: https://www.pcisecuritystandards.org/documents/PCI_DSS_v4-0_Summary_of_Changes.pdf

Q5: What cryptographic control is specifically mentioned in the material as a keyed hashing algorithm that can be used to ensure the complete unreadability of PAN?

A5: HMAC-SHA-256 is specifically mentioned in the material as a keyed hashing algorithm that can be used to ensure the complete unreadability of PAN data. The content provides this as a tip, noting that "to ensure the complete unreadability of PAN, it is necessary to utilize keyed cryptographic hashes of the entire PAN along with appropriate key management processes and procedures." HMAC-SHA-256 is a specific implementation of a keyed-hash message authentication code (HMAC) that uses the SHA-256 hash function. This algorithm provides a way to verify both the integrity and authenticity of data by combining a cryptographic hash function with a secret key. When properly implemented with strong key management practices, HMAC-SHA-256 can help organizations protect stored PAN data in compliance with PCI DSS requirements, making the data unreadable to unauthorized parties while maintaining its usability for legitimate business purposes.

Additional Resource: https://csrc.nist.gov/publications/detail/fips/198/1/final

Q6: Which of the following must be rendered unreadable according to Requirement 3? (Multiple Choice, select all that apply)

a) Digital media b) Backups c) Wireless network logs d) Network diagrams

A6: The correct answers are a) Digital media, b) Backups, and c) Wireless network logs.

According to the provided content for Requirement 3, "All digital media, backups, and wireless network logs should be rendered unreadable." This means that any PAN data stored in these locations must be protected using methods that make the data unreadable to unauthorized individuals. This typically involves using encryption, truncation, masking, or other methods outlined in the PCI DSS.

This requirement ensures that cardholder data is protected not just in primary storage locations, but also in secondary locations like backups and logs that might be overlooked. Digital media could include portable devices, storage media, and other physical media containing cardholder data. Network diagrams (option d) are not specifically mentioned in the content as requiring this treatment, though they should be protected as sensitive documents under other PCI DSS requirements.

Additional Resource: https://www.pcisecuritystandards.org/document_library/

Q7: Describe the concept of "split knowledge and dual control" as it relates to cryptographic keys in PCI DSS Requirement 3.

A7: "Split knowledge and dual control" is a security principle applied to cryptographic key management in PCI DSS Requirement 3. This concept involves dividing critical information or access among multiple individuals to prevent any single person from having complete control or knowledge.

Split knowledge refers to a condition where two or more people are required to reconstruct a cryptographic key because each person only possesses a part of the key. No single individual has access to all components needed to reconstruct the complete key.

Dual control means that at least two people are required to perform a sensitive operation. For cryptographic key management this ensures that no single individual can perform critical key management functions alone, such as key generation, transmission loading, storage, or destruction.

Together, these principles create a system of checks and balances where multiple authorized individuals must cooperate to access or manage cryptographic keys. This significantly reduces the risk of insider threats and unauthorized access to sensitive encryption keys that protect cardholder data.

For example, in a practical implementation, an organization might divide a cryptographic key into two parts, with each part held by a different key custodian. When the key needs to be used, both custodians must be present and provide their respective key components. This ensures that no single employee can compromise the encrypted cardholder data, even if they wanted to.

Additional Resource: https://www.nist.gov/publications/recommendation-key-management-part-1-general-0

Q8: When storing cardholder data that has become persistent, what is the crucial requirement mentioned in the content?

A8: When storing cardholder data that has become persistent, the crucial requirement mentioned in the content is to "ensure that all PCI-DSS requirements are met, including encryption of the stored data." This means that once data is stored in a persistent manner (i.e., it is retained beyond its immediate use for processing), it becomes subject to the full scope of PCI DSS protection requirements.

The content specifically emphasizes encryption as a key protection mechanism for persistent data. Encryption transforms the readable cardholder data into an unreadable format that requires cryptographic keys to decrypt, thus protecting it from unauthorized access even if the storage medium is compromised.

Beyond encryption, the "all PCI-DSS requirements" reference means organizations must implement comprehensive protection measures for persistent data, including:

- Proper key management for encryption keys
- Access controls restricting who can access the stored data
- Monitoring and logging of access attempts
- Secure disposal when the data is no longer needed
- Regular testing of security systems protecting the data

This requirement acknowledges that persistent data represents an ongoing security risk that must be continuously managed according to PCI DSS standards to prevent unauthorized access and potential data breaches.

Additional Resource: https://www.pcisecuritystandards.org/documents/Protecting_Telephone_Based_Payment_Card_Data_v3-0_nov_2018.pdf

Q9: Which technologies should NOT be used to send unprotected PAN according to Requirement 4? (Multiple Choice, select all that apply)

a) Email b) Instant messaging c) SMS d) Secure FTP e) All of the above

A9: The correct answer is a) Email, b) Instant messaging, and c) SMS.

According to Requirement 4, organizations should "never send unprotected PAN using technologies used by end users that are not secure, such as e-mail, instant messaging, or SMS." These communication channels are specifically identified as insecure for transmitting unprotected PAN data because they:

1. Typically lack end-to-end encryption by default
2. May store copies of messages on multiple servers along the transmission path
3. Often retain messages on devices indefinitely

4. Can be easily intercepted during transmission

5. Are accessible to multiple individuals (especially in corporate environments)

Secure FTP (option d) is not specifically mentioned in the provided content as a prohibited technology. In fact, when properly configured with encryption, SFTP can be an acceptable method for secure file transfers, though it would still need to meet the strong cryptography requirements of PCI DSS.

If PAN data must be sent using these end-user technologies, it should first be encrypted using strong cryptography before transmission, or the communication channel itself should be encrypted (such as using secure email protocols).

Additional Resource: https://www.pcisecuritystandards.org/documents/Guidance-PCI-DSS-Scoping-and-Segmentation_v1.pdf

Q10: What is the recommended version of Transport Layer Security (TLS) according to PCI DSS 4.0?

A10: According to PCI DSS 4.0, the recommended versions of Transport Layer Security (TLS) are 1.2 or higher (specifically 1.2 or 1.3). The content explicitly states that "to ensure that your customers' CHD is transmitted safely and securely over open, public networks, such as the internet, Wi-Fi, Bluetooth, NFC and GPRS, it is essential to use a strong version of TLS, e.g., 1.2 or 1.3 protocols."

This recommendation reflects the current security standards for data encryption during transmission. Earlier versions of TLS (1.0 and 1.1) and the predecessor SSL (Secure Sockets Layer) are considered vulnerable to various security exploits and attacks. TLS 1.2 and 1.3 provide stronger security through:

- More secure cipher suites
- Improved handshake processes
- Resistance to known cryptographic attacks
- Better performance in some cases (especially TLS 1.3)

TLS 1.3, released in 2018, offers additional security improvements over 1.2, including a simplified handshake process and the removal of older, less secure cryptographic algorithms. While PCI DSS 4.0 recommends TLS 1.2 as a minimum, organizations should consider implementing TLS 1.3 where possible for maximum security of transmitted cardholder data.

Additional Resource: https://www.pcisecuritystandards.org/documents/Migrating-from-SSL-Early-TLS-Info-Supp-v1_1.pdf

Q11: Explain how PAN transmissions can be safeguarded according to PCI DSS Requirement 4.

A11: According to PCI DSS Requirement 4, PAN (Primary Account Number) transmissions can be safeguarded through multiple complementary approaches:

1. **Encrypting the information before transmission**: This involves encrypting the PAN data itself before sending it, regardless of the transmission channel used. This method ensures that even if the transmission is intercepted, the PAN data remains protected by encryption.

2. **Encrypting the transmission channel**: This involves using secure protocols (like TLS 1.2 or 1.3) to create an encrypted tunnel through which the data travels. This protects all data sent through the channel, not just the PAN.

3. **Implementing both methods**: While not explicitly required by PCI DSS, the content notes that "it's strongly advised" to use both levels of protection for maximum security.

The content specifically states that "PAN transmissions can be safeguarded by encrypting the information before it's sent, or by encrypting the channel through which the data is transmitted, or even both."

Additional safeguards mentioned include:

- Tracking all keys and certificates used for encryption
- Ensuring expired or revoked certificates are not used
- Using properly issued self-signed certificates only when necessary (and only if issued by an internal certificate authority)
- Avoiding insecure technologies like email, instant messaging, or SMS for sending unprotected PAN
- Never using Wired Equivalent Privacy (WEP) for Wi-Fi networks

These layered approaches to security reflect the defense-in-depth principle, which is fundamental to effective information security practices and PCI DSS compliance.

Additional Resource: https://www.pcisecuritystandards.org/documents/PCI_DSS_v4-0_ROC_Reporting_Template.pdf

Q12: True or False: According to PCI DSS 4.0, self-signed certificates are never permitted for encrypting cardholder data transmissions.

A12: False. According to the provided content, self-signed certificates can be used under specific conditions. The material states: "A self-signed certificate can be used if necessary, but only if it's been issued by an internal certificate authority (CA) within the organization."

This means that self-signed certificates are permitted for encrypting cardholder data transmissions, but with important restrictions:

1. They must be issued by an internal certificate authority that is controlled by the organization
2. They should only be used "if necessary" - implying that commercially-signed certificates from trusted public CAs are preferred
3. They must still provide strong encryption that meets PCI DSS requirements

Self-signed certificates issued by an internal CA can provide adequate security when properly managed within a controlled environment. However, they lack the third-party validation that commercially-signed certificates offer, which means organizations must implement additional controls to ensure their security and validity.

It's important to note that while self-signed certificates might be technically permitted in certain situations, they may introduce additional complexity for compliance validation and may not be suitable for public-facing applications where trust relationships with external entities are important.

Additional Resource: https://www.pcisecuritystandards.org/documents/PCI-DSS-v4-0-SAQ-D_Merchant.pdf

Q13: What wireless security protocol should NEVER be used according to PCI DSS Requirement 4?

A13: According to PCI DSS Requirement 4, Wired Equivalent Privacy (WEP) should NEVER be used for Wi-Fi networks. The content explicitly states: "Never use Wired Equivalent Privacy (WEP) for Wi-Fi."

WEP is an old security protocol for wireless networks that was introduced in 1997 as part of the original IEEE 802.11 standard. It has been deprecated because of significant security vulnerabilities:

1. WEP uses weak encryption (RC4 algorithm with static keys)
2. It has flawed authentication mechanisms
3. The protocol has known key management issues
4. WEP can be easily cracked using readily available tools

Instead of WEP, organizations should implement more secure wireless protocols such as:

- WPA2 (Wi-Fi Protected Access 2) with AES encryption
- WPA3, which offers even stronger protection

The prohibition of WEP reflects PCI DSS's requirement for strong cryptography during the transmission of cardholder data over open, public networks. Using WEP would create a significant vulnerability in the organization's security posture and would result in non-compliance with PCI DSS requirements.

Additional Resource: https://www.pcisecuritystandards.org/documents/Wireless-Guidelines-Info-Supplement.pdf

Q14: In a retail environment, what is the primary reason for the "if you don't need it, don't store it" approach regarding cardholder data?

A14: In a retail environment, the primary reason for the "if you don't need it, don't store it" approach regarding cardholder data is to reduce the risk and impact of potential data breaches. This approach is fundamental to PCI DSS Requirement 3 because it addresses the root cause of many security issues by eliminating unnecessary data storage.

The content specifically mentions that "this easy-to-follow rule can help organizations keep their cardholder data safe and secure" and compares it to keeping fortress gates locked when they don't need to be opened. The reasoning behind this approach includes

1. **Risk Reduction**: Every piece of cardholder data stored represents a potential target for attackers. By minimizing stored data, retailers reduce their attack surface.
2. **Scope Limitation**: Less stored cardholder data means a smaller PCI DSS scope, potentially simplifying compliance efforts and reducing costs.
3. **Breach Impact Mitigation**: If a breach does occur, having less cardholder data stored limits the potential damage and

liability.

4. **Protection from Unauthorized Access**: As the content states, this approach "can ensure that their valuable cardholder account data is not exposed to unauthorized individuals."

The real-world example provided in the content reinforces this reasoning by describing how a retail company storing customer PANs without proper protection could face financial losses and reputation damage if that data is compromised. By not storing unnecessary data in the first place, retailers can significantly reduce these risks while still meeting their business needs.

Additional Resource: https://www.pcisecuritystandards.org/documents/Prioritized-Approach-for-PCI-DSS-v4_0.pdf

Q15: Which of the following is NOT a method mentioned in the content for protecting PAN data? (Multiple Choice)

a) Cryptographic hashes with appropriate key management b) Masking the PAN's first six and last four digits c) Rendering digital media unreadable d) Triple DES encryption with 128-bit keys

A15: The correct answer is d) Triple DES encryption with 128-bit keys.

This option is not mentioned in the provided content as a method for protecting PAN data. While Triple DES (3DES) is a valid encryption algorithm recognized by PCI DSS in some contexts, the specific implementation with 128-bit keys is not mentioned in the content, and typical 3DES implementations use different key lengths.

The other options are all mentioned in the content:

a) Cryptographic hashes with appropriate key management - The content specifically mentions "keyed cryptographic hashes of the entire PAN along with appropriate key management processes and procedures" and gives HMAC-SHA-256 as an example.

b) Masking the PAN's first six and last four digits - The content states that "PAN data should be masked, displaying only the PAN's first six and last four digits."

c) Rendering digital media unreadable - The content notes that "All digital media, backups, and wireless network logs should be rendered unreadable."

Understanding the specific methods approved for protecting PAN data is critical for implementing proper security controls and achieving PCI DSS compliance.

Additional Resource: https://www.pcisecuritystandards.org/documents/PCI-DSS-v4-0-SAQ-A.pdf

Q16: What is the significance of strong cryptography in Requirement 4 of PCI DSS 4.0?

A16: Strong cryptography is a cornerstone of Requirement 4 in PCI DSS 4.0, playing a vital role in protecting cardholder data during transmission over open, public networks. Its significance includes:

1. **Data Protection During Transit**: Strong cryptography ensures that cardholder data cannot be read or intercepted while being transmitted across vulnerable public networks like the internet, Wi-Fi, Bluetooth, NFC, and GPRS. The requirement explicitly states that organizations "must encrypt transmitted cardholder data when traveling across public networks."

2. **Defense Against Interception**: Without strong cryptography, transmitted cardholder data could be captured through various attack methods like packet sniffing or man-in-the-middle attacks. Strong cryptography renders such intercepted data unusable to attackers.

3. **Specific Protocol Requirements**: The content emphasizes using TLS 1.2 or 1.3 as the recommended protocols for implementing strong cryptography, reflecting the need for up-to-date security standards.

4. **Comprehensive Protection**: The content notes that PAN transmissions can be protected either by "encrypting the information before it's sent, or by encrypting the channel through which the data is transmitted, or even both," with the dual-layer approach being strongly advised.

5. **Certificate and Key Management**: The requirement extends to proper management of cryptographic materials, stating that "it's important to keep track of all keys and certificates" and that expired or revoked certificates should not be used.

Strong cryptography is not merely a technical checkbox but a fundamental security principle that helps maintain the confidentiality and integrity of cardholder data throughout its transmission journey, protecting both merchants and consumers from financial fraud and identity theft.

Additional Resource: https://www.pcisecuritystandards.org/documents/Penetration_Testing_Guidance_March_2015.pdf

Q17: A company discovers they have been inadvertently storing sensitive authentication data (SAD) along with transaction records. What does PCI DSS Requirement 3 mandate regarding this data?

A17: According to PCI DSS Requirement 3, Sensitive Authentication Data (SAD) must be unrecoverable. The content explicitly states that "all SAD must be unrecoverable." This means that upon discovery of inadvertently stored SAD, the company must take immediate action to securely delete this data in a manner that ensures it cannot be recovered.

Sensitive Authentication Data includes security-related information such as card verification codes/values, full magnetic stripe data (or equivalent on a chip), and PINs/PIN blocks. This information is particularly sensitive because it is used to authenticate cardholders and authorize transactions.

The requirement for unrecoverability means that:

1. The company must permanently delete the SAD using secure deletion methods that prevent forensic recovery

2. Simply marking the data as deleted or moving it to trash/recycle bins is insufficient

3. The deletion method must render the data completely unrecoverable even with specialized forensic tools

4. The company should document the discovery, the extent of the issue, and the actions taken to remediate

Additionally, the company should:

- Investigate how the SAD was being stored when it shouldn't have been

- Identify and correct the processes or systems that allowed SAD storage

- Implement controls to prevent future inadvertent storage of SAD

- Perform a thorough review of all systems to ensure no other instances of inappropriate SAD storage exist

This strict requirement underscores the high risk associated with SAD retention and the importance of having proper data handling procedures in place from the outset.

Additional Resource: https://www.pcisecuritystandards.org/documents/PCI_DSS_V4-0_Attestation_of_Compliance.pdf

Q18: What responsibilities do key custodians have according to the content on Requirement 3?

A18: According to the content on Requirement 3, key custodians have a specific and crucial responsibility: "Key custodians have a responsibility to protect the data by protecting the keys." This straightforward but profound statement encapsulates the essential role that key custodians play in the cryptographic key management lifecycle.

This responsibility entails several important aspects:

1. **Safeguarding Cryptographic Keys**: Key custodians must protect the cryptographic keys from unauthorized access, misuse, or compromise, as these keys provide access to protected cardholder data.

2. **Implementing Split Knowledge and Dual Control**: The content mentions that "Cryptographic keys must be securely stored using split knowledge and dual control." Key custodians are responsible for participating in this process, where no single individual has complete access to the full key.

3. **Following Key Management Procedures**: Custodians must adhere to documented key management policies and procedures, including proper key generation, distribution, storage, and destruction practices.

4. **Maintaining Key Secrecy**: Custodians must keep their portion of the key secret and secure, understanding that a compromised key could lead to compromised data.

5. **Participating in Key Rotation and Updates**: When keys need to be rotated or updated, custodians must follow secure procedures to maintain data protection throughout the process.

The emphasis on key custodians' responsibilities highlights the human element in cryptographic security. Even the strongest encryption is only as secure as the management of its keys, making the role of key custodians critical to the overall security posture of an organization handling cardholder data.

Additional Resource: https://www.pcisecuritystandards.org/documents/PCI-DSS-v4-0-ROC-Template-Excel.xlsx

Q19: Fill in the blank: When displaying a PAN, only the ______________ and ______________ can be shown.

A19: When displaying a PAN, only the first six digits and last four digits can be shown.

This is explicitly stated in the provided content: "When displaying a PAN, only the first six and last four digits can be shown." This requirement is part of PCI DSS Requirement 3, which focuses on protecting stored account data.

The first six digits of a payment card number (PAN) are known as the Issuer Identification Number (IIN) or Bank Identification Number (BIN), which identifies the card issuer. The last four digits are commonly used for verification purposes. The middle digits, which must be masked, contain unique account information specific to the individual cardholder.

This masking requirement helps protect cardholders from identity theft and fraud while still allowing merchants and service providers to identify the card type and verify the card with the customer when necessary. The requirement applies to all displays of PAN data, including on receipts, screens, paper records, and digital representations. It's important to note that this is specifically about displaying the PAN - storage requirements may be different and might require full encryption or other protection methods for the complete PAN.

Additional Resource: https://www.pcisecuritystandards.org/documents/PCI_DSS-QRG-v4_0.pdf

Q20: Which of the following statements about PCI DSS requirements for wireless networks is correct? (Multiple Choice)

a) WEP encryption is acceptable if no other options are available b) Authentication credentials can be sent in plaintext over wireless networks if they are temporary c) Organizations should never use wireless networks for transmitting cardholder data d) Wireless networks must use approved encryption protocols for transmitting cardholder data

A20: The correct answer is d) Wireless networks must use approved encryption protocols for transmitting cardholder data.

According to the content provided about Requirement 4, organizations must protect cardholder data during transmission over various networks, including wireless networks. The content specifically states: "Never use Wired Equivalent Privacy (WEP) for Wi-Fi." Additionally, under the Key Takeaways section, it mentions: "If you have a wireless network, ensure that authentication credentials aren't sent in plain text and data is encrypted using approved protocols."

Let's examine why the other options are incorrect:

a) WEP encryption is acceptable if no other options are available - This is incorrect because the content explicitly prohibits the use of WEP under any circumstances.

b) Authentication credentials can be sent in plaintext over wireless networks if they are temporary - This is incorrect as the content specifically states that authentication credentials should not be sent in plaintext.

c) Organizations should never use wireless networks for transmitting cardholder data - This is incorrect because the content does not prohibit the use of wireless networks; it only requires proper security measures when using them.

The correct implementation of wireless security for cardholder data transmission requires both the protection of authentication credentials and the encryption of the data itself using approved protocols such as WPA2/WPA3 with AES encryption.

Additional Resource: https://www.pcisecuritystandards.org/documents/Multi-Factor-Authentication-Guidance-v1_0.pdf

Q21: What approach should be taken regarding internal transmissions of cardholder data according to Requirement 4?

A21: According to the Key Takeaways section of Requirement 4, organizations should "consider using encryption for internal transmissions as well" when it comes to cardholder data. This suggests that while the primary focus of Requirement 4 is on protecting data transmitted over open, public networks, extending similar protections to internal networks is considered a best practice.

This approach recognizes that internal threats can be just as significant as external ones. Internal networks, although typically considered more secure than public networks, still face various risks:

1. **Insider threats**: Employees or contractors with malicious intent might attempt to intercept unencrypted cardholder data on internal networks.

2. **Compromised internal systems**: If an attacker gains access to the internal network, unencrypted data transmissions would be vulnerable.

3. **Segmentation bypasses**: Weaknesses in network segmentation could expose cardholder data to parts of the internal network where it shouldn't be accessible.

4. **Defense-in-depth**: Encrypting internal transmissions provides an additional layer of security beyond network-level controls.

The recommendation to consider encryption for internal transmissions aligns with the defense-in-depth security principle, which advocates for multiple, overlapping security controls rather than relying on a single security measure. While PCI DSS doesn't mandate encryption for all internal transmissions in all environments, the guidance suggests that organizations should evaluate their internal risk environment and implement encryption where appropriate to protect cardholder data throughout its entire transmission path, both externally and internally.

Additional Resource: https://www.pcisecuritystandards.org/documents/PCI_DSS_v4-0_Summary_of_Changes.pdf

Q22: Describe how cryptographic key management is addressed in Requirement 3 of PCI DSS 4.0.

A22: Cryptographic key management is addressed comprehensively in Requirement 3 of PCI DSS 4.0, with multiple aspects covered to ensure the security of keys that protect cardholder data:

1. **Secure Storage**: The content explicitly states that "Cryptographic keys must be securely stored using split knowledge and dual control." This means no single individual should have access to the complete key, reducing the risk of insider threats.

2. **Key Management Policies and Procedures**: The content mentions that key management policies and procedures are discussed, including "making strong keys, distributing them securely, and storing them securely." This indicates a requirement for documented processes that cover the entire key lifecycle.

3. **Key Custodian Responsibilities**: The material notes that "Key custodians have a responsibility to protect the data by protecting the keys." This establishes clear accountability for individuals involved in key management.

4. **Service Provider Guidance**: For environments where keys are shared between organizations, "service providers must provide guidance on best practices for managing shared keys." This ensures consistent security practices across organizational boundaries.

5. **Documentation Requirements**: The content states that "The PCIP will document security policies and operational procedures to protect cryptographic keys and ensure the safety of PAN data." This emphasizes the importance of formal documentation of key management practices.

6. **Appropriate Key Management for Hashing**: When using keyed cryptographic hashes (like HMAC-SHA-256), the content notes that these must be used "along with appropriate key management processes and procedures."

These elements collectively establish a framework for secure cryptographic key management that protects the confidentiality and integrity of the encryption keys, which in turn protect the cardholder data. Proper key management is essential because even the strongest encryption algorithm becomes vulnerable if its keys are not properly secured throughout their lifecycle.

Additional Resource: https://csrc.nist.gov/publications/detail/sp/800-57-part-1/rev-5/final

Q23: True or False: According to PCI DSS 4.0, it is mandatory to use strong cryptography at both the data level and channel level when transmitting PAN data.

A23: False. According to the provided content about Requirement 4, it is not mandatory to use strong cryptography at both the data level and channel level when transmitting PAN data, although it is strongly recommended.

The content specifically states: "PAN transmissions can be safeguarded by encrypting the information before it's sent, or by encrypting the channel through which the data is transmitted, or even both. Although it's not mandatory to use robust cryptography at both levels, it's strongly advised."

This means organizations have three compliant options for protecting PAN data during transmission:

1. Encrypt the PAN data itself before transmission (data-level encryption), regardless of the security of the transmission channel
2. Encrypt the transmission channel (channel-level encryption, such as TLS 1.2/1.3), which protects the data as it travels
3. Implement both data-level and channel-level encryption for maximum security (the recommended approach)

While implementing both levels of encryption provides the strongest protection through defense in depth, PCI DSS 4.0 recognizes that either method alone can provide sufficient protection if properly implemented. The standard gives organizations flexibility to choose the approach that best fits their technical environment and risk profile, while strongly encouraging the use of both methods for optimal security.

Additional Resource: https://www.pcisecuritystandards.org/documents/Best-Practices-Securing-Ecommerce_v1.0.pdf

Q24: A retail company is developing a new point-of-sale system. According to the content on Requirements 3 and 4, what approach should they take regarding data retention and transmission?

A24: Based on the content covering Requirements 3 and 4, the retail company developing a new point-of-sale system should implement a comprehensive approach to data retention and transmission that includes:

Data Retention Approach:

1. Follow the "if you don't need it, don't store it" principle as the foundation of their data retention strategy
2. Conduct a thorough analysis to determine the minimum cardholder data elements required for business purposes
3. Implement documented data retention and disposal policies that specify what data is stored, how long it's kept, and how it's securely deleted
4. For any PAN data that must be stored:

- Render it unreadable through encryption with strong cryptographic keys
- Implement proper key management with split knowledge and dual control
- Consider using index tokens instead of the actual PAN where possible
- Ensure all digital media and backups containing cardholder data are protected

5. Never store Sensitive Authentication Data (SAD) after authorization
6. If displaying PAN data in the system, mask it to show only the first six and last four digits

Data Transmission Approach:

1. Implement strong cryptography (TLS 1.2 or 1.3) for all cardholder data transmitted over public networks
2. Consider encrypting the data itself before transmission for additional security
3. Ensure wireless communications use secure protocols (never WEP)
4. Track and maintain all cryptographic certificates and keys used for transmission
5. Restrict the technologies used to transmit cardholder data to necessary, secure methods only
6. Never allow unprotected PAN to be sent via end-user messaging technologies like email or SMS
7. Consider encrypting internal network transmissions for protection against insider threats
8. Implement documented operational procedures for maintaining transmission security

This comprehensive approach addresses the key requirements while providing multiple layers of protection for cardholder data throughout its lifecycle in the point-of-sale system. The company should also ensure these security measures are built into the system from the design phase rather than added later, following the principle of security by design.

Additional Resource: https://www.pcisecuritystandards.org/documents/PCI_DSS_for_Large_Organizations_v1.pdf

Q25: Explain how Requirements 3 and 4 work together to provide comprehensive protection for cardholder data.

A25: Requirements 3 and 4 of PCI DSS 4.0 work together to provide comprehensive protection for cardholder data by addressing two critical and complementary aspects of data security: protection of stored data (Requirement 3) and protection of data in transit (Requirement 4). Together, they create a complete security envelope around cardholder data throughout its lifecycle.

Comprehensive Protection Through Complementary Coverage:

1. **Complete Data Lifecycle Protection**: Requirement 3 focuses on protecting cardholder data when it's at rest (stored), while Requirement 4 protects it when it's in motion (transmitted). This ensures that cardholder data is protected regardless of its state.
2. **Layered Security Approach**: Both requirements implement the concept of defense in depth:

- Requirement 3 emphasizes minimizing data storage ("if you don't need it, don't store it"), and when storage is necessary, using encryption, masking, and proper key management
- Requirement 4 emphasizes strong cryptography for transmission channels, with the option of additional data-level encryption

3. **Consistent Cryptographic Standards**: Both requirements emphasize the importance of strong cryptography and proper key management, creating a consistent security approach:
   - Requirement 3 mandates secure storage of cryptographic keys using split knowledge and dual control
   - Requirement 4 requires tracking all keys and certificates and ensuring they're not expired or revoked
4. **Addressing Different Threat Vectors**: Together, they address different potential attack vectors:
   - Requirement 3 protects against data breaches of storage systems, insider threats, and improper data disposal
   - Requirement 4 protects against network sniffing, man-in-the-middle attacks, and interception of data in transit
5. **Policy and Procedure Emphasis**: Both requirements highlight the importance of documented policies and procedures:
   - Requirement 3 emphasizes data retention policies and key management procedures
   - Requirement 4 emphasizes operational procedures for maintaining transmission security

In the real world, these requirements work together to create a secure environment. For example, when a customer makes a purchase, Requirement 4 ensures their card data is protected as it's transmitted from the point-of-sale to the payment processor, while Requirement 3 ensures that if any of that data needs to be stored for future use (like for recurring billing), it's properly protected in storage. This comprehensive approach significantly reduces the risk of cardholder data compromise regardless of where or how an attacker might attempt to access it.

Additional Resource: https://www.pcisecuritystandards.org/documents/PCI_DSS_v4-0_Resource_Guide.pdf

22

Control Objective 3 - Question Set

Maintain a Vulnerability Management Program

Q1: Which of the following is NOT mentioned as a type of malware in the context of PCI DSS Requirement 5?

A) Ransomware B) Botnets C) Polymorphic malware D) Spyware

A1: The correct answer is D) Spyware.

The content specifically mentions several types of malware: adware, botnets, crypto-jacking, malvertising, polymorphic malware, and ransomware. Spyware, while a common type of malware, is not explicitly mentioned in the provided content. Ransomware is described as a particularly nasty type of malware that holds valuable files, data, or information for ransom. Botnets are described as versatile malware that can adapt quickly and use other infected computers to help spread. Polymorphic malware is noted for its ability to change appearance to avoid detection.

Additional resource: https://www.pcisecuritystandards.org/pci_security/maintaining_payment_security

Q2: True or False: According to PCI DSS Requirement 5, systems considered "Not at Risk" do not need to be monitored after being documented as such.

A) True B) False

A2: False.

According to the provided content, systems considered "Not at Risk" should be "identified, documented, and confirmed as not at risk by their manufacturer\vendor. Plus, continually monitored, just in case!" This clearly indicates that even systems deemed not at risk require ongoing monitoring. This is an important security principle - continuous verification rather than a one-time assessment, as the risk landscape constantly changes and new vulnerabilities may emerge.

Additional resource: https://blog.pcisecuritystandards.org/pci-dss-v4-0-resource-hub

Q3: What does the CIA triad refer to in the context of security that malware can compromise?

A3: The CIA triad refers to the three fundamental principles of information security: Confidentiality, Integrity, and Availability.

As mentioned in the content, malware can "wreak havoc both in your business and personal life, compromising the security triad of Confidentiality, Integrity, and Availability (CIA) of your data." Confidentiality ensures that sensitive information is accessible only to authorized individuals. Integrity guarantees that data remains accurate and unaltered by unauthorized parties. Availability ensures that systems and data are accessible when needed. Malware can threaten all three aspects by stealing confidential data, corrupting data integrity, or disrupting system availability through attacks like ransomware.

Additional resource: https://www.pcisecuritystandards.org/documents/PCI_DSS_v4-0_Summary_of_Changes.pdf

Q4: According to PCI DSS Requirement 5, which of the following is required for anti-phishing protection?

A) Only automated filters B) Only security awareness training C) Both automated filters and security awareness training D) Either automated filters or security awareness training

A4: C) Both automated filters and security awareness training.

The content explicitly states: "you should also have some anti-phishing protection in place; this must include security awareness training." It further mentions that "an automated filter or dedicated security system can help keep you safe from these kinds of scams." The key takeaway also reinforces this by stating there is "a new requirement that you need to fulfill to protect yourself from phishing attacks. This calls for implementing technical defenses and automated solutions to stop these cyber attacks. And remember, this requirement applies even if you have already undergone security training." This indicates that both components are necessary, not just one or the other.

Additional resource: https://www.pcisecuritystandards.org/merchants/process/

Q5: Describe how ransomware affects the Confidentiality, Integrity, and Availability components of the security triad. Provide specific examples for each component.

A5: Ransomware impacts all three components of the CIA security triad:

Confidentiality: While ransomware primarily targets availability, it can also compromise confidentiality. Modern ransomware attacks often employ a "double extortion" technique where attackers not only encrypt data but also exfiltrate it before encryption. They then threaten to publish sensitive data unless a ransom is paid. For example, the Maze ransomware group became notorious for stealing data before encryption and leaking portions of it to prove their access if victims refused to pay.

Integrity: Ransomware attacks compromise data integrity by altering files through encryption. Even after decryption (if possible), there's no guarantee that the data remains unchanged from its original state. Some ransomware variants deliberately corrupt data even after ransom payment. Additionally, if an organization restores from backups, there could be data loss between the last backup and the infection, further compromising data integrity.

Availability: This is the most obvious impact of ransomware. By encrypting files and systems, ransomware directly prevents access to critical data and services. Healthcare organizations hit by ransomware have had to turn away patients or revert to manual processes. Financial institutions may lose access to transaction systems, and manufacturing companies might experience production line shutdowns because operating systems become unavailable.

The comprehensive impact on all three security pillars makes ransomware particularly devastating and explains why PCI DSS Requirement 5 emphasizes strong anti-malware defenses including regular scanning, continuous behavioral analysis, and keeping anti-malware solutions updated.

Additional resource: https://www.pcisecuritystandards.org/pci_security/standard_overview

Q6: Which of the following terms refers to a framework for developing secure software with security integrated throughout the development process?

A) SLC B) SDLC C) S-SDLC D) WAF

A6: C) S-SDLC

The content mentions various acronyms related to software development processes. S-SDLC stands for Secure Software Development Lifecycle, which specifically refers to a development framework with security integrated throughout the process. The content states: "Requirement 6: Develop and Maintain Secure Systems and Software is about having a Software Lifecycle (SLC), also known as a Software or System Development Lifecycle (SDLC) in place, or better still – a Secure Software Development Lifecycle (S-SDLC)." The "S" prefix indicates the security focus, making it the most appropriate answer among the options. WAF (Web Application Firewall) is a different technology used to protect web applications, not a development methodology.

Additional resource: https://www.pcisecuritystandards.org/document_library/

Q7: True or False: According to PCI DSS requirements, anti-malware defenses can be disabled without documentation if they're re-enabled quickly.

A) True B) False

A7: False.

The content clearly states: "Stay one step ahead of malicious threats and attacks, enable Anti-malware defenses on all systems, and only disable them with full change approval, ensuring all are fully documented. Re-enable these defense mechanisms as soon as possible."

This indicates that even temporary disabling of anti-malware defenses requires both full change approval and complete documentation. While the guidance does emphasize re-enabling the defenses as soon as possible, this doesn't eliminate the need for proper documentation and approval before disabling them. This requirement helps maintain security accountability and ensures that all changes to security controls are tracked and justified.

Additional resource: https://www.pcisecuritystandards.org/pci_security/maintaining_payment_security

Q8: What is recommended as an appropriate solution to protect internet-facing web applications according to Requirement 6?

A8: A Web Application Firewall (WAF) is specifically recommended as an appropriate solution for protecting internet-facing web applications.

The content states: "internet-facing web applications must be protected by an automated technical solution. A Web Application Firewall (WAF) would be an appropriate solution." WAFs work by filtering, monitoring, and blocking HTTP traffic to and from web applications, providing protection against various attacks like SQL injection, cross-site scripting (XSS), and other vulnerabilities. This is particularly important for applications that process, store, or transmit cardholder data. The requirement emphasizes the need for automated technical solutions rather than manual monitoring, with WAF being explicitly mentioned as a suitable option.

Additional resource: https://blog.pcisecuritystandards.org/just-published-pci-dss-v4-0

Q9: Which of the following is NOT mentioned as a component of anti-malware solutions in the content?

A) Network-based controls B) Host-based controls C) End-point-based controls D) Cloud-based controls

A9: D) Cloud-based controls.

The content specifically mentions that "Anti-malware solutions come in various forms, including a mix of network, host, and end-point-based controls." It does not mention cloud-based controls as one of the components. While cloud-based anti-malware solutions do exist in the industry, they are not explicitly listed in the provided content. Understanding the different types of anti-malware controls is important for implementing comprehensive protection as required by PCI DSS Requirement 5.

Additional resource: https://www.pcisecuritystandards.org/merchants/process/

Q10: Explain the relationship between Software Lifecycle (SLC) and patch management programs as described in Requirement 6. Why are they described as "two sides of the same coin"?

A10: The relationship between Software Lifecycle (SLC) and patch management programs is described as complementary and essential for maintaining a secure environment. They are "two sides of the same coin" because they address different but related aspects of software security throughout its existence.

The Software Lifecycle (SLC) focuses on the proactive aspect of security, ensuring that software is designed, developed, and implemented with security in mind from the beginning. It provides a framework for developing secure software and systems, incorporating security at every stage from requirements gathering through design, development, testing, and deployment. This proactive approach helps minimize vulnerabilities in new or modified software.

On the other hand, patch management is reactive in nature, addressing vulnerabilities that are discovered after software is deployed. It involves the process of identifying, acquiring, testing, and installing updates (patches) for software systems to address security vulnerabilities and other bugs. As the content states, "With a patch management program in place, you are keeping up to date with vulnerabilities in your system, quickly identifying and patching them."

Together, these components create a comprehensive approach to software security:

- SLC ensures new software is built securely from the ground up
- Patch management ensures existing software remains secure as new vulnerabilities are discovered

This combination provides continuous protection throughout the entire software lifecycle - from initial development through ongoing maintenance. One creates secure software, while the other keeps it secure over time. Hence, they are like "two sides of the same coin, working together to ensure your system remains safe and secure."

Additional resource: https://www.pcisecuritystandards.org/documents/PCI_DSS_v4-0_Summary_of_Changes.pdf

Q11: True or False: PCI DSS Requirement 6 applies only to software specifically created for payment card processing.

A) True B) False

A11: False.

According to the content, Requirement 6 applies more broadly to "All (bespoke and custom) software created by or for the entity's own use, whether made specifically for them or customized from existing software." It further clarifies that "if the entity has a program that helps them with their work or a system that's been tailored to fit their needs, this requirement applies."

This indicates that the requirement covers all custom software used by the organization, not just software specifically for payment card processing. This broader scope ensures that vulnerabilities in any custom software can't be exploited as a pathway to eventually access cardholder data, following the defense-in-depth principle. Security should be implemented consistently across all custom applications within the cardholder data environment.

Additional resource: https://www.pcisecuritystandards.org/merchants/process/

Q12: Which testing methodologies are mentioned as forms of consistent validation for secure coding practices?

A) SAST only B) DAST only C) Both SAST and DAST D) Neither SAST nor DAST

A12: C) Both SAST and DAST.

The content mentions both Static Automated Security Testing (SAST) and Dynamic Automated Security Testing (DAST) as forms of consistent validation for secure coding practices. Specifically, it states that code must be "reviewed and fixed before production, ideally with consistent validation such as Static Automated Security Testing (SAST) and\or Dynamic Automated Security Testing (DAST) as well as other forms of testing, e.g. pen testing."

SAST analyzes source code or compiled versions of code to identify potential security vulnerabilities without executing the application. DAST, on the other hand, tests applications in their running state, identifying vulnerabilities that might only appear during execution. Both approaches provide complementary methods for identifying different types of security issues in software.

Additional resource: https://blog.pcisecuritystandards.org/pci-dss-v4-0-resource-hub

Q13: Describe the characteristics of polymorphic malware and explain why it poses a particular challenge for detection.

A13: Polymorphic malware is characterized by its ability to change its appearance or code structure while maintaining its malicious functionality. As described in the content, it "can change its appearance to try and avoid detection, but it still does the same bad things to your computer."

The key characteristics of polymorphic malware include:

1. Metamorphic capability: It can alter its code structure, appearance, or signature with each infection or iteration
2. Persistent functionality: Despite these changes in appearance, its malicious functions remain the same
3. Evasion focus: Its primary purpose for changing is to evade detection by security tools

Polymorphic malware poses particular challenges for detection because:

1. Signature-based detection becomes ineffective: Traditional antivirus programs that rely on recognizing known malware signatures struggle to identify polymorphic malware since its signature constantly changes
2. Each instance appears unique: Security tools may see each variant as a new, unknown threat rather than recognizing it as part of a known malware family
3. Rapid evolution: The malware can change faster than signature databases are updated
4. Resource intensity: Detecting polymorphic malware often requires more advanced methods like behavioral analysis, heuristics, or machine learning, which are more resource-intensive

This is why the content emphasizes both "regularly scanning for viruses" and "continuous behavioral analysis" as methods to detect malware. While scanning can catch known variants, behavioral analysis is particularly important for detecting polymorphic malware by identifying suspicious activities rather than relying solely on signatures.

Additional resource: https://www.pcisecuritystandards.org/pci_security/maintaining_payment_security

Q14: According to PCI DSS Requirement 6, which of the following environments was previously known as "Development & Test"?

A) Production environment B) Pre-Production environment C) Staging environment D) Quality Assurance environment

A14: B) Pre-Production environment.

The content explicitly states: "Tip: Pre Production was previously known as Development & Test. Production is the live environment." This terminology change is important to understand when interpreting PCI DSS requirements and documentation. The pre-production environment is where software is tested and validated before being deployed to the production environment. Understanding the distinction between these environments is crucial for implementing proper security controls and separation of duties as required by PCI DSS.

Additional resource: https://www.pcisecuritystandards.org/document_library/

Q15: True or False: According to PCI DSS, anti-malware logs must be retained for at least one year.

A) True B) False

A15: True.

The content states in the key takeaways section: "It's also crucial to keep logs of the anti-malware activities for a year and guard them against unauthorized access." This one-year retention requirement ensures that organizations maintain sufficient historical data to support security investigations, identify patterns of attacks, and verify compliance with PCI DSS requirements. Protecting these logs from unauthorized access is equally important to maintain their integrity and confidentiality.

Additional resource: https://blog.pcisecuritystandards.org/just-published-pci-dss-v4-0

Q16: Describe a comprehensive anti-malware strategy that would satisfy PCI DSS Requirement 5. Include specific components and explain how they work together.

A16: A comprehensive anti-malware strategy to satisfy PCI DSS Requirement 5 would include the following components:

1. Multi-layered Defense Approach:
    - Network-based controls: Implement gateway anti-malware solutions that scan traffic at network entry/exit points
    - Host-based controls: Install anti-malware software directly on servers processing cardholder data
    - Endpoint-based controls: Deploy anti-malware protection on all workstations, especially those that might access cardholder data
2. Regular Malware Scanning:
    - Schedule automatic scans of all systems to detect known malware signatures
    - Implement on-access scanning to check files when they're created, opened, or modified
    - Conduct periodic deep scans of entire systems
3. Continuous Behavioral Analysis:
    - Deploy solutions that monitor system behavior for suspicious activities
    - Implement heuristic analysis to detect unknown malware based on behavior patterns
    - Use machine learning-based detection for identifying new malware variants
4. Anti-Phishing Protection:
    - Implement email filtering solutions to detect and block phishing attempts
    - Deploy web filtering to prevent access to known malicious sites

- Utilize link protection technologies that scan URLs before allowing access
- Conduct regular security awareness training for all employees

5. Maintenance and Updates:
   - Ensure automatic updates of anti-malware definitions and engines
   - Regularly check for and apply software updates to anti-malware solutions
   - Maintain formal change management processes for any modifications to anti-malware configurations

6. Documentation and Monitoring:
   - Document systems considered "not at risk" with vendor confirmation
   - Continue monitoring these systems despite their "not at risk" designation
   - Maintain documented approval for any temporary disabling of anti-malware controls
   - Re-enable protection as quickly as possible when disabled

7. Logging and Retention:
   - Configure comprehensive logging of all anti-malware activities
   - Retain logs for at least one year as required by PCI DSS
   - Protect logs from unauthorized access or modification
   - Regularly review logs for indicators of compromise

These components work together by creating defense-in-depth. If malware evades one layer (such as network filtering), host-based protection might catch it. If it has an unknown signature, behavioral analysis can identify suspicious activities. Regular updates ensure protection against new threats, while logging and monitoring provide visibility into potential security incidents. The anti-phishing components specifically target one of the most common malware delivery vectors. Documentation ensures that all systems are protected appropriately, and any exceptions are properly justified and monitored.

This multi-faceted approach addresses all aspects of Requirement 5, providing comprehensive protection against various types of malware including ransomware, botnets, and polymorphic malware that might otherwise compromise the confidentiality, integrity, and availability of cardholder data.

Additional resource: https://www.pcisecuritystandards.org/pci_security/standard_overview

Q17: Which characteristic of botnets is highlighted in the content as making them particularly dangerous?

A) They can steal financial data directly B) They can adapt quickly and use other infected computers to spread C) They target specifically PCI DSS environments D) They are impossible to detect with conventional anti-malware

A17: B) They can adapt quickly and use other infected computers to spread.

The content specifically states that botnets "are really versatile and can adapt quickly to try and get past your computer's defenses. They can even use other infected computers to help spread their malware!" This distributed nature and adaptability make botnets particularly dangerous threats. By leveraging networks of already-compromised machines (the "bot" network), they can amplify their attack capabilities and spread more efficiently than malware that operates in isolation. This networked approach makes them more resilient and difficult to completely eradicate.

Additional resource: https://www.pcisecuritystandards.org/merchants/process/

Q18: What is the difference between Static Automated Security Testing (SAST) and Dynamic Automated Security Testing (DAST)? When would each be most valuable in the secure software development lifecycle?

A18: Static Automated Security Testing (SAST) and Dynamic Automated Security Testing (DAST) are complementary security testing approaches that differ in their methodology and timing within the secure software development lifecycle:

SAST (Static Automated Security Testing):

- Analyzes source code, bytecode, or binary code without executing the application
- Examines code from the "inside out" perspective
- Identifies vulnerabilities by analyzing code syntax, structure, and data flow
- Can detect issues like buffer overflows, SQL injection vulnerabilities, and other coding flaws
- Most valuable during the development phase, before code is compiled and deployed
- Can find issues early in the development cycle, reducing the cost of remediation
- Example tools include Fortify, Checkmarx, and SonarQube

DAST (Dynamic Automated Security Testing):

- Tests applications in their running state
- Examines the application from the "outside in" perspective
- Identifies vulnerabilities by simulating attacks against a running application
- Can detect issues like authentication problems, server configuration issues, and runtime vulnerabilities
- Most valuable during the testing phase, after the application is deployed in a test environment
- Can find issues that only emerge during execution or through interaction with other systems
- Example tools include OWASP ZAP, Burp Suite, and Acunetix

When each is most valuable:

SAST is most valuable:

- Early in the development process when code is being written
- When doing code reviews before submission
- For catching issues before they reach testing environments
- When developing security-critical components that need thorough review

DAST is most valuable:

- Later in the development cycle when applications can be executed
- When testing integrated systems where components interact
- For identifying issues that only manifest during runtime
- When testing applications in environments similar to production

Both approaches are recommended as part of a comprehensive security testing strategy, as mentioned in the content: "ideally with consistent validation such as Static Automated Security Testing (SAST) and\or Dynamic Automated Security Testing (DAST) as well as other forms of testing, e.g. pen testing." Together, they provide more complete coverage than either approach alone, catching different types of vulnerabilities at different stages of development.

Additional resource: https://www.pcisecuritystandards.org/document_library/

Q19: True or False: If a vendor confirms a system is "Not at Risk" for malware, it can be permanently excluded from anti-malware requirements.

A) True B) False

A19: False.

According to the content, systems considered "Not at Risk" should be "identified, documented, and confirmed as not at risk by their manufacturer\vendor. Plus, continually monitored, just in case!" The phrase "continually monitored, just in case" clearly indicates that even systems deemed not at risk cannot be permanently excluded from oversight and must remain under ongoing monitoring.

This approach recognizes that risk assessments are time-bound - what is considered secure today may not remain so as new vulnerabilities are discovered or as the threat landscape evolves. Systems that are initially deemed "not at risk" could become vulnerable later due to new attack vectors, changes in the environment, or newly discovered vulnerabilities. The requirement for continued monitoring ensures that organizations maintain vigilance even for systems previously considered secure.

Additional resource: https://blog.pcisecuritystandards.org/pci-dss-v4-0-resource-hub

Q20: How should lower-risk vulnerabilities be handled according to PCI DSS Requirement 6?

A) They can be ignored as they pose minimal risk B) They must be fixed immediately regardless of severity C) They should have defined correction timeframes after budget discussions with stakeholders D) They should be documented but require no further action

A20: C) They should have defined correction timeframes after budget discussions with stakeholders.

The content states: "Lower-risk vulnerabilities can have defined correction timeframes after budget discussions with stakeholders." This approach recognizes that while all vulnerabilities should be addressed, organizations need to prioritize remediation efforts based on risk levels. High-risk vulnerabilities would typically require immediate attention, while lower-risk issues can be addressed according to an established schedule that balances security needs with practical resource constraints.

This risk-based approach allows organizations to make informed decisions about vulnerability management while ensuring that even lower-risk issues have a clear plan and timeline for resolution rather than being indefinitely postponed or ignored.

Additional resource: https://www.pcisecuritystandards.org/documents/PCI_DSS_v4-0_Summary_of_Changes.pdf

Q21: Describe a comprehensive strategy for defending against phishing attacks that would satisfy PCI DSS requirements. Include both technical and human elements in your answer.

A21: A comprehensive anti-phishing strategy that satisfies PCI DSS requirements would include both technical defenses and human-focused elements:

Technical Defenses:

1. Email Filtering Solutions:
    - Implement advanced email security gateways that can detect and block phishing attempts
    - Use technologies that analyze email headers, content, and sender reputation
    - Deploy solutions that can detect spoofed sender addresses and domain names
    - Implement DMARC, SPF, and DKIM email authentication protocols
2. URL/Link Protection:
    - Deploy systems that scan links in emails before allowing users to visit them
    - Implement real-time URL scanning that checks destinations when links are clicked
    - Use browser plugins or extensions that warn users about potentially malicious websites
3. Attachment Scanning:
    - Implement solutions that scan all email attachments for malware
    - Use sandboxing technology to detonate suspicious attachments in isolated environments

- Block high-risk attachment types that commonly deliver malware

4. Web Filtering:
    - Deploy web filtering solutions to prevent access to known phishing sites
    - Implement DNS filtering to block resolution of malicious domains
    - Use browser isolation technology for high-risk web browsing activities
5. Multi-factor Authentication (MFA):
    - Require MFA for all access to sensitive systems and data
    - Implement MFA especially for email accounts to prevent account takeover
    - Use MFA methods resistant to phishing (like hardware tokens or push notifications)

Human Elements:

1. Security Awareness Training:
    - Conduct regular, mandatory phishing awareness training for all employees
    - Include role-specific training for employees with access to sensitive data
    - Cover recognition of phishing attempts, proper reporting procedures, and safe practices
2. Phishing Simulation Exercises:
    - Regularly conduct simulated phishing campaigns to test employee awareness
    - Provide immediate feedback and additional training for employees who fall for simulations
    - Track improvement metrics over time to measure program effectiveness
3. Clear Reporting Mechanisms:
    - Establish simple procedures for employees to report suspected phishing attempts
    - Create dedicated reporting channels (email addresses or buttons in email clients)
    - Provide timely feedback to reporters to reinforce positive security behavior
4. Security Culture Development:
    - Foster an environment where security is everyone's responsibility
    - Recognize and reward employees who identify and report phishing attempts
    - Ensure leadership visibly supports and participates in security initiatives

Integration and Continuous Improvement:

1. Incident Response Integration:
    - Link anti-phishing controls to broader incident response procedures
    - Ensure rapid response to reported phishing attempts
    - Conduct post-incident analysis to improve defenses
2. Metrics and Reporting:
    - Track key metrics like phishing simulation failure rates, reported attempts, and successful attacks
    - Regularly report on program effectiveness to management
    - Use metrics to identify areas needing improvement
3. Continuous Updates:
    - Regularly update technical controls to address emerging phishing tactics
    - Keep training content current with examples of recent phishing techniques
    - Adjust the program based on industry trends and organization-specific attacks

This comprehensive approach satisfies PCI DSS requirements by implementing both the required "technical defenses and automated solutions to stop these cyber attacks" and security awareness training. As emphasized in the content, the technical controls are required "even if you have already undergone security training," highlighting that both components are necessary for a complete defense strategy.

Additional resource: https://www.pcisecuritystandards.org/pci_security/maintaining_payment_security

Q22: True or False: The PCI DSS requires anti-malware software to be installed on all systems, regardless of the system's risk profile.

A) True B) False

A22: False.

The content indicates that there is a process for identifying systems that are "Not at Risk." Specifically, it states that "Systems considered Not at Risk should be identified, documented, and confirmed as not at risk by their manufacturer\vendor. Plus, continually monitored, just in case!" This suggests that not all systems necessarily need anti-malware software installed if they can be properly documented as not at risk.

However, it's important to note that even systems identified as "Not at Risk" must still be:

1. Formally documented as such
2. Confirmed by their manufacturer/vendor as not being at risk

3. Continually monitored despite their "not at risk" designation

This nuanced approach allows organizations to focus their anti-malware efforts on systems that truly need protection while ensuring that exceptions are properly justified, documented, and monitored.

Additional resource: https://blog.pcisecuritystandards.org/just-published-pci-dss-v4-0

Q23: Which of the following is the most accurate statement about access to production code according to PCI DSS Requirement 6?

A) Access to production code should be limited to the development team B) Access to production code on application servers should be restricted C) Production code access should be available to all IT staff D) There are no specific requirements for production code access

A23: B) Access to production code on application servers should be restricted.

The content explicitly states: "The importance of restricting access to production code on application servers is highlighted, suggesting using different accounts for work in the production and development environments as a mitigation strategy." This aligns with the principle of least privilege, ensuring that only personnel who absolutely require access to production code have it. This separation of duties and access control helps prevent unauthorized or accidental changes to production systems that could introduce vulnerabilities or disrupt operations.

Additional resource: https://www.pcisecuritystandards.org/merchants/process/

Q24: Explain why it's recommended to use different accounts for development and production environments. What security principle does this reflect?

A24: Using different accounts for development and production environments is recommended because it implements the principle of separation of duties and least privilege, which are fundamental security concepts.

As stated in the content: "Companies can keep their customers' information safe by making sure that only the right people can access the code on their servers. Make sure you are using different accounts for development and production."

This separation provides several security benefits:

1. Containment of compromises: If a development account is compromised, the attacker doesn't automatically gain access to production systems where sensitive data resides.

2. Prevention of accidental changes: Developers working in development environments cannot accidentally make changes directly to production systems, which could cause outages or introduce vulnerabilities.

3. Audit trail clarity: When separate accounts are used, it's easier to track who made changes to which environment, enhancing accountability.

4. Least privilege implementation: This approach ensures individuals only have the access they need to perform their specific job functions - developers need development access but typically don't need production access for their daily work.

5. Reduction of insider threat risk: It creates an additional barrier for malicious insiders who would need to obtain separate

production credentials to cause harm.

This recommendation reflects the principle of separation of duties, which prevents any single individual from controlling all aspects of a critical process, and least privilege, which restricts access rights to only what is necessary for users to complete their assigned tasks. Together, these principles form a cornerstone of information security and are particularly important in environments handling sensitive payment card data.

Additional resource: https://www.pcisecuritystandards.org/document_library/

Q25: Describe how continuous behavioral analysis helps detect malware that might evade traditional signature-based detection. Include examples of suspicious behaviors that might indicate malware infection.

A25: Continuous behavioral analysis is an advanced malware detection approach that focuses on identifying suspicious activities and behaviors rather than relying solely on known malware signatures. As mentioned in the content, this is one of the recommended methods to "detect any hidden malware that might have slipped past our defenses."

How continuous behavioral analysis works:

1. Runtime monitoring: Unlike signature-based detection that scans files before execution, behavioral analysis monitors systems during operation, observing how programs behave when running.
2. Baseline establishment: The system establishes normal behavior patterns for the environment, applications, and users.
3. Anomaly detection: Deviations from these normal patterns trigger alerts for investigation, even if the specific malware variant has never been seen before.
4. Contextual analysis: Behaviors are evaluated within the context of the environment, reducing false positives by understanding what's normal for specific systems.

This approach is particularly effective against:

1. Zero-day threats: New malware without known signatures
2. Polymorphic malware: As mentioned in the content, malware that "can change its appearance to try and avoid detection"
3. Fileless malware: Threats that operate entirely in memory without writing files to disk
4. Advanced persistent threats: Sophisticated attacks designed to remain undetected

Examples of suspicious behaviors that might indicate malware infection:

1. Unusual system calls or API usage:
    - Programs making calls to encryption functions unexpectedly (potential ransomware)
    - Applications attempting to disable security tools
    - Unusual memory manipulation techniques

2. Abnormal network activities:
    - Communication with known command and control servers
    - Unexpected data exfiltration attempts
    - DNS requests to suspicious domains
    - Unusual scanning of internal network resources
3. File system anomalies:
    - Mass file type conversions (typical of ransomware)
    - Unexpected creation of executable files in temporary directories
    - High rates of file reads/writes (potential data harvesting)
    - Modifications to system files
4. Privilege and account behavior:
    - Attempts to escalate privileges
    - Creation of unexpected user accounts
    - Authentication attempts outside normal working hours
    - Unusual lateral movement between systems
5. Process anomalies:
    - Legitimate Windows processes spawning unexpected child processes
    - Processes injecting code into other processes
    - Unusual process parent-child relationships
    - System processes running from non-standard locations

By continuously monitoring for these types of behaviors, security systems can detect sophisticated malware that evades traditional signature-based detection methods. This approach is particularly important for protecting cardholder data environments as required by PCI DSS Requirement 5, as it provides a more robust defense against advanced threats like the botnets and polymorphic malware mentioned in the content.

Additional resource: https://www.pcisecuritystandards.org/pci_security/standard_overview

23

Control Objective 4 - Question Set

Implement Strong Access Control Measures

Q1: What is the primary purpose of Requirement 7 in PCI DSS?

A1: The primary purpose of Requirement 7 is to restrict access to system components and cardholder data on a "business need-to-know" basis. This requirement implements administrative controls that ensure only authorized individuals with a legitimate business need can access cardholder data. By applying the principle of least privilege, organizations limit access rights to only what is necessary for individuals to perform their job functions. This significantly reduces the risk of unauthorized access to sensitive data and helps ensure that cardholder data is used responsibly and appropriately. The requirement applies to all personnel who might interact with cardholder data, including employees, contractors, consultants, vendors, and third-party service providers, as well as to service accounts used by applications and systems.

Additional resources: https://www.pcisecuritystandards.org/document_library/

Q2: True or False: The concept of "least privilege" means giving all employees equal access to all systems to ensure work efficiency.

A2: False. The concept of "least privilege" is the exact opposite of giving all employees equal access. Least privilege means giving people access only to the specific data and systems they need to perform their job functions – no more, no less. This approach minimizes risk by ensuring that employees cannot access sensitive information that is not necessary for their roles. By implementing least privilege, organizations reduce the potential for data breaches from both external attackers who might compromise an account and from internal threats. Regular reviews of access privileges help maintain this principle by preventing privilege creep over time. This targeted approach to access control is a cornerstone of effective data security governance.

Additional resources: https://www.sans.org/security-resources/policies/general/pdf/principle-of-least-privilege

Q3: Multi-factor authentication (MFA) is required in which of the following scenarios according to PCI DSS? (Select all that apply)

a) For consumer cardholder accounts accessing their own data b) For all non-console access to the CDE for personnel with administrative access c) For all access to the CDE d) For personnel remotely accessing the CDE from outside the trusted network

A3: The correct answers are b) For all non-console access to the CDE for personnel with administrative access, c) For all access to the CDE, and d) For personnel remotely accessing the CDE from outside the trusted network.

PCI DSS Requirement 8 mandates that MFA must be implemented for all non-console (remote) access to the CDE for personnel with administrative access rights. Additionally, it requires MFA protection for all access to the CDE. This includes administrators, standard users, third parties, and vendors who are accessing the CDE remotely from outside the trusted network.

It's important to note that consumer or cardholder accounts (option a) are not governed by Requirement 8. This means that while implementing MFA for customer accounts might be a good security practice, it is not specifically mandated by PCI DSS Requirement 8.

Additional resources: https://blog.pcisecuritystandards.org/multi-factor-authentication-for-everyone

Q4: Describe the three main categories of PCI DSS requirements related to physical access controls and explain how they differ in scope.

A4: PCI DSS Requirement 9 categorizes physical access controls into three distinct scopes:

1. **Sensitive Areas Only**: These requirements apply exclusively to designated sensitive areas where cardholder data is processed, stored, or transmitted. These areas have higher security needs due to the direct presence of cardholder data or critical systems. Controls might include more stringent authentication methods, specialized monitoring, or restricted personnel access lists.

2. **Cardholder Data Environment (CDE)**: These requirements apply to the entire CDE, which encompasses all people, processes, and technologies that store, process, or transmit cardholder data or sensitive authentication data, as well as any sensitive areas contained within the CDE. The CDE includes connected systems that could impact the security of payment processing.

3. **Facility-Wide**: These requirements apply to the physical boundary of the business premises, such as buildings, office areas, or perimeters. These controls exist outside of the CDE and sensitive areas and might include measures like guard desks that check visitor identification, general facility access controls, or overall security policies that govern the entire facility.

This tiered approach ensures that security measures are appropriately matched to the risk level of different physical areas, providing comprehensive protection while allowing practical business operations.

Additional resources: https://www.pcisecuritystandards.org/documents/PCI_DSS_v4_0_SAQ_D_Merchant.pdf

Q5: Which of the following statements correctly describes authorization controls as specified in Requirement 7?

a) Authorization controls ensure all employees have access to all data b) Authorization controls ensure that access to cardholder data is granted only to those who need it and only when absolutely necessary c) Authorization controls are only needed for external contractors, not employees d) Authorization controls are primarily focused on physical access restrictions

A5: The correct answer is b) Authorization controls ensure that access to cardholder data is granted only to those who need it and only when absolutely necessary.

Requirement 7 emphasizes that authorization controls should create a secure environment where each user is given access tailored to their specific role and responsibilities. This helps protect sensitive information by ensuring that only individuals with a legitimate business need can access cardholder data. The requirement uses the analogy of having "a key that fits the exact lock it needs to open - no more, no less."

This approach contrasts with option a), which would create significant security risks by giving everyone access to everything. Option c) is incorrect because authorization controls apply to all personnel who might interact with cardholder data, including employees, contractors, consultants, vendors, and third-party service providers. Option d) is incorrect because authorization controls in Requirement 7 focus on administrative and logical access, while physical access restrictions are primarily covered in Requirement 9.

Additional resources: https://www.pcisecuritystandards.org/pci_security/maintaining_payment_security

Q6: What does PCI DSS require regarding the use of shared or generic user IDs?

A6: PCI DSS Requirement 8 explicitly prohibits the use of shared or generic user IDs for system access. Each user must be assigned a unique user ID that specifically identifies that individual. This requirement ensures accountability and traceability by making it possible to link actions performed on critical systems to specific individuals.

When everyone uses their own unique identification, it becomes possible to:

- Track who accessed what data and when
- Identify who made specific changes to systems or data
- Investigate security incidents more effectively
- Apply appropriate access controls based on individual roles
- Maintain accurate audit trails for compliance purposes

The prohibition on shared accounts helps prevent situations where multiple people know the same credentials, which would make it impossible to determine who performed a specific action. This requirement applies to all personnel with access to system components, including administrators, standard users, and third parties. It's worth noting that system and application accounts (service accounts) have different considerations, but even these should be carefully controlled and not used for regular interactive logins by users.

Additional resources: https://www.pcisecuritystandards.org/documents/Guidance-PCI-DSS-Scoping-and-Segmentation_v1.0.pdf

Q7: How should an organization manage access to physical media containing cardholder data according to Requirement 9?

A7: According to PCI DSS Requirement 9, organizations must maintain strict control over the storage and accessibility of all physical media containing cardholder data. This applies to both paper records (such as printed reports, receipts, or forms) and digital media (like USB drives, external hard drives, backup tapes, or CD/DVDs).

Key management practices include:

1. **Secure Storage**: Media must be stored in a physically secure location with restricted access, such as a locked drawer, cabinet, or dedicated secure room. Alternatively, a specialized tape management organization might be used to collect and store media.

2. **Inventory Management**: Organizations must maintain logs to track which media has been sent, where it has gone, and who has access to it. This includes properly labeling media to identify it as containing cardholder data.

3. **Access Controls**: Access to media storage areas should be restricted to authorized personnel with a business need to know.

4. **Secure Disposal**: When no longer needed, media must be destroyed or rendered unrecoverable using secure methods. For paper records, this might include cross-cut shredding, incineration, or pulping. For electronic media, this might include secure wiping, degaussing, or physical destruction.

5. **Transportation Security**: When media needs to be moved, it should be secured during transport and tracked with appropriate logs and accountability measures.

These measures help ensure that cardholder data remains protected throughout its lifecycle, reducing the risk of data breaches through physical means.

Additional resources: https://www.pcisecuritystandards.org/documents/PCI_DSS_for_Small_Merchants_Resource_Guide.pdf

Q8: True or False: Under PCI DSS requirements, it is acceptable to hardcode credentials into code or configuration files as long as the files are encrypted.

A8: False. PCI DSS specifically prohibits hardcoding credentials into code or configuration files under any circumstances, even if the files are encrypted. This practice creates significant security risks because:

1. Hardcoded credentials often exist in multiple places, making it difficult to update them when needed

2. They may be visible to anyone who has access to the code or configuration files

3. They are likely to be included in backups, version control systems, and development environments

4. They may be overlooked during security reviews or credential rotation processes

Instead, credentials for system accounts should be stored securely using appropriate credential management solutions, changed periodically, and configured with appropriate complexity. Organizations should implement proper methods for applications to access credentials securely at runtime, such as secure credential vaults, environment variables protected by access controls, or other secure credential management systems.

This requirement helps prevent unauthorized access to systems and applications by protecting sensitive authentication credentials from exposure in source code or configuration files.

Additional resources: https://owasp.org/www-community/vulnerabilities/Hard-coded_password

Q9: Which of the following are appropriate controls for Point of Interaction (POI) devices according to Requirement 9? (Select all that apply)

a) Maintaining an inventory including make, model, location, and serial number b) Conducting periodic inspections to check for tampering or substitution c) Training personnel to identify and report suspicious devices d) Allowing public access to device storage areas for customer convenience

A9: The correct answers are a) Maintaining an inventory including make, model, location, and serial number, b) Conducting periodic inspections to check for tampering or substitution, and c) Training personnel to identify and report suspicious devices.

PCI DSS Requirement 9, specifically sub-requirement 9.5.1 and its related controls, requires organizations to protect physical payment devices (Point of Interaction devices) from tampering and substitution. This includes:

- Maintaining a current list of devices with details including make, model, location, and serial number to ensure organizations can verify that the devices being used are legitimate
- Conducting regular inspections to identify signs of tampering (like unusual attachments or damage) or substitution (unauthorized replacement with a fraudulent device)
- Training personnel who work with these devices to identify suspicious behavior and report security issues

Option d) is incorrect because allowing public access to device storage areas would compromise security. Instead, these areas should have restricted access limited to authorized personnel only.

These controls work together to prevent attackers from installing skimming devices or replacing legitimate payment devices with fraudulent ones that could capture cardholder data.

Additional resources: https://blog.pcisecuritystandards.org/preventing-terminal-tampering-protecting-the-payments-ecosystem

Q10: Explain how the principle of "business need to know" differs from the concept of "least privilege" in the context of PCI DSS.

A10: While closely related and often used together, "business need to know" and "least privilege" represent distinct but complementary aspects of access control in PCI DSS:

Business Need to Know (emphasized in Requirement 7) refers to the justification for why an individual should have access to specific cardholder data or systems. It focuses on whether there is a legitimate business reason for a person to have access to particular information. This concept asks the question: "Does this person need this information to perform their job responsibilities?" Access should only be granted when there is a clear, documented business purpose.

Least Privilege refers to the level or extent of access that should be granted once a business need has been established. It focuses on providing the minimum permissions necessary to perform the required job functions. This concept ensures that even when someone has a legitimate need to access a system, they only receive the specific privileges required for their role – no more, no less.

For example, a customer service representative might have a business need to know certain customer account information (justifying some access), but the principle of least privilege would ensure they can only view relevant fields, not edit sensitive data or access system administration functions.

Together, these principles create a comprehensive approach: business need to know determines who should have access, while least privilege determines what specific access they should have. Both are essential for creating a secure environment that protects cardholder data.

Additional resources: https://www.nist.gov/blogs/cybersecurity-insights/zero-trust-cybersecurity-never-trust-always-verify

Q11: What role do video cameras play in physical security according to Requirement 9, and where should they be implemented?

A11: According to PCI DSS Requirement 9, video cameras play a critical role in physical security by monitoring and recording access to sensitive areas where cardholder data is stored, processed, or transmitted. These surveillance systems serve multiple purposes:

1. **Deterrence**: The visible presence of cameras discourages unauthorized access attempts and inappropriate behavior
2. **Detection**: Cameras help identify unauthorized access or suspicious activities in real-time
3. **Documentation**: Recorded footage provides evidence for investigating security incidents
4. **Compliance verification**: Video records demonstrate adherence to physical security requirements

Cameras should be implemented to monitor access to sensitive areas within the cardholder data environment (CDE). However, the requirement specifically excludes public-facing areas from this camera monitoring mandate. This means areas like retail floors where customers are present don't require the same level of video surveillance as back-office areas where cardholder data is processed or stored.

The video monitoring system should be configured to retain footage for a sufficient period to support investigations, and access to the monitoring system itself should be restricted to authorized personnel. Additionally, cameras should be positioned to capture entry and exit points, server rooms, data centers, and other areas where cardholder data might be physically accessible.

This surveillance requirement complements other physical security controls like access cards, visitor logs, and physical barriers to create a comprehensive physical security strategy.

Additional resources: https://www.pcisecuritystandards.org/documents/PCI_DSS_v4_0_ROC_Reporting_Template.pdf

Q12: Which of the following statements is TRUE regarding interactive logins for system accounts according to PCI DSS?

a) Interactive logins for system accounts are encouraged to improve system management efficiency b) Interactive logins for system accounts should ideally be blocked via technical controls c) Interactive logins for system accounts are prohibited only for third-party vendors d) Interactive logins for system accounts are required to have simple passwords for emergency access

A12: The correct answer is b) Interactive logins for system accounts should ideally be blocked via technical controls.

PCI DSS Requirement 8 addresses system and application accounts, which are highly privileged accounts that need special protection to prevent compromise. The standard specifically states that interactive logins for system accounts should ideally be blocked through technical controls.

If interactive logins for system accounts must be used by regular users, there are precise requirements that must be followed:

- The use must be restricted
- Proper approval is required
- All use must be documented
- Access must be disabled when the work is completed

Additionally, credentials for system accounts should not be hardcoded into code or configuration files, and passwords should be changed periodically with appropriate complexity.

Options a), c), and d) are all incorrect and would introduce security vulnerabilities if implemented. Encouraging interactive logins, only restricting them for vendors, or using simple passwords would all increase the risk of system compromise.

Additional resources: https://www.pcisecuritystandards.org/documents/PCI_DSS_v4-0.pdf

Q13: How does PCI DSS define the Cardholder Data Environment (CDE) and why is this definition important for implementing Requirements 7, 8, and 9?

A13: PCI DSS defines the Cardholder Data Environment (CDE) as the people, processes, and technologies that store, process, or transmit cardholder data or sensitive authentication data, as well as any connected systems that could impact the security of payment processing.

This definition is crucial for implementing Requirements 7, 8, and 9 because it establishes the scope of where access controls must be applied:

For **Requirement 7** (Restrict access on a business need-to-know basis), understanding the CDE helps organizations identify which systems contain cardholder data and therefore require strict access controls. This allows them to properly implement administrative controls and apply the least privilege principle to the right systems and data.

For **Requirement 8** (Identify users and authenticate access), the CDE definition clarifies where stronger authentication controls like MFA are required. For example, all non-console access to the CDE for personnel with administrative access must be protected by multi-factor authentication, so organizations must clearly understand which systems are within the CDE boundary.

For **Requirement 9** (Restrict physical access), the CDE definition helps organizations determine which physical areas need enhanced protection. Different physical security controls apply to sensitive areas within the CDE versus the broader facility, so properly defining the CDE is essential for implementing appropriate physical safeguards.

By clearly defining the CDE, organizations can ensure they apply the right controls to the right systems, avoiding both security gaps and unnecessary controls on out-of-scope systems.

Additional resources: https://www.pcisecuritystandards.org/documents/PCI_DSS_v4-0_Prioritized_Approach.xlsx

Q14: What should an organization do when reviewing access privileges according to the principle of least privilege?

A14: When reviewing access privileges according to the principle of least privilege, an organization should conduct a systematic evaluation process that includes:

1. **Regular Reviews**: Establish a formal schedule for access privilege reviews (typically quarterly or at least annually) to prevent "privilege creep" over time.
2. **Role-Based Assessment**: Review each role in the organization and determine the minimum access required for individuals to perform their job functions effectively.
3. **Current Need Verification**: Confirm that existing access rights still align with current job responsibilities, especially for employees who have changed roles within the organization.
4. **Excess Privilege Identification**: Look for instances where users have more access than necessary for their current responsibilities and document these cases.
5. **Privilege Adjustment**: Promptly remove or reduce excessive access rights identified during the review process.
6. **Special Access Scrutiny**: Pay particular attention to administrative or privileged accounts, ensuring they are only granted to those with a clear business justification.
7. **Documentation**: Maintain records of all reviews, including who conducted them, what was examined, what changes were made, and approvals for any exceptions.
8. **Automation Consideration**: Where possible, implement automated tools to help identify excessive privileges and streamline the review process.
9. **Integration with HR Processes**: Ensure the review process is connected to personnel changes like role transitions, promotions, or departures to trigger immediate access adjustments.

This systematic approach helps ensure that access rights remain aligned with business needs while minimizing the risk of unauthorized access to cardholder data.

Additional resources: https://csrc.nist.gov/publications/detail/sp/800-53/rev-5/final

Q15: True or False: Consumer or cardholder accounts (the accounts customers use to access their own information) must comply with all the authentication requirements in PCI DSS Requirement 8.

A15: False. Consumer or cardholder accounts (the accounts customers use to access their own information) are not governed by PCI DSS Requirement 8. This is explicitly mentioned in the provided content with the note: "Consumer or Cardholder accounts are not governed by requirement 8."

Requirement 8 focuses on identification and authentication controls for users who have access to the organization's systems and cardholder data environment (CDE), such as employees, administrators, third-party vendors, and service accounts. These users could potentially access multiple customer accounts or backend systems, which is why they need stronger controls.

The authentication requirements for consumer-facing accounts (where customers access only their own data) may be addressed by other security standards or best practices, but they fall outside the scope of PCI DSS Requirement 8. This distinction is important for organizations to understand when implementing their authentication controls and preparing for PCI DSS assessments.

That said, implementing strong authentication for consumer accounts is still a good security practice, even if not specifically mandated by Requirement 8.

Additional resources: https://blog.pcisecuritystandards.org/pci-dss-v4-0-resource-hub

Q16: Which of the following approaches would satisfy the PCI DSS requirements for protecting service accounts? (Select all that apply)

a) Using the same password for all service accounts to simplify management b) Changing passwords for system accounts periodically with appropriate complexity c) Hardcoding credentials in encrypted configuration files d) Blocking interactive logins for system accounts via technical controls e) Implementing proper approval and documentation for any interactive use of system accounts

A16: The correct answers are b) Changing passwords for system accounts periodically with appropriate complexity, d) Blocking interactive logins for system accounts via technical controls, and e) Implementing proper approval and documentation for any interactive use of system accounts.

PCI DSS places specific emphasis on protecting service accounts (system and application accounts) because they often have elevated privileges and access to sensitive systems. The standard recommends:

- Changing passwords for system accounts periodically and ensuring they have appropriate complexity to resist brute force attacks
- Ideally blocking interactive logins for system accounts through technical controls to prevent misuse
- If interactive use is necessary, requiring proper approval, documentation, and disabling access when work is complete

Options a) and c) represent insecure practices that would violate PCI DSS requirements:

- Using the same password for multiple accounts creates a significant security risk, as compromise of one account would affect all accounts
- Hardcoding credentials in configuration files is explicitly prohibited, even if the files are encrypted, as this practice makes credential management difficult and increases the risk of exposure

Service accounts require special attention in access control strategies because they often have privileged access to critical systems and may not be associated with individual users, making accountability more challenging.

Additional resources: https://www.sans.org/blog/secure-service-account-management/

Q17: Describe the importance of identification versus authentication in access control, and how PCI DSS Requirement 8 addresses both concepts.

A17: Identification and authentication are two distinct but complementary components of access control that work together to secure systems:

Identification is the process of determining who is attempting to use a system. It answers the question, "Who are you?" This typically involves a user claiming an identity by providing a username or user ID. Identification establishes which entity (person or program) is attempting to gain access.

Authentication is the process of verifying that the claimed identity is legitimate. It answers the question, "Can you prove you are who you say you are?" This typically involves validating credentials like passwords, security tokens, or biometric factors.

PCI DSS Requirement 8 addresses both concepts:

For **identification**, the requirement mandates that:

- Each user must have a unique user ID (not shared or generic)
- System and application accounts must be identifiable and managed appropriately
- User identification must be implemented for all access to system components

For **authentication**, the requirement specifies that:

- Authentication credentials must have substantial length and complexity
- Multi-factor authentication (MFA) must be implemented for specific access scenarios
- No shared authentication credentials are allowed
- Authentication methods must verify that the entity is actually who they claim to be

The requirement specifically emphasizes that passwords alone are sometimes insufficient for authentication because they can be compromised. That's why PCI DSS requires stronger authentication methods like MFA in high-risk scenarios, such as remote administrative access to the CDE.

By addressing both identification and authentication, Requirement 8 ensures that organizations not only know who is accessing their systems but also have reasonable assurance that the identities are legitimate.

Additional resources: https://csrc.nist.gov/publications/detail/sp/800-63/3/final

Q18: A retail company is implementing PCI DSS requirements for its point-of-sale environment. Which of the following would be the MOST effective way to protect POI (Point of Interaction) devices according to Requirement 9?

a) Installing antivirus software on all POI devices b) Maintaining an inventory of devices and conducting periodic inspections for tampering c) Requiring customers to show ID before using payment terminals d) Encrypting all network traffic from POI devices

A18: The correct answer is b) Maintaining an inventory of devices and conducting periodic inspections for tampering.

PCI DSS Requirement 9.5.1 specifically addresses the protection of physical payment devices (POI devices) from tampering and substitution. The most effective approach according to this requirement includes:

1. Maintaining a complete inventory of devices that includes make, model, location, and serial number of each device
2. Conducting periodic inspections to identify signs of tampering (such as unexpected attachments or damage) or substitution (unauthorized replacement with fraudulent devices)
3. Training personnel to be aware of suspicious behavior and to report tampering or substitution of devices

While the other options may provide some security benefits, they don't address the specific physical security concerns targeted by Requirement 9:

- Option a) (antivirus software) addresses malware but not physical tampering
- Option c) (customer ID verification) might help with fraudulent card use but not device tampering
- Option d) (network encryption) protects data in transit but not the physical devices themselves

The real-world example provided in the content specifically highlights a scenario where a retail store experienced a data breach due to a compromised POI device because they did not implement proper controls such as regular inspections and inventory management. This underscores why option b) is the most effective approach according to PCI DSS Requirement 9.

Additional resources: https://blog.pcisecuritystandards.org/5-reasons-to-protect-pos-systems-and-terminals

Q19: Explain how multi-factor authentication (MFA) enhances security compared to single-factor authentication, and in which scenarios PCI DSS requires its implementation.

A19: Multi-factor authentication (MFA) significantly enhances security compared to single-factor authentication by requiring two or more independent verification methods from different categories of authentication factors:

1. **Something you know** (knowledge factor): passwords, PINs, security questions
2. **Something you have** (possession factor): mobile phones, security tokens, smart cards
3. **Something you are** (inherence factor): fingerprints, facial recognition, voice recognition

The security advantage of MFA is that even if one factor is compromised (such as a password being stolen), an attacker still cannot gain access without the additional factor(s). This creates multiple layers of security that are significantly harder to breach simultaneously.

According to PCI DSS, MFA must be implemented in the following scenarios:

1. **All non-console (remote) access to the CDE for personnel with administrative access rights** - This applies to administrators accessing systems remotely, as these accounts have elevated privileges that could cause significant damage if compromised.
2. **All access to the CDE** - The requirement specifies that all access to the cardholder data environment must be protected by multi-factor authentication.
3. **All remote access from outside the entity's network to the CDE** - This includes administrators, standard users, third parties, and vendors who are accessing the CDE remotely from outside the trusted network.

The standard emphasizes that even if there is no possibility of directly accessing cardholder data, MFA should still be implemented for remote access that could potentially impact or gain access to the CDE or related systems. This is because compromised remote access could be used as a stepping stone to eventually reach cardholder data.

PCI DSS does not require MFA for consumer or cardholder accounts (the accounts customers use to access their own information), though implementing it for these accounts may still be a security best practice.

Additional resources: https://www.pcisecuritystandards.org/documents/Multi-Factor-Authentication-Guidance-v1.pdf

Q20: What are the key differences between how PCI DSS Requirements 7, 8, and 9 approach access control?

A20: PCI DSS Requirements 7, 8, and 9 collectively establish a comprehensive access control framework, with each requirement focusing on a different dimension of access:

Requirement 7: Administrative Access Controls

- Focuses on *who* should have access and why
- Implements the "business need to know" principle
- Addresses access rights and permissions based on job roles
- Emphasizes policy-based controls and access governance
- Concerns the administrative decisions about who gets access to what
- Applies the principle of least privilege to limit access to only what's necessary
- Examples: Role definitions, access request processes, approval workflows

Requirement 8: Technical Access Controls

- Focuses on *how* users prove their identity to gain access
- Implements user identification and authentication mechanisms
- Addresses the technical means of verifying user identities
- Emphasizes credentials, authentication factors, and account management
- Concerns the systems and methods used to validate legitimate users
- Examples: Unique IDs, password requirements, multi-factor authentication, account lockout

Requirement 9: Physical Access Controls

- Focuses on *where* cardholder data can be physically accessed
- Implements protections for physical spaces and media
- Addresses the physical security of locations containing cardholder data
- Emphasizes barriers, monitoring, and physical restrictions
- Concerns the protection of tangible assets and physical access points
- Examples: Badge systems, video monitoring, visitor procedures, media protection

These requirements work together to create a defense-in-depth approach:

- Requirement 7 ensures only the right people are granted access
- Requirement 8 ensures those people are properly identified and authenticated
- Requirement 9 ensures physical protections complement the logical controls

By addressing administrative, technical, and physical dimensions of access control, these requirements create a robust security framework that protects cardholder data from multiple angles.

Additional resources: https://www.pcisecuritystandards.org/documents/Prioritized-Approach-for-PCI_DSS-v4_0.pdf

Q21: True or False: According to PCI DSS, the same physical security controls must be applied uniformly throughout an entire facility where cardholder data is present.

A21: False. According to PCI DSS Requirement 9, physical security controls are not applied uniformly throughout an entire facility but instead are implemented based on a tiered approach with different requirements for different areas.

The content specifically outlines three distinct categories of physical security controls:

1. **Sensitive Areas Only**: Some requirements apply exclusively to designated sensitive areas where cardholder data is processed, stored, or transmitted. These areas have more stringent security requirements due to the direct presence of cardholder data.

2. **Cardholder Data Environment (CDE)**: Some requirements apply to the entire CDE, which includes all people, processes, and technologies that store, process, or transmit cardholder data, as well as any sensitive areas contained within it.

3. **Facility-Wide**: Some requirements apply to the physical boundary of the business premises, such as a building, office area, or perimeter. These controls exist outside of the CDE and sensitive areas, and may include measures like a guard desk that checks identification of visitors.

This tiered approach allows organizations to implement appropriate security controls based on risk levels and operational needs. For example, public-facing areas (like retail floors) have different requirements than back-office areas where cardholder data is processed. Areas with the highest sensitivity receive the most stringent controls, while general facility controls provide a baseline level of security.

This risk-based approach to physical security is more practical and effective than applying uniform controls everywhere, as it concentrates resources where they're most needed.

Additional resources: https://www.pcisecuritystandards.org/documents/PCI_DSS_v4-0_Summary_of_Changes.pdf

Q22: Which of the following is NOT a requirement for system and application accounts (service accounts) according to PCI DSS?

a) Passwords should be changed periodically with appropriate complexity b) Interactive logins should ideally be blocked via technical controls c) Credentials should not be hardcoded into code or configuration files d) All service accounts must use biometric authentication

A22: The correct answer is d) All service accounts must use biometric authentication.

PCI DSS does not require biometric authentication for service accounts. While biometric authentication may be one possible factor in a multi-factor authentication scheme, it is not specifically mandated for service accounts.

The actual requirements for system and application accounts (service accounts) according to PCI DSS include:

- Passwords should be changed periodically with appropriate complexity to ensure they remain secure
- Interactive logins for system accounts should ideally be blocked via technical controls to prevent misuse
- If interactive logins must be used, they require proper approval, documentation, and should be disabled when the work is complete
- Credentials should not be hardcoded into code or configuration files, as this creates security risks

Service accounts require special attention because they often have elevated privileges and are not associated with individual users, making accountability more challenging. The requirements focus on securing these accounts through proper credential management, restricted use, and elimination of risky practices like hardcoding passwords.

Additional resources: https://www.cisecurity.org/insights/white-papers/security-primer-service-account-management

Q23: As a security administrator, you're implementing PCI DSS requirements for a retail environment. Describe how you would apply the concept of "least privilege" to protect cardholder data.

A23: Implementing the concept of "least privilege" in a retail environment to protect cardholder data involves a systematic approach to access control:

Assessment and Role Definition:

1. Identify all roles that interact with the cardholder data environment (CDE), such as cashiers, managers, IT staff, accounting personnel, and vendors.
2. For each role, determine the minimum level of access needed to perform job functions effectively.
3. Document these access requirements clearly, including systems, data, and functions needed.

Access Implementation:

1. Configure point-of-sale systems so cashiers can process transactions but cannot access full card numbers or export customer data.
2. Grant store managers limited administrative functions (like transaction voids or returns) but not access to backend databases or configuration settings.
3. Restrict IT staff access based on specialization - payment application administrators don't need access to network equipment configuration, and vice versa.
4. Provide accounting staff with access to transaction totals and settlement data but not individual cardholder details.

5. Configure vendor access with time-limited credentials and access only to specific systems they need to support.

Technical Controls:

1. Implement role-based access control (RBAC) in all systems containing cardholder data.
2. Use function-specific logins for point-of-sale terminals rather than shared registers.
3. Configure database controls to mask or tokenize card data for most users.
4. Implement application controls that limit data export capabilities.
5. Use network segmentation to restrict access to the CDE from other business systems.

Administrative Processes:

1. Require documented approval for all access requests with business justification.
2. Implement a periodic access review process (quarterly) to identify and remove excessive privileges.
3. Create procedures for immediate access revocation when employees change roles or leave.
4. Maintain audit logs of all access changes for accountability.
5. Develop a process for emergency access that includes temporary elevation with proper documentation and revocation.

This comprehensive approach ensures that employees can perform their jobs effectively while minimizing the risk of unauthorized access to cardholder data, whether through external attacks or insider threats.

Additional resources: https://www.nist.gov/cyberframework/implementation-tiers-and-profiles

Q24: What measures should be taken to protect physical media containing cardholder data when it needs to be transported or shipped offsite?

A24: When physical media containing cardholder data needs to be transported or shipped offsite, several critical security measures must be implemented according to PCI DSS Requirement 9:

Pre-Transport Preparation:

1. **Classification and Labeling**: Properly classify media as containing cardholder data, but without labeling that would identify it as valuable to potential thieves.
2. **Inventory Management**: Record what media is being transported, its contents, destination, and expected delivery timeframe.
3. **Secure Packaging**: Use tamper-evident packaging or containers that would reveal if the media was accessed during transit.
4. **Data Minimization**: When possible, redact, truncate, or tokenize cardholder data to minimize the risk if the media is compromised.

5. **Encryption**: For electronic media, encrypt the data using strong cryptography before transport.

Transport Procedures:

1. **Authorized Couriers**: Use only trusted, authorized couriers or delivery services with tracking capabilities.
2. **Chain of Custody**: Implement a formal chain of custody process with signatures at each transfer point.
3. **Secure Transport Methods**: Use secure transport methods that can be tracked, such as bonded couriers or secure shipping services.
4. **Split Shipments**: For highly sensitive data, consider splitting the information across multiple shipments so that no single lost package contains complete data sets.
5. **Transport Logs**: Maintain detailed logs of all media transportation, including sender, recipient, courier details, and tracking information.

Recipient Procedures:

1. **Verification Process**: Establish procedures for the recipient to verify the integrity of received media.
2. **Confirmation Requirements**: Require confirmation of receipt to complete the chain of custody.
3. **Secure Storage**: Ensure the recipient has appropriate secure storage facilities.

Management Oversight:

1. **Approval Process**: Require management approval for any offsite transport of media containing cardholder data.
2. **Risk Assessment**: Conduct a risk assessment for regular transport routes or methods.
3. **Incident Response Plan**: Develop specific response procedures for lost or delayed media shipments.
4. **Audit Trail**: Maintain complete records of all media transfers for audit purposes.

These measures help ensure that cardholder data remains protected throughout the transportation process, reducing the risk of data breaches through physical means. The goal is to maintain the security, tracking, and accountability of the media from origin to destination.

Additional resources: https://csrc.nist.gov/publications/detail/sp/800-88/rev-1/final

Q25: How do Requirements 7, 8, and 9 work together to implement strong access control measures, and what might happen if one of these requirements is neglected?

A25: Requirements 7, 8, and 9 work together as a comprehensive access control framework that protects cardholder data through complementary layers of security:

How They Work Together:

1. **Requirement 7 (Administrative Controls)** determines WHO should have access based on business need-to-know and

least privilege principles. It establishes the policies and procedures for granting appropriate access based on job roles and responsibilities.

2. **Requirement 8 (Technical Controls)** verifies THAT USERS ARE WHO THEY CLAIM TO BE through proper identification and authentication. It ensures that only legitimate users can access systems through unique IDs, strong authentication methods like MFA, and proper credential management.
3. **Requirement 9 (Physical Controls)** restricts WHERE cardholder data can be physically accessed. It protects the physical environment, media, and devices that store or process cardholder data through measures like facility access controls, media protection, and device monitoring.

These requirements create a defense-in-depth approach where multiple layers of protection must be breached to compromise cardholder data. They address different aspects of the same problem - unauthorized access to cardholder data.

Consequences of Neglecting a Requirement:

If **Requirement** 7 is neglected:

- Users might have excessive privileges beyond what they need
- Access rights might not be reviewed regularly, allowing former employees to retain access
- Service accounts might have unnecessarily broad permissions
- Result: Even properly authenticated users could access or modify data they shouldn't have access to

If **Requirement 8** is neglected:

- Weak authentication could allow credential theft or brute force attacks
- Shared accounts would eliminate accountability
- Lack of MFA would remove a critical security layer for sensitive access
- Result: Unauthorized users could impersonate legitimate users to gain access

If **Requirement 9** is neglected:

- Physical devices could be tampered with or substituted
- Unauthorized individuals could access secure areas
- Media containing cardholder data could be stolen
- Result: Attackers could bypass logical controls through physical access

The real-world example provided in the content illustrates this interconnection: a retail store experienced a data breach due to a compromised point of interaction device because they neglected physical security controls from Requirement 9. This shows how a failure in one area (physical security) can undermine the entire security posture, even if the other requirements are well-implemented.

A comprehensive approach implementing all three requirements creates a robust security posture that protects cardholder data from multiple attack vectors.

Additional resources: https://www.pcisecuritystandards.org/documents/PCI_DSS_v4.0_At_A_Glance.pdf

24

Control Objective 5 - Question Set

Test and Monitor All Network Systems

Q1: What is the primary purpose of PCI-DSS Requirement 10?

A1: The primary purpose of PCI-DSS Requirement 10 is to establish systems for logging and monitoring all access to system components and cardholder data. This requirement mandates that organizations implement comprehensive logging mechanisms that create tamper-proof records of activities within the cardholder data environment (CDE). These logs must be collected from all devices covered by the standard, stored securely, and analyzed regularly for security events and suspicious activities. The requirement emphasizes that log monitoring should be integrated into day-to-day security operations and paired with incident response processes that can be activated when necessary. Through proper implementation of Requirement 10, organizations can track user activities, detect potential security breaches, and maintain an audit trail that supports security investigations and compliance verification.

Additional Resource: https://www.pcisecuritystandards.org/document_library/

Q2: Which of the following is NOT a key component of Requirement 10? (Multiple Choice)

a) Automated reviews of logs b) Time synchronization across systems c) Quarterly scanning of systems for vulnerabilities d) Tracking and monitoring all access to network resources and cardholder data

A2: The correct answer is c) Quarterly scanning of systems for vulnerabilities.

Quarterly vulnerability scanning is actually a component of Requirement 11 (Testing Security of Systems and Networks Regularly), not Requirement 10. Requirement 10 focuses specifically on logging and monitoring access to systems and cardholder data. The key components of Requirement 10 include automated reviews of logs (10.4.1.1), time synchronization across systems using protocols like NTP (10.6.2), and tracking and monitoring all access to network resources and cardholder data. Requirement 10 is about maintaining visibility into who is accessing what and when, whereas vulnerability scanning in Requirement 11 is about identifying security weaknesses in systems and networks.

Additional Resource: https://blog.pcisecuritystandards.org/pci-dss-requirement-10-tracking-and-monitoring

Q3: True or False: Requirement 10 applies to consumer and cardholder activity.

A3: False. According to the provided content, "Requirement 10 does not apply to consumers or cardholder activity." This means that the logging and monitoring requirements specified in Requirement 10 are focused on tracking system access, administrative actions, and potential security events within the cardholder data environment, rather than tracking the activities of individual consumers or cardholders. The requirement is designed to monitor those who have access to the systems that process or store cardholder data, not the cardholders themselves. This distinction is important from both a compliance and privacy perspective, as it ensures organizations focus their security monitoring on appropriate targets while respecting consumer privacy.

Additional Resource: https://www.pcisecuritystandards.org/pci_security/maintaining_payment_security

Q4: Explain the importance of time synchronization in the context of PCI-DSS Requirement 10 and describe the controls that must be implemented.

A4: Time synchronization is crucial in the context of PCI-DSS Requirement 10 because it ensures consistent and accurate timestamps across all systems in the cardholder data environment. This consistency is essential for several reasons:

1. It enables proper correlation of events across multiple systems during security investigations
2. It provides reliable chronological evidence of actions taken before, during, and after security incidents
3. It supports accurate audit trails that can withstand scrutiny in forensic analysis
4. It helps prevent disputes about the sequence of events during incident response

According to Requirement 10.6.2, organizations must implement specific controls for time synchronization including:

1. Having a formal time server designated as the authoritative time source
2. Restricting access to time settings to only authorized personnel
3. Configuring all systems to use the Network Time Protocol (NTP) or similar technology
4. Ensuring time settings are receiving time signals from industry-accepted time sources

Without proper time synchronization, log analysis becomes significantly more challenging, as events occurring across different systems cannot be reliably sequenced or correlated. This could hamper security investigations and potentially allow attackers to exploit timing discrepancies to conceal their activities.

Additional Resource: https://www.pcisecuritystandards.org/pdfs/pci_ssc_quick_guide.pdf

Q5: When will automated log reviews (Requirement 10.4.1.1) become mandatory only for service providers? (Multiple Choice)

a) March 2023 b) March 2024 c) March 2025 d) March 2026

A5: The correct answer is c) March 2025.

According to the provided content, automated log reviews under requirement 10.4.1.1 "was mandatory for all organizations until March 2025, after which it became a requirement for service providers only." This timeline indicates that while all organizations subject to PCI-DSS must implement automated log reviews until March 2025, after this date, only service providers will be required to maintain this control. This change reflects the evolving nature of the PCI-DSS standard and its recognition of the different risk profiles and security capabilities between service providers and other organizations. Service providers typically have access to multiple merchants' cardholder data, which justifies the continued stringent requirement for automated log reviews.

Additional Resource: https://www.pcisecuritystandards.org/about_us/process_for_changes

Q6: List and describe the steps that must be taken after a security breach according to Requirement 10.7.3.

A6: According to Requirement 10.7.3, the following steps must be taken after a security breach:

1. **Restore Security**: Organizations must take immediate action to contain the breach and restore security controls to prevent further unauthorized access or damage. This includes patching vulnerabilities, isolating affected systems, or implementing additional security measures.

2. **Document the Recovery Process**: A detailed record must be maintained of all actions taken during the recovery process. This documentation serves as evidence of the organization's response and helps identify areas for improvement in security controls and incident response procedures.

3. **Take Required Actions**: Organizations must execute all necessary remediation activities based on the nature and scope of the breach. This may include notifying affected parties, engaging with law enforcement, implementing compensating controls, or making systemic changes to prevent similar breaches.

4. **Restart Monitoring**: If monitoring systems were disabled or compromised during the breach, they must be reestablished to ensure continuous visibility into system activity. This ensures that security teams can detect any persistent threats or follow-up attack attempts.

These steps form a comprehensive approach to breach recovery that not only addresses the immediate security concern but also ensures proper documentation, appropriate remediation, and the restoration of ongoing monitoring capabilities to prevent future incidents.

Additional Resource: https://www.pcisecuritystandards.org/documents/PCI_DSS_v4-0_SAQ_D_ServiceProvider.pdf

Q7: What is the primary challenge associated with implementing PCI-DSS Requirement 11, and why is it still considered necessary?

A7: The primary challenge associated with implementing PCI-DSS Requirement 11 is that it is resource-intensive, requiring considerable planning and a significant portion of an organization's budget, particularly for engaging an Approved Scanning Vendor (ASV). The requirement involves comprehensive security testing activities such as vulnerability scans, penetration testing, and subsequent remediation tasks, all of which demand specialized expertise, tools, and time.

Despite these challenges, Requirement 11 is considered necessary because it provides critical assurance that all in-scope systems and applications remain secure on an ongoing basis. Regular testing helps organizations:

1. Identify and address vulnerabilities before they can be exploited by attackers

2. Verify that security controls are functioning effectively

3. Ensure that changes to the environment haven't introduced new security weaknesses

4. Maintain vigilance against evolving threats and attack techniques

5. Provide evidence of due diligence in protecting cardholder data

As stated in the material, "The importance of Requirement 11 cannot be overstated," and "with proper planning and budgeting, Requirement 11 can be a powerful tool for keeping your organization's data safe and secure." This highlights that while the requirement is demanding in terms of resources, its value in preventing data breaches and protecting cardholder information justifies the investment.

Additional Resource: https://www.pcisecuritystandards.org/documents/Penetration_Testing_Guidance_March_2015.pdf

Q8: Fill in the blank: According to the provided content, the customized approach is ___________ to Requirement 11.

A8: The correct answer is "not applicable".

According to the provided content, "The customized approach is not applicable to requirement 11." This means that organizations must follow the prescribed methods and controls outlined in Requirement 11 without deviation or substitution with alternative controls. Unlike some other PCI-DSS requirements where organizations might have flexibility to implement compensating controls or customized approaches that meet the same security objectives, Requirement 11 must be implemented exactly as specified in the standard. This strict approach reflects the critical nature of regularly testing security systems and networks, and ensures that all organizations maintain a consistent minimum level of security testing to protect cardholder data environments.

Additional Resource: https://blog.pcisecuritystandards.org/pci-dss-v4-0-resource-guide

Q9: Which of the following systems should be employed at the perimeter of the CDE and other critical points according to Requirement 11? (Multiple Choice)

a) Network Time Protocol (NTP) systems b) File Integrity Management (FIM) systems c) Intrusion Detection and Prevention Systems (IDS/IPS) d) Automated Security Vendors (ASV)

A9: The correct answer is c) Intrusion Detection and Prevention Systems (IDS/IPS).

According to the provided content, "intrusion detection and prevention systems (IDS/IPS) should be employed at the perimeter of the CDE and other critical points." These systems are designed to monitor network traffic for suspicious activity and potential attacks, and in the case of IPS, can also take automated actions to block detected threats. Placing these systems at the perimeter of the Cardholder Data Environment and other critical points creates a security boundary that can detect and potentially prevent unauthorized access attempts before they reach sensitive systems or data. While the other options listed are important components of PCI-DSS compliance (NTP for time synchronization, FIM for change detection, and ASV for vulnerability scanning), they are not specifically prescribed for deployment at the CDE perimeter.

Additional Resource: https://www.pcisecuritystandards.org/documents/PCI_DSS_v4-0.pdf

Q10: True or False: Internal vulnerability scans are only required on a quarterly basis under PCI-DSS Requirement 11.

A10: False. While quarterly internal vulnerability scans are a baseline requirement, the provided content specifically states that internal vulnerability scans must be conducted "after any significant changes, regardless of the regular three-month scan cycle." This means that in addition to the regular quarterly scanning schedule, organizations must perform additional internal vulnerability scans whenever significant changes are made to the environment. These significant changes might include network modifications, new system components, upgrades to applications, or changes to security controls. This requirement ensures that new vulnerabilities potentially introduced by changes are promptly identified and addressed, rather than waiting for the next scheduled quarterly scan.

Additional Resource: https://www.pcisecuritystandards.org/documents/ASV_Program_Guide_v3.1.pdf

Q11: Describe the requirements for file integrity monitoring (FIM) according to PCI-DSS, including frequency and response to unauthorized changes.

A11: File Integrity Monitoring (FIM) requirements in PCI-DSS are designed to detect unauthorized modifications to critical system files, configuration files, or content files. According to the provided content:

1. **Frequency**: Critical files must be checked using change-detection tools at least weekly. The requirement specifies that this verification must occur "at least once every seven days."
2. **Scope**: The FIM system should monitor system-critical files that could affect the security of the cardholder data environment or the functionality of security controls.
3. **Response to Unauthorized Changes**: When unauthorized changes are detected, they "should be handled appropriately." This means organizations must:
    - Investigate the cause of the change
    - Determine if the change was authorized but not properly documented
    - Assess the potential impact on security
    - Remediate any unauthorized changes
    - Update documentation and change management processes if needed
    - Consider whether the unauthorized change represents a security incident requiring escalation
4. **Implementation**: The requirement mentions using "change-detection/file integration management (FIM) system" to detect and manage changes.

For e-commerce merchants, there are additional requirements specific to payment pages. They must implement "a detection mechanism... for unauthorized changes on payment pages" with checks occurring at least once every seven days or more frequently based on targeted risk analysis.

The FIM capabilities serve as a critical detective control that helps organizations maintain the integrity of their systems and quickly identify potential security compromises or unauthorized modifications that could lead to data breaches.

Additional Resource: https://www.pcisecuritystandards.org/documents/PCI-DSS-v3.2.1-SAQ-D.pdf

Q12: What is the primary purpose of time synchronization in PCI-DSS Requirement 10, and what protocol is commonly used to achieve this? (Short Answer)

A12: The primary purpose of time synchronization in PCI-DSS Requirement 10 is to ensure consistent and accurate timestamps across all systems in the cardholder data environment, which enables proper correlation of events during security analysis and investigations. The Network Time Protocol (NTP) is the commonly used protocol to achieve this synchronization. Time synchronization makes it possible to establish the precise sequence of events across multiple systems during security incidents, ensuring that audit logs have reliable timestamps that can be trusted for forensic analysis and compliance verification.

Additional Resource: https://www.nist.gov/publications/network-time-protocol-best-practices

Q13: If an organization chooses to conduct penetration testing using their own team under Requirement 11, what conditions must be met? (Multiple Choice, select all that apply)

a) The team must be certified by the Payment Card Industry Security Standards Council b) The team must be qualified and independent from the system owner c) The team must document their process for meeting the testing methodology d) The team must be from a third-party provider e) The team must conduct testing at least quarterly

A13: The correct answers are b) The team must be qualified and independent from the system owner, and c) The team must document their process for meeting the testing methodology.

According to the provided content, if an organization decides to conduct penetration testing using their own team, they must "ensure they are qualified and independent and document their process for meeting the methodology." This means that internal penetration testers must have appropriate qualifications and skills to conduct effective testing, must be organizationally independent from those responsible for the systems being tested (to avoid conflicts of interest), and must follow a documented methodology that aligns with industry standards for penetration testing.

There is no specific requirement that the team must be certified by the PCI SSC (though certifications may be part of demonstrating qualification), nor is there a requirement that penetration testing must be conducted by third-party providers or performed quarterly.

Additional Resource: https://www.pcisecuritystandards.org/documents/Penetration-Testing-Guidance-v1_1.pdf

Q14: Explain the significance of automated log reviews in PCI-DSS Requirement 10 and when this requirement will change for different types of organizations.

A14: Automated log reviews, as specified in PCI-DSS Requirement 10.4.1.1, are a critical component of security monitoring that enables organizations to efficiently analyze large volumes of log data to detect potential security incidents. The significance of automated log reviews includes:

1. The ability to process and analyze logs from numerous systems and devices in near real-time

2. Consistent application of detection rules without human error or oversight

3. 24/7 monitoring capability that doesn't rely on analyst availability

4. The capacity to correlate events across multiple systems to identify complex attack patterns

5. Prompt alerting when suspicious activities are detected, enabling faster incident response

According to the provided content, the requirement for automated log reviews has a significant timeline change: it "was mandatory for all organizations until March 2025, after which it became a requirement for service providers only." This means that after March 2025, only service providers (entities that process, store, or transmit cardholder data on behalf of other entities) will be required to maintain automated log review capabilities.

This change reflects a risk-based approach to compliance, recognizing that service providers typically represent a higher concentration of risk due to their access to multiple merchants' cardholder data. For non-service provider organizations after March 2025, while automated log reviews may still be recommended as a security best practice, they will no longer be explicitly required for PCI-DSS compliance.

Additional Resource: https://www.pcisecuritystandards.org/documents/PCI_DSS_v4-0_Summary_of_Changes.pdf

Q15: What additional requirement do service providers have regarding malware detection compared to other organizations under Requirement 11? (Short Answer)

A15: Under Requirement 11, service providers have the additional requirement to detect covert malware communication channels. This means they must implement systems and processes capable of identifying hidden or encrypted communications that malware might use to communicate with command and control servers, exfiltrate data, or receive instructions. This requirement recognizes the higher risk profile of service providers who typically have access to multiple merchants' cardholder data, making them attractive targets for sophisticated attacks that may use covert channels to avoid detection by traditional security controls.

Additional Resource: https://www.pcisecuritystandards.org/documents/PCI_DSS_v4-0_ROC_Reporting_Template.pdf

Q16: When establishing an incident response plan in accordance with PCI-DSS Requirements, what should be done whenever an alert is received?

A16: According to the provided content, whenever an alert is received, it "should be followed up on and partnered with an incident response process that is ready to take action if necessary." This means that organizations should have established procedures for:

1. Promptly reviewing and analyzing the alert to determine its validity and severity

2. Escalating legitimate alerts to the appropriate personnel or teams

3. Conducting initial investigation to understand the scope and nature of the potential incident

4. Activating the broader incident response process if warranted based on the findings

5. Documenting the alert, investigation steps, and outcomes

6. Taking appropriate remedial actions based on the type and severity of the event

7. Ensuring that the incident response team is prepared with the necessary tools, authority, and procedures to respond effectively

This approach ensures that alerts aren't simply acknowledged but are integrated into a comprehensive security response framework that can effectively address potential security incidents. The emphasis on having an incident response process "ready to take action" highlights the importance of preparation and established procedures rather than ad-hoc responses to security events.

Additional Resource: https://www.pcisecuritystandards.org/documents/responding_to_a_breach.pdf

Q17: Which of the following statements about e-commerce merchants and PCI-DSS Requirement 11 is correct? (Multiple Choice)

a) E-commerce merchants are exempt from Requirement 11 b) E-commerce merchants must check payment pages for unauthorized changes at least monthly c) E-commerce merchants must have a detection mechanism for unauthorized changes on payment pages, checked at least once every seven days d) E-commerce merchants can use a customized approach for Requirement 11

A17: The correct answer is c) E-commerce merchants must have a detection mechanism for unauthorized changes on payment pages, checked at least once every seven days.

According to the provided content, "E-commerce merchants must have a detection mechanism in place for unauthorized changes on payment pages, checked at least once every seven days or more frequently based on targeted risk analysis." This requirement is specific to e-commerce merchants because their payment pages are directly accessible from the internet and are common targets for attacks such as web skimming or formjacking, where attackers modify the page code to capture payment card data. Regular checking helps ensure that any unauthorized modifications are quickly detected.

The content also explicitly states that "The customized approach is not applicable to requirement 11," which means option d is incorrect. There is no mention of e-commerce merchants being exempt from Requirement 11 (option a), and the required frequency is weekly (every seven days), not monthly (option b).

Additional Resource: https://blog.pcisecuritystandards.org/protecting-against-web-skimming-attacks

Q18: True or False: Under PCI-DSS Requirement 10, storing audit logs is optional if real-time monitoring is in place.

A18: False. According to the provided content, it is "necessary to store all of these audit logs and analyze them for security events and other suspicious activity." The requirement explicitly states that organizations must both collect and store audit logs from all devices covered by the standard. Real-time monitoring alone is not sufficient for compliance with Requirement 10.

Storing audit logs is crucial because:

1. It provides historical evidence for forensic investigation if a breach is discovered later
2. It allows for trend analysis and detection of slow-developing attack patterns
3. It supports compliance verification during assessments
4. It enables post-incident review to improve security controls

5. It may be required for legal proceedings related to security incidents

The requirement for both storing and analyzing logs emphasizes the complementary nature of these activities in maintaining effective security monitoring within the cardholder data environment.

Additional Resource: https://www.pcisecuritystandards.org/documents/PCI_DSS_V4_0_SAQ_A.pdf

Q19: Which of the following describes the proper sequence of actions after a security breach according to Requirement 10.7.3? (Multiple Choice)

a) Document recovery, restore security, restart monitoring, take required actions b) Take required actions, restore security, document recovery, restart monitoring c) Restore security, document recovery, take required actions, restart monitoring d) Restart monitoring, restore security, document recovery, take required actions

A19: The correct answer is c) Restore security, document recovery, take required actions, restart monitoring.

According to the provided content, requirement 10.7.3 outlines the necessary steps that must be taken after a breach in this specific order: "restoring security, documenting the recovery process, taking required actions, and restarting monitoring if it was stopped."

This sequence is logical from a security perspective:

1. First, restore security to prevent further unauthorized access and contain the breach
2. Document the recovery process while it's happening to maintain accurate records
3. Take required actions based on the nature of the breach (which may include notifications, additional controls, etc.)
4. Finally, restart monitoring systems if they were disabled during the incident

Following this prescribed order ensures that the immediate security risk is addressed first, while still ensuring proper documentation and follow-up actions occur.

Additional Resource: https://www.pcisecuritystandards.org/documents/incident-response-guide.pdf

Q20: What is the purpose of an Approved Scanning Vendor (ASV) in the context of PCI-DSS Requirement 11? (Short Answer)

A20: An Approved Scanning Vendor (ASV) is a security vendor that has been validated by the PCI Security Standards Council to conduct external vulnerability scanning services for PCI-DSS compliance. The purpose of an ASV in the context of Requirement 11 is to perform regular, independent external vulnerability scans of an organization's internet-facing systems and networks to identify security weaknesses that could be exploited by attackers. ASVs use specialized tools and methodologies to detect vulnerabilities, misconfigurations, and other security issues, and provide reports that help organizations remediate these findings. The requirement for ASV scanning is resource-intensive and requires budgeting, as mentioned in the content: "organizations will take considerable planning and a significant amount of an organization's budget to pay for an Automated Security Vendor (ASV)." Using an ASV ensures that vulnerability assessments are conducted by qualified third parties with no conflicts of interest, providing an objective evaluation of an organization's external security posture.

Additional Resource: https://www.pcisecuritystandards.org/assessors_and_solutions/approved_scanning_vendors

Q21: Describe the relationship between Requirement 10 (logging and monitoring) and incident response processes.

A21: The relationship between Requirement 10 (logging and monitoring) and incident response processes is both complementary and interdependent, creating a complete security operations cycle. According to the provided content, "Whenever an alert is received, it should be followed up on and partnered with an incident response process that is ready to take action if necessary."

This relationship can be described as follows:

1. **Detection and Alerting**: Requirement 10 establishes the mechanisms for collecting, storing, and analyzing logs from all systems in the cardholder data environment. These logs serve as the primary source of security alerts when suspicious or unauthorized activities are detected.

2. **Activation of Response**: When monitoring systems generate an alert, this triggers the incident response process. The alert serves as the initial indicator that an investigation and potentially a full incident response may be required.

3. **Investigation Support**: The detailed logs required by Requirement 10 provide the forensic evidence needed by incident responders to investigate the nature, scope, and impact of potential security incidents. Without comprehensive logging, incident response would be severely hampered.

4. **Post-Incident Actions**: Requirement 10.7.3 specifically outlines steps to be taken after a security breach, including "restoring security, documenting the recovery process, taking required actions, and restarting monitoring if it was stopped." These steps are integral components of the incident response process.

5. **Continuous Improvement Cycle**: Analysis of security incidents identified through logging and monitoring helps organizations refine both their monitoring capabilities (improving alert rules, adding new log sources) and their incident response procedures.

This relationship highlights that effective security operations require both robust monitoring capabilities to detect potential incidents and well-defined response processes to address them when they occur. Neither component is sufficient on its own – they must work together as an integrated security framework.

Additional Resource: https://www.pcisecuritystandards.org/documents/PCI_DSS_v4-0_Summary_of_Changes.pdf

Q22: What requirements must be met when retesting after vulnerability remediation according to PCI-DSS Requirement 11? (Multiple Choice, select all that apply)

a) Retesting must be performed by the same individual who performed the original test b) Retesting must verify that vulnerabilities have been resolved c) Retesting must be conducted within 7 days of remediation d) Third-party providers must conduct retesting to confirm issues have been fixed e) Retesting must include a full system scan, not just the remediated vulnerabilities

A22: The correct answers are b) Retesting must verify that vulnerabilities have been resolved, and d) Third-party providers must conduct retesting to confirm issues have been fixed.

According to the provided content, "If you hire a third-party provider, ensure that they will retest to confirm that any issues have been fixed." This directly supports option d. The purpose of retesting is inherently to "verify that vulnerabilities have been resolved" (option b), which is the fundamental goal of the retesting process.

The content does not specify that retesting must be performed by the same individual who performed the original test (option a), nor does it mandate a specific timeframe of 7 days for retesting (option c). Additionally, there is no requirement mentioned that retesting must include a full system scan rather than focusing on the remediated vulnerabilities (option e).

The requirement for third-party providers to conduct retesting ensures that there is independent verification of remediation efforts, providing greater assurance that security issues have been properly addressed.

Additional Resource: https://www.pcisecuritystandards.org/documents/Penetration_Testing_Guidance_March_2015.pdf

Q23: If an organization uses internal staff for penetration testing, what two key requirements must they meet according to PCI-DSS Requirement 11?

A23: According to the provided content, if an organization uses internal staff for penetration testing under PCI-DSS Requirement 11, they must meet two key requirements:

1. The team must be qualified and independent from the system owner

2. The team must document their process for meeting the testing methodology

The qualification requirement ensures that the internal penetration testers have the necessary skills, knowledge, and experience to effectively identify security vulnerabilities. This might include relevant certifications, training, or demonstrated expertise in penetration testing techniques.

The independence requirement is crucial to avoid conflicts of interest and ensure objective testing. The penetration testers should not be the same individuals responsible for designing, implementing, or maintaining the systems being tested, as this could compromise their objectivity or create blind spots in testing.

The documentation requirement ensures that the testing follows a structured, repeatable methodology that aligns with industry standards and covers all necessary aspects of security testing. This documentation provides evidence that the testing was conducted thoroughly and professionally, which is important for demonstrating compliance during PCI-DSS assessments.

These requirements help ensure that internal penetration testing is as effective and objective as testing conducted by third-party specialists, while still allowing organizations the flexibility to use their own staff when appropriate.

Additional Resource: https://www.pcisecuritystandards.org/documents/PCI-Penetration-Testing-Guidance.pdf

Q24: Essay Question: Compare and contrast the key objectives, components, and implementation challenges of PCI-DSS Requirements 10 and 11, and explain how they complement each other in securing cardholder data environments.

A24: **Comparing and Contrasting PCI-DSS Requirements 10 and 11**

PCI-DSS Requirements 10 and 11 represent two critical pillars of payment card security, each with distinct focuses but complementary objectives in protecting cardholder data environments (CDE). This essay examines their key objectives, components, implementation challenges, and how they work together to create a comprehensive security framework.

Key Objectives

Requirement 10 primarily focuses on visibility and detection through logging and monitoring. Its core objective is to ensure that all access to system components and cardholder data is tracked, recorded, and analyzed, creating accountability and enabling the detection of unauthorized activities. As stated in the content, it "should be a primary task for any organization and must be part of its day-to-day security activities." The requirement aims to establish an audit trail that can be used to reconstruct events, identify anomalies, and support incident investigations.

Requirement 11, in contrast, centers on proactive identification and remediation of vulnerabilities before they can be exploited. Its objective is to "ensure that all in-scope systems and applications remain secure from one day to the next" through regular security testing. This requirement takes an offensive security approach by actively testing systems for weaknesses that attackers might exploit.

Key Components

Requirement 10 comprises several key components:

1. Comprehensive logging of all access to systems and cardholder data
2. Time synchronization across systems using NTP to ensure consistent timestamps
3. Secure storage and protection of audit logs
4. Automated reviews of logs for security events (10.4.1.1)
5. Periodic reviews of system components (10.4.2)
6. Procedures for responding to detected security events
7. Specific recovery steps after security breaches (10.7.3)

Requirement 11 includes different but equally important components:

1. Regular vulnerability scanning (both internal and after significant changes)
2. Penetration testing to identify exploitable vulnerabilities
3. Deployment of intrusion detection and prevention systems (IDS/IPS)
4. Change detection/file integrity monitoring (FIM)
5. Detection of unauthorized wireless access points
6. Special monitoring for e-commerce payment pages
7. Detection of covert malware communication channels (for service providers)

Implementation Challenges

The challenges in implementing Requirement 10 primarily involve technical complexity and operational overhead. Organizations must deploy and configure logging across numerous systems, establish time synchronization, implement secure log storage, and develop automated analysis capabilities. The volume of log data can be overwhelming, making effective analysis difficult without proper tools and expertise. Additionally, distinguishing between normal activities and genuine security events requires sophisticated detection rules and experienced security analysts.

Requirement 11 presents different challenges, primarily centered on resources and expertise. The content explicitly states that these activities "are resource intensive and will take considerable planning and a significant amount of an organization's budget." Vulnerability scanning and penetration testing require specialized skills and tools, and may temporarily impact system performance. Remediation of identified vulnerabilities can be complex, especially in legacy systems or environments with strict change management requirements. The requirement for regular testing creates an ongoing operational burden that must be sustained over time.

Complementary Relationship

Requirements 10 and 11 complement each other through a defense-in-depth approach that combines proactive and detective controls:

1. **Temporal Complementarity**: Requirement 11 focuses on identifying and addressing vulnerabilities before exploitation, while Requirement 10 detects and responds to attacks that occur despite preventive measures.
2. **Validation Cycle**: Vulnerability remediation activities from Requirement 11 can be verified through the monitoring capabilities established in Requirement 10, creating a continuous improvement loop.
3. **Coverage Enhancement**: While Requirement 11 might identify known vulnerabilities, Requirement 10 can detect novel attack patterns or zero-day exploits through behavioral analysis of logs.
4. **Incident Response Support**: Alerts generated through Requirement 10 monitoring activate incident response processes, while the testing conducted under Requirement 11 helps simulate and prepare for various attack scenarios.
5. **Comprehensive Security Posture**: Together, these requirements address both the "find and fix" aspects of security (Requirement 11) and the "watch and respond" components (Requirement 10), creating a more robust security posture than either would provide alone.

Conclusion

PCI-DSS Requirements 10 and 11 represent complementary approaches to securing cardholder data environments. Requirement 10 establishes visibility through comprehensive logging and monitoring, enabling detection and response to security events. Requirement 11 focuses on proactive identification and remediation of vulnerabilities through regular testing and scanning. While they present different implementation challenges—technical complexity and operational overhead for Requirement 10, and resource intensity and specialized expertise for Requirement 11—they work together to create a security framework that is both proactive in preventing breaches and responsive in detecting and addressing security incidents. This complementary relationship exemplifies the defense-in-depth principle that is fundamental to effective information security programs.

Additional Resource: https://www.pcisecuritystandards.org/documents/PCI_DSS_v4-0_ROC_Reporting_Template.pdf

Q25: What critical function does Network Time Protocol (NTP) serve in the context of PCI-DSS Requirement 10, and what controls must be implemented around time servers? (Short Answer)

A25: Network Time Protocol (NTP) serves the critical function of synchronizing time across all systems in the cardholder data environment, ensuring consistent and accurate timestamps on all audit logs. This synchronization is essential for proper correlation of security events across multiple systems during incident investigation and analysis. According to Requirement 10.6.2, the controls that must be implemented around time servers include: having a formal time server designated as the authoritative time source, restricting access to time settings to only authorized personnel, and ensuring that time data is received from industry-accepted time sources. These controls prevent potential manipulation of timestamps that could be used to hide unauthorized activities and ensure that log data maintains its integrity and evidentiary value for security investigations.

Additional Resource: https://csrc.nist.gov/publications/detail/white-paper/2016/11/22/securing-network-time-protocol/final

25

Control Objective 6 - Question Set

Maintain a Security Policy

Q1: What are the main components covered in PCI-DSS Requirement 12? (Multiple Choice)

A) Policy and procedure documentation, annual risk assessments, security awareness training, incident response plans, and third-party due diligence B) Network security, firewall configurations, and data encryption only C) Password requirements, user access controls, and physical security measures D) Software development, testing procedures, and change management

A1: The correct answer is A) Policy and procedure documentation, annual risk assessments, security awareness training, incident response plans, and third-party due diligence.

Requirement 12 of PCI-DSS focuses on supporting information security with organizational policies and programs. It ensures that all personnel follow the highest level of security practices through comprehensive documentation, regular risk assessments, proper training, established incident response protocols, and thorough vetting of third-party service providers. This requirement serves as the foundation for an organization's security governance structure.

Additional resource: https://www.pcisecuritystandards.org/document_library/

Q2: True or False: PCI-DSS Requirement 12 only focuses on employee security awareness training.

A2: False.

While security awareness training is an important component of Requirement 12, it is just one aspect of a much broader requirement. Requirement 12 encompasses a comprehensive approach to information security that includes policy and procedure documentation, annual risk assessments, incident response planning, third-party due diligence, and employee screening, among other elements. The requirement aims to establish a complete organizational framework for information security rather than focusing solely on training.

Additional resource: https://www.pcisecuritystandards.org/document_library/

Q3: Explain the importance of an incident response plan as outlined in Requirement 12. (Short Answer)

A3: According to Requirement 12, a robust incident response plan is essential because it enables organizations to respond effectively and quickly to security breaches or incidents. The plan should be developed comprehensively and tested periodically to ensure its effectiveness.

The importance of such a plan includes:

1. Minimizing damage during security incidents
2. Providing clear procedures for staff to follow during emergencies
3. Ensuring proper communication channels during incidents
4. Helping to maintain business continuity
5. Meeting compliance requirements
6. Establishing protocols for evidence preservation and incident documentation
7. Facilitating post-incident analysis to prevent future occurrences

The real-world example provided in the content illustrates this importance: if a small business had an effective incident response plan before a third-party payment processor breach, they could have minimized the damage and responded more effectively to protect customer data.

Additional resource: https://www.pcisecuritystandards.org/document_library/

Q4: By what date will additional requirements for working with third-party companies be implemented? (Multiple Choice)

A) January 2024 B) March 2024 C) January 2025 D) March 2025

A4: The correct answer is D) March 2025.

As mentioned in the key takeaways of the provided content, "As of March 2025, everyone will have to learn more about how to stay safe when working with other companies." This refers to new requirements in PCI-DSS v4.0 that will become mandatory by this date, particularly focusing on third-party risk management and additional security measures for organizations working with external service providers like payment processors.

Additional resource: https://www.pcisecuritystandards.org/document_library/

Q5: Describe the key elements of a comprehensive security policy according to Requirement 12. (Essay)

A5: According to PCI-DSS Requirement 12, a comprehensive security policy should include several key elements to effectively protect an organization's data and systems:

1. **Documented Policies and Procedures**: Organizations must maintain detailed documentation of all security policies and procedures. These documents should be clear, accessible to relevant personnel, and cover all aspects of information security.
2. **Regular Updates**: Security policies should not be static documents. They must be regularly reviewed and updated to address new threats, vulnerabilities, and changes in the business or technological environment.
3. **Rigorous Enforcement**: Having policies is insufficient if they are not enforced. Organizations must implement mechanisms to ensure compliance with security policies across all levels of the organization.
4. **Risk Assessment Framework**: The policy should include provisions for conducting annual risk assessments to identify vulnerabilities and threats to the organization's information security.
5. **Security Awareness Training**: A comprehensive security policy should mandate regular security awareness training for all personnel to ensure they understand their responsibilities in maintaining information security.
6. **Incident Response Planning**: The policy should outline procedures for responding to security incidents, including roles and responsibilities, communication protocols, and steps for containment, eradication, and recovery.
7. **Third-Party Management**: Guidelines for managing and monitoring third-party service providers, ensuring they comply with the organization's security requirements.
8. **Pre-Employment Screening**: Procedures for screening employees before hiring to ensure they do not pose a security risk.
9. **Assignment of Security Responsibilities**: Clear designation of individuals responsible for key security tasks within the organization.
10. **Critical Technology Policies**: Specific policies governing the use of critical technologies within the organization to minimize security risks.

These elements work together to create a robust security framework that protects the organization's data from potential threats. The policy should be tailored to the organization's specific needs and risk profile while ensuring compliance with PCI-DSS requirements. A well-implemented security policy serves as the foundation for an organization's overall security posture and demonstrates a commitment to protecting sensitive cardholder data.

Additional resource: https://www.pcisecuritystandards.org/document_library/

Q6: What should organizations do regarding third-party managed service providers (MSPs) according to Requirement 12? (Multiple Choice)

A) Trust them implicitly as they have their own security protocols B) Only verify their compliance during the initial contract C) Carefully manage and monitor them to ensure their compliance with security policies D) Avoid using MSPs entirely due to inherent security risks

A6: The correct answer is C) Carefully manage and monitor them to ensure their compliance with security policies.

Requirement 12 emphasizes the importance of third-party due diligence. Organizations must carefully manage and continuously monitor their third-party managed service providers to ensure they comply with the organization's security policies and PCI-DSS requirements. This includes performing proper due diligence before engaging with an MSP, establishing clear security expectations in contracts, regularly assessing their compliance, and maintaining oversight throughout the relationship. The requirement recognizes that third parties can introduce significant security risks if not properly managed.

Additional resource: https://www.pcisecuritystandards.org/document_library/

Q7: What is the significance of the sub-requirement that appears at the end of each requirement? (Short Answer)

A7: The sub-requirement that appears at the end of each PCI-DSS requirement addresses policy documentation. As explicitly stated in the provided content: "At the end of each requirement, there is always a sub-requirement addressing policy documentation."

This is significant because it emphasizes the critical importance of documenting all security policies and procedures related to each requirement. Proper documentation ensures:

1. Consistency in security practices across the organization
2. Clear guidance for all personnel on security expectations
3. Evidence of compliance during assessments and audits
4. A reference point for training new employees
5. A basis for updating and improving security measures
6. Continuity of security practices despite personnel changes

This pattern in the PCI-DSS standard highlights how documentation serves as the foundation for implementing, maintaining, and demonstrating compliance with each requirement. Without proper documentation, even well-designed security controls may be inconsistently applied or difficult to verify during compliance assessments.

Additional resource: https://www.pcisecuritystandards.org/document_library/

Q8: True or False: According to Requirement 12, organizations are not responsible for the security practices of their third-party payment processors.

A8: False.

According to Requirement 12, organizations are indeed responsible for ensuring that their third-party payment processors maintain adequate security practices. The content explicitly states that "if you work with other companies to process payments, they need to show that they are following the rules too" and "before you start working with a new payment company, you need to ensure they follow the rules too."

The requirement emphasizes third-party due diligence, which places the responsibility on organizations to carefully vet, manage, and monitor their payment processors and other service providers. This includes verifying their compliance with PCI-DSS requirements and ensuring they maintain appropriate security measures.

The real-world example provided in the content reinforces this point: a small business owner was held liable for damages caused by a security breach at their third-party payment processor. This illustrates that organizations cannot transfer security responsibility simply by outsourcing payment processing; they remain accountable for protecting their customers' data throughout the payment chain.

Additional resource: https://www.pcisecuritystandards.org/document_library/

Q9: Explain the real-world implications of not properly vetting a third-party payment processor. (Essay)

A9: Failing to properly vet a third-party payment processor can have severe and far-reaching implications for an organization, as illustrated by the real-world example provided in the content about Requirement 12.

Financial Consequences: The most immediate impact is often financial. As demonstrated in the example, when a payment processor experiences a security breach, the business that engaged them may be held liable for damages. These can include regulatory fines (such as those imposed by card brands or regulatory bodies), legal fees, settlement costs from lawsuits, and penalties for PCI-DSS non-compliance. For small businesses especially, these unexpected costs can be devastating and potentially lead to bankruptcy.

Reputational Damage: Beyond direct financial impacts, organizations face significant reputational damage. Customers whose sensitive payment card information has been compromised often lose trust in the business, regardless of whether the breach occurred at a third-party processor. This loss of trust frequently translates to:

- Decreased customer retention
- Reduced new customer acquisition
- Negative publicity and reviews
- Diminished brand value
- Long-term revenue decline

Operational Disruption: A breach at a payment processor can cause substantial operational disruption for the associated business. This may include:

- Temporary inability to process payments
- Need to quickly implement alternative payment methods
- Diversion of staff resources to handle the crisis
- Time spent on investigations and remediation
- Requirement to notify affected customers
- Obligation to provide credit monitoring services to affected individuals

Legal and Regulatory Consequences: Organizations may face legal action from multiple parties:

- Class-action lawsuits from affected customers
- Lawsuits from business partners affected by the breach
- Regulatory investigations and enforcement actions
- Contractual disputes with the processor itself

Long-term Compliance Burden: After experiencing such an incident, organizations typically face enhanced scrutiny and more stringent compliance requirements, including:

- More frequent and thorough PCI-DSS assessments
- Additional documentation requirements
- Potentially higher merchant level classification
- More extensive security controls

Prevention Through Proper Vetting: As highlighted in Requirement 12, organizations can mitigate these risks by:

- Conducting thorough due diligence before engaging payment processors
- Verifying their PCI-DSS compliance status
- Reviewing their security policies and procedures
- Checking their incident response capabilities
- Establishing clear security responsibilities in contracts
- Implementing ongoing monitoring of the processor's security posture
- Requiring regular compliance attestations

The real-world example effectively illustrates how Requirement 12's emphasis on third-party due diligence is not merely a compliance checkbox but a critical business protection measure. By following the policy documentation, risk assessment, security awareness, and third-party management aspects of Requirement 12, organizations can significantly reduce their exposure to these devastating consequences.

Additional resource: https://www.pcisecuritystandards.org/document_library/

Q10: What should be done with security policies according to Requirement 12? (Multiple Choice)

A) Create them once and maintain them without changes B) Update them only after a security incident occurs C) Establish, regularly update, and rigorously enforce them D) Develop them but keep them flexible with minimal enforcement

A10: The correct answer is C) Establish, regularly update, and rigorously enforce them.

According to the provided content on Requirement 12, "a comprehensive security policy should be established, regularly updated, and rigorously enforced." This three-part approach ensures that security policies remain relevant, address emerging threats, and are actually followed throughout the organization. Static policies quickly become outdated in the rapidly evolving cybersecurity landscape, while unenforced policies, no matter how well-written, fail to provide actual protection for cardholder data and other sensitive information.

Additional resource: https://www.pcisecuritystandards.org/document_library/

Q11: How does Requirement 12 address the hiring process? (Short Answer)

A11: Requirement 12 addresses the hiring process by emphasizing the importance of pre-employment screening. According to the content provided, "employees should be thoroughly screened before hiring" as part of an organization's comprehensive approach to information security.

This pre-employment screening serves several security purposes:

1. Helps identify potential security risks before individuals gain access to sensitive cardholder data
2. Verifies the credentials and background of potential employees
3. Reduces the risk of insider threats within the organization
4. Ensures that individuals with appropriate trustworthiness are handling payment card information
5. Establishes a foundation of trust and security from the beginning of employment

This requirement recognizes that people are often the weakest link in security, and proper vetting during the hiring process is a crucial first step in maintaining a secure environment. The screening process should be documented as part of the organization's security policies and consistently applied to all relevant positions that may have access to cardholder data or security systems.

Additional resource: https://www.pcisecuritystandards.org/document_library/

Q12: What is required of payment companies regarding security issues? (Multiple Choice)

A) They must inform their clients only about major security breaches B) They need to scan for problems and fix them C) They are solely responsible for security with no obligations to share information D) They must handle security internally with no external scanning requirements

A12: The correct answer is B) They need to scan for problems and fix them.

According to the key takeaways in the provided content, "You also need to ensure the payment company is scanning for problems and fixing them." Additionally, the content mentions that "the payment company has to give you the information you need to stay safe too," indicating that they have dual responsibilities of both actively identifying and remedying security issues and providing necessary security information to their clients. This reflects PCI-DSS Requirement 12's emphasis on comprehensive security management and third-party accountability.

Additional resource: https://www.pcisecuritystandards.org/document_library/

Q13: True or False: Virtual environments require the same security verification as physical environments under Requirement 12.

A13: True.

According to the provided content, specifically in the key takeaways section, "It's essential to check that everything stays safe even if it's on a computer that's not really there." This statement refers to virtual environments, indicating that they require the same level of security verification as physical environments.

Requirement 12 recognizes that security risks exist regardless of whether systems are implemented in physical or virtual environments. Organizations must ensure that their security policies, procedures, and controls extend to all environments where cardholder data is stored, processed, or transmitted, including virtualized infrastructure.

This is increasingly important as many organizations migrate to cloud-based and virtualized environments. The requirement emphasizes that virtualization does not exempt any system from security requirements, and organizations must maintain consistent security standards across all types of environments to ensure comprehensive protection of cardholder data.

Additional resource: https://www.pcisecuritystandards.org/document_library/

Q14: Discuss the relationship between risk assessments and security policies as outlined in Requirement 12. (Essay)

A14: PCI-DSS Requirement 12 establishes a crucial interdependent relationship between risk assessments and security policies, creating a dynamic framework that enhances an organization's overall security posture.

Risk Assessments Informing Security Policies:

According to Requirement 12, organizations must conduct annual risk assessments as part of their security program. These assessments serve as the foundation for developing and refining security policies by:

1. **Identifying Vulnerabilities and Threats:** Risk assessments systematically identify potential security weaknesses and

threats specific to the organization's environment, payment card processing systems, and business operations.

2. **Prioritizing Risks:** Not all risks carry equal weight. Assessments help quantify and prioritize risks based on their potential impact and likelihood, allowing organizations to focus their security policies on the most critical areas.

3. **Establishing Baseline Requirements:** Risk assessments establish a baseline understanding of the organization's security needs, which directly informs the minimum requirements that should be addressed in security policies.

4. **Justifying Security Investments:** The findings from risk assessments provide concrete evidence to justify investments in security controls, procedures, and technologies that are subsequently documented in security policies.

Security Policies Guiding Risk Management:

Conversely, well-structured security policies provide the framework for effective risk management by:

1. **Formalizing Risk Responses:** Security policies document the organization's official response to identified risks, including risk acceptance, mitigation, avoidance, or transfer strategies.

2. **Standardizing Security Practices:** Policies ensure consistent application of security controls across the organization, reducing the likelihood that risks will be addressed differently by different departments or personnel.

3. **Establishing Accountability:** Security policies clearly define roles and responsibilities for risk management, ensuring that specific individuals are accountable for addressing identified risks.

4. **Setting Compliance Requirements:** Policies translate risk assessment findings into specific compliance requirements that personnel must follow, creating a direct path from risk identification to risk mitigation.

The Cyclical Relationship:

The relationship between risk assessments and security policies in Requirement 12 is cyclical rather than linear:

1. Initial risk assessments inform the development of security policies.

2. Implemented security policies reduce certain risks but may introduce others.

3. Subsequent risk assessments evaluate the effectiveness of existing policies and identify new or changing risks.

4. Security policies are then updated based on these new findings.

5. The cycle continues, ensuring security policies remain relevant and effective.

Real-World Application:

The content's real-world example illustrates this relationship. When a small business owner faces a breach at their third-party payment processor, proper risk assessment would have identified the risks associated with that processor. This assessment would then inform security policies regarding third-party due diligence, which would have potentially prevented the partnership with an insecure processor.

Documentation Requirements:

Requirement 12 emphasizes that both risk assessments and security policies must be thoroughly documented. This documentation serves as evidence of compliance during audits and assessments while also providing a historical record of how the organization's security approach has evolved in response to changing risks.

In conclusion, Requirement 12 establishes risk assessments and security policies as complementary components of an effective security program. Risk assessments provide the intelligence and justification for security policies, while security policies provide the structure and direction for addressing identified risks. This symbiotic relationship ensures that an organization's approach to security remains both evidence-based and operationally effective.

Additional resource: https://www.pcisecuritystandards.org/document_library/

Q15: What is a key takeaway from Requirement 12 regarding other companies you work with? (Multiple Choice)

A) You should limit partnerships to minimize security risks B) You need to check that other companies you work with are also following the rules C) Other companies' security practices are their own responsibility D) You should only work with the largest, most established companies

A15: The correct answer is B) You need to check that other companies you work with are also following the rules.

This is explicitly stated in the key takeaways section of the provided content: "This includes things like making sure everyone knows how to stay safe online, having a plan for when things go wrong, and checking that other companies you work with are also following the rules." The content further emphasizes this point by stating, "If you work with other companies to process payments, they need to show that they are following the rules too."

Requirement 12 places significant emphasis on third-party due diligence, recognizing that an organization's security is only as strong as its weakest link, which often includes external partners and service providers. The organization must verify that all third parties who handle cardholder data or could impact the security of cardholder data are compliant with relevant PCI-DSS requirements.

Additional resource: https://www.pcisecuritystandards.org/document_library/

Q16: Explain what organizations should do before partnering with a new payment company. (Short Answer)

A16: According to Requirement 12, before partnering with a new payment company, organizations should ensure the company follows PCI-DSS rules and security requirements. As stated in the provided content: "Before you start working with a new payment company, you need to ensure they follow the rules too."

This pre-partnership verification process should include:

1. Verifying the payment company's PCI-DSS compliance status, including reviewing their Attestation of Compliance (AOC) or other compliance documentation

2. Assessing their security policies and practices to ensure they meet your organization's security requirements

3. Reviewing their incident response capabilities and history of security incidents

4. Checking their scanning and vulnerability management practices

5. Confirming they have proper documentation of their security procedures

6. Establishing clear contractual terms regarding security responsibilities

7. Verifying they have appropriate security measures for both physical and virtual environments

This due diligence process is crucial because, as demonstrated in the real-world example provided, organizations can be held liable for breaches that occur at their third-party payment processors. Thorough vetting before establishing the partnership can significantly reduce this risk.

Additional resource: https://www.pcisecuritystandards.org/document_library/

Q17: True or False: According to Requirement 12, incident response plans should be developed but don't need to be tested.

A17: False.

According to the provided content on Requirement 12, "a robust incident response plan should be developed and tested periodically to ensure its effectiveness." This clearly indicates that merely developing an incident response plan is insufficient – regular testing is also required.

Testing incident response plans serves several critical purposes:

1. Verifies that the plan works as intended in various scenarios

2. Identifies gaps or weaknesses in the response procedures

3. Ensures that team members understand their roles and responsibilities

4. Builds muscle memory so that responses become more automatic during actual incidents

5. Helps maintain compliance with PCI-DSS requirements

6. Demonstrates due diligence in security preparedness

Without periodic testing, an incident response plan may look good on paper but fail when actually needed during a security incident. Testing can take various forms, including tabletop exercises, simulations, and full-scale drills, all of which help ensure the organization is genuinely prepared to respond effectively to security incidents.

Additional resource: https://www.pcisecuritystandards.org/document_library/

Q18: How does Requirement 12 contribute to the overall security posture of an organization? (Essay)

A18: Requirement 12 serves as the foundational framework for an organization's security governance, playing a pivotal role in establishing, maintaining, and continuously improving the overall security posture. Its contribution can be analyzed across several dimensions:

1. Establishing a Security-Focused Organizational Culture

Requirement 12 mandates comprehensive security policies and programs that permeate throughout the organization. By requiring documented policies, security awareness training, and clear assignment of security responsibilities, it transforms security from an IT department concern into an organization-wide priority. This cultural shift ensures that security becomes embedded in daily operations rather than treated as an afterthought or compliance checkbox.

The requirement's emphasis on thorough employee screening before hiring further reinforces this culture by ensuring that personnel trustworthiness is established from the outset of employment. This creates a foundation where security is valued at all organizational levels.

2. Providing Governance Structure and Accountability

One of Requirement 12's most significant contributions is establishing clear governance for security efforts. By requiring:

- Documented policies and procedures
- Assignment of individuals to key security tasks
- Regular policy updates and enforcement
- Annual risk assessments

It creates a framework where responsibilities are clearly defined, and accountability is established. This governance structure prevents security measures from being implemented haphazardly and ensures consistent application of controls across the organization.

3. Enabling Risk-Based Security Decision Making

The annual risk assessment requirement ensures that security efforts are aligned with actual threats and vulnerabilities rather than perceived risks or compliance checkboxes. This risk-based approach allows organizations to:

- Prioritize security investments based on actual risk levels
- Adapt security controls to changing threat landscapes
- Allocate resources more effectively
- Justify security expenditures based on quantifiable risks

This contributes significantly to a mature security posture by ensuring efforts are focused where they provide the greatest risk reduction.

4. Extending Security Beyond Organizational Boundaries

Requirement 12's emphasis on third-party due diligence recognizes that modern organizations operate within complex ecosystems of partners and service providers. By mandating careful management and monitoring of third parties:

- Security extends to the entire supply chain
- Vulnerabilities introduced by external entities are identified and addressed

- Contractual security requirements enforce consistent controls across partnerships
- Third-party incidents are less likely to impact the organization

The real-world example provided in the content perfectly illustrates this benefit – proper third-party due diligence could have prevented a small business from partnering with a vulnerable payment processor, thereby avoiding a breach and subsequent liability.

5. Providing Incident Preparedness

The requirement for a robust, periodically tested incident response plan significantly enhances an organization's ability to withstand and recover from security incidents. This preparedness:

- Minimizes damage when incidents occur
- Reduces recovery time and associated costs
- Maintains business continuity
- Preserves customer trust through proper incident handling
- Demonstrates due care in security management

Rather than focusing solely on prevention, this aspect of Requirement 12 acknowledges that incidents will occur and ensures organizations can respond effectively when they do.

6. Ensuring Adaptability Through Documentation and Regular Updates

The documentation requirements throughout Requirement 12 create an organizational memory that:

- Preserves security knowledge despite personnel changes
- Provides a baseline for measuring security improvements
- Enables consistent application of security controls
- Facilitates training of new personnel
- Supports compliance verification during assessments

The requirement for regular updates ensures that this documentation remains relevant as technologies, threats, and business needs evolve.

7. Creating Comprehensive Coverage Through Policy Requirements

The content notes that "At the end of each requirement, there is always a sub-requirement addressing policy documentation." This pattern ensures that policies exist for every aspect of PCI-DSS, creating comprehensive coverage without security gaps. This holistic approach prevents the common problem of strong security in some areas but vulnerabilities in others.

8. Preparing for Future Security Challenges

The content mentions new requirements coming in March 2025 related to working with third-party companies. This forward-looking aspect of Requirement 12 ensures organizations continuously evolve their security posture to address emerging threats and changing compliance landscapes.

In conclusion, Requirement 12 contributes to an organization's security posture not merely through specific controls but by establishing the foundational elements necessary for effective security governance. It creates the organizational structures, policies, awareness, and accountability needed to support all other security efforts. While other PCI-DSS requirements may address specific technical controls, Requirement 12 provides the framework that ensures those controls are properly implemented, maintained, and evolved over time – making it perhaps the most crucial requirement for long-term security effectiveness.

Additional resource: https://www.pcisecuritystandards.org/document_library/

Q19: What information must payment companies provide according to Requirement 12? (Multiple Choice)

A) Only information about confirmed breaches B) Technical details about their security infrastructure C) The information organizations need to stay secure D) Financial compensation details in case of breaches

A19: The correct answer is C) The information organizations need to stay secure.

According to the key takeaways in the provided content: "Finally, the payment company has to give you the information you need to stay safe too." This indicates that payment companies have an obligation to share relevant security information with the organizations they serve, enabling those organizations to maintain appropriate security measures.

This information sharing might include details about security practices, vulnerability notifications, compliance attestations, incident notifications, security recommendations, and other information necessary for the organization to properly secure their cardholder data environment and meet their PCI-DSS compliance obligations. This requirement recognizes that effective security requires transparency and collaboration between payment companies and the organizations they serve.

Additional resource: https://www.pcisecuritystandards.org/document_library/

Q20: What is the purpose of conducting annual risk assessments as mentioned in Requirement 12? (Short Answer)

A20: According to Requirement 12, annual risk assessments serve to identify vulnerabilities, threats, and potential security gaps in an organization's systems and processes. The purpose of these assessments is to:

1. Systematically identify and document potential security risks to cardholder data
2. Evaluate the likelihood and potential impact of identified risks
3. Prioritize risks based on their severity and the organization's risk tolerance
4. Inform updates to security policies and procedures
5. Guide resource allocation for security controls and improvements
6. Establish a baseline for measuring security progress over time

7. Ensure that security measures remain appropriate as technologies and threats evolve

8. Provide documentation of due diligence in security management

9. Support compliance with PCI-DSS requirements

10. Identify risks associated with third-party relationships and technologies

The content specifically mentions annual risk assessments as a key component of Requirement 12, indicating their importance in maintaining an effective security program. By conducting these assessments regularly, organizations can maintain a proactive rather than reactive approach to security, addressing vulnerabilities before they can be exploited by malicious actors.

Additional resource: https://www.pcisecuritystandards.org/document_library/

Q21: Which of the following is NOT a component of Requirement 12? (Multiple Choice)

A) Security awareness training B) Incident response planning C) Network segmentation testing D) Third-party due diligence

A21: The correct answer is C) Network segmentation testing.

Based on the provided content, Requirement 12 covers "policy and procedure documentation, annual risk assessments, security awareness training, incident response plans, and third-party due diligence." Network segmentation testing is not mentioned as a component of Requirement 12.

Network segmentation testing is typically associated with other PCI-DSS requirements that focus more on technical security controls and network architecture, rather than the organizational policies and programs that are the focus of Requirement 12. While network segmentation is an important security control that might be referenced in policies developed under Requirement 12, the testing of network segmentation itself is not a primary component of this specific requirement.

Additional resource: https://www.pcisecuritystandards.org/document_library/

Q22: True or False: Employee screening is an important aspect of Requirement 12.

A22: True.

According to the provided content, "employees should be thoroughly screened before hiring" is explicitly mentioned as one of the steps organizations should take as part of Requirement 12. This pre-employment screening is considered an important aspect of creating a secure environment for data protection.

Employee screening helps organizations:

1. Verify the identity and background of potential employees

2. Identify potential security risks before granting access to sensitive systems or data

3. Confirm the qualifications and integrity of individuals who will be handling cardholder data

4. Reduce the risk of insider threats

5. Demonstrate due diligence in personnel security

By including employee screening as part of Requirement 12, PCI-DSS recognizes that people are often the weakest link in security and proper vetting is an essential component of a comprehensive security program.

Additional resource: https://www.pcisecuritystandards.org/document_library/

Q23: Explain how a small business can implement the principles of Requirement 12 to protect customer data. (Essay)

A23: # Implementing PCI-DSS Requirement 12 in a Small Business Environment

Small businesses often face unique challenges when implementing comprehensive security requirements like PCI-DSS Requirement 12. With limited resources, expertise, and time, they must nevertheless protect customer payment card data effectively. The following approach offers a practical roadmap for small businesses to implement the key principles of Requirement 12.

Developing Right-Sized Security Policies

Start with Templates: Small businesses can leverage policy templates specifically designed for their scale rather than creating complex documents from scratch. The PCI Security Standards Council provides small merchant resources that include sample policy templates.

Focus on Relevance: Policies should address only the payment card processes and systems actually used by the business. For example, a small retail shop with a single point-of-sale terminal needs simpler policies than a business with multiple payment channels.

Use Clear Language: Policies should be written in straightforward language that all employees can understand, avoiding technical jargon when possible.

Implementation Steps:

1. Document how payment cards are accepted, processed, and stored
2. Create a simple security policy that addresses these specific processes
3. Outline clear rules for employee handling of payment information
4. Establish password requirements appropriate for the business
5. Document procedures for granting and revoking system access

Practical Risk Assessment Approach

Simplified Annual Assessment: Small businesses can conduct streamlined risk assessments focused specifically on payment card operations.

Checklist Method: Using a checklist-based approach can make risk assessments more manageable while still identifying key vulnerabilities.

Implementation Steps:

1. Create an inventory of all systems that store, process, or transmit cardholder data
2. Identify potential threats to these systems (theft, unauthorized access, etc.)
3. Evaluate basic security controls (physical security, passwords, etc.)
4. Document findings and create a simple action plan for addressing gaps
5. Review this assessment annually or when significant changes occur

Right-Sized Security Awareness

Informal Training: Small businesses can implement security awareness through regular team meetings and practical demonstrations rather than formal training programs.

Relevant Content: Focus training on the specific security threats relevant to the business's payment operations.

Implementation Steps:

1. Hold quarterly security discussions during staff meetings
2. Create simple reminders about security practices to post in relevant areas
3. Share real examples of payment card fraud that could affect the business
4. Provide hands-on guidance for secure payment handling
5. Document attendance and topics covered as evidence of training

Manageable Incident Response

Simplified Plan: A small business incident response plan can be straightforward while still covering essential elements.

Clear Communication Chain: Establish who employees should contact immediately if they suspect a security incident.

Implementation Steps:

1. Create a one-page incident response procedure with clear steps
2. Identify key contacts (owner, IT support, payment processor, etc.)
3. Document steps for containing common incidents
4. Maintain a list of external resources for incident assistance
5. Practice the response to a simulated incident annually

Practical Third-Party Management

Focused Due Diligence: Small businesses should concentrate due diligence efforts on their payment processor and any vendors with access to payment systems.

Leverage Attestations: Request and maintain compliance documentation from service providers rather than conducting complex assessments.

Implementation Steps:

1. Maintain a simple list of all service providers involved in payment processing
2. Request PCI-DSS compliance attestations annually
3. Document security expectations in contracts, even if simplified
4. Verify that the payment processor scans for vulnerabilities
5. Confirm the processor will notify the business of security issues

Employee Screening for Small Teams

Basic Background Checks: Even with limited resources, implement fundamental screening for employees who handle payments.

Defined Access Limits: Clearly establish which employees should have access to payment systems and data.

Implementation Steps:

1. Conduct reference checks for all new hires
2. Consider basic background screening for positions with payment access
3. Document which positions require screening and what checks are performed
4. Limit payment system access to essential personnel only
5. Maintain records of screening activities

Technology Use Policies

Focus on Payment Technologies: Small businesses should develop simple policies specifically for technologies used in payment processing.

Practical Security Measures: Implement basic but effective controls for payment devices and systems.

Implementation Steps:

1. Document approved payment devices and software

2. Create simple rules for secure use of payment technologies

3. Establish procedures for updating and maintaining payment systems

4. Define acceptable use of business computers and devices

5. Implement basic controls like screen timeouts and session limits

Documentation and Maintenance

Simplified Documentation: Maintain essential records without creating overwhelming paperwork.

Regular Reviews: Schedule annual reviews of all security policies and procedures.

Implementation Steps:

1. Create a simple filing system for security documentation

2. Use a calendar reminder for annual policy reviews

3. Document any security incidents and the response taken

4. Maintain records of employee acknowledgment of policies

5. Keep service provider compliance attestations on file

Real-World Application

The small business in the provided example could have prevented issues with their third-party payment processor by:

1. Requesting and reviewing the processor's compliance attestation

2. Documenting security expectations in their agreement

3. Periodically verifying continued compliance

4. Having an incident response plan ready in case of processor breaches

5. Limiting cardholder data exposure in their own systems

By implementing these practical approaches to Requirement 12, small businesses can achieve meaningful security improvements and PCI-DSS compliance without overwhelming their limited resources. The key is focusing on the specific payment card risks relevant to their operations and implementing right-sized controls that provide effective protection while remaining manageable for a small organization.

Additional resource: https://www.pcisecuritystandards.org/document_library/

Q24: What should organizations do with their security policies according to Requirement 12? (Multiple Choice)

A) Create them only when specifically requested by auditors B) Establish, regularly update, and rigorously enforce them C) Develop them but allow flexibility in enforcement D) Update them only after security incidents occur

A24: The correct answer is B) Establish, regularly update, and rigorously enforce them.

According to the provided content, "a comprehensive security policy should be established, regularly updated, and rigorously enforced." This three-part approach ensures that security policies are not only created but remain relevant to emerging threats and are actually followed throughout the organization. Security policies that are not regularly updated quickly become outdated as threats evolve, while policies that are not enforced provide little actual protection regardless of how well they are written.

Additional resource: https://www.pcisecuritystandards.org/document_library/

Q25: How does Requirement 12 address the use of critical technologies? (Short Answer)

A25: According to the provided content, Requirement 12 addresses the use of critical technologies by stating that "policies for the use of critical technologies should be implemented." This indicates that organizations must develop and maintain specific policies governing how critical technologies are used within the organization.

These policies for critical technologies should:

1. Define what constitutes "critical technologies" within the organization's environment
2. Establish clear rules and procedures for their secure usage
3. Outline access controls and authentication requirements
4. Define monitoring and logging requirements
5. Specify secure configuration standards
6. Include procedures for patching and updates
7. Detail backup and recovery requirements
8. Address vendor management for technology providers
9. Include employee training requirements specific to these technologies
10. Establish incident response procedures for technology-related incidents

The purpose of these policies is to ensure that technologies that could significantly impact the security of cardholder data are used in a secure manner. This includes technologies directly involved in processing payments as well as those that could provide access to cardholder data environments. By implementing specific policies for critical technologies, organizations can reduce the risk of security breaches resulting from improper use or configuration of these systems.

Additional resource: https://www.pcisecuritystandards.org/document_library/

26

Compensating Controls - Question Set

Q1: What are compensating controls in the context of PCI DSS?

A1: Compensating controls are alternative security measures implemented when an organization cannot meet specific PCI DSS requirements due to legitimate technical or business constraints. They serve as security substitutes that must provide protection equivalent to the original requirement. Compensating controls are not shortcuts or workarounds, but rather carefully designed alternatives that maintain the same level of security and rigor as the original requirement. They allow organizations to achieve PCI DSS compliance while accommodating their unique circumstances, provided they undergo proper risk assessment and validation by a Qualified Security Assessor (QSA).

For more information: https://www.pcisecuritystandards.org/documents/Prioritized-Approach-for-DSS.pdf

Q2: Which of the following is NOT a valid reason to implement compensating controls?

A2: The correct answer is "disagreeing with a PCI DSS requirement." Compensating controls are only appropriate for legitimate technical or business constraints that prevent an organization from implementing the original requirement. The content explicitly states that compensating controls are not for disagreeing with a PCI-DSS requirement or for retroactively addressing missed requirements. They are specifically designed for situations where legitimate constraints make implementation of the original requirement impossible or impractical. Organizations must demonstrate that they have a valid reason beyond preference or convenience.

For more information: https://www.pcisecuritystandards.org/documents/Understanding_SAQs_PCI_DSS_v3.pdf

Q3: True or False: A compensating control must provide equivalent security to the original PCI DSS requirement.

A3: True. The content explicitly states that compensating controls "must provide equivalent security to the original requirement, maintaining the same level of protection and rigor." This is a fundamental principle of compensating controls. They must address the same security concerns and provide the same level of protection as the original requirement, just through alternative means. A compensating control that provides less security than the original requirement would not be acceptable under PCI DSS. The effectiveness of the compensating control in providing equivalent security must be validated by a QSA.

For more information: https://www.pcisecuritystandards.org/documents/PCI_DSS_v3-2-1.pdf

Q4: Describe the process for implementing a valid compensating control.

A4: The process for implementing a valid compensating control involves several key steps:

1. Identify the specific PCI DSS requirement that cannot be met and document the legitimate technical or business constraint preventing implementation.
2. Conduct a thorough risk assessment to understand the security objectives of the original requirement and the risks that need to be addressed.
3. Design a compensating control that provides equivalent security to the original requirement.
4. Document how the compensating control addresses the same security concerns and maintains the same level of protection.
5. Implement the compensating control according to best practices.
6. Have the compensating control reviewed and validated by a PCI Qualified Security Assessor (QSA).
7. Monitor the effectiveness of the compensating control and reassess regularly to determine if the original constraint still exists.

This process ensures that compensating controls are implemented only when necessary and provide appropriate security protections.

For more information: https://www.pcisecuritystandards.org/documents/Guidance-PCI-DSS-Scoping-and-Segmentation.pdf

Q5: When evaluating a compensating control, what must a PCI QSA verify?

A5: When evaluating a compensating control, a PCI Qualified Security Assessor (QSA) must verify several critical elements:

1. That there is a legitimate technical or business constraint preventing implementation of the original requirement
2. That the compensating control provides equivalent security to the original requirement
3. That a thorough risk assessment was conducted to identify and address all relevant risks
4. That the compensating control maintains the same level of protection and rigor as the original requirement
5. That the compensating control is properly implemented and functioning as intended
6. That the compensating control is not being used simply because the organization disagrees with or wants to avoid the original requirement
7. That appropriate documentation exists explaining the constraint and justifying the compensating control

The QSA's validation is essential for the compensating control to be considered valid under PCI DSS.

For more information: https://www.pcisecuritystandards.org/documents/PCI_DSS_QSA_Guidelines_v3.pdf

Q6: List three examples of compensating controls mentioned in the content.

A6: The content specifically mentions three examples of compensating controls:

1. Network segmentation - Isolating systems that store, process, or transmit cardholder data from other systems to reduce the attack surface and limit potential exposure.

2. Encryption - Using cryptographic techniques to protect data beyond what may be specifically required, potentially compensating for other security controls.

3. Regular audits - Implementing frequent and comprehensive security audits to detect and address potential vulnerabilities or unauthorized access attempts.

Additionally, the content mentions two specific scenarios: using a third-party payment processor as a compensating control when encryption software is unaffordable, and implementing a VPN with strong encryption and strict access controls when legacy software cannot support multi-factor authentication.

For more information: https://www.pcisecuritystandards.org/documents/PCI_DSS_Risk_Assmt_Guidelines_v1.pdf

Q7: What is the relationship between risk assessment and compensating controls?

A7: Risk assessment plays a crucial role in the implementation of compensating controls. The relationship between the two can be described as follows:

1. Risk assessment is a prerequisite for implementing compensating controls. The content explicitly states that implementing compensating controls "requires a thorough risk assessment to ensure they are as effective as the original requirement in mitigating risk."

2. Risk assessment helps identify the security objectives of the original requirement and the specific risks that need to be addressed by the compensating control.

3. Through risk assessment, organizations can determine whether a proposed compensating control provides equivalent security to the original requirement.

4. Risk assessment provides the evidence and justification needed to demonstrate to a QSA that the compensating control is appropriate and effective.

5. Ongoing risk assessment helps organizations monitor the effectiveness of compensating controls and determine if they need to be adjusted or if the original constraint has been resolved.

Without a thorough risk assessment, organizations cannot properly design, implement, or validate compensating controls.

For more information: https://www.pcisecuritystandards.org/documents/Prioritized-Approach-for-DSS.pdf

Q8: In what circumstances are compensating controls NOT appropriate?

A8: According to the content, compensating controls are NOT appropriate in the following circumstances:

1. When an organization disagrees with a PCI DSS requirement - Compensating controls cannot be used simply because an organization does not like or agree with a specific requirement.

2. For retroactively addressing missed requirements - Compensating controls are not meant to be used as a remedy for requirements that were overlooked or ignored during implementation.

3. When there is no legitimate technical or business constraint - If an organization can feasibly implement the original requirement but chooses not to for convenience or preference, compensating controls are not appropriate.

4. When the proposed alternative does not provide equivalent security - If a potential compensating control cannot provide the same level of protection and rigor as the original requirement, it is not appropriate.

Compensating controls are specifically designed for situations with legitimate constraints and must maintain the security objectives of the original requirements.

For more information: https://www.pcisecuritystandards.org/documents/Understanding_SAQs_PCI_DSS_v3.pdf

Q9: For a small business that cannot afford high-end encryption software, what compensating control was suggested in the content?

A9: The content specifically mentions that for a small online business that cannot afford high-end encryption software, a suggested compensating control would be "using a third-party payment processor." This approach transfers the responsibility for securing the payment card data to a specialized service provider who already has robust security measures in place, including encryption.

By using a third-party payment processor, the small business avoids having to store, process, or transmit cardholder data directly, which significantly reduces their PCI DSS scope and security requirements. The payment processor, which specializes in secure transactions, would handle the encryption and other security measures required to protect the cardholder data. This serves as an effective compensating control because it addresses the security concern (protecting cardholder data) through an alternative means that is more feasible for the small business while maintaining equivalent security.

For more information: https://www.pcisecuritystandards.org/documents/Small_Merchant_Guide_to_Safe_Payments.pdf

Q10: What compensating control could be used if legacy software cannot support multi-factor authentication?

A10: According to the content, if legacy software cannot support multi-factor authentication, an appropriate compensating control could be "a VPN with strong encryption and strict access controls." This compensating control addresses the security objective of multi-factor authentication (preventing unauthorized access) through alternative means.

The VPN with strong encryption creates a secure tunnel for accessing the system, ensuring that communications are protected from interception. The strict access controls limit who can access the system and what they can do once connected. Together, these measures provide layered security that compensates for the inability to implement multi-factor authentication directly in the legacy software.

This example illustrates how compensating controls can use different security technologies and approaches to achieve equivalent security outcomes when the original requirement cannot be implemented due to legitimate technical constraints.

For more information: https://www.pcisecuritystandards.org/documents/Multi-Factor-Authentication-Guidance-v1_0.pdf

Q11: Multiple Choice: Who must review compensating controls for them to be valid under PCI DSS?

A11: The correct answer is "A PCI Qualified Security Assessor (QSA)."

The content explicitly states that "a compensating control must be reviewed by a PCI QSA to be valid." This review and validation by a qualified independent assessor is crucial to ensure that the compensating control truly provides equivalent security to the original requirement. The QSA evaluates whether the compensating control addresses the same security concerns and maintains the same level of protection as the original requirement.

Other roles such as internal security teams, compliance officers, or even the Chief Information Security Officer, while important for implementing security measures, do not have the authority to validate compensating controls for PCI DSS compliance purposes. Only a properly qualified QSA can make this determination.

For more information: https://www.pcisecuritystandards.org/documents/PCI_DSS_QSA_Guidelines_v3.pdf

Q12: True or False: Compensating controls are appropriate for retroactively addressing missed requirements.

A12: False. The content explicitly states that "compensating controls are not for retroactively addressing missed requirements." Compensating controls are specifically designed for situations where legitimate technical or business constraints prevent an organization from implementing a specific PCI DSS requirement as written.

They are not meant to be used as a remedy for requirements that were overlooked, ignored, or not properly implemented in the past. Organizations cannot simply claim they are using compensating controls to address requirements they failed to implement previously.

Compensating controls must be planned and implemented with proper justification based on legitimate constraints, not as an afterthought to address compliance gaps discovered during an assessment.

For more information: https://www.pcisecuritystandards.org/documents/PCI_DSS_v3-2-1.pdf

Q13: Explain the concept of "equivalent security" in the context of compensating controls.

A13: "Equivalent security" is a fundamental principle of compensating controls in PCI DSS. It means that while the compensating control may use different methods or technologies than the original requirement, it must provide the same level of protection against the risks that the original requirement was designed to address.

Key aspects of equivalent security include:

1. The compensating control must address the same security objectives as the original requirement.

2. It must protect against the same threats and vulnerabilities.

3. It must maintain the same level of protection and rigor as the original requirement.

4. It cannot result in a lower security posture than would be achieved by implementing the original requirement.

5. It must be demonstrably effective at mitigating the identified risks.

For example, if the original requirement calls for encryption of stored cardholder data, a compensating control might use a combination of network segmentation, access controls, and monitoring to provide equivalent protection against unauthorized access to that data.

Equivalent security ensures that while organizations have flexibility in how they implement security measures, they cannot compromise on the level of protection provided to cardholder data.

For more information: https://www.pcisecuritystandards.org/documents/Guidance-PCI-DSS-Scoping-and-Segmentation.pdf

Q14: What role does documentation play in implementing compensating controls?

A14: Documentation plays a crucial role in implementing compensating controls for PCI DSS compliance. Proper documentation is essential for:

1. Justification: Documenting the legitimate technical or business constraint that prevents implementation of the original requirement.

2. Risk Assessment: Documenting the thorough risk assessment performed, including identified risks, vulnerabilities, and how the compensating control addresses them.

3. Design and Implementation: Providing detailed information about how the compensating control is designed and implemented.

4. Equivalence Demonstration: Explaining how the compensating control provides equivalent security to the original requirement.

5. Validation: Providing the necessary information for a QSA to review and validate the compensating control.

6. Ongoing Compliance: Maintaining records of testing, monitoring, and updates to the compensating control.

7. Historical Record: Creating a historical record that can be referenced during future assessments or if questions arise.

Without comprehensive documentation, organizations cannot demonstrate the appropriateness and effectiveness of their compensating controls, potentially leading to compliance issues during assessments. Documentation serves as evidence that the compensating control was implemented with proper consideration and not as a convenience or shortcut.

For more information: https://www.pcisecuritystandards.org/documents/PCI_DSS_v3-2-1.pdf

Q15: Multiple Choice: What is required before implementing compensating controls?

A15: The correct answer is "A thorough risk assessment."

The content explicitly states that implementing compensating controls "requires a thorough risk assessment to ensure they are as effective as the original requirement in mitigating risk." This risk assessment is a critical prerequisite for implementing compensating controls because it:

1. Identifies the security objectives of the original requirement
2. Evaluates the risks that need to be addressed
3. Determines whether the proposed compensating control provides equivalent security
4. Provides the foundation for justifying the compensating control to a QSA

Without a thorough risk assessment, organizations cannot properly design, implement, or validate compensating controls. The risk assessment ensures that the compensating control addresses the same security concerns and provides the same level of protection as the original requirement.

For more information: https://www.pcisecuritystandards.org/documents/PCI_DSS_Risk_Assmt_Guidelines_v1.pdf

Q16: Describe a scenario where implementing a compensating control would be appropriate, including the constraint and solution.

A16: Scenario: A hospital uses a critical legacy medical records system that stores payment card information for patient billing. This system cannot be easily upgraded or replaced, and it cannot implement the PCI DSS requirement for encrypting stored cardholder data.

Constraint: The legacy medical records system is essential for patient care operations and cannot be replaced in the short term due to high costs, complex integration with other medical systems, and the risk of disruption to patient care. The system's architecture does not support encryption of stored data.

Proposed Compensating Control Solution:

1. Implement network segmentation to isolate the legacy system on a separate, highly secured network segment
2. Deploy enhanced access controls requiring multiple levels of authorization for accessing the system
3. Implement comprehensive logging and real-time monitoring of all access to the system
4. Conduct more frequent vulnerability scans and penetration tests for the network segment
5. Apply strict firewall rules limiting connectivity to only essential systems
6. Implement data loss prevention (DLP) technology to detect and prevent unauthorized data exfiltration
7. Conduct additional security awareness training for all staff with access to the system

This compensating control provides equivalent security to encryption by creating multiple layers of protection around the unencrypted data, significantly reducing the risk of unauthorized access or data exposure while accommodating the legitimate technical constraint.

For more information: https://www.pcisecuritystandards.org/documents/Guidance-PCI-DSS-Scoping-and-Segmentation.pdf

Q17: True or False: Network segmentation is an example of a compensating control.

A17: True. The content specifically mentions network segmentation as an example of a compensating control. Network segmentation involves separating networks and systems that store, process, or transmit cardholder data from other networks and systems within an organization.

As a compensating control, network segmentation can help organizations reduce their PCI DSS scope and provide additional security protections when specific requirements cannot be met. By isolating cardholder data environments from other networks, organizations can implement stricter access controls, more focused monitoring, and create additional barriers against potential attackers.

Network segmentation can serve as a compensating control for various PCI DSS requirements by providing an additional layer of protection against unauthorized access and potential data breaches, even when other specific security measures cannot be implemented due to legitimate constraints.

For more information: https://www.pcisecuritystandards.org/documents/Guidance-PCI-DSS-Scoping-and-Segmentation.pdf

Q18: Multiple Choice: What level of security must compensating controls provide compared to the original requirement?

A18: The correct answer is "Equivalent security."

The content explicitly states that compensating controls "must provide equivalent security to the original requirement, maintaining the same level of protection and rigor." This is a fundamental principle of compensating controls in PCI DSS.

Compensating controls cannot provide less security than the original requirement, as this would create vulnerabilities and decrease the overall security posture. While providing higher security might seem beneficial, the requirement is specifically for equivalent security - the compensating control must address the same security concerns and provide the same level of protection as the original requirement.

This equivalence must be demonstrated through thorough risk assessment and validated by a Qualified Security Assessor (QSA) to ensure that the compensating control truly meets the security objectives of the original requirement.

For more information: https://www.pcisecuritystandards.org/documents/PCI_DSS_v3-2-1.pdf

Q19: What distinguishes a legitimate compensating control from an inappropriate workaround?

A19: Several key factors distinguish a legitimate compensating control from an inappropriate workaround:

1. Legitimate Constraint: A legitimate compensating control addresses a genuine technical or business constraint that prevents implementation of the original requirement, while a workaround might be implemented out of convenience or

preference.

2. Equivalent Security: A legitimate compensating control provides security equivalent to the original requirement, maintaining the same level of protection and rigor. A workaround often results in reduced security.
3. Thorough Risk Assessment: Legitimate compensating controls are based on comprehensive risk assessments that identify and address all relevant risks. Workarounds typically lack this foundation.
4. Proper Documentation: Legitimate compensating controls are well-documented, including the constraint, risk assessment, and security equivalence. Workarounds often lack proper documentation.
5. QSA Validation: Legitimate compensating controls are reviewed and validated by a PCI QSA. Workarounds typically avoid this scrutiny.
6. Addressing Security Intent: Legitimate compensating controls address the security intent of the original requirement through alternative means. Workarounds often ignore or minimize the security objectives.
7. Ongoing Monitoring: Legitimate compensating controls include provisions for ongoing monitoring and testing. Workarounds rarely include such measures.

A legitimate compensating control is a carefully designed alternative security measure that maintains the security objectives of the original requirement while accommodating legitimate constraints. An inappropriate workaround is an attempt to avoid implementing proper security measures.

For more information: https://www.pcisecuritystandards.org/documents/PCI_DSS_QSA_Guidelines_v3.pdf

Q20: How do business constraints differ from technical constraints when justifying compensating controls?

A20: Business constraints and technical constraints differ in several important ways when justifying compensating controls:

Business Constraints:

1. Related to organizational limitations such as budget, resources, or operational requirements
2. Example: A small business unable to afford high-end encryption software
3. Often involve financial considerations or business model restrictions
4. May be temporary and resolvable with changes in business priorities or growth
5. Require demonstration that the business truly cannot accommodate the requirement, not just that it is inconvenient

Technical Constraints:

1. Related to technological limitations such as legacy systems, software incompatibilities, or architectural issues
2. Example: Legacy software that cannot support multi-factor authentication
3. Often involve inherent limitations in existing systems that cannot be easily modified

4. May be more persistent until systems can be upgraded or replaced

5. Require demonstration that the technical limitation is genuine and cannot be overcome through configuration changes

Both types of constraints must be legitimate to justify compensating controls. Organizations must demonstrate that they cannot reasonably implement the original requirement due to these constraints, and that the proposed compensating control provides equivalent security. The nature of the constraint often influences the design of the compensating control - business constraints might lead to outsourcing solutions (like third-party payment processors), while technical constraints might lead to additional layers of security controls around the limited system.

For more information: https://www.pcisecuritystandards.org/documents/PCI_DSS_Risk_Assmt_Guidelines_v1.pdf

Q21: Essay Question: Compare and contrast the two example scenarios of compensating controls provided in the content.

A21: The content provides two distinct scenarios illustrating the implementation of compensating controls, each addressing different types of constraints:

Scenario 1: Small Online Business with Financial Constraints

This scenario involves a small online business that cannot afford high-end encryption software, presenting a business constraint based on financial limitations. The compensating control solution is to use a third-party payment processor.

Scenario 2: Organization with Legacy Software Limitations

This scenario involves an organization using legacy software that cannot support multi-factor authentication, presenting a technical constraint based on system limitations. The compensating control solution is implementing a VPN with strong encryption and strict access controls.

Similarities:

1. **Legitimate Constraints:** Both scenarios present genuine constraints that prevent implementation of specific PCI DSS requirements - one financial, one technical.

2. **Security Equivalence:** Both compensating controls aim to provide equivalent security to the original requirements through alternative means.

3. **Risk Mitigation:** Both address the fundamental security concerns (protecting cardholder data and preventing unauthorized access) despite not implementing the original requirements.

4. **Alternative Approaches:** Both leverage alternative technologies or services to achieve security objectives.

Differences:

1. **Nature of Constraints:** Scenario 1 features a business/financial constraint, while Scenario 2 involves a technical/legacy system constraint.

2. **Implementation Approach:** Scenario 1 uses an external service provider (third-party payment processor) to address the constraint, effectively transferring responsibility for the security control. Scenario 2 implements additional internal controls

(VPN with encryption and access controls) to compensate for the limitation.

3. **Control Ownership:** The first scenario shifts some security responsibility to a third party, while the second maintains security responsibility internally but uses different methods.
4. **Scope Impact:** Using a third-party payment processor potentially reduces the overall PCI DSS scope for the organization, while implementing a VPN maintains the scope but adds additional security layers.
5. **Long-term Considerations:** The financial constraint might be temporary as the business grows, potentially allowing for future implementation of encryption software. The technical constraint with legacy software might require a more significant system overhaul or replacement to resolve.

These scenarios demonstrate how compensating controls can be tailored to address different types of constraints while maintaining equivalent security. They illustrate the flexibility within PCI DSS to accommodate legitimate limitations while still ensuring appropriate protection of cardholder data. In both cases, a thorough risk assessment would be required to ensure the compensating controls adequately address the security objectives of the original requirements, and a QSA would need to validate their appropriateness and effectiveness.

For more information: https://www.pcisecuritystandards.org/documents/Prioritized-Approach-for-DSS.pdf

Q22: What technical or business constraints might legitimately prevent an organization from implementing a specific PCI DSS requirement?

A22: Several legitimate technical or business constraints might prevent an organization from implementing specific PCI DSS requirements:

Technical Constraints:

1. Legacy systems that cannot be easily upgraded or modified to support modern security features
2. Proprietary software with closed architecture that doesn't allow for implementation of specific security controls
3. Technical incompatibilities between required security measures and essential business applications
4. Hardware limitations that prevent implementation of certain security technologies
5. Custom-built applications that would require significant redevelopment to incorporate security features
6. Embedded systems or specialized equipment with fixed functionality

Business Constraints:

1. Financial limitations, particularly for small businesses, that make certain security technologies unaffordable
2. Operational requirements that conflict with specific security controls (e.g., 24/7 availability requirements)
3. Contractual obligations that limit system modifications
4. Resource limitations in terms of expertise or personnel to implement certain security measures

5. Business models that require specific workflows incompatible with certain security requirements

6. Regulatory conflicts where other compliance requirements conflict with specific PCI DSS implementations

Both types of constraints must be genuine and demonstrably prevent implementation of the original requirement. Organizations must document these constraints thoroughly and demonstrate that they have explored all reasonable options for implementing the original requirement before proposing a compensating control. The constraint cannot be based on preference, convenience, or disagreement with the requirement.

For more information: https://www.pcisecuritystandards.org/documents/PCI_DSS_v3-2-1.pdf

Q23: True or False: If a compensating control is approved by a QSA, it never needs to be reassessed.

A23: False. Although the content doesn't explicitly state this, it's an important principle in PCI DSS compliance that compensating controls, even after being approved by a QSA, require ongoing reassessment. This is because:

1. The technical or business constraint that initially justified the compensating control might change over time. For example, a small business might grow and have more resources, or a legacy system might eventually be replaced.

2. New threats and vulnerabilities emerge constantly, potentially affecting the effectiveness of previously approved compensating controls.

3. PCI DSS itself evolves with new versions and requirements, which may impact the validity of existing compensating controls.

4. The organization's environment and systems change over time, which could affect how compensating controls function.

Compensating controls should be reassessed during each compliance cycle to ensure they still provide equivalent security to the original requirement and that the constraint still exists and is legitimate. This ongoing validation is an essential part of maintaining effective security and compliance.

For more information: https://www.pcisecuritystandards.org/documents/PCI_DSS_QSA_Guidelines_v3.pdf

Q24: How do compensating controls relate to the concept of defense-in-depth in information security?

A24: Compensating controls and defense-in-depth are closely related concepts in information security:

Defense-in-depth is a security strategy that employs multiple layers of security controls to protect sensitive data and systems, with the understanding that no single control is infallible. If one layer fails, others remain to continue protecting the assets.

Compensating controls often embody the defense-in-depth principle in several ways:

1. Alternative Protection: When a specific security control cannot be implemented, compensating controls provide alternative means of protection, ensuring there isn't a gap in the security architecture.

2. Multiple Layers: Compensating controls frequently involve implementing multiple security measures to achieve equivalent security to the original requirement. For example, if encryption can't be implemented, a combination of network

segmentation, access controls, and monitoring might be used instead.

3. Risk Mitigation: Both concepts focus on effectively mitigating risks rather than adhering rigidly to a specific implementation method.

4. Comprehensive Protection: Both emphasize the importance of overall security posture rather than individual controls in isolation.

5. Adaptability: Both recognize that security solutions may need to be adapted to specific environments and constraints while maintaining effective protection.

In practice, many compensating controls represent excellent examples of defense-in-depth implementation. For instance, the example in the content of using "a VPN with strong encryption and strict access controls" when multi-factor authentication can't be implemented demonstrates layering multiple security controls to achieve equivalent protection. Similarly, implementing network segmentation as a compensating control adds additional security boundaries that embody the defense-in-depth philosophy.

For more information: https://www.pcisecuritystandards.org/documents/Guidance-PCI-DSS-Scoping-and-Segmentation.pdf

Q25: Multiple Choice: What is the main purpose of compensating controls in PCI DSS compliance?

A25: The main purpose of compensating controls in PCI DSS compliance is:

B) To provide alternative security measures when specific requirements can't be met due to legitimate constraints.

The content clearly states that "compensating controls are alternative security measures used when an organization cannot meet specific PCI DSS requirements due to technical or business constraints." Their purpose is to provide equivalent security through alternative means when legitimate constraints prevent the implementation of specific requirements as written.

Compensating controls allow organizations to maintain PCI DSS compliance while accommodating their unique circumstances and limitations. They provide flexibility in how security objectives are achieved while ensuring that cardholder data remains protected with the same level of security that would be provided by implementing the original requirements.

This flexibility is important because organizations vary widely in their environments, technologies, and resources, but all must achieve the same security outcomes to protect cardholder data effectively.

For more information: https://www.pcisecuritystandards.org/documents/PCI_DSS_v3-2-1.pdf

27

The Appendix - Question Set

Q1: What is the primary purpose of appendices in the PCI DSS framework? (Multiple Choice)

A) They replace the core PCI DSS Requirements for specific entity types B) They provide additional requirements tailored to different types of entities C) They are optional guidelines that don't affect compliance D) They only apply to Level 1 merchants

A1: The correct answer is B) They provide additional requirements tailored to different types of entities.

Appendixes in the PCI DSS framework serve as supplementary requirements that work in conjunction with the core PCI DSS Requirements. They don't replace the main requirements but rather add specific controls based on the type of entity or implementation scenario. As stated in the provided content, "Appendixes apply to different types of entities and are in addition to the PCI-DSS Requirements." This allows organizations to build a secure and compliant customer environment tailored to their specific circumstances. The appendixes enable a customized security approach while maintaining the fundamental security principles of PCI DSS.

For more information: https://www.pcisecuritystandards.org/document_library/

Q2: Appendix A of PCI DSS v4.0.1 focuses exclusively on securing payment terminals. (True/False)

A2: False.

Appendix A covers "Additional PCI DSS Requirements" and includes a broader scope than just payment terminals. According to the provided content, Appendix A contains "additional requirements for different types of entities, including regular monitoring and testing of networks, maintaining an information security policy, and more." This appendix addresses various security aspects across different entity types and is not limited to payment terminals only. It provides supplemental requirements that entities must implement based on their specific roles in the payment ecosystem.

For more information: https://docs.pcisecuritystandards.org/

Q3: Explain the concept of "Compensating Controls" in PCI DSS and when they might be implemented. (Short Answer)

A3: Compensating Controls, covered in Appendix B of PCI DSS, are alternative security measures that organizations can implement when they cannot meet specific PCI DSS requirements through the primary prescribed controls due to legitimate technical or documented business constraints.

These controls serve as security substitutes that must meet the intent and rigor of the original requirement while providing a similar level of defense. For compensating controls to be valid, an organization must:

1. Have legitimate technological or documented business constraints that prevent implementation of the original requirement
2. Define controls that address the same risk as the original requirement
3. Ensure the compensating control goes above and beyond other PCI DSS requirements
4. Ensure the control is commensurate with the additional risk imposed by not adhering to the original requirement

Organizations must document compensating controls using the Compensating Controls Worksheet (Appendix C) and have them validated by a qualified assessor. Compensating controls are not permanent solutions but temporary measures until full compliance can be achieved.

For more information: https://blog.pcisecuritystandards.org/how-to-use-compensating-controls

Q4: Which of the following is NOT an area covered in the Compensating Controls Worksheet? (Multiple Choice)

A) Constraints B) Definition of compensating controls C) Identified risks D) Implementation timeline E) Validation of compensating controls

A4: The correct answer is D) Implementation timeline.

According to the provided content, the Compensating Controls Worksheet (Appendix C) includes areas such as:

- Constraints (documenting the legitimate technical or business constraints)
- Definition of compensating controls (detailing the alternative security measures)
- Identified risks (analyzing potential vulnerabilities created by not following the original requirement)
- Validation of compensating controls (verifying the effectiveness of the alternative measures)

An implementation timeline is not mentioned as a standard component of the Compensating Controls Worksheet. While timeline may be useful for project management purposes, they are not a required element of the formal documentation needed fo compensating controls under PCI DSS.

For more information: https://www.pcisecuritystandards.org/documents/Prioritized-Approach-for-PCI_DSS-v4_0.pdf

Q5: Describe the "Customized Approach" outlined in Appendix D of PCI DSS v4.0.1 and how it differs from the traditional approach to compliance. (Essay)

A5: The Customized Approach, detailed in Appendix D of PCI DSS v4.0.1, represents a significant evolution in how organizations can achieve PCI DSS compliance while adapting to their unique operational environments.

Unlike the traditional "Defined Approach" (previously the only method available in earlier versions of PCI DSS), which requires organizations to implement specific controls exactly as prescribed in the standard, the Customized Approach provides flexibility by focusing on the security outcomes rather than prescriptive methods. This approach allows organizations to design and implement their own controls that satisfy the intent of the PCI DSS requirements, provided they can demonstrate that these controls achieve the same security objectives.

Key characteristics of the Customized Approach include:

1. **Outcome-based focus**: Organizations must clearly articulate how their custom controls meet or exceed the security intent of the original requirement.

2. **Risk assessment**: A thorough risk analysis must be conducted to identify potential threats and vulnerabilities that the custom control addresses.

3. **Validation requirements**: More rigorous testing procedures are required to validate that custom controls are properly designed, implemented, effective, and in place at all times.

4. **Documentation burden**: Organizations must maintain detailed documentation of their custom controls, including technical design, implementation details, and effectiveness measures.

5. **Target objective**: Each custom control must directly address the target objective of the original requirement.

Appendix D provides guidance on implementing this approach, while Appendix E offers sample templates to support documentation and validation efforts. The Customized Approach requires more effort in documentation and validation but offers greater flexibility for organizations with complex environments or innovative security solutions.

This approach is particularly valuable for organizations that:

- Have mature security programs with advanced controls that may exceed standard requirements
- Operate in unique technological environments where standard controls may not be applicable
- Seek to integrate PCI DSS compliance more seamlessly into their existing security frameworks

The Customized Approach represents a maturation of the PCI DSS framework, acknowledging that security can be achieved through various means while maintaining the core objective of protecting cardholder data.

For more information: https://blog.pcisecuritystandards.org/pci-dss-v4-0-implementing-the-customized-approach

Q6: Appendix F of PCI DSS v4.0.1 focuses on leveraging which framework to support Requirement 6? (Multiple Choice)

A) NIST Cybersecurity Framework B) ISO 27001 C) PCI Software Security Framework D) COBIT Framework E) CIS Controls

A6: The correct answer is C) PCI Software Security Framework.

Appendix F specifically focuses on "Leveraging the PCI Software Security Framework to Support Requirement 6." As noted in the provided content, this appendix provides "Guidance on how to use the PCI Software Security Framework to support Requirement 6 of PCI DSS."

Requirement 6 in PCI DSS deals with developing and maintaining secure systems and applications. The PCI Software Security Framework (SSF) includes both the Secure Software Standard and Secure Software Lifecycle (Secure SLC) Standard, which are designed to help organizations develop and maintain secure payment software. By leveraging these standards, merchants and service providers can implement more effective controls for secure software development and maintenance, which directly supports compliance with Requirement 6.

For more information: https://www.pcisecuritystandards.org/pci_security/software_security_framework/

Q7: Appendix G of PCI DSS v4.0.1 provides sample templates for implementing compensating controls. (True/False)

A7: False.

According to the provided content, Appendix G is the "PCI DSS Glossary of Terms, Abbreviations, and Acronyms" - a comprehensive reference guide for terminology used throughout the PCI DSS standard. It does not provide templates for implementing compensating controls.

The appendix that provides templates is Appendix E, which contains "Sample Templates to Support Customized Approach." These templates help organizations document their implementation of the Customized Approach to PCI DSS compliance. Meanwhile, Appendix C is the "Compensating Controls Worksheet," which provides documentation guidance for compensating controls.

This distinction is important for PCIP candidates as they need to understand the purpose and content of each appendix to correctly apply them in practical compliance scenarios.

For more information: https://listings.pcisecuritystandards.org/documents/PCI-DSS-v4_0.pdf

Q8: When do the PCI DSS appendixes apply to an organization, and how do they relate to the core requirements? (Short Answer)

A8: PCI DSS appendixes apply to organizations based on their specific entity type, implementation scenario, or compliance approach, and they function as additional requirements that complement the core PCI DSS requirements rather than replacing them.

As stated in the provided content, "Appendixes apply to different types of entities and are in addition to the PCI-DSS Requirements." This means that all organizations must comply with the applicable core PCI DSS requirements, and then additionally implement the controls specified in relevant appendixes based on their particular circumstances.

For example:

- Multi-tenant service providers would need to implement core requirements plus specific controls from applicable appendixes
- Organizations using SSL/early TLS for card-present POS POI terminal connections would need to address specialized requirements in the relevant appendix
- Entities seeking to implement a customized approach to compliance would use Appendix D and E to document their alternative controls
- Organizations that cannot meet a specific requirement due to legitimate constraints would use Appendixes B and C to document compensating controls

The relationship is supplementary and additive - the core requirements establish the foundation of security controls, while the appendixes provide specialized requirements to address specific risk scenarios or implementation approaches. This combined approach ensures a comprehensive security posture tailored to each organization's unique environment.

For more information: https://www.pcisecuritystandards.org/document_library/?category=pcidss&document=pci_dss

Q9: Which appendix would be most relevant for an organization that cannot implement a specific PCI DSS requirement due to legitimate business constraints? (Multiple Choice)

A) Appendix A: Additional PCI DSS Requirements B) Appendix B: Compensating Controls C) Appendix D: Customized Approach D) Appendix F: Leveraging the PCI Software Security Framework E) Appendix G: PCI DSS Glossary

A9: The correct answer is B) Appendix B: Compensating Controls.

Appendix B outlines the framework for implementing compensating controls, which are specifically designed for situations where organizations face legitimate technical or documented business constraints that prevent them from implementing a PCI DSS requirement as written. As stated in the provided content, "This section outlines compensating controls that can be used to meet specific PCI DSS requirements when primary controls are not feasible."

When an organization cannot meet a specific requirement as prescribed, Appendix B provides guidance on how to develop alternative security controls that achieve the same intent and level of security as the original requirement. These compensating controls must meet certain criteria, including addressing the same risk, going beyond other PCI DSS requirements, and being commensurate with the additional risk imposed by not adhering to the original requirement.

Additionally, organizations would use Appendix C (the Compensating Controls Worksheet) to document these controls for assessment purposes.

For more information: https://www.pcisecuritystandards.org/glossary/compensating-controls/

Q10: Analyze the relationship between PCI DSS core requirements and appendixes in creating a comprehensive security posture for organizations handling payment card data. (Essay)

A10: The relationship between PCI DSS core requirements and appendixes represents a layered, adaptive approach to security that balances standardization with flexibility to create a comprehensive security posture for diverse organizations handling payment card data.

Foundation and Specialization

The core PCI DSS requirements (organized in the 12 requirement domains) establish the fundamental security foundation that all entities must implement. These core requirements address universal security needs such as network security, data protection, access control, vulnerability management, and security monitoring. They represent the non-negotiable baseline that every organization must achieve.

The appendixes, however, recognize that organizations operate in different contexts with unique challenges and implementation scenarios. As noted in the provided content, "Appendixes apply to different types of entities and are in addition to the PCI-DSS Requirements." This additive relationship means that appendixes don't replace core requirements but enhance them with specialized controls tailored to specific situations.

Complementary Security Functions

The appendixes serve several complementary functions in relation to the core requirements:

1. **Adaptation Function:** Appendixes B and C (Compensating Controls) allow organizations to adapt when they cannot implement a core requirement exactly as written due to legitimate constraints, ensuring the security intent is still met.
2. **Customization Function:** Appendixes D and E (Customized Approach) enable organizations to implement alternative controls that achieve the same security outcomes as prescriptive requirements, allowing for innovation and integration with existing frameworks.
3. **Specification Function:** Appendix A provides additional requirements for specific entity types, addressing unique risks in specialized environments.
4. **Integration Function:** Appendix F shows how organizations can leverage the PCI Software Security Framework to support Requirement 6, demonstrating how PCI standards can work together.
5. **Clarification Function:** Appendix G provides terminology clarification to ensure consistent understanding across all requirements.

Building a Security Fortress

As metaphorically described in the content, "With the right combination of PCI-DSS Requirements and Appendix, you can create a fortress of security for your customer's data." This fortress analogy aptly captures how the core requirements provide the main structure and walls of defense, while appendixes reinforce vulnerable points, add specialized defenses, or provide alternative defensive measures where the standard design cannot be implemented.

Strategic Implementation Considerations

Organizations must approach PCI DSS implementation by:

1. First identifying which core requirements apply to their cardholder data environment
2. Then determining which appendixes are relevant based on their entity type and implementation scenarios
3. Implementing both sets of controls in a coordinated manner
4. Ensuring documentation adequately demonstrates how both core requirements and appendix controls work together

Compliance and Security Balance

This layered approach helps strike a balance between compliance and security. Rather than viewing compliance as a checkbox exercise, the combination of requirements and appendixes encourages organizations to focus on the security outcomes while providing flexibility in how those outcomes are achieved. This promotes a security-first mindset where compliance becomes a natural byproduct of proper security implementation.

The relationship between core requirements and appendixes ultimately enables organizations of different sizes, industries, and technical environments to achieve equivalent security postures while acknowledging their operational realities. This adaptive framework ensures that PCI DSS remains both rigorous in its security expectations and realistic in its implementation approach.

For more information: https://www.pcisecuritystandards.org/pci_security/maintaining_payment_security/

Q11: Appendix E provides guidance on how to interpret the PCI DSS glossary of terms. (True/False)

A11: False.

According to the provided content, Appendix E contains "Sample Templates to Support Customized Approach." These are templates and guidelines designed to help organizations document and implement their customized approach to meeting PCI DSS requirements. The appendix provides structured formats for organizations to demonstrate how their alternative controls satisfy the security objectives of the standard requirements.

The guidance on terminology is actually found in Appendix G, which is described as the "PCI DSS Glossary of Terms, Abbreviations, and Acronyms." This appendix provides definitions and explanations of the specialized vocabulary used throughout the PCI DSS standard.

Understanding the correct purpose of each appendix is crucial for PCIP candidates, as it helps determine which resources to consult when addressing different aspects of PCI DSS compliance.

For more information: https://www.pcisecuritystandards.org/documents/PCI_DSS_v4-0_Summary_of_Changes.pdf

Q12: What is the primary purpose of Appendix D in PCI DSS v4.0.1, and how does it benefit organizations seeking compliance? (Short Answer)

A12: The primary purpose of Appendix D in PCI DSS v4.0.1 is to provide guidance on the "Customized Approach" to implementing PCI DSS requirements, which allows organizations to develop alternative security controls that achieve the same security outcomes as the defined requirements.

This appendix benefits organizations seeking compliance in several ways:

1. **Flexibility in Implementation**: Rather than following prescriptive controls exactly as written in the standard, organizations can design controls that better align with their existing security architecture and business processes.

2. **Innovation Enablement**: Organizations can leverage innovative security technologies and methodologies that may provide equal or better protection than traditional approaches.

3. **Operational Efficiency**: By integrating PCI DSS controls with existing security frameworks and tools, organizations can reduce duplicate efforts and streamline security operations.

4. **Risk-Based Focus**: The Customized Approach emphasizes understanding the security objective behind each requirement and implementing controls that address the underlying risks, promoting a more thoughtful security posture.

5. **Adaptability for Complex Environments**: Organizations with unique or complex IT environments can develop controls that address their specific context while still meeting the security intent of PCI DSS.

However, organizations choosing this approach must provide robust documentation and validation that their customized controls achieve the same level of security as the defined requirements. Appendix D works in conjunction with Appendix E, which provides sample templates to support this documentation process.

For more information: https://blog.pcisecuritystandards.org/pci-dss-v4-0-resource-guide

Q13: Multi-tenant service providers must comply with which of the following additional requirements from the PCI DSS appendixes? (Multiple Choice)

A) Only Appendix A requirements B) Only Appendix B requirements C) Only Appendix D requirements D) A combination of requirements from multiple appendixes based on their specific implementation E) No additional requirements beyond the core PCI DSS requirements

A13: The correct answer is D) A combination of requirements from multiple appendixes based on their specific implementation.

Multi-tenant service providers must comply with additional requirements from the PCI DSS appendixes that are relevant to their specific service offerings and implementation scenarios. The provided content states that "The PCI-DSS has several appendices that provide additional requirements for multi-tenant service providers," among other entity types.

However, the specific appendixes that apply will depend on various factors:

1. If the service provider has legitimate technical or business constraints preventing implementation of certain requirements, they may need to use Appendix B (Compensating Controls) and document those controls using Appendix C (Compensating Controls Worksheet).

2. If they choose to implement alternative controls to achieve the security objectives, they may leverage Appendix D (Customized Approach) and use templates from Appendix E.

3. If their services involve software development related to payment applications, Appendix F may be relevant.

4. As a multi-tenant provider, certain additional requirements from Appendix A would likely apply specifically to their service model.

This highlights the importance of understanding the complete set of appendixes and determining applicability based on the specific circumstances of the service provider's environment, rather than assuming a one-size-fits-all approach.

For more information: https://www.pcisecuritystandards.org/documents/Multi-tenant-environments-info-supp-v2-0.pdf

Q14: Explain the considerations for entities using SSL/early TLS for card-present POS POI terminal connections as referenced in the PCI DSS appendixes. (Essay)

A14: The use of SSL (Secure Sockets Layer) and early TLS (Transport Layer Security) in payment environments represents a significant security concern within the PCI DSS framework due to known vulnerabilities in these older protocols. The PCI DSS appendixes provide specific guidance for entities that continue to use these protocols for card-present Point of Sale (POS) Point of Interaction (POI) terminal connections.

Background on SSL/early TLS Vulnerabilities

SSL and early TLS (1.0 and in some cases 1.1) protocols have been demonstrated to have multiple security vulnerabilities, including POODLE, BEAST, CRIME, and Heartbleed, that could allow attackers to decrypt protected communications and access sensitive cardholder data. Due to these vulnerabilities, PCI DSS has generally required that organizations migrate away from these protocols to more secure versions like TLS 1.2 or higher.

Special Considerations for Card-Present POS POI Terminals

While the general requirement is to discontinue the use of vulnerable protocols, PCI DSS recognizes through its appendixes that certain legacy card-present POS POI terminals may have legitimate technical constraints that prevent immediate migration. These terminals often have firmware that supports only SSL/early TLS, and in some cases cannot be updated or replaced immediately without significant business disruption or cost.

Requirements Outlined in PCI DSS Appendixes

For entities that must continue using SSL/early TLS for card-present POS POI terminal connections, the PCI DSS appendixes typically require:

1. **Risk Mitigation Plan**: Entities must develop and implement a formal risk mitigation and migration plan that details:
    - The known vulnerabilities these protocols pose
    - The specific POI devices that use these protocols
    - The business justification for continued use
    - The additional security controls implemented to minimize risk
    - Clear timelines for migration to secure protocols
2. **Compensating Controls**: Using the guidance in Appendix B and the worksheet format in Appendix C, entities must document compensating controls that mitigate the risk of using vulnerable protocols. These might include:
    - Network segmentation to isolate POI devices

- Enhanced monitoring of SSL/TLS traffic
- Implementation of additional encryption layers
- More frequent vulnerability scanning and penetration testing
- Point-to-point encryption (P2PE) solutions

3. **Secure Configuration**: Even when using SSL/early TLS, entities must ensure:
   - The implementation uses the strongest available cipher suites
   - The protocols are configured to support only secure connections
   - Regular patching of other components in the payment chain
   - Disabling fallback to even less secure protocol versions
4. **Documentation Requirements**: Using templates similar to those found in Appendix E, entities must thoroughly document:
   - The inventory of all POI devices using vulnerable protocols
   - Evidence of the technical constraints preventing immediate migration
   - Testing results demonstrating the effectiveness of compensating controls
   - Executive-level sign-off acknowledging the risks and approving the mitigation strategy

Migration Timeline Expectations

While PCI DSS may allow for continued use of SSL/early TLS in these specific scenarios, it's critical to note that this is considered a temporary exception, not a permanent solution. Entities must demonstrate ongoing progress toward:

1. Working with POI vendors to obtain firmware updates
2. Developing a terminal replacement schedule for devices that cannot be updated
3. Testing and certifying newer protocol implementations
4. Gradually phasing out vulnerable devices according to business risk

Compliance Assessment Considerations

During PCI DSS assessments, entities using SSL/early TLS for card-present POI connections can expect:

- More scrutiny of their risk mitigation strategies
- Detailed examination of compensating controls
- Verification that only the minimum necessary systems use vulnerable protocols

- Review of progress against migration timelines
- Validation that new POI deployments do not introduce additional vulnerable implementations

This balanced approach recognizes the practical challenges faced by merchants with legacy POI terminals while still maintaining the security focus that is central to PCI DSS. By providing specific guidance through its appendixes, PCI DSS enables organizations to manage the transition to more secure protocols in a risk-based, pragmatic manner without compromising on the ultimate goal of protecting cardholder data.

For more information: https://blog.pcisecuritystandards.org/migrating-from-ssl-and-early-tls

Q15: The PCI Software Security Framework referenced in Appendix F is primarily designed to replace Requirement 6 of PCI DSS. (True/False)

A15: False.

The PCI Software Security Framework (SSF) referenced in Appendix F is not designed to replace Requirement 6 but rather to support and complement it. As stated in the provided content, Appendix F focuses on "Leveraging the PCI Software Security Framework to Support Requirement 6."

The appendix outlines "how merchants and organizations can use custom software that follows the PCI SSC Secure Software Standard and Secure SLC Standard to meet secure systems and software requirements." This indicates that the Software Security Framework provides a methodology and standards that organizations can use to satisfy the secure development requirements outlined in Requirement 6, not replace them.

The relationship is complementary - Requirement 6 defines what security controls must be in place for secure systems and applications, while the Software Security Framework provides a structured approach to implementing those controls, particularly for custom-developed payment software. Organizations that follow the SSF standards may find it easier to demonstrate compliance with Requirement 6, but they must still address all aspects of the requirement.

For more information: https://www.pcisecuritystandards.org/pci_security/software_security_framework/

Q16: What does the validation of compensating controls involve according to the Compensating Controls Worksheet (Appendix C)? (Short Answer)

A16: The validation of compensating controls, as outlined in the Compensating Controls Worksheet (Appendix C), involves a comprehensive assessment process to verify that the alternative security measures effectively mitigate the risks associated with not implementing the original PCI DSS requirement as written.

This validation process typically includes:

1. **Testing Effectiveness**: Assessors must verify through testing that the compensating control actually addresses the risk that the original requirement was designed to mitigate.
2. **Evaluating Implementation**: The assessment examines whether the control is properly implemented according to its documented design.

3. **Verifying Scope Coverage**: Validation confirms that the compensating control covers all systems and components that were in scope for the original requirement.

4. **Assessing Control Strength**: The process evaluates whether the control provides a level of defense that is at least as strong as the original requirement would have provided.

5. **Confirming Additional Protection**: Since compensating controls must go "above and beyond" other PCI DSS requirements, validation verifies this additional protection is in place.

6. **Reviewing Documentation**: Assessors examine the complete documentation of the control, including the business or technical constraints that necessitated the compensating control.

7. **Evaluating Risk Analysis**: The validation reviews the organization's analysis of residual risks and confirms that these risks are appropriately managed.

8. **Ensuring Maintenance Procedures**: The process checks that procedures are in place to maintain the compensating control over time.

The validated compensating controls must collectively address the same risk and provide similar protection as the original requirement would have provided, while accounting for the additional risk introduced by not implementing the requirement as written.

For more information: https://www.pcisecuritystandards.org/documents/Prioritized-Approach-for-PCI_DSS-v4_0.pdf

Q17: In the context of PCI DSS compensating controls, "identified risks" refers to: (Multiple Choice)

A) All potential security vulnerabilities in an organization's environment B) Risks specifically associated with not implementing the original PCI DSS requirement as written C) Only risks related to payment card data breaches D) Risks identified during annual risk assessments E) Risks that cannot be mitigated through any controls

A17: The correct answer is B) Risks specifically associated with not implementing the original PCI DSS requirement as written.

According to the provided content, the Compensating Controls Worksheet includes "identified risks" as one of its key areas. In the context of PCI DSS compensating controls, "identified risks" specifically refers to the vulnerabilities and threats that may arise from not implementing a particular PCI DSS requirement exactly as written.

When an organization cannot meet a specific requirement due to legitimate technical or business constraints, they must identify and document the security risks that could result from this non-standard implementation. These identified risks form the foundation for designing appropriate compensating controls that will address these specific vulnerabilities.

The documentation of identified risks serves several purposes:

1. It demonstrates the organization's understanding of the security intent behind the original requirement

2. It shows awareness of what could go wrong if the requirement isn't implemented as written

3. It provides the basis for evaluating whether the proposed compensating controls adequately address all the relevant risks

This focused approach to risk identification ensures that compensating controls are directly aligned with the security objectives of the original requirement, rather than addressing general security concerns.

For more information: https://www.pcisecuritystandards.org/glossary/compensating-controls/

Q18: Discuss how organizations can effectively combine PCI DSS Requirements and Appendixes to "create a fortress of security" for customer data. Provide specific examples of this integration. (Essay)

A18: # Creating a Security Fortress: Integrating PCI DSS Requirements and Appendixes

The metaphor of creating a "fortress of security" for customer data aptly captures the comprehensive protection that can be achieved when organizations strategically integrate PCI DSS core requirements with the specialized guidance provided in its appendixes. This integration creates multiple layers of defense that collectively provide robust protection for cardholder data throughout its lifecycle.

Foundation: Core Requirements as the Fortress Walls

The 12 core PCI DSS requirements serve as the primary walls of the security fortress, establishing the fundamental controls that every organization must implement:

1. **Network Security** (Requirements 1, 2, 4): These requirements establish the perimeter defenses, including firewalls, secure configurations, and transmission encryption—equivalent to the outer walls and moat of a fortress.

2. **Data Protection** (Requirements 3, 4): These controls focus on protecting stored cardholder data and data in transit—similar to securing the valuable treasures within the fortress's inner chambers.

3. **Vulnerability Management** (Requirements 5, 6, 11): These requirements ensure continuous monitoring for weaknesses and swift remediation—comparable to guards patrolling the fortress walls, looking for structural weaknesses.

4. **Access Control** (Requirements 7, 8, 9): These controls restrict access to systems and physical areas—functioning like the fortress gatekeepers who verify identities before granting entry.

5. **Monitoring and Response** (Requirements 10, 11): These requirements ensure detection of security incidents—similar to watchtowers with vigilant sentries.

6. **Security Management** (Requirement 12): This establishes governance and policies—equivalent to the fortress commander who ensures all defenses work in concert.

Reinforcements: Appendixes as Specialized Defenses

The appendixes provide specialized reinforcements that strengthen the fortress in specific areas or address unique architectural needs:

1. **Appendix A (Additional Requirements)**: Adds specialized defenses for particular entity types, such as service providers who must implement more rigorous monitoring and oversight controls. For example, multi-tenant service providers must implement stronger isolation between customer environments—similar to adding internal compartmentalization within the fortress to prevent a breach in one area from compromising the entire structure.

2. **Appendixes B and C (Compensating Controls)**: Provide alternative defensive mechanisms when standard defenses cannot be implemented. For instance, an organization unable to implement traditional network segmentation might implement enhanced monitoring, stricter access controls, and additional data-level encryption—comparable to compensating

for a weakness in one section of the fortress wall by adding additional guards, traps, and internal barriers.

3. **Appendixes D and E (Customized Approach)**: Enable organizations to design defenses tailored to their unique environment while achieving the same security outcomes. For example, a cloud-native organization might implement API-based security controls rather than traditional network controls—similar to adapting fortress designs to the specific terrain and available building materials while maintaining defensive strength.

4. **Appendix F (Software Security Framework)**: Strengthens application security by integrating with specialized standards for secure software development. This is like ensuring that the weapons and tools used by the fortress defenders are themselves secure and won't fail during an attack.

5. **Appendix G (Glossary)**: Ensures consistent understanding of security terminology—ensuring all fortress defenders speak the same language and interpret commands consistently.

Integration Examples: Building the Fortress in Practice

Let's examine specific examples of how organizations can integrate requirements and appendixes:

Example 1: E-commerce Platform Provider

An e-commerce platform provider serving multiple merchants would integrate:

- **Core Requirement 1** (Network Security): Implementing network segmentation between merchants
- **Appendix A**: Adding service provider-specific controls for continuous monitoring of all customer environments
- **Appendix F**: Leveraging the Software Security Framework to ensure their payment application meets Requirement 6 for secure coding
- **Appendix D**: Using the Customized Approach to implement cloud-native security controls that achieve the same outcomes as traditional controls

This integration creates a defense system where the core segmentation is enhanced by service provider-specific monitoring, the payment application itself is secured through specialized standards, and the entire architecture is adapted to the cloud environment while maintaining security outcomes.

Example 2: Legacy Retail Environment

A retailer with some legacy POS systems might integrate:

- **Core Requirement 2** (Secure Configurations): Hardening all systems according to standards
- **Appendix B/C**: Documenting compensating controls for legacy POS terminals that cannot support the latest TLS version
- **Core Requirement 11** (Testing): Implementing more frequent vulnerability scanning
- **Appendix A**: Adding enhanced monitoring specifically focused on the legacy systems

This integration acknowledges the reality of the legacy components while surrounding them with additional defenses and monitoring to compensate for their inherent limitations.

Example 3: Financial Institution with Custom Payment Processing

A financial institution with proprietary payment processing systems might integrate:

- **Core Requirements 3, 4** (Data Protection): Implementing encryption for stored and transmitted data
- **Appendix D/E**: Using the Customized Approach to document how their proprietary encryption exceeds the standard requirements
- **Core Requirement 6** (Secure Development): Following secure coding practices
- **Appendix F**: Adopting the Secure Software Lifecycle practices for their development team

This integration allows the organization to leverage their advanced security capabilities while demonstrating how they meet or exceed the intent of the standard requirements.

Synergistic Protection: The Fortress Effect

The true power of integrating requirements and appendixes comes from the synergistic protection they provide:

1. **Defense in Depth**: Multiple layers of controls mean that a failure in one defense doesn't compromise the entire security posture.
2. **Adaptability**: The flexibility to implement controls appropriate to specific environments ensures practical security without unnecessary constraints.
3. **Comprehensive Coverage**: Together, requirements and appendixes address technological, procedural, and human aspects of security.
4. **Risk-Based Focus**: The integration encourages organizations to understand the security objectives rather than just implementing checklist items.
5. **Continuous Improvement**: The framework encourages organizations to evolve their security controls as threats and technologies change.

When properly integrated, PCI DSS requirements and appendixes create not just a static fortress but an adaptive, intelligent defense system that protects cardholder data throughout its lifecycle while accommodating the practical realities of diverse business environments.

For more information: https://www.pcisecuritystandards.org/document_library/

Q19: Implementation of the requirements specified in PCI DSS appendixes is always optional for all organizations. (True/False)

A19: False.

The implementation of requirements specified in PCI DSS appendixes is not always optional. As stated in the provided content, "Appendixes apply to different types of entities and are in addition to the PCI-DSS Requirements." This means that when an appendix applies to a particular entity type or scenario, the requirements within that appendix become mandatory for those organizations, not optional.

For example:

- Multi-tenant service providers must implement the additional requirements specified for their entity type
- Organizations using SSL/early TLS for card-present POS POI terminal connections must follow the specific requirements in the relevant appendix
- Designated entities requiring supplemental validation must comply with the additional validation requirements

The appendixes provide targeted requirements that apply based on specific criteria, and when those criteria are met, the requirements become mandatory components of PCI DSS compliance. Organizations must first determine which appendixes apply to their environment based on their entity type, implementation scenarios, and compliance approach, and then implement all applicable requirements from both the core standard and the relevant appendixes.

Only in cases where the appendix clearly doesn't apply to an organization's environment would the requirements within that appendix not be mandatory for that specific organization.

For more information: https://www.pcisecuritystandards.org/documents/PCI_DSS_v4-0_ROC_Reporting_Template.pdf

Q20: Explain what is meant by "designated entities requiring supplemental validation" in the context of PCI DSS appendixes. (Short Answer)

A20: "Designated entities requiring supplemental validation" refers to specific organizations that have been identified as needing to perform additional validation steps beyond the standard PCI DSS assessment requirements due to their role in the payment ecosystem, transaction volume, or risk profile.

These entities, typically designated by payment brands or acquirers, must implement and validate a more rigorous set of controls outlined in the relevant PCI DSS appendix. The supplemental validation requirements typically include:

1. **More frequent assessments**: These entities may need to conduct assessments more frequently than the standard annual cycle.
2. **Additional testing procedures**: Beyond the standard testing procedures, these entities must undergo more in-depth testing of their security controls.
3. **Enhanced evidence collection**: More comprehensive documentation and evidence must be gathered to demonstrate compliance.

4. **Targeted control areas**: The supplemental validation often focuses on specific high-risk areas like continuous monitoring, threat detection capabilities, and response procedures.

5. **Executive oversight**: Higher levels of management involvement and attestation may be required.

6. **Independent reviews**: Additional independent review of security measures beyond the standard assessment process.

This designation is typically applied to:

- Service providers processing large volumes of transactions
- Entities that have experienced significant security breaches
- Organizations with complex environments that present elevated risk
- Entities providing critical payment infrastructure services

The supplemental validation ensures that organizations with elevated risk or significance in the payment ecosystem implement stronger controls and undergo more thorough verification, providing additional assurance regarding their security posture.

For more information: https://www.pcisecuritystandards.org/documents/PCI-DSS-v4-0-Designated-Entities-Supplemental-Validation.pdf

Q21: Which of the following best describes "constraints" as documented in the Compensating Controls Worksheet? (Multiple Choice)

A) Financial limitations that prevent implementing security controls B) Time restrictions that delay security implementations C) Legitimate technical or documented business constraints that prevent meeting the original requirement D) Staffing shortages that impact security implementation E) Vendor limitations in product functionality

A21: The correct answer is C) Legitimate technical or documented business constraints that prevent meeting the original requirement.

According to the provided content, the Compensating Controls Worksheet includes "constraints" as one of its key areas. In the context of PCI DSS, "constraints" specifically refers to the legitimate technical or documented business constraints that prevent an organization from implementing a PCI DSS requirement exactly as written.

These constraints must be documented and validated to justify the use of compensating controls. It's important to note that not all limitations qualify as legitimate constraints. For a constraint to be considered legitimate, it must:

1. Be based on documented technical limitations or business objectives that cannot reasonably be altered

2. Not simply be a matter of cost or convenience

3. Be thoroughly documented with supporting evidence

4. Be validated by a qualified assessor

Examples of legitimate constraints might include:

- Legacy systems that cannot support current encryption standards and cannot be immediately replaced
- Regulatory requirements in certain jurisdictions that conflict with specific PCI DSS requirements
- Technical limitations in specialized hardware that cannot be modified or updated

The documentation of constraints is a critical first step in the compensating controls process, as it establishes the foundation for why alternative controls are necessary.

For more information: https://www.pcisecuritystandards.org/glossary/compensating-controls/

Q22: Explain the importance of Appendix G (PCI DSS Glossary of Terms, Abbreviations, and Acronyms) and how it contributes to effective PCI DSS implementation. (Essay)

A22: # The Strategic Value of Appendix G: Beyond Simple Definitions

Appendix G of the PCI DSS, the "Glossary of Terms, Abbreviations, and Acronyms," might appear at first glance to be merely a reference tool. However, its importance extends far beyond providing simple definitions. This appendix serves as a foundational element that enables consistent understanding, precise implementation, and effective compliance with the entire PCI DSS framework.

Establishing a Common Language for Security

At its core, Appendix G creates a standardized vocabulary that ensures all stakeholders interpret PCI DSS requirements consistently. This common language function serves several critical purposes:

1. Precision in Technical Implementation

Security is an inherently technical domain where precision matters. Appendix G defines technical terms with exact meanings, eliminating ambiguity that could lead to implementation errors. For example, understanding the precise PCI DSS definition of "network segmentation" versus "isolation" can make the difference between a compliant and non-compliant implementation. Similarly, terms like "strong cryptography," "multi-factor authentication," and "out-of-band management" have specific meanings within PCI DSS that may differ slightly from general industry usage.

When security professionals implement controls based on shared, precise definitions, they avoid the dangerous gaps that can emerge from terminology misinterpretations. This precision is particularly crucial when organizations leverage the Customized Approach (Appendix D), as they must demonstrate that their alternative controls satisfy the exact intent of requirements.

2. Cross-Functional Communication

PCI DSS compliance requires collaboration across multiple organizational functions—IT, security, risk management, legal, executive leadership, and often third-party service providers. Appendix G ensures these diverse stakeholders, who may come from different professional backgrounds, share a common understanding of requirements:

- Business executives can understand technical requirements without specialized knowledge

- Legal teams can accurately interpret compliance obligations
- IT teams can translate business requirements into technical specifications
- Auditors and assessors can evaluate controls against consistent criteria
- Third-party service providers can align their services with client needs

This cross-functional alignment reduces miscommunication that could lead to compliance gaps or inefficient security investments.

3. Global Consistency

As an international standard implemented across diverse linguistic and cultural contexts, PCI DSS requires uniform interpretation globally. Appendix G enables consistent application of the standard worldwide by:

- Providing clear definitions that can be accurately translated
- Clarifying concepts that might have different regional interpretations
- Establishing universal abbreviations and acronyms
- Defining specialized payment industry terminology that might not have direct equivalents in all languages

This global consistency ensures that multinational organizations can implement cohesive security programs across geographically dispersed operations.

Enabling Accurate Compliance Assessment

Beyond implementation, Appendix G plays a crucial role in the assessment and validation process:

1. Objective Evaluation Criteria

The glossary provides precise definitions that serve as objective criteria against which compliance can be measured. For Qualified Security Assessors (QSAs) and internal assessment teams, these definitions establish clear boundaries for determining whether a control satisfies a requirement. This objectivity reduces disagreements during assessments and ensures consistent evaluation across different assessors and organizations.

2. Documentation Standardization

Organizations documenting their compliance posture for assessment must use terminology consistently. Appendix G ensures that documentation precisely reflects implemented controls using standardized language that assessors can evaluate against the requirements. This standardization is particularly important when completing formal documents like the Self-Assessment Questionnaire (SAQ) or Report on Compliance (ROC).

3. Evidence Classification

During assessments, organizations must provide evidence demonstrating compliance. The glossary helps both organizations and assessors properly classify and evaluate evidence by defining what constitutes appropriate documentation for different requirements. For example, understanding the precise definition of "policy," "procedure," "process," and "standard" ensures that the right type of documentation is provided for each requirement.

Supporting Advanced Compliance Approaches

As organizations mature in their security programs, Appendix G becomes increasingly valuable for supporting advanced compliance approaches:

1. Compensating Controls Development

When developing compensating controls (Appendixes B and C), organizations must demonstrate that these controls address the same risk and provide a similar level of defense as the original requirement. Precise understanding of terminology is essential for:

- Accurately identifying the risk the original requirement addresses
- Designing controls that mitigate that specific risk
- Documenting how the compensating control satisfies the requirement's intent

Without the clear definitions in Appendix G, organizations might misinterpret the requirement's purpose and develop inadequate compensating controls.

2. Customized Approach Implementation

Organizations leveraging the Customized Approach (Appendix D) must demonstrate that their alternative controls satisfy the security objectives of the original requirements. This requires precise understanding of:

- The security intent behind each requirement
- The specific risks each requirement addresses
- The expected outcomes of properly implemented controls

Appendix G provides the definitional foundation that enables organizations to design customized controls that truly meet the security objectives rather than merely appearing to satisfy the letter of the requirement.

3. Integration with Other Security Frameworks

Many organizations implement PCI DSS alongside other security frameworks like ISO 27001, NIST CSF, or SOC 2. Appendix G helps security professionals map PCI DSS requirements to these frameworks by clarifying exactly what each term means in the PCI DSS context, enabling more efficient control integration and reducing duplication of effort.

Educational and Training Foundation

Finally, Appendix G serves as an educational resource that supports effective training and knowledge transfer:

1. Onboarding New Personnel

Organizations can use the glossary to quickly onboard new security and compliance personnel, providing them with the foundational knowledge needed to understand PCI DSS requirements. This accelerates the learning curve and ensures new team members contribute effectively to compliance efforts.

2. Training Program Development

Training programs for staff with security responsibilities can use Appendix G as a curriculum foundation, ensuring that all personnel share a common understanding of key concepts. This is particularly important for organizations implementing security awareness programs required by PCI DSS Requirement 12.

3. Certification Preparation

For professionals pursuing certifications like PCIP (Payment Card Industry Professional), Appendix G serves as a study resource that establishes the precise terminology they'll need to master for examination success.

Conclusion: The Glossary as a Strategic Asset

Far from being a mere reference document, Appendix G serves as a strategic asset that enables precise implementation, consistent assessment, and effective communication across the entire PCI DSS ecosystem. Organizations that thoroughly understand and leverage this glossary can:

- Implement more accurate and effective security controls
- Reduce compliance gaps stemming from misinterpretation
- Improve cross-functional collaboration
- Streamline assessment processes
- Develop more effective training programs
- Better integrate PCI DSS with other security frameworks

By establishing a common language for security, Appendix G creates the foundation upon which the entire PCI DSS compliance structure rests, making it an indispensable component of the standard rather than an afterthought.

For more information: https://www.pcisecuritystandards.org/glossary/

Q23: Custom software that follows the PCI SSC Secure Software Standard automatically satisfies all aspects of Requirement 6 of PCI DSS. (True/False)

A23: False.

Custom software that follows the PCI SSC Secure Software Standard does not automatically satisfy all aspects of Requirement 6 of PCI DSS. According to the provided content, Appendix F outlines "how merchants and organizations can use custom software that follows the PCI SSC Secure Software Standard and Secure SLC Standard to meet secure systems and software requirements."

This indicates that the Software Security Framework provides a methodology that can help organizations satisfy aspects of Requirement 6, but it doesn't guarantee complete compliance with all components of the requirement. Requirement 6 covers a broad range of controls related to secure systems and applications, including:

1. Vulnerability management processes
2. Secure software development processes
3. Security patch management
4. Change management controls
5. Separation of development and production environments
6. Secure coding practices
7. Software security testing
8. Application security training

While the PCI SSC Secure Software Standard addresses many aspects of secure software development, organizations must still implement and maintain all the controls specified in Requirement 6, and use Appendix F as guidance for how the Software Security Framework can support these efforts. The appendix helps organizations leverage the framework as part of their overall approach to Requirement 6, not as a complete replacement for it.

For more information: https://blog.pcisecuritystandards.org/pci-software-security-framework-what-you-need-to-know

Q24: How does Appendix F help organizations meet the secure systems and software requirements outlined in Requirement 6 of PCI DSS? (Short Answer)

A24: Appendix F helps organizations meet Requirement 6 of PCI DSS by providing guidance on how to leverage the PCI Software Security Framework (SSF) as part of their secure systems and software development practices. This appendix creates a bridge between the core PCI DSS requirements and the specialized software security standards.

Specifically, Appendix F:

1. **Maps Framework Controls to Requirements**: It shows how controls from the Secure Software Standard and Secure Software Lifecycle (Secure SLC) Standard align with specific Requirement 6 controls, allowing organizations to understand which framework elements satisfy which PCI DSS requirements.

2. **Provides Implementation Guidance**: The appendix offers practical guidance on how to implement the Software Security Framework in a way that supports PCI DSS compliance, including specific considerations for different types of payment software.

3. **Establishes Validation Methods**: It outlines how organizations can validate and document that their software development practices, when following the framework, meet the intent of Requirement 6.

4. **Clarifies Scope Considerations**: The appendix helps organizations understand which software components fall within the scope of both Requirement 6 and the Software Security Framework.

5. **Addresses Custom Software Development**: It specifically guides organizations that develop custom payment software on how to implement secure development practices aligned with both standards.

6. **Supports Emerging Technologies**: The appendix helps organizations apply secure development principles to newer technologies and methodologies, such as cloud-native applications and DevOps practices.

By following the guidance in Appendix F, organizations can implement a more comprehensive and effective approach to secure software development that satisfies Requirement 6 while also aligning with industry best practices for secure payment software development.

For more information: https://www.pcisecuritystandards.org/pci_security/software_security_framework/

Q25: Which of the following best represents the relationship between PCI DSS core requirements and appendixes? (Multiple Choice)

A) Appendixes replace core requirements for certain entity types B) Core requirements and appendixes are completely independent of each other C) Appendixes provide additional requirements that work in conjunction with core requirements D) Organizations must choose between implementing core requirements or appendixes E) Appendixes only apply to Level 1 merchants

A25: The correct answer is C) Appendixes provide additional requirements that work in conjunction with core requirements.

As stated directly in the provided content, "Appendixes apply to different types of entities and are in addition to the PCI-DSS Requirements." This clearly establishes that the relationship between core requirements and appendixes is complementary and additive, not substitutive or exclusive.

The content further emphasizes this relationship by noting that "They provide additional requirements tailored to different entities, allowing you to build a secure and compliant customer environment." This indicates that the appendixes work alongside the core requirements to create a comprehensive security approach.

The metaphor used in the content also supports this understanding: "With the right combination of PCI-DSS Requirements and Appendix, you can create a fortress of security for your customer's data." This imagery of a "combination" and "fortress" implies that both elements work together to create a strong, unified security posture.

This relationship is fundamental to understanding the PCI DSS framework, as organizations must implement all applicable core requirements and then additionally implement any relevant appendix requirements based on their specific entity type and implementation scenario.

For more information: https://www.pcisecuritystandards.org/document_library/?category=pcidss&document=pci_dss

28

Self Assessment Questionnaires (SAQ's) - Question Set

Q1: What are PCI-DSS Self-Assessment Questionnaires (SAQs) primarily designed to do?

A) They are validation tools that assist merchants and service providers in:

- Self-evaluating their compliance with the PCI-DSS requirements
- Determining which security controls apply to their environment
- Documenting their compliance status
- Serving as a navigational map to guide organizations to compliance

SAQs function as a structured framework to help organizations systematically assess their payment card environment against PCI-DSS requirements. Each SAQ is specifically designed for different merchant types and payment processing environments. They not only help merchants identify their compliance status but also guide them toward remediation steps if necessary.

Resource: https://www.pcisecuritystandards.org/documents/SAQ-InstrGuidelines-v3_2_1.pdf

Q2: True or False: PCI-DSS compliance is a one-time event that, once achieved, covers an organization for a full year until the next assessment.

A2: FALSE. This is an important misconception to correct. PCI-DSS compliance is an ongoing process, not a one-time event.

The content explicitly states: "PCI-DSS Compliance is not a one-time event - it is an ongoing process! It must be part of your business-as-usual (BAU) day-to-day operation."

Organizations must maintain their compliance continuously throughout the year. If a data breach occurs, forensic investigators will examine whether the organization was compliant at the time of the breach, not merely whether they had previously achieved compliance. An attestation from six months prior won't matter if compliance wasn't maintained.

This continuous compliance requirement ensures that cardholder data environments remain protected at all times, not just during assessment periods.

Resource: https://blog.pcisecuritystandards.org/5-reasons-to-make-pci-dss-business-as-usual

Q3: Which of the following is a key eligibility criterion for most SAQ types (except SAQ D)?

a) Having a third-party process all payments b) Using only P2PE solutions c) No electronic storage of cardholder data (CHD) d) Having fewer than 6 million transactions annually

A3: c) No electronic storage of cardholder data (CHD)

The content explicitly states: "To be eligible for any of the SAQ's, apart from SAQ D, there must be no electronic storage of cardholder data (CHD)."

This is a critical distinction that determines which SAQ a merchant can use. Electronic storage of cardholder data significantly increases risk and compliance requirements, which is why merchants who electronically store CHD must complete the more comprehensive SAQ D. This requirement helps merchants understand the importance of minimizing data storage to reduce their compliance burden and security risk.

Resource: https://www.pcisecuritystandards.org/documents/Understanding_SAQs_PCI_DSS_v3.pdf

Q4: Describe the key characteristics and requirements for merchants eligible to complete SAQ A.

A4: SAQ A is designed for card-not-present merchants (e-commerce or mail/telephone order) who have completely outsourced all cardholder data functions. Key characteristics include:

1. All cardholder data functions must be fully outsourced to PCI DSS-validated third-party service providers
2. The merchant does not electronically store, process, or transmit any cardholder data
3. For e-commerce merchants, customers are redirected from the merchant's website to a PCI-compliant third-party payment processor
4. No elements of the payment page originate from the merchant's website (typically using an iframe or URL redirect)
5. The merchant must verify and validate that their third-party providers are PCI-compliant
6. SAQ A contains approximately 20+ questions
7. It does NOT apply to face-to-face merchants
8. Any "not applicable" answers require full explanation

SAQ A represents the lowest complexity level for PCI compliance since the merchant has effectively outsourced their payment card handling responsibilities. However, merchants must remember that they still retain ultimate responsibility for ensuring their customers' card data is properly protected, even when using third-party providers.

Resource: https://www.pcisecuritystandards.org/documents/PCI-DSS-v3_2_1-SAQ-A.pdf

Q5: Which SAQ type is specifically designed for e-commerce merchants who partially outsource their payment processing but maintain administration of the websites that link to it?

a) SAQ A b) SAQ A-EP c) SAQ B d) SAQ C

A5: b) SAQ A-EP

SAQ A-EP is specifically designed for e-commerce merchants who partially outsource their payment processing but maintain administration of the websites that link to it. This SAQ applies when either:

- The merchant's website creates a payment form that posts directly to a PCI-compliant third-party processor
- The merchant's website redirects to a PCI-compliant processor, but some elements of the payment page come from the merchant's website

This represents a higher level of risk than SAQ A because the merchant's website is more directly involved in the payment process, making it a potential target for hackers. With approximately 190+ questions, SAQ A-EP is significantly more comprehensive than SAQ A, reflecting the increased security responsibilities of merchants in this category.

Resource: https://www.pcisecuritystandards.org/documents/PCI-DSS-v3_2_1-SAQ-A-EP.pdf

Q6: Compare and contrast SAQ A and SAQ A-EP, explaining the key differences in their applicability, requirements, and security implications.

A6: SAQ A and SAQ A-EP both apply to e-commerce merchants but differ significantly in several ways:

Applicability:

- SAQ A: Applies to e-commerce merchants who completely outsource all cardholder data functions
- SAQ A-EP: Applies to e-commerce merchants who partially outsource payment processing but maintain administration of websites that link to it

Website Involvement:

- SAQ A: Customers are fully redirected from the merchant's website to a third-party payment processor with no elements of the payment page originating from the merchant's site
- SAQ A-EP: Either the merchant's website creates a payment form, or some elements of the payment page come from the merchant's website

Complexity:

- SAQ A: ~20+ questions, simplest form of validation
- SAQ A-EP: ~190+ questions, much more comprehensive

Security Implications:

- SAQ A: Lower risk as merchant's systems are completely removed from the payment flow
- SAQ A-EP: Higher risk as the merchant's website becomes a potential target for hackers who might attempt to introduce malicious code to steal data before redirecting to the service provider

Benefits vs. Drawbacks:

- SAQ A: Simpler compliance requirements but less control over the payment experience
- SAQ A-EP: Allows for highly configurable payment forms with better branding and user experience, but requires significantly more security controls

Security Recommendations for A-EP:

- Active monitoring for changes to the website
- Implementation of a Web Application Firewall (WAF)
- Prevention of hackers from capturing payment card details before redirection

The fundamental difference is the level of involvement the merchant has in the payment process. With SAQ A, the merchant is completely hands-off, while with SAQ A-EP, the merchant maintains some control over the payment form or elements, which increases both flexibility and security responsibility.

Resource: https://blog.pcisecuritystandards.org/understanding-saq-options-for-ecommerce-merchants

Q7: True or False: SAQ B can be used for e-commerce transactions.

A7: FALSE. SAQ B cannot be used for e-commerce transactions.

The content clearly states: "SAQ (B) This SAQ only applies to mail\telephone orders (MOTO) or face-to-face transactions; it can't be used for eCommerce transactions."

SAQ B is specifically designed for merchants who process payments through:

- Mail/telephone orders (MOTO)
- Face-to-face transactions using imprint machines
- Standalone dial-out terminals

The key distinction is that SAQ B applies to payment methods that either use physical terminals connected only to telephone lines or manual imprint machines. These payment methods do not involve online transactions through websites or internet-connected payment applications, which would require different SAQ types with more extensive security controls.

Resource: https://www.pcisecuritystandards.org/documents/PCI-DSS-v3_2_1-SAQ-B.pdf

Q8: What were "Knuckle Busters" in the context of payment processing, and which SAQ type would apply to merchants using them?

a) Early versions of chip and PIN devices covered by SAQ B-IP b) Manual imprint machines covered by SAQ B c) Virtual terminals covered by SAQ C-VT d) Mobile payment devices covered by SAQ P2PE

A8: b) Manual imprint machines covered by SAQ B

"Knuckle Busters" was the colloquial name given to manual credit card imprint machines, primarily used in the 1980s through the early 2000s. They were nicknamed "Knuckle Busters" because users would often scrape their knuckles on the machine when pulling the roller across to make an imprint of the credit card.

These devices worked by:

- Placing the credit card face-up on the device
- Putting carbon receipt paper on top
- Manually pulling a roller across to create an impression of the raised numbers
- Creating a carbon copy receipt

Merchants using these imprint machines would fall under SAQ B requirements. The content notes that while these devices are increasingly rare, merchants who still use them must pay particular attention to physical security controls, especially regarding the storage and handling of the carbon receipts which contain complete cardholder data.

Resource: https://www.pcisecuritystandards.org/glossary/knuckle-buster/

Q9: What are the key requirements for a merchant to be eligible for SAQ B-IP?

A9: For a merchant to be eligible for SAQ B-IP, they must meet the following key requirements:

1. The merchant must not store cardholder data (CHD) in digital format
2. They must use only IP-based, PTS-approved Point-of-Interaction (POI) devices
3. These POI devices must be standalone and connected to the payment processor via the internet
4. The devices must be validated and listed on the PCI SSC website
5. The payment devices must not be connected to any other systems in the merchant's environment (achieved through network segmentation)
6. Payment information must be transmitted only from the approved devices directly to the payment processor
7. The PTS POI devices must not depend on other devices (computers, mobile phones, tablets) to connect to the payment processor

SAQ B-IP is applicable to merchants handling both card-present (brick-and-mortar) and card-not-present (MOTO) transactions, but it does not apply to e-commerce channel merchants. Merchants completing this SAQ are required to respond to approximately 80+ questions.

The key distinction between SAQ B and SAQ B-IP is the connection method: SAQ B applies to terminals connected via telephone lines, while SAQ B-IP applies to terminals connected via the internet, which introduces additional security considerations.

Resource: https://www.pcisecuritystandards.org/documents/PCI-DSS-v3_2_1-SAQ-B-IP.pdf

Q10: How are IP-connected payment devices typically secured within a merchant environment according to the material?

a) By using VPN connections to encrypt all traffic b) By isolating them on a separate network segment with a fixed IP address range c) By implementing multi-factor authentication for all device access d) By requiring manual authorization for all transactions over a certain amount

A10: b) By isolating them on a separate network segment with a fixed IP address range

According to the material, IP-connected payment devices are secured primarily through network segmentation. The content states: "Internet Protocol (IP) connected devices are allocated a fixed IP address by the Network or IT Security team. They will designate a range of IP addresses for use in these devices. This range of IPs will be segmented and protected from the wider network, thus reducing the PCI-DSS scope."

This approach creates a separate, protected network environment specifically for payment processing, which is described as a "fortress" in the content. By isolating these devices from the rest of the network, merchants can:

- Reduce their PCI-DSS scope
- Minimize the attack surface for potential breaches
- Create a more secure environment for payment processing
- Prevent lateral movement if other systems are compromised

This network segmentation is a critical security control for merchants using IP-connected payment devices under SAQ B-IP.

Resource: https://www.pcisecuritystandards.org/documents/Guidance-PCI-DSS-Scoping-and-Segmentation_v1.pdf

Q11: Explain the key security considerations and best practices for merchants using virtual terminal solutions who fall under SAQ C-VT requirements.

A11: Merchants using virtual terminal solutions under SAQ C-VT face unique security considerations requiring specific best practices:

Environment and Implementation:

- The virtual terminal must be Internet-based and hosted by a PCI DSS-validated third-party service provider

- Transactions must be entered manually, one at a time, via keyboard
- The solution must be accessed using an Internet-connected web browser
- The computing device must be isolated in a single location, not connected to other systems
- No software or hardware that captures/stores account data should be installed

Call Recording Considerations:

- Payment calls should not be recorded, as this would extend the PCI-DSS network scope
- Technical solutions to pause call recording during payment collection should be implemented
- This prevents exposing customer payment information and maintains a limited PCI-DSS scope

Scope Reduction Benefits:

- Properly implemented, this approach significantly reduces the PCI-DSS network scope
- With proper configuration and protection, it creates a safer environment
- The isolated nature of the setup minimizes exposure to other systems

Typical Implementation Contexts:

- Customer service departments
- Dedicated call centers
- Mail-order organizations
- Anywhere operators take card details over the phone and manually enter them

Security Controls:

- The computing device should be dedicated solely to payment processing
- Regular security updates and patches should be applied
- Access controls should limit who can use the virtual terminal
- Physical security measures should protect the device location
- Staff should be trained on secure handling of payment information

This approach balances security with practical business needs, providing a relatively straightforward compliance path for merchants who manually process individual transactions through a hosted solution.

Resource: https://www.pcisecuritystandards.org/documents/PCI-DSS-v3_2_1-SAQ-C-VT.pdf

Q12: True or False: It's acceptable for merchants using virtual terminals (SAQ C-VT) to record phone calls during which payments are taken, as long as the recordings are encrypted.

A12: FALSE. Recording phone calls during which payments are taken is not acceptable for SAQ C-VT merchants, regardless of encryption.

The content explicitly states: "Make sure these types of payment calls are not recorded. Recording them would extend your PCI-DSS network scope."

Instead of recording calls that include payment information, the material recommends implementing technical solutions that allow operators to pause call recording while payments are taken. This approach:

1. Prevents the expansion of PCI-DSS scope
2. Protects customers' personal payment information
3. Reduces the organization's risk and compliance burden
4. Demonstrates that the organization values customer privacy and security

Even with encryption, recorded calls containing payment card information would significantly expand the PCI-DSS scope and introduce additional requirements that would likely make the merchant ineligible for SAQ C-VT. The recommended approach is to eliminate the recording of sensitive authentication data entirely rather than attempting to secure recordings.

Resource: https://www.pcisecuritystandards.org/documents/Protecting_Telephone_Based_Payment_Card_Data_v3-0_nov_2018.pdf

Q13: Which SAQ type applies to merchants who process cardholder data via point-of-sale (POS) systems connected to the internet but are not connected to other systems within the merchant's environment?

a) SAQ B b) SAQ B-IP c) SAQ C d) SAQ C-VT

A13: c) SAQ C

SAQ C applies to merchants who process cardholder data (CHD) via point-of-sale (POS) or other payment application systems connected to the internet. Key characteristics that make SAQ C applicable include:

1. The merchant uses an installed payment processing application on a computer, laptop, tablet, in stores, or on a till
2. The device has both a payment application system and an Internet connection
3. The payment application system is not linked to any other systems in the merchant's environment (achieved through network segmentation)
4. The POS environment is physically isolated from other premises or locations
5. Any LAN is used only for a single store

SAQ C applies to merchants handling both card-present (brick-and-mortar) and card-not-present (MOTO) transactions, but it cannot be used for eCommerce transactions. Merchants completing SAQ C must respond to approximately 160+ questions.

The key distinction from SAQ B-IP is that SAQ C involves installed payment applications on multi-purpose devices, rather than standalone payment terminals.

Resource: https://www.pcisecuritystandards.org/documents/PCI-DSS-v3_2_1-SAQ-C.pdf

Q14: What are the key requirements for merchants to qualify for SAQ P2PE, and approximately how many questions must they answer?

A14: For merchants to qualify for SAQ P2PE, they must meet the following key requirements:

1. They must be using a PCI-validated Point-to-Point Encryption (P2PE) solution that is listed on the PCI SSC website
2. The P2PE solution must be correctly implemented according to the solution provider's requirements
3. They can handle both card-present (brick-and-mortar) and card-not-present (MOTO) transactions, including taking orders over the phone and keying card information directly into a PCI-listed P2PE payment terminal
4. They must not store electronic cardholder data
5. This SAQ does not cover E-commerce channels, so merchants must not be processing e-commerce transactions

Merchants qualifying for SAQ P2PE must respond to approximately 30+ questions, making it one of the shorter SAQs. For any questions that do not apply to their business environment, merchants must provide explanations.

The P2PE solution creates a significant reduction in PCI DSS scope because the cardholder data is encrypted at the point of interaction and can only be decrypted by the solution provider, meaning the merchant never has access to the clear-text cardholder data.

Resource: https://www.pcisecuritystandards.org/documents/PCI-DSS-v3_2_1-SAQ-P2PE.pdf

Q15: What type of encryption does P2PE utilize, and what are the primary benefits of implementing a P2PE solution?

a) Symmetrical encryption; reduced audit scope and time b) Asymmetrical encryption; reduced audit scope and time c) Symmetrical encryption; enhanced user experience d) Asymmetrical encryption; elimination of all PCI requirements

A15: b) Asymmetrical encryption; reduced audit scope and time

According to the material, P2PE (Point-to-Point Encryption) utilizes a secure form of asymmetrical encryption to protect cardholder data. The content describes it as being "locked at the Chip & PIN device point of collection and only unlocked at its final destination."

The primary benefits of implementing a P2PE solution include:

1. Significantly reduced PCI-DSS scope, since the merchant environment never has access to unencrypted cardholder data

2. Reduced audit time - the material states that implementation "can reduce the time required to perform a full PCI-DSS audit to just a few days"

3. Enhanced security throughout the payment journey

4. Third-party management of patches and updates (the solution is "fully managed and patched by a third-party solution provider")

5. Simplified compliance for merchants who don't want to deal with technical complexities

However, the material also notes that P2PE solutions are "expensive to implement" and are "aimed at medium to large retail chains," making them less suitable for smaller merchants despite their security advantages.

Resource: https://www.pcisecuritystandards.org/programs/point-to-point-encryption-program/

Q16: True or False: SAQ D should be the first choice for merchants looking to simplify their PCI-DSS compliance.

A16: FALSE. SAQ D should not be the first choice for merchants looking to simplify their PCI-DSS compliance.

The content explicitly advises against this approach, stating: "TIP: An SAQ D should be avoided if at all possible by any merchant."

SAQ D is the most comprehensive and complex self-assessment questionnaire, requiring merchants to comply with all 12 PCI-DSS requirements and its 300+ sub-requirements. This makes it significantly more burdensome than other SAQ types that are tailored to specific payment environments.

Instead, merchants should:

1. Examine their payment channels to determine how they handle payment card information

2. Make changes to secure their cardholder data environment (CDE)

3. Potentially reduce their PCI-DSS scope by implementing more secure payment methods

4. Select the most appropriate SAQ based on their actual payment environment

Only when no other SAQ type is applicable should merchants resort to SAQ D. The one exception mentioned is when merchants have multiple payment channels requiring multiple SAQs with significant overlap - in this case, completing a single SAQ D might be simpler than multiple separate SAQs.

Resource: https://www.pcisecuritystandards.org/documents/Understanding_SAQs_PCI_DSS_v3.pdf

Q17: Under which circumstances must a merchant complete SAQ D? (Select all that apply)

a) When they accept cardholder data on their websites b) When they electronically store cardholder data c) When they don't store cardholder data electronically but don't meet criteria for another SAQ type d) When they process fewer than 6 million transactions annually

A17: a) When they accept cardholder data on their websites b) When they electronically store cardholder data c) When they don't store cardholder data electronically but don't meet criteria for another SAQ type

According to the material, SAQ D must be completed by merchants in several scenarios:

1. When they accept cardholder data on their websites
2. When cardholder data is stored electronically by merchants
3. When merchants do not store cardholder data electronically but do not meet the criteria of another SAQ type
4. When merchants may meet the criteria of another SAQ type but have additional PCI-DSS requirements

The content explicitly states: "An SAQ D is your only option if none of the SAQs already mentioned meet your organization's criteria." Additionally, it notes: "If you store cardholder data (CHD) digitally, you must complete SAQ D."

The number of transactions processed (option d) is not mentioned as a criterion for determining SAQ type in this material. SAQ eligibility is based on how payment card data is handled, not transaction volume.

Resource: https://www.pcisecuritystandards.org/documents/PCI-DSS-v3_2_1-SAQ-D-Merchant.pdf

Q18: Describe strategies merchants can use to reduce their PCI-DSS scope and potentially qualify for simpler SAQ types.

A18: Merchants can implement several strategies to reduce their PCI-DSS scope and qualify for simpler SAQ types:

1. Eliminate Electronic Storage of Cardholder Data (CHD)

- Avoid storing CHD electronically, as this immediately makes SAQ D the only option
- Implement data retention policies that minimize storage duration
- Consider tokenization solutions that replace CHD with non-sensitive tokens

2. Outsource Payment Processing

- Fully outsource payment processing to qualified third-party service providers (potentially qualifying for SAQ A)
- Use hosted payment pages where the customer is redirected to a third-party's site for payment
- Ensure third-party providers are PCI-compliant and request their Attestation of Compliance

3. Implement Network Segmentation

- Isolate payment systems from other business networks
- For IP-connected devices, allocate a fixed IP address range that's segmented from the wider network
- Implement proper firewall controls between segments

4. Adopt Secure Payment Technologies

- Implement PCI-validated P2PE solutions (qualifying for SAQ P2PE with only 30+ questions)
- Use standalone payment terminals connected only to telephone lines (qualifying for SAQ B)
- Consider IP-based point-of-interaction devices with proper segmentation (qualifying for SAQ B-IP)

5. Modify Payment Channel Operations

- For call centers, implement call recording pausing during payment collection
- Use dedicated, isolated computers for virtual terminal access (qualifying for SAQ C-VT)
- Physically isolate POS environments from other locations

6. Review Payment Flows Across Channels

- Examine how payment card data flows through your organization
- Identify unnecessary touchpoints where data is handled or stored
- Redesign processes to minimize exposure to cardholder data

7. Consolidate Payment Channels When Appropriate

- If you have multiple payment channels with significant overlap in requirements, consider using SAQ D for all channels
- However, if channels can be cleanly separated, use the simplest applicable SAQ for each

By strategically implementing these approaches, merchants can significantly reduce their compliance burden while maintaining or even enhancing payment security.

Resource: https://www.pcisecuritystandards.org/documents/Guidance-PCI-DSS-Scoping-and-Segmentation_v1.pdf

Q19: What are the key differences between SAQ D for Merchants and SAQ D for Service Providers?

A19: While both SAQ D for Merchants and SAQ D for Service Providers require compliance with all 12 PCI-DSS requirements and 300+ sub-requirements, there are several key differences:

1. Applicability:

- SAQ D for Merchants: Applies to merchants who don't qualify for other SAQ types, particularly those who accept cardholder data on websites or store cardholder data electronically
- SAQ D for Service Providers: The only SAQ option available to service providers

2. Service Scope Flexibility:

- SAQ D for Merchants: Typically covers all of the merchant's payment channels
- SAQ D for Service Providers: Providers can decide which of their services are to be compliant, which is especially relevant for hosting providers offering multiple services

3. Additional Requirements:

- Service providers have additional requirements beyond what merchants must address, including:
  - More stringent network security controls
  - Specific service provider responsibilities
  - Requirements for managing client relationships and responsibilities

4. Documentation Differences:

- While both require answering all questions, the documentation expectations for service providers may be more extensive due to their role in serving multiple clients

5. Responsibility Scope:

- Merchants: Primarily responsible for their own environment
- Service Providers: Responsible for securing environments that may impact multiple clients' cardholder data

The material specifically notes that "service providers are entitled to decide which of their services are to be compliant," providing flexibility that merchants typically don't have. This allows service providers to segment their offerings and only bring specific services into PCI DSS scope.

Resource: https://www.pcisecuritystandards.org/documents/PCI-DSS-v3_2_1-SAQ-D-ServiceProvider.pdf

Q20: Which of the following statements about storing cardholder data (CHD) is correct according to the material?

a) Merchants can store CHD electronically as long as it's encrypted and still qualify for SAQ A b) Only storing CHD for less than 24 hours exempts merchants from SAQ D requirements c) Storing CHD electronically requires merchants to complete SAQ D d) Service providers can store CHD on behalf of merchants without PCI-DSS validation

A20: c) Storing CHD electronically requires merchants to complete SAQ D

According to the material, the electronic storage of cardholder data (CHD) is a critical factor in determining which SAQ type applies to a merchant. The content explicitly states:

"To be eligible for any of the SAQ's, apart from SAQ D, there must be no electronic storage of cardholder data (CHD)."

Furthermore, the content reinforces this point with: "If you store cardholder data (CHD) digitally, you must complete SAQ D."

This requirement exists because the electronic storage of cardholder data significantly increases the security risks and compliance responsibilities for merchants. SAQ D is the most comprehensive questionnaire, requiring compliance with all 12 PCI-DSS requirements and 300+ sub-requirements, reflecting the increased security controls necessary when cardholder data is stored electronically.

None of the other options are supported by the material. There are no exemptions based on storage duration mentioned, and service providers must be PCI-DSS validated if they store CHD on behalf of merchants.

Resource: https://www.pcisecuritystandards.org/documents/Protecting_Telephone_Based_Payment_Card_Data_v3-0_nov_2018.pdf

Q21: True or False: Service providers must make all of their services PCI-DSS compliant when completing SAQ D.

A21: FALSE. Service providers do not need to make all of their services PCI-DSS compliant when completing SAQ D.

The content explicitly states: "However, it's worth pointing out that service providers are entitled to decide which of their services are to be compliant. This is especially applicable for hosting providers that provide many different services, and it may well be the case that not all services are required to be compliant."

This flexibility allows service providers to:

1. Determine which specific services involve payment card data or support payment card processing
2. Define the scope of their PCI-DSS compliance program accordingly
3. Focus compliance efforts and resources on services that actually require them
4. Potentially offer both PCI-compliant and non-PCI-compliant service options to clients with different needs

This approach is particularly relevant for hosting providers or technology companies that offer a wide range of services, only some of which may involve cardholder data. By limiting the scope to relevant services, providers can manage compliance more efficiently while maintaining appropriate security for payment card data.

Resource: https://www.pcisecuritystandards.org/documents/PCI_DSS_v4-0_ROC_Reporting_Template.pdf

Q22: Who ultimately bears the responsibility for PCI-DSS compliance when a merchant outsources their card data processing to a third-party provider?

A22: The merchant ultimately bears the responsibility for PCI-DSS compliance, even when card data processing is outsourced to a third-party provider.

The content explicitly states: "The responsibility for compliance sits with the merchant. What do I mean? So, even though the organization has outsourced its entire card data processing, the data is stored with a third-party provider. PCI-DSS states that the responsibility sits with the merchant."

This means that merchants:

1. Cannot transfer their compliance responsibility by outsourcing
2. Must verify that their third parties do not present a threat
3. Need to validate that their service providers are PCI-compliant
4. Should request and review their service providers' Attestation of Compliance (AoC)
5. Remain accountable if a breach occurs through their third-party provider

This principle applies across all SAQ types, including SAQ A where all cardholder data functions are outsourced. While outsourcing can reduce the merchant's direct security burden, it does not eliminate their ultimate responsibility for ensuring the protection of their customers' cardholder data throughout the entire payment process.

Resource: https://www.pcisecuritystandards.org/documents/Third_Party_Security_Assurance_Info_Supp.pdf

Q23: Which of the following best describes the nature of PCI-DSS compliance according to the material?

a) A project with a defined beginning and end b) A one-time certification that provides safe harbor protection c) An ongoing process that must be part of business-as-usual operations d) A quarterly assessment requirement

A23: c) An ongoing process that must be part of business-as-usual operations

The material explicitly describes PCI-DSS compliance as an ongoing process rather than a one-time event. The content states: "PCI-DSS Compliance is not a one-time event - it is an ongoing process! It must be part of your business-as-usual (BAU) day-to-day operation."

The material emphasizes this point with a scenario: "If you suffer a breach and the forensic investigators are called in, they will be interested to know if you were compliant at the time of the breach. It won't matter if you start waving your PCI-DSS accreditation in their face, dated six months ago! No, it's whether you have maintained your PCI-DSS compliance throughout."

This ongoing nature of compliance means organizations must:

1. Continuously monitor their systems and processes
2. Regularly validate security controls
3. Maintain compliance between formal assessment periods
4. Integrate security practices into everyday operations
5. Keep documentation and evidence of compliance current

The material uses the metaphor of PCI-DSS being "like a vigilant sentry, always on guard" to reinforce that compliance requires constant attention and maintenance.

Resource: https://blog.pcisecuritystandards.org/5-reasons-to-make-pci-dss-business-as-usual

Q24: Explain the security challenges and considerations specifically associated with e-commerce payment channels under SAQ A-EP, and describe the recommended security controls to address these risks.

A24: E-commerce payment channels under SAQ A-EP present unique security challenges that require specific controls:

Security Challenges:

1. **Website Vulnerability**: Unlike SAQ A where customers are completely redirected, merchants under SAQ A-EP have

websites that either create payment forms or contribute elements to the payment page, making them prime targets for attackers.

2. **Code Injection Risk**: Hackers may attempt to introduce malicious code into the merchant's website to:
   - Steal payment data before redirection to the service provider
   - Inject illegitimate advertisements
   - Compromise the customer's session
3. **Form Control Complexity**: The highly configurable nature of payment forms that improve customer experience also increases security responsibilities.
4. **Scope Expansion**: The merchant's webserver becomes part of the cardholder data environment, significantly expanding PCI-DSS scope.
5. **Integration Vulnerabilities**: The connection points between the merchant's website and the payment processor create potential security gaps.

Recommended Security Controls:

1. **Web Application Firewall (WAF)**: The material specifically recommends implementing a WAF to help "detect and prevent these attacks" by filtering malicious traffic before it reaches the website.
2. **Active Monitoring for Changes**: Merchants should continuously monitor their websites for unauthorized modifications to detect compromise quickly.
3. **Change Prevention Controls**: Implement technical controls that prevent unauthorized changes to website code, particularly for payment-related components.
4. **Secure Development Practices**: Follow secure coding guidelines when developing website components that interact with payment processes.
5. **Network Segmentation**: Isolate web servers that connect to payment systems from other parts of the network.
6. **Vulnerability Management**: Regularly scan for and remediate vulnerabilities in the website code and infrastructure.
7. **Security Testing**: Conduct penetration testing specifically focused on the payment flow.

The material emphasizes that "protecting the webserver that links to the payment processing system is essential to ensure the success of any e-Commerce business." Without these security measures, the business risks data breaches, fraud, and other malicious activities that could severely impact operations.

Resource: https://www.pcisecuritystandards.org/documents/SAQ-A-EP-Guidelines-v3_2_1.pdf

Q25: How many different SAQ types exist for merchants and service providers according to the material, and what are they?

a) 6 total: A, B, C, C-VT, D for Merchants, and D for Service Providers b) 7 total: A, B, C, P2PE, D for Merchants, and D for Service Providers c) 8 total: A, A-EP, B, B-IP, C, C-VT, P2PE, and D d) 9 total: A, A-EP, B, B-IP, C, C-VT, P2PE, D for Merchants, and D for Service Providers

A25: d) 9 total: A, A-EP, B, B-IP, C, C-VT, P2PE, D for Merchants, and D for Service Providers

According to the material, there are eight SAQs for merchants (labeled A through D) and a separate SAQ D for service providers, making nine total SAQ types:

For Merchants:

1. SAQ A - For card-not-present merchants with fully outsourced cardholder data functions
2. SAQ A-EP - For e-commerce merchants with partially outsourced payment processing
3. SAQ B - For merchants using imprint machines or standalone dial-out terminals
4. SAQ B-IP - For merchants using IP-based, PTS-approved POI devices
5. SAQ C-VT - For merchants using Internet-based virtual terminal solutions
6. SAQ C - For merchants using payment application systems connected to the internet
7. SAQ P2PE - For merchants using PCI-validated Point-to-Point Encryption solutions
8. SAQ D for Merchants - For merchants who don't qualify for other SAQ types

For Service Providers: 9. SAQ D for Service Providers - The only option available for service providers

The material explicitly states: "There are eight SAQs, labeled SAQ-A through to SAQ-D for Merchants. For Service Providers, there is a separate SAQ-D."

Understanding the different SAQ types and their applicability is crucial for determining which validation approach is appropriate for a particular payment environment.

Resource: https://www.pcisecuritystandards.org/documents/SAQ-InstrGuidelines-v3_2_1.pdf

29

AoC & RoC Compliance - Question Set

Q1: What is an Attestation of Compliance (AoC) in the context of PCI-DSS?

A1: An Attestation of Compliance (AoC) is a formal certification document that specifies an organization's PCI-DSS compliance status. It is completed and verified by a Qualified Security Assessor (QSA) and serves as documented proof that an organization adheres to security best practices required by the Payment Card Industry Data Security Standard. The AoC is essentially a powerful written statement that assures stakeholders that the organization has completed a valid Self-Assessment Questionnaire (SAQ) or PCI assessment specifically tailored to their cardholder data environment. This document is often requested by business partners, acquiring banks, or payment brands as evidence of compliance with PCI-DSS requirements.

Additional resource: https://www.pcisecuritystandards.org/document_library/

Q2: True or False: A Report on Compliance (RoC) is only required for merchants who process fewer than 6 million card transactions annually.

A2: False. A Report on Compliance (RoC) is required for Level 1 merchants, which are defined as those processing more than 6 million Visa or Mastercard transactions annually. The RoC is not required for lower-level merchants who typically complete Self-Assessment Questionnaires instead. Level 1 merchants undergo more rigorous compliance validation procedures due to the higher volume of cardholder data they process, which presents greater risk to the payment ecosystem.

Additional resource: https://www.pcisecuritystandards.org/merchants/

Q3: Who is responsible for completing and verifying an Attestation of Compliance (AoC)?

A3: A Qualified Security Assessor (QSA) is responsible for completing and verifying an Attestation of Compliance (AoC). QSAs are security professionals who have been certified by the PCI Security Standards Council to validate an entity's adherence to PCI-DSS. They have the expertise and knowledge to assess compliance with the standard's requirements and provide an independent verification of an organization's security posture. The QSA conducts the assessment, reviews evidence, validates controls, and ultimately signs off on the AoC, certifying that the organization meets the applicable PCI-DSS requirements.

Additional resource: https://www.pcisecuritystandards.org/assessors_and_solutions/qualified_security_assessors/

Q4: What defines a Level 1 merchant according to the PCI-DSS?

A4: A Level 1 merchant, according to PCI-DSS, is primarily defined as a retailer that processes more than 6 million Visa or Mastercard transactions annually. It's important to note that this threshold applies to each card brand individually, not collectively. This means that reaching 6 million transactions with just one card brand (Visa, Mastercard, American Express, etc.) is sufficient to classify a merchant as Level 1.

Additionally, other factors can result in a merchant being classified as Level 1 regardless of transaction volume:

1. Having experienced a data breach that resulted in cardholder data compromise
2. Card brand discretion (any payment card brand can designate a merchant as Level 1 based on risk assessment)
3. Risk factors that might increase the potential exposure of cardholder data

Level 1 merchants are subject to the most rigorous compliance validation requirements, including an annual on-site assessment by a QSA and quarterly network scans by an Approved Scanning Vendor (ASV).

Additional resource: https://www.pcisecuritystandards.org/documents/PCI-DSS-v4-0-ROC-Reporting-Template.pdf

Q5: In the PCI compliance process, what happens after a QSA creates a Report on Compliance (RoC)?

A5: After a Qualified Security Assessor (QSA) creates a Report on Compliance (RoC), the following process occurs:

1. The completed RoC is presented to the merchant's acquiring bank (acquirer).
2. The acquirer reviews the RoC to ensure it is complete and meets all requirements.
3. Once the acquirer has accepted the RoC, they forward it to the relevant payment brand(s) (Visa, Mastercard, etc.) for verification.
4. The payment brand reviews the RoC and may request additional information or clarification.
5. Once verified by the payment brand, the compliance status is updated in their records.

This process ensures that multiple stakeholders validate the compliance assessment, maintaining the integrity of the PCI-DSS program and providing appropriate oversight of the compliance validation process.

Additional resource: https://www.pcisecuritystandards.org/documents/PCI_DSS_v4-0.pdf

Q6: What is the primary difference between an Attestation of Compliance (AoC) and a Report on Compliance (RoC)?

A6: The primary difference between an Attestation of Compliance (AoC) and a Report on Compliance (RoC) lies in their purpose, content, and level of detail:

An Attestation of Compliance (AoC):

- Is a certification document that summarizes an organization's compliance status
- Serves as a declaration that the organization has met the PCI-DSS requirements
- Is a shorter form document that confirms compliance without extensive details
- Can accompany either a completed Self-Assessment Questionnaire or a full RoC
- Functions as a high-level assurance document for partners and stakeholders

A Report on Compliance (RoC):

- Is a comprehensive, detailed document that outlines the full assessment results
- Documents the organization's security posture, environment, systems, and cardholder data protection measures
- Provides in-depth information about how each PCI requirement is being met
- Includes specific testing procedures, evidence examined, and findings
- Is required specifically for Level 1 merchants
- Contains significantly more technical and procedural details about compliance

In essence, the AoC is a summary attestation of compliance status, while the RoC is the detailed evidence and documentation of how compliance was achieved and validated.

Additional resource: https://www.pcisecuritystandards.org/document_library/?category=pcidss&document=pci_dss

Q7: Multiple Choice: Which of the following statements about a merchant being classified as Level 1 is NOT correct?

A) A merchant processing 6.5 million Visa transactions annually would be classified as Level 1. B) A merchant processing 4 million Mastercard and 3 million Visa transactions annually would automatically be classified as Level 1. C) A merchant that has suffered a data breach may be classified as Level 1 regardless of transaction volume. D) Card brands have the discretion to classify any merchant as Level 1 based on risk assessment.

A7: The correct answer is B) A merchant processing 4 million Mastercard and 3 million Visa transactions annually would automatically be classified as Level 1.

This statement is incorrect because the threshold of 6 million transactions applies to each card brand individually, not collectively. In this scenario, the merchant processes 4 million Mastercard transactions and 3 million Visa transactions, neither of which reaches the 6 million threshold for any single card brand. Therefore, this merchant would not automatically be classified as Level 1 based solely on transaction volume.

All other statements are correct:

- Statement A is correct: 6.5 million Visa transactions exceeds the 6 million threshold for a single brand.
- Statement C is correct: Merchants that have experienced a data breach may be elevated to Level 1 status regardless of their

transaction volume.

- Statement D is correct: Card brands maintain discretion to classify merchants as Level 1 based on their risk assessment, even if the transaction volume is below the threshold.

However, it's worth noting that the merchant in scenario B could still be classified as Level 1 if other factors were present, such as a previous data breach or card brand discretion based on risk factors.

Additional resource: https://www.pcisecuritystandards.org/merchants/

Q8: Fill in the blank: After the acquirer has accepted the RoC, it then sends it to the ________________ for verification.

A8: After the acquirer has accepted the RoC, it then sends it to the payment brand for verification.

The payment brand (such as Visa, Mastercard, American Express, Discover, or JCB) is the final authority in the verification process. Each payment brand has its own compliance program and requirements based on PCI-DSS, and they need to verify that their participating merchants are properly securing cardholder data according to the standard. The payment brands have a vested interest in ensuring compliance since they bear significant risk from data breaches. Once the payment brand verifies the RoC, the merchant's compliance status is updated in their records, completing the formal compliance validation process.

Additional resource: https://www.pcisecuritystandards.org/about_us/payment_brands/

Q9: Describe the complete process flow from PCI assessment to final verification of compliance.

A9: The complete process flow from PCI assessment to final verification of compliance follows these steps:

1. **Preparation Phase**:
    - The organization determines its compliance requirements based on merchant level, transaction volume, and card brands accepted.
    - The organization engages a Qualified Security Assessor (QSA) for Level 1 merchants or prepares for self-assessment for lower levels.
2. **Assessment Phase**:
    - The QSA (or internal assessor for self-assessments) reviews the cardholder data environment.
    - Testing of controls is conducted to verify that security measures meet PCI-DSS requirements.
    - Documentation of processes and evidence of compliance is collected.
    - Gaps or non-compliance issues are identified and remediated.
3. **Documentation Phase**:
    - For Level 1 merchants, the QSA creates a detailed Report on Compliance (RoC) documenting the results of the assessment.

- The QSA also completes an Attestation of Compliance (AoC) certifying the organization's compliance status.
- For lower-level merchants, an appropriate Self-Assessment Questionnaire (SAQ) and AoC are completed.

4. **Submission Phase**:
   - The completed RoC and AoC are presented to the merchant's acquiring bank (acquirer).
   - The acquirer reviews the documentation for completeness and accuracy.
5. **Verification Phase**:
   - Once the acquirer has accepted the compliance documentation, it forwards the RoC and AoC to the relevant payment brand(s).
   - The payment brand reviews the documentation to verify compliance.
   - The payment brand may request additional information or clarification if needed.
6. **Completion Phase**:
   - Upon verification, the payment brand updates the merchant's compliance status in their records.
   - The merchant is officially recognized as PCI-DSS compliant for that assessment cycle.
   - The organization begins preparation for the next compliance cycle, as PCI-DSS compliance is an ongoing process requiring annual reassessment.

This process ensures multiple layers of review and verification, maintaining the integrity of the PCI-DSS compliance program and providing appropriate oversight throughout the compliance validation process.

Additional resource: https://www.pcisecuritystandards.org/documents/PCI_DSS_v4-0.pdf

Q10: True or False: An Attestation of Compliance (AoC) can only be completed after a full Report on Compliance (RoC) has been prepared.

A10: False. An Attestation of Compliance (AoC) is not exclusively tied to a Report on Compliance (RoC) and can be completed without a full RoC being prepared. The AoC can accompany different types of compliance validation documentation depending on the merchant level and assessment approach:

1. For Level 1 merchants who undergo a full PCI-DSS assessment by a QSA, the AoC would accompany the RoC.
2. For merchants at Levels 2-4 who typically complete Self-Assessment Questionnaires (SAQs), the AoC would accompany the completed SAQ rather than an RoC.

The AoC serves as a summary certification of compliance status regardless of which assessment method was used. It's a versatile document that provides a standardized way for organizations to attest to their compliance status whether they completed a full on-site assessment resulting in an RoC or a self-assessment resulting in a completed SAQ.

Additional resource: https://www.pcisecuritystandards.org/document_library/?category=saqs

Q11: Multiple Choice: What written document assures that an organization has completed a valid SAQ or PCI assessment tailored to their cardholder environment?

A) PCI-DSS Report B) Attestation of Compliance (AoC) C) Report on Compliance (RoC) D) Payment Card Verification (PCV)

A11: The correct answer is B) Attestation of Compliance (AoC).

The Attestation of Compliance (AoC) is the written document that assures an organization has completed a valid Self-Assessment Questionnaire (SAQ) or PCI assessment tailored to their cardholder environment. As stated in the provided content, "An AoC is a powerful written statement that assures your organization has completed a valid SAQ or PCI assessment tailored to your cardholder environment."

The AoC serves as a formal declaration of compliance status and is typically signed by an officer of the company (for self-assessments) or by a Qualified Security Assessor (for on-site assessments). It provides a standardized way for organizations to attest to their compliance with PCI-DSS requirements and can be shared with business partners, acquiring banks, and payment brands as evidence of compliance.

Options A and D are incorrect as they are not standard PCI-DSS documentation terms. Option C, the Report on Compliance (RoC), is a detailed document that outlines the assessment results but is not the document that specifically assures completion of an SAQ or assessment.

Additional resource: https://www.pcisecuritystandards.org/document_library/?category=aocs

Q12: What are the primary contents of a Report on Compliance (RoC)?

A12: A Report on Compliance (RoC) is a comprehensive document that contains detailed information about an organization's PCI-DSS assessment. The primary contents of a RoC include:

1. **Organization Information**: Details about the assessed entity, including company name, address, contact information, and business description.

2. **Scope of Assessment**: Definition of the cardholder data environment (CDE), including network diagrams, cardholder data flows, and a description of in-scope and out-of-scope components.

3. **Security Posture**: Detailed analysis of the organization's overall security posture, security policies, and governance structure.

4. **Environment Description**: Comprehensive documentation of the systems, applications, networks, and technologies that store, process, or transmit cardholder data.

5. **Cardholder Data Protection Measures**: Detailed descriptions of the controls implemented to protect cardholder data, including encryption, access controls, and monitoring mechanisms.

6. **Requirement-by-Requirement Assessment**: For each of the PCI-DSS requirements and sub-requirements, the RoC documents:

- The testing procedures performed
- Evidence examined
- Observations made
- Compliance status (compliant, non-compliant, not applicable)
- Compensating controls (if applicable)

7. **Findings and Recommendations**: Documentation of any gaps or vulnerabilities identified during the assessment and recommendations for remediation.

8. **Supporting Documentation**: References to policies, procedures, and other evidence examined during the assessment.

9. **Attestation Section**: Formal statements by the QSA regarding the compliance status of the organization.

The RoC provides a thorough examination of how an organization meets each PCI-DSS requirement and serves as the primary evidence of compliance for Level 1 merchants. It's a detailed technical document that guides both the assessed organization and the reviewing parties (acquirers and payment brands) in understanding the organization's compliance posture.

Additional resource: https://www.pcisecuritystandards.org/documents/PCI-DSS-v4-0-ROC-Reporting-Template.pdf

Q13: Scenario-based question: A retailer processes 5 million Visa transactions and 5 million Mastercard transactions annually. They have never experienced a data breach. Would they be classified as a Level 1 merchant? Explain your answer.

A13: Based on the information provided, this retailer would NOT automatically be classified as a Level 1 merchant based solely on transaction volume.

The key point from the content is: "The definition of a Level 1 merchant should note that the transaction threshold applies to each card brand individually." This means that a merchant must process more than 6 million transactions with a single card brand (Visa OR Mastercard OR American Express, etc.) to be classified as Level 1 based on volume.

In this scenario:

- The retailer processes 5 million Visa transactions annually (below the 6 million threshold)
- The retailer processes 5 million Mastercard transactions annually (below the 6 million threshold)
- They have never experienced a data breach

Since neither card brand's transactions exceed the 6 million threshold individually, and there is no history of a data breach, the retailer would likely be classified as a Level 2 merchant (typically defined as processing between 1-6 million transactions annually).

However, it's important to note that this classification could still change if:

1. Any card brand exercises its discretion to classify them as Level 1 based on risk factors

2. Their transaction volume increases in the future

3. They experience a data breach

4. They process over 6 million transactions with any other card brand not mentioned in the scenario

Merchants should always confirm their merchant level with their acquiring bank and each payment card brand they work with, as requirements can vary.

Additional resource: https://www.pcisecuritystandards.org/merchants/

Q14: What factors beyond transaction volume can cause a merchant to be classified as Level 1? Select all that apply:

A) Geographic location of the merchant B) Having experienced a data breach C) Card brand discretion based on risk assessment D) Age of the merchant's payment systems E) Number of physical locations

A14: The correct answers are B) Having experienced a data breach and C) Card brand discretion based on risk assessment.

According to the provided content: "Even if your volume is low, risk matters. Brands want control over who gets top-tier scrutiny. It's not just about numbers, it's about trust and exposure." The content specifically mentions these two factors that can elevate a merchant to Level 1 status regardless of transaction volume:

B) Having experienced a data breach - The content states: "A data breach? You're in." This means that merchants who have suffered a security incident resulting in compromised cardholder data may be elevated to Level 1 status regardless of their transaction volume.

C) Card brand discretion based on risk assessment - The content states: "Card brand discretion? That works as well." This means that payment card brands (like Visa, Mastercard, etc.) have the authority to designate any merchant as Level 1 based on their assessment of risk factors.

Options A (geographic location), D (age of payment systems), and E (number of physical locations) might be factors that card brands consider in their risk assessment, but they are not explicitly mentioned in the provided content as automatic triggers for Level 1 classification.

Additional resource: https://www.pcisecuritystandards.org/merchants/

Q15: Who is responsible for creating the final Report on Compliance (RoC) after testing an organization's controls and collecting documentation?

A15: A PCI auditor, specifically a Qualified Security Assessor (QSA), is responsible for creating the final Report on Compliance (RoC) after testing an organization's controls and collecting documentation.

As stated in the provided content: "Following the testing of your controls and the collection of documentation of your processes, a PCI auditor (QSA) creates a final PCI RoC (Report on Compliance)."

QSAs are security professionals who have been certified by the PCI Security Standards Council to perform PCI-DSS assessments. They have the expertise, training, and authorization to evaluate an organization's compliance with the PCI-DSS requirements. The

QSA conducts the assessment, examines evidence, tests controls, interviews personnel, and then documents their findings in the RoC.

It's important to note that the QSA must be independent from the organization being assessed to ensure an objective evaluation. The QSA's role is to provide an unbiased assessment of the organization's compliance status, documenting both compliant areas and any deficiencies that need to be addressed.

Additional resource: https://www.pcisecuritystandards.org/assessors_and_solutions/qualified_security_assessors/

Q16: Put the following steps in the correct order for the RoC verification process:

1. Payment brand verifies the RoC
2. QSA creates the RoC
3. Merchant's acquirer reviews the RoC
4. Acquirer sends the RoC to the payment brand
5. Controls are tested and documentation is collected

A16: The correct order for the RoC verification process is:

1. Controls are tested and documentation is collected
2. QSA creates the RoC
3. Merchant's acquirer reviews the RoC
4. Acquirer sends the RoC to the payment brand
5. Payment brand verifies the RoC

This order follows the logical flow described in the content:

First, the organization's PCI controls are tested and documentation of processes is collected as part of the assessment. As stated: "Following the testing of your controls and the collection of documentation of your processes..."

Second, based on this assessment, "a PCI auditor (QSA) creates a final PCI RoC (Report on Compliance)."

Third, the RoC is presented to the merchant's acquiring bank for review. As stated: "A Report on Compliance is a document that documents the detailed results of an assessment of PCI-DSS compliance; it is then presented to the merchant's acquirer."

Fourth, once the acquirer accepts the RoC, they forward it to the payment brand. As stated: "As soon as the acquirer has accepted the RoC, it then sends it to the payment brand for verification."

Finally, the payment brand completes the process by verifying the RoC and updating the merchant's compliance status.

This process ensures multiple levels of review and validation before compliance status is finalized.

Additional resource: https://www.pcisecuritystandards.org/documents/PCI_DSS_v4-0.pdf

Q17: True or False: An Attestation of Compliance (AoC) and a Report on Compliance (RoC) serve the same purpose and contain the same level of detail.

A17: False. An Attestation of Compliance (AoC) and a Report on Compliance (RoC) do not serve the same purpose and do not contain the same level of detail.

The Attestation of Compliance (AoC) is a certification document that specifies an organization's PCI-DSS compliance status. It serves as a summary declaration that confirms the organization has met the applicable PCI-DSS requirements. The AoC is relatively brief and provides a high-level assurance of compliance without extensive technical details.

In contrast, the Report on Compliance (RoC) is a comprehensive, detailed document that outlines an organization's security posture, environment, systems, and cardholder data protection measures. It documents the detailed results of a PCI-DSS assessment, including specific findings for each requirement, testing procedures performed, evidence examined, and compliance status for each control.

While both documents are part of the PCI compliance validation process, the RoC provides in-depth evidence and documentation of how compliance was achieved, whereas the AoC serves as a formal attestation that compliance has been achieved. The RoC is much more extensive and technical in nature compared to the AoC.

The relationship between these documents is that an AoC often accompanies a RoC when submitted to acquirers and payment brands, with the AoC serving as the executive summary and formal declaration, while the RoC provides the supporting evidence and details.

Additional resource: https://www.pcisecuritystandards.org/document_library/?category=aocs

Q18: What does the acronym QSA stand for in the context of PCI-DSS, and what is their role in the compliance process?

A18: QSA stands for Qualified Security Assessor in the context of PCI-DSS.

A Qualified Security Assessor is a security professional who has been certified by the PCI Security Standards Council to validate an entity's adherence to the Payment Card Industry Data Security Standard (PCI-DSS).

The role of a QSA in the compliance process includes:

1. **Assessment Planning**: Working with the organization to determine the scope of the assessment and the applicable PCI-DSS requirements.

2. **Control Evaluation**: Testing and evaluating the organization's security controls against PCI-DSS requirements to determine if they are properly implemented and functioning effectively.

3. **Evidence Collection**: Gathering and reviewing documentation, interviewing personnel, and examining system configurations to validate compliance.

4. **Gap Identification**: Identifying areas where the organization may not fully meet PCI-DSS requirements and providing guidance on remediation.

5. **Documentation Creation**: Creating the Report on Compliance (RoC) that documents the detailed results of the assessment.

6. **Attestation**: Completing and verifying the Attestation of Compliance (AoC) that certifies the organization's compliance status.

7. **Reporting**: Presenting the findings to the organization and assisting with the submission of compliance documentation to acquiring banks and payment brands.

As mentioned in the provided content, QSAs are responsible for completing and verifying the Attestation of Compliance and for creating the Report on Compliance following the testing of controls and collection of documentation. They serve as independent assessors who provide an objective evaluation of an organization's compliance with PCI-DSS requirements.

Additional resource: https://www.pcisecuritystandards.org/assessors_and_solutions/qualified_security_assessors/

Q19: Multiple Choice: According to the provided content, which statement best describes the purpose of an Attestation of Compliance (AoC)?

A) It is a detailed report that documents all security vulnerabilities found during an assessment. B) It is a certification that specifies an organization's PCI-DSS compliance status. C) It is a technical document that outlines network configurations for cardholder data environments. D) It is a remediation plan for addressing non-compliance issues identified during an audit.

A19: The correct answer is B) It is a certification that specifies an organization's PCI-DSS compliance status.

This answer directly aligns with the definition provided in the content: "The Attestation of Compliance (AoC) is a certification that specifies an organization's PCI-DSS compliance status and is completed and verified by a Qualified Security Assessor (QSA)."

Option A is incorrect because a detailed report documenting security vulnerabilities would be part of the Report on Compliance (RoC), not the AoC. The AoC is a more concise certification document rather than a detailed vulnerability report.

Option C is incorrect because technical documentation of network configurations would be included in the RoC or other supporting documentation, not in the AoC itself. The AoC does not typically contain detailed technical configurations.

Option D is incorrect because a remediation plan for addressing non-compliance issues would be a separate document, not the AoC. The AoC is focused on certifying compliance status rather than outlining remediation steps.

The AoC serves as a formal attestation that an organization has met the applicable PCI-DSS requirements, providing assurance to business partners, acquiring banks, and payment brands that the organization is following security best practices for protecting cardholder data.

Additional resource: https://www.pcisecuritystandards.org/document_library/?category=aocs

Q20: Essay question: Compare and contrast the Attestation of Compliance (AoC) and Report on Compliance (RoC) in terms of purpose, content, and when each is required in the PCI-DSS compliance process.

A20: # Comparing Attestation of Compliance (AoC) and Report on Compliance (RoC)

Purpose

Attestation of Compliance (AoC) The AoC serves as a formal certification document that declares an organization's compliance status with PCI-DSS requirements. Its primary purpose is to provide a standardized, executive-level attestation that an organization has met the applicable security requirements. The AoC functions as a compliance "seal of approval" that can be shared with business partners, acquiring banks, and payment brands as evidence of compliance without revealing sensitive security details.

Report on Compliance (RoC) The RoC's purpose is to document the detailed results of a comprehensive PCI-DSS assessment. It serves as the evidentiary foundation that supports the compliance claims made in the AoC. The RoC aims to provide a thorough analysis of an organization's security controls, testing procedures, findings, and compliance status for each PCI-DSS requirement. It offers transparency into how an organization protects cardholder data and meets the standard's requirements.

Content

Attestation of Compliance (AoC) The AoC is a relatively concise document that includes:

- Basic organization information
- Assessment details (date, type of assessment)
- Compliance status declarations
- Scope of the assessment
- Brief summary of compliance status for each PCI-DSS requirement
- Attestation statements
- QSA or internal assessor signatures

The AoC does not contain detailed technical information or specific evidence of compliance. It is designed to be a high-level certification document that can be shared without disclosing sensitive security information.

Report on Compliance (RoC) The RoC is a comprehensive, detailed document that includes:

- Extensive organization information
- Detailed description of the cardholder data environment
- Network diagrams and data flow diagrams
- Complete inventory of in-scope systems and components
- Detailed security posture analysis
- Specific testing procedures performed for each requirement
- Evidence examined for each requirement

- Findings and observations for each requirement
- Compliance status for each sub-requirement
- Details of compensating controls (if applicable)
- Documentation of non-compliance issues
- Supporting evidence and technical details

The RoC provides an exhaustive record of the assessment process and findings, often running to hundreds of pages with technical appendices.

When Required

Attestation of Compliance (AoC) An AoC is required in all PCI-DSS compliance validation scenarios. It accompanies:

- A completed Self-Assessment Questionnaire (SAQ) for merchants at Levels 2-4
- A Report on Compliance (RoC) for Level 1 merchants
- Compliance documentation for service providers

The AoC must be completed annually as part of the regular compliance validation cycle. It serves as the formal declaration of compliance regardless of the type of assessment performed.

Report on Compliance (RoC) A RoC is specifically required for:

- Level 1 merchants (processing more than 6 million transactions of a single card brand annually)
- Merchants that have experienced a data breach (regardless of volume)
- Merchants designated as Level 1 by card brand discretion
- Level 1 service providers

Lower-level merchants typically complete Self-Assessment Questionnaires instead of a full RoC. The RoC must be prepared by a Qualified Security Assessor (QSA) based on an on-site assessment, whereas lower-level assessments may be conducted internally.

Integration in the Compliance Process

The AoC and RoC work together in the compliance validation process, particularly for Level 1 entities. The detailed findings in the RoC support the compliance claims made in the AoC. The QSA first completes the comprehensive assessment and documents the results in the RoC. Then, based on those findings, they complete the AoC as a summary certification.

Both documents follow a standardized format prescribed by the PCI Security Standards Council to ensure consistency across assessments. The AoC provides a quick reference for compliance status, while the RoC provides the detailed evidence that would be examined in case of a dispute or audit.

In conclusion, while both documents are part of the PCI-DSS compliance validation framework, they serve complementary but distinct purposes. The AoC provides a formal declaration of compliance status, while the RoC provides the detailed evidence and documentation that supports that declaration.

Additional resource: https://www.pcisecuritystandards.org/document_library/?agreement=pcidss

Q21: In which situations might a merchant with a low transaction volume still be classified as a Level 1 merchant? (Select all that apply)

A) If they operate in multiple countries B) If they have experienced a data breach C) If a card brand uses its discretion based on risk assessment D) If they accept multiple card brands E) If they have high-risk factors despite low volume

A21: The correct answers are B) If they have experienced a data breach, C) If a card brand uses its discretion based on risk assessment, and E) If they have high-risk factors despite low volume.

According to the provided content: "Even if your volume is low, risk matters. Brands want control over who gets top-tier scrutiny. It's not just about numbers, it's about trust and exposure."

The content specifically mentions:

- "A data breach? You're in." (option B)
- "Card brand discretion? That works as well." (option C)

Option E is also correct because the content states: "It's not just about numbers, it's about trust and exposure," indicating that high-risk factors can lead to Level 1 classification despite low transaction volume.

Options A and D are not mentioned in the content as specific factors that would cause a merchant with low transaction volume to be classified as Level 1. While operating in multiple countries (A) might potentially increase risk, and accepting multiple card brands (D) might affect overall transaction volume, neither is explicitly stated as a trigger for Level 1 classification in the provided material.

The key takeaway is that risk factors and card brand discretion play significant roles in merchant level classification, beyond just transaction volume thresholds.

Additional resource: https://www.pcisecuritystandards.org/merchants/

Q22: Which of the following is NOT mentioned as a component of a Report on Compliance (RoC) in the provided content?

A) An organization's security posture B) The organization's cardholder data environment C) Systems used to process transactions D) Names of all employees with access to cardholder data E) Cardholder data protection measures

A22: The correct answer is D) Names of all employees with access to cardholder data.

According to the provided content, a Report on Compliance (RoC) "outlines an organization's security posture, environment, systems, and cardholder data protection." The content does not specifically mention that a RoC includes the names of all employees with access to cardholder data.

The other options are all mentioned as components of a RoC:

- Option A (An organization's security posture) is explicitly mentioned: "outlines an organization's security posture..."
- Option B (The organization's cardholder data environment) is implied by "environment" in the description
- Option C (Systems used to process transactions) is covered by "systems" in the description
- Option E (Cardholder data protection measures) is explicitly mentioned: "...and cardholder data protection"

While a RoC might include information about access control policies and procedures, and might document roles that have access to cardholder data, listing the specific names of all employees with such access would be unusual in a RoC and is not mentioned in the provided content. Such detailed personnel information would typically be maintained in internal access control documentation rather than in the RoC itself.

Additional resource: https://www.pcisecuritystandards.org/documents/PCI-DSS-v4-0-ROC-Reporting-Template.pdf

Q23: What is the relationship between transaction volume and merchant levels in PCI-DSS?

A23: The relationship between transaction volume and merchant levels in PCI-DSS is primarily defined by specific transaction thresholds for each card brand, with higher volumes resulting in higher merchant levels and more rigorous compliance requirements.

According to the provided content, Level 1 merchants are defined as retailers that process more than 6 million Visa or Mastercard transactions annually. This threshold applies to each card brand individually, not collectively. This means that if a merchant processes 6 million transactions with just one card brand (Visa, Mastercard, American Express, etc.), they would be classified as Level 1.

Key aspects of this relationship include:

1. **Individual Brand Thresholds**: The content emphasizes that "the transaction threshold applies to each card brand individually." This means a merchant must exceed the threshold with at least one specific card brand to trigger the higher classification.

2. **Higher Volume = Higher Level = More Scrutiny**: Level 1 is the highest merchant level with the most rigorous compliance requirements, including mandatory Report on Compliance (RoC) preparation by a QSA.

3. **Brand-Specific Definitions**: Each payment card brand (Visa, Mastercard, American Express, etc.) sets its own transaction thresholds and level definitions. While the content mentions 6 million as the threshold for Level 1, it's important to note that this could vary between brands.

4. **Beyond Volume**: While transaction volume is the primary determinant, the content also notes that other factors can override volume considerations: "Even if your volume is low, risk matters." This indicates that the relationship between volume and merchant level is not absolute.

5. **Risk-Based Considerations**: Card brands retain discretion to elevate merchants to higher levels based on risk assessment, regardless of transaction volume. Experience of a data breach also automatically elevates a merchant to Level 1 status.

The relationship serves as a risk-based approach to compliance validation, where organizations handling larger volumes of transactions (and thus presenting greater potential risk to the payment ecosystem) are subject to more comprehensive assessment requirements.

Additional resource: https://www.pcisecuritystandards.org/merchants/

Q24: Fill in the blank: A Report on Compliance is a document that documents the detailed results of an assessment of PCI-DSS compliance; it is then presented to the _______________.

A24: A Report on Compliance is a document that documents the detailed results of an assessment of PCI-DSS compliance; it is then presented to the merchant's acquirer.

This answer comes directly from the provided content, which states: "A Report on Compliance is a document that documents the detailed results of an assessment of PCI-DSS compliance; it is then presented to the merchant's acquirer."

The merchant's acquirer (also known as the acquiring bank or payment processor) is the financial institution that processes credit and debit card transactions for merchants. In the PCI-DSS compliance process, the acquirer serves as the first level of review for compliance documentation before it is forwarded to the payment brands.

The content further explains that "As soon as the acquirer has accepted the RoC, it then sends it to the payment brand for verification." This highlights the sequential flow of the compliance validation process, where the merchant's acquirer reviews the RoC first, and only after accepting it does the acquirer forward it to the relevant payment brand(s) for final verification.

This process ensures that multiple stakeholders validate the compliance documentation, providing appropriate oversight of the assessment results before compliance status is formally recognized.

Additional resource: https://www.pcisecuritystandards.org/about_us/payment_brands/

Q25: True or False: The transaction threshold that defines a Level 1 merchant applies to the combined total of transactions across all card brands accepted by the merchant.

A25: False. The transaction threshold that defines a Level 1 merchant does NOT apply to the combined total of transactions across all card brands; instead, it applies to each card brand individually.

According to the provided content: "The definition of a Level 1 merchant should note that the transaction threshold applies to each card brand individually. Visa, Mastercard, Amex, they all set their own limits. Hitting the number with just one brand can push you into Level 1."

This means that a merchant is classified as Level 1 if they process more than 6 million transactions annually with ANY SINGLE card brand, not based on the combined total across all brands. For example:

- A merchant processing 7 million Visa transactions but only 2 million Mastercard transactions would be classified as Level 1 because they exceed the threshold for Visa.
- A merchant processing 5 million Visa transactions and 5 million Mastercard transactions (10 million total) would NOT automatically be classified as Level 1 based on transaction volume because they don't exceed the 6 million threshold for any single brand.

This distinction is important because it means merchants need to monitor their transaction volumes by individual card brand rather than in aggregate. Exceeding the threshold with just one card brand is sufficient to trigger Level 1 classification and the associated requirement for a Report on Compliance (RoC) prepared by a Qualified Security Assessor.

Additional resource: https://www.pcisecuritystandards.org/merchants/

30

Prioritized Approach Tool (PAT) - Question Set

Q1: What is the primary purpose of the Prioritized Approach Tool (PAT) in PCI-DSS compliance?

A1: The primary purpose of the Prioritized Approach Tool (PAT) is to help organizations prioritize their PCI-DSS compliance efforts by identifying quick wins and establishing a structured approach to implementation. The tool enables organizations to track their progress against each PCI-DSS control, document advancements in their compliance program, identify gaps, and determine areas requiring additional focus. By breaking down compliance into manageable security milestones, the PAT provides a systematic method to reduce the risk of data breaches while working toward full compliance. This is especially valuable for PCIPs who may not have project management expertise but need to chart and monitor compliance progress effectively.

Additional resources: https://www.pcisecuritystandards.org/documents/Prioritized-Approach-for-PCI-DSS.pdf

Q2: True or False: The Prioritized Approach Tool is primarily designed for experienced project managers.

A2: False. The content specifically states that the Prioritized Approach Tool (PAT) is "a valuable tool for you as a PCIP, as you may not necessarily be a project manager." The tool is designed to be accessible and useful for PCIPs regardless of their project management experience. It provides structure and guidance for compliance efforts, making it particularly valuable for professionals who need assistance with organizing and tracking their PCI-DSS compliance journey without requiring specialized project management skills.

Additional resources: https://www.pcisecuritystandards.org/document_library/

Q3: Which of the following is NOT one of the six priority areas in the Prioritized Approach Tool?

A3: Based on the content provided, the six priority areas of the Prioritized Approach Tool are:

1. Data retention limitation and removal of sensitive authentication data (SAD)

2. Protection of systems and networks in case of a data breach

3. Applications that securely accept payment cards

4. Monitoring and controlling access to systems

5. Protection of cardholder data

6. Completion of remaining compliance efforts and ensuring all controls are in place

A choice that would NOT be among these six priority areas would be "Establishing a security awareness training program." While security awareness training is important in the broader context of PCI-DSS compliance, it is not specifically listed as one of the six priority areas in the Prioritized Approach Tool as described in the provided content.

Additional resources: https://www.pcisecuritystandards.org/prioritized_approach_tool/

Q4: What is the first priority area according to the Prioritized Approach Tool?

A4: According to the Prioritized Approach Tool, the first priority area is limiting data retention and removing sensitive authentication data (SAD) from the system as soon as possible. This is considered the most important area because it directly reduces risk by minimizing the amount of sensitive data stored in the environment. When sensitive authentication data is promptly removed and overall cardholder data storage is limited, the potential impact of a data breach is significantly reduced. This "data minimization" approach is fundamental to information security principles and represents a critical first step in protecting payment card environments.

Additional resources: https://www.pcisecuritystandards.org/documents/PCI_DSS_v4_Prioritized_Approach.pdf

Q5: How does the Prioritized Approach Tool help PCIPs in their role?

A5: The Prioritized Approach Tool helps PCIPs in their role by:

1. Providing a structured approach to compliance without requiring project management expertise

2. Enabling them to identify and implement "quick wins" to make immediate security improvements

3. Offering a systematic way to track progress against each PCI-DSS control

4. Helping identify gaps in the compliance program that need attention

5. Establishing clear security milestones to lower the risk of a data breach

6. Documenting progress against controls, which aids in reporting and demonstrating compliance efforts

7. Prioritizing activities into six logical areas in order of importance, creating a roadmap for implementation

8. Allowing PCIPs to focus resources on the highest-risk areas first

9. Creating a framework for communicating progress to stakeholders

The tool essentially serves as a roadmap and tracking mechanism that enables PCIPs to navigate the complexity of PCI-DSS compliance in a methodical, risk-based manner.

Additional resources: https://www.pcisecuritystandards.org/pci_security/

Q6: Multiple Choice: Which of the following best describes the second priority area in the PAT?

a) Protecting cardholder data b) Ensuring systems and networks are protected in case of a data breach c) Monitoring and controlling access to systems d) Applications that securely accept payment cards

A6: The correct answer is b) Ensuring systems and networks are protected in case of a data breach.

According to the provided content, the second priority area in the Prioritized Approach Tool focuses on ensuring that systems and networks are protected in case of a data breach. This area emphasizes implementing security measures that can contain and mitigate the impact if a breach occurs. This might include network segmentation, encryption, firewalls, and other controls that create multiple layers of defense. This priority acknowledges that while organizations should strive to prevent breaches (addressed in other priority areas), they must also be prepared for scenarios where preventive controls fail.

Additional resources: https://www.pcisecuritystandards.org/documents/Prioritized-Approach-Tool-v4_0.xlsx

Q7: What are the six priority areas of the Prioritized Approach Tool in the correct order?

A7: The six priority areas of the Prioritized Approach Tool in the correct order of importance are:

1. Data retention should be limited, and sensitive authentication data (SAD) should be removed from the system as soon as possible.
2. Ensure that your systems and networks are protected in case of a data breach.
3. Applications that securely accept payment cards.
4. It is important to monitor and control who has access to your systems.
5. It is important to protect the data pertaining to cardholders.
6. The remaining compliance efforts need to be completed, and all controls need to be in place.

This order reflects a risk-based approach, starting with data minimization (reducing what could be stolen), then implementing protective measures, securing applications, controlling access, protecting the data that must be retained, and finally addressing any remaining compliance requirements.

Additional resources: https://www.pcisecuritystandards.org/documents/PCI_DSS_v4_0.pdf

Q8: True or False: The Prioritized Approach Tool eliminates the need for a complete PCI-DSS implementation.

A8: False. The Prioritized Approach Tool does not eliminate the need for a complete PCI-DSS implementation. Instead, it provides a structured methodology to organize and prioritize compliance efforts. The sixth priority area specifically states: "The remaining compliance efforts need to be completed, and all controls need to be in place." This clearly indicates that full compliance with all PCI-DSS requirements remains the ultimate goal. The tool simply helps organizations approach this goal in a systematic way, focusing first on the areas that provide the greatest risk reduction, while still working toward comprehensive compliance with all PCI-DSS controls.

Additional resources: https://www.pcisecuritystandards.org/about_us/

Q9: Explain how the Prioritized Approach Tool supports the concept of risk reduction in PCI-DSS compliance.

A9: The Prioritized Approach Tool supports risk reduction in PCI-DSS compliance by organizing security controls in a sequence that addresses the highest risks first. This risk-based methodology is evident in several ways:

1. Data minimization first: The highest priority is given to limiting data retention and removing sensitive authentication data (SAD), which directly reduces the potential impact of a breach by limiting what data could be compromised.
2. Defense-in-depth approach: The sequential priorities build layers of protection, starting with removing unnecessary data, then protecting systems and networks, securing applications, controlling access, and protecting remaining cardholder data.
3. Focus on critical vulnerabilities: By prioritizing security milestones, organizations address the most critical vulnerabilities first, providing immediate risk reduction while working toward full compliance.
4. Gap identification: The tool helps identify compliance gaps, allowing organizations to assess their risk exposure and allocate resources to the most significant security issues.
5. Incremental security improvement: Rather than treating compliance as a binary state (compliant/non-compliant), the tool encourages progressive security improvements that continuously reduce risk over time.
6. Practical implementation: By breaking down compliance into manageable components, organizations can make steady progress rather than being overwhelmed by the full set of requirements, which could lead to delays in implementing any security improvements.

This approach ensures that even before achieving full compliance, organizations have addressed their most significant security risks, substantially reducing the likelihood and potential impact of data breaches during the compliance journey.

Additional resources: https://www.pcisecuritystandards.org/merchants/

Q10: Which of the following statements best describes how the Prioritized Approach Tool helps with tracking compliance progress?

a) It automatically implements PCI-DSS controls for the organization b) It eliminates the need for documentation in the compliance process c) It helps organizations track compliance against each PCI-DSS control and document progress d) It replaces the need for qualified security assessors

A10: The correct answer is c) It helps organizations track compliance against each PCI-DSS control and document progress.

According to the provided content, "Using this tool, the business can keep track of its compliance against each PCI-DSS control and document its progress against those controls." The Prioritized Approach Tool serves as a tracking mechanism that allows organizations to methodically document where they stand in relation to each control requirement and monitor their progress over time. This tracking capability provides visibility into the compliance journey, helps demonstrate efforts to auditors and stakeholders, and enables more effective resource allocation by clearly showing which areas still need attention.

Additional resources: https://www.pcisecuritystandards.org/assessors_and_solutions/

Q11: What does the acronym "SAD" stand for in the context of the Prioritized Approach Tool, and why is its removal prioritized?

A11: In the context of the Prioritized Approach Tool, "SAD" stands for Sensitive Authentication Data. SAD includes security-critical data such as full magnetic stripe data, card verification values/codes (CVV/CVC), and PINs/PIN blocks that are used to authenticate cardholders during payment transactions.

The removal of SAD is prioritized (appearing in the first priority area) because:

1. Risk reduction: SAD presents particularly high risk as it contains the essential elements needed for payment card fraud or counterfeiting.
2. PCI-DSS requirement: PCI-DSS explicitly prohibits storing SAD after authorization, even if encrypted (with very limited exceptions).
3. Data minimization: Removing unnecessary sensitive data is a fundamental security principle that immediately reduces risk exposure.
4. Breach impact reduction: If SAD is not present in systems, it cannot be stolen during a data breach, significantly reducing the potential damage.
5. Quick win opportunity: Removing SAD can often be accomplished relatively quickly compared to other compliance efforts, providing immediate risk reduction.

By addressing SAD removal first, organizations eliminate one of the highest-risk elements in their environment, making this a logical starting point for compliance efforts.

Additional resources: https://www.pcisecuritystandards.org/glossary/

Q12: Fill in the blank: The third priority area in the Prioritized Approach Tool focuses on ____________.

A12: The third priority area in the Prioritized Approach Tool focuses on applications that securely accept payment cards.

This priority area addresses the security of the applications used for payment card transactions. After minimizing data retention (priority 1) and protecting systems and networks (priority 2), securing the actual applications that handle card data becomes the next logical focus. This may include ensuring applications are developed according to secure coding practices, are properly authenticated, utilize encryption for transmission of cardholder data, and are regularly tested for vulnerabilities. Secure applications are crucial as they are often the direct interface with payment card data and represent a common attack vector for criminals seeking to compromise cardholder data.

Additional resources: https://www.pcisecuritystandards.org/programs/

Q13: Describe at least three ways the Prioritized Approach Tool can benefit an organization's PCI-DSS compliance program.

A13: The Prioritized Approach Tool can benefit an organization's PCI-DSS compliance program in several significant ways:

1. Risk-Based Implementation: The tool structures compliance efforts according to risk, ensuring that the most critical security controls are implemented first. This means organizations achieve substantial risk reduction early in their compliance journey, rather than addressing requirements in a random or convenience-based order.

2. Progress Tracking and Documentation: The tool enables organizations to systematically track compliance against each PCI-DSS control and document their progress. This creates a clear record of compliance efforts, which is valuable for internal reporting, demonstrating due diligence, and providing evidence during assessments.

3. Gap Identification: By mapping out all requirements and tracking progress, the tool helps identify compliance gaps and areas needing attention. This prevents important requirements from being overlooked and ensures a comprehensive approach to compliance.

4. Resource Optimization: With clear prioritization, organizations can allocate their often limited security resources more effectively, focusing on high-impact areas first and planning resource allocation for remaining requirements.

5. Milestone Achievement: Breaking down compliance into six priority areas creates achievable milestones, which can help maintain momentum and demonstrate progress to stakeholders, even when full compliance may take time to achieve.

6. Accessible Project Management: For PCIPs who may not have project management expertise, the tool provides a structured framework for organizing the compliance effort without requiring specialized project management skills.

7. Communication Aid: The tool and its prioritization framework offer a common language and structure for communicating about compliance status and progress with executives, auditors, and other stakeholders.

These benefits collectively enable a more efficient, effective, and risk-focused approach to achieving and maintaining PCI-DSS compliance.

Additional resources: https://www.pcisecuritystandards.org/blog/

Q14: Multiple Choice: Which of the following is the correct sequence for the last three priority areas in the Prioritized Approach Tool?

a) Monitoring system access, protecting cardholder data, completing remaining compliance efforts b) Protecting cardholder data, monitoring system access, completing remaining compliance efforts c) Completing remaining compliance efforts, monitoring system access, protecting cardholder data d) Monitoring system access, completing remaining compliance efforts, protecting cardholder data

A14: The correct answer is a) Monitoring system access, protecting cardholder data, completing remaining compliance efforts.

According to the provided content, the six priority areas in order are:

1. Data retention limitation and SAD removal

2. System and network protection

3. Secure payment card acceptance applications

4. Monitoring and controlling system access

5. Protecting cardholder data

6. Completing remaining compliance efforts

Therefore, the last three priority areas (4-6) are: monitoring and controlling system access, protecting cardholder data, and completing the remaining compliance efforts with all controls in place.

Additional resources: https://www.pcisecuritystandards.org/pci_security/maintaining_payment_security

Q15: Why might a PCIP who isn't a project manager find the Prioritized Approach Tool particularly valuable?

A15: A PCIP who isn't a project manager would find the Prioritized Approach Tool particularly valuable for several reasons:

1. Structured Framework: The tool provides a ready-made structure for organizing compliance efforts without requiring formal project management knowledge or experience. As the content explicitly states, "The Prioritised Approach Tool (PAT) is a valuable tool for you as a PCIP, as you may not necessarily be a project manager."

2. Simplified Planning: The six priority areas create a logical sequence for implementation, eliminating the need to develop a complex project plan from scratch.

3. Progress Tracking: The tool's built-in tracking mechanisms allow PCIPs to monitor compliance progress without needing to create custom tracking systems.

4. Risk-Based Prioritization: The tool has already determined the risk-based priority of different controls, saving the PCIP from having to make these complex risk assessments themselves.

5. Clear Milestones: The priority areas create natural milestones that help PCIPs demonstrate progress to stakeholders.

6. Gap Identification: The tool helps identify compliance gaps, making it easier for non-project managers to ensure comprehensive coverage of all requirements.

7. Resource Allocation Guidance: The prioritization helps PCIPs make informed decisions about where to focus limited resources without extensive project management experience.

8. Communication Tool: The structured approach gives PCIPs a framework for communicating with technical teams, management, and other stakeholders about compliance status and plans.

In essence, the tool provides project management structure and guidance for professionals whose expertise may be more focused on security, compliance, or payment card technologies rather than project management methodologies.

Additional resources: https://www.pcisecuritystandards.org/faq/

Q16: True or False: According to the Prioritized Approach Tool, protecting cardholder data is considered a higher priority than monitoring and controlling system access.

A16: False. According to the provided content on the Prioritized Approach Tool, monitoring and controlling system access (priority area 4) is considered a higher priority than protecting cardholder data (priority area 5).

The six priority areas in order are:

1. Data retention limitation and SAD removal
2. System and network protection
3. Secure payment card acceptance applications
4. Monitoring and controlling system access
5. Protecting cardholder data
6. Completing remaining compliance efforts

This prioritization reflects a risk-based approach where controlling who has access to systems is addressed before implementing additional protections for the cardholder data itself. The logic is that restricting access helps prevent unauthorized users from reaching the data in the first place, creating an important security layer before focusing on the specific protections for the data that legitimate users can access.

Additional resources: https://www.pcisecuritystandards.org/supportors/

Q17: Scenario-based question: A company has just begun its PCI-DSS compliance journey and has limited resources. They want to use the Prioritized Approach Tool effectively. Which of the following actions should they take FIRST according to the tool's prioritization?

a) Implement a comprehensive logging and monitoring solution b) Deploy encryption for all cardholder data c) Remove sensitive authentication data and limit data retention d) Update all applications to the latest secure versions

A17: The correct answer is c) Remove sensitive authentication data and limit data retention.

According to the Prioritized Approach Tool, the first priority area is "Data retention should be limited, and sensitive authentication data (SAD) should be removed from the system as soon as possible." This represents the starting point for organizations beginning their compliance journey, especially those with limited resources.

This is prioritized first because:

- It directly reduces risk by minimizing the data that could potentially be compromised
- SAD (like CVV codes and magnetic stripe data) presents particularly high risk if compromised
- PCI-DSS specifically prohibits storing SAD after authorization

- Data minimization often requires fewer resources to implement than complex technical controls
- It represents a "quick win" that can significantly reduce risk early in the compliance process

For a company just starting with limited resources, focusing on data minimization and SAD removal would provide the greatest immediate risk reduction while setting the foundation for subsequent compliance efforts.

Additional resources: https://www.pcisecuritystandards.org/get_started/

Q18: What role does gap identification play in the Prioritized Approach Tool, and how does it benefit compliance efforts?

A18: Gap identification plays a crucial role in the Prioritized Approach Tool and provides several benefits to compliance efforts:

Role in the Prioritized Approach Tool:

- The tool explicitly helps "identify gaps in your compliance program and areas where you may need to focus your efforts"
- It provides a structured framework against which organizations can compare their current state
- It enables systematic tracking of compliance status for each PCI-DSS control
- It highlights requirements that haven't been addressed or are only partially implemented

Benefits to compliance efforts:

1. Comprehensive Coverage: Gap identification ensures no requirements are overlooked, preventing blind spots in the compliance program.
2. Resource Allocation: By clearly identifying gaps, organizations can allocate resources more effectively to areas of greatest need.
3. Risk Management: Understanding compliance gaps helps organizations assess their risk exposure and prioritize remediation efforts based on risk impact.
4. Realistic Planning: Clear visibility into gaps enables more accurate planning, scheduling, and budgeting for remediation activities.
5. Progress Measurement: Gap analysis provides a baseline against which progress can be measured over time.
6. Stakeholder Communication: Gap reports can effectively communicate compliance status and needs to management and other stakeholders.
7. Preparation for Assessments: Identifying gaps before formal assessments allows organizations to address issues proactively rather than reactively.
8. Continuous Improvement: Regular gap identification supports a cycle of continuous improvement in the security program.

Through systematic gap identification, the Prioritized Approach Tool transforms compliance from a vague goal into a concrete set of actionable items, making the compliance process more manageable and effective.

Additional resources: https://www.pcisecuritystandards.org/documents/Self-Assessment_Questionnaire_Instructions_and_Guidelines_v4_0.pdf

Q19: Multiple Choice: What is the main goal of the six security milestones in the Prioritized Approach Tool?

a) To extend the timeline for achieving PCI-DSS compliance b) To reduce the number of required PCI-DSS controls c) To lower the risk of a data breach while working toward compliance d) To simplify the PCI-DSS requirements for small businesses

A19: The correct answer is c) To lower the risk of a data breach while working toward compliance.

According to the provided content, "The tool aims to assist you with your compliance journey, through a set of security milestones designed to lower the risk of a data breach." This statement directly connects the purpose of the security milestones to risk reduction.

The Prioritized Approach Tool doesn't reduce or simplify the requirements (options b and d), nor does it aim to extend the compliance timeline (option a). Instead, it organizes the existing requirements into a risk-based sequence that helps organizations address the most critical security concerns first, thereby reducing breach risk even before full compliance is achieved. This approach acknowledges that compliance is a journey and ensures that the journey itself provides increasing security benefits along the way.

Additional resources: https://www.pcisecuritystandards.org/documents/PCI_DSS_V4_0_SAQ_A.pdf

Q20: Explain the relationship between "quick wins" and the Prioritized Approach Tool in PCI-DSS compliance.

A20: The relationship between "quick wins" and the Prioritized Approach Tool in PCI-DSS compliance is integral to the tool's value and effectiveness:

1. Explicit Purpose: The opening statement of the provided content identifies that "Organizations can prioritize compliance efforts by identifying quick wins by utilizing the Prioritised Approach Tool." This establishes quick wins as a core function of the tool.

2. Strategic Implementation: The tool is structured to identify and prioritize actions that can deliver significant security improvements with relatively lower effort or resource investment – the essence of "quick wins."

3. Risk-Based Sequencing: The prioritization sequence itself is designed to place higher emphasis on controls that can provide immediate risk reduction (quick wins) before moving to more complex, longer-term compliance efforts.

4. Momentum Building: Quick wins generate visible progress early in the compliance journey, building momentum and demonstrating value to stakeholders, which can help secure continued support for the compliance program.

5. Early Risk Reduction: By focusing on quick wins like data minimization and SAD removal first, organizations achieve substantial risk reduction early, rather than waiting until all requirements are implemented.

6. Resource Optimization: The identification of quick wins helps organizations use limited resources effectively, achieving

maximum security benefit from initial investments.

7. Gap Closure Targeting: The tool helps identify gaps where quick wins might be possible, allowing targeted efforts on high-impact, readily achievable improvements.
8. Practical Approach: The quick win philosophy acknowledges the real-world constraints organizations face, offering a practical path forward rather than an all-or-nothing approach to compliance.

The Prioritized Approach Tool essentially operationalizes the concept of quick wins by providing a structured framework that identifies, prioritizes, and tracks these high-value, achievable security improvements as part of a broader compliance strategy.

Additional resources: https://www.pcisecuritystandards.org/documents/PCI_DSS_v4_Quick_Reference_Guide.pdf

Q21: Which of the following statements about the sixth priority area in the Prioritized Approach Tool is most accurate?

a) It focuses exclusively on documentation requirements b) It addresses remaining compliance efforts and ensuring all controls are in place c) It deals primarily with penetration testing requirements d) It emphasizes employee security awareness training

A21: The correct answer is b) It addresses remaining compliance efforts and ensuring all controls are in place.

According to the provided content, the sixth priority area is described as: "The remaining compliance efforts need to be completed, and all controls need to be in place." This clearly indicates that this final priority area encompasses all remaining compliance requirements that haven't been addressed in the previous five priority areas, with the goal of ensuring that all PCI-DSS controls are ultimately implemented.

While documentation, penetration testing, and security awareness training may be among the components addressed in this final priority area, the description is broader and more comprehensive than any of these specific elements alone. The sixth priority area serves as a "catch-all" to ensure that after addressing the highest-risk areas in priorities 1-5, organizations complete the full set of PCI-DSS requirements for comprehensive compliance.

Additional resources: https://www.pcisecuritystandards.org/documents/PCI_DSS_v4-0_Summary_of_Changes.pdf

Q22: True or False: The Prioritized Approach Tool is primarily focused on reducing the total number of PCI-DSS requirements an organization must meet.

A22: False. The Prioritized Approach Tool does not reduce the total number of PCI-DSS requirements an organization must meet. Instead, it provides a structured methodology for organizing and prioritizing the implementation of the full set of PCI-DSS requirements.

The provided content states that the tool helps "track the progress of your PCI-DSS compliance program" and that the sixth priority area involves ensuring "all controls need to be in place." This clearly indicates that comprehensive compliance with all PCI-DSS requirements remains the ultimate goal.

The tool's purpose is to:

- Prioritize compliance efforts based on risk

- Track progress against each PCI-DSS control
- Identify gaps in the compliance program
- Document progress toward full compliance
- Provide a structured approach to implementation

Rather than reducing requirements, the tool helps organizations approach the full set of requirements in a logical, risk-based sequence, focusing first on those that provide the greatest security benefit while still working toward complete compliance with all PCI-DSS controls.

Additional resources: https://www.pcisecuritystandards.org/documents/PCI_DSS_v4-0.pdf

Q23: How does the fourth priority area (monitoring and controlling system access) contribute to the overall security objectives of PCI-DSS?

A23: The fourth priority area of the Prioritized Approach Tool, "monitoring and controlling who has access to your systems," contributes significantly to the overall security objectives of PCI-DSS in multiple ways:

1. Access Control Implementation: This priority area ensures that only authorized individuals can access cardholder data and systems, implementing the principle of least privilege where users have only the access needed for their job functions.
2. Authentication Mechanisms: It addresses the implementation of strong authentication methods to verify user identities before granting system access, reducing the risk of unauthorized access through credential theft or misuse.
3. Audit Trail Creation: By monitoring system access, organizations create audit trails that document who accessed what data and when, which is essential for detection, forensic investigation, and accountability.
4. Anomaly Detection: Continuous monitoring enables the detection of unusual access patterns or behavior that might indicate a security incident in progress.
5. Insider Threat Mitigation: Access controls and monitoring help manage the risk posed by malicious insiders who might misuse their legitimate access privileges.
6. Separation of Duties: This area helps implement segregation of duties, ensuring that no single individual has excessive access that could enable fraudulent activities.
7. Third-Party Management: It addresses the monitoring and control of access by vendors and service providers who may need limited access to systems containing cardholder data.
8. Incident Response Support: Access monitoring provides early warning of potential security incidents, supporting faster incident response and containment.

This priority area creates a critical security layer by controlling the human element of security—determining who can access sensitive systems and data, under what circumstances, and ensuring this access is properly monitored. It addresses the fact that even with technical protections in place, inappropriate access privileges can undermine the entire security program.

Additional resources: https://www.pcisecuritystandards.org/documents/PCI_DSS_v4-0_ROC_Reporting_Template.pdf

Q24: Match each priority area of the Prioritized Approach Tool with its most relevant security principle:

A24: Matching priority areas with their most relevant security principles:

1. "Data retention should be limited, and sensitive authentication data (SAD) should be removed from the system as soon as possible."
    - Security Principle: Data Minimization This priority area directly applies the principle of data minimization, which holds that organizations should collect and retain only the minimum amount of sensitive data necessary for business purposes. By removing SAD and limiting overall data retention, organizations reduce their attack surface and potential breach impact.
2. "Ensure that your systems and networks are protected in case of a data breach."
    - Security Principle: Defense in Depth This priority area implements the defense in depth principle by establishing multiple layers of security controls to protect systems and networks, ensuring that if one control fails, others are in place to continue protecting assets.
3. "Applications that securely accept payment cards."
    - Security Principle: Secure by Design This area focuses on ensuring that applications handling payment card data incorporate security from the ground up, rather than as an afterthought, embodying the secure by design principle.
4. "It is important to monitor and control who has access to your systems."
    - Security Principle: Least Privilege This priority area implements the principle of least privilege, ensuring that users only have the minimum access rights necessary to perform their job functions, combined with accountability through monitoring.
5. "It is important to protect the data pertaining to cardholders."
    - Security Principle: Data Protection This area focuses on implementing controls specifically designed to protect the confidentiality and integrity of cardholder data that must be retained, applying the fundamental principle of data protection.
6. "The remaining compliance efforts need to be completed, and all controls need to be in place."
    - Security Principle: Comprehensive Security This final priority area embodies the principle of comprehensive security, recognizing that a complete security program must address all aspects of protection rather than focusing on isolated controls.

These mappings demonstrate how the Prioritized Approach Tool aligns with fundamental information security principles while providing a practical implementation sequence.

Additional resources: https://www.pcisecuritystandards.org/documents/PCI_DSS_v4-0_SAQ_D_Merchant.pdf

Q25: Describe how an organization might use the Prioritized Approach Tool to communicate progress to senior management and other stakeholders.

A25: An organization can effectively use the Prioritized Approach Tool to communicate progress to senior management and other stakeholders in several strategic ways:

1. Milestone-Based Reporting: The six priority areas provide natural milestones for reporting. Organizations can communicate progress in terms of "We've completed Priority Areas 1-3 and are 60% through Priority Area 4," providing a clear sense of advancement through a recognized framework.
2. Risk Reduction Narrative: Rather than simply reporting on control implementation, the tool enables a risk-focused narrative: "By completing Priority Areas 1 and 2, we've addressed our highest-risk exposures by removing sensitive authentication data and implementing multiple layers of network protection."
3. Visual Progress Tracking: The tool's tracking capabilities can be translated into visual dashboards or progress charts showing completion percentages across priority areas, providing at-a-glance status updates for executives.
4. Gap Analysis Presentations: Organizations can present identified gaps alongside remediation plans, demonstrating both awareness of issues and a structured approach to addressing them.
5. Resource Justification: When requesting resources, teams can tie requests directly to specific priority areas: "To complete Priority Area 3, we need investment in secure application development tools and training."
6. Comparative Benchmarking: Progress can be presented in the context of industry benchmarks or previous assessments, showing improvement over time and comparative standing.
7. Compliance Journey Mapping: The tool allows organizations to create a compliance roadmap with projected completion dates for each priority area, helping set expectations about the overall timeline.
8. Business Impact Alignment: Communications can connect priority areas to business objectives: "Completing Priority Area 4 will enable us to safely launch our new e-commerce platform while maintaining compliance."
9. Audit Preparation Status: Updates can include readiness assessments for upcoming audits based on progress through the priority areas.
10. Executive Summaries: The prioritized structure facilitates creating concise executive summaries that highlight key achievements, current focus areas, and critical gaps requiring attention.

By leveraging the structured, risk-based approach of the Prioritized Approach Tool in stakeholder communications, security and compliance teams can transform technical details into strategic narratives that resonate with management concerns about risk reduction, resource allocation, and compliance status.

Additional resources: https://www.pcisecuritystandards.org/documents/PCI_DSS_v4-0_ROC_Template.xlsx

31

User Authentication and Password Security - Question Set

Q1: What are the three categories of authentication methods used to secure cardholder data?

A1: The three categories of authentication methods for securing cardholder data are:

1. Something you know: The most common form of authentication that requires users to provide information only they should know, such as usernames, passwords, or passphrases.
2. Something you have: This method requires users to possess physical items like token devices, smart cards, or digital certificates that verify their identity.
3. Something you are: This authentication method uses biometric identifiers unique to the individual, such as fingerprints or facial scans.

These three authentication categories, when used in combination as multi-factor authentication, provide a robust security approach for protecting cardholder data by requiring multiple forms of verification before granting access.

Additional resource: https://www.pcisecuritystandards.org/documents/Multi-Factor-Authentication-Guidance-v1.0.pdf

Q2: According to PCI-DSS, what is the minimum required length for passwords and passphrases?

A2: According to PCI-DSS, passwords and passphrases must be at least twelve (12) characters long and include both alphabetic and numeric characters. This requirement ensures stronger passwords that are more resistant to brute force attacks and other password-cracking techniques.

However, PCI-DSS does provide an exception for legacy systems that cannot support 12-character passwords. In these cases, a minimum of eight characters is allowed, though organizations should implement additional compensating controls to address the reduced security that comes with shorter passwords.

The 12-character minimum, combined with complexity requirements, significantly increases the mathematical difficulty of guessing or cracking passwords compared to shorter alternatives.

Additional resource: https://www.pcisecuritystandards.org/documents/PCI_DSS_v4.pdf

Q3: True or False: Shared or generic user IDs are acceptable in a cardholder data environment as long as they have strong passwords.

A3: False. According to PCI-DSS requirements, all shared, generic, and default passwords are explicitly prohibited in a cardholder data environment. Each user must be assigned a unique ID before being allowed to access systems connected to the cardholder data environment.

The requirement for unique user IDs ensures:

- Individual accountability for actions taken within the system
- Ability to trace activities to specific individuals
- More effective access control management
- Better security through elimination of shared credentials

This requirement applies regardless of password strength - even with a strong password, shared IDs create security vulnerabilities and accountability issues that violate PCI-DSS standards.

Additional resource: https://www.pcisecuritystandards.org/documents/Guidance-PCI-DSS-Requirement-8-3.pdf

Q4: After how many failed login attempts should a user ID be locked out according to PCI-DSS?

A4: According to PCI-DSS requirements, a user ID should be locked out after ten (10) failed login attempts. This security measure helps prevent unauthorized access through brute force attacks, where an attacker might attempt multiple password combinations to gain access to a system.

Once locked out, the user ID should remain locked for at least 30 minutes or until an administrator manually enables it again. This lockout duration creates a significant obstacle for automated attack tools and helps protect the cardholder data environment from unauthorized access attempts.

This control works alongside other authentication requirements to create a comprehensive defense against password-based attacks

Additional resource: https://www.pcisecuritystandards.org/documents/PCI_DSS_v4_Account_Lockout.pdf

Q5: Which type of authentication is required for all access to the Cardholder Data Environment (CDE)?

A5: Multi-factor authentication (MFA) is required for all access to the Cardholder Data Environment (CDE). This means that regardless of whether the access is remote or onsite, users must authenticate using at least two different types of authentication factors from the three categories (something you know, something you have, and something you are).

This comprehensive MFA requirement ensures that every entry point to the CDE is protected by multiple layers of security significantly reducing the risk of unauthorized access and potential data breaches. The implementation of MFA for all CDE access represents a critical security control in protecting sensitive cardholder data.

Even if one authentication factor is compromised (such as a password), an attacker would still need to overcome additional authentication barriers to gain access to cardholder data.

Additional resource: https://www.pcisecuritystandards.org/documents/Multi-Factor-Authentication-Guidance-v1.0.pdf

Q6: How often should passwords or passphrases be changed according to PCI-DSS requirements?

A6: According to PCI-DSS requirements, passwords or passphrases must be changed at least once every 90 days (approximately every three months). This requirement is designed to limit the window of opportunity for attackers who may have obtained user credentials through various means.

Regular password changes help mitigate several security risks:

- They limit the usefulness of stolen credentials
- They reduce the impact of undetected security breaches
- They help maintain a strong security posture for the cardholder data environment

Organizations may implement more stringent password change policies, requiring changes more frequently than every 90 days, but they must at minimum comply with this 90-day requirement specified by PCI-DSS.

Additional resource: https://www.pcisecuritystandards.org/documents/Password_Security_Guidelines.pdf

Q7: What action is required when a terminal or session has been inactive for more than 15 minutes?

A7: When a terminal or session has been inactive for more than 15 minutes, the user must be required to re-authenticate to reactivate the terminal or session. This requirement helps prevent unauthorized access when legitimate users leave their workstations unattended.

Some organizations may implement stricter controls by setting the idle time to less than 15 minutes, and this may include the activation of a screensaver, but re-authentication is still required to resume the session.

This security measure is important because unattended, authenticated sessions present an opportunity for unauthorized users to access sensitive cardholder data without having to bypass authentication controls.

Additional resource: https://www.pcisecuritystandards.org/documents/Session_Management_Guidelines.pdf

Q8: When should access for terminated users be revoked according to PCI-DSS?

A8: According to PCI-DSS requirements, access for terminated users must be revoked immediately upon termination. This immediate revocation requirement is critical for maintaining the security of the cardholder data environment because former employees or contractors no longer have a legitimate need for access and could potentially misuse their access privileges if they remain active.

Immediate revocation helps prevent several security risks:

- Unauthorized access by former employees who may have malicious intent

- Accidental misuse of systems by individuals who no longer work for the organization
- Compliance issues related to inappropriate access rights

Organizations should have processes in place to ensure coordination between Human Resources, IT, Security, and other departments to ensure a smooth and secure offboarding process with prompt access removal.

Additional resource: https://www.pcisecuritystandards.org/documents/User_Access_Management_Guidelines.pdf

Q9: What is a digital certificate in the context of authentication, and what requirement must it meet to be effective?

A9: A digital certificate is an electronic credential that serves as a form of "something you have" authentication, verifying the identity of users and securing communications through cryptographic techniques. Digital certificates contain information about the identity of the certificate holder, a public key, digital signature, and other data that helps establish trust in digital environments.

For a digital certificate to be effective as an authentication method, the key requirement is that it must be personalized and unique to the individual user - it cannot be shared with others. This personal nature ensures that the authentication process maintains its integrity by confirming that the person using the certificate is indeed the authorized individual.

Digital certificates are commonly used in secure communications, encrypted connections, and as part of multi-factor authentication systems to enhance security beyond passwords alone.

Additional resource: https://www.pcisecuritystandards.org/documents/Digital_Certificate_Implementation.pdf

Q10: Within what timeframe should inactive user accounts be removed or disabled according to PCI-DSS?

A10: According to PCI-DSS requirements, inactive user accounts should be removed or disabled within 90 days of inactivity. This requirement helps to reduce the risk associated with dormant accounts that might be compromised or used maliciously if left active.

Inactive accounts present several security risks:

- They may belong to former employees whose departure wasn't properly processed
- They provide potential entry points for attackers that might not be closely monitored
- They can contribute to "access creep" where unused privileges accumulate over time

Regular review and management of user accounts, including the timely removal or disabling of inactive accounts, is an important security practice that helps maintain the integrity of the cardholder data environment and reduces the overall attack surface.

Additional resource: https://www.pcisecuritystandards.org/documents/Account_Management_Best_Practices.pdf

Q11: What is "Just in Time" (JIT) access and why is it recommended for third-party user IDs?

A11: "Just in Time" (JIT) access is a security approach where access privileges are granted to users only when needed and for the specific duration required to complete a task, rather than providing permanent access. The access is temporary and expires automatically after a predetermined period.

JIT access is recommended for third-party user IDs because it significantly reduces security risks by:

1. Limiting the window of opportunity for potential misuse or compromise of credentials
2. Reducing the attack surface by minimizing the time that credentials are active
3. Enhancing monitoring capabilities since access events are more distinctly defined
4. Improving access control by ensuring administrators know exactly when third parties are accessing systems
5. Minimizing risk of credential theft or misuse since credentials are only valid for short periods

Since third-party users typically don't require constant access to systems within the cardholder data environment, providing them with permanent access creates unnecessary security exposure. JIT access, combined with monitoring of third-party user ID usage, creates a comprehensive security approach for managing external access to sensitive systems.

Additional resource: https://www.pcisecuritystandards.org/documents/Third_Party_Access_Management.pdf

Q12: True or False: A minimum password length of 8 characters is acceptable for all systems according to PCI-DSS.

A12: False. According to PCI-DSS requirements, passwords and passphrases must be at least twelve (12) characters long, including both alphabetic and numeric characters. The 8-character minimum is only an exception allowed specifically for legacy systems that have technical limitations preventing them from supporting 12-character passwords.

This exception is noted in the content: "Note that a minimum of eight characters is allowed if legacy systems don't support using such long passwords or passphrases."

Organizations should implement the full 12-character minimum wherever technically possible and should consider implementing additional compensating controls for legacy systems that can only support 8-character passwords. The goal should be to either upgrade these legacy systems when possible or implement additional security measures to compensate for the reduced password strength.

Additional resource: https://www.pcisecuritystandards.org/documents/PCI_DSS_v4_Password_Requirements.pdf

Q13: According to PCI-DSS, how many previous passwords should be prohibited from being reused?

A13: According to PCI-DSS requirements, users should not be allowed to submit a new password or passphrase that is the same as any of the last four (4) passwords or passphrases they have previously used. This requirement is designed to prevent users from cycling through a small set of passwords, which would undermine the security benefits of regular password changes.

By enforcing password history, organizations ensure:

- Users create genuinely new passwords when changes are required
- The risk of password reuse is reduced
- The overall password security posture is strengthened

This password history requirement works in conjunction with other password controls, such as complexity requirements and regular password changes, to create a comprehensive approach to password security in the cardholder data environment.

Additional resource: https://www.pcisecuritystandards.org/documents/Password_Management_Guidelines.pdf

Q14: What form of authentication is required for non-console (remote) access to the CDE for personnel with administrative access rights?

A14: Multi-factor authentication (MFA) is required for all non-console (remote) access to the CDE for personnel with administrative access rights. This means that administrators accessing the cardholder data environment remotely must authenticate using at least two different authentication factors from the three categories (something you know, something you have, and something you are).

This requirement is particularly important because:

- Administrative accounts typically have elevated privileges that could lead to significant security breaches if compromised
- Remote connections may traverse untrusted networks
- Remote access points could be more vulnerable to interception
- Remote administrative sessions might originate from potentially compromised devices

By requiring MFA for remote administrative access, PCI-DSS ensures that even if one authentication factor (such as a password) is compromised, unauthorized users still cannot gain administrative access to the cardholder data environment without the additional authentication factors.

Additional resource: https://www.pcisecuritystandards.org/documents/Administrative_Access_Security.pdf

Q15: Which of the following would meet PCI-DSS password complexity requirements? (Select the best answer)

A) "password" (8 characters, all lowercase) B) "Password1" (9 characters, mixed case with number) C) "P@ssw0rd!123" (13 characters, mixed case with numbers and special characters) D) "12345678" (8 characters, all numbers)

A15: The correct answer is C) "P@ssw0rd!123" (13 characters, mixed case with numbers and special characters).

PCI-DSS requires passwords and passphrases to be at least twelve characters long and include both alphabetic and numeric characters. Option C meets these requirements with its 13-character length and inclusion of both alphabetic and numeric characters It also includes special characters, which further strengthens the password.

Options A, B, and D all fail to meet the requirements:

- Option A: Only 8 characters (below 12-character minimum) and doesn't contain any numeric characters
- Option B: Only 9 characters (below 12-character minimum)
- Option D: Only 8 characters (below 12-character minimum) and doesn't include any alphabetic characters

However, it's important to note that while "P@ssw0rd!123" technically meets the PCI-DSS requirements, it's not a good password choice in practice because it's a variation of a commonly known pattern. PCI-DSS guidance advises against using commonly known passwords such as "LetMeIn123" or "Password1234".

Additional resource: https://www.pcisecuritystandards.org/documents/Strong_Password_Guidelines.pdf

Q16: For how long should a user ID be locked out after reaching the maximum number of failed login attempts?

A16: According to PCI-DSS requirements, a user ID should be locked out for at least 30 minutes after reaching the maximum number of failed login attempts (which is 10 attempts). Alternatively, the account can remain locked until an administrator explicitly enables it.

This lockout duration serves several security purposes:

1. It creates a significant time penalty for attackers attempting to guess passwords
2. It helps prevent automated brute force attacks from being effective
3. It provides time for security teams to potentially detect attack patterns
4. It gives legitimate users who may have forgotten their password time to use proper account recovery methods

The combination of limiting failed attempts to 10 and imposing a minimum 30-minute lockout creates an effective defense against password guessing attacks while still allowing legitimate users to recover access through appropriate channels.

Additional resource: https://www.pcisecuritystandards.org/documents/Account_Lockout_Implementation.pdf

Q17: Which of the following is an example of "something you have" as an authentication method?

A) Password B) PIN code C) Digital certificate D) Fingerprint

A17: The correct answer is C) Digital certificate.

Authentication methods are categorized into three types:

- "Something you know" - knowledge-based authentication like passwords or PINs
- "Something you have" - possession-based authentication like smart cards or digital certificates
- "Something you are" - inherence-based authentication using biometric identifiers

A digital certificate is an electronic credential that a user possesses, making it a "something you have" authentication factor. Digital certificates contain cryptographic keys and identity information that verify the user's identity during the authentication process.

Options A (password) and B (PIN code) are both examples of "something you know" authentication methods, as they are information stored in a user's memory. Option D (fingerprint) is an example of "something you are" - a biometric identifier inherent to the individual.

Additional resource: https://www.pcisecuritystandards.org/documents/Authentication_Factors_Guide.pdf

Q18: What action is required for passwords or passphrases that are being used for the first time or after being reset?

A18: According to PCI-DSS requirements, passwords and passphrases must be changed immediately after the first use when they are being used for the first time or after being reset. This requirement applies to initially assigned passwords and any password resets.

This security practice ensures that:

1. Only the intended user knows their operational password
2. Administrators or help desk staff who set up the initial password or performed the reset don't retain knowledge of the user's credentials
3. The password is unique and known only to the authorized user

The content states: "You should require passwords and passphrases to be reset for first-time use, as well as when they are reset, make sure a unique value is used for each user. The user should change them immediately after the first use."

This practice is part of good password hygiene and helps maintain the security of the cardholder data environment by ensuring that only authorized users have knowledge of their credentials.

Additional resource: https://www.pcisecuritystandards.org/documents/Password_Reset_Procedures.pdf

Q19: True or False: Biometric authentication (such as fingerprint or facial scan) is categorized as "something you know" in the authentication framework.

A19: False. Biometric authentication (such as fingerprint or facial scan) is categorized as "something you are" in the authentication framework, not "something you know."

The three categories of authentication factors are:

1. Something you know - knowledge-based factors like passwords or PINs
2. Something you have - possession-based factors like smart cards or tokens
3. Something you are - inherence-based factors like biometric identifiers

Biometric authentication relies on unique physical or behavioral characteristics inherent to an individual, making it a clear example of the "something you are" category. These physical attributes are intrinsic to the person and cannot be forgotten or easily transferred to others, unlike knowledge-based factors which can be shared or stolen.

Understanding the correct categorization of authentication factors is essential for properly implementing multi-factor authentication requirements, especially in secure environments like those handling cardholder data.

Additional resource: https://www.pcisecuritystandards.org/documents/Biometric_Authentication_Guide.pdf

Q20: What should happen to inactive user accounts according to PCI-DSS requirements?

A20: According to PCI-DSS requirements, inactive user accounts must be removed or disabled within 90 days of inactivity. The content specifically states: "Remove, or Disable inactive user accounts within 90 days."

This requirement helps to reduce security risks associated with dormant accounts, which include:

1. Potential unauthorized access if the account credentials were compromised but not detected
2. Increased attack surface through unnecessary active accounts
3. Difficulty in maintaining accurate access control when unused accounts remain active
4. Potential privilege escalation opportunities for attackers

Organizations should implement processes to regularly identify inactive accounts approaching the 90-day threshold and take appropriate action to either remove them completely or disable them to prevent their use. This may involve automated monitoring systems that track account usage and generate reports or alerts when accounts approach the inactivity threshold.

Regular account management, including the timely handling of inactive accounts, is an important component of maintaining a secure cardholder data environment.

Additional resource: https://www.pcisecuritystandards.org/documents/Account_Lifecycle_Management.pdf

Q21: What two specific examples of passwords should not be used according to password hygiene best practices mentioned in the content?

A21: According to the password hygiene best practices mentioned in the content, two specific examples of passwords that should not be used are "LetMeIn123" and "Password1234". These are considered commonly known passwords that are easily guessable and frequently targeted in password attacks.

The content explicitly states: "It is strongly advised that you do not use any commonly known passwords such as LetMeIn123 or Password1234."

Using such predictable passwords significantly weakens security, even if they technically meet length and complexity requirements. These passwords:

1. Are included in common password dictionaries used by attackers
2. Follow obvious patterns that are easy to guess

3. Appear frequently in data breaches

4. Provide minimal security despite meeting technical requirements

Organizations should encourage users to create unique, complex passwords that are not based on common patterns or words. Password managers can help users generate and store strong, unique passwords for different systems and applications.

Additional resource: https://www.pcisecuritystandards.org/documents/Common_Password_Vulnerabilities.pdf

Q22: Explain how multi-factor authentication enhances security compared to single-factor authentication.

A22: Multi-factor authentication (MFA) significantly enhances security compared to single-factor authentication by requiring users to verify their identity using multiple independent verification methods, creating multiple layers of defense against unauthorized access.

Key ways MFA enhances security include:

1. Defense in Depth: MFA implements the security principle of defense in depth by requiring multiple different verification factors. If one factor is compromised (like a password), additional barriers remain in place.

2. Protection Against Credential Theft: Even if credentials like passwords are stolen through phishing, data breaches, or keylogging, attackers still cannot access the system without the additional factors.

3. Mitigation of Common Attack Vectors: MFA effectively neutralizes many common attack methods:

    - Phishing attacks may capture passwords but not physical tokens
    - Stolen passwords alone become insufficient for access
    - Brute force attacks against passwords become ineffective
    - Social engineering becomes significantly more difficult

4. Complementary Security Strengths: Each authentication factor has different security characteristics:

    - Knowledge factors (passwords) can be complex but might be shared
    - Possession factors (tokens) are tangible but might be lost
    - Inherence factors (biometrics) are unique but not changeable

5. By combining factors, the weaknesses of one are compensated by the strengths of others.

6. Increased Attack Complexity: Attackers must compromise multiple different types of authentication mechanisms, dramatically increasing the difficulty, cost, and time required for a successful breach.

In the context of PCI-DSS, MFA is required for all access to the CDE and for non-console administrative access, reflecting its critical importance in protecting sensitive cardholder data from unauthorized access.

Additional resource: https://www.pcisecuritystandards.org/documents/Multi-Factor-Authentication-Benefits.pdf

Q23: What are the requirements for user IDs in a cardholder data environment?

A23: In a cardholder data environment, user IDs must meet several specific requirements according to PCI-DSS:

1. Uniqueness: Each user ID must be unique within the organization. This ensures accountability and traceability of actions to specific individuals.
2. Distinctiveness: The user ID must be different from the user's name and other identifiers. This adds a layer of security by not making the identifier obvious.
3. No Sharing: Shared, generic, or default user IDs are explicitly prohibited. Each individual must have their own unique identifier.
4. Proper Lifecycle Management:
    - Access for terminated users must be revoked immediately
    - Inactive user accounts must be removed or disabled within 90 days
    - Third-party access should use "Just in Time" (JIT) access methods
5. Proper Authentication: The user ID must be used in conjunction with appropriate authentication methods, including complex passwords and multi-factor authentication where required.

These requirements collectively ensure that access to cardholder data can be properly controlled, monitored, and audited, with clear accountability for all actions taken within the cardholder data environment.

Additional resource: https://www.pcisecuritystandards.org/documents/User_Identification_Requirements.pdf

Q24: True or False: The activation of a screensaver alone is sufficient to meet the requirement for re-authentication after an idle session of 15 minutes.

A24: False. According to PCI-DSS, the activation of a screensaver alone is not sufficient to meet the requirement for re-authentication after an idle session of 15 minutes.

The content states: "In some organizations, the allowed idle time could be less than the 15-minute requirement and include activation of the screensaver." This indicates that while screensavers may be part of an organization's approach to handling idle sessions, they must be accompanied by a re-authentication requirement.

When a session has been idle for more than 15 minutes, the user must re-authenticate to reactivate the terminal or session. The screensaver may activate as a visual indication that the session is locked, but the security control that actually satisfies the requirement is the re-authentication process, not the screensaver itself.

The re-authentication requirement ensures that if a user leaves their workstation unattended, another person cannot simply move the mouse or press a key to gain access to the session and potentially to cardholder data.

Additional resource: https://www.pcisecuritystandards.org/documents/Session_Security_Implementation.pdf

Q25: Which of the following statements about complex passwords and passphrases is correct according to PCI-DSS?

A) They must be at least 8 characters long in all cases B) They must include alphabetic characters but numeric characters are optional C) They must be at least 12 characters long and include both alphabetic and numeric characters D) They must be changed at least once every 60 days

A25: The correct answer is C) They must be at least 12 characters long and include both alphabetic and numeric characters.

According to PCI-DSS requirements, passwords and passphrases must be at least twelve characters long and include both alphabetic and numeric characters. The content specifically states: "PCI-DSS requires passwords and passphrases to be at least twelve characters long, and they must include both alphabetic and numeric characters."

Option A is incorrect because the standard requirement is 12 characters, not 8. The 8-character minimum is only allowed as an exception for legacy systems that cannot support longer passwords.

Option B is incorrect because numeric characters are not optional - they are required alongside alphabetic characters.

Option D is incorrect because the password change requirement is 90 days, not 60 days.

The 12-character minimum with both alphabetic and numeric characters creates mathematically complex passwords that are more resistant to brute force attacks and other password-cracking techniques, helping to secure the cardholder data environment.

Additional resource: https://www.pcisecuritystandards.org/documents/Password_Complexity_Requirements.pdf

32

PCI DSS Changes: A Lifecycle Overview - Question Set

Q1: What is the total duration of the PCI-DSS Lifecycle?

A1: The PCI-DSS Lifecycle has a total duration of 36 months (3 years). This three-year cycle ensures that the standards remain current with evolving technologies and emerging security threats. The cycle is structured into eight distinct stages, with each stage having specific timelines, objectives, and deliverables. This methodical approach allows organizations sufficient time to implement changes, provide feedback, and prepare for new versions while ensuring the payment card industry maintains robust security standards. The three-year timeframe strikes a balance between maintaining stability for implementing organizations and ensuring standards don't become outdated in the rapidly evolving cybersecurity landscape.

For more information: https://www.pcisecuritystandards.org/document_library/

Q2: True or False: New PCI-DSS standards become effective immediately after they are published.

A2: False. New PCI-DSS standards do not become effective immediately after publication. According to the PCI-DSS Lifecycle, standards are published in Stage 1 (in October after the Council's annual Community Meetings), but they don't become effective until Stage 2, which occurs on January 1 of Year 1. This deliberate gap between publication and effective date gives stakeholders time to understand the changes and prepare for implementation. During this period, organizations have the option to implement the new standards, but it is not mandatory until the effective date.

For more information: https://www.pcisecuritystandards.org/document_library/

Q3: List and briefly explain the eight stages of the PCI-DSS Lifecycle.

A3: The eight stages of the PCI-DSS Lifecycle are:

1. Standards Published (October): New standards are released after the Council's annual Community Meetings, marking the beginning of a fresh cycle.

2. Standards Effective (January 1 of Year 1): New standards officially become effective, and stakeholders should start using them, though old standards are grandfathered for 14 months.

3. Market Implementation (Throughout Year 1): The market fully embraces the new standards, evaluating how changes affect cardholder data environments.

4. Feedback Begins (November to March of Year 2): Stakeholders provide feedback on new standards and suggest improvements.

5. Old Standards Retired (Last day of December in Year 2): The outdated PCI-DSS standards are officially retired.

6. Feedback Review (April through August of Year 2): Feedback from Participating Organizations is collected and evaluated, categorized into clarifications, additional guidance, and evolving requirements.

7. Draft Revisions (November to April in Year 3): The PCI SSC drafts new standards based on research, analysis, and stakeholder input, with Technical Working Group preparing drafts.

8. Final Review (May through July of Year 3): Drafts are reviewed and adjusted by the Council and Board of Advisors, with a "summary of changes" document provided to stakeholders.

For more information: https://www.pcisecuritystandards.org/document_library/

Q4: During which stage of the PCI-DSS Lifecycle do stakeholders begin providing feedback on the standards?

A4: Stakeholders begin providing feedback on the PCI-DSS standards during Stage 4 of the Lifecycle, which is aptly named "Feedback Begins." This stage occurs from November to March of Year 2 of the cycle. During this critical phase, stakeholders are invited to provide their insights on the new standards and suggest potential improvements. This feedback mechanism is essential as it allows organizations that are actively implementing the standards to share their practical experiences, challenges, and recommendations. The Council values this input and considers it carefully for future revisions of the standards. This collaborative approach ensures that the standards remain relevant, practical, and effective in addressing real-world security challenges in the payment card industry.

For more information: https://www.pcisecuritystandards.org/document_library/

Q5: Explain the importance of the PCI-DSS Lifecycle Model and how it contributes to payment security standards evolution.

A5: The PCI-DSS Lifecycle Model is fundamental to maintaining effective payment security standards for several key reasons:

First, it establishes a systematic and predictable process for standards development, allowing organizations to plan their compliance activities with confidence. The 36-month cycle provides stability while ensuring standards don't become outdated.

Second, the model incorporates structured stakeholder feedback, creating an inclusive approach that considers real-world implementation challenges. This feedback loop helps refine requirements to be more practical and effective, balancing security with operational feasibility.

Third, the lifecycle addresses emerging threats and technologies through its regular update process. As payment technologies evolve and new attack vectors emerge, the standards can adapt accordingly, maintaining their relevance in protecting cardholder data.

Fourth, the grandfathering period (14 months) provides organizations with reasonable time to transition between versions, reducing operational disruption while maintaining security.

Fifth, the model creates transparency through clearly defined stages and deliverables. Stakeholders understand what changes are coming and when, allowing for proper resource allocation and implementation planning.

Finally, the lifecycle model reinforces the PCI SSC's role as a collaborative industry body rather than just a regulatory entity. By involving stakeholders throughout the process, it fosters a collective responsibility for payment security across the ecosystem.

This methodical approach ensures that PCI-DSS remains a living standard that evolves with the threat landscape while providing the stability needed for effective implementation across diverse organizations.

For more information: https://www.pcisecuritystandards.org/document_library/

Q6: True or False: Old PCI-DSS standards are retired on January 1 of Year 2 in the lifecycle.

A6: False. According to the PCI-DSS Lifecycle, old standards are not retired on January 1 of Year 2. They are officially retired in Stage 5, which occurs on the last day of December in Year 2 (December 31 of Year 2). This timing is significant because it marks the end of the grandfathering period and the complete transition to the new standards. The precise timing allows organizations approximately two years from when new standards are published (in October before Year 1) until old standards are retired, providing ample time for implementation and adjustment to the new requirements.

For more information: https://www.pcisecuritystandards.org/document_library/

Q7: How long are old PCI-DSS standards grandfathered for compliance validation after new standards become effective?

A7: Old PCI-DSS standards are grandfathered for 14 months for compliance validation after new standards become effective. This grandfathering period begins when new standards become effective (January 1 of Year 1) and allows organizations to continue using the previous version of the standards for their compliance assessments during this transition period.

However, the content specifically notes that while this grandfathering period exists, it is recommended that organizations transition to the new standards as quickly as possible, especially for critical control requirements. This approach ensures that organizations maintain robust security controls while having reasonable time to implement changes required by the new standards.

The grandfathering period serves as a practical accommodation to the reality that organizations may need time to adjust their systems, processes, and documentation to meet new requirements, while not compromising on the ultimate goal of enhancing payment security.

For more information: https://www.pcisecuritystandards.org/document_library/

Q8: During Stage 6 of the PCI-DSS Lifecycle, feedback from Participating Organizations is categorized into which three types?

A8: During Stage 6 (Feedback Review) of the PCI-DSS Lifecycle, which occurs from April through August of Year 2, feedback from Participating Organizations is categorized into the following three types:

1. Clarifications: These focus on ensuring that the wording of requirements is concise and accurately portrays the intended meaning. Clarifications help remove ambiguity and make the standards easier to understand and implement correctly.
2. Additional Guidance: This category provides supplementary information on specific topics to help organizations better understand how to implement requirements. It doesn't change the requirements themselves but offers more context and implementation advice.
3. Evolving Requirements: This category addresses the need to update standards to keep pace with emerging threats and changes in the payment technology market. These represent substantive changes to ensure the standards remain effective against new security challenges.

This structured categorization helps the PCI SSC systematically address different types of feedback and make appropriate revisions to the standards, ensuring they remain clear, helpful, and current with evolving security needs.

For more information: https://www.pcisecuritystandards.org/document_library/

Q9: Describe the "Market Implementation" stage of the PCI-DSS Lifecycle and explain its significance for organizations that handle payment card data.

A9: The "Market Implementation" stage (Stage 3) of the PCI-DSS Lifecycle spans throughout Year 1 after new standards become effective. This critical phase represents the period when the payment card industry fully embraces and operationalizes the new standards.

During Market Implementation, organizations evaluate how the changes in PCI-DSS affect their specific cardholder data environment. This assessment is crucial as it helps organizations understand the gap between their current security posture and the new requirements. Organizations must determine what new controls need to be implemented, which existing controls need modification, and what documentation must be updated.

The significance of this stage for organizations that handle payment card data is multifaceted:

1. Operational Integration: Organizations must integrate new requirements into their daily operations, which may involve changes to business processes, technical configurations, and security controls.
2. Resource Allocation: Based on the assessment of changes, organizations allocate appropriate resources (financial, personnel, technological) to implement necessary modifications.
3. Training and Awareness: Staff must be trained on new requirements to ensure proper implementation and maintenance of controls.
4. Compliance Planning: Organizations develop timelines and project plans to achieve compliance with the new standards before the old standards are retired.
5. Risk Management: The implementation phase allows organizations to address new security requirements that mitigate evolving threats, thereby reducing their overall risk exposure.
6. Competitive Advantage: Early and effective implementation can become a market differentiator, demonstrating a commitment to data security to customers and partners.

The Market Implementation stage ensures a smooth and gradual integration of necessary updates, allowing organizations to maintain continuous compliance while enhancing their security posture in line with industry best practices and requirements.

For more information: https://www.pcisecuritystandards.org/document_library/

Q10: Where can one find the official PCI-DSS Lifecycle Model documentation?

A10: The official PCI-DSS Lifecycle Model documentation can be found in the PCI SSC document library, which is accessible at https://www.pcisecuritystandards.org/document_library/.

As specified in the content, when searching for the Lifecycle Model in this library, one should type "lifecycle" in the search window and check the "Show Archived Documents" option to ensure all relevant documents appear in the search results.

This document library is maintained by the Payment Card Industry Security Standards Council (PCI SSC) and contains all official documentation related to PCI standards, including the PCI-DSS, PA-DSS, and other related standards and guidance documents. It serves as the authoritative source for organizations seeking to understand and implement PCI compliance requirements correctly.

For more information: https://www.pcisecuritystandards.org/document_library/

Q11: When are new PCI-DSS standards typically published?

A11: New PCI-DSS standards are typically published in October, immediately following the Council's annual Community Meetings. This publication marks Stage 1 of the PCI-DSS lifecycle and the beginning of a fresh three-year cycle for PCI-DSS.

The timing is strategic for several reasons:

1. It follows the Community Meetings where industry stakeholders gather and discuss payment security issues
2. It provides organizations with approximately three months to familiarize themselves with the new standards before they become effective on January 1
3. It establishes a consistent and predictable schedule that organizations can plan around

While the standards are published at this time, implementation is not immediately mandatory. Organizations have the option to implement the new standards right away, but they are not required to do so until the standards become effective in Stage 2 (January 1 of Year 1). This approach gives organizations flexibility while encouraging early adoption of enhanced security measures.

For more information: https://www.pcisecuritystandards.org/document_library/

Q12: True or False: The PCI SSC communicates how stakeholder feedback will be incorporated into future versions of the standards.

A12: True. According to the information provided, during Stage 4 (Feedback Begins) of the PCI-DSS Lifecycle, the Council not only invites stakeholders to provide feedback on new standards and suggest improvements but also explicitly "will then carefully consider all feedback submitted and communicate how it will be incorporated into future versions of the standards." This communication creates transparency in the standards development process and helps stakeholders understand how their input influences the evolution of PCI-DSS. This collaborative approach reinforces the PCI SSC's commitment to developing standards that reflect real-world implementation experiences and challenges faced by organizations across the payment card industry.

For more information: https://www.pcisecuritystandards.org/document_library/

Q13: Explain the recommended approach for transitioning from old to new PCI-DSS standards and why this approach is advised.

A13: The PCI SSC recommends that organizations transition from old to new PCI-DSS standards as quickly as possible, even though there is a 14-month grandfathering period for compliance validation after new standards become effective. This expedited transition is particularly emphasized for critical control requirements.

The recommended approach involves several key steps:

1. Early Familiarization: Organizations should begin reviewing and understanding new standards as soon as they are published in Stage 1 (October), before they become effective.
2. Gap Analysis: Conduct a thorough assessment to identify differences between current implementations and new requirements.
3. Prioritized Implementation: Focus first on implementing critical control requirements that address significant security risks.
4. Phased Transition: Develop a structured plan to implement all changes, starting with the most important security controls
5. Documentation Updates: Revise policies, procedures, and compliance documentation to reflect the new standards.

This approach is strongly advised for several compelling reasons:

1. Enhanced Security: New standards typically address emerging threats and vulnerabilities. Faster implementation means better protection against current attack vectors.
2. Risk Reduction: Critical control requirements usually target high-risk areas; implementing these quickly reduces organizational exposure to data breaches.
3. Operational Efficiency: Gradual, planned implementation is less disruptive than last-minute compliance efforts.
4. Resource Management: Spreading implementation over time allows better allocation of technical resources and budget.
5. Competitive Advantage: Early compliance can be a market differentiator, demonstrating security leadership to customers and partners.
6. Compliance Confidence: Proactive implementation reduces the risk of non-compliance when old standards are retired.
7. Adaptation Period: Early adoption provides more time to address any implementation challenges that may arise.

While the grandfathering period exists to provide flexibility, relying on it extensively could leave organizations with significant security gaps and a compressed timeline for addressing new requirements before the old standards are retired on December 31 of Year 2.

For more information: https://www.pcisecuritystandards.org/document_library/

Q14: During which months of the PCI-DSS Lifecycle does the Draft Revisions stage (Stage 7) occur?

A14: The Draft Revisions stage (Stage 7) of the PCI-DSS Lifecycle occurs from November of Year 2 through April of Year 3. During this critical six-month period, the PCI SSC works on drafting new standards based on thorough research, analysis, and input received from stakeholders.

This stage involves the Technical Working Group, which prepares drafts that are then circulated internally for review by the Council. The timing of this stage is significant as it follows the Feedback Review stage (Stage 6) that concludes in August of Year 2, allowing a short break before beginning the drafting process in November.

The Draft Revisions stage represents the practical application of all the feedback and analysis from earlier stages, transforming stakeholder input and security research into concrete proposed changes to the standards. This work forms the foundation for the Final Review stage that follows.

For more information: https://www.pcisecuritystandards.org/document_library/

Q15: What is the primary purpose of Stage 8 (Final Review) in the PCI-DSS Lifecycle?

A15: The primary purpose of Stage 8 (Final Review) in the PCI-DSS Lifecycle is to review and adjust the draft standards before their official publication. This stage occurs from May through July of Year 3 and involves several key activities:

1. Review and adjustment of drafts by both the Council and Board of Advisors to ensure quality, clarity, and appropriateness of the proposed standards
2. Creation of a "summary of changes" document that is provided to stakeholders, helping them understand what has changed from the previous version
3. Preparation of the final versions of standards for publication at the upcoming Community Meetings

This stage represents the culmination of the three-year lifecycle, where all the feedback, research, and development work comes together in a finalized set of standards. It ensures that the new version of PCI-DSS has undergone thorough review at multiple levels before being released to the payment card industry.

Upon completion of Stage 8, the new standards are ready for publication in October, which will mark the beginning of a new three-year lifecycle.

For more information: https://www.pcisecuritystandards.org/document_library/

Q16: True or False: When new PCI-DSS standards are published, stakeholders have the option to implement them immediately but are not required to do so until the standards become effective.

A16: True. According to the information provided about Stage 1 (Standards Published) of the PCI-DSS lifecycle, "As a stakeholder, you have the freedom to implement the new standards immediately, but it is not mandatory until they become effective." This gives organizations flexibility in their implementation approach while encouraging early adoption. The standards become mandatory in Stage 2 (Standards Effective), which occurs on January 1 of Year 1. This approach allows organizations approximately three months (from October to January) to understand the changes, plan their implementation strategy, and make preparations before the standards become mandatory. This flexibility is designed to facilitate a smoother transition to new requirements while not compromising security through unnecessarily delayed implementation.

For more information: https://www.pcisecuritystandards.org/document_library/

Q17: When a new three-year PCI-DSS Lifecycle begins, where are the final standards first published?

A17: When a new three-year PCI-DSS Lifecycle begins, the final standards are first published on the PCI Security Standards Council's website. This occurs in October, right after the Council's annual Community Meetings, marking Stage 1 (Standards Published) of the new lifecycle.

The Community Meetings serve as an important venue where the PCI SSC discusses the new standards with industry stakeholders, but the official publication happens on the Council's website, making the standards accessible to all organizations that need to implement them.

This publication on the website ensures that the standards are widely available, allowing organizations to begin reviewing and planning for implementation immediately, even though the standards don't become mandatory until January 1 of the following year (Stage 2: Standards Effective).

For more information: https://www.pcisecuritystandards.org/document_library/

Q18: Describe the role of the Technical Working Group during Stage 7 (Draft Revisions) of the PCI-DSS Lifecycle.

A18: During Stage 7 (Draft Revisions) of the PCI-DSS Lifecycle, which occurs from November of Year 2 through April of Year 3, the Technical Working Group plays a pivotal role in shaping the evolution of the standards.

The Technical Working Group's primary responsibilities include:

1. Preparation of Draft Standards: They take the lead in crafting the drafts of new standards based on the research, analysis, and stakeholder input collected during earlier stages of the lifecycle.
2. Technical Expertise Application: As a specialized group with deep knowledge of payment security technologies and practices, they translate security requirements into clear, implementable technical controls.
3. Incorporation of Feedback: They integrate the categorized feedback (clarifications, additional guidance, and evolving requirements) from Stage 6 into coherent draft standards.
4. Risk Assessment: They evaluate proposed changes in the context of evolving threats and vulnerabilities to ensure the standards address current security challenges.
5. Consistency Review: They ensure that new or modified requirements maintain consistency with the overall framework and philosophy of PCI-DSS.
6. Documentation Development: Beyond the standards themselves, they may contribute to supporting materials that will help organizations understand and implement requirements.

7. Internal Circulation: They prepare materials that are circulated within the Council for review, refinement, and validation.

The Technical Working Group's efforts during this stage are crucial because they transform conceptual security needs and stakeholder feedback into practical, implementable standards. Their work forms the foundation for the subsequent Final Review stage, where the Council and Board of Advisors will make final adjustments before publication.

The expertise of this group ensures that PCI-DSS remains technically sound, practically implementable, and effective at protecting cardholder data across the payment ecosystem.

For more information: https://www.pcisecuritystandards.org/document_library/

Q19: What document is provided to stakeholders during Stage 8 (Final Review) and what purpose does it serve?

A19: During Stage 8 (Final Review) of the PCI-DSS Lifecycle, a "summary of changes" document is provided to stakeholders. This document serves several important purposes:

1. Clear Communication: It explicitly outlines what has changed between the current and upcoming version of the PCI-DSS standards, making the revisions transparent and accessible.
2. Implementation Planning: It helps organizations quickly identify which aspects of the standards have changed, allowing them to focus their planning efforts on those specific areas rather than reviewing the entire standard for changes.
3. Resource Allocation: By understanding the scope and nature of changes, organizations can better allocate resources (budget, personnel, time) for compliance efforts.
4. Gap Analysis Facilitation: The document enables stakeholders to conduct more efficient gap analyses between their current implementations and the new requirements.
5. Training Focus: It helps organizations target their training and awareness programs on the new or modified requirements.
6. Compliance Strategy: It informs the development of strategic approaches to achieving compliance with the updated standards.
7. Risk Assessment: It allows security teams to evaluate how the changes affect their organization's risk profile.

This document is a critical communication tool that bridges the final development work of the Council with the practical implementation needs of the stakeholder community. By providing this summary, the PCI SSC demonstrates transparency in its standards development process and helps facilitate smoother transitions to new versions of PCI-DSS.

For more information: https://www.pcisecuritystandards.org/document_library/

Q20: During which months of Year 2 does the Feedback Review stage (Stage 6) of the PCI-DSS Lifecycle take place?

A20: The Feedback Review stage (Stage 6) of the PCI-DSS Lifecycle takes place from April through August of Year 2. During these five months, the PCI Security Standards Council collects and evaluates feedback received from Participating Organizations during the earlier Feedback Begins stage (Stage 4).

This timing is significant within the overall lifecycle because:

1. It follows the Feedback Begins stage (November to March of Year 2) and the Old Standards Retired milestone (December 31 of Year 2)
2. It provides adequate time (5 months) for thorough analysis of all feedback received
3. It precedes the Draft Revisions stage (November of Year 2 to April of Year 3), ensuring that feedback can be incorporated into the next version of the standards

During this period, feedback is methodically categorized into three types: clarifications, additional guidance, and evolving requirements. This structured approach ensures that all aspects of potential improvements to the standards are considered systematically before moving to the drafting phase.

For more information: https://www.pcisecuritystandards.org/document_library/

Q21: True or False: The PCI-DSS Lifecycle includes opportunities for stakeholder input that directly influences future versions of the standards.

A21: True. The PCI-DSS Lifecycle explicitly incorporates opportunities for stakeholder input that directly influences future versions of the standards. This is primarily evident in Stages 4 and 6 of the lifecycle:

During Stage 4 (Feedback Begins), which occurs from November to March of Year 2, stakeholders are specifically invited to provide feedback on new standards and suggest improvements. The content explicitly states that "The Council will then carefully consider all feedback submitted and communicate how it will be incorporated into future versions of the standards."

Stage 6 (Feedback Review), occurring from April through August of Year 2, is entirely dedicated to collecting and evaluating feedback from Participating Organizations. This feedback is systematically categorized into clarifications, additional guidance, and evolving requirements, which directly shapes how the standards will evolve.

This stakeholder involvement continues to influence the standards during Stage 7 (Draft Revisions) when the Technical Working Group incorporates the analyzed feedback into draft standards.

This collaborative approach ensures that PCI-DSS evolves based not only on security research and threat analysis but also on practical implementation experience from organizations across the payment card industry, making the standards more effective and implementable.

For more information: https://www.pcisecuritystandards.org/document_library/

Q22: Explain how stakeholder feedback is categorized during Stage 6 of the PCI-DSS Lifecycle and why this categorization is important for standards development.

A22: During Stage 6 (Feedback Review) of the PCI-DSS Lifecycle, stakeholder feedback is systematically categorized into three distinct types:

1. Clarifications: This category focuses on improving the wording of requirements to ensure they are concise and accurately convey the intended meaning. These changes don't alter what is required but make it clearer how to interpret and implement the requirements.

2. Additional Guidance: This encompasses supplementary information on specific topics that helps organizations better understand implementation approaches. This category adds context and explanation without changing the core requirements themselves.

3. Evolving Requirements: This addresses substantive changes needed to keep the standards current with emerging threats and technological changes in the payment card industry. These represent actual modifications to what organizations must do to maintain compliance.

This structured categorization is critically important for standards development for several reasons:

First, it enables targeted and appropriate responses to different types of feedback. Minor wording issues can be addressed without overhauling requirements, while significant security gaps can trigger more substantial revisions.

Second, it helps prioritize changes based on security impact. Evolving requirements that address new threats can be given higher priority than clarifications that don't affect security outcomes.

Third, it maintains the integrity of the standards by distinguishing between clarifying existing intent (clarifications) and creating new requirements (evolving requirements). This prevents scope creep and ensures changes are purposeful.

Fourth, it facilitates communication with stakeholders about how their feedback influenced the standards. Organizations can see which of their suggestions led to clarifications versus substantial changes.

Fifth, it supports implementation planning by helping organizations understand which changes require new controls versus those that simply clarify existing practices.

Sixth, it creates a structured knowledge management approach, organizing institutional knowledge about standards implementation challenges that can inform future versions.

Finally, it demonstrates the PCI SSC's commitment to continuous improvement through a methodical, transparent process that balances stability with necessary evolution.

This systematic approach ensures that PCI-DSS remains clear, relevant, and effective at protecting cardholder data while being practically implementable across diverse organizational environments.

For more information: https://www.pcisecuritystandards.org/document_library/

Q23: What happens immediately after the completion of Stage 8 (Final Review) in the PCI-DSS Lifecycle?

A23: Immediately after the completion of Stage 8 (Final Review), which occurs from May through July of Year 3, the final versions of the PCI-DSS standards are prepared for publication at the upcoming Community Meetings in October. This publication marks the beginning of a new three-year lifecycle.

The transition from Stage 8 to the new lifecycle involves several key activities:

1. Finalization of Documents: All standard documents, supporting materials, and guidance are finalized based on the reviews conducted during Stage 8.

2. Publication Preparation: Technical preparation of documents for official release on the PCI SSC website.

3. Communication Planning: Development of communication strategies to inform the payment card industry about the new standards.

4. Community Meeting Preparation: Organization of presentations and materials to introduce the new standards at the annual Community Meetings.

5. Implementation Resources: Finalization of resources that will help organizations implement the new standards.

This transition represents both the conclusion of one lifecycle and the beginning of another, demonstrating the continuous nature of the PCI-DSS evolution. The cycle ensures that standards are regularly reviewed and updated to address emerging security threats and changing payment technologies while providing a predictable framework for organizations to plan their compliance activities.

For more information: https://www.pcisecuritystandards.org/document_library/

Q24: When new PCI-DSS standards become effective, what is the recommended approach regarding critical control requirements?

A24: When new PCI-DSS standards become effective, the recommended approach regarding critical control requirements is to implement them as quickly as possible, rather than relying on the grandfathering period. According to the content, while old standards are grandfathered for 14 months for compliance validation after new standards become effective, "it's recommended to transition to the new standards quickly, especially for critical control requirements."

Critical control requirements typically address significant security vulnerabilities or emerging threats that could put cardholder data at risk. Delaying implementation of these controls, even when technically permitted during the grandfathering period, could leave organizations exposed to security risks that the new standards are specifically designed to address.

This recommendation reflects the PCI SSC's emphasis on security effectiveness over mere technical compliance. While the grandfathering period exists to provide implementation flexibility and prevent operational disruption, organizations should prioritize security controls that mitigate significant risks, particularly those identified as critical in the new standards.

A best practice approach would be to conduct a gap analysis immediately when new standards become effective, identify which new requirements are considered critical, and prioritize the implementation of those controls while developing a comprehensive plan to address all other changes before the grandfathering period expires.

For more information: https://www.pcisecuritystandards.org/document_library/

Q25: True or False: The PCI-DSS Lifecycle Model was created primarily to help payment card brands enforce compliance among merchants.

A25: False. According to the provided content, the PCI-DSS Lifecycle Model was created primarily to help the PCI Security Standards Council (PCI SSC) assess its current PCI-DSS standards, not to help payment card brands enforce compliance among merchants. The content specifically states: "The PCI-DSS Lifecycle Model helps the PCI SSC assess its current PCI-DSS standards. This assessment is done through reviews, updates, and revisions."

The Lifecycle Model is described as a framework for the ongoing development and improvement of the standards themselves, ensuring they remain relevant to evolving technologies and emerging threats. It provides a structured approach for gathering feedback, reviewing the effectiveness of current standards, and implementing necessary changes to keep the PCI-DSS current and effective.

While the resulting standards are indeed used by payment card brands and others for compliance assessment and enforcement, the Lifecycle Model itself is focused on the standards development process rather than compliance enforcement activities. It represents the PCI SSC's methodology for maintaining and evolving the standards in a systematic, transparent manner that incorporates stakeholder feedback and addresses emerging security challenges.

For more information: https://www.pcisecuritystandards.org/document_library/

33

Additional Technology Information - Question Set

Q1: What is the primary focus of integrating PCI-DSS into Business As Usual processes?

A) Meeting annual compliance requirements only
B) Maintaining both compliance and security continuously
C) Reducing the cost of annual assessments
D) Limiting the scope of PCI-DSS requirements

A1:

The correct answer is B) Maintaining both compliance and security continuously.

The content emphasizes that "PCI-DSS is much more than just monitoring once a year and getting ready for a point-in-time test day at the end of the year." It also explicitly states that "compliance does not necessarily indicate security, so focus on your organization's compliance and security aspects."

By integrating security into standard business processes, organizations can maintain a PCI-DSS-compliant environment between assessments, making it a continuous effort rather than an annual event. This ongoing approach ensures that security remains effective throughout the year rather than just during assessment periods.

For more information: https://www.pcisecuritystandards.org/bau-resources

Q2: True or False: Network segregation primarily increases the scope of PCI-DSS assessments.

A2:

False.

According to the content, "the first thing to mention about network segregation is that implementing it will limit or reduce the scope of PCI-DSS assessments." Network segregation allows organizations to focus on critical aspects of their business, particularly ensuring that the Cardholder Data Environment (CDE) is secure.

By dividing the network into separate zones, organizations can isolate the CDE from other parts of the network, thereby reducing the number of systems that fall within the scope of PCI-DSS assessment. This not only reduces compliance costs but also makes it easier to identify and troubleshoot security incidents.

For more information: https://www.pcisecuritystandards.org/network-segregation-guidance

Q3: Explain how tokenization can reduce PCI-DSS compliance scope and what limitations exist with this approach.

A3:

Tokenization reduces PCI-DSS compliance scope by replacing sensitive data like Primary Account Numbers (PANs) with unique, non-sensitive surrogate values called tokens. By storing tokens instead of PANs, organizations can reduce the amount of cardholder data in their environment, which directly reduces the scope of PCI-DSS compliance.

However, tokenization has important limitations:

1. It does not completely eliminate the need for PCI-DSS compliance - the tokenization system itself must be secure and compliant.
2. "High-value tokens" that can be used to retrieve PANs or perform transactions have the same sensitivity as PANs and therefore still fall under PCI-DSS scope.
3. Organizations must carefully evaluate tokenization solutions to ensure they meet specific security and functionality requirements.
4. The tokenization process itself must be properly secured to prevent compromise during the token creation and exchange process.

For effective implementation, organizations should conduct thorough risk analysis when selecting a tokenization solution to ensure it adequately protects cardholder data while meeting business needs.

For more information: https://www.pcisecuritystandards.org/tokenization-guidance

Q4: Which of the following best describes Point to Point Encryption (P2PE) in the context of credit card transactions?

A) Encryption of data at rest within the merchant environment
B) Encryption of data at one designated device with decryption only at a second designated device
C) Encryption of data with the possibility of decryption at various points during transmission
D) Encryption of customer information during the checkout process

A4:

The correct answer is B) Encryption of data at one designated device with decryption only at a second designated device.

In the context of a P2PE solution, card transactions are encrypted at one designated and independently validated encryption device (the point of origin). The encrypted ciphertext is then sent to a second designated and independently validated device capable of decryption (the destination point).

Throughout the entire transmission process between these two points, the data remains encrypted with "no possibility of decryption at any point along the way." This end-to-end encryption approach ensures that cardholder data is protected throughout its journey from the point of capture to the secure processing environment, making it an effective protection against data breaches during transmission.

For more information: https://www.pcisecuritystandards.org/p2pe-solutions

Q5: What are the primary benefits of implementing network segregation in a PCI-DSS environment? (Select all that apply)

A) Reducing the scope of PCI-DSS assessments
B) Making it easier to identify and troubleshoot security incidents
C) Eliminating the need for PCI-DSS compliance altogether
D) Reducing the complexity of implementing security controls
E) Better controlling access to sensitive data

A5:

The correct answers are A, B, D, and E.

Network segregation provides multiple benefits in a PCI-DSS environment:

A) Reducing the scope of PCI-DSS assessments - The content explicitly states that "implementing it will limit or reduce the scope of PCI-DSS assessments."

B) Making it easier to identify and troubleshoot security incidents - The content notes that "it also makes it easier to identify and troubleshoot security incidents. In the event of a breach, only one section of the network might be affected."

D) Reducing the complexity of implementing security controls - The content mentions that "implementing network segregation can reduce the complexity associated with implementing and maintaining PCI-DSS security controls."

E) Better controlling access to sensitive data - The content states that "by dividing your network into separate zones, you can better control access to sensitive data and mitigate risks to your organization."

Option C is incorrect because network segregation reduces scope but does not eliminate the need for PCI-DSS compliance.

For more information: https://www.pcisecuritystandards.org/network-security-best-practices

Q6: Why might a "high-value token" still fall under the scope of PCI-DSS despite the use of tokenization?

A6:

A "high-value token" still falls under the scope of PCI-DSS because it can be used to retrieve the original Primary Account Number (PAN) or perform financial transactions. As the content explains: "Beware of a token called a 'high-value token.' This token category can be used to retrieve PAN or perform transactions. Accordingly, a high-value token could have the same sensitivity as PAN and, therefore, fall under the scope of PCI-DSS."

Unlike standard tokens that cannot be reversed to obtain the original PAN, high-value tokens essentially retain the functional value of the original cardholder data, making them just as sensitive from a security and compliance perspective. Therefore, systems storing or processing high-value tokens must adhere to the same PCI-DSS requirements as those handling actual PANs.

Organizations implementing tokenization should be careful to understand the distinction between different types of tokens and ensure appropriate security controls are applied based on the token's value and capability.

For more information: https://www.pcisecuritystandards.org/tokenization-security-guide

Q7: Describe the concept of virtualization in the context of PCI-DSS compliance and explain the key considerations when implementing virtualization in a cardholder data environment.

A7:

Virtualization is the separation of applications, desktops, machines, networks, data, and services from their corresponding physical constraints. In the context of PCI-DSS compliance, virtualization allows multiple applications and services to run on a single physical server, increasing the efficiency of computing resources while potentially providing security benefits.

Key considerations when implementing virtualization in a cardholder data environment include:

1. **PCI-DSS Applicability**: The content explicitly states, "Remember that PCI-DSS still applies when applying virtualization technologies to your cardholder data environment." Virtualization does not exempt any component from compliance requirements.

2. **Risk Assessment**: "As with any evolving technology, there are associated risks." Organizations must conduct thorough risk analysis to understand the specific vulnerabilities and threats introduced by virtualization.

3. **Compliance Impact**: "When virtualizing a cardholder data environment, it is crucial to consider the impact of virtualization on PCI-DSS compliance." This includes understanding how virtualization affects security controls, segmentation, and access management.

4. **Isolation and Segmentation**: Proper configuration is necessary to ensure that virtual environments containing cardholder data are adequately isolated from other virtual environments.

5. **Hypervisor Security**: The hypervisor (virtualization management layer) must be properly secured as it represents a potential single point of failure for all virtual environments.

Virtualization acts as a "bridge between the physical and digital worlds," combining physical server power with cloud flexibility. While it offers significant benefits like resource efficiency and potential security improvements through isolation, organizations must carefully address these considerations to maintain PCI-DSS compliance.

For more information: https://www.pcisecuritystandards.org/virtualization-guidance

Q8: What security limitation of mobile devices must be addressed when implementing mobile payment solutions?

A) Mobile devices cannot connect to secure networks
B) Mobile devices are not designed to provide secure input or storage of cardholder information
C) Mobile devices process transactions too slowly
D) Mobile devices cannot implement encryption

A8:

The correct answer is B) Mobile devices are not designed to provide secure input or storage of cardholder information.

The content explicitly states: "it is essential to remember that they [mobile devices] are not designed to provide secure input or storage of cardholder information." This inherent limitation means that additional security measures must be implemented when using mobile devices for payment processing.

To address this limitation, the content recommends using other methods such as encryption and tokenization to protect sensitive information. Additionally, merchants should use approved PIN Entry Devices (PEDs) or Secure Card Readers (SCRs) that are specifically designed to capture and encrypt cardholder information safely and securely.

This approach allows merchants to leverage the convenience of mobile payment solutions while still maintaining the security of cardholder data and compliance with PCI-DSS requirements.

For more information: https://www.pcisecuritystandards.org/mobile-payment-security

Q9: True or False: When implementing Wi-Fi networks for credit card transactions, WPA2 or higher encryption is required by PCI-DSS.

A9:

True.

The content explicitly states: "PCI-DSS requires that any Wi-Fi networks used for credit card transactions be secured using strong encryption methods. This means using WPA2 or higher encryption protocols and implementing strong passwords and other security measures."

This requirement addresses the significant security risk associated with wireless networks - the potential for unauthorized access and interception of sensitive cardholder data during transmission. Older protocols like WEP (Wired Equivalent Privacy) are insufficient for protecting payment card data due to known vulnerabilities.

In addition to implementing WPA2 or higher encryption, organizations must also use strong passwords and regularly monitor their networks for unauthorized access or suspicious activity to maintain compliance with PCI-DSS and protect customer data.

For more information: https://www.pcisecuritystandards.org/wireless-security-guidance

Q10: Which of these is a characteristic of Near Field Communication (NFC) technology as used in credit card transactions?

A) It requires physical insertion of the card into a reader
B) It uses satellite technology for payment processing
C) It allows contactless payments through RFID technology
D) It only works with mobile phones, not cards

A10:

The correct answer is C) It allows contactless payments through RFID technology.

The content explains that "NFC-enabled credit cards use radio frequency identification (RFID) technology to transmit payment information wirelessly between the card and the payment terminal." This allows customers to simply tap their card on the terminal to make a payment without having to swipe or insert their card.

NFC is a short-range wireless communication technology that enables two devices to exchange information when they are brought into close proximity (typically a few centimeters). In payment scenarios, this creates a convenient "tap-to-pay" experience, but also introduces security considerations that must be addressed to protect the wirelessly transmitted payment information.

For more information: https://www.pcisecuritystandards.org/contactless-payment-security

Q11: Compare and contrast tokenization and encryption as methods for protecting cardholder data.

A11:

Tokenization and encryption are both methods for protecting cardholder data, but they work differently and have distinct characteristics:

Tokenization:

- Replaces sensitive data (like PANs) with unique, non-sensitive surrogate values called tokens
- The original data and token typically have no mathematical relationship
- The original data cannot be derived from the token (except with high-value tokens)
- Reduces the amount of cardholder data in the environment
- Reduces the scope of PCI-DSS compliance
- Tokens (except high-value tokens) generally don't fall under PCI-DSS scope
- Often used for data at rest

Encryption:

- Scrambles data so it can only be accessed with the correct key
- The original data and encrypted data have a mathematical relationship
- The original data can be retrieved with the proper decryption key
- Encrypted cardholder data still falls within PCI-DSS scope
- Particularly useful for protecting data in transit (as in P2PE solutions)
- Requires careful key management
- Often used for data in transit

In practice, these methods are often used together as complementary approaches. For example, a transaction might be encrypted during transmission (using P2PE) and then tokenized for storage in the merchant's systems. This combined approach provides protection throughout the data lifecycle while reducing the scope of systems that need to handle actual cardholder data.

For more information: https://www.pcisecuritystandards.org/data-protection-methods

Q12: What types of Bluetooth POS devices are mentioned in the content, and what considerations should be made when selecting them?

A) Desktop and laptop models, selected based on processing speed
B) Handheld terminals and countertop models, selected based on business needs and security features
C) Tablet and smartphone models, selected based on cost
D) Fixed and mobile models, selected based on battery life

A12:

The correct answer is B) Handheld terminals and countertop models, selected based on business needs and security features.

The content specifically mentions: "These devices range from handheld terminals to countertop models, each with unique features and benefits. Handheld terminals are ideal for mobile businesses or those with limited counter space, while countertop models are better suited for larger establishments."

Additionally, the content notes that when selecting Bluetooth POS devices, businesses should consider both their specific operational needs and security requirements. Important security considerations include whether the devices offer "advanced security features such as encryption and tokenization to safeguard sensitive information further."

The selection should balance business functionality with the need to ensure the security of customer data while complying with PCI-DSS requirements for wireless technology.

For more information: https://www.pcisecuritystandards.org/bluetooth-pos-security

Q13: What is the primary advantage of biometric authentication for securing cardholder data environments?

A13:

The primary advantage of biometric authentication for securing cardholder data environments is that it is much harder to hack or replicate than traditional authentication methods like passwords or PINs.

As stated in the content: "Biometric authentication is becoming increasingly popular because it is much harder to hack or replicate than traditional passwords or PINs. Biometric authentication is one of the strongest authentication methods available."

Biometric authentication uses unique physical characteristics such as fingerprints, facial features, voice patterns, or even typing behaviors to verify a person's identity. These characteristics are inherently tied to the individual, making them significantly more difficult to forge or steal compared to knowledge-based credentials.

In the context of PCI-DSS compliance, biometric authentication provides a powerful layer of security for controlling access to sensitive cardholder data environments and card production facilities, helping to ensure that only authorized personnel can access these critical areas.

For more information: https://www.pcisecuritystandards.org/biometric-authentication-guide

Q14: Describe the key components necessary for offering secure mobile payment options according to the content.

A14:

According to the content, the key components necessary for offering secure mobile payment options include:

1. **Point of Interaction (POI)** - This is the starting point for secure mobile payments and serves as the interface where cardholder data is initially captured.
2. **Approved PIN Entry Devices (PEDs)** - These are specialized devices designed to securely capture and encrypt cardholder PIN information.
3. **Secure Card Readers (SCRs)** - These devices safely capture card information and encrypt it immediately upon acquisition.
4. **Validated Encryption Devices** - The content emphasizes that POI devices "must be specifically designed to safely and securely capture and encrypt cardholder data."
5. **PCI SSC Validation** - Devices used should be validated and approved, with the content noting that "a list of approved devices and P2PE solutions will be available on the PCI SSC website as soon as they become validated."
6. **Additional Security Methods** - The content recommends using "other methods, such as encryption and tokenization, to protect sensitive information" to compensate for the inherent security limitations of mobile devices.

These components work together to create a secure mobile payment ecosystem that addresses the fundamental challenge that mobile devices "are not designed to provide secure input or storage of cardholder information." By implementing these specialized components and security methods, merchants can offer the convenience of mobile payments while maintaining the security of cardholder data.

For more information: https://www.pcisecuritystandards.org/mobile-payment-security-requirements

Q15: Which of the following statements about integrating PCI-DSS into Business As Usual (BAU) processes is NOT accurate?

A) PCI-DSS is much more than just monitoring once a year
B) Everyone in the organization plays a role in maintaining compliance
C) Security should be integrated into standard business processes
D) Annual compliance automatically ensures security

A15:

The correct answer is D) Annual compliance automatically ensures security.

This statement contradicts the content, which explicitly states: "Compliance does not necessarily indicate security, so focus on your organization's compliance and security aspects." This highlights that merely achieving compliance, particularly as a point-in-time annual exercise, does not automatically guarantee that an organization is secure.

The other statements accurately reflect the content:

- "PCI-DSS is much more than just monitoring once a year and getting ready for a point-in-time test day at the end of the year."
- "Remember that the people in your organization also play an essential role in maintaining your PCI-DSS-compliant status."
- "By integrating security into standard business processes, organizations can maintain a PCI-DSS-compliant environment between PCI-DSS assessments."

The key takeaway is that PCI-DSS compliance should be viewed as an ongoing, integrated part of business operations with a focus on both compliance and actual security outcomes, rather than a periodic checkbox exercise.

For more information: https://www.pcisecuritystandards.org/continuous-compliance-guidance

Q16: True or False: High-value tokens require the same level of protection as the original Primary Account Numbers (PANs) they replace.

A16:

True.

The content explicitly states: "Beware of a token called a 'high-value token.' This token category can be used to retrieve PAN or perform transactions. Accordingly, a high-value token could have the same sensitivity as PAN and, therefore, fall under the scope of PCI-DSS."

High-value tokens are a special category of tokens that, unlike standard tokens, retain the functional capability to either retrieve the original PAN or to conduct financial transactions directly. This functional equivalence to actual PANs means they present the same level of risk if compromised and therefore require the same level of protection under PCI-DSS.

Organizations implementing tokenization must be careful to understand the distinction between different types of tokens and ensure appropriate security controls are applied based on the token's value and capability. Systems storing or processing high-value tokens remain fully in scope for PCI-DSS compliance.

For more information: https://www.pcisecuritystandards.org/token-security-classification

Q17: How does virtualization potentially improve security in a PCI-DSS environment?

A17:

Virtualization can potentially improve security in a PCI-DSS environment in several ways:

1. **Isolation of Applications and Data**: As the content states, virtualization "provides an extra layer of security, isolating applications and data from each other so that if one application or service is compromised, the rest remain secure." This compartmentalization helps contain security breaches.

2. **Resource Efficiency**: By increasing the efficiency of computing resources, virtualization allows organizations to allocate more resources to security functions and controls, potentially strengthening the overall security posture.

3. **Simplified Deployment of Security Controls**: Virtualization enables consistent application of security controls across multiple virtual environments through centralized management.

4. **Improved Disaster Recovery**: Virtual environments can be more easily backed up and restored, improving resilience and reducing downtime in case of security incidents.

5. **Enhanced Monitoring Capabilities**: Virtualization platforms often provide additional monitoring capabilities at the hypervisor level, allowing for detection of unusual activities that might indicate security issues.

However, the content also cautions that "as with any evolving technology, there are associated risks" and reminds that "PCI-DSS still applies when applying virtualization technologies to your cardholder data environment." Organizations must carefully consider these risks and ensure that their virtualized environments are properly configured and secured to maintain compliance.

For more information: https://www.pcisecuritystandards.org/virtualization-security-guide

Q18: What security risk is specifically associated with NFC-enabled credit cards?

A) Battery depletion in the card
B) Physical damage to the embedded chip

C) Interception of wirelessly transmitted payment information
D) Inability to process transactions in rural areas

A18:

The correct answer is C) Interception of wirelessly transmitted payment information.

The content states: "Hackers can use specialized equipment to intercept and steal the payment information transmitted by NFC-enabled cards." This risk arises from the wireless nature of NFC transactions, where payment data is transmitted over radio frequency waves between the card and the payment terminal.

This security risk is why "PCI-DSS requires merchants to implement additional security measures when processing NFC transactions" to protect the cardholder data being transmitted wirelessly. These measures typically include encryption, tokenization, and transaction limits to mitigate the risk of data interception and reduce the potential impact of any compromised transactions.

For more information: https://www.pcisecuritystandards.org/nfc-security-requirements

Q19: What are three best practices for effectively integrating PCI-DSS into business-as-usual processes?

A19:

Based on the content, three best practices for effectively integrating PCI-DSS into business-as-usual processes are:

1. **Recognize PCI-DSS as a Continuous Process**: "PCI-DSS is much more than just monitoring once a year and getting ready for a point-in-time test day at the end of the year." Organizations should view compliance as an ongoing responsibility rather than a periodic assessment.

2. **Focus on Both Compliance and Security**: "Compliance does not necessarily indicate security, so focus on your organization's compliance and security aspects." This dual focus ensures that organizations don't just check boxes but actually implement meaningful security measures.

3. **Integrate Security into Standard Business Processes**: "By integrating security into standard business processes, organizations can maintain a PCI-DSS-compliant environment between PCI-DSS assessments." This integration helps make security a natural part of everyday operations rather than a separate activity.

A fourth best practice mentioned in the content is to "make sure everyone in your organization is aware of their role" in maintaining PCI-DSS compliance, recognizing that people play an essential role in maintaining a compliant status.

These practices collectively help organizations maintain continuous compliance and effective security, rather than experiencing compliance as a cyclical exercise with potential gaps between assessment periods.

For more information: https://www.pcisecuritystandards.org/bau-implementation-guide

Q20: In a properly implemented P2PE solution, where can encrypted card data be decrypted?

A) At multiple points during transmission
B) Only at the second designated and independently validated device
C) At any point with proper authentication
D) At the merchant's discretion

A20:

The correct answer is B) Only at the second designated and independently validated device.

According to the content: "In the context of a P2PE solution, card transactions are encrypted at one designated and independently validated encryption device. To decrypt the data, the encrypted ciphertext is sent to a second designated and independently validated device capable of decrypting the unreadable ciphertext."

The content further emphasizes that "While the data is in transit between the source and the destination, it remains encrypted, with no possibility of decryption at any point along the way." This strict end-to-end encryption approach ensures that cardholder data remains protected throughout its entire journey from the point of capture to the secure processing environment.

This architecture is fundamental to the security provided by P2PE solutions, as it eliminates opportunities for data compromise during transmission by ensuring that decryption can only occur at the designated endpoint.

For more information: https://www.pcisecuritystandards.org/p2pe-implementation-guide

Q21: What are the primary benefits of network segregation in a PCI-DSS environment? Provide a real-world example of how it might be implemented.

A21:

According to the content, the primary benefits of network segregation in a PCI-DSS environment include:

1. **Reduced Scope**: "Implementing it will limit or reduce the scope of PCI-DSS assessments," allowing organizations to focus on the most critical aspects of their business.

2. **Cost Savings**: There are "obvious cost savings associated with a reduced assessment" since fewer systems need to be evaluated for compliance.

3. **Reduced Complexity**: Network segregation "can reduce the complexity associated with implementing and maintaining PCI-DSS security controls."

4. **Better Access Control**: "By dividing your network into separate zones, you can better control access to sensitive data and mitigate risks to your organization."

5. **Easier Incident Management**: "It also makes it easier to identify and troubleshoot security incidents. In the event of a breach, only one section of the network might be affected, making it easier to contain and resolve the issue quickly."

Real-world example from the content: "Imagine you run a small online retail store. You accept credit card payments through your website but use a tablet in-store to process payments. By implementing network segregation, you can ensure that only the devices and payment channels in scope are adequately secured and compliant with PCI-DSS."

In this example, the merchant could create three separate network segments:

- A cardholder data environment (CDE) segment for the website payment processing
- A separate CDE segment for the in-store tablet payment system
- A general business network for other operations (email, inventory management, etc.)

This approach isolates payment processing systems from general business operations, reducing the scope of PCI-DSS compliance to only those segments that actually handle cardholder data, while also limiting the potential impact of a security breach.

For more information: https://www.pcisecuritystandards.org/network-segmentation-guidance

Q22: Which types of authentication factors does biometric authentication represent?

A) Something you know
B) Something you have
C) Something you are
D) Somewhere you are

A22:

The correct answer is C) Something you are.

Biometric authentication falls under the "something you are" category of authentication factors because it uses unique physical or behavioral characteristics inherent to an individual. As described in the content, biometric authentication "uses unique physical characteristics to verify a person's identity. This can include fingerprints, facial recognition, voice recognition, and even the way a person types on a keyboard."

These physical and behavioral traits are intrinsic to the person being authenticated, unlike:

- "Something you know" (knowledge factors like passwords or PINs)
- "Something you have" (possession factors like ID cards or security tokens)
- "Somewhere you are" (location factors like GPS coordinates)

The content notes that biometric authentication is "becoming increasingly popular because it is much harder to hack or replicate than traditional passwords or PINs" and describes it as "one of the strongest authentication methods available" precisely because these inherent characteristics are difficult to forge or steal.

For more information: https://www.pcisecuritystandards.org/authentication-factors-guide

Q23: Compare how network segregation, tokenization, and P2PE each contribute to reducing PCI-DSS scope.

A23:

Network segregation, tokenization, and P2PE each contribute to reducing PCI-DSS scope in different but complementary ways:

Network Segregation:

- Physically or logically divides the network into separate zones, isolating the cardholder data environment (CDE)
- Limits the systems and components that need to comply with PCI-DSS
- As stated in the content: "Implementing it will limit or reduce the scope of PCI-DSS assessments"
- Reduces complexity by containing cardholder data to specific network segments
- Makes it easier to identify which systems are in scope for compliance

Tokenization:

- Replaces sensitive cardholder data (PANs) with non-sensitive tokens
- The content states: "If you choose to store tokens instead of PANs, you can reduce the amount of cardholder data in your environment and simultaneously reduce the scope of your PCI-DSS compliance"
- Systems that only handle non-high-value tokens may be removed from scope
- Maintains business functionality while reducing compliance obligations
- Particularly effective for reducing scope in data storage scenarios

Point to Point Encryption (P2PE):

- Encrypts data at the point of capture (e.g., payment terminal)
- Keeps data encrypted throughout transmission until it reaches the secure decryption point
- Systems that only handle encrypted data and have no ability to decrypt it may be removed from scope
- Particularly effective for reducing scope in data transmission scenarios
- Provides protection against interception during transit

Each of these technologies addresses different aspects of cardholder data protection:

- Network segregation controls where the data can go
- Tokenization protects data at rest

- P2PE protects data in transit

When implemented together as part of a comprehensive security strategy, these technologies can significantly reduce the scope of PCI-DSS assessments while maintaining strong protection for cardholder data throughout its lifecycle.

For more information: https://www.pcisecuritystandards.org/scope-reduction-strategies

Q24: What key security consideration must be addressed when using Wi-Fi networks for payment card transactions?

A) Wi-Fi networks must be powered down at night
B) Wi-Fi networks must use WPA2 or higher encryption protocols
C) Wi-Fi networks must be renamed monthly
D) Wi-Fi networks must be public for customer convenience

A24:

The correct answer is B) Wi-Fi networks must use WPA2 or higher encryption protocols.

The content explicitly states: "PCI-DSS requires that any Wi-Fi networks used for credit card transactions be secured using strong encryption methods. This means using WPA2 or higher encryption protocols and implementing strong passwords and other security measures."

This requirement addresses the significant security risk of unauthorized access to sensitive information. As the content explains, "If someone gains access to your Wi-Fi network, they could potentially intercept credit card data as it's being transmitted."

In addition to implementing WPA2 or higher encryption, the content also mentions implementing strong passwords and regularly monitoring the network for signs of unauthorized access or suspicious activity. These combined measures help ensure that wireless networks used for payment card transactions remain secure and compliant with PCI-DSS requirements.

For more information: https://www.pcisecuritystandards.org/wireless-network-security

Q25: Describe the security challenges associated with mobile payment acceptance and how merchants can address them while remaining PCI-DSS compliant.

A25:

Mobile payment acceptance presents several significant security challenges that merchants must address to remain PCI-DSS compliant:

Key Security Challenges:

1. **Device Security Limitations**: As stated in the content, mobile devices "are not designed to provide secure input or storage of cardholder information." They lack the built-in security controls of purpose-built payment terminals.
2. **Wireless Transmission Risks**: Mobile payments typically rely on wireless technologies (Wi-Fi, Bluetooth, NFC) which

can be vulnerable to interception if not properly secured.

3. **Physical Security Concerns**: Mobile payment devices are portable and therefore at higher risk of theft, loss, or tampering compared to fixed terminals.

4. **Multiple Technologies**: The content mentions various technologies used in mobile payments (NFC, Bluetooth, Wi-Fi) each with their own security considerations.

Solutions to Address These Challenges:

1. **Use Validated Hardware**: The content recommends using "approved PIN entry devices (PEDs) or secure card readers (SCRs)" that are "specifically designed to capture and encrypt cardholder data safely and securely." These should be validated devices listed on the PCI SSC website.

2. **Implement Encryption**: The content emphasizes that "encryption is a powerful tool for protecting data and ensuring privacy" and recommends using P2PE solutions to protect data in transit.

3. **Apply Tokenization**: The content suggests that "by choosing to store tokens instead of PANs, you can reduce the amount of cardholder data in your environment" which enhances security and reduces compliance scope.

4. **Secure Wireless Communications**: For Wi-Fi, the content specifies using "WPA2 or higher encryption protocols and implementing strong passwords." For Bluetooth, it recommends devices with "advanced security features such as encryption and tokenization."

5. **Choose the Right Equipment for Business Needs**: The content notes that different types of mobile payment devices (handheld terminals vs. countertop models) are suited for different business contexts, and merchants should select appropriate devices that balance security with operational requirements.

By implementing these solutions, merchants can offer the convenience of mobile payments while maintaining the security of cardholder data and compliance with PCI-DSS requirements. The key is using specialized secure components to compensate for the inherent security limitations of mobile devices.

For more information: https://www.pcisecuritystandards.org/mobile-payment-compliance-guide

34

PCI DSS v4.0.1 Requirement 6.4.3 - Question Set

Q1: What is the primary purpose of PCI DSS Requirement 6.4.3?

A1: The primary purpose of PCI DSS Requirement 6.4.3 is to protect web-based cardholder data entry points by implementing security controls that detect if payment pages have been altered or tampered with after deployment. This requirement specifically focuses on detecting unauthorized modifications to payment pages that consumers interact with in their browsers, particularly from external sources like malicious scripts injected into third-party code (such as Magecart attacks). The objective is to ensure rapid detection of any changes made to online payment pages (in seconds, not days) so that immediate action can be taken before customer cardholder data is exposed, stolen, or sold. Early detection is crucial as it stops potential damage before it begins, protecting both consumers and businesses from data breaches.

Additional resource: https://www.pcisecuritystandards.org/document_library

Q2: Which of the following is NOT considered a form of tampering that Requirement 6.4.3 aims to detect?

A) Injected JavaScript for skimming credit cards B) Redirects sending users' card details elsewhere C) Modified form actions posting sensitive info outside your environment D) Regular scheduled updates to payment page content by authorized developers

A2: The correct answer is D) Regular scheduled updates to payment page content by authorized developers. Requirement 6 .4.3 focuses on detecting unauthorized changes to payment pages, particularly malicious modifications that could compromise cardholder data. While the system should detect all changes (including authorized ones), the requirement's primary concern is identifying malicious tampering such as injected skimming scripts, unauthorized redirects, and modified form actions that send data to unauthorized destinations. Authorized updates are legitimate changes managed through proper change control procedures, not the tampering activities this requirement aims to prevent. However, good implementations should still detect these authorized changes but would recognize them as approved modifications through change management processes.

Additional resource: https://blog.pcisecuritystandards.org/

Q3: True or False: Requirement 6.4.3 applies to merchants who redirect customers completely away from their website to a third-party payment processor's page for payment entry.

A3: False. Requirement 6.4.3 does NOT apply when card capture is handled entirely off-site via redirect links managed solely by validated PSP/gateway providers (e.g., PayPal-hosted payments not loading content inside the merchant domain). In these cases, the responsibility for maintaining change and tamper detection on those payment pages shifts to the third-party providers' compliance programs. However, merchants still maintain due diligence obligations per Requirement 12 regarding vendor management and risk assessments. This requirement specifically targets merchants who host payment pages on their own domains or embed third-party iFrames within their domains.

Additional resource: https://www.pcisecuritystandards.org/faq/

Q4: List and briefly explain four specific methods that can be used for implementing change detection mechanisms on payment pages.

A4: Four specific methods for implementing change detection mechanisms on payment pages include:

1. File Integrity Monitoring (FIM) - This solution continuously monitors files for unexpected changes by comparing current file states against known good baselines, typically using cryptographic hash comparisons to detect any modifications to critical payment page files.

2. Subresource Integrity (SRI) checks - This web standard allows browsers to verify that resources loaded from external sources (like CDNs) haven't been tampered with by comparing cryptographic hashes embedded in HTML tags with the actual loaded resources.

3. Content Security Policy (CSP) reporting mode with monitoring - CSP restricts which resources can be loaded and executed, while reporting mode sends alerts when policy violations occur, helping detect unauthorized script execution or resource loading.

4. Hash validation against known-good versions - Similar to FIM but may be implemented differently, this approach involves regular calculation of cryptographic hashes of payment page components and comparing them against verified baseline versions to identify unauthorized changes.

These solutions should monitor all files involved in rendering client-side components of checkout/payment forms, including HTML, JavaScript, CSS, and especially third-party resources loaded at runtime.

Additional resource: https://www.pcisecuritystandards.org/document_library?category=pcidss&document=pci_dss

Q5: What is the required timeframe for detecting changes to payment pages according to Requirement 6.4.3?

A) Within 24 hours B) During weekly scheduled scans C) Monthly during security reviews D) In real-time or near-real-time

A5: D) In real-time or near-real-time. Requirement 6.4.3 explicitly states that detection must happen fast—in seconds, not days—to prevent damage. The requirement emphasizes that alerts must occur in real-time or near-real-time, not just during scheduled scans days later. This immediacy is critical because payment card skimming attacks can start capturing cardholder data immediately after a successful breach, and delays in detection can lead to significant data exposure. The requirement is designed to ensure organizations can respond rapidly to unauthorized modifications before substantial damage occurs.

Additional resource: https://blog.pcisecuritystandards.org/pci-dss-v4-0-resource-hub

Q6: A merchant uses a third-party analytics tool on their e-commerce site, including the checkout page where customers enter payment information. What specific risk does Requirement 6.4.3 address regarding this scenario?

A6: Requirement 6.4.3 addresses the risk that the third-party analytics tool could be compromised and used as a vector for injecting malicious code into the payment page, specifically "Magecart-style" attacks. In this scenario, attackers might target the third-party analytics provider, inject card-skimming JavaScript into their legitimate code, and then wait for this malicious code to be automatically distributed to all merchant sites using the service.

Since the analytics tool has legitimate access to the checkout page, the injected malicious code could capture payment card details as customers enter them, sending this sensitive data to attacker-controlled servers while the legitimate transaction proceeds normally. The customer and merchant might remain unaware of the breach. Requirement 6.4.3 mandates implementing change and tamper detection specifically to identify these types of modifications to the payment page, including changes that come through trusted third-party services like analytics tools. This enables rapid detection and response before significant data theft occurs.

Additional resource: https://www.pcisecuritystandards.org/blog/magecart-what-you-need-to-know/

Q7: Which of the following personnel should receive alerts when unauthorized modifications to payment pages are detected?

A) Any available IT staff member B) The company CEO only C) Staff trained to investigate, assess risk, and act quickly D) External auditors

A7: C) Staff trained to investigate, assess risk, and act quickly. Requirement 6.4.3 specifically states that alerts must go to personnel who are trained to investigate the potential incident, assess the associated risk, and take appropriate action quickly. These individuals should understand the technical aspects of the payment page environment, be able to determine whether a change is legitimate or malicious, and know how to initiate incident response procedures when necessary. Sending alerts to untrained staff, executives without technical knowledge, or external parties like auditors would delay the critical immediate response needed to mitigate potential data breaches. The requirement emphasizes that the right people must receive notifications quickly to enable effective response.

Additional resource: https://www.pcisecuritystandards.org/document_library?document=incident_response

Q8: True or False: If a merchant embeds a third-party hosted iFrame for payment card entry within their domain, they are exempt from Requirement 6.4.3.

A8: False. According to the scope clarification in Requirement 6.4.3, the requirement explicitly applies to "Third-party hosted iFrames embedded within merchant-controlled domains." Even though the actual payment form might be hosted and managed by a third party within the iFrame, the merchant is still responsible for implementing change and tamper detection mechanisms for the payment pages on their domain that contain these iFrames. This is because attackers could potentially modify the surrounding page to interfere with the iFrame or inject malicious code that intercepts data before it reaches the protected iFrame. The merchant maintains responsibility for the security of the overall payment experience that occurs within their domain, including pages that embed third-party components.

Additional resource: https://www.pcisecuritystandards.org/document_library?category=pcidss&document=pci_dss

Q9: What should a QSA expect to see as evidence of compliance with Requirement 6.4.3 during an assessment? (Select all that apply)

A) Inventory list identifying monitored URLs/resources B) Screenshots/configuration evidence proving active monitoring system setup C) Sample alert messages sent upon test triggers D) Incident response records linked to actual events captured

A9: All options (A, B, C, and D) are correct. A Qualified Security Assessor (QSA) will expect comprehensive evidence demonstrating both the technical implementation AND operational effectiveness of change and tamper detection mechanisms over time. This includes:

A) An inventory list identifying all monitored URLs and resources that are in scope for the requirement, showing complete coverage of payment pages.

B) Screenshots and configuration evidence proving that monitoring systems are actively configured and operational.

C) Sample alert messages generated during testing, demonstrating that the system successfully detects changes and notifies appropriate personnel.

D) Incident response records that document actual events captured by the system, showing the full lifecycle from detection through resolution.

This combination of evidence demonstrates not just that a system exists but that it functions effectively as required to detect and respond to unauthorized changes to payment pages.

Additional resource: https://www.pcisecuritystandards.org/document_library?document=qsa_qualification_requirements

Q10: What are the five steps in the compliance pathway for implementing Requirement 6.4.3?

A10: The five steps in the compliance pathway for implementing Requirement 6.4.3 are:

1. Identify which web applications/pages collect cardholder data (CHD) or Primary Account Numbers (PAN) directly through end-user interaction.

2. Catalog every component/resource involved in delivering these interfaces, including core site code, CDNs, scripts, images, and fonts.

3. Select suitable change/tamper detection method(s) such as file scanning tools, real-time behavioral anomaly engines, or browser-integrated protection.

4. Configure automated alerts tied closely with incident response playbooks to ensure proper notification and action.

5. Test regularly by simulating benign but detectable changes and verifying whether they're caught properly by the imple-

mented detection systems.

These steps provide a systematic approach to achieving compliance with the requirement, starting with scope definition, progressing through implementation, and concluding with validation testing to ensure operational effectiveness.

Additional resource: https://www.pcisecuritystandards.org/document_library?category=pcidss&document=pci_dss

Q11: A merchant has implemented a file integrity monitoring solution for their payment pages. During a monthly review, they discover the solution is only scanning files once per day. How does this implementation fail to meet Requirement 6.4.3?

A11: This implementation fails to meet Requirement 6.4.3 because it does not provide real-time or near-real-time detection of changes to payment pages. The requirement explicitly states that "detection must happen fast—in seconds, not days—to prevent damage" and that "alerts must occur in real-time or near-real-time, not just during scheduled scans days later."

A once-daily scan creates a potentially dangerous 24-hour window during which an attacker could inject malicious code, capture numerous customers' payment card data, and potentially remove the evidence before detection occurs. During a busy shopping day, hundreds or thousands of transactions could be compromised before the daily scan identifies the tampering.

To meet the requirement, the merchant would need to reconfigure their file integrity monitoring solution to perform continuous monitoring or very frequent checks (minutes, not hours or days) and generate immediate alerts when changes are detected. Additionally, they should implement complementary controls that can provide more immediate detection, such as real-time behavioral monitoring or client-side detection technologies.

Additional resource: https://www.pcisecuritystandards.org/document_library?document=best_practices_for_securing_ecommerce

Q12: Which of the following is NOT a recommended method for implementing change detection on payment pages?

A) File Integrity Monitoring (FIM) B) Subresource Integrity checks (SRI) C) Annual penetration testing D) Content Security Policy reporting mode with monitoring

A12: C) Annual penetration testing is NOT a recommended method for implementing change detection on payment pages for Requirement 6.4.3. While penetration testing is a valuable security practice required by other PCI DSS requirements, it is performed periodically (typically annually) and does not provide the continuous, real-time detection capabilities required by 6.4.3.

The requirement specifically calls for mechanisms that can detect changes as they occur, allowing for immediate notification and response. The other options—File Integrity Monitoring, Subresource Integrity checks, and Content Security Policy reporting—are all valid methods explicitly mentioned in the requirement documentation as they provide ongoing monitoring and can detect changes in real-time or near-real-time.

Annual penetration testing might identify vulnerabilities that could allow tampering, but it cannot detect actual tampering events that occur between testing intervals, making it inadequate as a primary change detection mechanism.

Additional resource: https://www.pcisecuritystandards.org/document_library?document=best_practices_securing_web

Q13: Describe how Content Security Policy (CSP) can be used to meet the change and tamper detection requirements for payment pages.

A13: Content Security Policy (CSP) can be used to meet the change and tamper detection requirements for payment pages in the following ways:

1. Restrictive Policy Definition: CSP allows organizations to define which sources of content are allowed to load on payment pages. By creating a strict whitelist of approved sources for scripts, images, styles, and other resources, any attempt to load unauthorized content (such as injected malicious scripts) would be blocked by the browser.

2. Reporting Mode: CSP can be implemented in reporting mode, where policy violations are reported to a designated endpoint while still allowing the content to load. This provides visibility into potential tampering attempts without disrupting legitimate functionality during initial implementation.

3. Real-time Violation Detection: When an unauthorized script attempts to execute or a resource attempts to load from an unapproved domain, CSP generates violation reports in real-time that can be sent to a monitoring service.

4. Integration with Monitoring Systems: These CSP violation reports can be integrated with SIEM tools or dedicated monitoring platforms to trigger immediate alerts to security personnel when violations occur.

5. Tamper Evidence: CSP reports include detailed information about the blocked resource, including its source and the specific policy violation, providing valuable forensic data about tampering attempts.

To fully implement this approach, an organization would:

- Develop a comprehensive CSP that covers all legitimate resources used on payment pages
- Set up a reporting endpoint to collect violation data
- Implement monitoring and alerting on the collected reports
- Regularly review and update the policy as legitimate resources change

This approach satisfies 6.4.3 by providing real-time detection of unauthorized script execution or resource loading, which are common methods used in payment page tampering attacks.

Additional resource: https://content-security-policy.com/

Q14: What common attack method is Requirement 6.4.3 specifically designed to help detect?

A) SQL injection B) Distributed Denial of Service (DDoS) C) Magecart attacks D) Password brute force attempts

A14: C) Magecart attacks. Requirement 6.4.3 is specifically designed to help detect Magecart attacks, which are explicitly mentioned in the requirement description. Magecart attacks involve injecting malicious JavaScript code into web pages, particularly payment pages, to skim credit card data in real-time as customers enter it. These attacks often target third-party components like analytics tools, plugins, or other external resources that are loaded on payment pages.

The requirement's focus on change and tamper detection mechanisms for payment pages directly addresses this threat model, as it requires organizations to detect when unexpected modifications occur to these pages—exactly what happens during a Magecart attack. The other attack methods listed (SQL injection, DDoS, and password brute force) are addressed by different PCI DSS requirements and don't specifically involve tampering with payment page content to steal card data during entry.

Additional resource: https://www.pcisecuritystandards.org/blog/skimming-prevention-best-practices/

Q15: True or False: When implementing Requirement 6.4.3, it's recommended to rely on a single detection method rather than multiple layers of detection.

A15: False. The requirement documentation explicitly recommends combining multiple layers of detection for stronger assurance rather than relying on a single method. The provided guidance states: "Combine multiple layers (e.g., a WAF watching traffic patterns plus local file monitors) for stronger assurance." This layered approach creates defense-in-depth, where if one detection mechanism fails or is bypassed, others may still identify the tampering. Different detection technologies may also be better at identifying different types of tampering. For example, file integrity monitoring may detect changes to static files, while behavioral analysis might better detect dynamic script injection. Using complementary technologies provides more comprehensive coverage and reduces the risk of undetected tampering.

Additional resource: https://www.pcisecuritystandards.org/document_library?document=best_practices_for_implementing_security

Q16: What should be included in an inventory list for Requirement 6.4.3 compliance? (Select all that apply)

A) Core website code files B) Third-party scripts loaded from CDNs C) Employee performance reviews D) External images and fonts loaded on payment pages E) iFrames embedded within payment pages

A16: Options A, B, D, and E should be included in an inventory list for Requirement 6.4.3 compliance. The requirement specifically states that organizations should "catalog every component/resource involved in delivering these interfaces (core site code, CDNs, scripts, images, fonts)." This means:

A) Core website code files - These are the primary files that make up the payment page functionality. B) Third-party scripts loaded from CDNs - These external resources are common attack vectors for Magecart-style attacks. D) External images and fonts loaded on payment pages - These resources could potentially be manipulated or replaced with malicious alternatives. E) iFrames embedded within payment pages - These components, even if hosted by third parties, are specifically mentioned as being in scope.

Option C (Employee performance reviews) is not relevant to payment page security and would not be included in the inventory list for this requirement. The inventory should focus exclusively on the technical components that could affect the security of cardholder data entry on payment pages.

Additional resource: https://www.pcisecuritystandards.org/document_library?document=pci_dss_resources

Q17: A merchant wants to implement Requirement 6.4.3 for their e-commerce site. Which of these pages must have change and tamper detection mechanisms? (Select all that apply)

A) The product listing page B) The shopping cart page where users review items before checkout C) The checkout page where customers enter their credit card details D) The order confirmation page that displays after payment processing E) The "Contact Us" form

A17: C) The checkout page where customers enter their credit card details is the only page that must have change and tamper detection mechanisms implemented. Requirement 6.4.3 specifically applies to "web-based cardholder data entry points, specifically, payment pages that consumers interact with in their browsers." This means only pages where customers directly enter their payment card information fall under this requirement.

The product listing page (A), shopping cart review page (B), order confirmation page after payment (D), and contact form (E) do not involve direct entry of cardholder data and therefore would not require change and tamper detection mechanisms under Requirement 6.4.3. However, it's worth noting that implementing similar protections on these pages might be part of a defense-in-depth strategy, especially if these pages are part of the checkout flow and could potentially be manipulated to affect the actual payment page.

Additional resource: https://www.pcisecuritystandards.org/document_library?document=prioritized_approach

Q18: What types of alerts are required by Requirement 6.4.3 when unauthorized modifications to payment pages are detected?

A18: Requirement 6.4.3 requires real-time or near-real-time alerts that reach the appropriate personnel quickly when unauthorized modifications to payment pages are detected. These alerts must:

1. Be generated immediately upon detection of unauthorized modifications to payment pages
2. Be directed to staff who are specifically trained to investigate, assess risk, and act quickly
3. Contain sufficient information to enable rapid investigation and response
4. Be delivered through channels that ensure timely receipt and acknowledgment

The requirement documentation mentions several common integration options for these alerts, including:

- SIEM (Security Information and Event Management) tools
- Messaging platforms such as Slack or Microsoft Teams
- Email alert systems
- Mobile push notifications

The critical aspect is that these alerts must occur in real-time or near-real-time, not during scheduled scans or reviews that might happen days later. This immediacy is essential because payment card skimming attacks can begin capturing data as soon as the tampering occurs, making rapid detection and response critical to minimizing exposure.

Additional resource: https://www.pcisecuritystandards.org/document_library?document=incident_response_plan

Q19: You are implementing a File Integrity Monitoring (FIM) solution for PCI DSS Requirement 6.4.3. Which of the following file types should be monitored? (Select all that apply)

A) HTML files that render the payment form B) JavaScript files loaded on the payment page C) CSS files that style the payment page D) Database backup files E) Server log files

A19: A, B, and C are the correct answers. When implementing File Integrity Monitoring (FIM) for Requirement 6.4.3, you should monitor all files involved in rendering the client-side components of checkout/payment forms. The requirement specifically mentions:

A) HTML files that render the payment form - These files define the structure of the payment page and form fields.

B) JavaScript files loaded on the payment page - JavaScript is the primary attack vector for card skimming attacks and must be monitored for unauthorized changes.

C) CSS files that style the payment page - While less common as attack vectors, CSS files can potentially be used for malicious purposes and are part of the client-side components.

Options D (database backup files) and E (server log files) are not directly involved in rendering the client-side components of the payment form that customers interact with in their browsers. While these files may be important to monitor for other PCI DSS requirements, they are not specifically required for 6.4.3, which focuses on detecting tampering with the actual payment pages that customers see and interact with.

Additional resource: https://www.pcisecuritystandards.org/document_library?document=file_integrity_monitoring

Q20: A merchant has implemented a system that performs daily file integrity checks on their payment pages and sends alerts to the security team when changes are detected. What aspect of this implementation falls short of meeting Requirement 6.4.3?

A20: The aspect of this implementation that falls short of meeting Requirement 6.4.3 is the frequency of the file integrity checks. The requirement explicitly states that "detection must happen fast—in seconds, not days—to prevent damage" and that "alerts must occur in real-time or near-real-time, not just during scheduled scans days later."

Daily file integrity checks create a significant window of vulnerability where unauthorized modifications could remain undetected for up to 24 hours. During this time, attackers could capture cardholder data from numerous transactions before the organization becomes aware of the breach. For busy e-commerce sites, this could mean thousands of compromised payment card details.

To comply with Requirement 6.4.3, the merchant would need to:

1. Increase the frequency of file integrity checks to continuous monitoring or very frequent intervals (minutes rather than days)
2. Implement additional real-time detection mechanisms such as CSP violation reporting or client-side detection
3. Ensure that alerts are generated and sent immediately when changes are detected

4. Configure the system to notify personnel who can take immediate action

This approach would significantly reduce the detection window and better protect cardholder data from skimming attacks.

Additional resource: https://www.pcisecuritystandards.org/document_library?document=real_time_monitoring

Q21: What is Subresource Integrity (SRI) and how does it help satisfy Requirement 6.4.3?

A21: Subresource Integrity (SRI) is a security feature that enables browsers to verify that resources they fetch (such as JavaScript files, CSS stylesheets, or other assets) are delivered without unexpected manipulation. It works by allowing web developers to include a cryptographic hash with each external resource, which the browser then uses to validate the resource before executing it.

SRI helps satisfy Requirement 6.4.3 in the following ways:

1. Tamper Detection: When a resource is modified from its expected state (whether maliciously or accidentally), the cryptographic hash will no longer match, and the browser will refuse to load or execute the resource. This provides immediate, client-side detection of modifications to critical resources used on payment pages.

2. Third-Party Resource Protection: SRI is particularly valuable for resources loaded from CDNs or other third-party sources, which are common targets for Magecart-style attacks. Even if the third-party source is compromised, browsers will reject the modified resources.

3. Real-Time Protection: SRI provides protection in real-time, directly in the user's browser, preventing execution of tampered scripts before they can do harm.

Implementation involves adding an "integrity" attribute to script and link tags, containing a base64-encoded cryptographic hash of the expected file content:

```
<script src="https://example.com/script.js"

    integrity="sha384-oqVuAfXRKap7fdgcCY5uykM6+R9GqQ8K/uxy9rx7HNQlGYl1kPzQho1wx4JwY8wC"

    crossorigin="anonymous"></script>
```

When combined with other change detection mechanisms, SRI provides a robust layer of protection that helps satisfy the requirement's goal of detecting unauthorized modifications to payment pages quickly.

Additional resource: https://developer.mozilla.org/en-US/docs/Web/Security/Subresource_Integrity

Q22: A merchant implements change detection on their payment pages but excludes all third-party scripts loaded from trusted vendors. How does this approach fail to meet Requirement 6.4.3?

A22: This approach fails to meet Requirement 6.4.3 because it creates a significant security gap by excluding third-party scripts, which are actually one of the primary attack vectors for payment page tampering. The requirement explicitly states that solutions "should monitor all files involved in rendering the client-side components of your checkout/payment forms," and specifically mentions "anything loaded at runtime via CDNs or third-party scripts."

Magecart attacks (which are specifically mentioned in the requirement) commonly target trusted third-party services precisely because:

1. They provide a single point of compromise that affects multiple merchants
2. Changes to these scripts might face less scrutiny because they come from "trusted" sources
3. The compromised third-party provider might unwittingly distribute the malicious code to all its customers

By excluding these scripts from monitoring, the merchant would miss detecting one of the most common attack scenarios: a trusted third-party service being compromised and serving malicious code that skims payment card data. The requirement specifically notes that "if it touches the form, track it," emphasizing that all components, regardless of source, must be monitored if they interact with the payment page.

To properly comply, the merchant must extend their change detection to include all third-party scripts and resources loaded on their payment pages, even those from trusted vendors.

Additional resource: https://www.pcisecuritystandards.org/document_library?document=third_party_security

Q23: Which of the following is the best example of testing the effectiveness of a change detection mechanism for Requirement 6.4.3?

A) Reviewing the configuration documentation annually B) Making a controlled, benign change to a payment page and verifying the system detects it C) Having developers self-certify that the system works D) Checking that the detection software license is current

A23: B) Making a controlled, benign change to a payment page and verifying the system detects it is the best example of testing the effectiveness of a change detection mechanism for Requirement 6.4.3. This approach provides actual evidence that the system works as intended in a real-world scenario.

The requirement explicitly recommends: "Test regularly! Simulate benign but detectable changes and verify whether they're caught properly." This type of functional testing confirms that:

1. The detection mechanism is actively monitoring the correct files/resources
2. Changes are detected in a timely manner
3. Alerts are properly generated and sent to the appropriate personnel
4. The end-to-end process functions as designed

The other options are inadequate for various reasons:

- Reviewing configuration documentation (A) doesn't verify actual functionality
- Developer self-certification (C) doesn't provide objective evidence of effectiveness
- Checking license status (D) only confirms the software is licensed, not that it's properly implemented or functioning

By performing controlled tests with simulated changes, organizations can demonstrate the operational effectiveness of their change detection mechanisms, which is a key element of compliance with Requirement 6.4.3.

Additional resource: https://www.pcisecuritystandards.org/document_library?document=testing_security_controls

Q24: True or False: If a merchant uses a validated payment service provider's hosted payment page through an iFrame, but the merchant controls the parent page where the iFrame is embedded, the merchant has no responsibilities under Requirement 6.4.3.

A24: False. If a merchant uses a validated payment service provider's hosted payment page through an iFrame, but the merchant controls the parent page where the iFrame is embedded, the merchant DOES have responsibilities under Requirement 6.4.3.

The requirement scope clarification explicitly states that it "Applies To: Third-party hosted iFrames embedded within merchant-controlled domains." This means that even though the actual payment form is hosted and secured by the service provider within the iFrame, the merchant remains responsible for implementing change and tamper detection mechanisms for the parent page that hosts the iFrame.

This is important because attackers could potentially modify the parent page to:

1. Replace the legitimate iFrame with a malicious one
2. Overlay the legitimate iFrame with malicious content to capture card data
3. Modify how the iFrame is loaded or interacted with
4. Insert scripts that could potentially access data within the iFrame under certain conditions

The merchant must implement change detection mechanisms to identify unauthorized modifications to the page hosting the iFrame, even if they are not responsible for the content within the iFrame itself.

Additional resource: https://www.pcisecuritystandards.org/document_library?document=iframe_security

Q25: Describe a comprehensive strategy for implementing Requirement 6.4.3 for an e-commerce website, including specific technologies, processes, and documentation requirements.

A25: # Comprehensive Strategy for Implementing Requirement 6.4.3

Phase 1: Scoping and Inventory

1. **Identify Payment Pages**: Document all web pages where customers directly enter payment card information or that host iFrames for card entry.
2. **Catalog Components**: Create a comprehensive inventory of all resources that render these pages:
    - HTML files constituting the payment form structure
    - JavaScript files (both first-party and third-party)

- CSS stylesheets
- Images and media files
- External resources loaded from CDNs
- Third-party plugins and widgets
- iFrames and their sources

3. **Document Data Flows**: Map how data moves through the payment process to understand potential attack vectors.

Phase 2: Technical Implementation (Layered Approach)

Layer 1: Server-Side Monitoring

1. **File Integrity Monitoring (FIM)**:
   - Deploy enterprise FIM solution (e.g., Tripwire, OSSEC)
   - Create baselines of all files identified in inventory
   - Configure for continuous monitoring (not just scheduled scans)
   - Set up real-time alerting via integration with SIEM or messaging platforms
2. **Server Configuration Monitoring**:
   - Implement monitoring for web server configuration changes
   - Track changes to access controls, redirect rules, and security settings

Layer 2: Content Validation

1. **Subresource Integrity (SRI)**:
   - Add integrity attributes with SHA-384 hashes to all external scripts and stylesheets
   - Implement process to update hashes when legitimate changes occur

```
<script src="https://cdn.example.com/script.js"
    integrity="sha384-[hash]" crossorigin="anonymous"></script>
```

1.

2. **Version Control Integration**:
   - Automate comparison of production files against approved versions in repository

- Flag any discrepancies for immediate investigation

Layer 3: Runtime Protection

1. **Content Security Policy (CSP)**:
    - Develop strict policy allowing only authorized resource origins
    - Implement in report-only mode initially to identify legitimate resources
    - Configure violation reporting to centralized monitoring system
    - Transition to enforcement mode once baseline is established

<meta http-equiv="Content-Security-Policy" content="default-src 'self';

script-src 'self' https://trusted-cdn.com; report-uri /csp-reports">

1.

2. **Client-Side Scanning**:
    - Deploy JavaScript-based solution that checks DOM for unauthorized modifications
    - Validate loaded scripts against whitelist
    - Send alerts when unexpected elements are detected

Phase 3: Alert Configuration

1. **Real-Time Notification System**:
    - Integrate all detection layers with centralized alerting platform
    - Configure alerts to appropriate security personnel via multiple channels:
        - Security operations center dashboard
        - SMS/text messages for critical alerts
        - Email notifications
        - Integration with incident management system
2. **Alert Categorization**:
    - Develop severity ratings based on risk level of detected changes
    - Create response procedures for each severity level

- Ensure 24/7 coverage for critical alerts

Phase 4: Testing and Validation

1. **Controlled Testing**:
   - Develop test scenarios simulating various tampering methods
   - Perform regular tests by making controlled changes to payment pages
   - Document detection time, alert delivery, and response actions
2. **Penetration Testing**:
   - Conduct specialized testing attempting to bypass detection mechanisms
   - Address any identified gaps in coverage

Phase 5: Documentation and Evidence Collection

1. **System Documentation**:
   - Maintain detailed documentation of all implemented controls
   - Create architecture diagrams showing monitoring coverage
   - Document configuration settings for all detection mechanisms
2. **Evidence Repository**:
   - Establish secure storage for detection evidence:
     - Screenshots of alerts and dashboards
     - Configuration files and change logs
     - Test results demonstrating effectiveness
     - Records of actual events and responses
3. **Incident Response Integration**:
   - Link detection procedures with formal incident response plan
   - Document escalation paths and decision authority
   - Create playbooks specific to payment page tampering scenarios

Phase 6: Operational Procedures

1. **Change Management Integration**:
    - Develop procedures to update detection baselines when legitimate changes occur
    - Implement pre-approval process for payment page modifications
    - Create temporary exception process for emergency changes
2. **Regular Reviews**:
    - Schedule monthly reviews of detection system effectiveness
    - Analyze any false positives/negatives and tune accordingly
    - Update inventory as new components are added to payment pages

This comprehensive approach creates multiple layers of protection that work together to provide real-time detection of unauthorized changes to payment pages, satisfying Requirement 6.4.3 while building a robust defense against Magecart and similar attacks.

Additional resource: https://www.pcisecuritystandards.org/document_library?document=best_practices_for_ecommerce_security

35

PCI DSS v4.0.1 Requirement 11.6.1

Q1: What is the primary focus of Requirement 11.6.1 in the PCI DSS v4.0?

A1: The primary focus of Requirement 11.6.1 is the deployment of change-and-tamper-detection mechanisms on payment pages to alert personnel to unauthorized modifications. Specifically, it targets the detection of JavaScript injection attacks, such as Magecart-style skimming, where malicious code is injected into the browser environment to steal payment information directly from users during checkout. This requirement aims to provide real-time or near-real-time detection of unauthorized changes to payment pages, allowing organizations to respond rapidly to potential threats and minimize the risk of cardholder data compromise.

For more information, visit: https://pcidssguide.com/requirement-11-6-1-overview

Q2: True or False: Requirement 11.6.1 applies to all merchants regardless of how they process payment card data.

A2: False. Requirement 11.6.1 specifically applies to merchants who host or manage any part of the webpage where customers enter Primary Account Numbers (PANs) directly into forms rendered in their browsers. If a merchant uses redirect-only methods where all payment processing happens off-site through a validated service provider, this requirement may not apply. However, the standard warns that "redirecting doesn't always mean you're out of scope," and merchants should always confirm applicability with their QSA during scope validation rather than making assumptions.

For more information, visit: https://pcidssguide.com/requirement-11-6-1-applicability

Q3: Which attack technique is specifically mentioned as being detected by the controls required in 11.6.1? (Multiple choice)

A3: JavaScript injection attacks are specifically mentioned as being detected by the controls required in 11.6.1. These attacks, commonly used in Magecart-style skimming operations, involve injecting malicious code into payment pages that silently harvests payment information from unsuspecting users during the checkout process. The requirement focuses on detecting these types of attacks that compromise the browser environment to steal cardholder data before it's even transmitted to the merchant's servers.

For more information, visit: https://pcidssguide.com/javascript-injection-detection

Q4: In what timeframe should the change-and-tamper-detection mechanism be able to detect unauthorized modifications?

A4: The change-and-tamper-detection mechanism should be able to detect unauthorized modifications in real-time or near-real-time. As stated in the content, the objective is "to detect unauthorized changes in real time or near-real-time when a consumer lands on your website's payment page from their browser." This immediate detection is crucial for rapid incident response, allowing organizations to identify and address potential compromises before significant amounts of cardholder data are exposed.

For more information, visit: https://pcidssguide.com/real-time-detection-requirements

Q5: A merchant redirects customers to a third-party payment processor for all credit card transactions. The merchant never hosts forms where customers enter card data. Is this merchant required to implement controls under Requirement 11.6.1?

A5: Based on the information provided, this merchant may not be required to implement controls under Requirement 11.6.1, as they never host forms where customers enter card data. However, the content explicitly warns that "redirecting doesn't always mean you're out of scope." The merchant should not make assumptions about their exemption from this requirement. Instead, they should consult with their Qualified Security Assessor (QSA) during scope validation to confirm whether Requirement 11.6.1 applies to their specific implementation. The key determination is whether card data enters the merchant's environment at any point, even momentarily.

For more information, visit: https://pcidssguide.com/redirect-methods-and-scope

Q6: What is a primary benefit of implementing a change-and-tamper-detection mechanism as required by 11.6.1? (Multiple choice)

A6: A primary benefit of implementing a change-and-tamper-detection mechanism as required by 11.6.1 is providing real-time visibility into unauthorized script changes on payment pages. According to the content, this implementation "strengthens your defense against client-side attacks by providing real-time visibility into unauthorized script changes on payment pages." Additional benefits include facilitating rapid incident response, decreasing dwell time for attackers (reducing the time they have to harvest data), and aiding in maintaining compliance with PCI DSS standards aimed at securing online payment environments.

For more information, visit: https://pcidssguide.com/benefits-of-change-detection

Q7: The detection mechanism required by 11.6.1 must be capable of detecting modifications including what specific elements? (Fill in the blank)

A7: The detection mechanism required by 11.6.1 must be capable of detecting modifications including new or altered HTML elements, JavaScript files, and DOM manipulations that could affect how PAN input fields behave. These specific elements are mentioned in the content as modifications that must be detected automatically without human intervention first. This comprehensive detection capability ensures that various techniques attackers might use to compromise payment pages are identified promptly.

For more information, visit: https://pcidssguide.com/detectable-modifications

Q8: True or False: If a merchant uses a redirect method for payment processing, they are automatically exempt from Requirement 11.6.1.

A8: False. The content explicitly states that "redirecting doesn't always mean you're out of scope." Even if a merchant uses a redirect method for payment processing, they should not automatically assume they are exempt from Requirement 11.6.1. The standard advises merchants to "always confirm with your QSA during scope validation to be sure" rather than making assumptions about exemptions. The applicability depends on the specific implementation details and whether card data enters the merchant's environment at any point.

For more information, visit: https://pcidssguide.com/redirect-misconceptions

Q9: According to Requirement 11.6.1, what must happen when unauthorized changes are detected? (Multiple choice)

A9: According to Requirement 11.6.1, when unauthorized changes are detected, personnel must be alerted immediately. The content states that organizations must implement a solution capable of "alerting personnel immediately: When tampering occurs, or even suspected, you need alerts sent instantly so staff can investigate before customer data exposure happens at scale." Examples of appropriate alert mechanisms include email/SMS notifications or SIEM event triggers tied into incident response workflows. The key requirement is that alerts must enable rapid response to potential compromises.

For more information, visit: https://pcidssguide.com/alert-requirements

Q10: Explain the significance of Requirement 11.6.1 in the context of modern web-based attacks against e-commerce sites. Include examples of what types of attacks it helps prevent and how.

A10: Requirement 11.6.1 is significant because it addresses a critical vulnerability in modern e-commerce environments: client-side attacks that traditional security controls often miss. While many security measures focus on protecting server-side infrastructure and databases, 11.6.1 specifically targets threats that operate in the customer's browser environment.

The requirement is particularly important given the rise of sophisticated web skimming attacks, exemplified by Magecart campaigns. These attacks inject malicious JavaScript directly into payment pages, often through compromised third-party resources or direct website manipulation. Unlike traditional data breaches that target stored data, these attacks harvest card information in real-time as customers enter it, before it's encrypted or transmitted securely.

Types of attacks prevented include:

1. JavaScript injection through compromised third-party resources (analytics tools, chatbots, etc.)
2. Web skimming/formjacking attacks that silently copy card data during checkout
3. DOM manipulation attacks that alter form behavior to send data to attacker-controlled servers
4. Malicious modifications to legitimate scripts that introduce card-stealing functionality

The change-and-tamper-detection mechanism helps prevent these attacks by:

- Providing immediate visibility into unauthorized changes to payment page code
- Alerting security personnel in real-time when suspicious modifications occur
- Enabling rapid incident response before large-scale data theft occurs
- Reducing attacker "dwell time" and limiting the amount of compromised data

By focusing on detecting client-side tampering specifically on payment pages, this requirement addresses a significant attack vector that has been successfully exploited in numerous high-profile breaches affecting millions of customers worldwide.

For more information, visit: https://pcidssguide.com/modern-web-attacks-and-detection

Q11: Under what condition does Requirement 11.6.1 apply to a merchant? (Multiple choice)

A11: Requirement 11.6.1 applies to a merchant if they host or manage any part of the webpage where customers enter Primary Account Numbers (PANs) directly into forms rendered in their browsers. As stated in the content: "This applies only if you host or manage any part of the webpage where customers enter Primary Account Numbers (PANs) directly into forms rendered in their browsers. That means if the card data enters your environment, even for just a moment, this control is in effect." The key condition is that card data must enter the merchant's environment through web forms that the merchant hosts or manages, even if only momentarily.

For more information, visit: https://pcidssguide.com/applicability-conditions

Q12: A company uses an iframe from a validated service provider to collect payment information. The iframe is embedded in the company's checkout page, but the company's servers never receive the cardholder data. Does Requirement 11.6.1 apply to this company?

A12: This scenario requires careful analysis. Even though the company's servers never receive the cardholder data directly, they are still hosting the page that contains the iframe where payment information is collected. The applicability of Requirement 11.6.1 in this case is not clear-cut and would depend on specific implementation details.

The key consideration is whether the company "hosts or manages any part of the webpage where customers enter PANs." Since they host the checkout page containing the iframe, they might still be responsible for detecting tampering that could compromise the iframe or modify how it functions.

The company should consult with their QSA to determine if they're in scope for this requirement. As the content advises, "don't assume" and "always confirm with your QSA during scope validation to be sure." The QSA would evaluate whether the specific implementation creates responsibility for detecting changes to the page hosting the iframe, even if the company never directly processes the card data.

For more information, visit: https://pcidssguide.com/iframe-implementations

Q13: True or False: DOM manipulations that affect PAN input fields must be detected according to Requirement 11.6.1.

A13: True. According to the provided content, the change-and-tamper-detection mechanism must be capable of detecting "Any modification, including new/altered HTML elements, JavaScript files, DOM manipulations, that could affect how PAN input fields behave." DOM manipulations are specifically mentioned as one of the types of modifications that must be detected by the automated solution required under Requirement 11.6.1. This is important because attackers can use DOM manipulation techniques to alter how payment forms function without necessarily changing the underlying code files.

For more information, visit: https://pcidssguide.com/dom-manipulation-detection

Q14: Which of the following is an example of an alert mechanism that would satisfy Requirement 11.6.1? (Multiple choice)

A14: Examples of alert mechanisms that would satisfy Requirement 11.6.1 include email notifications, SMS notifications, and SIEM event triggers tied into incident response workflows. The content specifically mentions these examples as appropriate alerting methods. The key requirement is that these alerts must be "sent instantly so staff can investigate before customer data exposure happens at scale." Any mechanism that provides immediate notification to appropriate personnel when unauthorized changes are detected would satisfy this aspect of the requirement.

For more information, visit: https://pcidssguide.com/alert-mechanism-examples

Q15: What is the ultimate goal of implementing a change-and-tamper-detection mechanism on payment pages?

A15: The ultimate goal of implementing a change-and-tamper-detection mechanism on payment pages is to protect cardholder data by detecting unauthorized modifications before they can be successfully exploited to steal payment information. As stated in the objective, the goal is "early detection of malicious scripts added via third-party resources, modifications made by attackers post-deployment, and client-side code manipulation intended for credit card theft."

By spotting tampering quickly and catching injected scripts, altered fields, or suspicious code before damage is done, organizations can prevent the theft of customer payment information. The mechanism enables rapid incident response, minimizing the window of opportunity for attackers and reducing the potential impact of a compromise. Ultimately, this helps maintain the security of the online payment environment and protects customers' sensitive financial information.

For more information, visit: https://pcidssguide.com/detection-mechanism-goals

Q16: Match the following terms related to Requirement 11.6.1 with their correct descriptions: (Matching)

A16:

- Magecart-style skimming: Attacks where malicious code is injected into the browser environment to steal payment information during checkout

- Change-and-tamper-detection mechanism: An automated solution that detects unauthorized modifications to payment pages in real-time or near-real-time

- JavaScript injection: A common attack technique where malicious scripts are added to web pages to harvest payment information

- Client-side attacks: Threats that compromise the browser environment rather than server infrastructure

- DOM manipulation: Modifications to the Document Object Model that could affect how PAN input fields behave

Each of these terms represents key concepts related to Requirement 11.6.1 and understanding them is essential for proper implementation of the required controls.

For more information, visit: https://pcidssguide.com/key-terms-explained

Q17: What type of attack is "Magecart-style skimming" referring to in the context of Requirement 11.6.1? (Multiple choice)

A17: "Magecart-style skimming" refers to a type of client-side attack where malicious JavaScript code is injected into e-commerce websites to steal payment card information directly from users' browsers during the checkout process. This attack technique targets the client-side environment rather than the server, making it difficult to detect with traditional security controls.

The injected code typically captures form input data (such as credit card numbers, expiration dates, and CVV codes) as it's entered by customers and sends this information to attacker-controlled servers. Meanwhile, the normal checkout process continues uninterrupted, leaving users completely unaware that their payment information has been compromised. These attacks are named after "Magecart," a loose collection of threat groups that pioneered this technique in large-scale breaches affecting major e-commerce sites worldwide.

For more information, visit: https://pcidssguide.com/magecart-attack-explained

Q18: A QSA is assessing a merchant for compliance with Requirement 11.6.1. What should the QSA look for to verify proper implementation?

A18: When assessing compliance with Requirement 11.6.1, a QSA should look for:

1. Evidence that an automated change-and-tamper-detection solution has been deployed on all payment pages where customers enter PANs

2. Verification that the solution can detect various types of unauthorized modifications, including new/altered HTML elements, JavaScript files, and DOM manipulations that could affect PAN input fields

3. Confirmation that the solution operates in real-time or near-real-time when customers access payment pages

4. Documentation of alert mechanisms that notify personnel immediately when unauthorized changes are detected

5. Evidence that alerts are properly configured to reach appropriate personnel who can respond to potential incidents

6. Incident response procedures that address how the organization handles alerts from the detection system

7. Testing documentation showing that the solution effectively detects unauthorized changes

8. Evidence that the solution covers all in-scope payment pages and environments

The QSA should verify both the technical implementation of the detection mechanism and the operational processes surrounding alert handling and response to ensure comprehensive compliance with the requirement.

For more information, visit: https://pcidssguide.com/qsa-assessment-guidelines

Q19: True or False: Requirement 11.6.1 mandates that organizations prevent unauthorized modifications to payment pages.

A19: False. Requirement 11.6.1 mandates that organizations detect unauthorized modifications to payment pages and alert personnel, not prevent the modifications. The requirement specifically states that organizations must "deploy a change-and-tamper-detection mechanism" that "alerts personnel to unauthorized modification."

While prevention of unauthorized modifications is certainly desirable and may be implemented through other security controls (such as those addressed in other PCI DSS requirements), the specific focus of 11.6.1 is on detection and alerting. This distinction is important because even with strong preventive controls, detection remains necessary as a second line of defense against sophisticated attacks that might bypass preventive measures.

For more information, visit: https://pcidssguide.com/detection-vs-prevention

Q20: What characteristic makes the solution required by 11.6.1 different from a manual code review process?

A20: The solution required by 11.6.1 must be automated, detecting changes without human intervention first. As stated in the content, organizations must implement "an automated solution capable of detecting unauthorized changes" that operates in real-time or near-real-time.

This automated characteristic fundamentally differentiates the required solution from manual code review processes, which rely on human effort to identify changes and cannot provide continuous, real-time monitoring. Manual processes are inherently periodic rather than continuous, creating windows of vulnerability between reviews where unauthorized changes might go undetected for extended periods.

The automated nature ensures constant vigilance over payment pages, enabling immediate detection of unauthorized modifications as they occur and facilitating rapid incident response to potential compromises.

For more information, visit: https://pcidssguide.com/automated-detection-requirements

Q21: If a merchant uses a completely hosted payment solution where customers are redirected to the payment processor's site, what should the merchant do regarding Requirement 11.6.1? (Multiple choice)

A21: If a merchant uses a completely hosted payment solution where customers are redirected to the payment processor's site, the merchant should consult with their QSA during scope validation to determine if Requirement 11.6.1 applies to their specific implementation. The content explicitly warns that "redirecting doesn't always mean you're out of scope" and advises merchants "don't assume" exemption.

While this scenario might seem to place the merchant out of scope (since customers enter PANs on the payment processor's site rather than the merchant's), the specific implementation details matter. The merchant should not make unilateral determinations about applicability but should instead seek formal confirmation from their QSA that their particular redirect implementation exempts them from this requirement.

For more information, visit: https://pcidssguide.com/hosted-solutions-scope

Q22: Describe how Requirement 11.6.1 integrates with an organization's overall security program and incident response capabilities.

A22: Requirement 11.6.1 integrates with an organization's overall security program and incident response capabilities in several important ways:

First, it adds a specialized detection layer focused on client-side threats to payment pages, complementing traditional security controls that typically focus on server-side protections. This addresses a significant gap in many security programs that might otherwise miss sophisticated JavaScript injection attacks targeting the browser environment.

The real-time alerting mechanism required by 11.6.1 feeds directly into incident response workflows, enabling rapid detection and response to potential compromises. When the change-and-tamper-detection mechanism identifies suspicious modifications, it triggers immediate alerts to security personnel, activating incident response procedures specifically designed for potential payment page compromises.

From an incident response perspective, these alerts should initiate a defined sequence of actions:

1. Immediate assessment of the detected change
2. Containment actions if unauthorized changes are confirmed
3. Investigation to determine the source and extent of the compromise
4. Evidence preservation for forensic analysis
5. Remediation to address vulnerabilities that allowed the tampering
6. Notification to stakeholders if cardholder data was potentially exposed

The solution also provides valuable data for threat intelligence, helping organizations understand attack patterns targeting their payment pages and informing broader security strategies.

Additionally, this requirement encourages collaboration between security teams, development teams, and third-party service providers, as changes to payment pages need to be properly managed to distinguish between legitimate modifications and malicious tampering.

By integrating this client-side detection capability with existing security monitoring, vulnerability management, change management, and incident response processes, organizations create a more comprehensive security program that addresses the full spectrum of threats to cardholder data.

For more information, visit: https://pcidssguide.com/security-program-integration

Q23: According to the provided content, what is a result of implementing Requirement 11.6.1? (Multiple choice)

A23: According to the provided content, implementing Requirement 11.6.1 results in:

1. Strengthened defense against client-side attacks by providing real-time visibility into unauthorized script changes on payment pages
2. Facilitation of rapid incident response when potential tampering is detected
3. Decreased dwell time for attackers, reducing the window of opportunity for data theft
4. Maintenance of compliance with PCI DSS standards aimed at securing online payment environments

These results collectively enhance the security of payment pages and protect cardholder data from sophisticated client-side attacks that traditional security controls might miss. By implementing the change-and-tamper-detection mechanism required by 11.6.1, organizations improve their ability to detect and respond to threats targeting the browser environment where customers enter their payment information.

For more information, visit: https://pcidssguide.com/implementation-benefits

Q24: A merchant notices that their change-and-tamper-detection solution has flagged an unauthorized script being loaded on their payment page. What should be their immediate next steps?

A24: If a merchant notices that their change-and-tamper-detection solution has flagged an unauthorized script being loaded on their payment page, their immediate next steps should be:

1. Activate their incident response plan for potential cardholder data compromise
2. Quickly validate whether the alert is a true positive by examining the identified script
3. If confirmed as unauthorized, immediately contain the issue by taking the affected page offline or reverting to a known-good version to prevent further data exposure
4. Preserve evidence of the unauthorized script for forensic analysis (capture the script, logs, and other relevant data)
5. Determine the source and extent of the compromise (how the script was injected, how long it was active, what data might have been exposed)
6. After containment, work on remediation to fix the vulnerability that allowed the script to be injected
7. Assess whether notification to affected parties, payment brands, or regulators is required based on the findings
8. Document the incident and response actions taken for compliance purposes and future reference

The primary goal is to stop the potential data exposure as quickly as possible while preserving evidence needed for investigation. The speed of response is critical to limiting the amount of cardholder data that might be compromised.

For more information, visit: https://pcidssguide.com/incident-response-procedures

Q25: True or False: The change-and-tamper-detection mechanism required by 11.6.1 must be able to detect all types of changes to a payment page, including visual design changes that don't affect functionality.

A25: False. The change-and-tamper-detection mechanism required by 11.6.1 must specifically detect modifications "that could affect how PAN input fields behave," not all types of changes to a payment page. The content states that the solution must detect "Any modification, including new/altered HTML elements, JavaScript files, DOM manipulations, that could affect how PAN input fields behave."

Visual design changes that don't affect functionality or the security of cardholder data processing are not explicitly required to be detected under this requirement. The focus is on detecting changes that could compromise cardholder data security, particularly JavaScript injection attacks and similar tampering that could lead to card data theft. This targeted approach ensures that the detection mechanism focuses on security-relevant changes rather than generating alerts for benign modifications that don't pose a risk to cardholder data.

For more information, visit: https://pcidssguide.com/detection-scope-limitations

36

'TRUST, BUT VERIFY'

Ronald Reagan's famous quote, "Trust, but verify," is a wise reminder that we should not blindly rely on someone's word alone. This principle is especially important in the context of PCI-DSS and credit cards.

In this context, "Trust, but verify" means that while we may trust that a company is compliant with PCI-DSS, we must also verify it through regular audits and assessments. This helps ensure that the company maintains the necessary security measures to protect sensitive credit card information.

For example, let's say you are a small business owner who accepts credit card payments. You have implemented all the necessary security measures to comply with PCI-DSS standards, and you believe your system is secure. However, you cannot simply assume that everything is working as it should be. You must regularly verify your compliance through assessments and audits conducted by qualified third-party assessors.

In conclusion, "Trust, but verify" is an essential principle in the world of PCI-DSS v4.0 and credit cards. It reminds us that we cannot take anything for granted when protecting sensitive information. By regularly verifying compliance with PCI-DSS standards, we can help ensure that our customers' credit card data remains safe and secure.

About the Author

John Meah

John is a freelance writer, a PCIP, CISSP, CCSK, Sec+ Certified Cybersecurity Consultant, and a Full Member of the Chartered Institute of Information Security (CIIS). He works for an international offshore bank and previously spent many years working in Automotive Security, with the last twenty years in IT & Information Security within the Banking, Financial, and Logistics service sectors.

He successfully implemented PCI-DSS and a Secure-SDLC, and manages security for all projects, including governance, compliance, system design choices, implementations, vendor relationships, and so much more.

Before having a cybersecurity career, John spent many years attending crime scenes, specifically automotive crime, picking up the pieces with Law Enforcement and other emergency services. Initially, working as a security product specialist and incident responder, then as an incident manager across central London.

> 'At a deep level, security has always been top of mind for me; it's in my nature to ask questions, be curious, and be vigilant. This 'Security Mindset' translates into Zero tolerance for any crime, especially cybercrime, and a Zero Trust by design viewpoint.'

Today, John writes content for Techopedia and multiple technology companies in the U.S. and Canada. He's been featured in the InfoSec Magazine and Writers & Artists.co.uk.

John's writing journey enables him to present the Second Edition of the PCIP 4.0 Ultimate Study Guide from a practical, pragmatic, and resourceful viewpoint.

With a passion for creative writing, and a fascination for anything cyber-related, backed by his security background, his future projects include a cyber-thriller.

ALSO BY

John Meah

in

linkedin.com/in/johnmeah-cissp

Payment Card Industry Professional (PCIP) v4.0 Second Edition

Dyslexic Cybersecurity Superheroes: Turning Different Thinking into Digital Defense

CISSP 2025: Cybersecurity Word Search

Electric Dreams: The Future of Eco-Friendly Motorhomes & Campervans

The Cybersecurity Plus Advantage For Students & Professionals With Dyslexia

Certificate of Cloud Security Knowledge CCSK v5

CISSP 2025: Certified Information Systems Security Professional Study Guide

CCSKv4 - Cloud Security - Focused Exam Revision

CISSP Insider: Targeted Security Exam Study Guide 2024

Payment Card Industry Professional (PCIP) v4.0 First Edition

Payment Card Industry Professional (PCIP) v3.0

www.ingramcontent.com/pod-product-compliance
Lightning Source LLC
LaVergne TN
LVHW082023200926
848481LV00010B/2912
* 9 7 9 8 2 3 0 2 0 9 0 5 8 *